BAROQUE NAPLES
AND THE INDUSTRY OF PAINTING

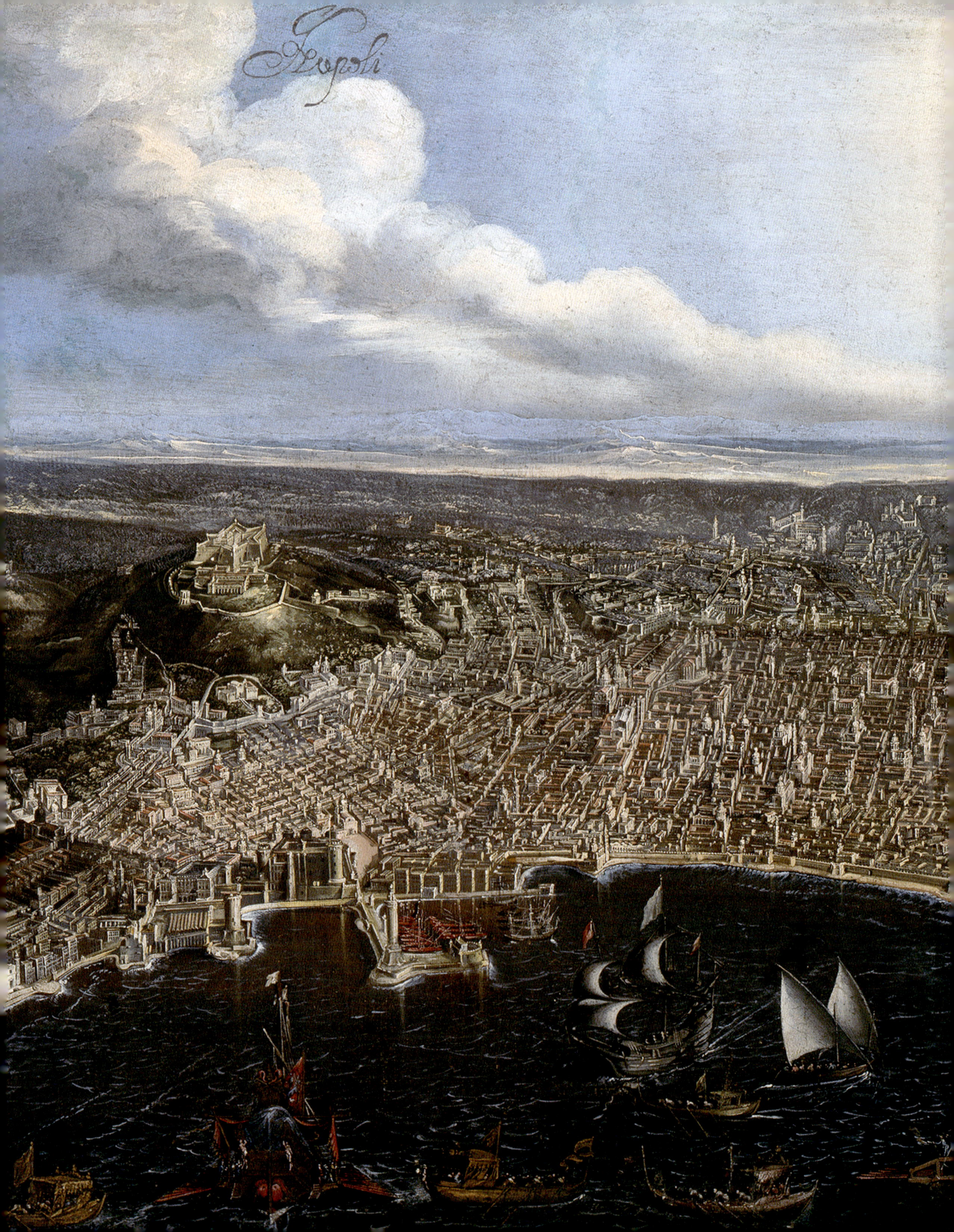
Napoli

CHRISTOPHER R. MARSHALL

BAROQUE NAPLES

AND THE INDUSTRY OF PAINTING

THE WORLD IN THE WORKBENCH

YALE UNIVERSITY PRESS • NEW HAVEN AND LONDON

Designed by Catherine Gaffney
Printed in China

Library of Congress Cataloging-in-Publication Data

Marshall, Christopher R., author.
Baroque Naples and the industry of painting : the world in the workbench / Christopher R. Marshall.
pages cm
Includes bibliographical references and index.
ISBN 978-0-300-17450-2 (cl : alk. paper)
1. Painting, Baroque – Italy – Naples. 2. Painting – Economic aspects – Italy – Naples – History – 16th century. 3. Painting – Economic aspects – Italy – Naples – History – 17th century. 4. Art and society – Italy – Naples – History – 16th century. 5. Art and society – Italy – Naples – History – 17th century. 6. Naples (Italy) – Economic conditions – 16th century. 7. Naples (Italy) – Economic conditions – 17th century. I. Title.
ND621.N2M374 2016
709.45'731--dc23

2015027965

A catalogue record for this book is available from the British Library

p. II Didier Barra, *Bird's-Eye View of Naples*, signed and dated 1647 (detail of fig. 149)

p. VII Viviano Codazzi and Domenico Gargiulo, *Barrel-vaulted Doric Palace Portico with Steps and an Archway, with Coastal View Beyond*, signed and dated 1641 (detail of fig. 64)

p. VIII Luca Giordano, *St Januarius Intercedes with the Virgin, Christ and the Eternal Father during the Plague of 1656*, 1660–61 (detail of fig. 175)

Contents

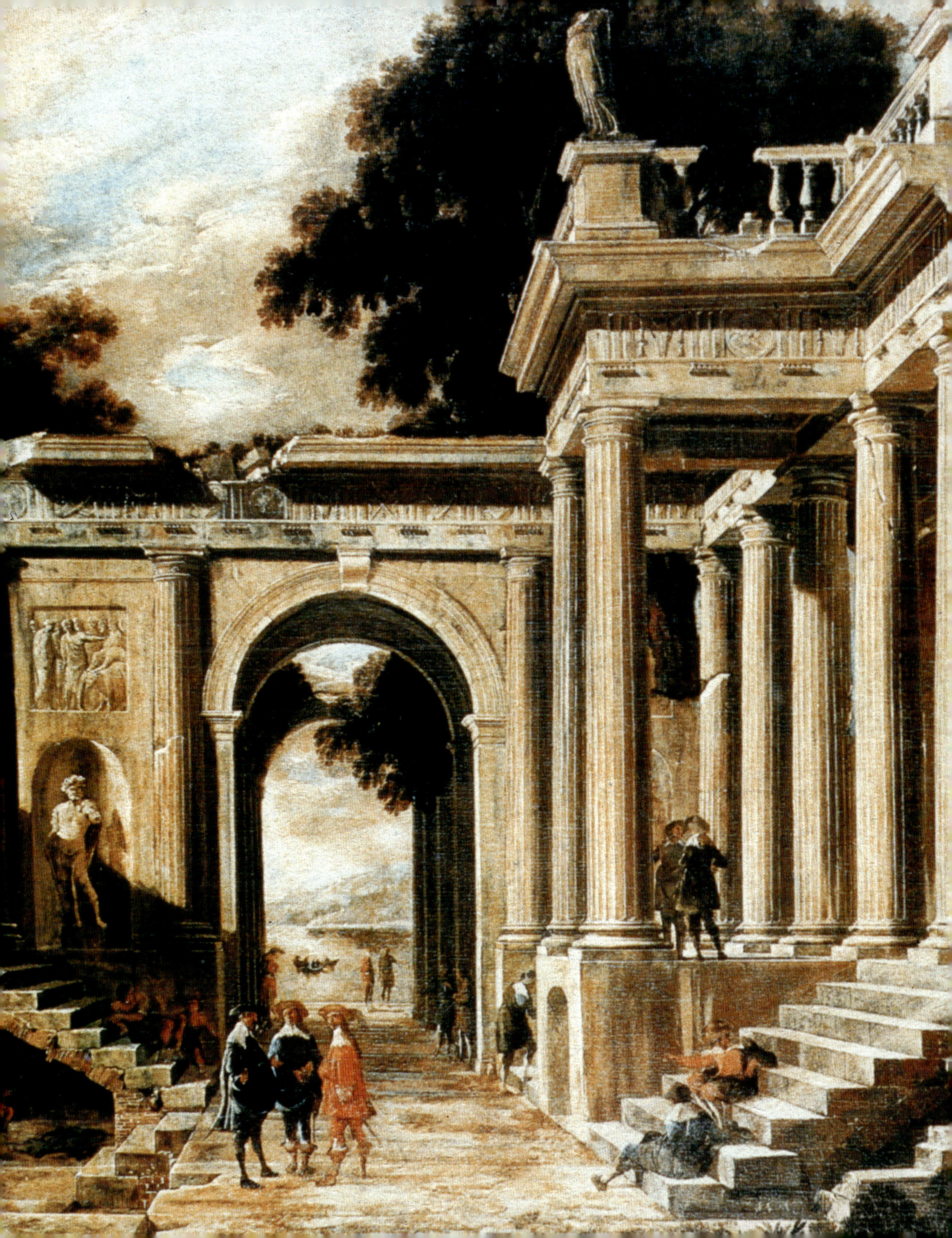

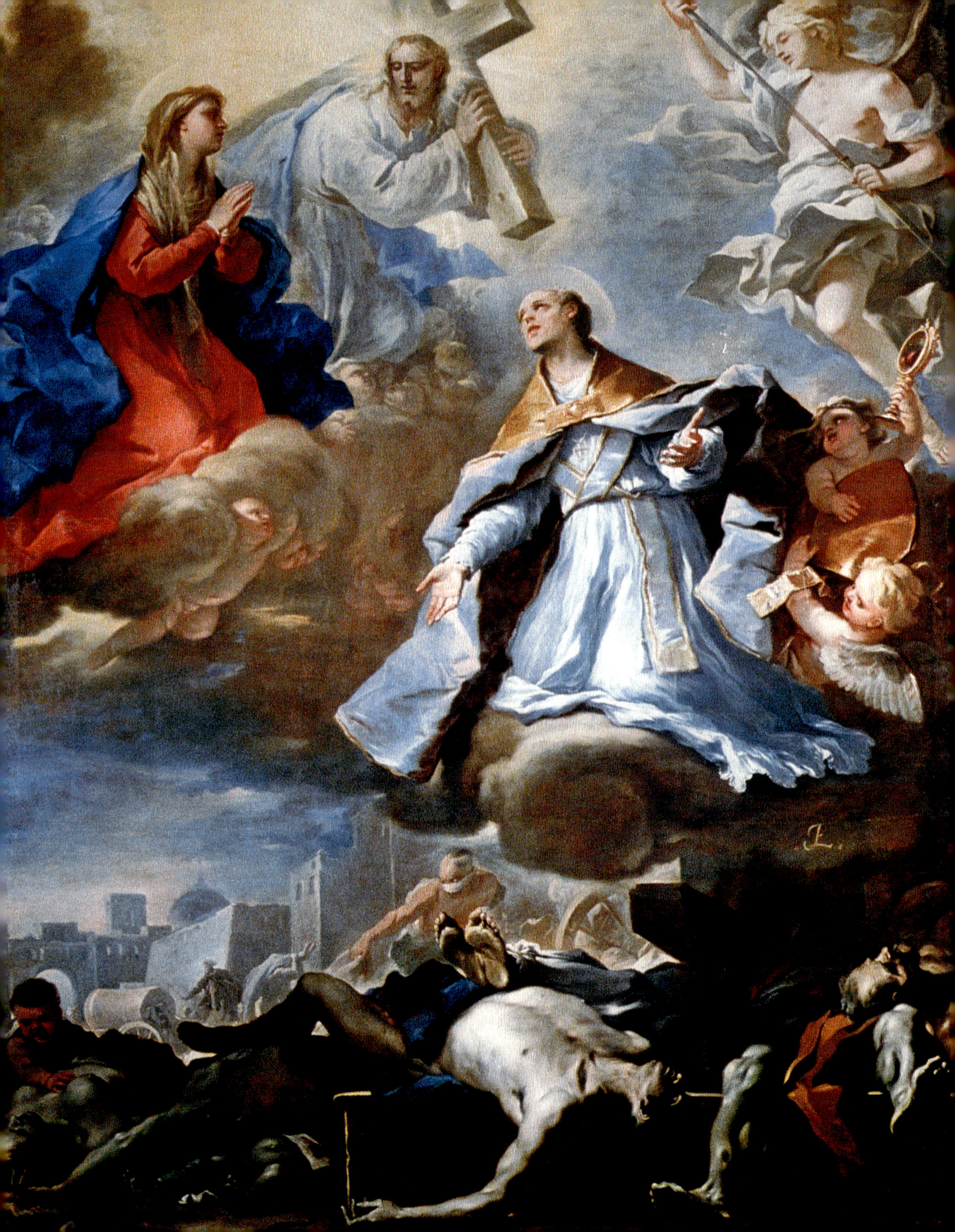

Acknowledgements

My *ringraziamenti* for this project stretch back many years. For his tutelage and advice, and for supervising my PhD thesis on the landscape painter Domenico Gargiulo, an undertaking that set me on the initial path to where I find myself today, I am greatly indebted to David R. Marshall. The encouragement of my other colleagues at the University of Melbourne has also proved invaluable, particularly the three successive heads of my School: Professors Margaret Manion, Jaynie Anderson and Rachel Fensham. My students have also stimulated my thinking and nourished my research in multiple ways that they might not have realized at the time. In particular, I am grateful to my PhD students, most of all perhaps to Callum Reid and Glenys Adams – the latter of whose work on the Oratorians proved particularly beneficial to my analysis of the collecting and patronage of the Neapolitan congregation in the present study.

This book could not have been written without the extraordinary legacy created by the legions of archival researchers whose patience and perspicacity have done so much to illuminate the dynamism and diversity of Neapolitan Baroque art and culture. It is with great pleasure that I here recognize the contributions of such scholars as Gennaro Borrelli, Antonio Delfino, Eduardo Nappi, Vincenzo Pacelli, Renato Ruotolo and Giuseppe de Vito. Their work builds in turn on the discoveries of previous researchers, such as Ulisse Prota Giurleo, Franco Strazzullo, Giambattista d'Addosio and Nunzio Federigo Faraglia, the last of whose publications on the Certosa di San Martino, for example, remain fundamental, despite dating back to 1885 and 1892. Other Neapolitan scholars – particularly those working at the Museo di Capodimonte and the Soprintendenza per i Beni Artistici e Storici di Napoli – have been extremely patient and generous with their time and resources in facilitating my research. In particular, I would like to thank Brigitte Daprà and Nicola Spinosa for their assistance and encouragement.

From among the expanded field of international scholars of Neapolitan Baroque art I must single out the contribution made by Gérard Labrot to our understanding of Neapolitan collections of art. Labrot's publications on seventeenth- and eighteenth-century inventories remain fundamental to the field, and the work of the Provenance Index of the Getty Information Institute in supporting and extending his contribution represents a vital ongoing initiative that remains globally accessible to scholars today via a very useful online database (see http://piprod.getty.edu/starweb/pi/servlet.starweb?path=pi/pi.web). Sebastian Schütze's study of Massimo Stanzione (undertaken in collaboration with Thomas Willette) and of Neapolitan patronage and culture more generally has also proved vital for my research, particularly for its emphasis on the intellectual and literary dimensions of Neapolitan art and culture. In Rome, I was able to profit from numerous conversations with Professor Schütze at the Bibliotheca Hertziana, to whose staff I am also most grateful, together with the staff of the Kunsthistorisches Institut, Florence, the Biblioteca Nazionale, Naples, the Frick Art Reference Library, the Witt Library of the Courtauld Institute of Art and my own research library, the Baillieu Library at the University of Melbourne. Research for this book was further supported by grants from the University of Melbourne Faculty of Arts Special Studies Program, and the Small Grant Program of the Australian Research Council.

I have benefited greatly from a constant dialogue of lively discussions and exchanges of ideas with other researchers working in related fields. They are too numerous to mention – but I nonetheless feel impelled to thank at least some of them by name, including Antonio Calabria, James Clifton, Charles Dempsey, Gabriele Finaldi, Gianluca Forgione, David Jaffé, Helen Langdon, Francesco Lofano, Joachim Meyer, Maria Rosario Nappi, Nicholas Penny, Ann Percy and Wendy Wassyng Roworth. I was also fortunate enough to be able to enjoy a period of extended time working on an initial conceptualization of this project at the Center for Advanced Study in the Visual Arts at the National Gallery of Art, Washington, DC, under the lively and supportive guidance of Peter M. Lukehart and Elizabeth Cropper, to whom I am most grateful.

Art-market research forms a particular focus of this investigation, and in this respect I have been fortunate to find myself coming under the aegis of Professors Hans van Miegroet and Neil de Marchi of Duke University. My participation in their project, *Mapping Markets for Paintings in Europe*, gave me an entrée into an expanded interdisciplinary field of researchers that I found greatly beneficial. A follow-up Fellowship at Duke University further cemented my deep respect and gratitude for their ongoing generosity and support. I have also been lucky enough to be able to collaborate with Richard E. Spear and Philip Sohm on their *Economic Lives of Italian Baroque Painters* project. This undertaking enabled me to team up with a lively field of international researchers and culminated in a particularly stimulating colloquium convened at the Clark Art Institute.

At Yale University Press, special thanks are owed to Gillian Malpass for her long and unwavering support of this project. Sincere thanks are also due to the anonymous reviewers of the manuscript for their generous yet probing reading of my work, together with Delia Gaze and Jacquie Meredith for assistance with copy editing and proofreading, and Catherine Gaffney for the design of the book. For patient checking of my Italian translations I am most grateful to Eleonora Rai, and for assistance with the photographs I am greatly indebted to the specialist assistance provided by Jane Brown and Ian Kendrick from the Visual Cultures Resource Centre of the University of Melbourne.

My parents – Vernon and Patricia Marshall – have continued to support and encourage me in this undertaking, as in all others. My final debt of gratitude, though, must go to Jane, Laura and Dominic, who have accompanied me on what has turned into a rather long journey but whose love and forbearance were nevertheless always strong and abiding enough to sustain it to the end.

A Note on Sources and Equivalences

This book draws heavily on the three-volume *Lives* of the Neapolitan artists compiled in the early eighteenth century by the artist/historian Bernardo de' Dominici. De' Dominici's critical stocks have waxed and waned over the years, even more so, it seems, than otherwise comparable authors such as Vasari and Malvasia. His trustworthiness as a source has gone from being fundamentally discredited in the later nineteenth and earlier twentieth centuries, to the current, more nuanced view that recognizes his fundamental significance, while understanding the need to check his assertions independently wherever possible and to interpret them within the context of the critical frameworks and rhetorical conventions of his own day.[1] I have used the standard facsimile edition of De' Dominici's *Vite*, as supplemented by the more recent, critical edition issued by Paparo in 2003–8, to which I have referred particularly in terms of the revisions and modifications of information contained in its footnotes. The translations from De' Dominici and other Italian sources are my own, except where otherwise indicated.

The standard Neapolitan form of measurement was the *palmo* – or hand. This has been converted at the rate of 1 *palmo* = approximately 26.37 centimetres, although recognizing at the same time its approximate value only as a unit of measurement, particularly when applied to paintings listed in early inventories.[2] Conversions of other conventions of measurement are explained wherever they occur in the text.

The international exchange rate for the Baroque Neapolitan ducat – particularly its relationship to the more stable scudo of neighbouring Rome – is a major issue, for which the reader should be referred to studies published elsewhere.[3] Foreign artists working in Naples very occasionally show themselves to have been aware of the periodically extreme devaluation of the Neapolitan ducat relative to the scudo. In 1620, for example, at the height of the Neapolitan currency crisis of the first decades of the century, Guido Reni secured an agreement with the deputies of the Tesoro di San Gennaro that he would be paid 100 Roman scudi per figure – payable at the local exchange rate of 130 Neapolitan ducats per figure (as discussed in Chapter Two).

For the most part, though, Neapolitan artists remained preoccupied by their own local contexts and were thus oblivious of such higher order issues of foreign exchange. From the Neapolitan perspective, the scudo/ducat was accordingly often regarded as being – at least notionally – equivalent 1–1 currencies. So, for example, in 1636 Falcone and his associates paid out exactly the same monthly fee for a life model in Neapolitan ducats as was paid in Roman scudi by the Accademia di San Luca in Rome (for which, see Chapter Four). Conversely, both Artemisia Gentileschi and De' Dominici, to cite two directly relevant examples, often use the term scudo/ducat interchangeably.[4]

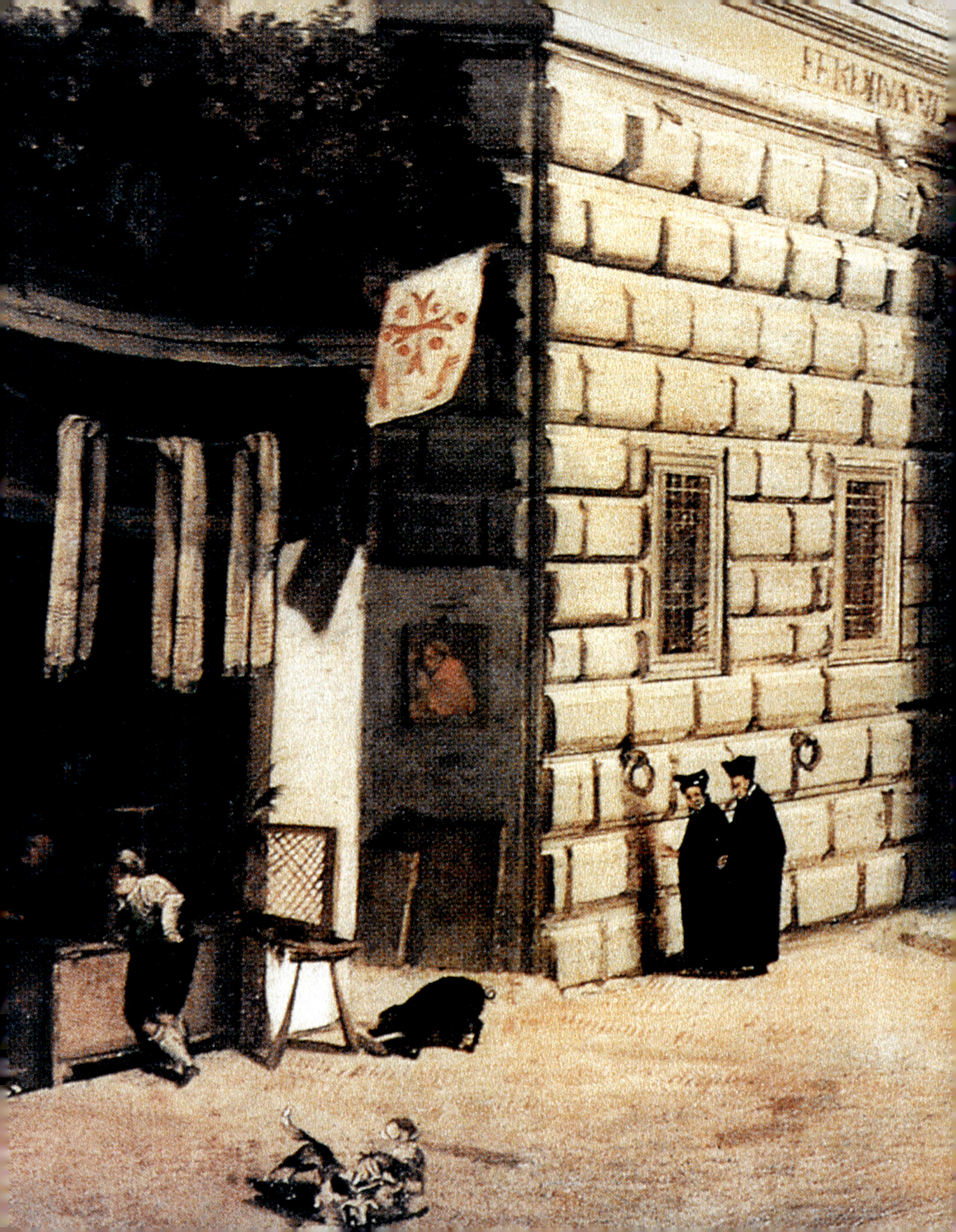

Introduction

The Neapolitan Baroque Art World: From Basement to Balcony

It is morning in the artists' quarter of Baroque Naples (figs 1, 70).[1] Two priests walk down the Via Monteoliveto alongside the Palazzo Gravina lost in conversation. Perhaps they are off to celebrate Mass in the nearby church of Sant'Anna dei Lombardi. If so, they would be able to pay their respects at the same time to three of the most important paintings by Caravaggio then to be seen in southern Italy, together with works by many of the area's local painters, including most of Caravaggio's early Neapolitan followers. Behind them, four mounted *cavalieri* can be seen approaching a passing carriage and an urchin leads a mule across the open space in front of the palace. Two fighting mongrels form a blur in the foreground, while a large black pig sniffs hopefully at a trestle table nearby.

This table belongs to a workshop, where two elderly men are seen talking animatedly to another figure who leans across the ledge that serves as the shop's counter. Perhaps they are haggling over the price of one of the shop's wares. But what are they selling exactly? The items on display offer some clues. Three bolts of fabric hang above the shop, beside three paintings that have been taken out from the back and placed onto the street, presumably in the hope of catching the attention of passers-by. Two are propped against the wall, while a third – showing a saint in profile – serves as an additional sign of the shop's wares. These incidental details thus vividly document the activities of the early Neapolitan art dealers – or *rivenditori* – who sold moderately priced paintings as part of their wider trade in fabrics, furniture and other new and used items of interior furnishing.

These dealers lived in close proximity to scores of artisans, whose shops and living quarters were similarly concentrated in the area. One such workshop further down the road announces its presence via a cluster of lutes suspended from rods. A master carver and his two assistants can also be seen hard at work at the edge of the open space in front of the palace, hammering and planing a carriage that is so large that it has had to be taken out into the street to be worked on. A painter's workshop is also evident just across the street. Its master has displayed two paintings, one propped on a table very like the dealer's across the way, and another beside the doorway itself. This workshop could be the one from which the painter and gilder Sebastiano Sellitto operated at the close of the sixteenth century.[2] This painter was the father of Carlo Sellitto, the first documented Neapolitan follower of Caravaggio, whose work hung in the church of Sant'Anna dei Lom-

1 Unidentified topographical painter in the circle of François de Nomé and Alessandro Baratta, *View of the Palazzo Gravina, Naples*, 1620s–1630s (detail)

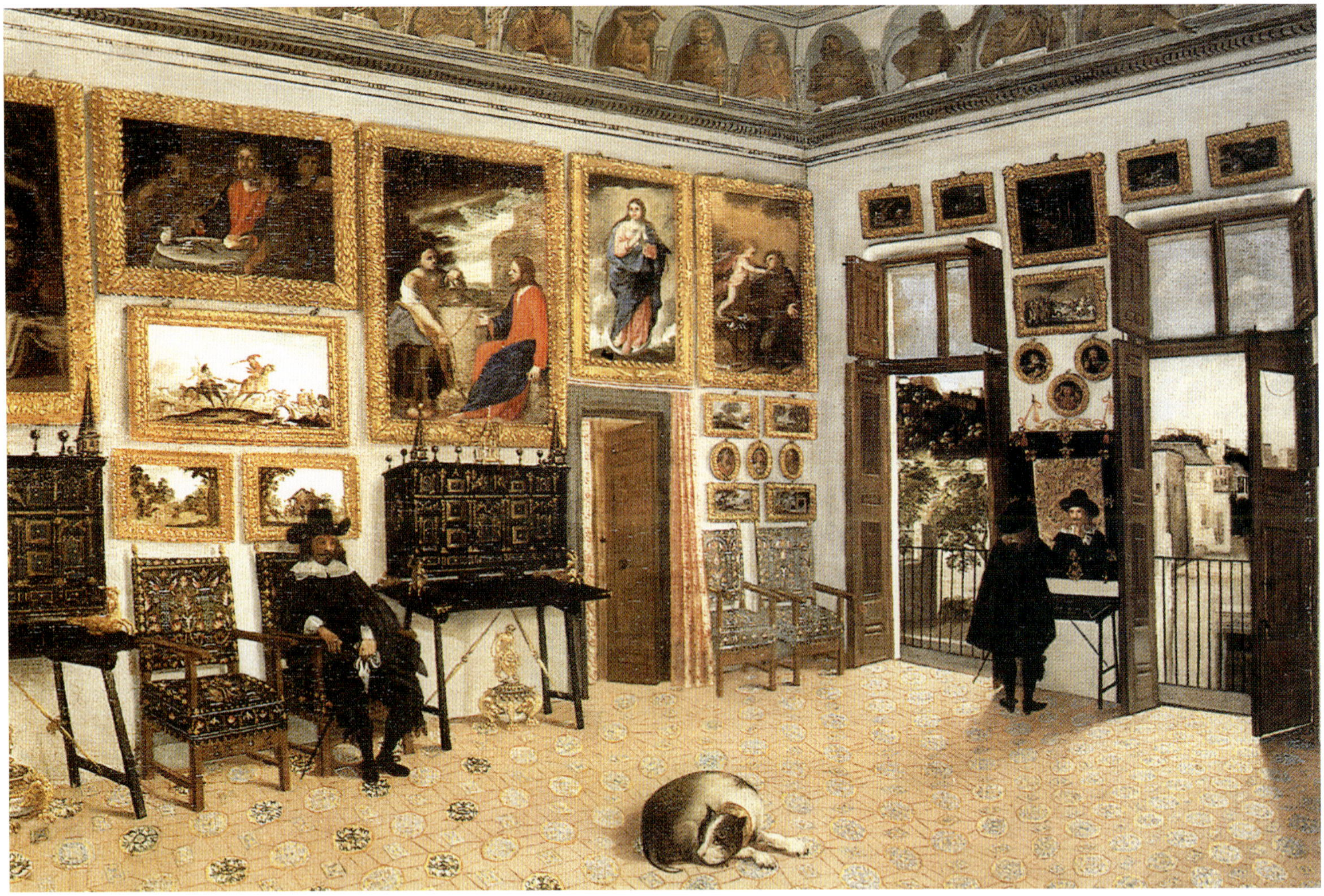

2 Michele Regolia, *Palace Interior, circa* 1675, signed (detail)

bardi just down the road. This unusually detailed Neapolitan *veduta* thus bears eloquent testimony to the intricately interconnected daily lives of painters, dealers and artisans in Baroque Naples.

The viewpoint shifts now from the bustle of the street to take in the view from the balcony above. Here one enters the rarefied realm of the *piano nobile* of an unidentified Neapolitan palace dating to the 1670s (figs 2, 65).[3] In this picture, two gentlemen can be seen waiting in a large antechamber filled with ornate furnishings. One contemplates his reflection idly in a gilt-encrusted ebony mirror, while a second stares vacantly into space from one of the embossed leather armchairs that line the room. These visitors must have been here some time already, since a giant, pug-faced mastiff has forgotten all about them and has flopped back down to sleep in the middle of the richly tiled floor. A servant peers surreptitiously from behind a brocaded dividing curtain – or *portiera* – to see if they are still there, while another servant advances bearing what appears to be a letter on a tray. Perhaps they will not have to wait much longer to attend to their business.

The silence that pervades the room is offset by the clamour of the furnishings. Lush tendrils on chair backs offer variants on the detailing of two ebony cabinets that incorporate gilding with compartments, small sculptures and decorative finials. These sit on folding console tables that have been placed above two ornate gilt-copper braziers for use during the colder months. Two golden clocks on top of the cabinets echo the gilt of the braziers below. All the colours, surfaces and outlines of this interior have thus been coordinated in an exuberant yet nonetheless carefully considered manner that extends further to encompass the paintings as well. Reading from left to right, three large dark Caravaggesque biblical narratives have been offset against a smaller and lighter unit of three copies after Callot's prints of contemporary events, while three brighter keyed devotional images have been hung further along the wall alongside three small heads of saints, which in turn have been juxtaposed with two rows of small landscapes that form a corresponding pair to the two chairs beneath them. A group of paintings on slate form their own unit on the other wall, juxtaposed, in turn, with three small *tondi* (roundels) of heads – including one of a soul in purgatory – that make a final play on the heads framed in the mirror below, including, at this very moment, one of the two visitors to this palace.

This book aims to chart the links between the two seemingly distant worlds evoked in these paintings. Its beginning point – and in a sense its final destination as well – is to propose that the rarefied ambience reflected in the mirror in the second painting is not, in fact, so far removed from the prosaic bustle of the street below as might at first appear. The dealers, painters and other artisans at work beneath the balcony (and perhaps the gentlemen can hear them now, as they take their rest) spend their working lives making and selling the objects that these visitors now have the luxury to regard. They are the producers and traders of the accumulated empire of things that the gentlemen in their palaces are now at leisure to consume. Yet the interconnections between these two worlds also go further.

It is not just a matter of the close physical proximity that was such a fact of life in the overheated congestion of Baroque Naples. By the mid-seventeenth century close to 400,000 people fought for space in a bustling port city whose boundaries were nonetheless restricted by the viceroys who ruled southern Italy on behalf of the Spanish crown. One aspect of this growth was an influx of people and business that created both social fluidity and friction as merchants, lawyers and the like sought increasing access to the prestige and influence traditionally enjoyed by the more established aristocratic families. This included their collecting many of the same objects found in the palace interior.

Yet even the Orsini di Gravina, whose palace was seen in the first painting – or any of the other venerable Neapolitan aristocratic families for that matter – were not so greatly distant from the world on the street in other senses as well. They helped, after all, to keep the local artists in business. Early inventories of the Palazzo Gravina list numerous works by most of the better-known artists of the neighbourhood – including Fabrizio Santafede, Giovanni Battista Caracciolo, Giovanni Bernardino Azzolino, Massimo Stanzione, Salvator Rosa, Juan Do, Bernardo Cavallino, Agostino Beltrano, Annella de Rosa and Pacecco de Rosa.[4] One artist in particular, Francesco Guarino, who came from the feudal Orsini town of Solofra in the Campania, seems even to have lived in the Palazzo Gravina as a retainer of the family during his extended stays in the city.[5] More fundamentally, though, many of the objects that made their way up the stairs and into this and other palaces did not remain there forever. Many found their way back into the secondary market as goods to be resold – even perhaps from the very workshop seen below the balcony of the Palazzo Gravina. So too did the artists and dealers seek at all times to remain responsive to – and sometimes to influence and pre-empt – the evolving tastes and interests of all those who acquired their work, including those in the palaces above.

How did these processes take place? Just what were the parameters of the Neapolitan Baroque art world and how did each sector operate in relation to the others? The study of Neapolitan Baroque painting has grown exponentially since the time of the landmark exhibition *Painting in Naples, 1606–1705: From Caravaggio to Giordano*, held in 1982–3, which was followed by the even more comprehensive *Civiltà del Seicento a Napoli* of 1984–5.[6] Numerous monographs, most of them accompanying major exhibitions devoted to the artists in question, have likewise significantly advanced our understanding of many of the significant painters of the period since that time.[7] A further group of surveys, exhibition catalogues and collections of essays devoted to the topic of Neapolitan Baroque painting more generally has also considerably enriched our knowledge of the field.[8] Added to these are the scores of articles that have appeared, for the most part, in *Ricerche sul '600 napoletano*, a journal that has constituted a goldmine of specialist research in the area since its inception in 1982.[9]

And yet, despite all the considerable advances that have been achieved as a result of this veritable explosion of interest in the field, none of the studies cited above addresses in any broadly based and synthetic way the full range of questions that this book sets out to investigate. This study will accordingly seek to pursue the kinds of questions that have been raised from time to time, but more or less in the margins of the literature as it now stands. In 1984, for example, Ann Percy wrote in the context of a study of Cavallino's work of the 1630s to 1650s that 'We do not understand exactly how the process of buying and selling cabinet pictures in the city was effected, nor do we know to what extent there might have been knowledgeable and enthusiastic individuals who patronized certain artists in the way Ferrante Spinelli, principe di Tarsia, for example, favored Aniello Falcone.'[10] Yet more recently, and as an indication of the ongoing gap in studies of what might be termed the industrial context to Neapolitan Baroque art, Javier Portús Pérez was similarly moved in 2005 to register his disappointment at the lack of consideration given in a new monograph on Ribera to such crucial ongoing questions as 'the little-known role of his workshop and the jungle of versions and copies of his paintings...[and] the crucial question of Ribera's clients and their expectations of his painting'.[11]

As a study of the working lives of Neapolitan Baroque painters, this book will pursue these kinds of issues against the wider backdrop of the seventeenth-century Neapolitan art world more generally. It will certainly be concerned as a result to chart the career trajectories of such well-known artists as Jusepe de Ribera, Luca Giordano, Bernardo Cavallino and Massimo Stanzione in a close-knit, over-stocked and highly competitive field. At the same time, though, this study will also highlight the necessarily historically contingent nature of such reputations – given that Cavallino, to take one example, was a struggling and, in fact, relatively little-known artist during his lifetime. The book will thus stress the need to go beyond the big names in order to reach, as well, such lesser-known painters as Onofrio de Anfora. This artist is known today only by virtue of the fact that he had the misfortune to be stabbed in a street brawl in 1644, thus making him the subject of an unusually detailed and revealing will describing the contents of his workshop taken from the middle of his career, rather than at the end as is more commonly the case.[12]

To give a clear and logical shape to such a broad and at times even sprawlingly complex landscape has been no easy task. In order to achieve at least a semblance of structure, the present study has been organized into three broad areas of investigation. The first section considers the world at the workbench by charting the activities of the painters' workshops of Baroque Naples, from the largest and most prestigious down to the more humble. The second addresses the industrial component of painting by considering the market for it in seventeenth-century Naples. This will include the activities of art dealers – who comprised both the *rivenditori* glimpsed in the *veduta* of fig. 1 and the painters themselves, who dealt in pictures as a matter of course – and the more prestigious and selective art merchants involved in the emerging trade in old master paintings as well as in the export of Giordano's canvases to foreign markets in the second half of the seventeenth century.

Finally, the study will consider the reception of Neapolitan painting most directly in the interests and concerns of Neapolitan patrons and collectors (Table 1). On the one hand, this will take in the most prestigious and public settings for the display of art – the Carthusians of Naples, for example, whose lavishly redecorated charterhouse still stands proudly pre-eminent at the foot of the Spanish fortress, Castel Sant'Elmo, overlooking the Bay of Naples. On the other, it will also be attentive to the influence of smaller and sometimes even notional collections that have long since been dispersed – such as that of the poet Giambattista Marino. Marino had hoped to assemble a major gallery of privately commissioned paintings following his return to Naples in 1624. He died before realizing his dream, but nonetheless still managed to exert a major influence on the development of private collecting in Naples via the publication of his widely read *Galeria* of 1619–20.

As shown in the rich and varied field of artists and initiatives indicated in Table 1, the study will emphasize the significant impact made by the public display of paintings in Baroque Naples more generally. This will include both those exhibited in especially influential private galleries and in public churches, the latter providing an important context for the diffusion and transmission of broader public awareness of foreign trends in art – from Raphael to Titian in the Renaissance, to contemporary artists like Domenichino, Vouet, Reni and Pietro da Cortona. The present study will, finally, also chart the rise of the flourishing culture of Neapolitan temporary exhibitions of painting. These provided major promotional opportunities for artists and their backers – ranging from merchants to viceroys – while also constituting significant arenas of public rivalry and competition.

Linking all this analysis will be a fundamental concern to understand the relationship of each element under examination to the whole. The varied outputs of Neapolitan painters will thus be traced as continuously circulating components of a vast and interconnected network of relations that extended from basement to street level to *piano nobile* and then back again. Copyists will thus be understood as working in relation to painters of original compositions, dealers and artisans as working in relation to painters, assistants in relation to masters, collectors in relation to their colleagues, and so on. The first step in this journey will be to leave the quiet luxury of the palace and to return to street level in order to trace the busy working lives of Neapolitan painters in more detail.

Overleaf Domenico Gargiulo, *Market in the Piazza del Mercato*, mid-1650s (detail of fig. 61)

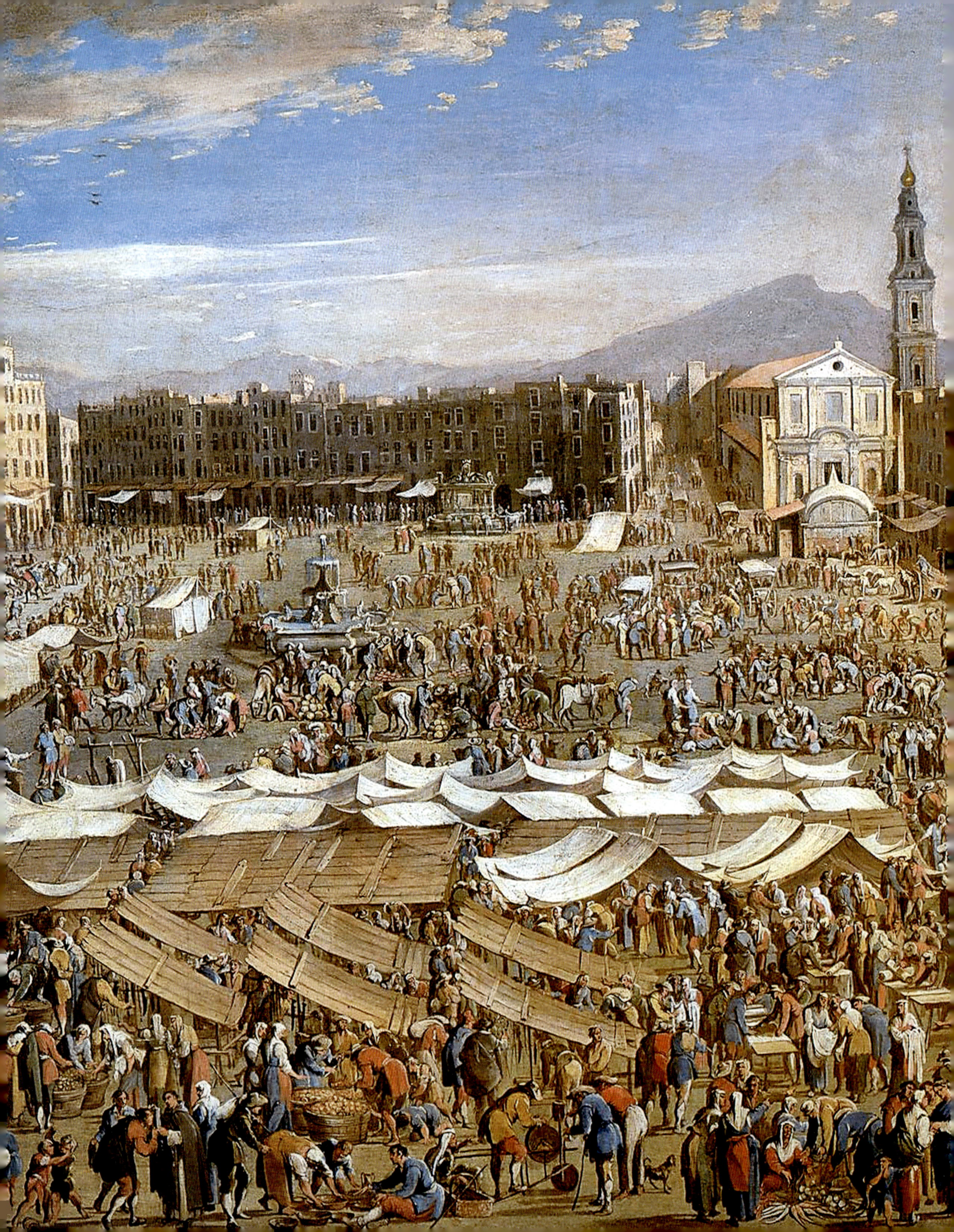

PART I

THE WORLD OF THE WORKSHOP

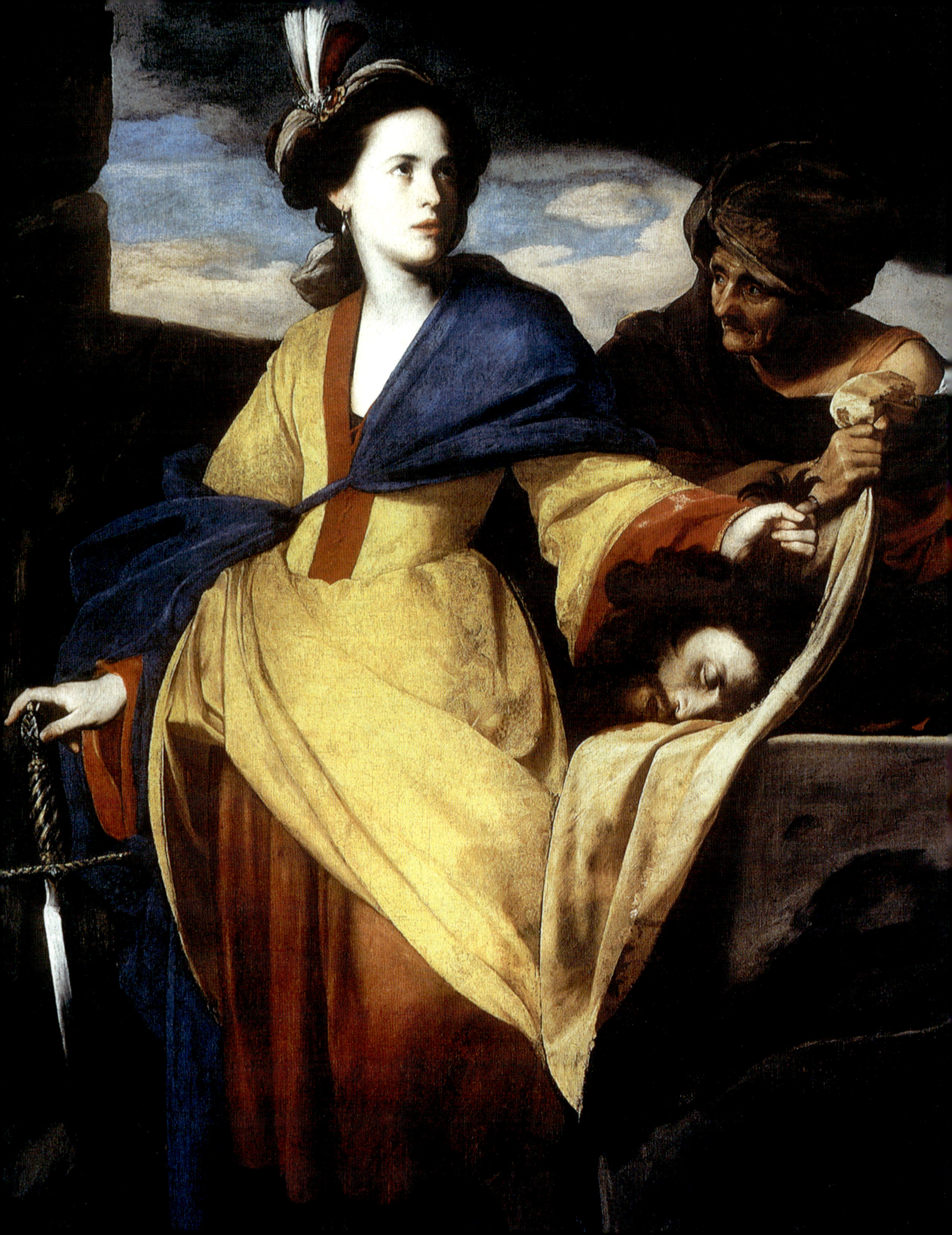

1

From the Street to the Studio

CONVENTION VERSUS CREATIVITY

In early 1618 the Neapolitan agent of Cosimo II de' Medici wrote to the grand duke's secretary concerning his negotiations with local artists. Cosimo del Sera had commissioned a picture of *Galatea* from the city's leading painter, Fabrizio Santafede (*circa* 1560–1624), but he remained unconvinced of Santafede's capabilities. The artist had visited him the previous day in order to show him a rough sketch of the composition and to discuss the subject, 'since they have not had much practice in these kinds of subjects here'.[1] Del Sera's comment on the Neapolitan unfamiliarity with mythologies is revealing in itself, and will be returned to presently. But Del Sera's reservations went deeper than this. He doubted that Santafede had the imagination and inventiveness necessary for paintings of this kind ('io non credo, che gl'habbia tanta bizzarria che basti').

Del Sera had no such doubts when it came to a younger artist named Jusepe de Ribera (1591–1652), who had arrived in Naples two years earlier. Ribera, he wrote, had painted for the viceroy three pictures of saints that were greatly esteemed and which demonstrated that he did not lack 'Bizzarria, e buone invenzioni' (originality and good invention). Del Sera lost no time in commissioning a painting from him. He was, in fact, so impressed with the artist's skill and inventiveness that he allowed him to choose the subject himself ('metta il quadro in ordine, per farlo a suo capriccio').[2]

This brief exchange illustrates vividly the changing mood of taste and patronage that was just then beginning to impact on Neapolitan painting. Santafede's late Mannerist style, already challenged by recent developments in Neapolitan Caravaggism, would soon be eclipsed by the rapidly increasing popularity of Ribera's rich and complex tenebrism (fig. 3). Yet there was more at stake than a simple matter of style. The distinction between the two painters also involved differing working practices and a different conception of the role of artistic creativity.

The young Ribera had initially migrated to Italy from Játiva in Valencia some time prior to 1611. He arrived in Naples in 1616 after periods of residence in Parma and several years in Rome, the epicentre of the Caravaggesque art world.[3] His background thus prepared him well to fulfil the expectations of the sophisticated Florentine connoisseur. Santafede's career, on the other hand, was based on his ability to cater to a markedly different set of expectations. His speciality was the devotional altarpiece, the *cona*, for which he is cited time and time again in documents (fig. 4).[4] Patrons of these altarpieces sought very different qualities from those required of narrative mythological paintings. Displays of inventiveness and imagination were subordinate in these contexts to an emphasis on clarity and hieratic formal-

Facing page Massimo Stanzione, *Judith and Holofernes*, *circa* 1640 (detail of fig. 8)

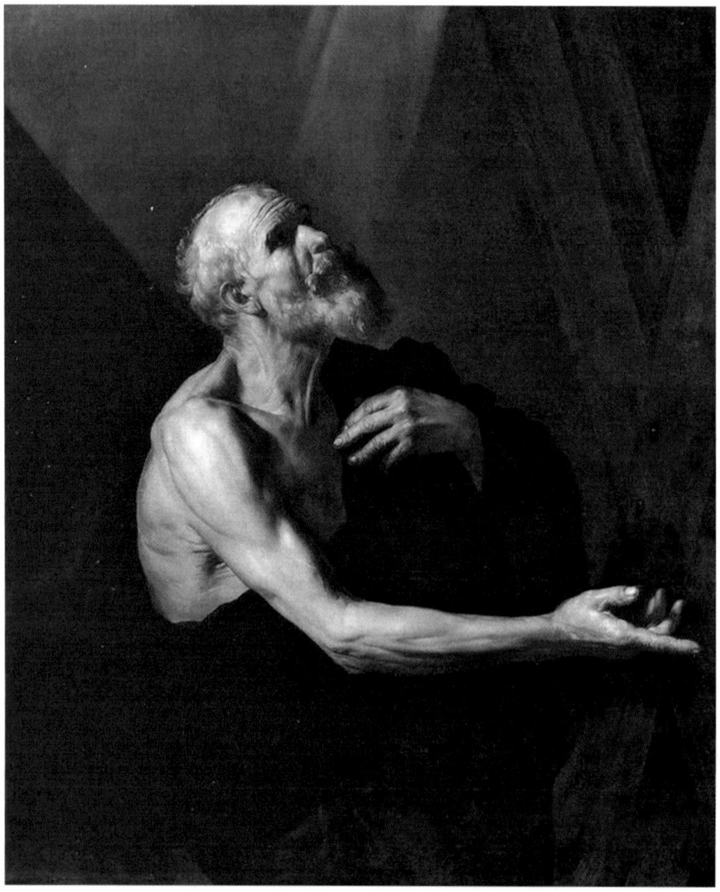

3 Jusepe de Ribera, *St Andrew*, *circa* 1617–18. Oil on canvas, 136 × 112 cm. Quadreria dei Girolamini, Naples

ity. Compositions and iconographic schemes, such as that of *Our Lady of the Rosary*, were developed into formulas that were then carried over with only minor variations from one commission to another. For an artist with a large workshop, such as the Flemish painter resident in Naples Dirck Hendricksz (1542/3–1618), better known by the Italianized form of Teodoro d'Errico, this resulted in numerous duplicates of popular compositional types.[5]

In a city that prided itself on its status as 'La Fedelissima' (the most faithful [city]), commissions for altarpieces were always a dominant feature of the local scene. They were particularly prominent in the late sixteenth and early seventeenth centuries, appearing with monotonous regularity in the published bank payments and contracts. Private secular commissions, by contrast, appear only rarely. The reasons for this, as will be seen, is that Neapolitan patronage operated according to a different dynamic from other major Italian centres, such as Rome and Florence. The viceroys, although in the main eager to enrich their collections, took these with them to Spain at the end of their term and were generally little interested in commissioning much art for Naples itself. There was thus no ruling household to set the standard for munificent patronage and no extended family to consolidate this, as was the case with the popes and their families. With no guiding programme of official patronage, it remained for individuals to commission works of art on their own.

This the Neapolitan aristocracy was slow to do, since it had moved en bloc to Naples only in the middle of the sixteenth century and had no significant local tradition of private patronage on which to draw.[6] The late sixteenth-century collection of the poet Berardino Ròta (1508–1575), which contained paintings attributed to Raphael, Francesco Salviati, Vasari, Correggio and others and which was housed in a palace with a façade painted by Giovanni Bernardo Lama and with ceiling paintings by Polidoro da Caravaggio, was thus exceptional for its day.[7] Those paintings that do appear in Neapolitan inventories of early seventeenth-century private collections tend to represent, instead, picture types that were relatively conservative by contemporary Roman standards. Portraits, devotional images and altarpieces were preferred over *istorie* and landscapes.[8] In the 1620s at least, Naples accordingly still felt as if it were some distance behind contemporary developments in Rome. A visiting Spanish painter, Jusepe Martínez (1600–1682), when taken by Ribera on a tour of the local private collections in 1625, was probably not too far from the truth when he commented: 'since I had come from Rome, everything seemed small to me, as in this city people are more concerned with military matters and horsemanship than with the art of painting'.[9]

PAINTERS AND ARTISANS

The integrated altarpiece that so dominated painting commissions at the end of the sixteenth century provides a powerful visualization of the close and sustained relations that existed between painters and artisans during this period. The considerable collaborative effort that must have gone into creating these opulent aids to devotion is plainly evident in those altarpieces that still retain their original frames. Giovanni Balducci's *Annunciation*, for example, in the Chiesa dell'Annunziata in Piedimonte d'Alife (fig. 5), which dates from the 1590s, is made up of two paintings – a major panel and an upper portion that is often described in documents as a *cimasa*.[10] Here painting forms

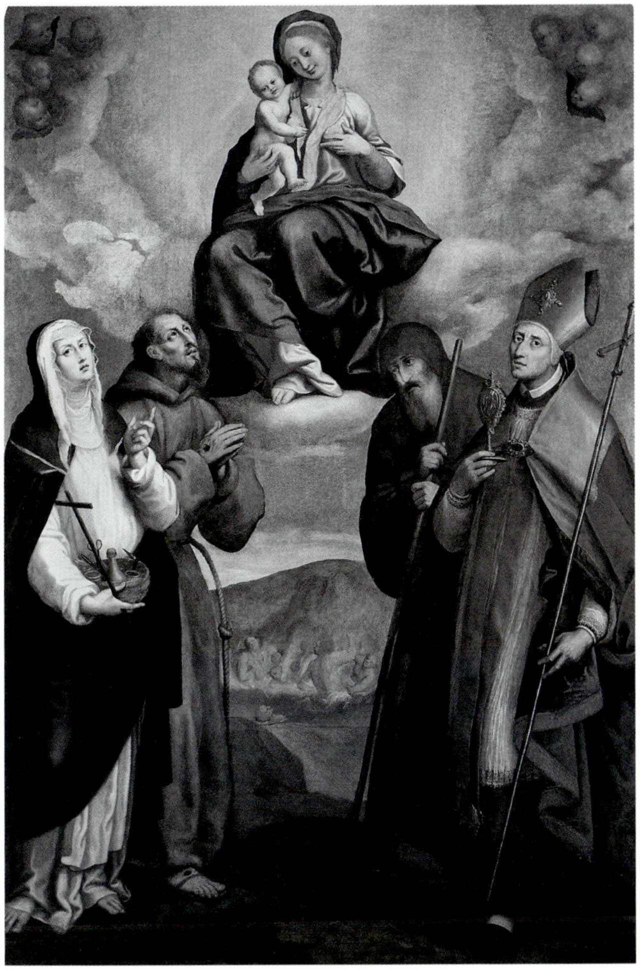

4 Fabrizio Santafede. *Our Lady of Grace with Sts Sophia, Francis of Assisi, Francesco di Paola and Januarius*, 1580s–1590s. Oil on panel, 228 × 150 cm. Museo Diocesano, Naples, on deposit from the Congrega di Santa Sofia

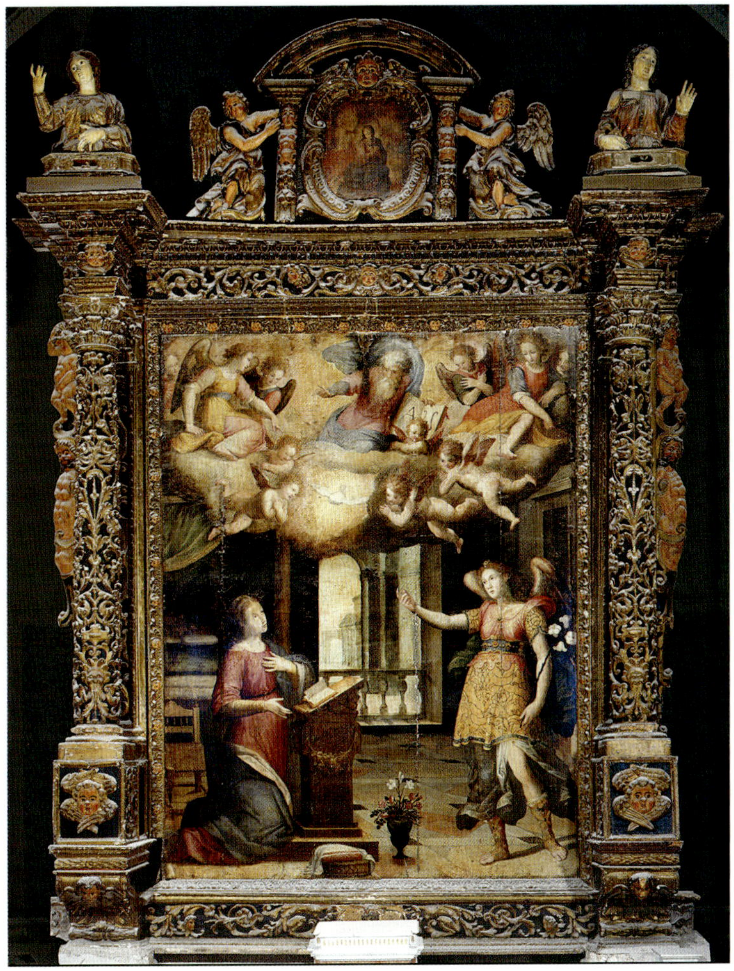

5 Giovanni Balducci, *Annunciation* altarpiece, late 1590s. Oil on panel, 453 × 340 cm. Chiesa dell'Annunziata, Piedimonte d'Alife

only one element of an elaborate decorative ensemble, as carved and gilded *putti*, herms and angels vie for the viewer's attention alongside a further two reliquaries of female saints that have been added to the tops of the columns. Documents of the period abound with like descriptions mentioning equally elaborate frames that were often to be executed by the carver following designs provided by either the artist or the patron.[11]

An unusually detailed sense of the complex process of collaboration involved in these constructions can be gained from the circumstances of a failed commission of 1588. In June of that year the painter Decio Tramontano (documented 1573–99) found himself involved in litigation with the Benedictine monastery of Santi Severino e Sossio.[12] In April of the previous year he had been commissioned to paint an altarpiece for which the monks were now tired of waiting. He had been given eight months to finish it, together with a down payment of 15 ducats and exemption from rent on his lodgings, which were owned by the abbey. Despite constant assurances that the altarpiece would soon be completed, he had never finished it and, to add insult to injury, had been seen in his workshop at work on other altarpieces. In his defence, Tramontano produced a physician to testify to a period of five months' illness and asked to be allowed to complete the commission now that his health had returned.

The proceedings include testimonies from four artisans involved in the commission who were quick to distance themselves from any potential blame for the delay. First to testify were the master gilders, Giannantonio Millone, Nardo de Lanno and Cesare Villano. Tramontano had employed them to lay in the panel's gesso ground, but its size had caused them problems (with the frame fitted, it came to a massive 4.75 × 3.69 m). As such, it was too large to fit in Tramontano's workshop and had to be worked on further and dried out of doors. It had not dried properly because of the dampness of the winter weather ('li tempi non erano naturali per essere Inverno et et [*sic*] humido'), which resulted in their losing both time and money.

Next to testify was the master carpenter, Paolo Cimino.[13] He had been commissioned, by the monastery rather than by Tramontano, to prepare the altarpiece and to carve its frame. He had prepared the panel, but was unable to complete the work because it had been left in a cellar before it had dried properly, and needed to be exposed to the sun for several months and turned continuously before it could be worked on further. Cimino is not specific about what his work entailed, but his procedures can be readily determined from other documents. His first task would have been to cut the panel to the required dimensions. He may have been given only a few days to complete this, since a week was the timeline set on another occasion for him to cut a panel and to send it on to the painter, who would have been expected to have it gessoed by gilders.[14] Cimino would then have carved the surrounding frame while the painter was honouring his part of the contract. He would finally have had to return to the project in order to fit the frame to the painted panel in either the painter's workshop or his own.[15] (It was at this stage that he appears to have experienced difficulties.)[16]

The case constitutes one of the very few instances in which the involvement of artisans in painting commissions is discussed, and these are the only Neapolitan documents known to the author in which Baroque artisans speak directly of their relations with painters. (None could write with confidence and Cimino could not sign his name.) They demonstrate that the production of Tramontano's altarpiece was a complicated, labour-intensive task involving three different specialists engaged in a complicated working quadrille that involved their intersecting on at least five stages of production. First, the carpenter prepared the panel that the gilders then gessoed. Next, the painter painted the altarpiece. Then the carpenter returned to fit the frame, and only then could the gilder return to gild its surfaces. When one worker failed to honour the contract, his co-workers on the commission were all directly affected.

In fact, in terms of division of labour and subcontracted payment, Tramontano's altarpiece constitutes one of the least-involved types of painting commission then in existence in Naples. Religious institutions sometimes took it upon themselves to hire and supervise the carvers and gilders of altarpieces, as the monks of Santi Severino e Sossio seem wisely to have decided in the case of Tramontano's altarpiece.[17] They just as often nevertheless delegated responsibility for the entire commission to the painter, including the frame.[18] It was even more common for private patrons to expect the painter to oversee all stages of production. As the other payments to Cimino attest, this added considerably to the artists' workloads. Tramontano and his colleagues would thus have been responsible not only for preparing and painting the panel but also for having it carved, for designing the frame, and for employing competent carpenters and gilders to carry out the work.[19]

This added complication of time and expense must have cut considerably into all these artists' earnings. The cost of framing and gilding an altarpiece was, after all, not inconsiderable and could in fact exceed the prices outlaid for the paintings themselves. In 1588, for example, one of Santafede's patrons paid 68 ducats out of his own pocket for the frame of an altarpiece that he was just then working on before paying an additional 115 ducats for its gilding and ultramarine.[20] The documentation for Santafede's part of the commission is lost in this instance, but during this period it is unlikely to have exceeded his upper limit of 60 ducats. The frame for Santafede's altarpiece would probably have thus cost more than three times the painting itself. For fresco contracts and large-scale decorative ensembles, of course, the division of labour and mode of payment could be still more complicated, as will be seen, with the addition of stucco workers, assistant frescoists and specialists to fresco the landscape and *grotteschi*. With very few exceptions, in the context of public commissions, these costs were all incurred by the painter.[21]

THE ARTISTS' QUARTER AND FAMILY CONNECTIONS

The deep and widespread associations between painters and artisans during this period grew naturally out of the close-knit Neapolitan artistic communities of the day. The Neapolitan professions each had their own district. A high proportion of painters, sculptors, carvers and gilders all lived together in the area around the Palazzo Gravina, illustrated in the *veduta* of the 1620s or 1630s (see fig. 70). This neighbourhood, centred on the Piazza della Carità and made up of lands traditionally held by the duca di Monteleone and the nearby monastery of Monteoliveto, was known as the Quartiere della Carità. It was a prime district of commerce – and thus also of art dealing – since it was situated between the seats of government, the court and the Spanish residents who represented the state. It also connected with the Via Toledo, a long, straight street created by vice-regal decree in the 1530s to facilitate expansion towards the port and still today one of the city's principal thoroughfares. Artists and artisans alike thronged here and in the adjoining *quartiere* of Spirito Santo.[22] Prota Giurleo accordingly describes this district as a veritable beehive of artists. Almost all the best-known painters of Naples (and many more besides) lived in the area down through the generations.

From the opening decades of the seventeenth century the district was thus home to the leading painter Fabrizio Santafede, together with dozens more painters, both established and aspiring alike. These included such well-known specialists in the devotional *cona* industry as Teodoro d'Errico, Loise Rodriguez, Cornelis Smet and Wensel Cobergher, as well as slightly less prominent artists such as Tommaso de Rosa, Giovanni Antonio Ardito, Loys Croys, Jacob Isaacsz. van Swanenburgh, Antonio Giusto, Matteo Cafaro, Domenico and Vito Greco, and Sebastiano Sellitto. From the next generation of early Neapolitan followers of Caravaggio, Carlo Sellitto is also encountered living here, together with Giovanni Battista Caracciolo, Giovanni Bernardino Azzolino and Filippo Vitale, as well as the sculptor Pietro Bernini. From the next generation of those painters active during the peak years of the 1630s and 1640s are also found the young Salvator Rosa, together with Juan Do, Bartolomeo Passante, Massimo Stanzione, Bernardo Cavallino, Agostino Beltrano, Diana de Rosa, Pacecco de Rosa, Giacomo Recco and Viviano Codazzi (the last of whom had moved to Naples from Rome).[23] Those painters, particularly foreigners, who were not able to find lodgings in the district formed a second colony outside the Porta Reale at the end of Via Toledo.[24]

Living and working in such close daily proximity naturally encouraged these artists to seek to strengthen their pre-existing professional associations via the common practice of intermarriage. In this clannish and tightly interconnected world, in fact, one soon finds that any given artist was likely to be related in some way or other to many of his or her contemporaries. Tracing the threads of any one of these personal-professional webs will accordingly involve the researcher in unravelling a mass of interconnections with other interlinked family histories. One instance should suffice to illustrate this common trend.

In 1597 the painter Tommaso de Rosa married Caterina de Mauro, sister of the painters Marcello and Cesare de Mauro. With this marriage Tommaso formalized his partnership within the De Mauro family business, and he worked alongside his brothers-in-law from that point onwards. In 1626 Tommaso's and Caterina's younger daughter, Grazia, in her turn married Ribera's pupil, Juan Do, with Ribera and Caracciolo serving as co-witnesses to the marriage. (Ten years earlier Ribera had himself married Caterina Azzolino, daughter of the painter Giovanni Bernardino Azzolino.) In this same year of 1626 Tommaso's and Caterina's eldest daughter, Diana (aka Annella), also married another young painter named Agostino Beltrano. Unusually for the time, both the bride and the groom were aspiring painters. Beltrano was cousin to Andrea Vaccaro, a follower of Caravaggio who went on to compete with Luca Giordano in a significant public commission during the early 1660s, and he himself would go on to work under Stanzione during the 1640s and 1650s. For her part, Diana also became an accomplished, if today frustratingly obscure painter, who also worked for a period in Stanzione's studio prior to her early death in 1643. Finally, Caterina's and Tommaso's only son, Francesco de Rosa, would also later become one of Stanzione's most able pupils under the better-known epithet of Pacecco de Rosa.

In 1610 Tommaso de Rosa died prematurely, aged forty. His widow waited two years before remarrying, aged thirty, this time to the early Neapolitan Caravaggesque painter Filippo Vitale, who was five or so years her junior. Vitale was then attached to the workshop of Carlo Sellitto just down the road, and this association must have been one of the principal attractions of the marriage, at least in terms of its potential to provide further stability and consolidation for both Caterina de Rosa herself as well as to the De Mauro-De Rosa family's fortunes more generally. Tommaso de Rosa seems to have been a reasonably successful painter, notwithstanding the fact that his one known work today has been characterized as 'prosaic ... unconvincing' and representative of 'an artist of not exceptional talent working in the late Mannerist tradition which extended well into the seventeenth century in Naples'.[25] While Caterina presumably would not have seen things this way, Vitale was nevertheless certainly well placed in terms of his future prospects, since Sellitto was then the leading painter of the new Caravaggesque style (fig. 6), a field that he led until his own early death in 1614; this was followed soon thereafter by Ribera's eclipsing of the Neapolitan Caravaggesque field following his arrival in the city in 1616. Vitale would likewise go on to become one of the leading Caravaggesque painters in the years following Sellitto's death (fig. 7), until he too was progressively edged out of the field of principal painters of the city following the ascendancy of Ribera and Stanzione from the 1620s.

With this marriage Vitale also became stepfather to Caterina's children, among them Diana and Francesco de Rosa (then aged eleven and six, respectively), who thus now had two artist father figures to follow in their vocations. The marriage produced further offspring and further matrimonial alliances in turn. In 1639 Caterina's and Filippo's only

6 Carlo Sellitto, *St Cecilia*, 1613. Oil on canvas, 245 × 184 cm. Museo e Gallerie Nazionali di Capodimonte, Naples

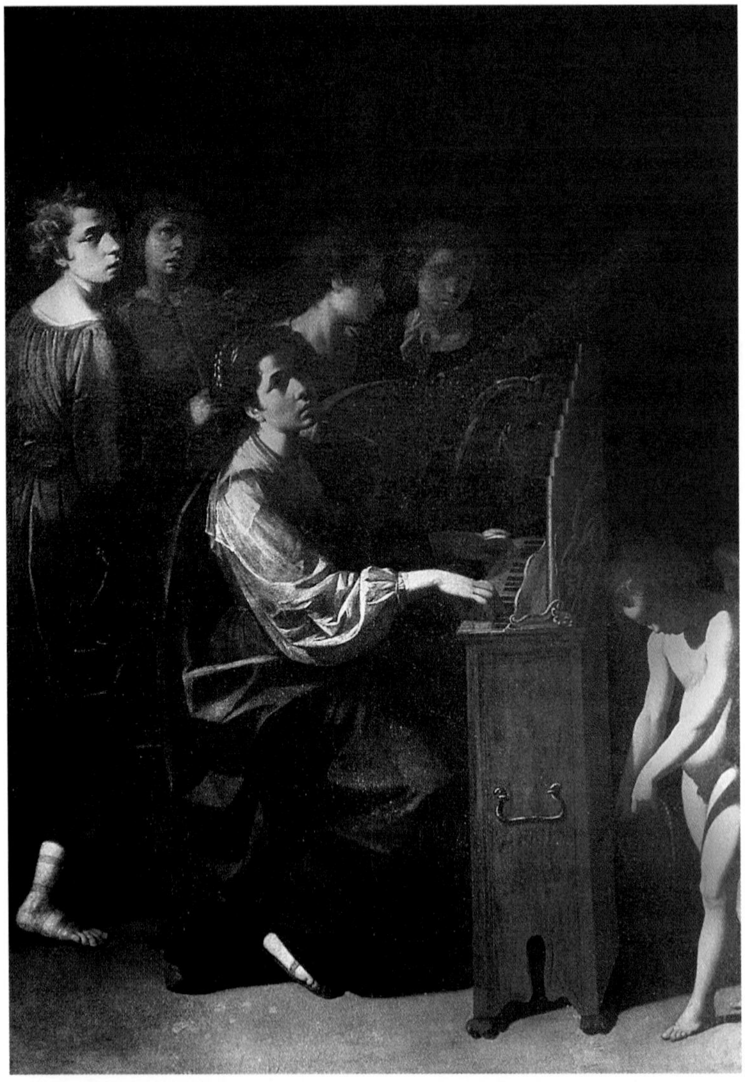

daughter, Orsola, married Aniello Falcone, who was just then instigating one of the earliest private life drawing academies in Naples. Twelve years later Aniello Falcone's sister, Candida, married Onofrio de Leone, himself a painter and also brother to one of Falcone's most gifted pupils, Andrea de Leone. Finally, in 1661, Grazia de Rosa's and Juan Do's eldest daughter Anna married the sculptor Michele Perrone. Towards the end of the seventeenth century the daughters of Anna Perrone (née Do) in turn married the painters Paolo de Matteis and Giovanni Battista Lama. Thus an intertwined network of business and family connections had been sustained over a period of four generations.[26]

The decision to send children into apprenticeships was also undertaken with equally tightly drawn family considerations in mind. Prior to their marriage in 1626, both Diana de Rosa and Agostino Beltrano had been employed simultaneously by another painter named Gaspare de Popolo. Beltrano, then aged fourteen, had undertaken a straightforward apprenticeship in which De Popolo had agreed to teach him the essentials of painting in return for his labour. Diana de Rosa, on the other hand, was then aged eighteen and so had already received some form of training in her stepfather's workshop. She accordingly entered into a more advanced, junior assistant's contract with De Popolo, who agreed to pay her 50 ducats per year as a result.[27] This contract must have been predetermined on Diana de Rosa's part a long time earlier, since Gaspare de Popolo was none other than her uncle. In 1602 he had begun his career by serving, in his turn, as apprentice to Diana's father, Tommaso de Rosa. By 1610, aged nineteen, he had progressed in the family's confidence to the point of marrying Tommaso's sister-in-law (Diana's aunt, in other words), Isabella de Mauro, shortly before Tommaso's death later in the year.[28]

This complex web of long-standing familial and professional relations extended further to encompass the next stage of the careers of the children of Caterina de Mauro and Tommaso de Rosa/Filippo Vitale, together with that of their new family member, Agostino Beltrano. At some stage from the late 1630s to the early 1640s both Diana and Pacecco de Rosa, together with Agostino Beltrano, all made the decision to become junior assistants in the workshop of Massimo Stanzione.[29] Caterina and Filippo Vitale can only have approved of the prospect of their son-in-law and two children now progressing from their first relatively modest master's workshop to that of one the two leading painters of the day. This move must have appeared particularly propitious given that Stanzione was just then receiving considerable acclaim for his development of a more refined and

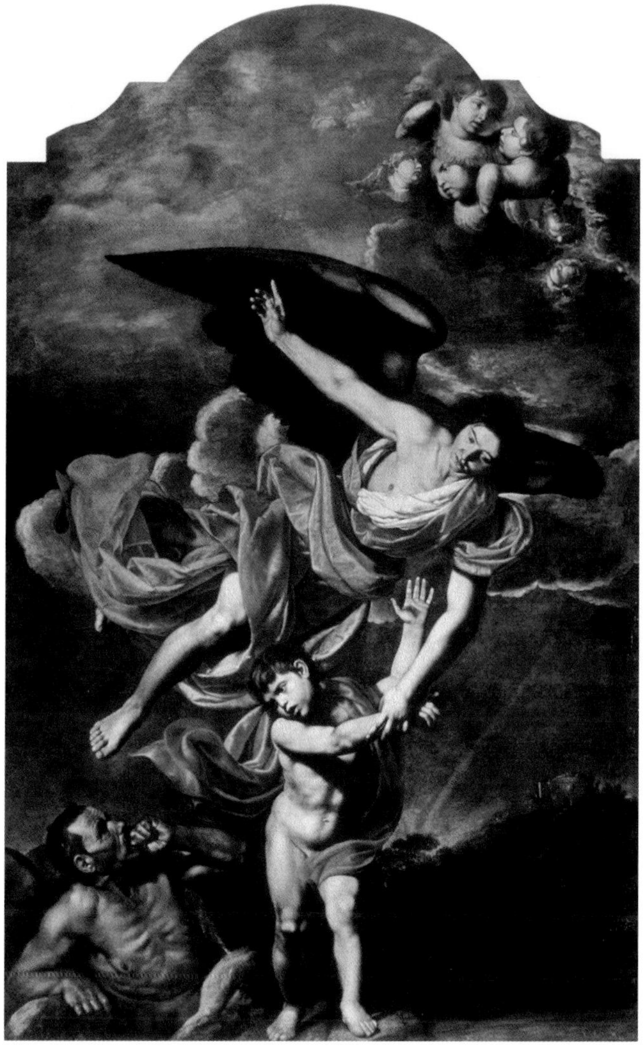

7 Filippo Vitale, *Guardian Angel*, *circa* 1612–13. Oil on canvas, 340 × 210 cm. Chiesa della Pietà dei Turchini, Naples

idealized version of Neapolitan Caravaggism, in tune with the emerging Neapolitan interest in Roman and Bolognese classicizing artists (fig. 8). But as with so much else in Neapolitan artistic practice, this step in their careers was also predetermined on the basis of long-standing personal affiliations. Stanzione had links back both to Gaspare de Popolo and to Caterina de Mauro's two brothers (and Gaspare de Popolo's brothers-in-law), Marcello and Cesare de Mauro. In 1615, six years before Diana de Rosa's and Agostino Beltrano's employment with De Popolo, he had already consented to act as godfather to Gaspare's and Isabella de Popolo née Mauro's first son. In 1620 and 1640 he also acted as godfather to Marcello and Cesare de Mauro's two sons. With this he thus became godfather not only to his two assistants' first master's son, but also to their two cousins!

DOWRIES AND ARTISTIC ALLIANCES

Through all this dense interlinking of the personal with the professional, the arrangement of marriages and the sometimes extremely complicated negotiations regarding dowries were regarded as pivotal and taken very seriously indeed. Orsola Vitale's dowry, for example, was the subject of seven years' protracted negotiations between Filippo Vitale and his relatives, on the one side, and the groom, Aniello Falcone, on the other. The negotiations involved Falcone and Vitale in drawing up a secret *albarano* on 1 May 1639 to replace the *capitoli matrimoniali* that were to be published the following day.[30]

The problems that could befall such negotiations also meant that arranged marriages could give rise to significant artistic tension. They certainly seem to have contributed to the breakdown of relations between the Carthusians of the Certosa di San Martino, then the city's most important public patrons of art, and the artist temporarily resident from Rome, Giovanni Lanfranco. In 1637 the Carthusians commissioned Lanfranco to produce a series of frescoes in the nave and presbytery of their church. The parties soon fell out, however, mainly over disagreements concerning Lanfranco's payments – a problem also experienced by many of the other artists employed by the Carthusians, as will be seen. Further exacerbating the situation, though, were issues of a more personal kind. In 1639 Lanfranco complained to his Roman patron that the monks of the Certosa were now ill disposed towards him because they had sided against his intentions by preferring to follow instead the wishes of a local architect and sculptor, Cosimo Fanzago. Fanzago was then the architect of the Certosa and he was also at that stage the city's most pre-eminent and influential artist-entrepreneur. Fanzago and the Carthusians wanted his son to marry Lanfranco's daughter, but Lanfranco had other ideas. He considered Fanzago's son to be 'troppo inferiore' and, in a decision that speaks volumes regarding his desire not to allow himself to become inextricably enmeshed within the local scene, had arranged instead to marry his daughter to the sculptor Giuliano Finelli, like him a foreigner who had also migrated from Rome to work in Naples.[31]

Although rarely commented on in the modern literature, the early eighteenth-century biographer Bernardo de' Dominici seems, therefore, to have been closer to the mark when he linked this marriage dispute with the eventual severing of Lanfranco's relations with the Carthusians via the flashpoint of a failed artistic commission.[32] This dis-

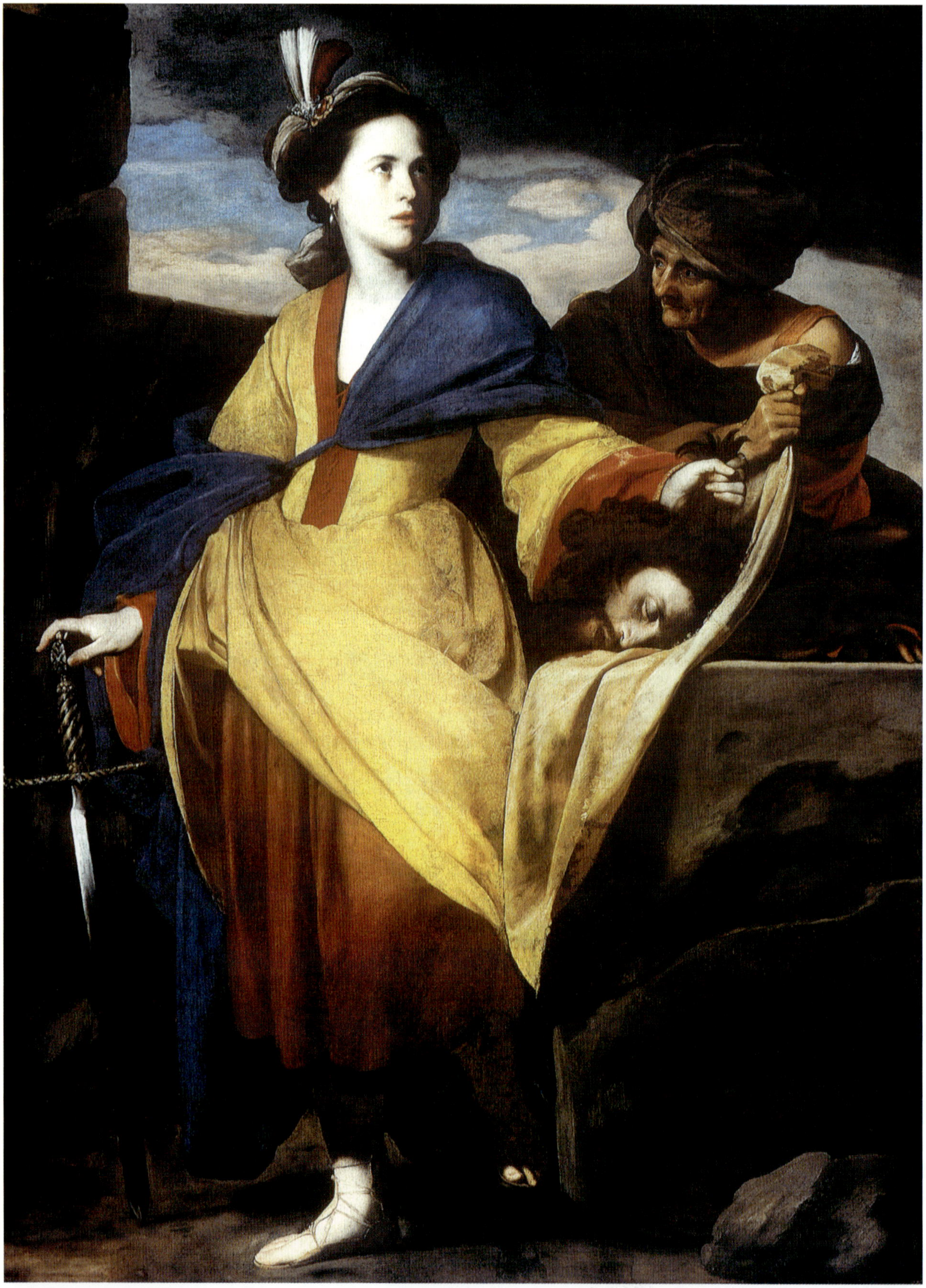

8 Massimo Stanzione, *Judith and Holofernes*, *circa* 1640. Oil on canvas, 199.4 × 146.1 cm. Metropolitan Museum of Art, New York

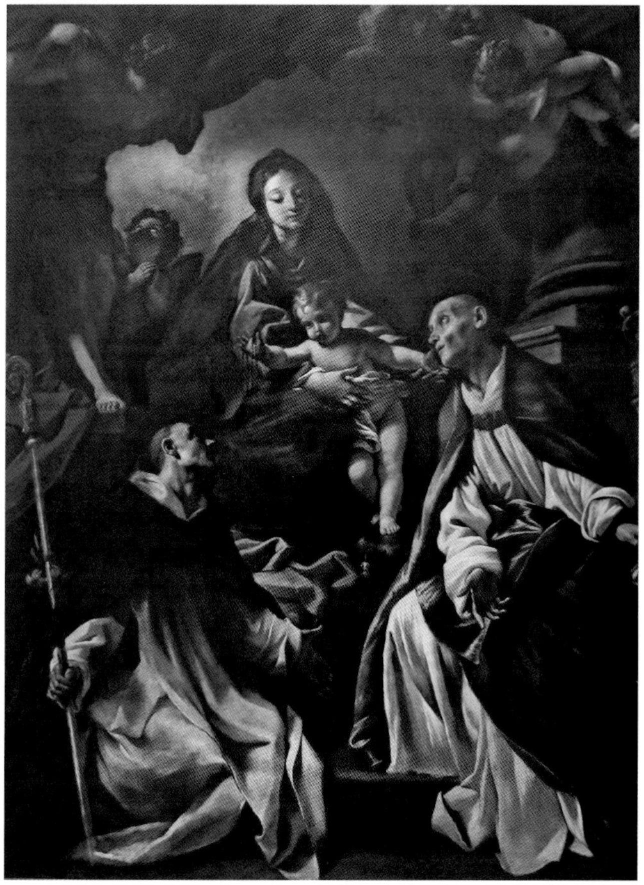

9 Giovanni Lanfranco, with subsequent additions by Luca Giordano, *Virgin and Child with Sts Dominic and Januarius* (originally *St Anselm of Canterbury and St Hugh of Lincoln*), *circa* 1638–44. Oil on canvas, 300 × 250 cm. Certosa di San Martino, Naples, on deposit from the Chiesa del Rosario, Afragola

puted commission was for one of Lanfranco's only Neapolitan altarpieces. No sooner was this completed than the Carthusians rejected it. Lanfranco's response was to make a statement of clannish allegiance: he repainted the saints in the altarpiece and donated it to the church of his 'own' nation, Sant'Anna dei Lombardi, the previously mentioned church in the heart of the artists' quarter, and one that contained important altarpieces by Caravaggio as well as by the local Caravaggesque practitioners Carlo Sellitto, Filippo Vitale and Caracciolo (fig. 9).[33]

Although accordingly Lanfranco may have exacerbated his problems with one of the city's most powerful artistic players and most important religious patrons, his desire to choose a groom for his daughter may nonetheless be considered sound, at least in professional and artistic terms. All that is heard of Fanzago's son, as it transpires, is his involvement in a brawl later in the century. Finelli, on the other hand, went on to become one of the leading Neapolitan sculptors of his day.[34] It was no doubt owing to his success that Finelli and his wife chose not to accompany Lanfranco in 1646 when he tired of the Neapolitan scene and elected to return to Rome for the final years of his career. They too, nonetheless, eventually succumbed to the expatriate's sense of displacement, and ultimately migrated back to Rome in 1651, only two years, as it transpired, prior to Finelli's death.

ARTISTS AS ARTISANS AND ARTISANS AS ARTISTS

Within such an interlinked artistic milieu, it was natural for early seventeenth-century Neapolitan painters to form close and long-standing professional and familial associations with artisans, particularly gilders and carpenters. These contacts can be seen frequently to have gone much deeper than the business dealings recorded in documents. A number of the more important Neapolitan painters of the seventeenth century were themselves sons of gilders. Filippo Vitale's father and two uncles were all gilders, for example, as was Carlo Sellitto's father, and so too was Agostino Beltrano's father, together with the father of Filippo Vitale's son-in-law, Aniello Falcone, who was also during the 1630s and 1640s one of the city's leading interpreters of contemporary trends in Roman and Bolognese classicism.[35]

Given that they lived in close proximity to each other, often worked together, and were commonly linked by long-standing family connections, it should thus also come as no surprise to find that a number of Neapolitan painters and artisans often shared work space. In the years prior to his marriage to Caterina de Mauro, for example, Tommaso de Rosa shared a workshop with the little-known painter and sometime gilder Giovanni Geronimo de Arena and with his brother, Matteo de Arena, who confined himself to gilding.[36] Sebastiano Sellitto's workshop was also close by, on Via Monteoliveto opposite the Palazzo Gravina. It bordered the workshop of the master carpenter Giovan Battista Vigliante (who is elsewhere documented carving a frame for one of Santafede's altarpieces).[37] When the occasion required, Sellitto collaborated with his neighbour Vigliante in the same way that Tramontano's disgruntled gilders shared their commission with Paolo Cimino.[38]

Within this environment of close working proximity it is also not uncommon to encounter artists and artisans swapping roles more fundamentally. Carlo Sellitto's father,

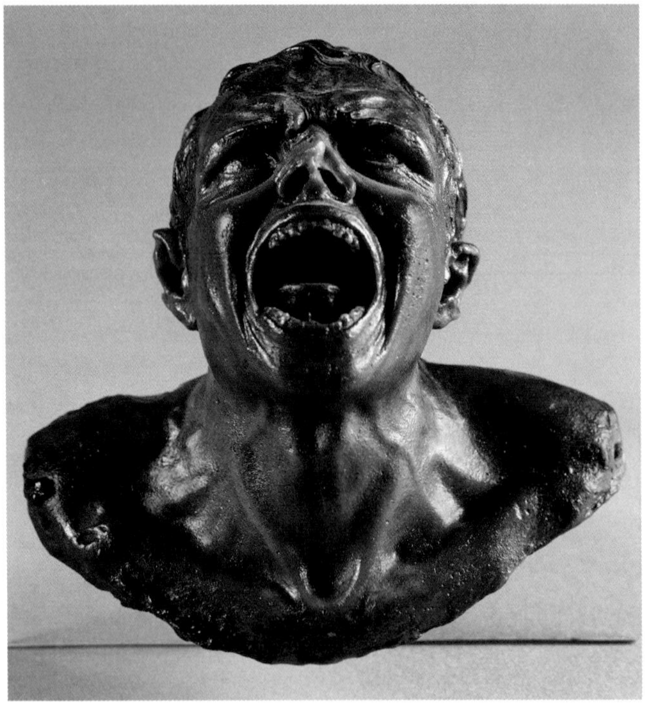

10 Giovanni Bernardino Azzolino, *Damned Soul*, 1610s–1620s. Polychrome wax, height 7 cm. Museo e Gallerie Nazionali di Capodimonte, Naples

Sebastiano, for example, is recorded in the documents as a 'pittore e indoratore'. This dual specialization enabled him to accept a commission to paint an altarpiece, in one instance, and then to gild one of Santafede's altarpieces, in another.[39] Giovanni Geronimo de Arena, for whom only one documented work exists, *St Charles Borromeo in Prayer* for the monastery of Monteoliveto,[40] is also documented earlier in his career as a gilder.[41] In the 1630s Aniello Falcone's colleague in his early life drawing academy, Honofrio Masturzo, was also both a gilder and painter, as were a number of Falcone's relatives.[42]

Just as there was no clear line drawn between artist and artisan, so too it was not unusual to find painters commonly undertaking work that today might be characterized anachronistically as artisanal, decorative, or somehow secondary to their major works. Besides painting altarpieces and gilding frames, Sebastiano Sellitto accordingly undertook, in 1584, to gild for the marchese di Laura a *travacca* (bed with baldacchino), 'excepting the little *putti* for which he will have to paint the skin tones'.[43] He was also happy to turn his hand to gilding a carriage when the opportunity presented itself.[44] In addition to his regular output as one of the leading early seventeenth-century specialists in altarpieces and devotional paintings, Loys Croys similarly painted coats of arms on standards and book miniatures.[45] Giovanni Bernardino Azzolino, Ribera's father-in-law and a highly regarded artist in his own right,[46] practised both as a painter and as a sculptor. His speciality appears to have been painted wax, stucco and relief sculpture (fig. 10).[47] In 1614, for example, he was paid for a relief sculpture of a *Crucifixion* and, in 1619, for 'tutta la pittura fatta a stucco' (all the painting made in stucco) for the Casa Professa of the Gesù.[48] Other commissions are known from the 1620s and 1640s.[49] Even the brilliant, albeit somewhat enigmatic, painter Giovanni Battista Spinelli seems to have worked on artisanal commissions on occasion. In 1607, for example, Lanfranco Massa paid him, perhaps on behalf of his master, Marcantonio Doria of Genoa, to make 150 gold rosaries.[50]

Artists combined their painting practices with these kinds of activities for the good reason that they wished to maintain viable and flourishing businesses. One should not, therefore, make the mistake of considering their works in these formats as being necessarily 'minor' in the sense of their being only small or cheap adjuncts to their careers. This is particularly clear for an artist like Onofrio de Leone, who was active during the 1630s and 1640s. In the early eighteenth century Bernardo de' Dominici dismissed this one-time assistant to Corenzio, and brother to the rather better-known battle painter Andrea de Leone, as 'not a painter of great worth'.[51] More recent analyses have not fundamentally challenged this interpretation (fig. 11).[52] But Onofrio de Leone was nonetheless proficient enough to be able to receive significant amounts of money for his creations.

In 1644, in fact, he is documented receiving no fewer than 612 ducats for his work. This constituted a princely sum, as will be discussed in Chapter Six. It was equivalent, for example, to three major gallery paintings by Ribera, Stanzione or any of the other leading figure painters of the day. De Leone's work, however, was for an altogether less 'princely' kind of product. He was, in actuality, paid for producing painted fans for export to Spain, and he must have made them in industrial quantities to command such fees. In 1643 he was paid 33.6 ducats for producing twenty-eight painted fans at a rate of 7 *carlini* (10 *carlini* making up a ducat) for each fan completed. On this basis, then, he would have had to produce no fewer than 800 fans to receive his payment in the next year.[53] Although there is no further documentation for this activity, one wonders, therefore, whether he might have subcontracted this work and thus have been receiving the money in his capacity as head of a workshop specializing in this kind of product.

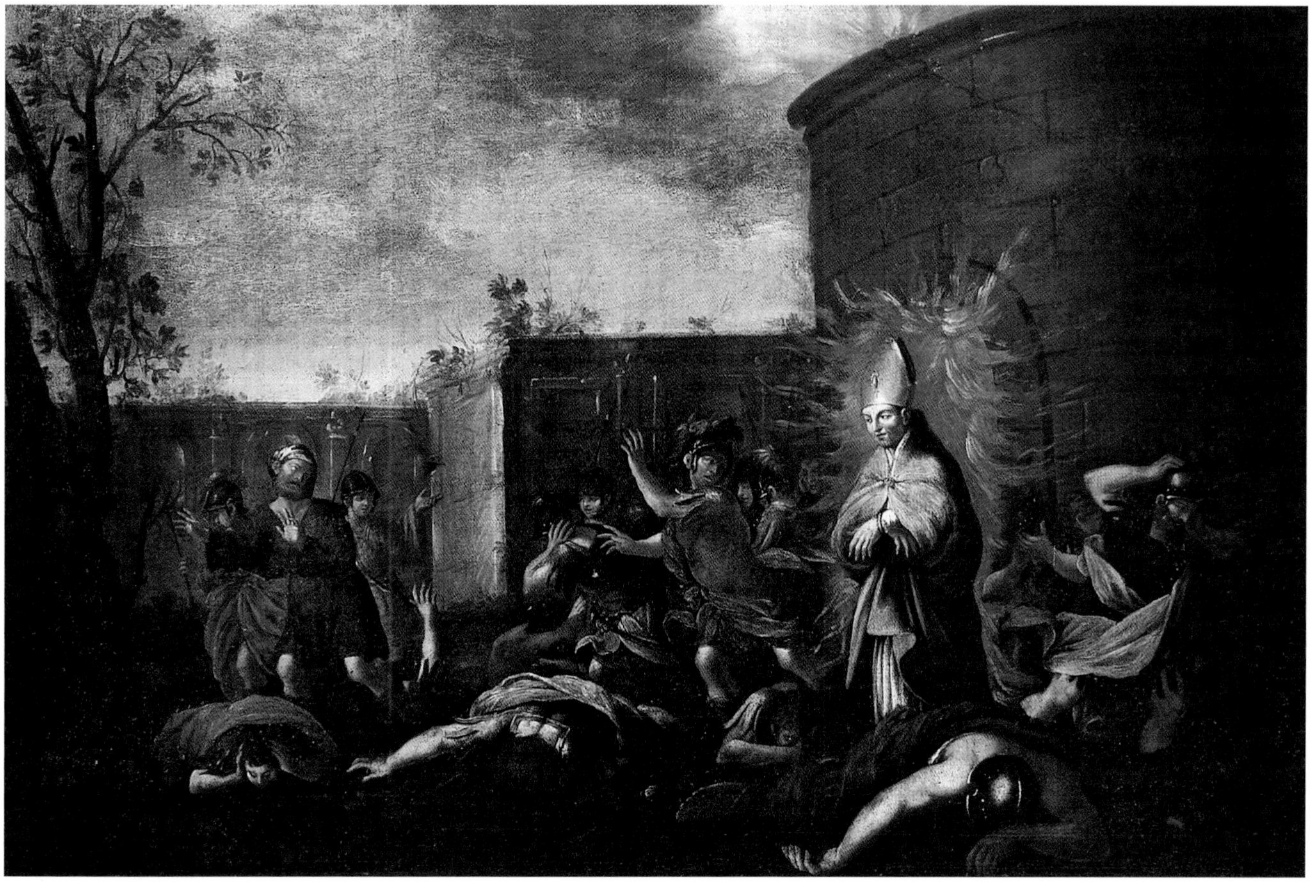

11 Onofrio de Leone, *St Januarius Emerging Unscathed from the Furnace*, *circa* 1642–5. Oil on canvas, 83 × 126 cm. Quadreria dei Girolamini, Naples

THE STATUS OF NEAPOLITAN PAINTING

When the clerk of the Vatican's Apostolic Chamber wrote in 1601 that 'Painting is a most noble profession, quite different from the mechanical crafts', he was restating a by then venerable central Italian tradition that identified painters as practitioners of a liberal art.[54] The line between artist and artisan, by contrast, was by no means as clearly drawn in early seventeenth-century Naples, as has been seen.

In addition to his workshop in Via Monteoliveto, Sebastiano Sellitto owned a residence at nearby Santa Maria Donnalbina. This indicates his attainment of an unusual degree of success and wealth. Fabrizio Santafede's much higher level of social and economic attainment is indicated by his collection of antiquities, which was said to be comparable in quality to those of the leading Neapolitan aristocratic collectors and antiquarians of the early seventeenth century.[55]

Santafede was very much the exception to the rule. His level of success and social advancement must have appeared spectacular compared to the vast majority of Neapolitan painters. Sellitto may have been fortunate enough to live separately from his work, but the plan of his workshop was in essence no different from that of any other Neapolitan artisan. Documents describe his workshop as 'consistente in una bottega con cantina e formale, e quattro appartamenti superiori' (consisting of a workshop with a cellar and formal area, and four rooms above). Such workshops were typical in Naples and are still to be seen there today. Although it does not specify the number of rooms, a document from his later years shows that Giovanni Battista Caracciolo lived and worked in quarters with essentially the same plan.[56]

Successful painters such as Sebastiano Sellitto could aspire to a marginally higher level of social and economic status than that of their craftsmen collaborators. Painters such as Decio Tramontano could further be addressed by the title *magnifico* rather than *maestro* used for artisans. Yet they remained locked into procedures that were little different from those of the artisans with whom they remained closely

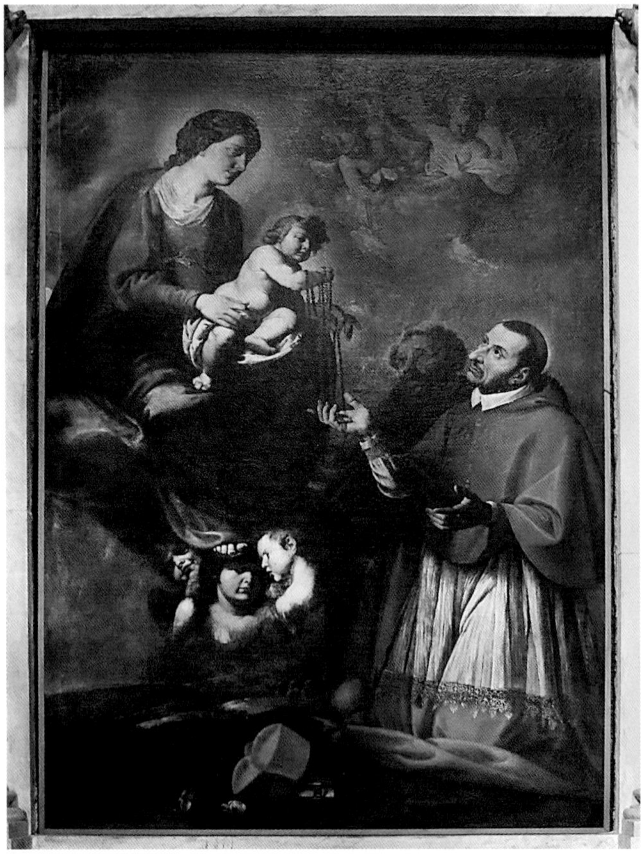

12 Filippo Vitale (and Pacecco de Rosa?), *Virgin and Child with Sts Dominic and Charles Borromeo*, 1640s. Oil on canvas, 200 × 170 cm. San Domenico Maggiore, Naples

associated. When Sebastiano Sellitto accepted the commission to gild and paint a bed with a baldacchino, he placed himself on the same level as the *trabaccari* whose workshops were concentrated not far distant from his in the Vicolo di San Giacomo. Gennaro Monte, one of the most successful silversmiths of the day, also lived in that street.[57]

The deep-seated connections between painting and the decorative arts were further formalized by the Neapolitan painters' professional association. Since 1521 painters had been grouped with gilders, playing card decorators, miniaturists and *rotellari* (either wheelwrights or painters of wheels)[58] in an association called the Corporazione dei Pittori. (Carpenters and other woodcarvers formed part of a separate guild, the Corporazione degli Scultori e Marmorari.)[59] This professional link between painters and gilders remained in place until 1650, when the demolition and restructuring of the Corporazione's oratory occasioned the gilders to strike out on their own. The Corporazione was then eventually reformed in 1664 as the Congregazione dei Pittori. It included the first 'public' Neapolitan life drawing academy and had the expressed aim (as related by De' Dominici in the early eighteenth century) of reinforcing the status of painting as 'la professione nobilissima' (a most noble profession).[60] Prior to this, and particularly during the first half of the seventeenth century, there was no such clear division between painting and the so-called decorative arts.

Neapolitan painters – and their colleagues in the related trades – were thus literally parochial, literally ghettoized and very tribal. They operated in a close-knit world that created strong links, together with efficient and closely related workshops. They also made it their business to look after their own. When viewing a late altarpiece by Filippo Vitale dating from the 1640s, for example, the observer may be struck by a certain stylistic disjunction that seems especially evident in the contrast between the harshly flattened *chiaroscuro* and gnarled, unidealized treatment of the face of St Charles Borromeo and the softer, lighter and more idealized treatment of the face of St Dominic (fig. 12). Here two divergent stylistic approaches appear to have been laid side by side – the one relatively harsh and unconstrainedly referring back to an earlier tradition of Neapolitan Caravaggesque realism, and the second containing the lessons of the more idealizing traditions of Stanzione and his ambience.

One answer to this stylistic conundrum – and one that has been reasonably proposed by Nicola Spinosa, Ferdinando Bologna and Stefano Causa – is that here the aged Vitale brought in his younger stepson Pacecco de Rosa to assist with the work.[61] If this were the case, then Vitale and De Rosa would only have been following the deep-set inclinations towards which all the interconnected relationships here outlined were directed. De Rosa was acting, in other words, in a similar way to that in which his uncle, Marcello de Mauro, had decades earlier stepped in to help complete the commissions already begun by his father, Tommaso de Rosa, following the latter's death.[62] Or how Filippo Vitale had himself stepped in to help complete work commenced by his earlier master, Carlo Sellitto, following Sellitto's premature death aged in his early thirties in 1614.[63]

This bedrock of physical proximity, inter-generational affiliation and artist to artisan linkage has significant implications for Neapolitan Baroque painting. It encouraged continuity and traditionalism even in a period of dynamic artistic change. It also enabled the development of interlocking constellations of tightly run and enormously productive artistic workshops. These workshops could be harshly resistant to the presence of outsiders, particularly when it came to famous Roman and Bolognese painters tempted to Naples by the lure of prestigious and well-paying commissions. Yet these artists could also be accommodating to those foreigners flexible enough to mould their practices and specializations to match the types of work that were not already so intensively covered – and coveted – by local artists and their cohorts. In so doing, though, the foreigners also learned to adapt their production to suit local exigencies. All this was undertaken within the dynamic field of Neapolitan workshop production, an area that will now be examined more directly.

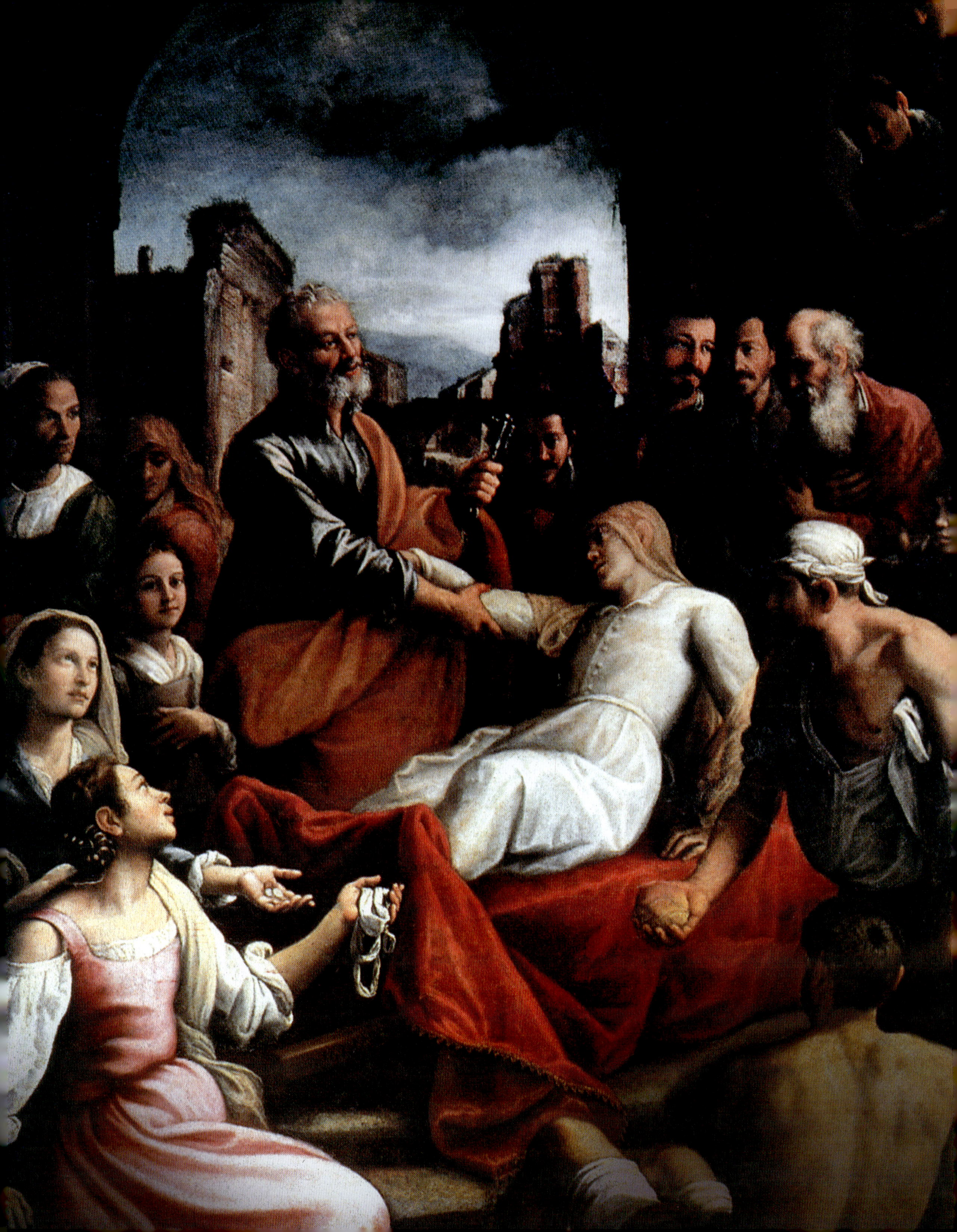

2

Altarpieces, Frescoes and the Larger Workshops 1580–1620

In 1608 the deputies of the Pio Monte della Misericordia turned their minds to the issue of who next to commission following the installation of their principal altarpiece painted by none other than Caravaggio in the previous months.[1] The catholic nature of their selections over the next few years suggests that, at this originary moment in the development of Neapolitan Caravaggism, these patrons at least did not feel the need to follow any clearly defined policy favouring either foreign artists or those working in a markedly contemporary style. Giovan Vincenzo Forlì and Fabrizio Santafede painted three of the remaining five altarpieces between them (figs 13, 98).[2] They were then nearing their sixties and were veterans of the tried and trusted, late Mannerist, Counter-Reformation-inspired style that was still dominant throughout southern Italy.

Carlo Sellitto (1581–1614), on the other hand, was half their age. An independent master from only the year before in 1608, he was just then developing the first Neapolitan response to Caravaggio's new style. When Sellitto nonetheless died before completing his work, the remaining two altarpieces were reassigned to the painter and sculptor Giovanni Bernardino Azzolino (soon to become Ribera's father-in-law), and to Giovanni Battista Caracciolo. Azzolino was then in his late thirties and was already demonstrating an impressive knack for bridging the tried and true formulae of late sixteenth-century artistic conventions with the new requirements of the Caravaggesque style. Caracciolo, on the other hand, was six years younger than Azzolino and, like Sellitto, had launched a career as an independent master only recently. His *Liberation of St Peter* of 1615, still *in situ* in the church of the Pio Monte della Misericordia, remains a fundamental document of this initial stage of Neapolitan Caravaggesque painting (fig. 14).[3]

Just around the corner from the Pio Monte della Misericordia there stands the cathedral of Naples. Here, during this same period, the deputies of the Cappella del Tesoro di San Gennaro likewise turned their attention to the matter of whom to commission for an extensive series of frescoes and altarpieces required for their recently completed treasury chapel dedicated to the city's principal patron saint. Their terms of reference for this prestigious commission, however, differed from those of their colleagues at the Pio Monte. In a letter of 1612 to the Spanish ambassador to the Holy See, the deputies made it quite clear that they did not want Neapolitans, 'for the scarcity that there is in this city of masters and artisans with the sufficient skills for a work of this quality'.[4]

The deliberations of the deputies of the Tesoro are routinely characterized as instances of an ingrained prejudice on the part of conservative and hidebound Neapolitan

Facing page Fabrizio Santafede, *The Raising of Tabitha*, 1611 (detail of fig. 13)

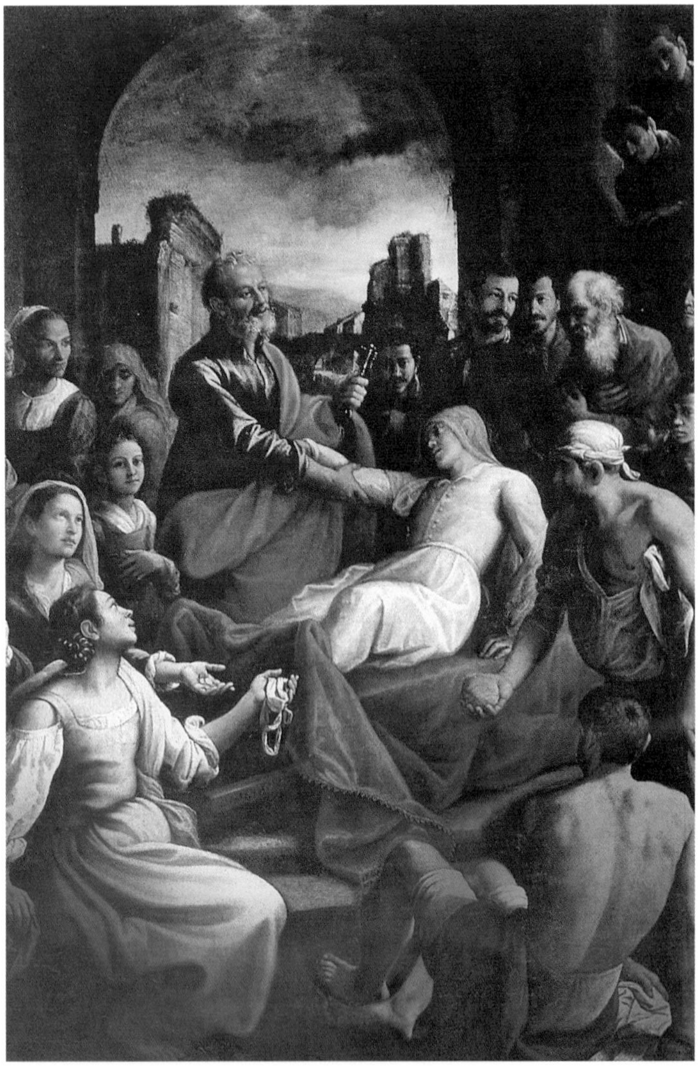

13 Fabrizio Santafede, *The Raising of Tabitha*, 1611. Oil on canvas, 306 × 205 cm. Chiesa del Pio Monte della Misericordia, Naples

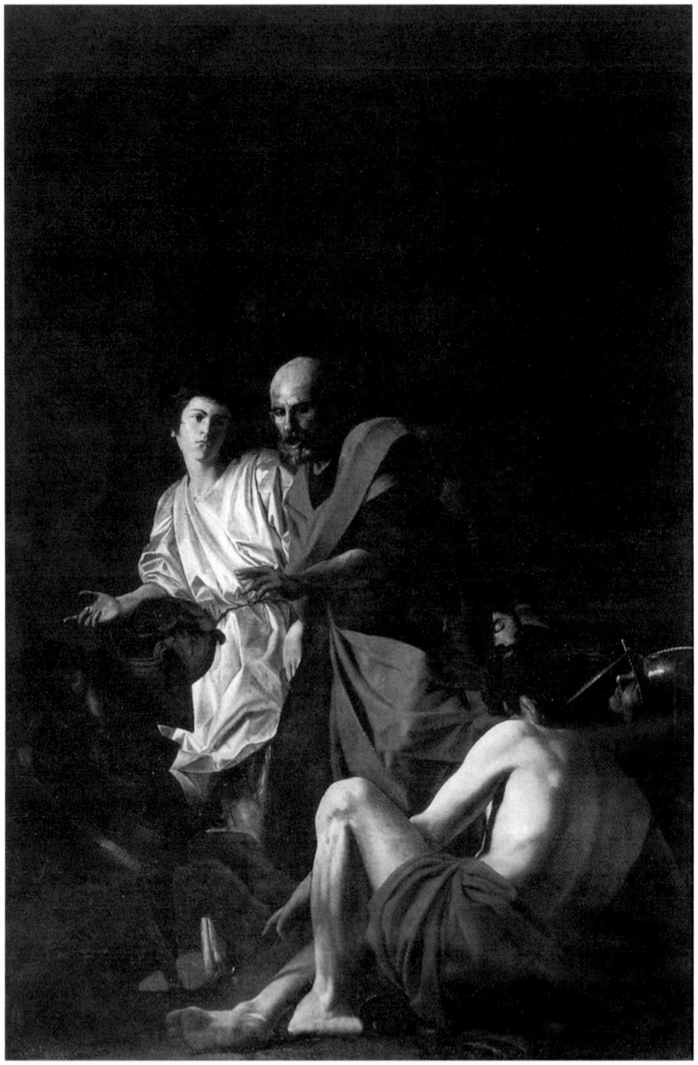

14 Giovanni Battista Caracciolo, *Liberation of St Peter*, 1615. Oil on canvas, 310 × 207 cm. Chiesa del Pio Monte della Misericordia, Naples

patrons against the manifest accomplishments of local painters.[5] In truth, however, the controversy created by the Tesoro commission was not so much the product of a deep-seated bias in Neapolitan patronage as a product of the particular course run by Neapolitan workshop traditions during the previous decades. In particular, it highlights the critical gap created by the lack of a strong local school of fresco painting. The power vacuum that this opened in the upper ranks of the Neapolitan art world would be exploited initially by those foreigners foolhardy (or uninformed) enough to accept the invitation to come to Naples. Ultimately, though, these challengers would be headed off by Massimo Stanzione's canny positioning of himself from the early 1630s onwards as the first viable Neapolitan practitioner of a new Baroque fresco style. At the same time, the decision at the Pio Monte della Misericordia to entrust altarpieces to younger painters such as Carlo Sellitto and Caracciolo, concurrently with work from older and better established artists, also raises the issue of just how Neapolitan artists of varying ages and artistic orientations might have been expected to progress through the ranks to being able to attract high-profile commissions for altarpieces such as these. It also questions on a wider level just how all these artists operated in relation to each other and how they divided the opportunities for work in the city between themselves.

EARLY BAROQUE PROLOGUE: THE *SOFFITTO CASSETTONATO*

To what extent was there an independent system in place for regulating the workings of the Neapolitan painting industry during this period? In principle, one might have envisaged a leading role for the professional association of the Corporazione dei Pittori in this respect. In reality, however, the opposite seems to have been the case, and the Corporazione appears to have functioned almost exclusively as a religious, social and charitable organization. Its statutes of 1562 and 1665 contain nothing in the way of professional stipulations, save for a single note in 1562 concerning the need for consuls (*consoles*) to donate to the Corporazione 2 per cent of their earnings made from appraising the works of other members (a similar arrangement, incidentally, as was set by the Accademia di San Luca in Rome).[6] The statutes limit themselves in all other respects to procedures for collecting dues and for maintaining the corporation's oratory (first at Sant'Agostino alla Zecca and then at the cloister of the Gesù Nuovo), together with the standard charitable functions and support to members in the form of visits to members in prison, burial services and dowries payable to daughters of impoverished members.[7]

This contrasts markedly with the statutes for related trades. Other Neapolitan corporations routinely required, for example, that those wishing to practise as masters should first be examined and 'approbati' (approved) by two elected consuls of the guild. Such was the case for the statutes of the Neapolitan embroiderers' guild of 1584,[8] the statutes of the Corporazione degli Architetti, Fabricatori, Pipernieri, Scarpellini e Tagliamonti of 1605,[9] and the statutes of the sculptors and marble workers of 1694 (the last stipulation having been expressly added to this guild's statutes after its omission from their earlier regulations of 1618).[10] The statutes of 1618 for the sculptors and marble workers also included prohibitions against masters taking on apprentices or assistants who were already employed by another master, and further identified that all arbitration disputes should be resolved by appraisals undertaken only by the guild's governors.[11] The guild laws of 1680 for the Neapolitan second-hand traders (the Corporazione di Rivenditori, who included art dealing in their concerns) are even more detailed. They contain injunctions concerning the need for prospective workshop heads not only to submit to an examination but also to provide accompanying documentation for their having served under a previous master. They also required foreigners wishing to operate in the city to submit to the same laws, and added stipulations concerning the number of workshops – and even the number and location of rooms – that *rivenditori* could lawfully maintain.[12]

In the absence of a comparable level of professional organization, it was thus left to the tightly knit world of the Neapolitan workshops to regulate itself. A vignette into the mutually sustaining accommodations routinely entered into as a result of this can be gained from the appraisal processes that were sometimes written into contracts as a requirement before final payment could be made. It is easy to see why these were never a standard feature of Neapolitan contracts. They would have added an extra layer of time, negotiation and financial uncertainty onto the proceedings for both the patron and the painter. Given further that painting sizes and subject matter were relatively standardized from an early date, it should not have been difficult in most instances for both parties to agree on a price at the beginning of the process rather than having to deal with the uncertainty of waiting until the end.

When valuations were nonetheless written into contracts they were generally done in the context of a recognition that both parties had already reached a rough estimate for the work. Thus, in 1602 Tommaso de Rosa (the first patriarch of the De Rosa-De Mauro artistic dynasty discussed in Chapter One) was paid 20 ducats on account for a privately commissioned painting, the final price for which was to be determined by a 'valuation carried out by two painters of his selection, which will not exceed the sum of around 50 ducats'.[13] Those patrons who did feel the need to bring in other painters to vet their contracts while they were still under way usually required them to act in a more generalized quality-control sense only. Thus in 1616 Andrea Genoino was paid 10 ducats towards an agreed total of 30 ducats for work that had to contain 'colori fini' and that was to be completed 'a lode di esperti' (so as to merit the praise of experts).[14]

The idea of an independent peer-review process governing the activities of Neapolitan painters (if this were ever contemplated) would have been almost impossible to implement, in any event, given the closely interconnected nature of the artists and their practices. In 1580, to take one documented example, the patrons of a parish church situated some 40 kilometres out of Naples contracted a local artist to authorize significant aspects of the commission on their behalf. Their caution is presumably attributable to their distance from Naples and relative unfamiliarity

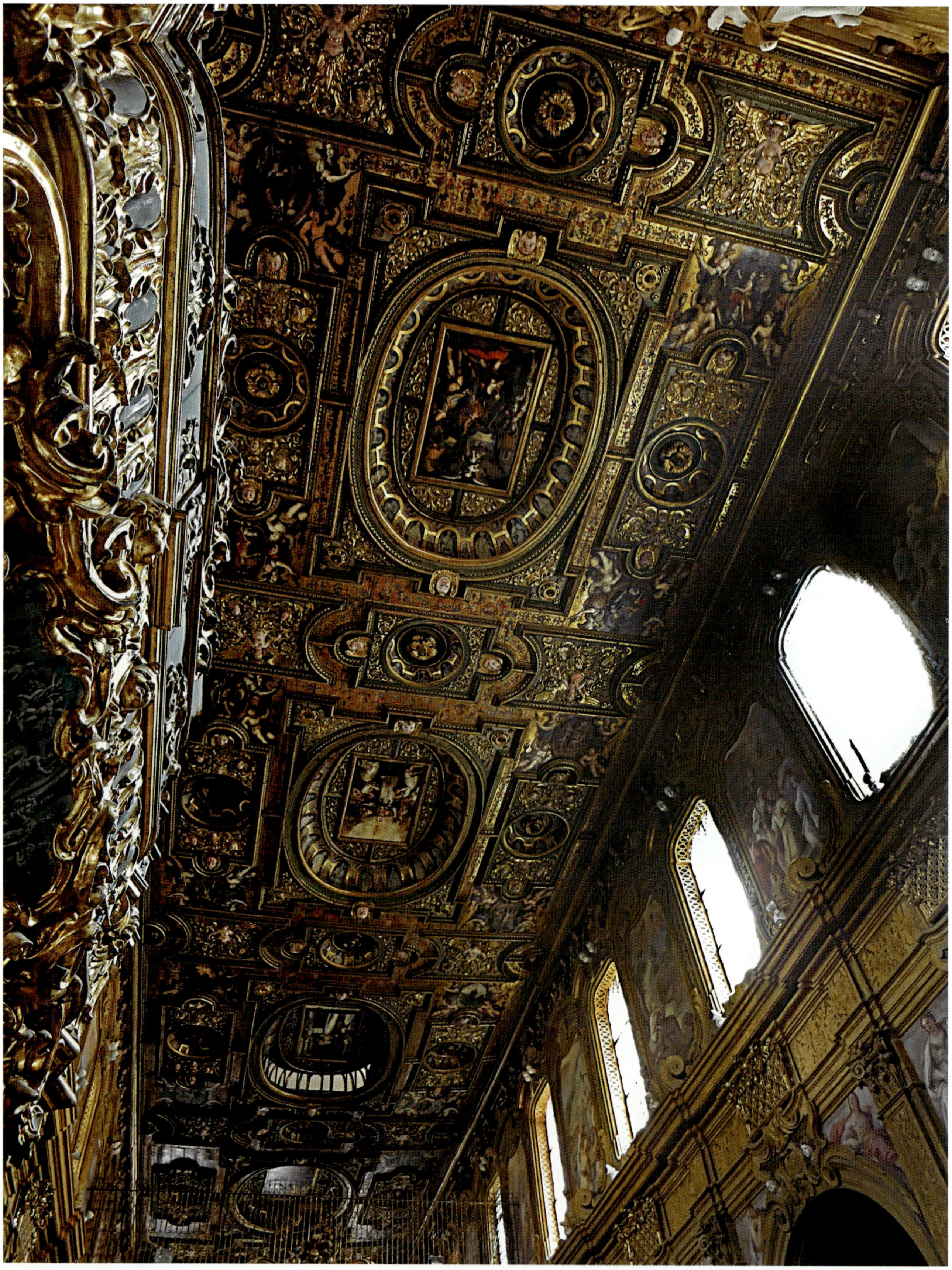

15 Dirck Hendricksz called Teodoro d'Errico, and workshop, *soffitto cassettonato* (nave ceiling), 1580–82. San Gregorio Armeno, Naples

with the art world as a result. So these patrons chose the painter and gilder Giovanni Andrea Magliuolo to liaise with the painter they had commissioned – a recently arrived Flemish resident in Naples, Dirck Hendricksz – and to vouchsafe the quality of his work before final payment could be made.[15] But if these patrons thought they were thus securing the services of an independent agent to look after their concerns they were almost certainly mistaken. In fact, Magliuolo was at that moment starting a very successful collaboration with this same artist. Hendricksz, better known by the Italianized form of Teodoro d'Errico, would work with Magliuolo over the next two decades at least. In 1594 he was elected alongside Magliuolo as one of the four consuls of the Corporazione dei Pittori (the other two being Forlì, author of one of the altarpieces at the Pio Monte della Misericordia, and a certain Cristiano de Noja).[16]

In between these moments, and starting from this very year of 1580, D'Errico set the seal on his career by embarking on a project to decorate the entire nave ceiling of the church of San Gregorio Armeno (fig. 15). This contract was almost certainly undertaken in partnership with Magliuolo, who seems to have used his background as a gilder and sometime goldsmith to design the elaborately carved and gilded ceiling into which the paintings were set. Carmela Vargas's research has underlined the probable importance in the patron's thinking of the richly ornamented gilded wooden reliquaries popular in Naples during that period as a prototype for this ceiling format.[17] Whatever the case, the commission inaugurated a trend for comparable works constructed over the next twenty years or so for most of the major nave projects. These included Santa Maria Donnaromita (1587–9), San Paolo Maggiore (1590–91, destroyed), the Chiesa dell'Annunziata (1592–4, destroyed), Santa Maria la Nova (1599–1602) (fig. 16), San Giovanni dei Fiorentini (1600–02, destroyed), and even the cathedral from as late as the early 1620s.[18] The longevity of this form of decoration is even evident as late as 1657–9, when it formed the basis for the elaborate ceiling of San Pietro a Maiella painted by Mattia Preti within frames designed by Fra Bonaventura Presti (figs 17–18).[19]

The *soffitto cassettonato*, as it came to be known, is paradigmatic of the collaborative nature of the larger turn-of-the-century projects. It was so large as naturally to require collaboration while at the same time it was easily subdivisible into individual panels that could be apportioned to a number of painters, worked on separately within each painter's workshop and then assembled on site into an integrated whole. This process can be documented in greater detail in the case of the Santa Maria Donnaromita ceiling, since it retains its accompanying account book itemizing all the work undertaken between 1587 and 1589.[20] From this one learns that Magliuolo was paid the high sum of 250 ducats 'for all the drawings that he has made and for his labour'. He accordingly seems to have acted as a kind of project manager responsible for designing the frame and then coordinating its construction and installation.[21]

Other payments indicate the apportioning of the painted components to Teodoro d'Errico and four other master painters. D'Errico was paid 150 ducats for the ceiling's three large central soffit paintings. Although this gave him the most prominent area of the ceiling to work on, it did

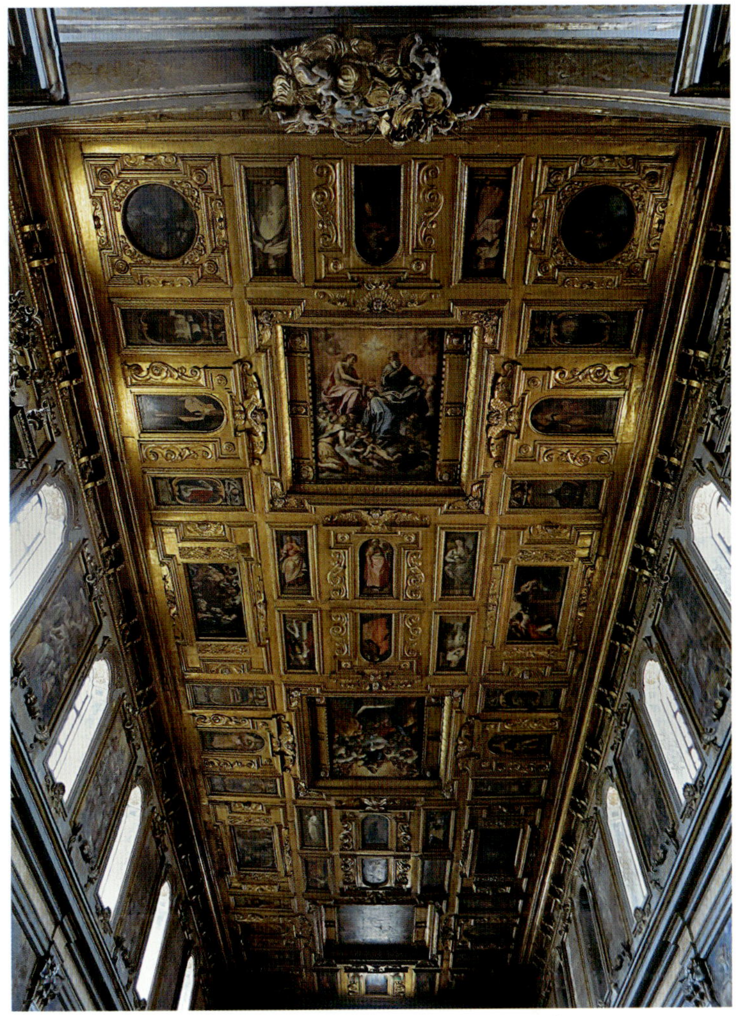

16 Dirck Hendricksz called Teodoro d'Errico, and workshop, *soffitto cassettonato* (nave ceiling), 1599–1602. Santa Maria la Nova, Naples

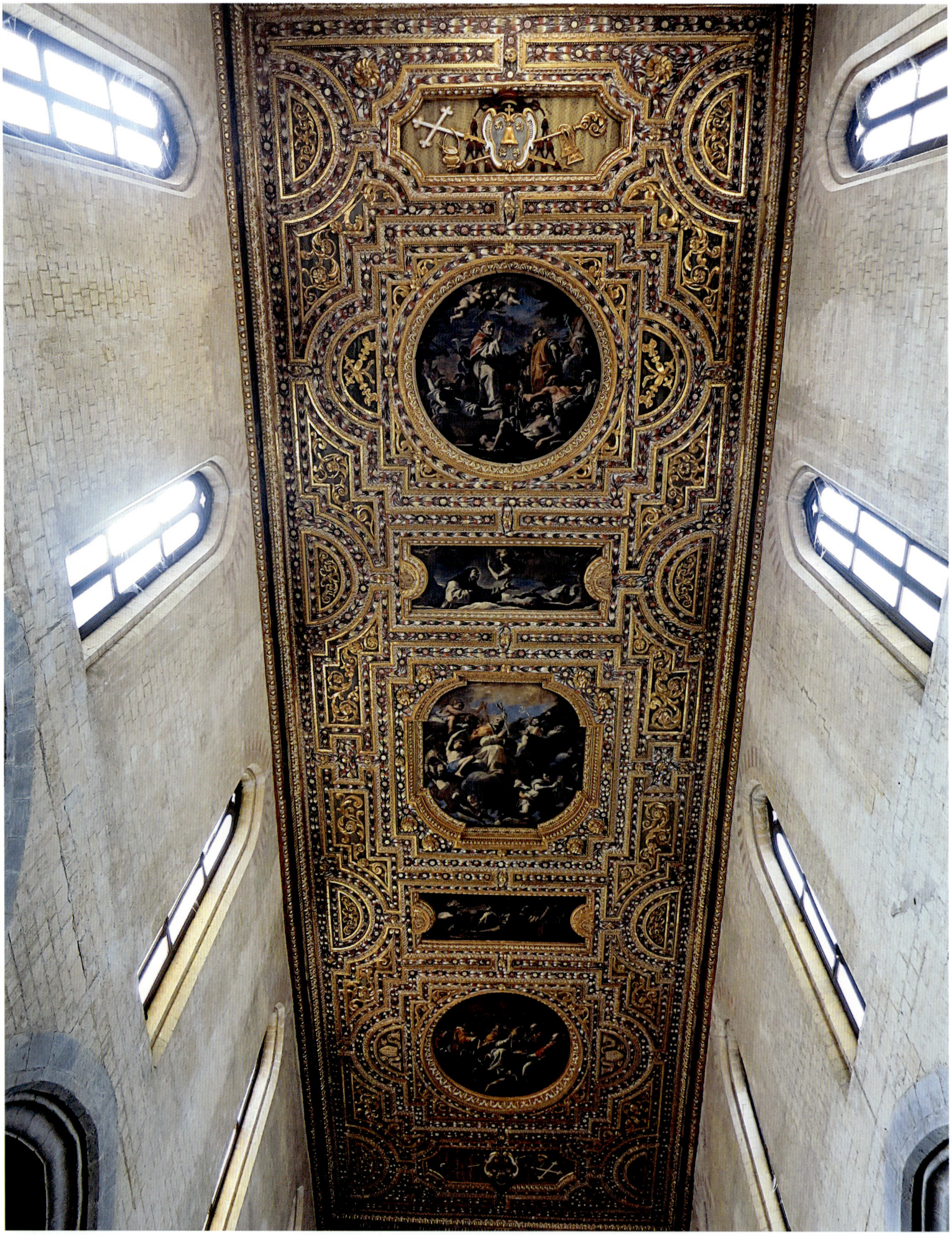

17 Mattia Preti, *soffitto cassettonato* (nave ceiling), 1657–9. San Pietro a Maiella, Naples

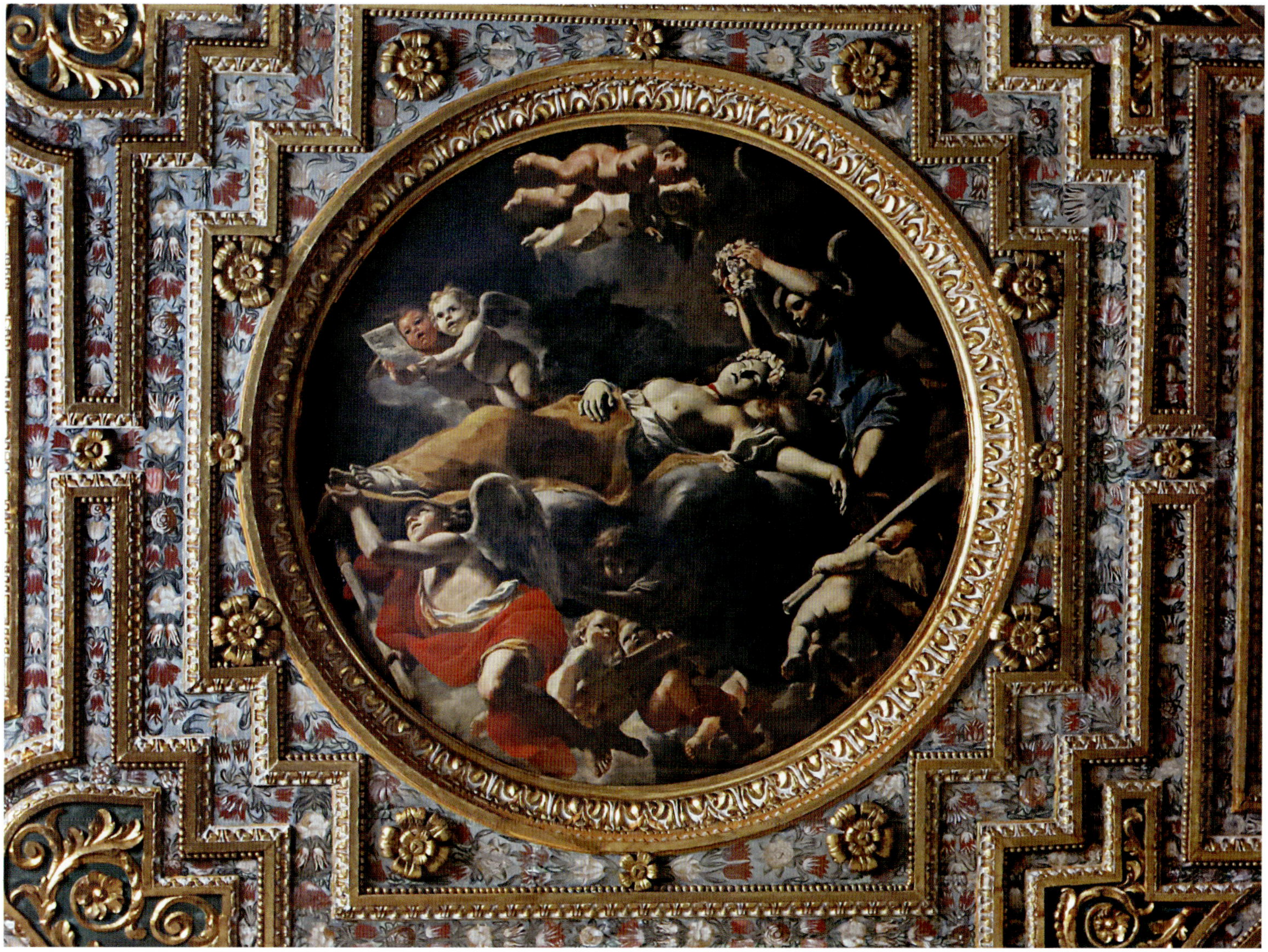

18 Mattia Preti, *soffitto cassettonato* (nave ceiling), 1657–9. San Pietro a Maiella, Naples

not necessarily mean that he was being recognized accordingly as the most senior painter of the consortium. Another painter, Girolamo Imparato, was paid 250 ducats to paint the eight slightly smaller square panels that still surround D'Errico's soffits, together with the high altarpiece for the sanctuary below the ceiling. Imparato had been receiving independent commissions for more than ten years prior to this date and was thus working as a fully matriculated independent painter cum co-partner in the enterprise rather than as a less-established junior assistant attached on a longer-term basis to D'Errico's workshop. A third component of the decoration was given to a certain 'pomponio pittore', probably a Northerner resident in the city, who was paid for the decorative friezes around and within the ceiling's frames. He too was probably also acting as a junior partner within the consortium rather than as an assistant to D'Errico, since he was paid directly by the abbess a comparable amount to that outlaid to D'Errico and Imparato. A fourth painter was paid in a similar manner for the dozens of heads of saints and *putti* around D'Errico's three soffits, together with eight 'istoriette' painted in the oval fields in the centre of Imparato's eight square panels.[22]

This joint-venture approach to managing the larger ecclesiastical projects provides one of the main reasons why Neapolitan painting remained at that stage a relatively diver-

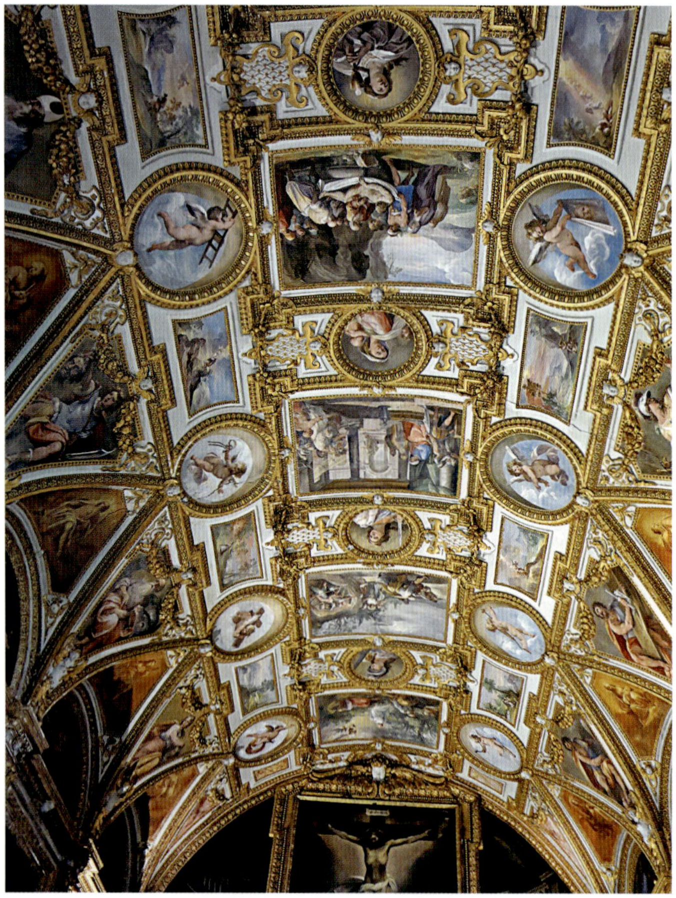

19 Cavalier d'Arpino, sacristy decoration, 1595–7. Fresco. Certosa di San Martino, Naples

sified field of comparable talents operating alongside one another. All this would change, eventually and as will be seen, with the greater stratification of the art world created by the consolidations of Ribera and Stanzione from the later 1620s onwards. Painters such as D'Errico, Azzolino, Santafede, Forlì, Francesco Curia and others of their ilk nonetheless each maintained their own successful outputs with no single artist dominating commissions and with the larger commissions tending to be subdivided between a number of painters acting in tandem. The space where one would imagine, on the other hand, a larger-scale, single-master-dominated approach to project management was in the area of fresco painting. But here again the relatively few frescoes commissioned in Naples during the late sixteenth century tended to mitigate against this, and the frescoes that were produced also operate according to a different set of criteria from those in Rome or Florence.

Frescoes were not, in fact, the norm in late sixteenth-century Naples and they would not come into prominence in Neapolitan church patronage until after the beginning of the seventeenth century. A significant exception was the important series of frescoes commissioned from the late 1580s onwards by the Carthusians of the Certosa di San Martino for their newly refurbished Gothic church overlooking the Bay of Naples, to be discussed in Chapter Eight. Any patron seeking major fresco specialists in the late 1580s would have been hard pressed to identify a Neapolitan painter versed enough in the idiom to compete for the commission. So the Carthusians looked to Rome, eventually enticing the young Cavalier d'Arpino (1568–1640) to work in the city on two sets of frescoes, in the choir of the church (from 1589–91) and then the sacristy (1595–7) (fig. 19).[23] D'Arpino was accompanied by his younger brother, Bernardino, who worked on frescoes in the passageway leading to the Sala Capitolare (chapter house) around the same time (1592–3).[24]

The form of these frescoes differs significantly in certain respects from projects undertaken by D'Arpino back in Rome during the same period. Like other Neapolitan frescoes, an emphatic armature of stucco bands and frames bisects the painted field into a series of separate *quadri riportati* (frescoes painted so as to resemble framed paintings inserted into the ceiling). These discreet fields are accordingly surrounded by richly moulded and gilded entablatures, almost to the point of being overwhelmed (from the point of view of more modern sensibilities at least). The result is a highly decorative, flattened surface effect that eschews the more unified and illusionistic painterly emphasis found in the painted frames and other architectural elements deployed concurrently by D'Arpino in Rome in the Olgiati chapel in Santa Prassede (1587–95) and in the wall frescoes of the Palazzo dei Conservatori (from 1595 onwards).

In Naples, richly stuccoed vaults continued to dominate the increasing number of ecclesiastical fresco commissions encountered in the opening decades of the seventeenth century. The Certosa di San Martino, for example, contains a series of stuccoed chapels dating well into the 1630s with fresco schemes by Giovanni Battista Caracciolo (the chapels of the Assumption and of St Januarius of 1631–2 and 1632–4, respectively), and Paolo Finoglio (chapel of St Martin, 1630–31) (fig. 20). The first Neapolitan to depart from this by now ingrained local tradition was, significantly enough, Massimo Stanzione. From 1630 he developed a more 'modern' unified pictorial field – minus the bisecting stucco frames – for his frescoes in the chapel of St Bruno at the Certosa (1630–37) (fig. 21) and again in the chapel of St John the Baptist (1642–56), as will be seen.

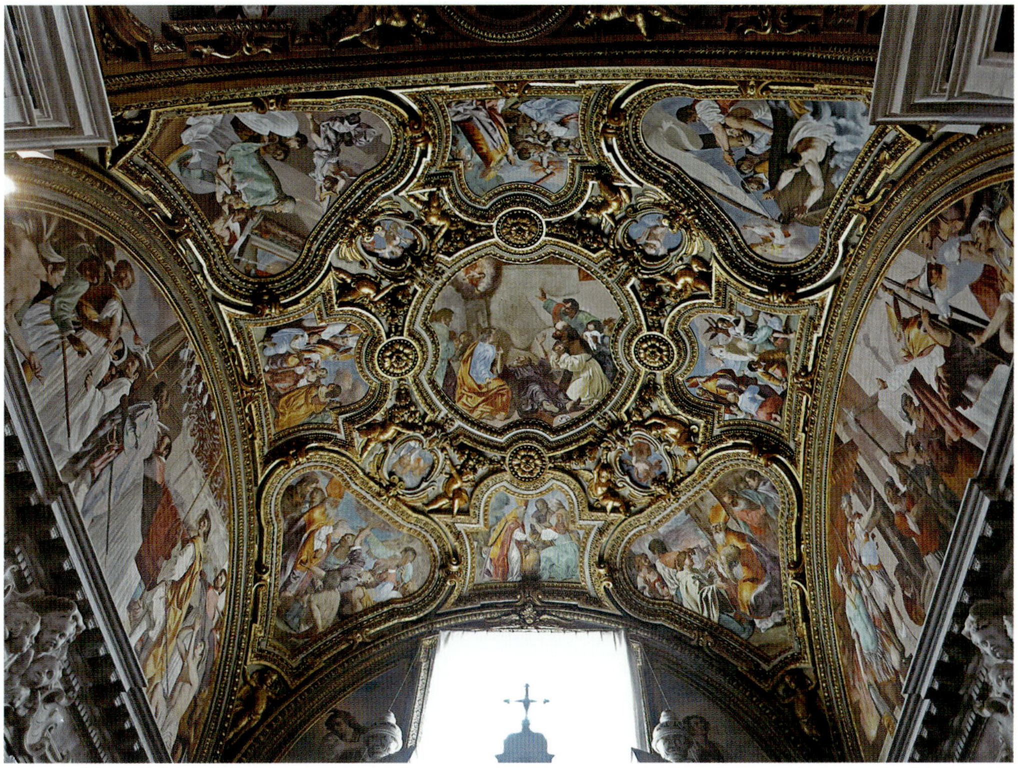

20 Paolo Finoglio, *Scenes from the Life of St Martin*, 1630–31. Fresco. Cappella di San Martino, Certosa di San Martino, Naples

21 Massimo Stanzione, Cappella di San Bruno, 1630–37. Fresco. Certosa di San Martino, Naples

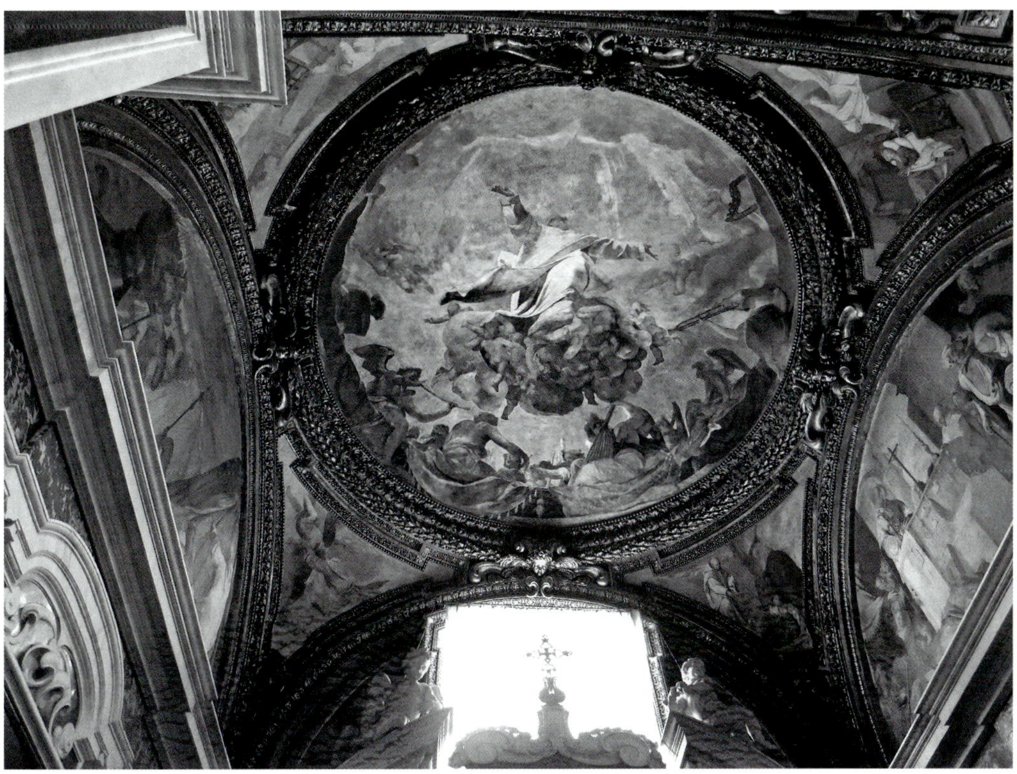

Back at the end of the sixteenth century, however, the heavily stuccoed frescoed vault was very much the norm, making these ceilings the equivalent, in visual terms, to the richly decorative effect achieved by the elaborate wooden constructions of the *soffitto cassettonato*. As a result, these frescoes also lent themselves to a similarly compartmentalized, collaborative approach to production. This can be seen particularly in the work of Belisario Corenzio (1558–1646), who probably learned fresco via an association with the workshop of D'Arpino in either Rome or Naples, although this is not documented.[25] From 1590 onwards Corenzio capitalized on the gap in local fresco production to become the pre-eminent Neapolitan frescoist of his generation (see Table 5 for examples). Occasionally, the documents register Corenzio acting in partnership with one of his colleagues in a joint fresco venture. This was the case, for example, in 1598, when he received payments for a series of frescoes in the church of the Annunziata in partnership with Avanzino Nucci, whom Corenzio identifies as 'Nucci Avanzino mio compagno'.[26]

More commonly, though, Corenzio used his evident logistical and administrative skills to assume responsibility for the entire commission and then to apportion work for frescoes among a series of specialists – often Flemish artists – brought in specially for the task. In 1609, for example, he was commissioned to paint an extensive series of frescoes in the monastery of Santi Severino e Sossio (the institution encountered in the litigation documents with Decio Tramontano, discussed in Chapter One). The contract stipulates that the frescoes must be by Corenzio's hand alone, with the sole exception that 'Belisario can arrange for others to execute only the friezes, landscapes and [architectural] perspective'.[27]

The division of labour permitted by this wording can be seen clearly in the frescoes in the Sala del Catasto Onciario (fig. 22). Corenzio's large figures dominate the three main ceiling compartments, the areas between and around the lunettes above the windows. The compartments are surrounded by elaborate borders (the 'frisi' referred to in the contract), which are filled with small grotesques. These were probably also painted by Northerners, perhaps by an artist like the 'Pomponio pittore' responsible for the decorative friezes at San Gregorio Armeno, since *grotteschi* were another Flemish specialization during this period.[28] One of the three main figure scenes on the ceiling, depicting the *Parable of the Mote and the Beam*, includes a prominent Paul Bril-inspired landscape that Corenzio would have also delegated to a Northern specialist.[29] Two smaller compartments on either side of the central scene depict similar landscapes with small figures that would probably have been executed by assistants in their entirety.

Two of the three ceiling frescoes, *Christ and the Woman Taken in Adultery* and the *Healing of the Paralytic*, also include prominent architectural backgrounds (the 'prospettiva' mentioned in the contract). Corenzio probably hired another Northern specialist for this task, since from the early eighteenth century onwards Corenzio was also identified as one of the first to contribute figures to architectural view paintings of these kinds. Chief among the candidates for his collaborators are the important, albeit somewhat enigmatic, painter of fantastic architectural scenes, François de Nomé, and the somewhat more conventional architectural view painter Didier Barra, who is probably identifiable with the 'Monsù Desiderio' mentioned by De' Dominici as a sometime collaborator of Corenzio.[30] In a similar vein, but under slightly different circumstances, another early Northern landscape specialist, Pietro Menens, was commissioned in 1594 to fresco landscapes and decorative borders for the monastery of Sant'Andrea delle Dame. The figures were to be painted by Corenzio at Menens's expense.[31] Although undocumented, the comparable landscapes in San Lorenzo Maggiore and the cloister of Santa Maria del Carmine were also probably by Northern specialists working under Corenzio's supervision.[32]

In 1590 Corenzio agreed to fresco the choir of the monastery of Sant'Andrea delle Dame for 200 ducats. A year later he undertook to fresco the chapel of St Agatha in the Certosa di San Martino for a total price of 220 ducats.[33] By contrast, the Cavalier d'Arpino commanded no fewer than 800 ducats for the first half only of his frescoes in the choir of the Certosa.[34] Admittedly, this was also to include a painting in oil of the *Crucifixion* flanked by a further two frescoed figures. Still, the sum of 800 ducats represents a hugely inflated price relative to Corenzio. Evidently, then, Corenzio's enormous success as a frescoist over the next several decades is attributable, at least in part, to his readiness to accept cut-price rates for his work relative to a bigger-name foreigner like D'Arpino. But while Corenzio's prices may seem ridiculously cheap by comparison to D'Arpino's, they were not, in fact, out of line with the other, relatively few Neapolitan painters receiving fresco contracts at this time. Azzolino and his partner, Giulio dell'Oca, for example, were quite happy to accept only 160 ducats for the contract

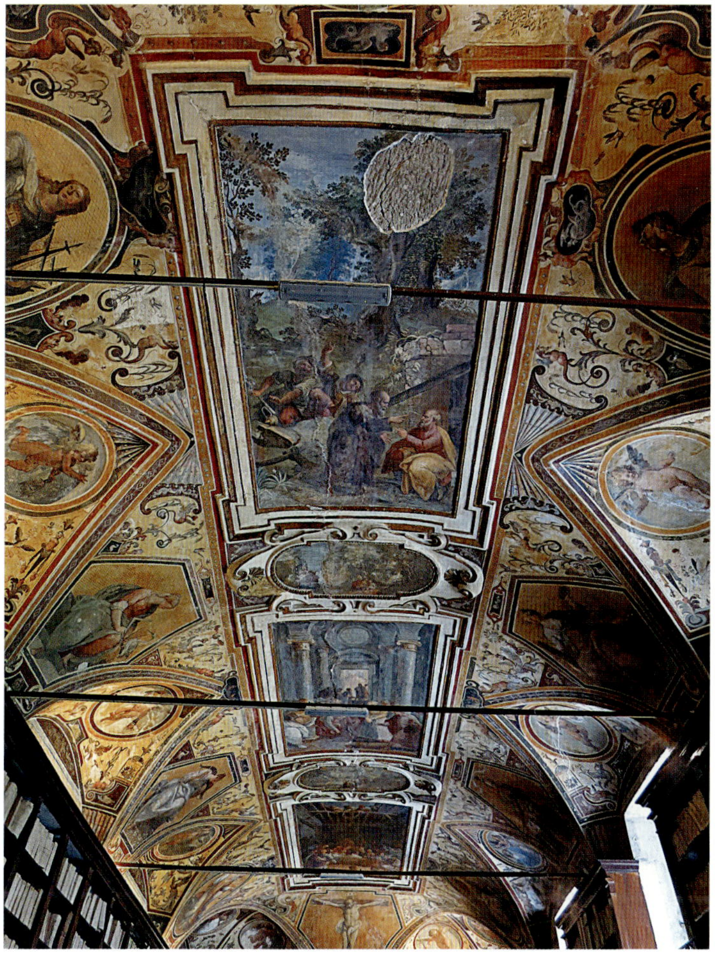

22 Belisario Corenzio and workshop, *Scenes from the Life of Christ*, 1609. Fresco. Sala del Catasto Onciario, Archivio di Stato (formerly Santi Severino e Sossio), Naples

for frescoing the entire cupola, pendentives included, of the church of Spirito Santo in 1599.[35]

These rates of payment constitute a further indication that the intellectual component of painting – whether in fresco or on panel – attracted no particular economic premium at this stage over and above what patrons were prepared to pay for applied art. In fact, in terms of price outlay, Neapolitan frescoes (as practised by Neapolitans at least) were often cheaper than the elaborate stucco surrounds that accompanied them. An unusually detailed indication of this is provided from the turn of the century by a series of valuations undertaken for the church of Sant'Anna del Lombardi involving Corenzio. In 1603 a disgruntled patron took the relatively unusual step of bringing the stuccoist Pietro Bigonio before the Gran Corte della Vicaria for not honouring the timely completion clause of his contract for the stucco-work in the chapel, which accompanied frescoes painted by Corenzio.[36] The drawn-out proceedings for this now-destroyed commission necessitated the appointment of no fewer than three independent appraisers (including the consul of the gilders' section of the Corporazione dei Pittori).

Leaving aside the variations in the appraisals – which progressively lowered the commission price and thus do not seem to have worked in the gilder's favour – it is nonetheless clear that painting was by no means the major cost involved in the project. Corenzio's work was valued separately by the three appraisers at 110 ducats, 124 ducats and 90 ducats, whereas the stucco-work was valued at 190, 185 and 115 ducats, and the gilding was valued at a further 85, 115 and 60 ducats. It is surely no coincidence, incidentally, that the highest valuation given to Corenzio was made by a fellow painter, Fabrizio Santafede, who would have known Corenzio very well during the course of his long career as one of the leading altarpiece painters of the day. The lowest appraisal, on the other hand, was made by the vice-regal engineer Constantino Avellone, whose relative independence of the painters' networks presumably left him freer in his deliberations than the other painters and gilders. In all three appraisals, nonetheless, the stucco and gilding accounted for more than twice the cost of the painting itself.

The documents for the Santa Maria Donaromita ceiling reveal a similar inversion of the cost of the decorative work over the frescoed figure painting and thus of what today might be regarded anachronistically as the most important element of the commission. These documents reveal that the paintings by Teodoro d'Errico and his colleagues were produced for a total cost of 837 ducats.[37] The surrounding frames of the ceiling, by contrast, amounted to almost double this at a grand total of 1,502 ducats. Materials for the frames alone accounted for almost the entire price of the paintings (356 ducats for the wood, 457 ducats for the gold leaf and its gilding), which was then added to by the cost of the carving (439 ducats), together with Magliuolo's fees for designing and overseeing the construction (250 ducats).[38]

From 1590 onwards Corenzio consolidated his position as the pre-eminent Neapolitan capable of taking on any and every commission of this type that began to appear in the wake of the Carthusians' fresco commissions. In this he was joined by a small number of painters, who, like him in fact, had come to Naples following extended periods of work in other cities, which had already provided them with opportunities for learning fresco techniques. This was the case, for example, for Giovanni Balducci, who moved to Naples in

1596 following more than twenty years of activity in Florence, working with Naldini and Federico Zuccari on some of the major fresco commissions of the period. Corenzio's 'compagno', Avanzino Nucci, likewise came originally from Umbria before assisting Niccolò Circignani on frescoes in Rome. Like Corenzio, he may also have benefitted from an early association with D'Arpino's Neapolitan workshop, since he seems also to have received one of the fresco commissions at the Certosa di San Martino in 1596, two years prior to his collaboration with Corenzio at the church of the Annunziata.[39]

Corenzio nonetheless dominated the field of Neapolitan fresco and he acquired an impressive list of commissions as the new century drew on. Accordingly, his workshop came to play a fundamental role in training the small number of Neapolitan painters interested in developing a proficiency in this emerging medium over the next thirty years. De' Dominici notes that Stanzione learned the art of fresco under Corenzio, a claim supposedly made on the basis of notes prepared by Stanzione himself and not subsequently disputed by later authors.[40] Caracciolo also benefitted from an early period working under Corenzio to become the only one of the first-wave Neapolitan *caravaggisti* to practise fresco. Corenzio's workshop was also fundamental for the rather more humble fresco practitioners Andrea and Onofrio de Leone.[41] In 1628 Andrea and Onofrio (who were both then aged in their late twenties) assisted Corenzio – now aged seventy and still going strong – on an important series of frescoes of scenes of vice-regal history in the Palazzo Reale (see fig. 164). Both painters subsequently used this training as the basis for their own sporadic work in fresco commissions of a smaller-scale and less prestigious nature.[42]

Corenzio's workshop also seems to have provided a training ground for Agostino Beltrano, as well as for Domenico Gargiulo (1609/10–1675), another of the artists associated with Aniello Falcone in the development of the so-called minor genres of painting to be discussed in Chapter Four. Gargiulo's career was based on the considerable success he enjoyed among private collectors from the mid-1630s onwards for his smaller easel paintings with expansive landscapes. He nonetheless also practised in fresco almost exclusively, as it transpired, for the Carthusians of San Martino, for whom he produced many series of frescoes starting from 1638. His entry point into what turned out to be one of the most prestigious and productive associations of his career appears to have been an early collaboration with Corenzio on a small series of frescoes depicting atrocities meted out against the Carthusians during the English Reformation.[43]

CRISIS AND CONFLICT: THE CONTRACT FOR THE CAPPELLA DEL TESORO DI SAN GENNARO

The eventual challenge to Corenzio's near-monopolization of the contracts for Neapolitan frescoes came in the legendary controversy concerning the ill-fated Tesoro di San Gennaro commission in Naples Cathedral (fig. 23). The genesis to this long and involved story occurred in 1612, at the time of the deputies' first correspondence with the Spanish ambassador to the Holy See and their statement that they did not wish the commission to go to Neapolitan artists. At that stage Guido Reni appears to have been the deputies' first choice. When he nonetheless ultimately failed to commit to the project, the deputies turned next, in late 1616, to the Cavalier d'Arpino, who finally arrived in Naples to begin work in 1618.

D'Arpino was a natural choice for the commission. Not only had he already proved himself on the local scene some fifteen years earlier, but he had also recently completed one of the highest-profile commissions of the day: an extensive series of designs for the mosaics in the cupola of St Peter's in Rome (1603–12).[44] Although they have not hitherto been connected with the Cappella del Tesoro commission, these mosaics must have provided an important precedent for the deputies' initial formulations. The cupola of the Cappella del Tesoro was ultimately painted in fresco, but at this early stage the deputies' stated preference was for cupola mosaics, frescoed pendentives and altarpieces painted in oil.[45] This made sense on an aesthetic level, since the dome at that stage had a very different appearance from the one that it eventually acquired following a remodelling some thirty years later. In his original design, Francesco Grimaldi had created a ribbed dome with a lantern, very much like a small version of the dome of St Peter's, in fact, a form that lent itself particularly well to the flattened and decorative emphasis of mosaic.[46]

Mosaic must have also seemed an apposite medium given the chapel's associations with the cathedral's venerable early Christian history and to the cult of St Januarius more specifically (the saint is depicted in a fourteenth-century mosaic in the basilica of Santa Restituta that forms part of the cathedral complex).[47] This preference must have made the local painters appear even less relevant to the deputies' concerns, since mosaic was virtually unknown in Naples – even more so than fresco, in fact. A similar outsourcing of work is found, for example, in the only other major Neapolitan mosaic project of the period: the altar commissioned

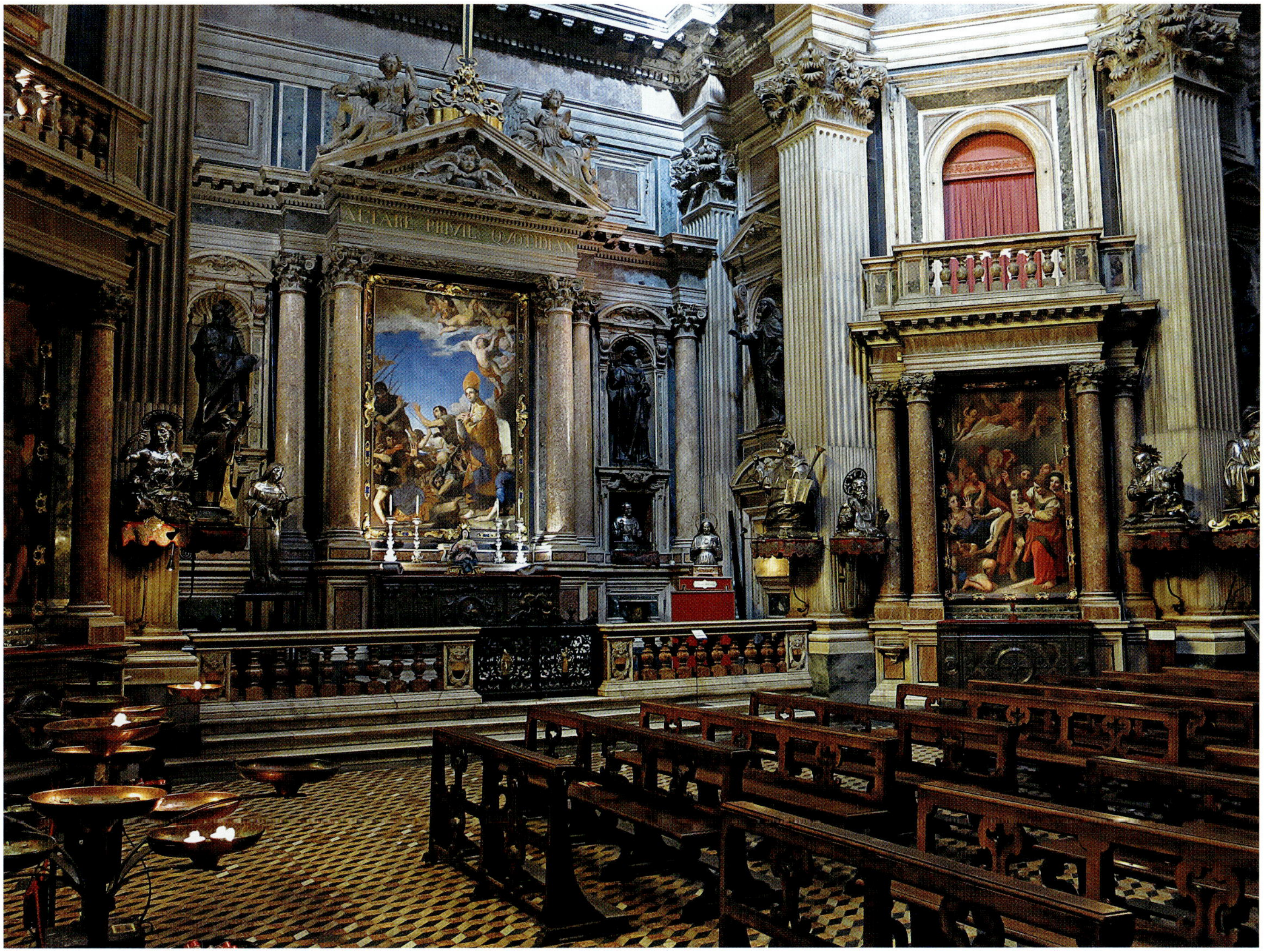

23 Interior view, Cappella del Tesoro di San Gennaro, Naples Cathedral

in the late 1630s and early 1640s by Cardinal Ascanio Filomarino for his family chapel in Santi Apostoli in Naples (to be discussed in Chapter Nine).

The decision to use mosaics rather than frescoes in the Cappella del Tesoro must have hit the local Neapolitan painters hard. And no one, it seems, took it harder than Corenzio himself. The mosaic context seems to have acted as a particular goad to this artist's perceived sense of injustice. Despite the fact that there exists no documented work of his in mosaic, Corenzio appears nonetheless to have regarded himself as a natural choice for the medium. He made a pitch along these very lines during the same period, as it transpires, to the monks of Montecassino, which was situated midway between Rome and Naples. In 1622 the Benedictines of Montecassino were also contemplating the choice of artist for an extensive series of redecorations, and they too wanted mosaic. They had already spent the considerable sum of 1,000 scudi acquiring Reni's cartoons for the mosaics of St Peter's completed ten years earlier, and they intended to use these now as the basis for their commission for mosaics in the cupola of the church. Corenzio petitioned them for the contract on the basis of his Greek heritage, noting that this background made mosaic his 'propria professione' (he appears to have emigrated to Naples from Krujë in present-day Albania).[48] The Benedictines rejected the offer, although ironically enough they did commission Corenzio several years later to paint frescoes in the cupola after they too ultimately decided against mosaic.[49] Here again, the success of Corenzio's career rested in large part on his evident tenacity and ability to stay in the picture long enough to emerge as the obvious candidate once all his competitors had given up and moved on to other projects.

As a result, though, Corenzio was prepared to take whatever steps he felt necessary to gain an upper hand in his dealings with clients and associates, come what may. Already in the later seventeenth century Carlo Celano recorded an accusation that Corenzio had murdered a former pupil, Loise Rodriguez, over a disputed contract, a charge repeated in the eighteenth century and not yet conclusively disputed in the modern literature.[50] These rumours of extreme criminality notwithstanding, Corenzio's attempts to undermine the Cappella del Tesoro commission have attained a yet more legendary notoriety. De' Dominici notes that Corenzio and his associates assaulted D'Arpino and his party soon after their arrival in Naples in 1618, so that they fled from the city.[51] While certainly conceivable, such a dramatic intervention appears to have become somewhat embellished in the retelling. D'Arpino was never to return to Naples, and the deputies, in fact, pursued him for several years after he had left with their down payment of 600 ducats – even to the extent of attempting to sequester his belongings in his home town of Arpino in Lazio.[52] This does not seem like the actions of a committee intent on mollifying an aggrieved artist hounded out of town by violent competitors. Instead, the real reason for D'Arpino's absconding from his work may have lain in his common tendency to overcommit himself with numerous simultaneous contracts (for example, he did not complete the frescoes for the Palazzo dei Conservatori in Rome until 1639, some forty-five years after the commission), combined with the natural greater priority that he assigned to his many pre-eminent Roman patrons over and above the far-distant Neapolitans.

By contrast, a more direct policy of threats and intimidation seems to have been felt necessary to dislodge the next aspirant for the Cappella del Tesoro contract. In this second stage of the commission, the deputies eventually persuaded Guido Reni to come to the city in 1620 in return for some favourable provisions and the highest rates of payment then set for painting in the city. He was promised board and lodgings, an advance of 1,200 scudi, an allowance of 100 scudi a month and a further payment of 100 scudi for each completed figure – payable at the local exchange rate of 130 Neapolitan ducats per figure. After five months in the city, however, Reni and his assistant Francesco Gessi fled to Rome following an incident in which a member of Reni's party was attacked and wounded by one of Corenzio's cronies. This notorious instance of anti-foreign labour agitation is independently confirmed by documents held in the archives of the Tesoro di San Gennaro and the Banco di Napoli. These show that Corenzio chose for the deed one of his frequent stucco-worker collaborators – a certain Giovanni Domenico Capuano – who eventually broke down and confessed under torture.[53] Although Corenzio was thus identified as the instigator of the scheme, he seems nonetheless characteristically to have escaped punishment, and he continued to receive commissions over the course of the next two decades that were to be counted among the most lucrative and prestigious of his career.

Back at the Tesoro, however, things went from bad to worse. First, the deputies vowed never again to let another Neapolitan painter work on the chapel. At the same time, they signalled the hollowness of their resolve by allowing an exception in the case of Fabrizio Santafede, who had, in fact, already been contracted to appraise D'Arpino's work and to assist him in painting half the altarpieces as far back as 1618. They even sent Santafede on a mission to Rome to persuade Reni to return or, failing this, to find 'some other person to do the painting who is talented and famous'.[54] It soon became clear, however, that neither D'Arpino nor Reni nor any other 'famoso' foreign painter was likely to set foot in Naples for the next few years (and one wonders, in fact, just how hard Santafede really tried to satisfy the deputies in this respect). As a result, though, in 1623 the deputies transferred the entire commission to Santafede himself – presumably at this time jettisoning their plans for mosaic and plumping for frescoes in the cupola instead. Santafede was authorized to select any painter he wanted to assist him in the task. He chose Caracciolo, thus ironically contracting an artist who had been trained in fresco by the very painter whose spoiling tactics had undone the deputies in the first place. The irony was further compounded by the subsequent appointment of another assistant, Francesco Gessi, who was himself a pupil of the by-now far-distant Reni.

As if this patched-up compromise was not inauspicious enough, Santafede died in 1624, inconveniently sending the deputies back to square one. At this stage they forgot their ostensible anti-Neapolitan bias and threw the commission open to anyone willing to paint the work, while reserving the right not to pay for it if it was not to their liking. By this stage Caracciolo had withdrawn, leaving the

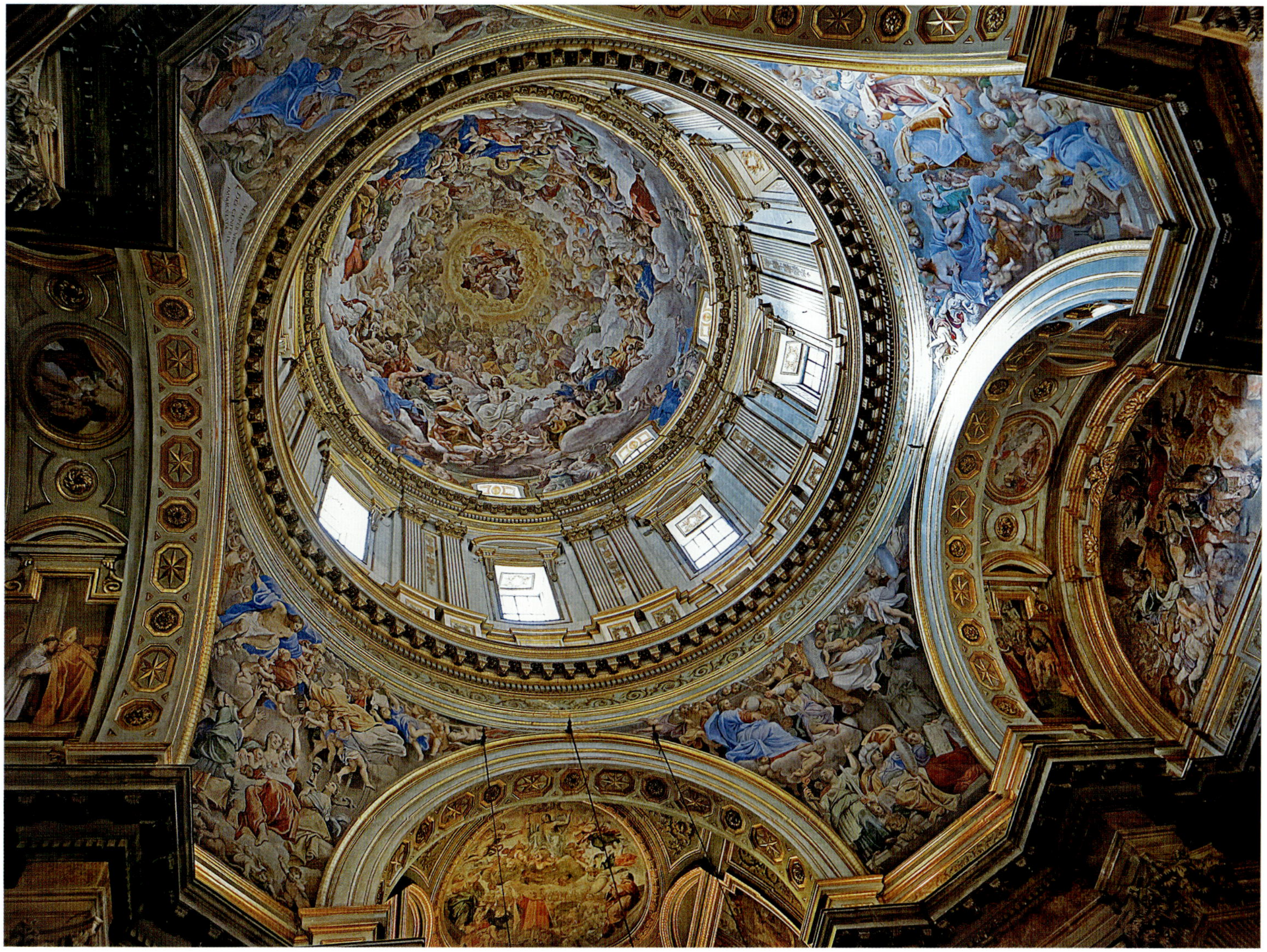

24 Domenichino, *Scenes from the Life of St Januarius* (pendentives), 1631–41; Giovanni Lanfranco, *Paradise* (cupola), 1643. Fresco. Cappella del Tesoro di San Gennaro, Naples Cathedral

field open to none other than Corenzio. This doggedly determined individual applied once again for the contract with a new partner in the form of one of his previous assistants, the by-now aged late Mannerist painter Simone Papa. It says a great deal for the deputies' disarray at this stage that they at first accepted Corenzio's offer, allowing him and Papa to paint first one pendentive, and then another, before ultimately deciding not to proceed with their work either.

Finally, in 1630, the fifth attempt at finding a suitable painter for the Tesoro bore fruit. Domenichino accepted the offer and moved to Naples, spending the last, increasingly pressured and anxiety-ridden ten years of his life there painting – yet not completing – an extensive series of frescoes and altarpieces (fig. 24). He too suffered from the intimidations of the Neapolitan painters. Already in 1632 he wrote to his Roman patron, Cassiano dal Pozzo, complaining of those 'with their teeth sharpened to damage me', and in 1634 he fled in fear of his life to Frascati, where he had to be much persuaded to return.[55] When he died in 1641, reputedly as a result of poisoning, in the opinions at least of Passeri and his widow, the cupola was still only half completed. Two of his six altarpieces were still to be started and another was only half finished.

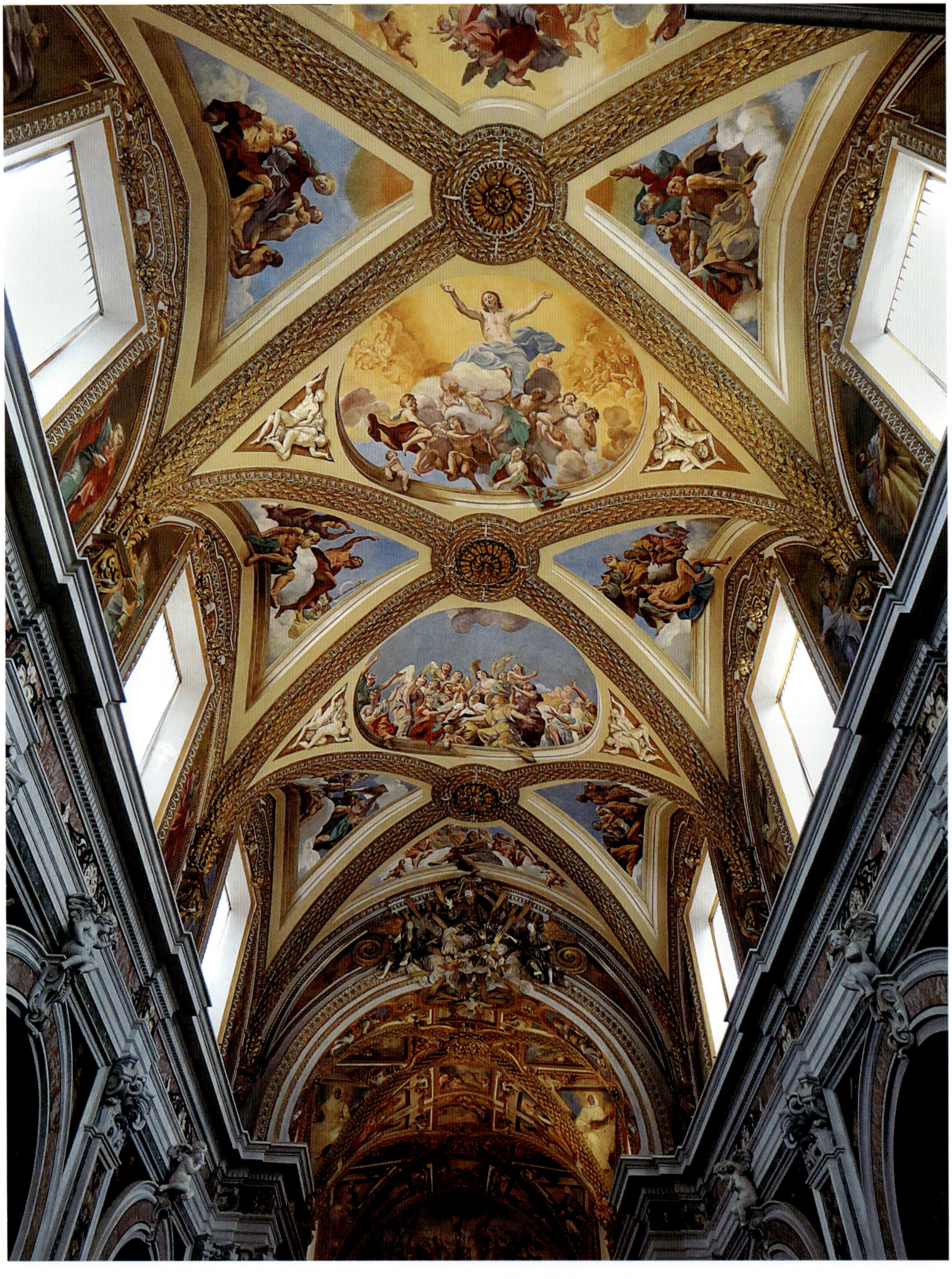

25 Giovanni Lanfranco, *Ascension, Angels, Apostles*, 1637–9. Fresco. Certosa di San Martino, Naples

The debacle of the Cappella del Tesoro commission opened a deep rift at the uppermost levels of Neapolitan public commissions that would take many years to heal. But if the enraged and underhanded local painters do not emerge from this tortuous history in a favourable light, then neither do their patrons. One might well argue that the Neapolitan patrons sowed the seeds for their own subsequent difficulties by virtue of their earlier predilection for the *soffitto cassettonato*, in combination with their continued liking for the most lavish manifestations of the work of the local *stuccatori*. This was then further compounded from 1610 to 1630 by the new taste for Caravaggesque painting on canvas – a taste that only added, incidentally, to the attractiveness of the model provided by Caravaggio himself as a spectacularly successful artist who had nonetheless not felt the need to develop a specialization in fresco. Be that as it may, the falling out on both sides that ensued from this lack of the creation of a viable local school of fresco created a vacuum of Neapolitan representation at the uppermost level of the major ecclesiastical decorative projects of the 1620s to 1640s.

To fill the void, a second prestigious painter was also lured down to Naples on the prospect of gaining the lion's share of a large series of prestigious public commissions that would simply not have been possible in the more crowded context of Roman fresco production. Giovanni Lanfranco moved to Naples in 1634, and spent the next twelve years there undertaking a feverishly productive sequence of major works. This included the cupola and pendentives of the Gesù Nuovo (1634–40, the cupola subsequently destroyed in an earthquake of 1688), the nave ceiling and end lunette of the choir of the Certosa di San Martino (1637–9) (fig. 25), the choir and Blessed Sacrament chapel of Pozzuoli Cathedral (1636–46, both destroyed), a particularly extensive series of frescoes in the nave and choir of the Theatine church of Santi Apostoli (1638–46), and even the cupola of the Cappella del Tesoro (1643) following the death of his old rival Domenichino. In between all this he also found the time to complete a number of altarpieces, together with three smaller fresco commissions at the Palazzo Arcivescovile (1645), the Palazzo Reale and at the Oratorio dei Nobili annexed to the Gesù Nuovo (the last two both in 1646).[56]

In marked contrast to Domenichino, Lanfranco seems not to have received any particular harassment from the locals during all this activity – a situation that he would most certainly have reported back in one of his many voluble letters to his Roman protector, Ferrante Carlo, if it had been the case. Those problems that he did encounter appear to have come, rather, from his patrons – and from the Carthusians of San Martino more particularly – who seem to have sought to undermine him in league with the architect and impresario Cosimo Fanzago (see pp. 15, 17).

In terms of his relations with local painters, though, Lanfranco appears to have integrated relatively well. His frescoes at the Certosa di San Martino were undertaken at the same time as major commissions by Ribera and Stanzione for the same patrons. Lanfranco also worked in tandem with these two painters at the Cappella del Tesoro di San Gennaro, painting frescoes in the cupola while they completed the altarpieces left unfinished at Domenichino's death. Finally, he collaborated with Ribera and Stanzione in 1645 when the three artists jointly agreed to appraise a large altarpiece of the *Purification of the Virgin* by another foreign artist working temporarily in Naples, Charles Mellin. On this occasion, Lanfranco, Ribera and Stanzione arrived at the extraordinarily high valuation of 600 ducats (three times the usual going rate for an altarpiece), which suggests that in this instance Lanfranco too was contributing to the common Neapolitan practice of colluding among his fellow artists in order to maintain favourable prices at the upper levels of public commissions.[57] The rancour of the Cappella del Tesoro commission seems, therefore, to have taught Neapolitans the all-important lesson that in future they would have to devise more productive and professional strategies than mere threats and intimidations when it came to the task of regaining lost ground in the competition for prestigious fresco contracts.

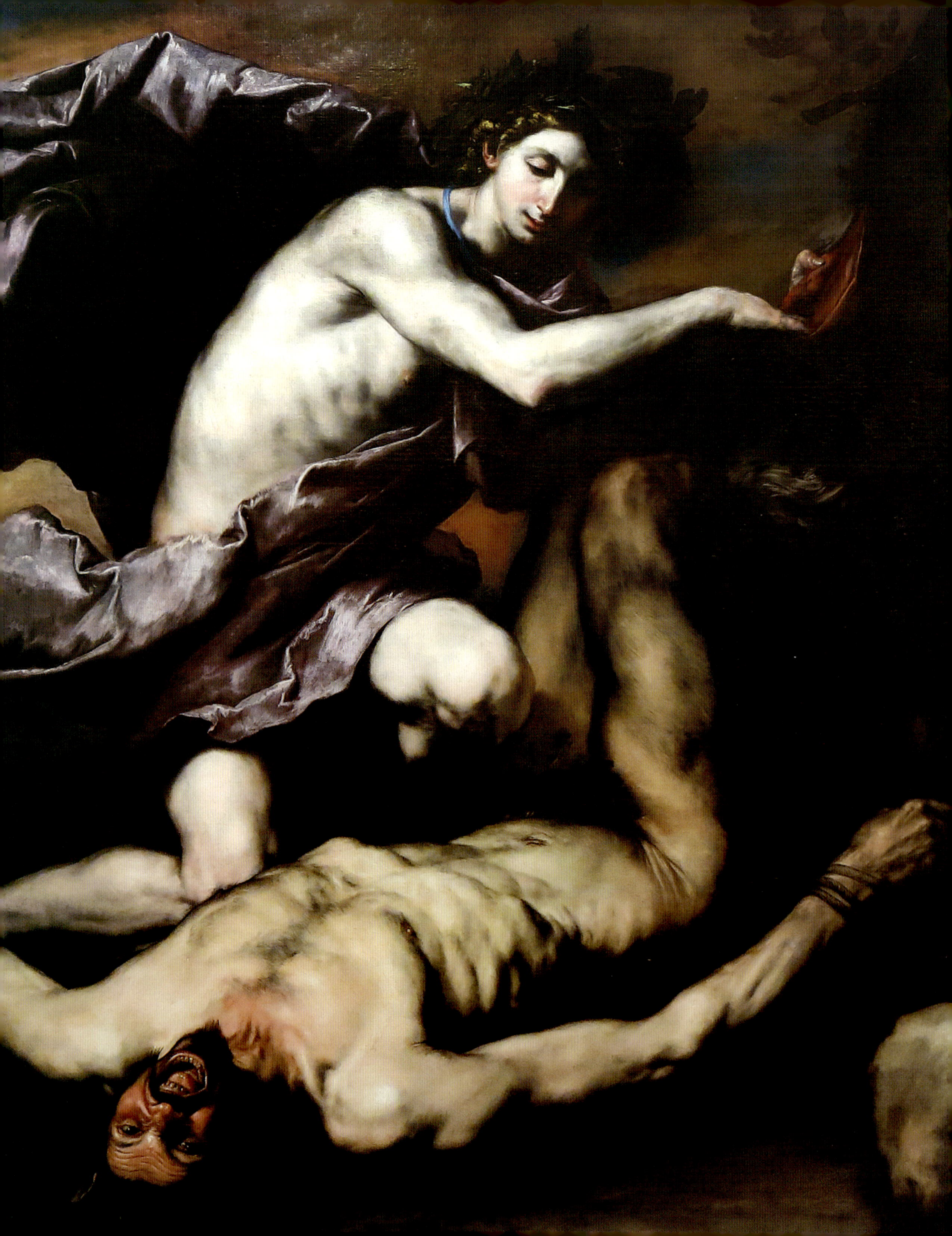

3

Stanzione, Ribera and the Years of Consolidation 1620–1656

Watching the events unfolding at the Cappella del Tesoro, initially from the sidelines, was Massimo Stanzione (1585–1656), whose early career coincides with the time of the project's first setbacks. In 1618 Stanzione is documented, characteristically enough, contributing a smaller, secondary canvas to one of the collaborative *soffitto cassettonato* commissions that were only then starting to appear somewhat retardataire in Naples, in this instance for a church outside the city.[1] Then aged thirty-three, and a little old under normal circumstances to be beginning a career in painting, he seems to have made his start on the local scene several years earlier by assisting Santafede, while at the same time working for Corenzio in a manner that enabled him to learn fresco techniques.

Fresco would not, however, figure as a prominent feature of Stanzione's career until many years later. It was not until 1624 that he received his first independent fresco commission, and then it was another six years before he received an extraordinary break in the form of an important chapel commission at the Certosa di San Martino. This second commission launched Stanzione on the wider stage as both a frescoist and a major player in the public commissions of the day. Before reaching this point, however, he was required to spend fifteen long years laying the groundwork by travelling and by learning from better-established artists and traditions, and by assiduously developing patronage networks, all of which he would ultimately bring to bear in varying combinations to advance his career to a position of unparalleled prominence.

Stanzione's career to the late 1620s is characteristic of this next phase of Neapolitan painting in that it developed largely in response to the new taste for Caravaggesque gallery paintings and altarpieces that arose following Caravaggio's two visits to the city in 1606–7 and 1609–10. The period accordingly represents something of an interregnum in Neapolitan painting, since the field for easel painting commissions remained relatively open in a manner that accommodated equally the steady continuation of the careers of older artists, such as Azzolino and Forlì, alongside that of emerging, younger artists working more directly in the new manner, like Ribera (who arrived in Naples in 1616), Filippo Vitale (1589–1650) and Paolo Finoglio (1590–1645). Caracciolo was the oldest of this group of first-wave Neapolitan *caravaggisti* – having been born in 1578 and active since the turn of the century. His greater age, together with his unusual expertise in fresco, gave him a slight edge over his younger colleagues and he enjoyed a higher proportion of public commissions over the course of the 1620s prior to his death in 1635.[2]

Seven years his junior, with no workshop to speak of and only a few sporadic public commissions to keep him in

Facing page Jusepe de Ribera, *Apollo and Marsyas*, signed and dated 1637 (detail of fig. 48)

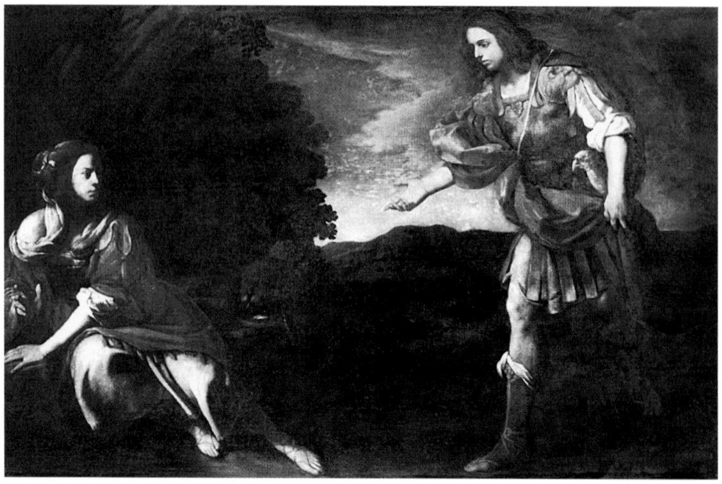

26 Massimo Stanzione, *Literary Subject*, late 1640s. Oil on canvas, 175 × 270 cm. Palazzo Montecitorio, Rome (on deposit)

Naples, Stanzione was freer to undertake a series of extended *viaggi di studio* to Rome, first in 1617–18 and then again in the later 1620s. Here he produced some scattered work of generally secondary importance while also studying at first hand recent trends in Roman Caravaggism. This was soon followed by interests in the latest developments in the classicism of the Carracci and then of the neo-Venetian style of the followers of Poussin as promoted by the Barberini and their entourage.[3] The subsequent break out of his career in the 1630s was based in large part on his ability to combine these modish external influences with the bedrock traditions of Neapolitan Caravaggesque realism. This effort would earn him the epithet of 'il Guido Napoletano', a phrase supposedly coined by Andrea Vaccaro in the 1630s and later patented, as it were, by De' Dominici in the early eighteenth century.[4]

Stanzione's efforts to build effective synergies between his fashionably up-to-date artistic interests and like-minded patrons accrued benefits from an early stage. In particular, and in the absence of significant church patronage, he was able to cultivate a series of fruitful associations with influential literati and aristocratic private collectors (fig. 26). These were centred upon the membership of the Accademia degli Oziosi (Academy of the Idlers). In 1621 he benefitted from these associations by becoming the first Neapolitan Baroque painter to receive a knighthood. In that year he was made a knight of the Order of the Golden Spur, an honour soon followed by two further knighthoods, one into the Order of Christ of Portugal (1627) and another into the Sacred Military Constantinian Order of St George (1623–30). Conferred in Rome, the applications for these titles all depended on the leverage of influential aristocratic promoters. Stanzione received the Order of St George, for example, via the intercession of the conde de Oñate in his capacity as the Spanish ambassador to the Holy See and prior to his eventual tenancy as viceroy of Naples from 1648 to 1653. Stanzione signed his work 'Eques Max' from this point on and he initiated a trend among his colleagues to seek comparable honours for themselves, including Ribera and Caracciolo, who both subsequently obtained knighthoods of the Order of Christ of Portugal in 1626 and 1629, respectively.[5]

None of this, of course, automatically brought any extra work Stanzione's way. Yet these honorifics helped to register the painter's ambition to look beyond the traditional boundaries set by the artist–artisan nexus that formed the basis of so much Neapolitan painting and patronage of the period. Instead, Stanzione signalled his intention to pursue avenues for conferring a higher status on his reputation and career that may have been time-honoured in Rome (as witness, for example, the Cavalier d'Arpino, or the case of Lanfranco, who was similarly inducted into the knighthood of the Order of Christ in 1628), but that were, in fact, very rare at that stage in Naples.[6]

All this eventually bore fruit in the commission in 1630 for the chapel of St Bruno in the Certosa di San Martino (fig. 27).[7] Prior to awarding him the commission, the Carthusians first took it upon themselves to check Stanzione's credentials as a frescoist with their Roman counterparts, thus further attesting to the misgivings still felt by Neapolitan patrons towards the capabilities of the local painters in the medium. A letter of June 1630 sent in response to their enquiries by a certain Father Carlo Felippo de Ferrariis reassured them. In the letter De Ferrariis confidently wrote that 'he did some work here that is truly excellent', before adding that 'in Naples you have excellent men who are expert in painting, but Stanzione is nonetheless significantly superior'.[8] De Ferrariis may have been referring to some now-lost frescoes by Stanzione for the Roman charterhouse of Santa Maria degli Angeli.[9] Either way, Stanzione's Roman years and contacts clearly proved indispensable to his gaining this all-important contract.

Another Roman context was necessitated by the iconography of the saint. St Bruno had been canonized only seven years earlier and his iconography was still quite new. The Carthusians at San Martino accordingly relied heavily for the imagery of their chapel on a series of recent prints that had been published in Rome in the run-up to the canonization after designs by Lanfranco. Stanzione was the perfect

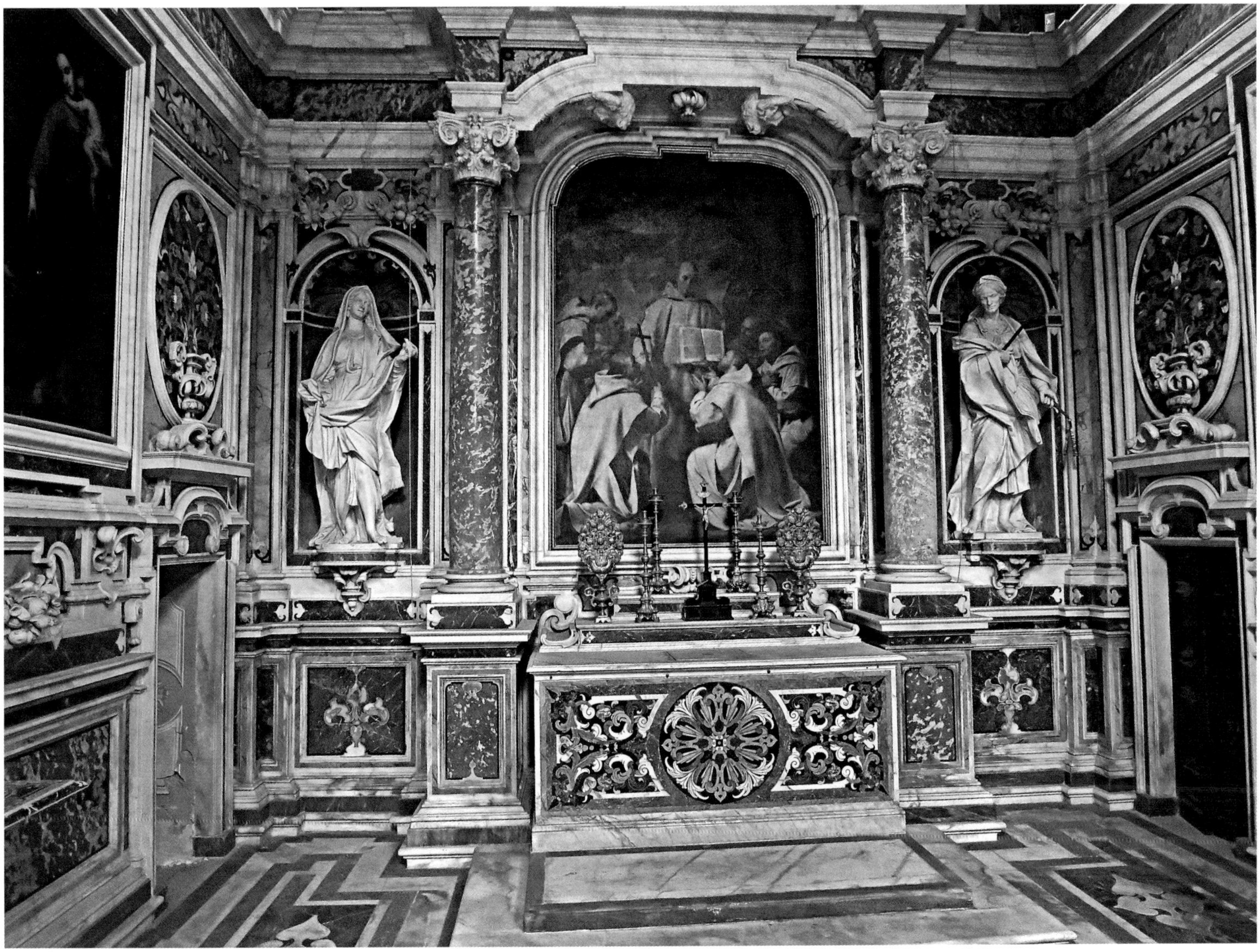

27 Massimo Stanzione, *Scenes from the Life of St Bruno*. Fresco and altarpieces. 1630–37. Cappella di San Bruno, Certosa di San Martino, Naples

artist to translate these images into a Neapolitan context. He sought precisely the same level of upper-tier patronage as Lanfranco had already achieved, and he sought to implement this moreover through a directly comparable process of modifying his earlier relatively unconstrained Neapolitan Caravaggesque realism in favour of a more heavily idealized Romano-Bolognese style.

Stanzione's resulting combination of the local and the international as applied particularly within the framework of a fashionably modern fresco style found immediate favour with patrons. The commission of the St Bruno chapel of 1630 set in train a succession of other important commissions for Neapolitan churches of the recently instituted Counter-Reformation orders, including choir frescoes for the Jesuits at the Gesù Nuovo (1639–40), a vast series of frescoes in the nave of the Theatine church of San Paolo Maggiore (1642–4) and an extensive series of frescoes for the recently canonized Giacomo della Marca in the Franciscan church of Santa Maria la Nova (1646–7). Stanzione was also called back to the Certosa di San Martino to work on a further two sets of frescoes, one of *circa* 1644–6 for the passageway leading to the sacristy – and a work, therefore, in direct comparison to the earlier scene in the Roman manner painted by the Cavalier d'Arpino and his workshop – and finally in the chapel of St John the Baptist, a commission begun in the mid-1640s but left incomplete at the time of Stanzione's death – aged seventy – in 1656.[10]

In between these points, Stanzione also took on an ever-increasing workload of public religious easel painting commissions. These included (to cite only a few of the most prominent examples) a *Pietà* of 1637–8 for the Certosa di San Martino that became his best-known composition (see fig. 178); two of the altarpieces left unfinished by Domenichino for the Cappella del Tesoro (1641–3); two immense canvases of the *Disputation* and the *Marriage Feast at Cana* painted for the choir of the church of the Annunziata (1640–42, subsequently destroyed); the Cacace chapel in San Lorenzo Maggiore (after 1649); canvases in the sacristy and a very large painting of the *Preparations for the Last Supper*, measuring 3.93 × 3.93 metres, painted in 1639 for the choir of the Certosa di San Martino; and a late altarpiece for the Merlino chapel in the Gesù Nuovo (after 1649).

THE CONTRIBUTIONS OF STANZIONE'S WORKSHOP

A detailed understanding of the activities of the efficient workshop that sprang up in the wake of all these demands is unfortunately hampered by two factors. The first results from the traditional lack of source documentation concerning workshop assistance, since an individual's contribution was subsumed into the collective identity of the workshop as directed by the master himself. Second, the very success of Stanzione's later style created the phenomenon from the mid-1630s onwards of a host of Neapolitan painters all imitating the successful blend of elements found in his work. This Stanzionesque so-called school of ennobled Neapolitan Caravaggesque naturalists is at times difficult to distinguish from those artists who can be characterized as workshop assistants in the stricter sense of the term. So, for example, Paolo Finoglio and Andrea Vaccaro have been identified not as true 'discepoli' of Stanzione, notwithstanding the fact that they are described as such by De' Dominici and other early sources.[11]

The process of excluding artists belonging to this latter category and of gathering together what is known about the rest nonetheless allows one to draw certain conclusions about the scope and chronology of Stanzione's workshop. Stanzione seems, in the first instance, to have divided it into at least three different types of assistant. The first corresponds to what might be called the long-time loyal subordinate. This term can be applied to those truly junior and subordinate painters who seem to have been more than happy to follow their master's lead strictly and at all times, and as a result to keep their contributions limited within the boundaries of his projects.

This group included Stanzione's own son, Giuseppe, who was born in 1616 and who is documented in his father's workshop from the mid- to late 1630s. Documents from this period show that Stanzione transferred a number of payments to Giuseppe.[12] The transferral of money paid initially to a master for specific work and then passed on to an assistant is generally taken as referring to payment for subordinate work on the commission in question. If this reading is applied to the documentation for Giuseppe Stanzione, he is accordingly found receiving 40 ducats out of a total of 300 paid out in 1635 for a now-lost, privately commissioned work of the *Rape of Persephone*. This was an evidently very large and elaborate mythology. Giuseppe was also paid 87 out of a total of 800 ducats in 1639 for a series of now-lost frescoes in San Lorenzo Maggiore. This was then followed in 1640 by a transferral of 90 ducats out of a total of 225 assigned to his father for a large painting of the *Annunciation* for another *soffitto cassettonato* commission, this time in the church of the convent of Santa Maria Regina Coeli. Giuseppe also received 200 of the 1,400 ducats agreed on as the total commission price for Stanzione's frescoes in the Gesù Nuovo during the same year, together with 50 out of the 300 ducats assigned for the total price of a very large altarpiece of the *Death of St Joseph* measuring 3.2 × 2.1 metres. All these transferrals from father to son represent small portions skimmed off the top of large contracts. They thus accord well with the rates of payment that might be expected for truly subordinate junior contributors to a wide range of the high-profile, mainly public commissions in both fresco and oil painting that Stanzione received during the period.

A second category of Stanzione's workshop, also first detectable from the mid-1630s, is what might be called the more marginal, splinter group collaborators. These slightly more independent and yet at the same time also more mysterious figures appear to have attached themselves to Stanzione at a relatively early point in their career trajectory, and they then seem to have gravitated towards certain compositions or aspects of Stanzione's work, before ultimately detaching themselves from his workshop within a few years. Bernardo Cavallino (1616–1656) is one such example. In the early 1640s to 1650s he maintained a moderately successful independent career as one of the most accomplished and unique practitioners of the niche market

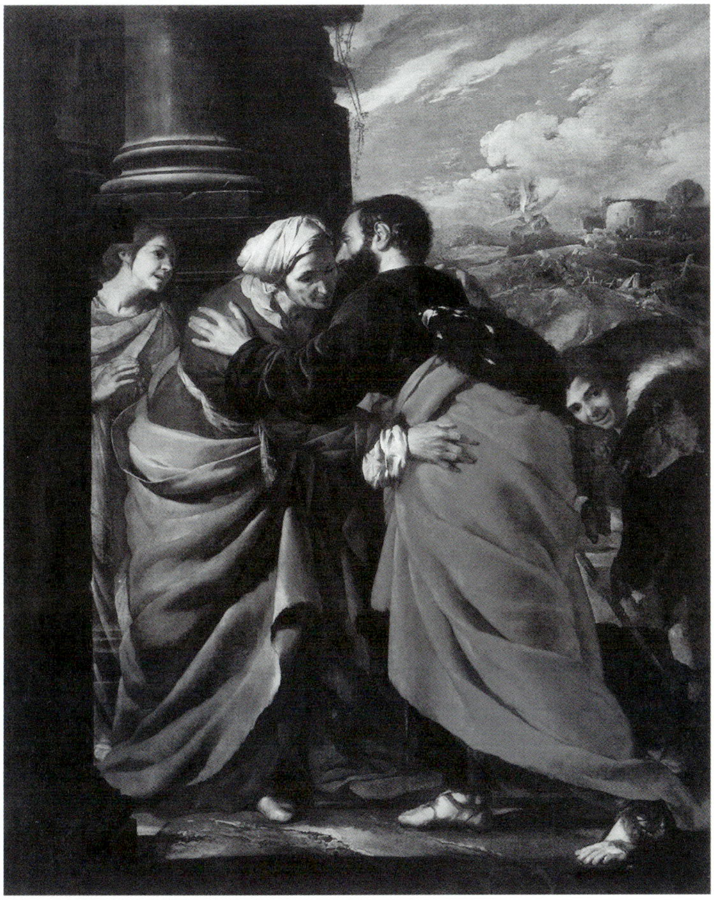

28 Bernardo Cavallino, *Meeting of Anna and Joachim at the Golden Gate*, mid-1630s. Oil on canvas, 229 × 178.5 cm. Szépművészeti Múzeum, Budapest

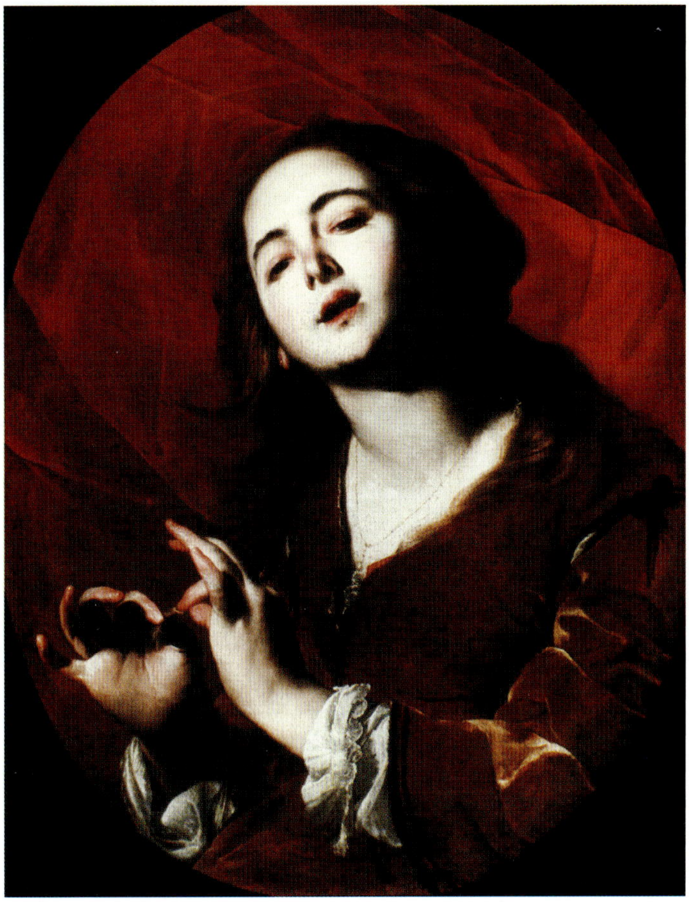

29 Bernardo Cavallino, *The Singer*, late 1640s. Oil on canvas, 75 × 64 cm. Museo e Gallerie Nazionali di Capodimonte, Naples

for private cabinet painting just then emerging and to be discussed in the next chapter. Before then, however, he appears to have spent some time in Stanzione's workshop during the early to mid-1630s (rather than in the early 1620s, as De' Dominici erroneously believed on the basis of inaccurate birth dates).[13]

Cavallino's career began during this period with a small group of mainly large figure paintings that struggle on an artistic level to assimilate the recent lessons of Stanzione and Ribera (albeit Ribera to a slightly lesser degree) (fig. 28).[14] By the later 1630s, however, Cavallino's style had developed into a more distinctive form that can be readily distinguished from Stanzione (fig. 29). If one follows De' Dominici in accepting that Cavallino worked under Stanzione at the outset of his career, then one is accordingly required to conclude that Stanzione did not employ him for very long. Cavallino seems also not to have assisted Stanzione on his frescoes, since none of the sources refers to Cavallino having ever practised in this medium during his later career. Cavallino was not then an all-round collaborator, but he seems to have been used to contribute certain elements to Stanzione's large easel painting commissions of the period, which he then used to develop further into distinctive elements of his subsequently independent career.

The second member of this splinter group remains one of the most tantalizing but at the same time also most obscure artistic personalities of the period. After decades of obscurity, only a handful of paintings, most notably a group of paintings depicting the *Life of the Virgin*, have been conclusively attached to the name of Annella (or Diana) de Rosa (1602–1643). This is despite the fact that this female painter is described enthusiastically in the early sources and is documented to at least some degree (fig. 30).[15] After an initial period spent learning the rudiments of the trade in the work-

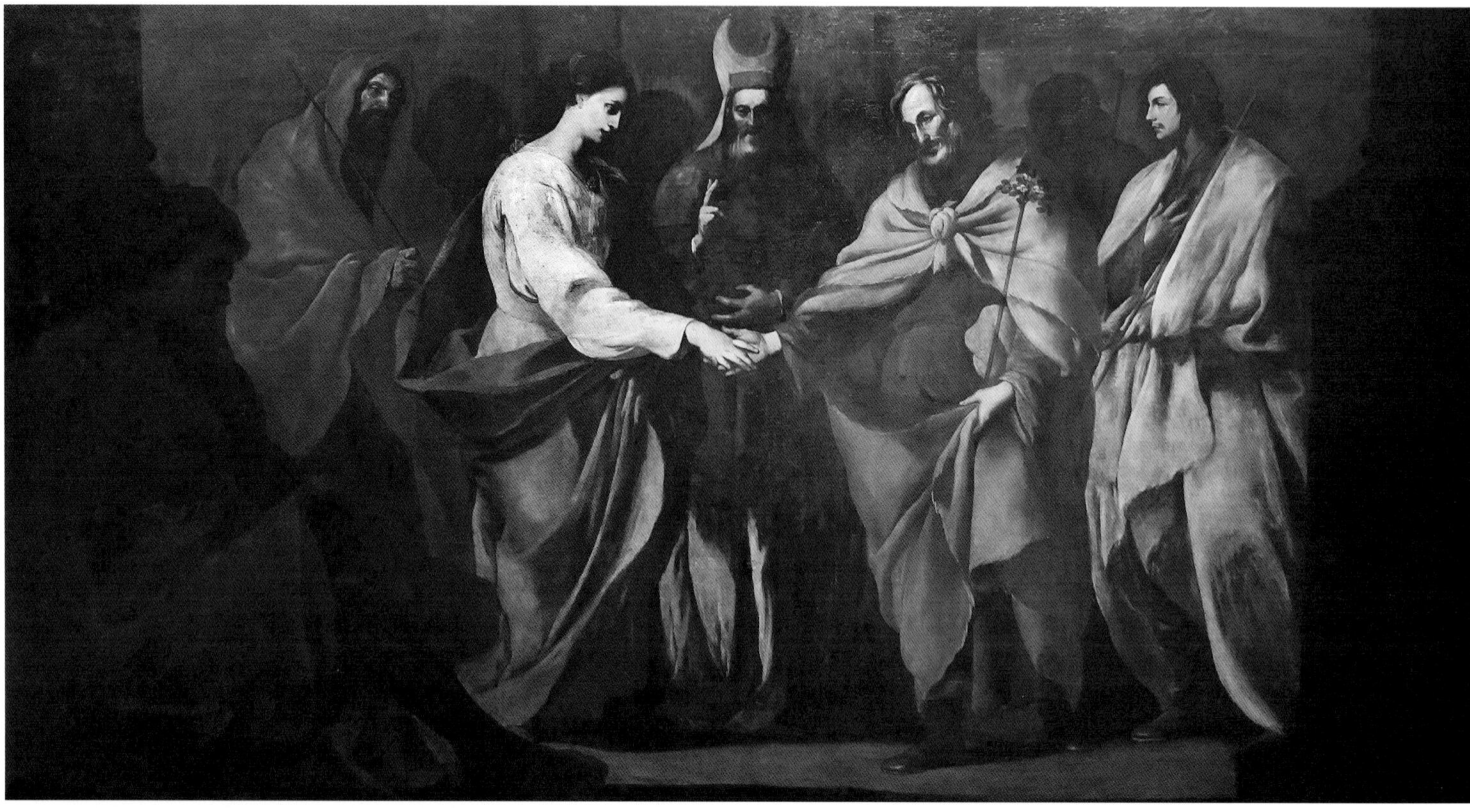

30 Annella de Rosa, *Marriage of the Virgin*, late 1630s. Oil on canvas, 135.5 × 250 cm. Museo Diocesano di Napoli, formerly San Giovanni Maggiore, Naples

shops of her father, Tommaso de Rosa, and then of her stepfather, Filippo Vitale, Annella de Rosa graduated in 1621 – aged eighteen – to an assistant's position in the workshop of her uncle Gaspare de Popolo. At some stage shortly after her marriage to Agostino Beltrano in 1626 she gravitated to the workshop of Stanzione.

Annella's participation in Stanzione's workshop seems to have been limited to a narrow band of compositions and picture types. The only indication of these works comes from early inventory references to works by her hand listed in Neapolitan private collections. The inventory of the collection of Giacomo Capece Zurlo of 1715, for example, refers to an *Annunciation* 'by Annella [coming] from Massimo copied after the Annunciation in Naples'.[16] This refers to Annella's copying a now-lost altarpiece painted by Stanzione in 1630. Other references document her specialization in generally smaller-scale paintings of virgin martyr saints, such as a reference in 1704 to 'two paintings measuring a *palmo* and one and a half *palmi* [approx. 26 × 39 cm] of two virgins with gilded frames by the hand of Annella retouched by Massimo'.[17]

Annella seems to have focused further on scenes of female protagonists involved in either acts of seduction (a *Lot and his Daughters* inventoried in 1698), or of violence (a *Beheading of St Catherine* inventoried in 1699), or in both aspects simultaneously (a *Herod and Herodias with the Head of St John the Baptist* cited in 1648 and 1649).[18] Most spectacular of all, it seems, was a large and gruesome painting of the *Martyrdom of St Agatha* mentioned in 1648 as 'created by the hand of Dianella, retouched by the hand of Massimo'. This painting probably derived, therefore, from a large composition of the subject, together with its slightly later variations, by Stanzione himself dating from the 1620s onwards.[19]

Even more so than Cavallino, then, Annella de Rosa appears to have used her experience in Stanzione's workshop as a means of focusing on a specialized 'splinter' niche specializing in virgins, martyrs and femmes fatales. Artemisia Gentileschi would, of course, specialize in a directly related field of imagery when she too came to Naples some time between either late 1629 or early 1630, and it seems that she also played an important role in encouraging Annella's specialization along these lines. For the present, though, Annella's input can be read as an important indication of Stanzione's apparent desire to delineate his workshop into different areas of production. While he and his other more conventional assistants worked on the larger altarpieces and frescoes, the young Bernardo Cavallino and Annella de Rosa helped to diversify the output by producing smaller and cheaper paintings for private collectors interested in more novel and individualistic reinterpretations of traditional subjects. This parallel production involving often quite diverse types of painting within the one large workshop helped to maintain Stanzione's clients' interest on a number of different levels – and it was just then becoming a standard feature of workshops specializing in paintings for the private sector of the market, as will be seen.

Annella's husband, Agostino Beltrano, by contrast, typifies the next category of Stanzione's workshop assistant, that of the more senior journeyman collaborator. Before his marriage in 1626, just short of his twentieth birthday, Beltrano's teenage years had been spent apprenticed to Gaspare de Popolo. He seems thereafter to have spent the next several years attached to the workshop of his new stepfather-in-law, Filippo Vitale, with also perhaps a brief, undocumented stretch working for Corenzio in a manner that also enabled him to learn fresco techniques.[20] Eventually, though, he joined Stanzione some time in the mid- to late 1630s. By then, Beltrano was already fully trained, highly experienced and nearly thirty years old. He had also spent at least some time acting as an independent master, a fact that is confirmed by his involvement in the extensive series of prominent altarpieces produced in 1634–5 for Pozzuoli Cathedral on the outskirts of Naples. Beltrano's *Martyrdom of St Januarius* from this commission provides a good documentation of his earlier style (fig. 31).[21] It owes little to Stanzione and reflects instead his earlier immersion within the ambience of such Riberesque painters as Hendrick van Somer, Pietro Novelli and Paolo Finoglio, not to mention Filippo Vitale himself.

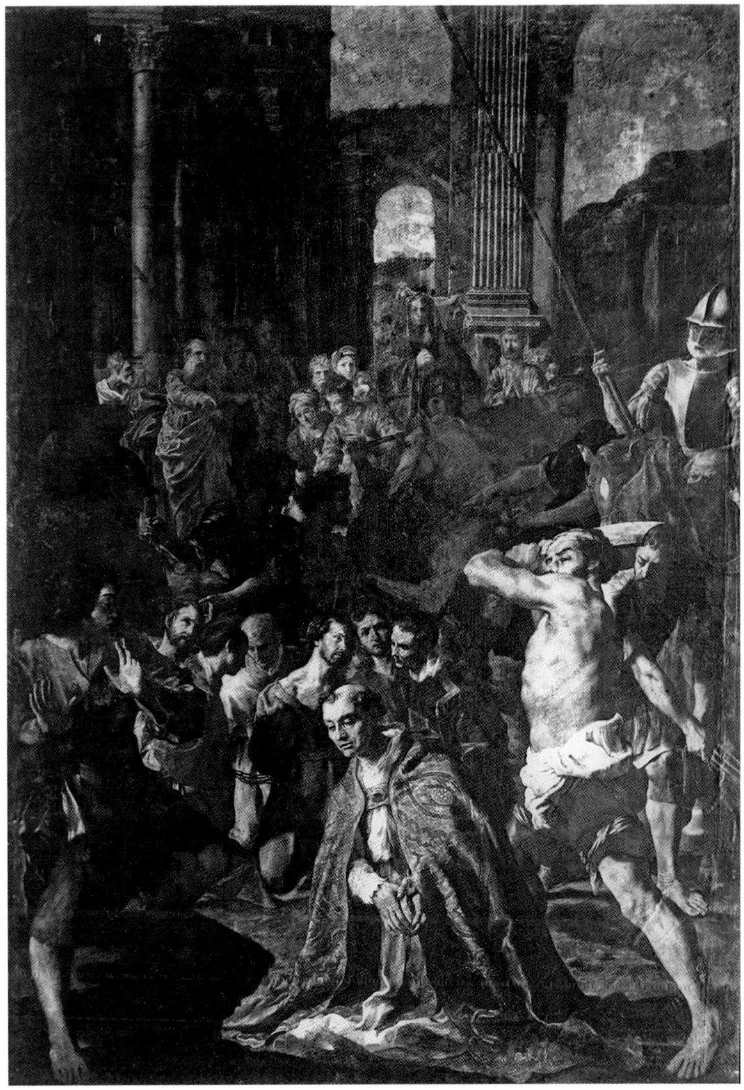

31 Agostino Beltrano, *Martyrdom of St Januarius*, 1634–5. Oil on canvas, 215 × 148 cm. Pozzuoli Cathedral, on deposit at the Museo Nazionale di San Martino, Naples

All this would change, however, over the next few years following Beltrano's initiation into the Stanzione enterprise. A signed painting of *Lot and his Daughters* dating to the mid-1640s has been characterized as a prime example on Beltrano's part of a moderate academic version of Stanzione's style (fig. 32).[22] It represents a slightly more independent variation on a composition also treated previously by Stanzione himself, which Beltrano probably copied as well (fig. 33).[23] One of Stanzione's chief attractions for Beltrano (as also for his wife, Annella de Rosa, whose lost *Lot and his Daughters* presumably would have related to this composition) was clearly the access that the master was able to provide to a 'sweeter' and more suave variant upon Neapolitan Caravaggism, which was just then finding favour with Neapolitan patrons.

At the same time, Beltrano was also expected to assist Stanzione across a wide range of public commissions. In 1644, for example, Stanzione transferred to Beltrano 100 ducats he had received for initial work on the San Paolo Maggiore frescoes.[24] Four years later the inventory of the collection of Don Giuseppe Carafa di Maddaloni further attests to Beltrano's involvement in this commission, since it lists a series of seventeen *bozzetti* (oil sketches) for the frescoes as painted by Beltrano after drawings provided by

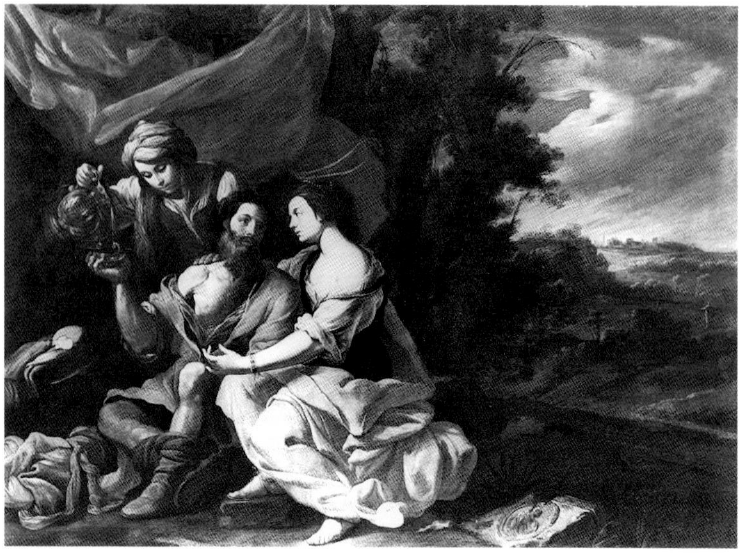

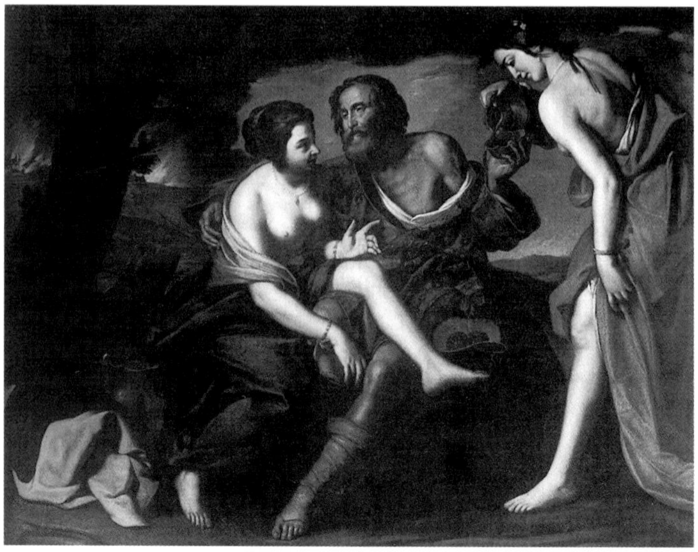

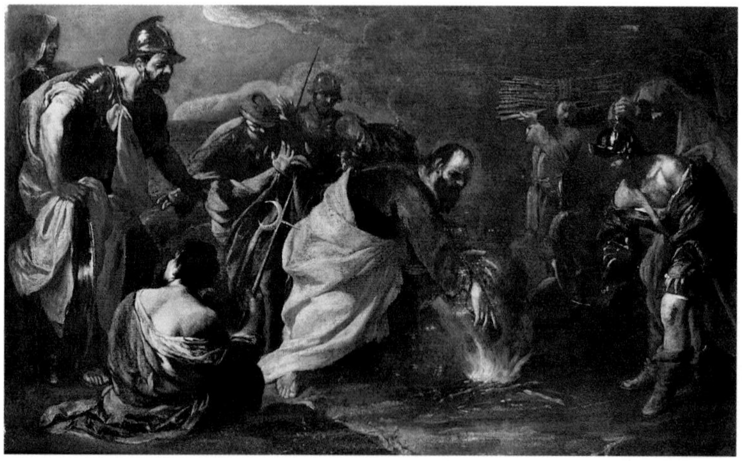

Above, left 32 Agostino Beltrano, *Lot and his Daughters*, mid-1640s, signed. Oil on canvas, 74 × 99 cm. Molinari Pradelli collection, Bologna

Above 33 Copy after Massimo Stanzione (Agostino Beltrano?), *Lot and his Daughters*, mid- to late 1640s. Oil on canvas, 183 × 237 cm. Palazzo Reale, Naples

Left 34 Agostino Beltrano after Massimo Stanzione, *St Paul on the Isle of Malta*, *circa* 1642–4. Oil on canvas, 48.2 × 74.2 cm. Whereabouts unknown

Stanzione.[25] The contract of 1642 for the San Paolo Maggiore frescoes had, in fact, allowed for precisely this kind of workshop intervention in its unusually specific stipulations concerning what was and was not to be painted by Stanzione himself. The master was to paint everything with his own hand 'except for the backgrounds and draperies, as well as the *bozzetti*, which he can have made by others'.[26] Here then is an unusually complete documentation of Stanzione's customary design process as translated across the varying levels of his workshop. It is possible that Beltrano may have performed the role of junior project manager in charge of carrying out Stanzione's directives across the workshop as a whole. A number of Beltrano's *bozzetti* after Stanzione's designs have appeared on the market, including one of *St Paul on the Isle of Malta* now in a private collection (fig. 34).[27]

BEYOND STANZIONE: ASSISTANTS AS MASTERS

The longevity and high productiveness of Stanzione's workshop seem partly attributable to Stanzione's willingness to allow for a certain degree of flexibility when it came to the outside activities of his more senior assistants. Beltrano, for example, is known to have received a number of independent commissions throughout the time he spent assisting Stanzione. Some of these appear to have stemmed directly from his association with the master. In 1644–5, for example, he frescoed the cupola and pendentives of the chapel of the Immaculate Conception in Santa Maria degli Angeli a Pizzofalcone. This represented an important step up for him and was undertaken at the also quite generous rate of 400 ducats.[28] Stanzione's altarpiece nonetheless sits on the high altar of this chapel; it may be that he had baulked at decorating the entire chapel, and that Beltrano was the patrons' second choice (Stanzione's altarpiece has also been dated on stylistic grounds to *circa* 1650–55, which suggests that he took longer than Beltrano to deliver the work, assuming that both altarpiece and frescoes were commissioned simultaneously).[29]

At the same time, though, Beltrano also received commissions for a number of generally secondary fresco cycles and cheaper altarpieces that do not appear to have had any direct connection with Stanzione.[30] These include chapel frescoes in the church of the Pietà dei Turchini (1645), painted by Beltrano in this instance for the lower price of 100 ducats;[31] a large altarpiece of *Our Lady of Purgatory* for a church outside Naples for 80 ducats (1646);[32] and some chapel frescoes and an altarpiece for the church of Sant'Agostino degli Scalzi produced also at the cheaper rate of 100 ducats (1649).[33] The summit of Beltrano's career as a frescoist appears to have been his work on the cupola of Santa Maria Donnaregina Nuova, completed in 1655 for the princely sum (for him at least) of 700 ducats.[34]

The same combination of dependent and semi-independent work appears to have characterized the participation of another of Stanzione's more senior journeyman assistants. Of Flemish origin, Niccolò de Simone is documented in Naples from 1636 to 1655 and he was dead by 1658 – thus making him in all likelihood one of the many artist victims of the plague of 1656.[35] He is not, in fact, identified as a 'discepolo' of Stanzione by De' Dominici and the other early sources, but since the mid-nineteenth century the close correspondences between his work and that of Stanzione during the 1640s and early 1650s have nonetheless led to his being more accurately identified as a sometime assistant.[36]

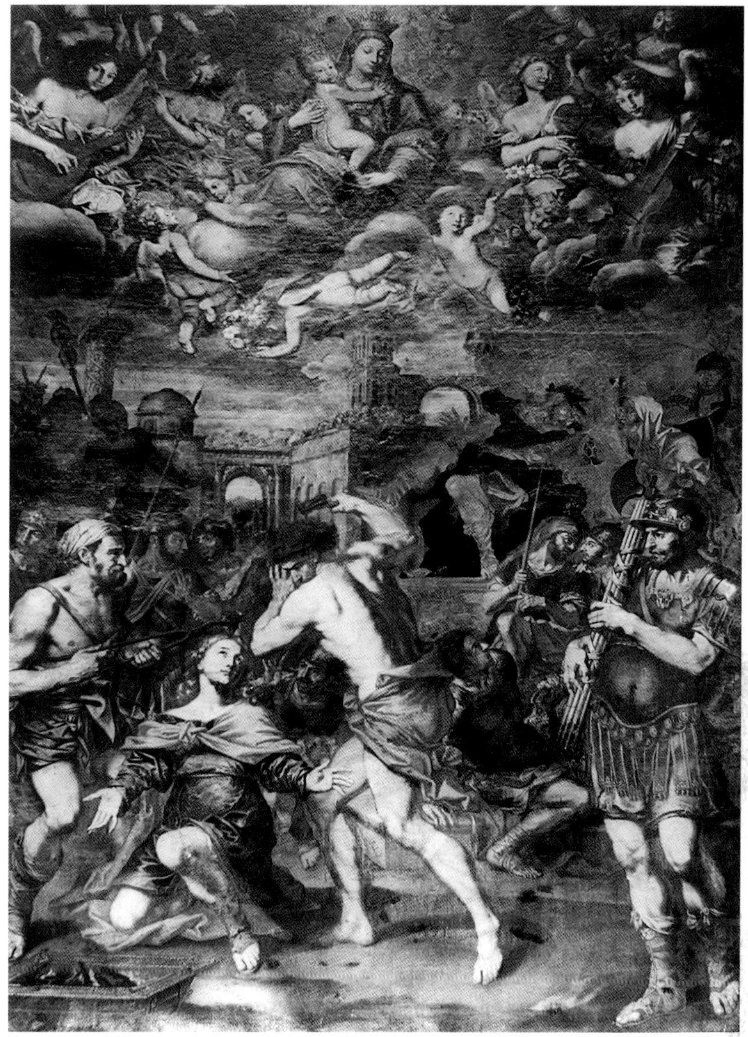

35 Niccolò de Simone, *Martyrdom of St Potito*, signed and dated 1654. San Potito, Naples

Like Beltrano, De Simone seems to have built on the platform provided by his presence in Stanzione's workshop as a means of attracting outside public commissions. He produced a number of altarpieces over the course of his career, including work for the Carmelite church of Madre di Dio e San Nicola in Lecce (1645),[37] two substantial altarpieces for the Neapolitan churches of Santa Maria Antescula (1655) and even the high altar of San Potito (1654) (fig. 35).[38] He also received a number of fresco contracts, including one at least that was unusually prestigious for an artist at his level. In 1642 he was paid the substantial sum of 600 ducats for an entire chapel – frescoes and altarpieces together – in the church of Santa Teresa degli Scalzi.[39] This represented something of a distinction, since the decision to entrust both the frescoes and altarpieces of a chapel to a single artist was generally made only with regard to the highest-ranked painters of the day, for example, Stanzione and Caracciolo at the Certosa di San Martino.[40]

The link between his contributions as an assistant to Stanzione and his work as a semi-independent master painting occasionally in his own right is seen most clearly in De Simone's cupola frescoes for the Cacace chapel in San Lorenzo Maggiore.[41] This was also a commission of some importance, since the chapel constitutes one of the most significant Neapolitan Baroque ensembles of the period (fig. 36). Its patron, Giovan Camillo Cacace, was *presidente* of the

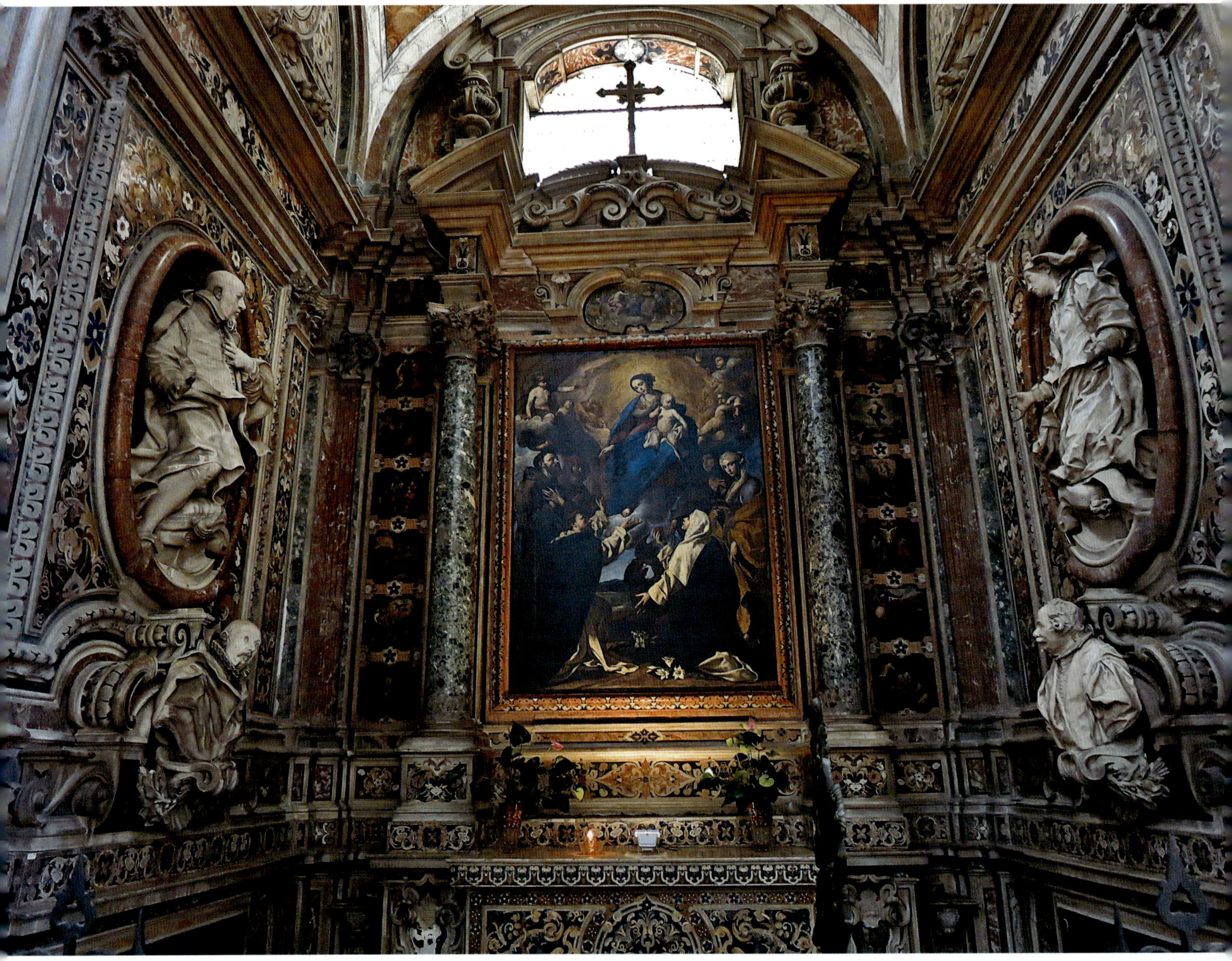

36 Cappella Cacace, San Lorenzo Maggiore, Naples, showing Andrea Bolgi, *Funerary Monuments to: Giusseppe de Caro and Francesco Antonio de Caro* (left wall); *Giovan Camillo Cacace and Vittoria de Caro* (right wall), 1652–54. Marble; Massimo Stanzione, *Our Lady of the Rosary with Sts Francis of Assisi, Francesco di Paola, Catherine of Siena, Lucy and Margaret of Antioch* (altarpiece), begun 1643, completed *circa* 1649–56. Oil on canvas, 265 × 190 cm; *The Mysteries of the Rosary* (panels surrounding altarpiece), Workshop of Massimo Stanzione, including Giuseppe Piscopo and Agostino Beltrano, 1651. Oil on copper, approx. 42 × 44 cm each

Regia Camera della Somaria and had been a founding member of the Accademia degli Oziosi in the opening decades of the century. He continued to play a leading role in the intellectual circles of the mid-century by virtue of his early support for the new sciences that were just then beginning to attract attention in Naples.[42] For his family chapel in San Lorenzo, Cacace commissioned extensive polychrome marble from 1642 onwards from the architect and entrepreneur Cosimo Fanzago.[43] He also commissioned portrait sculptures from Andrea Bolgi, former assistant to

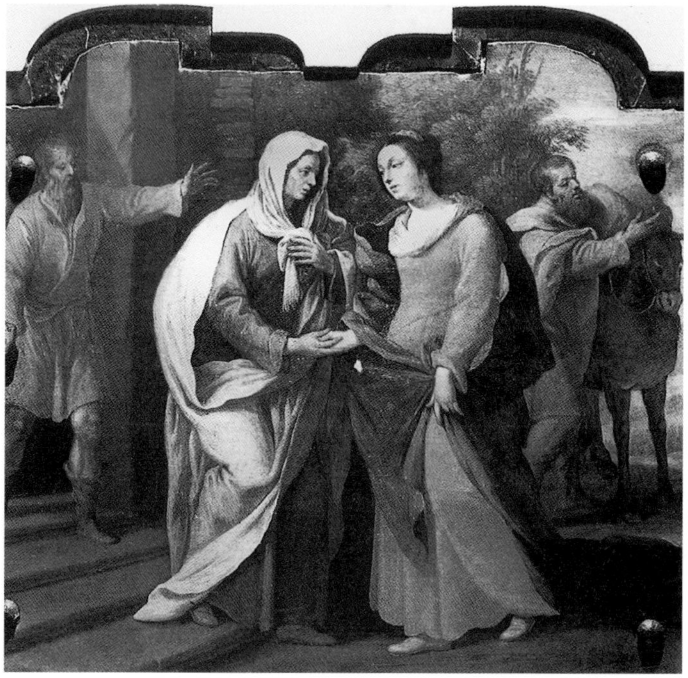

37 Agostino Beltrano, *Visitation*, 1651. Oil on copper, approx. 42 × 44 cm. Cappella Cacace, San Lorenzo Maggiore, Naples

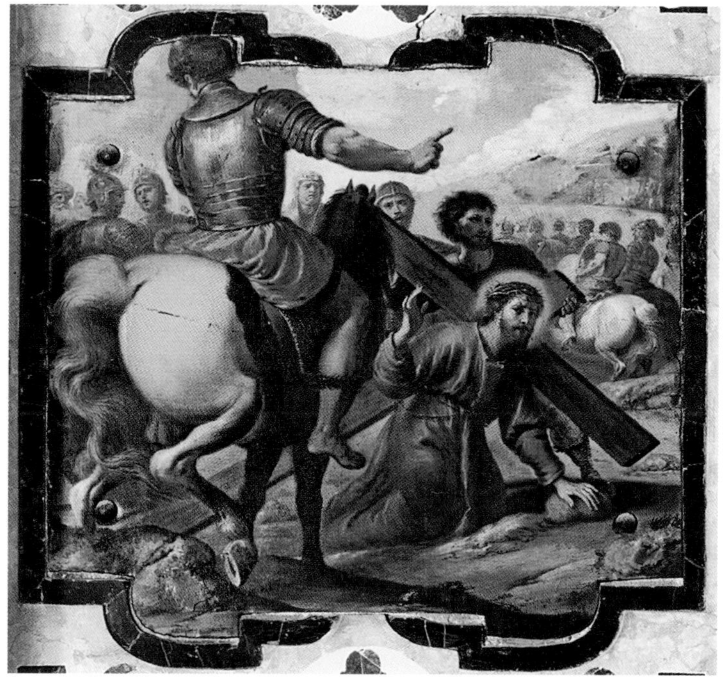

38 Giuseppe Piscopo, *Christ Falls for the First Time*, 1651. Oil on copper, approx. 42 × 44 cm. Cappella Cacace, San Lorenzo Maggiore, Naples

Bernini and creator of the celebrated *St Helena* sculpture for the crossing of St Peter's in Rome, whom he brought down to Naples especially for the purpose.[44]

Stanzione was also involved in the project and it was certainly via his association that De Simone gained access to Cacace's patronage. In 1643 Stanzione was commissioned to produce a large altarpiece of *Our Lady of the Rosary* for the Cacace chapel, which was to be surrounded by fifteen small paintings on copper depicting the *Mysteries of the Rosary*. Stanzione did not deliver the work, however, until sometime between 1649 and 1656, when the paintings are cited as being finally *in situ*.[45] The delay seems attributable, in part, to disagreements that arose concerning Stanzione's rates of pay, together with perceived difficulties involving the supervision of the commission. Cacace had initially wanted Stanzione to undertake the chapel frescoes as well (with architectural backgrounds to be provided by the *quadratura* specialist Viviano Codazzi), but he had perhaps unwisely left the supervision of this aspect to Fanzago, and had expected Fanzago to pay Stanzione out of the money he had already been allotted for his work. A sum of 258 ducats had been set aside for this purpose, but Stanzione declared himself unhappy both with the amount offered (he wanted 600 ducats) and the mode of payment. He complained that he would rather be paid by the patron directly, thus indicating that, unlike so many of his peers, he was no longer prepared to be treated like a mere *stuccatore* or some other slightly less senior collaborator being subcontracted out of the master artist's pay.[46]

Stanzione accordingly declined the commission, allowing it to pass in turn to his rather less discriminating assistant, Niccolò de Simone, who was willing to complete the work for 300 ducats, half Stanzione's asking price, while also consenting to the arrangement of being paid by Fanzago rather than Cacace. This proved fortuitous, since it recommended De Simone to Cacace who acted thereafter as an influential promoter of his work. Cacace's interest in De Simone even extended to his recommending the painter's services to the abbot of Montecassino in a hitherto unnoted rare, documented instance of Neapolitan *clientelismo*.[47]

The fifteen small copper panels surrounding Stanzione's altarpiece are still *in situ* in the chapel (figs 37–8). They are further revealing of Stanzione's approach to delegating work among his labour force, since they have long been recognized as slightly discontinuous in their styles. Schütze has further perceived within them an alternating juxtaposition of two distinct hands.[48] The style of one of the artists responsible is characterized by slightly tapering, elongated figures, whereas the figures in the panels by the second artist are fuller and more carefully delineated in a rather more conventionally idealized, Bolognese-inspired manner. The first artist is identifiable as Agostino Beltrano, while the second has now been identified as Giuseppe Piscopo – a little-known artist noted in the early sources as a pupil of both Stanzione and Falcone and, via Falcone, to a still little-understood period as a 'discepolo' of Falcone's pupil Domenico Gargiulo.[49]

At the time these clear differences of approach within a single workshop product would have been viewed in a negative sense, as a failing on the part of the master to integrate adequately his assistants' inputs into a unified finished product.[50] Here, however, Stanzione seems consciously to have played on the subtle distinctions between these two assistants in order to set up an alternating dialogue between their slightly different inflections of his style. The resulting comparison adds a liveliness to the scenes, since it contrasts Piscopo's slightly greater accomplishment in the area of musculature and academic nude studies – as witnessed particularly in his treatment of the scenes of Christ's Passion in the *Sorrowful Mysteries* – with Beltrano's particular effectiveness in deploying a rather more expressive and nervously energetic style to scenes of Christ and the Virgin in the *Joyful and Glorious Mysteries* (figs 37–8).[51]

As head of the largest workshop in Naples, then, Stanzione was quite prepared to acknowledge, even to emphasize on occasion, the differences in style and approach among his assistants. This readiness to allow for a certain degree of individuality and independence within the framework of such a well-organized and productive workshop reflects, in turn, the attitude that he appears to have adopted when it came to training his *discepoli* how to paint in his style. De' Dominici stresses the relative openness of Stanzione's workshop in this respect. He notes that Stanzione taught in a manner more akin to that of a private academy, as based particularly on the model of the Carracci's celebrated academy in Bologna. Stanzione's teaching is thus said to have encompassed the study of prints and drawings by and after the Carracci, Guido Reni and others. At the same time, though, Stanzione is also said to have imparted to his pupils a thorough grounding in more theoretical concerns – such as architecture and perspective – and above all in the need for artists to refer back constantly to the original literary sources on which biblical and mythological history paintings were based.[52]

De' Dominici had his own reasons for wishing to stress the academic, theoretical side of Stanzione's enterprise and

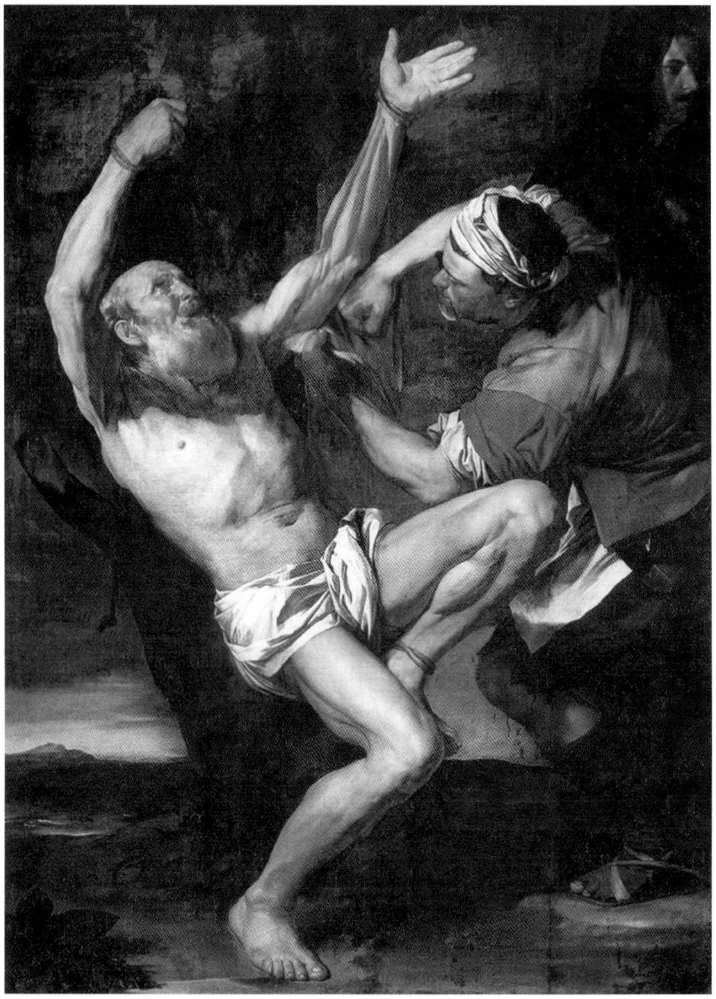

39 Jusepe de Ribera, *Martyrdom of St Bartholomew*, *circa* 1616–18. Oil on canvas, 179 × 139 cm. Colegiata de Osuna, Seville

it seems that his account here is embellished, at least to some degree. Even allowing for some exaggeration, though, the diverse nature of aspects of the workshop production does suggest a relatively open operation. A certain level of independent study and exploration of broader artistic influences and ideas were evidently encouraged, alongside a streamlined and productive approach that sought to keep the books balanced and the commissions flowing in.

RIBERA AND THE ARTISTS IN HIS SHADOW

Stanzione's attitude contrasts markedly with the more narrowly defined orientation of the other major workshop of the period. It would be misleading to oppose Ribera to Stanzione on the simplistic grounds of perceiving him as a mechanically minded workshop head with no interest in the wider intellectual or pedagogical challenges involved in artistic creation and communicating its principals to his pupils. As the most outstanding Caravaggesque painter of his generation, Ribera was every bit as complex and as theoretically engaged as Stanzione.[53] He was also actively interested in the idea of teaching, even to the extent of designing three plates in the early 1620s for a projected training manual on the rudiments of drawing.[54] It is significant, nonetheless, that Ribera abandoned this project long before bringing it to fruition. It is also true, moreover, that the work of his assistants remains much less clearly defined than Stanzione's, and as a result his workshop has proved resistant to individuation. This was already identified as an issue in the later seventeenth century and it has remained an open question in the more recent literature on the artist.[55] All this points to the very different nature of Ribera's workshop organization.

Ribera settled in Naples in 1616, aged twenty-five. His initial training in his home town of Valencia was followed by five years or so spent mainly in Rome but with shorter periods also in Parma, as well as probable trips down to Naples to prepare the ground for his eventual relocation there.[56] Unlike the peripatetic and somewhat uncertain early career of Stanzione, Ribera had already served his journeyman years by the time he reached Naples, and his activities from 1616 to the mid-1620s indicate a much more focused approach to establishing himself in the Neapolitan art world – and he was rapidly successful.

His first step was to secure an advantageous marriage to the daughter of Azzolino, then one of the leading painters of the previous generation. This arrangement had the added advantage of embedding Ribera, instantaneously as it were, within the heart of the all-important familial-professional networks discussed in Chapter One. During the next few years he built assiduously on his position as the most up-to-date and 'internationally' experienced translator of the new Caravaggesque idiom, a source of appeal that he combined with the strong national connections that he was able to cultivate with members of the Spanish administration and their circles. Within a few short years, then, Ribera had secured significant patronage from the viceroy of Naples and his wife, the duke and duchess of Osuna, together with numerous commissions from Cosimo del Sera, the agent to the grand duke of Tuscany mentioned in Chapter One, and equally important orders from the Neapolitan agent for Marcantonio Doria of Genoa. The steady exodus of Ribera's work out of the port of Naples in cargo bound for prestigious Spanish collections also began during this early period.[57]

The viceroy and vicereine had commissioned from Ribera a series of canvases intended for an integrated altarpiece in the presbytery of the Colegiata de Osuna in Seville (fig. 39).[58] This was not his first large-scale religious commission: as early as 1611 he had been commissioned by the Farnese to paint a large altarpiece of *St Martin and the Beggar* for a church in Parma (although this work is now lost). But while Ribera's combination of high piety and intense Caravaggesque drama was well suited to meeting the dictates of public religious settings, most of his output over the course of his career was directed more towards the ranks of private collectors. His trademark saints, ragged philosophers and allegorical series of the *Senses* all found immediate success from an early date. And while his work attracted numerous enthusiastic purchasers from Neapolitan aristocrats and emerging bourgeois collectors (including the influential Flemish merchant Gaspar Roomer, to be discussed in Chapter Seven), Ribera's Spanish heritage ensured that his work always remained a particular favourite among high-ranking Spanish dignitaries and those among their retinues seeking to enrich their collections or to make munificent donations to public institutions back home.[59]

Ribera frequently stressed the importance of this inheritance by signing his paintings as either 'Español' or 'Hispanis, Valentin', and he continued to find favour throughout his career with successive viceroys. They commissioned numerous works, frequently even before they reached Naples, during their earlier tenure often in Rome as ambassadors to the Holy See. The extent to which Ribera was sustained by this relatively closed patronage network is indicated by the references to his periods spent in residence in the Palazzo Reale, seat of the viceroys and their administration. It is known, for example, that he painted his celebrated canvas of *Magdalena Ventura with her Husband; or, The Bearded Woman* in 1631 (see fig. 165) while in residence at the Palazzo Reale following the request of the viceroy, the duque de Alcalá, and he is mentioned as in residence there once again in early 1646.[60] Ribera and his family also took refuge in the Palazzo Reale in 1647 during the Revolt of Masaniello.[61] De' Dominici is probably correct, therefore, in asserting that Ribera was appointed *pittore di corte* or court painter (the only Neapolitan painter mentioned as having enjoyed this position), a position that is said to have included a monthly salary of 60 doubloons, later increased to 80, which converts to the generous rate of 180 and 240 ducats per month.[62]

Ribera continued to identify his and his family's fortunes with the Spanish administration up until his death. He successfully obtained vice-regal military appointments for his two sons, both carrying various honours and stipends. His first-born son Antonio, moreover, used this as the basis for his subsequent career as a vice-regal functionary, eventually rising to a position as governor of the province of Lecce.[63] During the last months of his life, Ribera even petitioned Philip IV directly for a benefice to assist his recently widowed daughter Margarita (a request that the king eventually granted in the months following Ribera's death in September 1652).[64]

Back in the 1620s, though, this early success from such a unified sector of the market was certainly beneficial to Ribera in a number of ways. For one thing, it enabled him to raise his prices to a point where they soon equalled or even surpassed the uppermost pay scales of the period. Already in 1618, for example, he received 100 ducats for a painting of the *Martyrdom of St Bartholomew*, commissioned by another Florentine agent by the name of Vincenzo Vettori, and in 1623 his fees rose even higher to 150 ducats for a painting of the *Pietà* commissioned on behalf of Marcantonio Doria in Genoa.[65] This was about as high as prices for private commissions went at that date. Carlo Sellitto, for example, had enjoyed a brief moment of preeminence in the few years between Caravaggio's departure from Naples and Ribera's arrival. He would have been lucky to receive as much, since 114 ducats was his highest price, paid for an altarpiece of 1610, and 100 ducats was the going rate for both an altarpiece and a portrait commissioned separately from him in 1614.[66] By contrast, Stanzione remained a step behind both artists until 1630. In 1620, for example, he received 80 ducats for an altarpiece and then between 30 and 40 ducats for portraits commissioned in 1621 and 1622.[67]

Ribera's domination of the upper reaches of the private sector, combined with Stanzione's eventual ascendancy of the public field from 1630 onwards, came to exert a polarizing influence on the Neapolitan art world. These two artists' dominance of the field progressively scaled back its relative openness and fluidity of opportunities for painting contracts, such as those characterizing the first three decades of the century (for example, the simultaneous commissioning at the Pio Monte della Misericordia of the elder Santafede alongside the more junior Carlo Sellitto). During the 1630s to early 1650s, rather, there arose a more streamlined and also more stratified emphasis that tended to favour the work of a smaller number of larger workshops – as inclining particularly towards the twin peaks of Ribera and Stanzione, respectively.

This seems to have caused particular difficulties for the ongoing profiles of the other first-wave *caravaggisti*, such as Filippo Vitale and Paolo Finoglio, who had both stood on a more or less equal footing with Ribera and Stanzione at the beginning of their divergent trajectories. In 1618, for example, Vitale had received as much as 200 ducats for an altarpiece in the local artists' church of Sant'Anna dei Lombardi.[68] After the mid-1620s, however, he disappears almost entirely from the public record, and his later career and posthumous reputation would soon become almost as shadowy and difficult to determine as those of Ribera's workshop assistants soon to be discussed.[69]

The same is true of Paolo Finoglio, albeit for slightly different reasons. Finoglio enjoyed considerable success with his dramatic, vivid and tangibly present early Caravaggesque style during the 1620s. In the middle of the decade he painted an altarpiece of the *Circumcision*, together with a major series of ten lunettes of founders of religious orders, all for the chapter house of the Certosa di San Martino (fig. 40). In so doing, he demonstrated that he was equal in stature to Stanzione and Caracciolo, who were both then beginning their activity at the Certosa. This was further consolidated in 1629, when he painted an altarpiece of the *Immaculate Conception* for San Lorenzo Maggiore. This is now lost, but it must have been prominent since its ultramarine alone cost 38 ducats.[70] Finally, and at the end of the decade, he was given the signal honour of decorating an entire chapel – altarpieces and frescoes alike – in the church of the Certosa, that of St Martin, which he had completed by August 1631 (see fig. 20).[71]

This commission nonetheless ended on a frustrating and perhaps also inauspicious note for Finoglio's subsequent Neapolitan career. The final payment of 1631 records that the Carthusians had decided to return Finoglio's principal altarpiece for this chapel on the grounds that 'it did not succeed in pleasing the fathers', while also referring to an appraisal made by 'comuni esperti' (recognized experts). Evidently, then, a dispute over payment – and some aspect of Finoglio's rejected altarpiece – had also come to cloud the settling of accounts. Although it has not hitherto been connected to this settlement, an undated valuation of Finoglio's work in this chapel, jointly drawn up and signed by none other than Stanzione and Ribera, is clearly the appraisal to which this document refers.[72] In it the two artists carefully itemize every element in the chapel (minus the principal altarpiece, which had already been written out

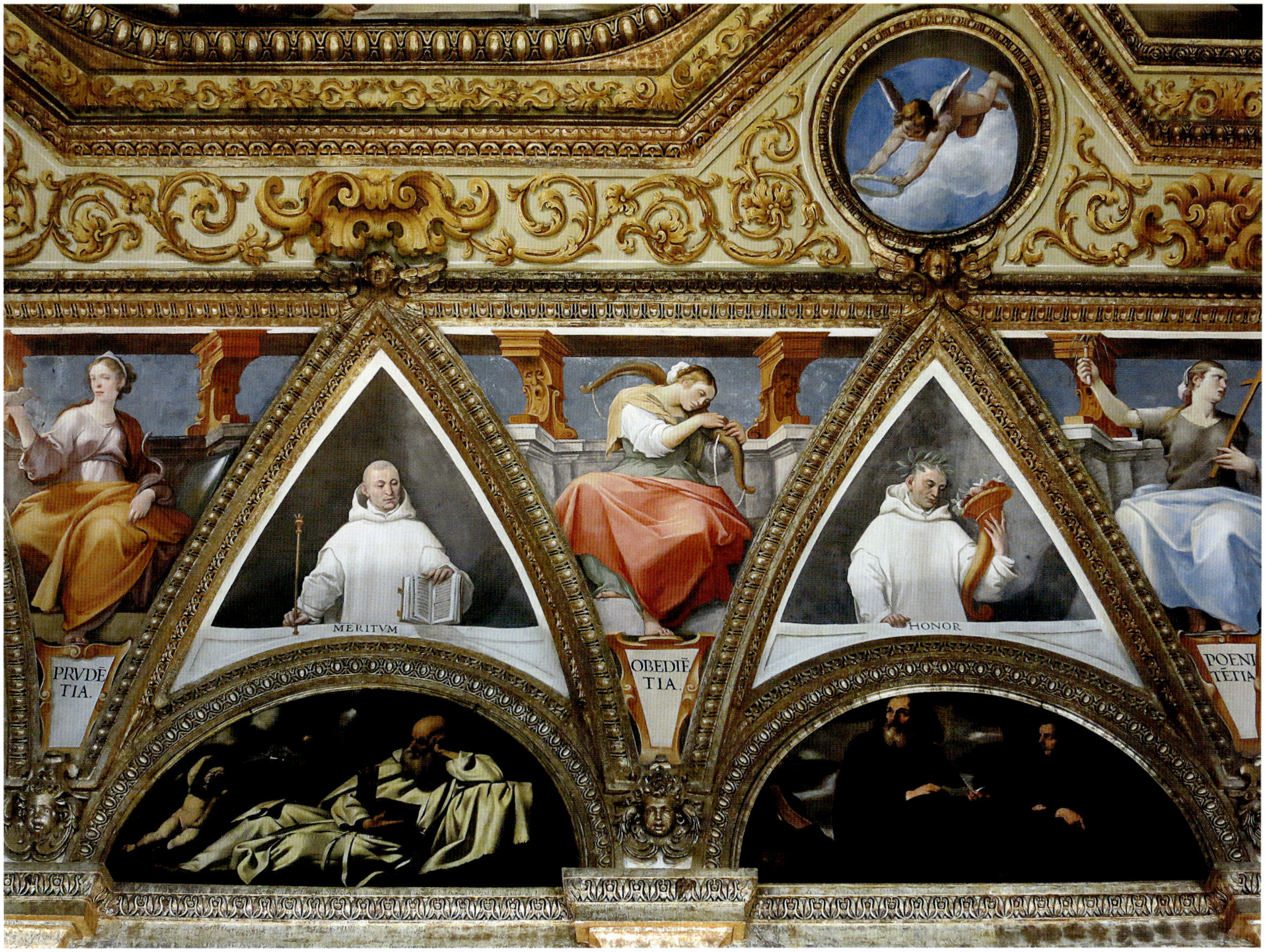

40 Paolo Finoglio, *St Romuald*; *St Francis of Paola*, 1624–25. Oil on canvas, 120 × 200 cm (each), Sala del Capitolo, Certosa di San Martino, Naples

of the project) before reaching a total valuation of 1,200 ducats (this figure was then used as the basis for the Carthusians' final settling of accounts in August 1631). This is a handsome sum compared to most other commissions of the period. Nonetheless, as Finoglio would surely have been aware, Stanzione was paid no fewer than 2,000 ducats at just this time for his decoration of the chapel of St Bruno in the same church.

Even if Ribera and Stanzione were colluding (with the support of the Carthusians) to keep Finoglio down to a payment level lower than that received by Stanzione in the sphere of public commissions, the discrepancy in prices remains: whatever the motivations, Finoglio was placed at a lower bracket than Stanzione for otherwise directly comparable work. Either way, Finoglio also begins to fade away from the documents at this point. First, he tried his hand at art dealing, establishing a partnership with another artist for this purpose in 1631 (to be discussed in Chapter Six). Eventually, though, he chose to leave Naples altogether. In 1635 he emigrated to the more conducive environment of Conversano, in Puglia, where he spent the last ten years of his life working for the court of Giangirolamo Acquaviva at what was then one of the most important political and cultural centres of the kingdom.[73] Whether or not Finoglio emigrated directly as a result of Stanzione's and Ribera's growing dominance of the upper levels of the market, his move nonetheless had the same effect, of removing one more potential competitor from their growing ascendancy of the field.

THE CONSEQUENCES OF RIBERA'S SUCCESS

There can be no doubting, therefore, that Ribera's relatively early and narrowly defined basis for success helped to raise him to an unprecedented level of pre-eminence in the Neapolitan art world. Yet, it can also be argued, in terms of the almost paradoxical manner in which such career trajectories can play out, that this also worked against him in the long run. It evidently encouraged a certain narrowing of his output. To be sure, Ribera was more than capable of original reinterpretations of traditional subjects and picture types (particularly his mythologies and psychological-physiognomical character studies), yet, as even the most cursory survey of his oeuvre will attest, these works were significantly outnumbered by a generally much more streamlined output oriented towards satisfying the unceasing demand for his squadrons of philosophers and saints, whether martyrs or anchorites (fig. 41).[74]

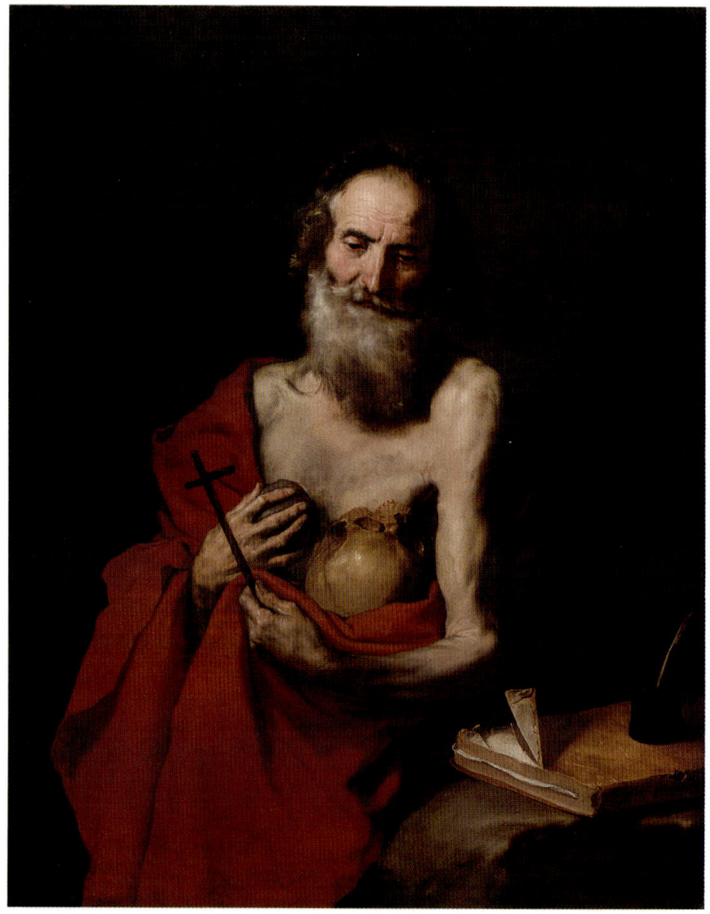

41 Jusepe de Ribera, *St Jerome*, *circa* 1639. Oil on canvas, 129 × 100 cm. The Cleveland Museum of Art

The religious instances of these trademark subjects and treatments worked equally well, moreover, in private settings, thus exempting Ribera of the customary need to modify his output significantly when switching between private and public idioms (although he did grade his work in terms of size and format). There are, in fact, relatively few examples in Ribera's oeuvre of compositions and picture types tailored specifically for public religious commissions (the series of *Patriarchs* and *Prophets* painted for the Certosa di San, to be discussed in Chapter Eleven, come to mind in this context), and very few instances of 'sacred conversation' altarpieces of the type so common in the work of Stanzione and his workshop.[75] Far more usual were picture types that Ribera was able to transfer from the private to the public setting without any major alteration of subject or composition. There is no particular distinction to be drawn, therefore, between one of Ribera's many versions of the *Martyrdom of St Bartholomew* painted for private collectors and those intended for public settings. The same could be said of his many treatments of the *Adoration of the Shepherds* and the *Pietà/Entombment*, or his numerous paintings of single saints.

As a result, Ribera's output, and that of the workshop that helped to sustain him, was less geared towards what might be termed product differentiation and segmentation of output than comparable artists, such as Stanzione. Rather, it lent itself inevitably to copying and to the serial repetition of a relatively narrow band of hallmark compositions. De' Dominici is the only early source to write in any depth on the activities of Ribera's *discepoli*. His account is revealing in that it highlights the practice of copying as central to the activities of this workshop. Thus Antonio Giordano – father of the much more famous Luca – is said to have specialized in copying Ribera's half-length saints, particularly *St Anthony*, which were then retouched by the master himself, presumably in order to be sold as originals. Similarly, Juan Do, the Spanish painter resident in Naples, is said to have copied Ribera's half-length philosophers and pictures of *St Jerome* so well that they were constantly confused as originals. Next, Enrico Fiammingo (identifiable from other sources as Hendrick van Somer) is mentioned as having specialized in copies after Ribera's *Apostles* that were so good that in De' Dominici's day they were still constantly confused with the work of the master, even by other painters. Finally, Bartolomeo Passante is said to have been so talented an imitator that Ribera had him execute many of his own commissions, particularly those ordered on behalf of foreign collectors.[76]

The essential accuracy of this account is confirmed by the continued difficulties experienced by contemporary scholars in their attempts to differentiate the work of this core group of Riberesque painters. These studies have sought to shed light on a complex series of intertwined connoisseurial problems that is further compounded by the paucity of independent information that could act as a reference point for the artists in question. The ultimate example of all this is Bartolomeo Passante. Until 1991 this artist was almost unknown and was identifiable only on the basis of a single signed work of secondary importance in the stores of the Prado in Madrid (although even this 'fact' is in itself uncertain, since the painting is actually signed Bassante rather than Passante). At that date, however, John T. Spike reasserted a long-dormant argument proposing that Passante might be identifiable, rather, as the author of a group of brilliant anonymous contemporary evocations of Ribera's style – as centred especially on vivid images of shepherds with their flocks. These had previously been grouped under the eponymous name of the Master of the Annunciation to the Shepherds (an argument that was based, in turn, on proposals advanced originally by August L. Mayer and Roberto Longhi) (fig. 42). This hypothesis has since been accepted by most writers, with the significant exception of Giuseppe de Vito, who has argued that the master should be identified as Juan Do.[77]

One of the main problems with the argument identifying Bartolomeo Passante as the Master of the Annunciation to the Shepherds is that a certain Bartolomeo Passante is documented in a Neapolitan marriage contract of 1636. This artist was born in Brindisi in 1618 and moved to Naples around 1629, before serving a probable apprenticeship with an otherwise unknown painter by the name of Pietro Beato, whose daughter he was marrying in 1636, aged eighteen. This same artist then died in 1648, aged thirty, so his work for Ribera would have had to be confined to a short period from the late 1630s to 1640s when he was still quite young.[78] For some writers, this compressed chronology seems difficult to reconcile with the stylistic elements inherent within the paintings by this master (which seem to indicate a dating earlier in the 1630s, if not several years earlier still).[79]

The issue is thus far from being resolved. Yet the lack of consensus is in itself significant since it continues the confusion concerning the true nature of this artist's identity that prevailed even within several decades of his presumed death. Thus in 1675 a Florentine merchant resident in Naples, Pietro Andrea Andreini, sent to Filippo Baldinucci a series of brief notes on local painters that included the following comments: 'Bartolomeo Passante who learned from and imitated closely the style of his master Jusepe de Ribera to the extent that, in fact, the copies made by his hand are almost impossible to distinguish from Jusepe's originals.'[80] A few years later, Carlo Celano continued to emphasize the problem when he noted that the paintings of Bartolomeo Passante were frequently confused with Ribera's and that very little, in fact, of his work remained in Naples since most had been exported for sale in Flanders.[81]

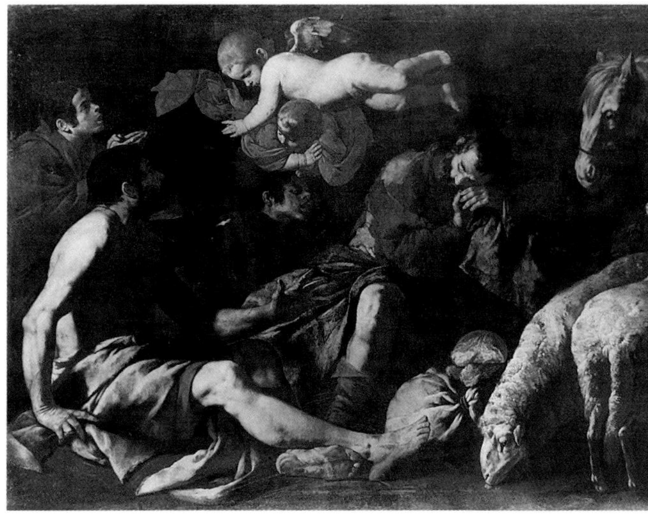

42 Master of the Annunciation to the Shepherds (Bartolomeo Passante?), *Annunciation to the Shepherds*, 1635–45. Oil on canvas, 180 × 261.5 cm. Museo e Gallerie Nazionali di Capodimonte, Naples

A similar level of confusion is evident – albeit to slightly varying degrees – for each of the three other painters in this group of Ribera's workshop assistants. Antonio Giordano is so obscure that none of his works has thus far been identified – although a tentative attempt has been made to identify Antonio and the young Luca as co-authors of two copies in the Prado after a series of lost works by Ribera of the Titans from the early 1630s.[82] An understanding of Juan Do's close variations on Ribera's style is similarly based on a mere handful of works – above all on an altarpiece of the *Adoration of the Shepherds* in the church of the Pietà dei Turchini in Naples that has been identified as by Do's hand from the time of De' Dominici onwards (fig. 43). De Vito's suggestion that this artist should nonetheless be identified as the Master of the Annunciation to the Shepherds has thrown even this fragile consensus into disarray. Finally, Hendrick van Somer is only now beginning to emerge from the margins as a painter of some significance – after many years of his work being confused, it seems, not only with other works by Ribera and his entourage but also with that of another artist with a similar name who was active, rather, in Amsterdam.[83]

The scant biographical information for these three artists adds further to the difficulties. Almost all the documents for Antonio Giordano, for example, postdate 1657 and concern his involvement in his son's booming enterprise until the time of his death in 1683.[84] A single exception for his own career is a modest payment of 7.5 ducats made out to him in 1637 for five paintings of *St Nicholas*. This suggests that Antonio's independent career – as launched presumably after a period spent in Ribera's workshop during the early 1630s – may have operated at a relatively modest level of the art world, working at the behest of dealers.[85] A little more is known about Juan Do (1604–1656), mainly as a result of his deposition made on the occasion of his marriage in 1626 to Grazia di Rosa – sister of Annella and Pacecco de Rosa. This shows that Do came from Ribera's home town of Játiva in Valencia and that he moved to Naples only in 1623. Ribera served as witness to this marriage, so the association of the two Valencians dated from at least this time, and, more likely, from many years earlier back in Spain. Do is accordingly probably to be counted as one of Ribera's earliest assistants, presumably active in his workshop from the late 1620s onwards. Two subsequent payments of 1633 and 1637 suggest a marginally higher economic attainment than Antonio Giordano, but still no documents for public commissions can be attached to his name, and the parameters of his career remain in other respects almost entirely obscure until the time of his death from the plague in 1656.[86] Finally, documentation of the career of Hendrick van Somer (1615–1684) remains an uncharted landscape save for a single public commission, for an altarpiece of the *Baptism* painted for the church of Santa Maria della Sapienza in 1641 for the relatively modest rate of 50 ducats.[87]

One of the few conclusions to be drawn from this hazy information is that, as De' Dominici perceptively noted, Ribera appears to have channelled his workshop's activities particularly into the production of head- to three-quarter-length, single-figure copies after his work. One may recall, in this respect, De' Dominici's observations concerning Antonio Giordano's half-length paintings of *St Anthony*, those by Juan Do of *Philosophers* and *St Jerome*, and Van Somer's *Apostles*. These comments further suggest that each assistant was given particular responsibility for producing multiple versions of one or more popular compositions or figure types. A number of these slightly reduced derivations from Ribera's larger saints have now been identified in a study of a further member of the workshop. Giovanni Ricca (active first half of the seventeenth century) is a painter whose reputation has similarly remained so marginal that already by the early eighteenth century he entirely escaped the attention of the otherwise exhaustive De' Dominici. His *Elijah* is a two-thirds-scale, reduced copy after a painting produced by Ribera for the internal façade of the Certosa di San Martino in 1638 (figs 44–5).[88] Ricca also produced multiple sets of smaller busts and heads of saints derived equally from Riberian prototypes.

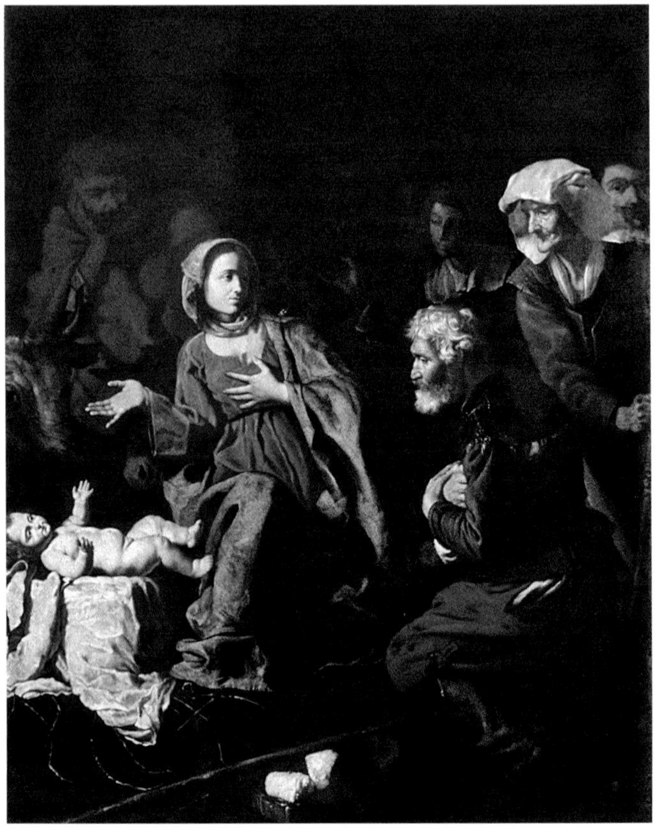

43 Juan Do, *Adoration of the Shepherds*, after 1626. Oil on canvas, 225 × 180 cm. Chiesa della Pietà dei Turchini, Naples

The production of these works seems to have been authorized by the master with an eye towards sales on the open market. They are typical of this kind of product in

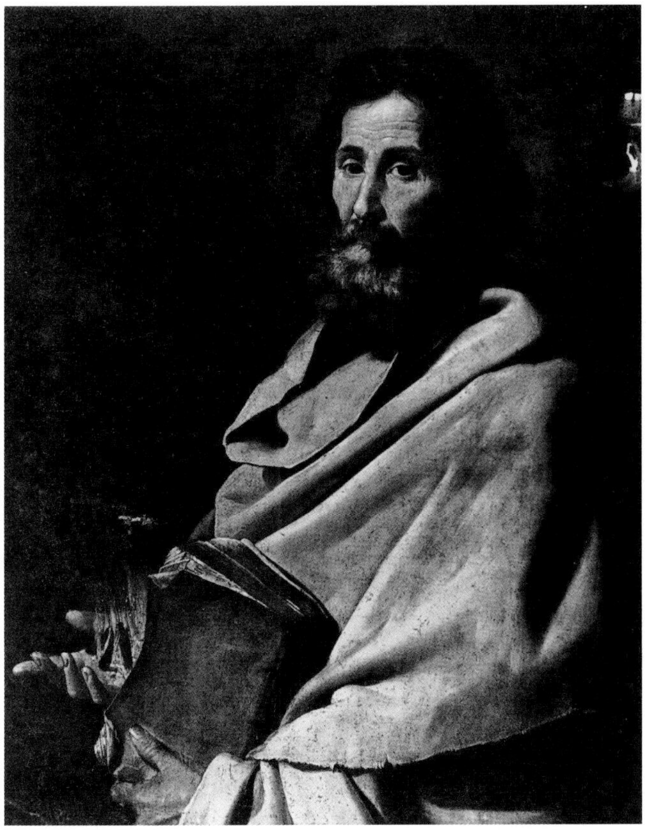

Above 44 Attributed to Giovanni Ricca, *Elijah*, *circa* 1638–40. Oil on canvas, 103 × 75 cm. Pinacoteca D'Errico, Matera

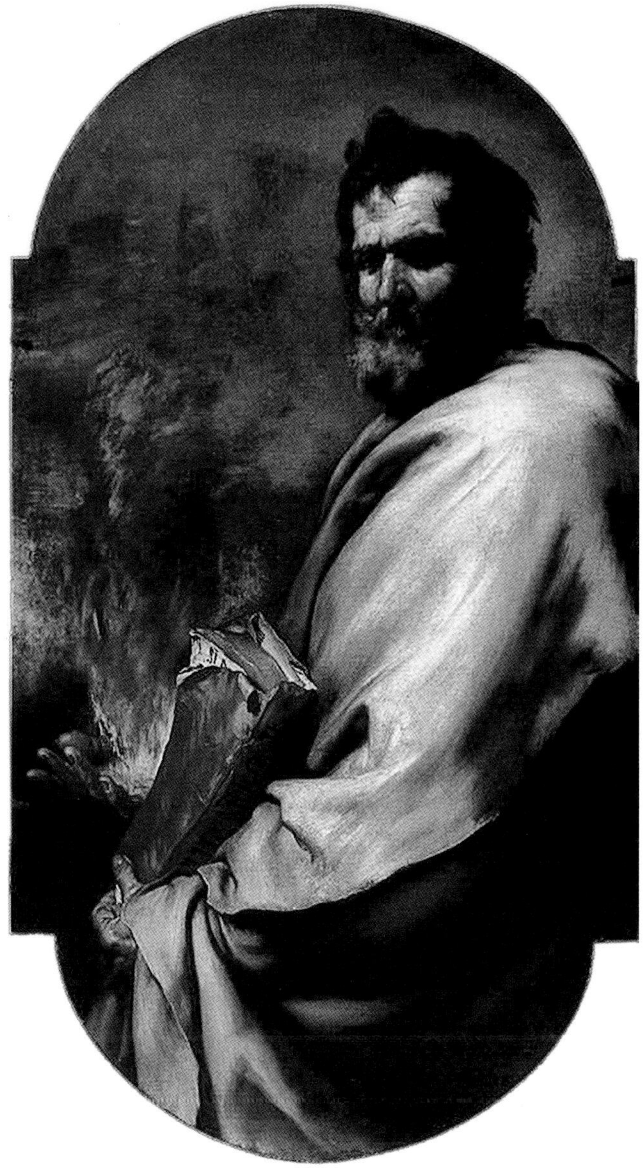

Right 45 Jusepe de Ribera, *Elijah*, 1638. Oil on canvas, 168 × 97 cm. Church of the Certosa di San Martino, Naples

that they constitute simple, standardized subjects and formats that could be produced speculatively without the need of a commission in advance. They could also be turned out relatively quickly in serial sets, and they would have been much cheaper to acquire than Ribera's more customary monumental figure paintings. Ribera's *Elijah* cost the Carthusians 50 ducats, or half of his standard public commission rate of 100 ducats per full-length figure.[89] Ricca's *Elijah*, by contrast, would have cost no more than a fifth of this amount, assuming, of course, that it was sold as a workshop piece and not as an original by the master himself.

This can be confirmed from an unusually detailed and carefully compiled inventory of the collection of Ettore Capecelatro, marchese di Torella, drawn up by Capecelatro's favourite artist, Domenico Gargiulo, in 1659.[90] This collection contained only one fully autograph painting by Ribera – a bust-length *St Simon* valued at the customary rate of 30 ducats for a work of this size. At the same time, Capecelatro owned no fewer than five paintings by Hendrick van Somer – all of half-length saints of the type described by De' Dominici. These were all slightly larger than Ribera's *St Simon* but were nonetheless each valued at the lower rate of 8 ducats, thus setting a comparative price for Ricca's equivalent work. Smaller reductions after Ribera's originals were cheaper still. A 'testa copia di Gioseppe di ribera piccola' (small head copied after Jusepe de Ribera) by Van Somer was valued at only 2 ducats, a price not so far distant from the 1.5 ducats per painting paid to Antonio Giordano in 1637 for his five versions of *St Nicholas*. The reduced-format versions of Riberesque compositions by Van Somer, Ricca, Antonio Giordano and other members of the

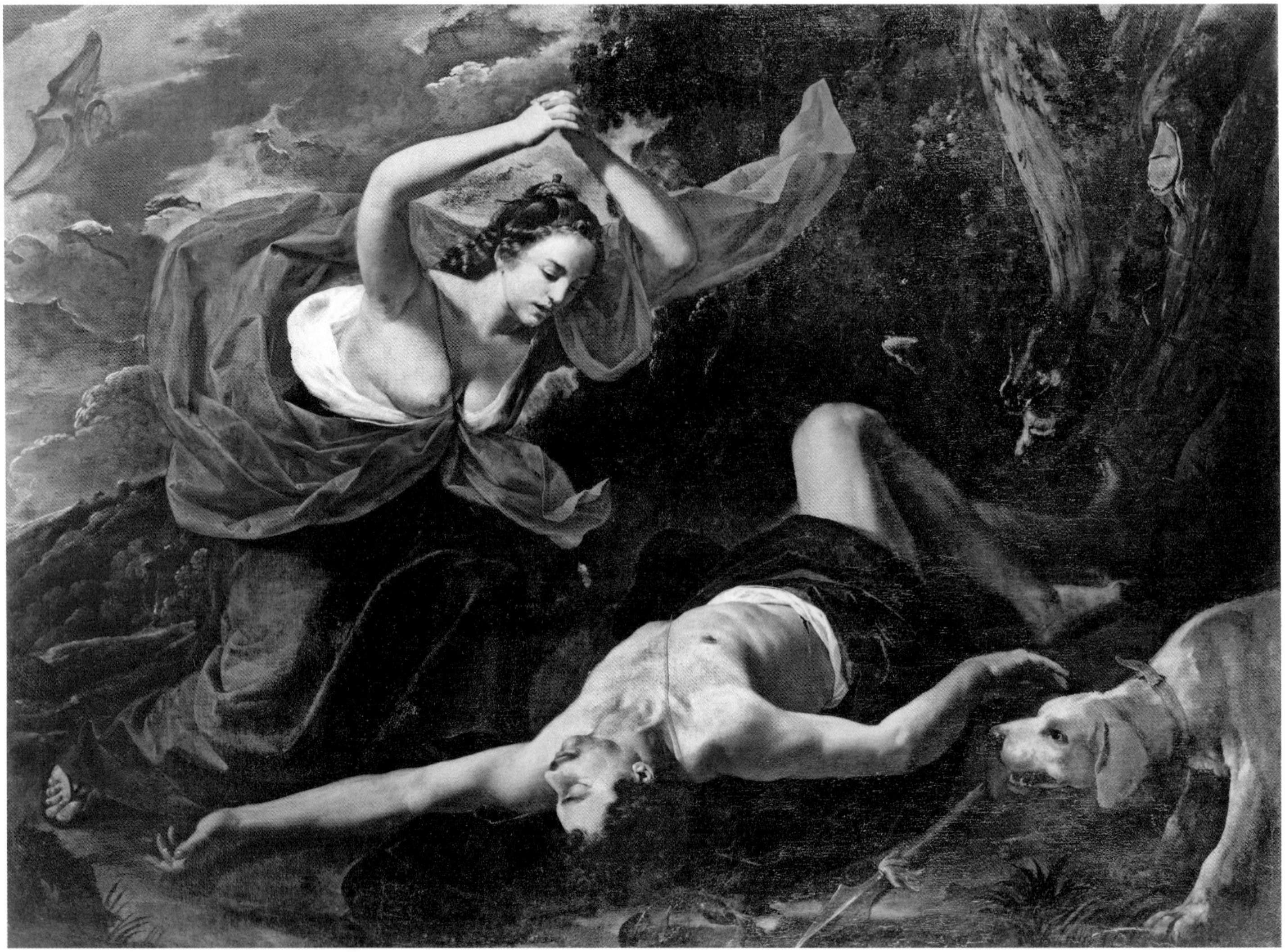

46 Attributed to Hendrick van Somer, *Venus and Adonis*, *circa* 1637–early 1640s. Oil on canvas, 162 × 212 cm. Private collection, Piacenza; formerly Sotheby's, New York

workshop would thus have appealed particularly to those more modest collectors like Capecelatro who were eager to own representative examples of the work of Ribera and his associates, but who were nonetheless not committed enough to part with the 200 ducats or thereabouts required to secure a major work by the master himself from the 1630s onwards.

Ribera thus seems to have conceived of his workshop above all else as a conduit for offering clients a cheaper, lower-end range to his output that could also be turned over more quickly than his larger and more laborious commissioned works. This would have had the added advantage of ensuring a steadier cash flow from walk-in customers while Ribera was waiting for the larger, but also more sporadic amounts of money paid to him by his other patrons. This is, once again, very different from Stanzione and it suggests a final point of distinction to be drawn between these two major workshops of the period.

The extent to which Stanzione spread his labour force across the entire range of his production has been noted: from Agostino Beltrano's assistance at the most extensive and prestigious public fresco commissions down to the smaller and cheaper adaptations of privately commissioned gallery paintings produced by Bernardo Cavallino and Annella de Rosa. But if this accordingly suggests a strategy of vertically integrating his workshop across all the varying levels of his production, then Ribera's organization, by contrast, points to a much more rigidly hierarchical, horizontal alignment of

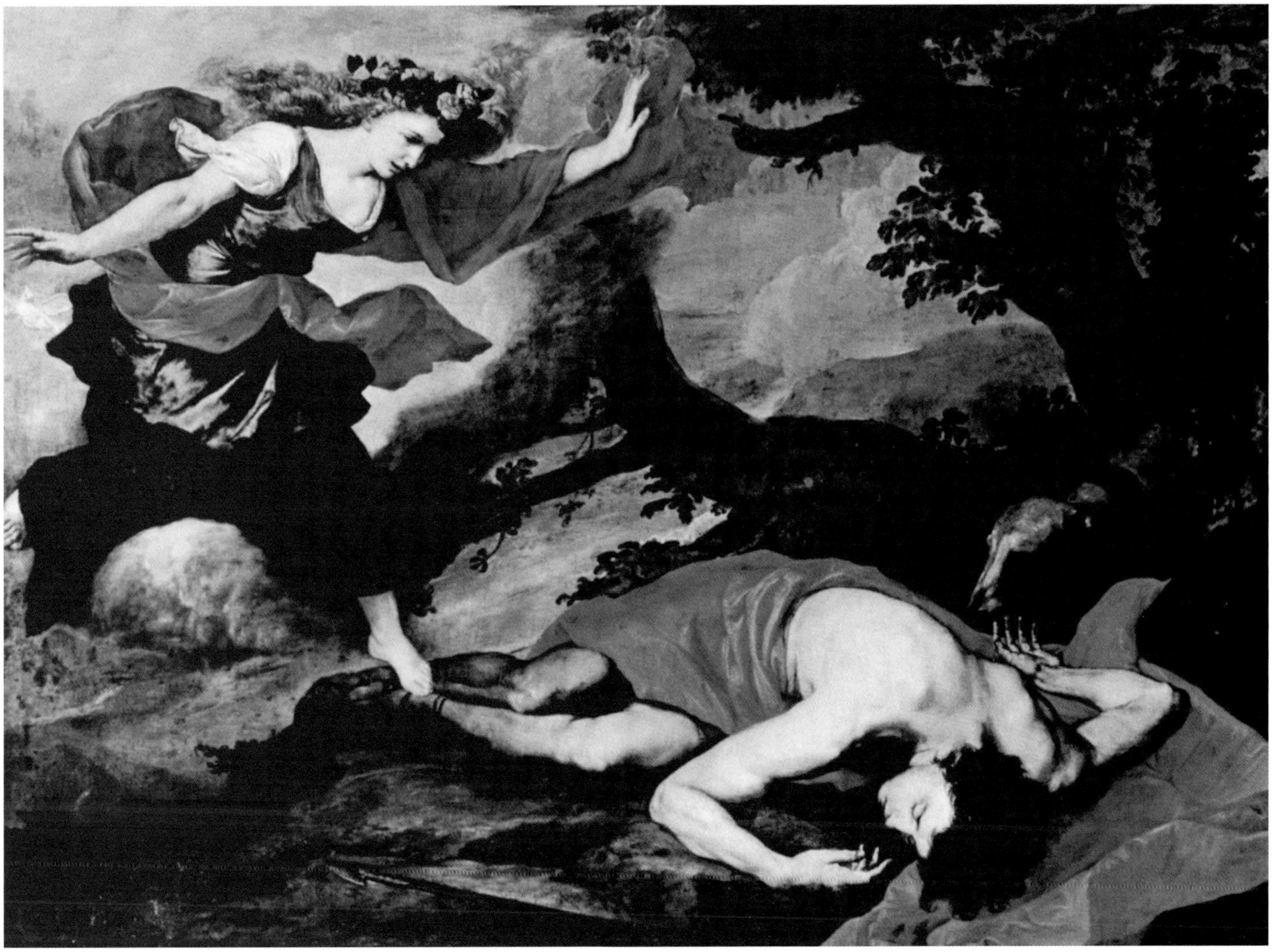

47 Jusepe de Ribera, *Venus and Adonis*, signed and dated 1637. Oil on canvas, 179 × 262 cm. Galleria Nazionale d'Arte Antica, Palazzo Corsini, Rome

the assistants' work. With a far less varied output to begin with, Ribera accordingly grouped his assistants for the most part beneath him, with their work concentrated towards the cheaper end of his output for private collectors.

Anonymity, confusions of identity and the submerging of the assistants' output within the margins of the master's work all follow inevitably from such a policy, and Ribera's senior assistants seem clearly to have been more affected by this than Stanzione's. Yet this group was nonetheless just as capable as Agostino Beltrano or Niccolò de Simone of rising above this customary mode of working in order to operate on a slightly more individualistic and semi-independent level. Presumably this would have occurred particularly during the later stages of their association with Ribera when, in the absence of any more specific information, they may be imagined as eventually drifting away from his workshop, particularly from the early to mid-1640s, in order to develop independent careers.

A painting of *Venus and Adonis*, now attributed to Hendrick van Somer, represents an example of this kind of presumably commissioned work. It is, to be sure, a variant on a famous composition by Ribera dating to the later 1630s (figs 46–7).[91] Yet it is nonetheless accomplished – even ambitious in its own way – and certainly compares favourably to Beltrano's variant on Stanzione's *Lot and his Daughters* (see fig. 32). The lack of any clear footprints left behind in the records by Van Somer strongly suggests that he was provided with very few of these kinds of opportunities, such as were afforded to the more senior assistants in Stanzione's workshop as a matter of course.

The comparison between Van Somer and De Simone seems especially pertinent in this respect. Both were Flemish immigrants who had moved to Naples at about the same time and who then sought to advance their careers by joining one of the leading workshops. Yet what a different experience De Simone had. His association with Stanzione facilitated multiple public commissions, for both altarpieces and frescoes, some of which fetched very high prices indeed in relative terms – 600 ducats in 1642 for the chapel in Santa Teresa degli Scalzi, and 300 ducats in the early 1650s for the Cacace chapel – as well as leading to important contacts with high-ranking patrons such as Giovanni Cacace. Van Somer's shadowy career suggests a very different story. His single known public commission was painted in 1641 for the much lower price of only 50 ducats, as compared, for example, with the 200 ducats paid to De Simone for his Lecce altarpiece of 1645.

It would be mistaken, nonetheless, to conclude from this that De Simone and Beltrano fared better in relative terms than Ribera's assistants because they were in some essential respect more talented or distinguished painters than Van Somer and his colleagues. In fact, in at least some instances the opposite seems to have been the case. Although the work of the Master of the Annunciation to the Shepherds was far less understood and prominent in his day, his output is nonetheless recognized now as of far greater originality and significance than Agostino Beltrano's or Niccolò de Simone's – indeed, it is probably fair to say that his work is also generally regarded as being of greater significance than Ribera's other assistants. Raffaello Causa, for example, described his paintings as 'absolutely personal and unmistakeable, full of spirit, vigour and with an intimate coherence of structure'.[92]

Herein lies the rub for this artist, however, since (if the argument identifying him as Passante is accepted for now) it was precisely this greater degree of artistic distinction that doomed him to obscurity. First Ribera recognized in his singular talent an artist whom he could delegate to produce, not just cheaper derivations after his work like Van Somer and Ricca, but also rather more prestigious and thus also more expensive productions. He was then able to sell these as his own commissioned work, particularly to foreign collectors not as knowledgeable about his oeuvre (this at least from De' Dominici). This process was subsequently picked up on and developed to a greater degree of efficiency by the Flemish merchant Gaspar Roomer, who began an export trade in his work (see pp. 128–30). The price of greater seniority and heightened talent in Ribera's workshop, then, was not to be given the opportunity to operate semi-independently for occasionally prestigious patrons in the assistant's own right. Rather, it was to be subsumed into the master's identity, with the added effect of having one's works sent further abroad.

THE CHALLENGES OF RIBERA'S FINAL YEARS

The orientation of Ribera's workshop thus seems not to have been as favourable as Stanzione's for the longer-term independent career development of his assistants. What, though, were the implications of this attitude to managing the output of the workshop for the master himself? The evidence, while admittedly scanty, is nonetheless suggestive. To begin with, it is curious that an artist with such a large and active workshop seems not to have been able to honour his contracts on a number of occasions.

In 1632 Ribera was required to return 100 ducats paid to him as an advance – or *caparra* – for a painting of the *Martyrdom of St Lawrence* commissioned by the high-ranking aristocrat and administrative functionary Giovanni d'Avalos, principe di Montesarchio.[93] The reason given for this reimbursement is only elliptically expressed in the document as 'Jusepe was not able to finish it', which gives no clue as to why this would have occurred for such an important patron. After all, the d'Avalos family had long been pre-eminent in Neapolitan Hispanic aristocratic circles – forebears had served the Spanish crown as governors of Milan and viceroy of Naples – while Giovanni d'Avalos had probably commissioned one of the most important paintings of Ribera's career – *Apollo and Marsyas*, now in the Capodimonte, painted in 1637 (fig. 48).[94]

Problems of this kind seem to have formed something of a pattern for Ribera, even before the effects of a long-term debilitating illness began to slow down his productivity from 1643 onwards. Another example concerns Giovanni Battista Pisante, prior of the Certosa di San Martino, who in 1638 commissioned two half-length saints from Ribera.[95] Pisante, likewise a patron of some significance, was at that stage supervising Ribera's commission for the previously mentioned *Elijah* and its pendant *Moses*, together with a monumental *Communion of the Apostles* for the choir of the church and an extensive series of *Prophets* and *Patriarchs* for the nave, which were not completed until 1643.[96] Yet it took

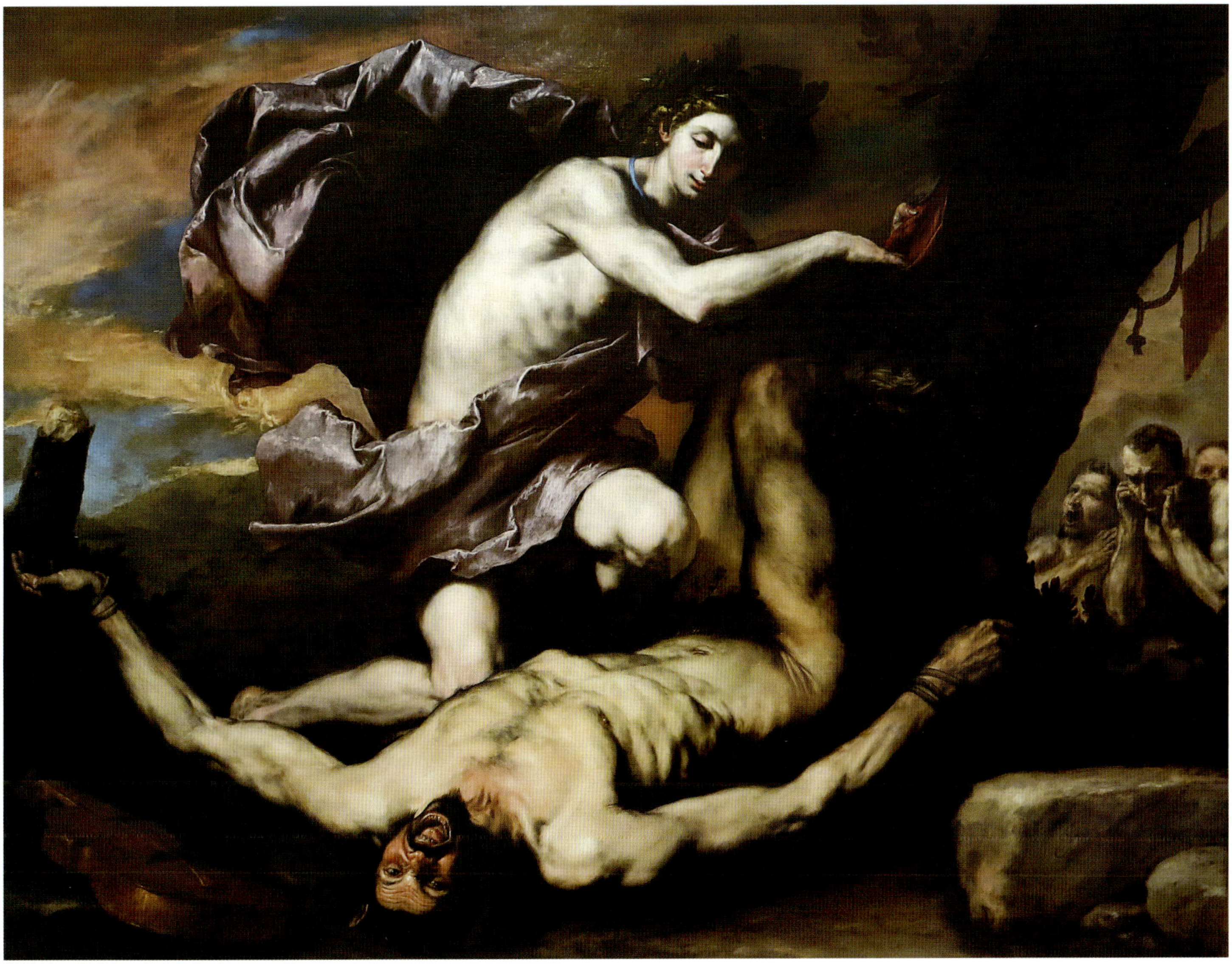

48 Jusepe de Ribera, *Apollo and Marsyas*, signed and dated 1637. Oil on canvas, 182 × 232 cm. Museo e Gallerie Nazionali di Capodimonte, Naples

Ribera some thirteen years to deliver the two half-lengths, in late 1651.[97] Similar problems stalled the timely completion of Ribera's *Communion of the Apostles*, commissioned in early 1638 but not delivered until September 1651 (fig. 49). Finally, in 1641, the protonotary of Palermo, Cristoforo Papa, commissioned a version of the *Adoration of the Shepherds* painted in the previous year for the viceroy, the duque de Medina de las Torres. For this he was prepared to pay the princely sum of 400 ducats, yet Ribera failed to complete it. On this occasion he was caught out and required by order of the court of the Vicaria in 1646 to return the 150 ducats paid by Papa as an advance.[98]

What can be inferred from this? One conclusion is that Ribera was not particularly good at delegating the workshop to assist him on prestigious local commissions, or perhaps he was not prepared to collaborate. Instances of collaborative works attributed to both Ribera and his workshop are, in fact, rare in the literature on this artist. An exception is the series of *Prophets* and *Patriarchs* for San Martino, some of which have been identified as probable workshop collaborations.[99] Yet this is readily understandable given the atypically large and extensive nature of this public commission, which must have placed an unusually intense strain on Ribera's customary mode of

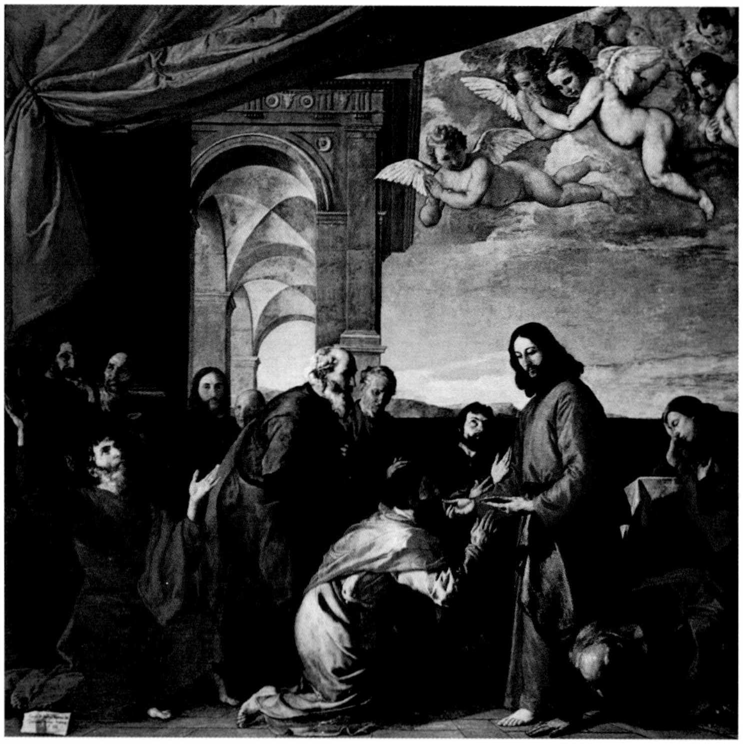

49 Jusepe de Ribera, *Communion of the Apostles*, signed and dated 1651. Oil on canvas, 400 × 400 cm. Church of the Certosa di San Martino, Naples

working. Hardly any other instances of this type of work have been identified – in fact, the opposite is the case since two paintings that were once attributed to Ribera and Juan Do together have since been reattributed to the master himself.[100]

This understanding of the relatively 'closed' nature of Ribera's autograph work may well need revising as future research emphasis shifts towards a more detailed analysis of the varying contributions made by each member of his workshop. In broad terms, though, the picture here outlined seems accurate enough. Ribera's occasional difficulties with completing contracts reinforce the prevailing impression that he did not make a habit of calling in workshop assistance for his own commissioned work. He did not, in other words, generally follow the standard practice of revising and completing workshop output for commissioned work by 'retouching' it and then selling it as his own, as so many other leading Baroque artists did as a matter of course, from Massimo Stanzione (as in the case of his dealings with Giuseppe Stanzione), to Ludovico Carracci, Guido Reni and beyond.[101] Instead, Ribera essentially divided his output into commissioned works painted by the master alone and works produced after his model and sold – presumably – as original, albeit cheaper productions. It is in this area of cheaper workshop output that Ribera seems more likely to have intervened by 'retouching' works before selling them (as De' Dominici noted in the context of Antonio Giordano).

The implications of all this for Ribera's productivity seem to have hit home particularly during the final decade of his career. From 1643 until his death in 1652 the artist is known to have suffered from a debilitating illness of some kind, which has been tentatively identified by Spinosa as a form of arterial hypertension.[102] Ribera remained active to a degree, and indeed completed a number of major contracts, including a monumental *Immaculate Conception* for the Cappella Reale (1646), *St Januarius Emerging Unscathed from the Furnace* for the Cappella del Tesoro of Naples Cathedral (1646) (fig. 50), and a *Pietà* painted for Don Antonio Ruffo of Messina in 1649–50, the last for the substantial sum of 270 ducats. Yet Ribera's productivity declined significantly during these years. Spinosa's catalogue of 2003 lists only seventy-five prime autograph compositions for the last twelve years of Ribera's life, whereas it records double this amount (or half Ribera's entire output) for the boom years of the 1630s. At the same time, Ribera's workshop seems also to have wound down progressively as his assistants grew older (or died, as in the case of Passante) and presumably drifted away towards their own somewhat struggling later careers.

Ribera was now painting at a rate of less than half of what he used to and generating fewer than half his annual earnings as a result. A further drain on his customary client base must undoubtedly have been the sharp decline in Spanish patronage caused by the disturbances of the Revolt of Masaniello of 1647–8 (a seismically disturbing, popular uprising directed particularly against the Spanish administration and all those associated with it).[103] Yet further deprived of the booming levels of productivity (and income) that had characterized his thriving workshop during the previous decade, Ribera now hit hard times. In early 1651 he petitioned the monks of the Certosa di San Martino to be given the opportunity once more to finish the monumental *Communion of the Apostles*, commissioned as far back as 1638. As a peace offering and sign of his continued abilities, he presented the new prior, Andrea Cancelliere, with the two long-delayed half-length saints, likewise commissioned back in 1638 (fig. 51).[104]

In response, the Carthusians sent their most trusted artists, Domenico Gargiulo and the silversmith Gennaro Monte

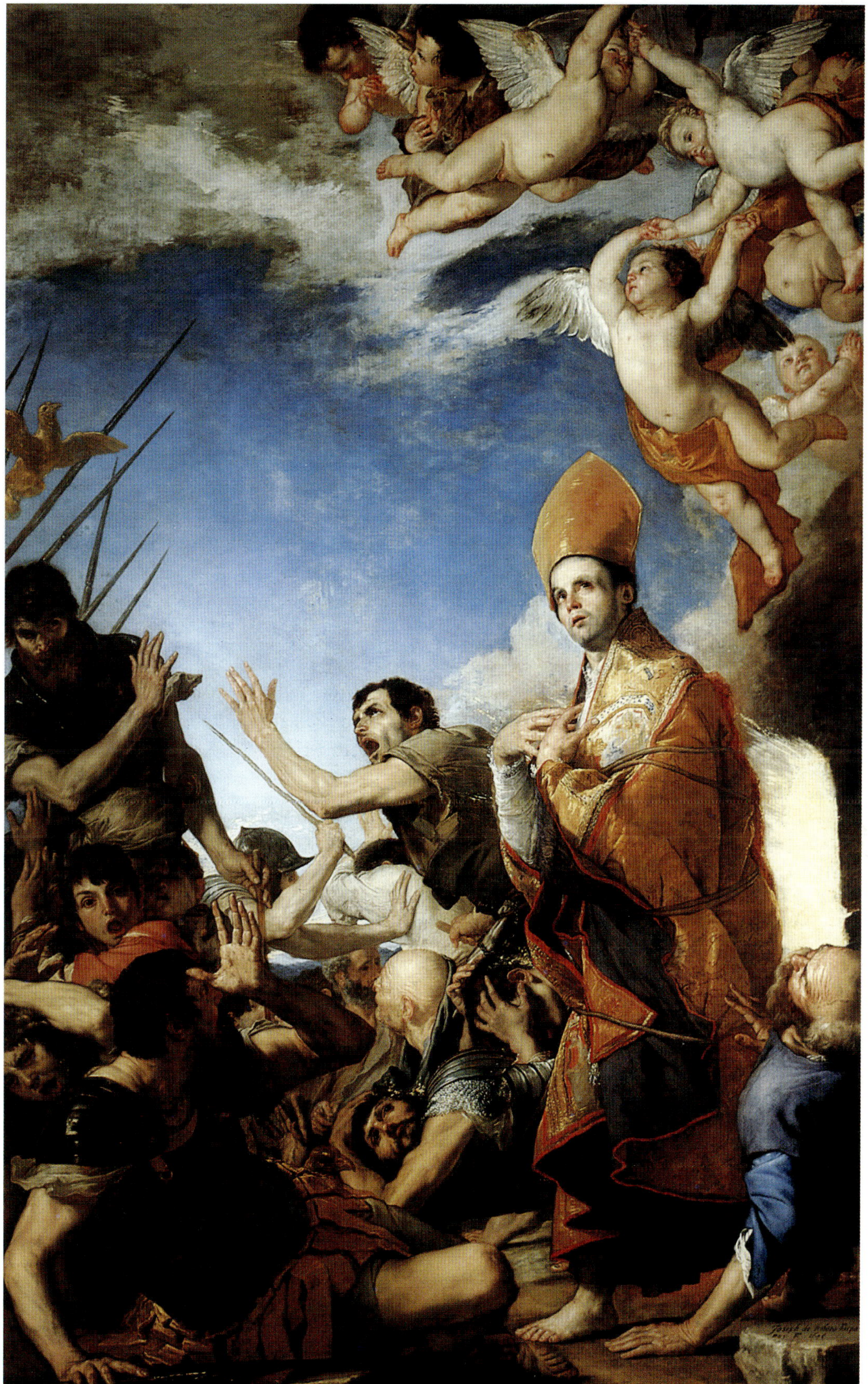

50 Jusepe de Ribera, *St Januarius Emerging Unscathed from the Furnace*, signed and dated 1646. Oil on copper, 320 × 200 cm. Cappella del Tesoro di San Gennaro, Naples Cathedral

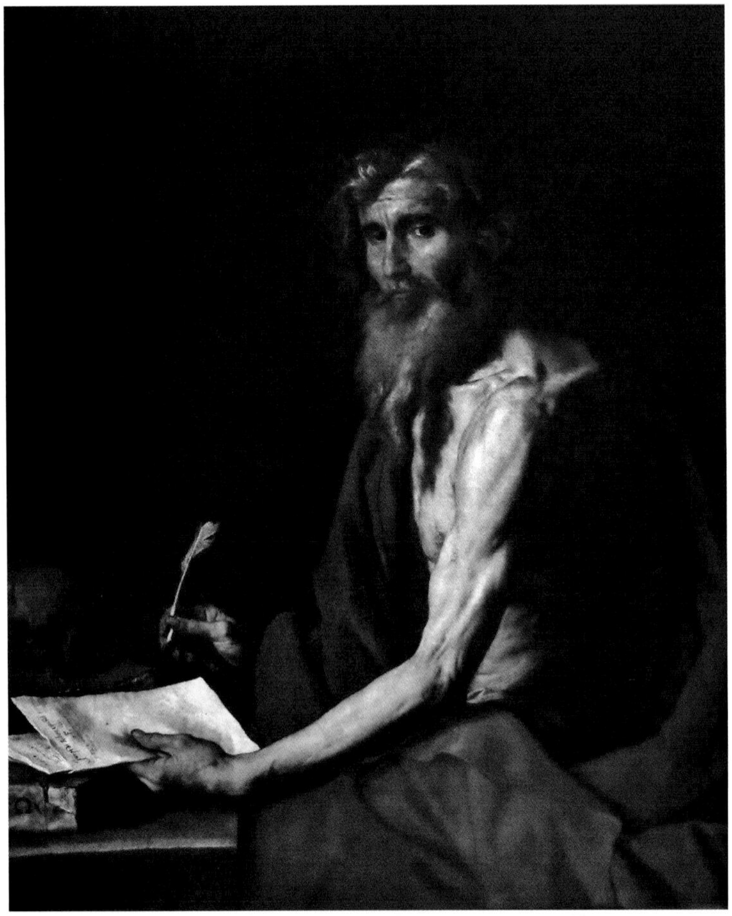

51 Jusepe de Ribera, *St Jerome*, signed and dated 1651. Oil on canvas, 125 × 100 cm. Museo di San Martino, Naples

(both of whom had worked at the Certosa for many years), on a fact-finding mission to Ribera's workshop in order to assess his ability to go ahead with the commission. They reported that it was worth proceeding, if only because Ribera had already received 300 ducats in hand in 1638. They also observed that Ribera now seemed motivated to complete the commission, 'to show the world that he was living and not dead, and to do it with pleasure so as to recuperate his extinct fame'.[105]

But while the two artists may have been thinking about Ribera's need to re-establish his reputation, Ribera himself seems to have been motivated by an urgent need for money. A series of letters that he dictated to be sent to the new prior makes for pathetic reading, since he alternately flatters, begs and complains to Cancelliere about his pressing domestic concerns and his need for a quicker and more generous series of cash advances than the Carthusians were prepared to give him. At one stage he went so far as to state outright: 'it would greatly alleviate my misery if you could bring me all the money together'.[106]

But the Carthusians did not satisfy his request, and chose, instead, to restrict Ribera's payments to a series of much smaller and also more regular advances made in conjunction with two to three weekly visits to his studio to check on progress. Evidently they did not entirely trust him, and while they had been content to pay Stanzione larger lump sums (500 ducats on one occasion, and 200 ducats on another) for the *Last Supper*, a companion painting to the *Communion of the Apostles* and also painted for the choir in 1639, they kept Ribera on a much tighter rein of smaller instalments to ensure his ongoing commitment.[107]

Ribera did eventually complete the *Communion of the Apostles*, within half a year of the commission's reactivation. Yet he still died on the verge of bankruptcy a few months later. This in turn set in train a drawn-out and ultimately mutually unsatisfactory legal struggle between Ribera's heirs and the Carthusians for money said to be owing on his work, all of which finally resulted in a cash settlement of 111 ducats in 1655 to finish the claim.[108]

So, at the end of the story, one can speculate whether or not Ribera might have prepared himself better for the professional downturns and financial challenges that added to the diminished reputation of his final years. Of course, a great many factors here – personal, familial, psychological and medical – are largely unknown. Nevertheless, the relatively narrow emphasis of Ribera's earlier career, combined with the particular orientation of his workshop, does not appear to have provided him with a flexible base from which to respond to the unexpected twists and turns of his later years. It seems, in short, that the late Ribera had neither the physical productivity, nor the workshop back-up, nor even the flexibility to create new areas of production to enable him to adapt to the changes in his situation. Ribera's late career, then, constitutes a classic case of what can go wrong when an artist becomes too narrowly defined and insufficiently diverse on a number of different levels of output to allow room to shift emphasis in response to changes in productivity and patronage.

None of these problems was liable to be incurred by the next great inheritor of Ribera's and Stanzione's mantle. Luca Giordano emerged in the early to mid-1650s in the brief interregnum between the end of Ribera's and Stanzione's careers and the reopening of the field for upper-level market dominance in Naples following their deaths. His early career also benefitted from the next phase of cultural and artistic renewal that began following the political and economic shocks to the kingdom created by the Revolt of Masaniello in 1647–8 and then even more so by the devastating plague in 1656.

Giordano's unprecedented success rested in great part on his ability to absorb and synthesize the lessons provided by his models. These lessons were not just artistic. In many respects his career development can be read as the culmination of a series of professional strategies modelled on Ribera, Stanzione and the wider scope of the Neapolitan art world more generally concerning the kinds of issues that have been charted here regarding patronage, productivity and the workshop. His manifest accomplishments in these respects had a particular orientation, nonetheless, and will be considered in due course in the context of a more specific account of the Neapolitan art market. The next chapter, however, examines the teeming world of the smaller workshops and above all the development of the field for cabinet painting that became such a crucial element in the renewal of Neapolitan Baroque painting from the 1630s onwards.

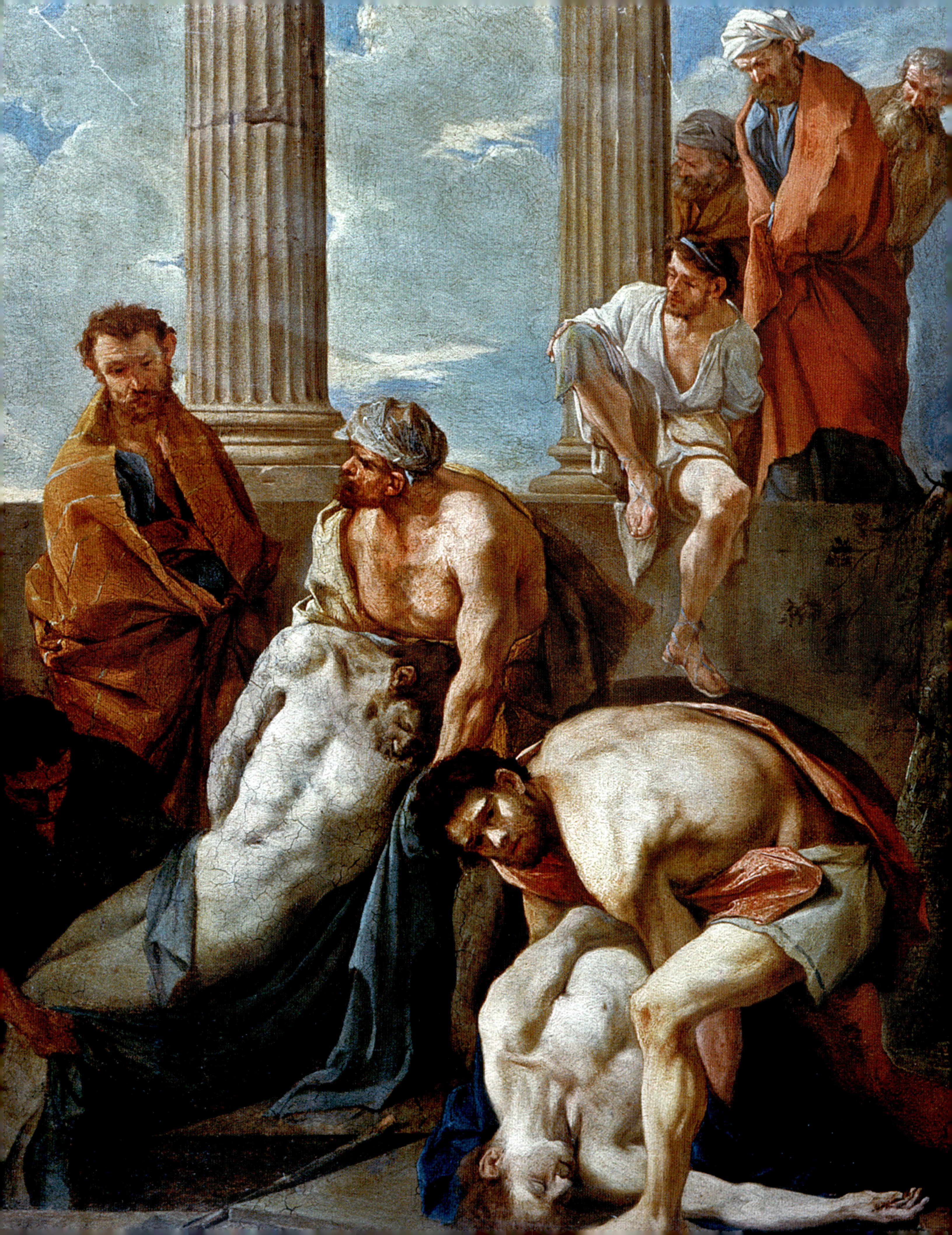

4

Aniello Falcone and the Rise of Neapolitan Cabinet Painting

LIFE DRAWING AND THE BIRTH OF THE NEAPOLITAN ACADEMY

In early 1636 Aniello Falcone (1607–1656) and two of his colleagues contracted a certain Paolo Savione to assist them in a new venture they were planning. On this occasion they agreed to pay Savione to pose as a life model in Falcone's residence every Monday, Wednesday and Friday for two hours per session from the end of January until April. Savione was to receive 12 *carlini* a month – equivalent to 1.2 ducats in total, or 1 *carlino* or 0.1 of a ducat for every two-hour session.[1] This was the same amount, incidentally (prior to Neapolitan devaluation at least), as the 1.2 Roman scudi paid monthly to the life model of the Accademia di San Luca in Rome, one of several factors suggesting Falcone's recent presence in Rome and probable attendance at the Accademia's life classes during that time.[2] The arrangement would no doubt have greatly benefitted the artists' practices. It would have regularized their life-drawing requirements and obviated the need to search beyond their workshops in order to find appropriate models to pose for their compositions. Carlo Celano, for example, speaks in this respect of Carlo Sellitto needing to rely on a particular life model for one of his altarpieces of *St Sebastian*,[3] while Artemisia Gentileschi complained to her patron, Don Antonio Ruffo of Messina, about the cost and difficulties involved in finding suitable female models for her history paintings.[4]

The agreement was also evidently tied to a yet more ambitious educational programme, since it explicitly documents the painters' intention to 'designare le lineature Conforme se sole fare nelle accademie de pittori' (delineate forms as is done in painters' academies). The idea of opening a private academy represented a new undertaking in Naples at that time. The only evidence of an earlier interest along these lines is an evidently embellished reference by De' Dominici concerning the young Massimo Stanzione's decision to leave Fabrizio Santafede's workshop in order to study life drawing under Giovanni Battista Caracciolo, on the basis of Caracciolo's earlier studies under the Carracci in Rome, an activity that would have occurred some twenty years earlier, if it could verified.[5] Of more direct relevance to the thinking of Falcone and his colleagues seems to have been the more recent model provided by Domenichino's private academy in Rome. Poussin, who was at the forefront of the current Neapolitan interest in neo-Venetian painting, had studied life drawing under Domenichino a few years earlier, and Falcone had presumably come to hear of the academy's activities during his presumed trip to Rome.[6] Domenichino was, moreover, then in Naples at work on the Cappella del Tesoro di San Gennaro in Naples Cathedral, although his strict

Facing page Andrea de Leone, *Tobit Burying the Dead*, late 1640s (detail of fig. 59)

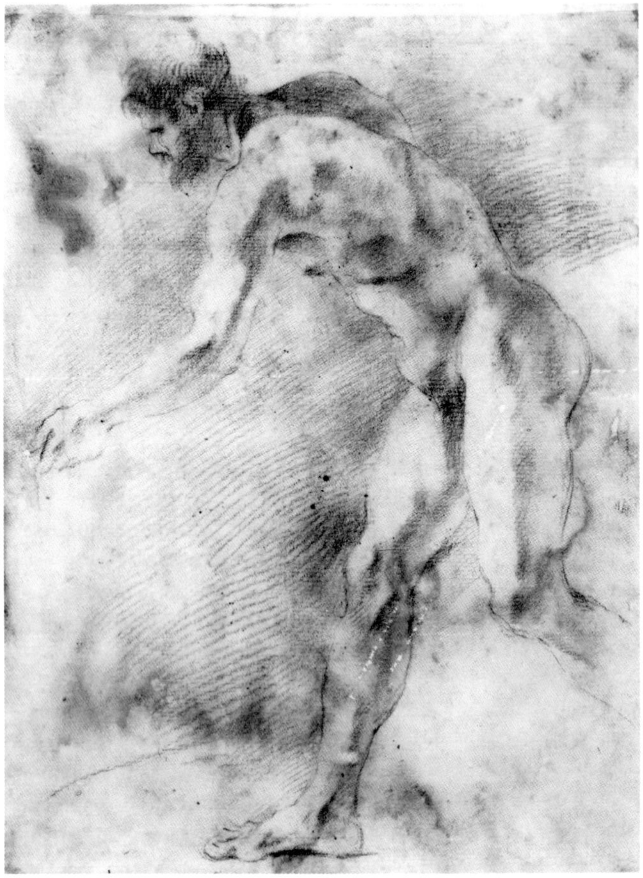

52 Aniello Falcone, *A Male Nude, Walking to the Left*, late 1630s. Red chalk, 250 × 190 mm. Sale Sotheby's, London, 3 July 2013, lot 36

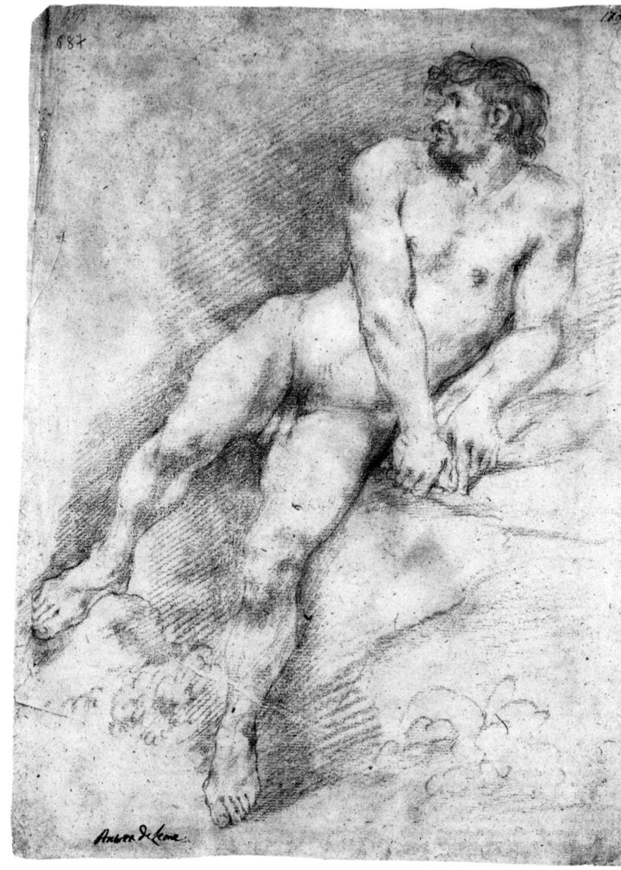

53 Andrea de Leone, *Life Study*, late 1630s. Red chalk, 339 × 230 mm. Museo e Gallerie Nazionali di Capodimonte, Gabinetto dei Disegni e delle Stampe, Naples

contract with the deputies of the Tesoro, as well as his fear of his Neapolitan enemies, render it very unlikely that he would have dared to run an open studio while in Naples.[7]

The activities of Falcone's Accademia are vividly documented in a series of red chalk drawings of landscapes, nudes and figure studies that are now split between the holdings of the Biblioteca Nacional, Madrid, and various public and private collections. These were valued highly soon after their creation, since a sizeable number were gathered together and acquired for the collection of the viceroy, the marques del Carpio, in the 1680s.[8] The drawings confirm the essential tenor of De' Dominici's observations regarding the Accademia's curriculum and demonstrate the effectiveness of Falcone's methods for teaching pupils to draw from the model and after prints, as well as to undertake periodic landscape sketching expeditions in the Neapolitan *campagna* (figs 52–4).[9] They document the early presence in Falcone's Accademia of Andrea de Leone,[10] Domenico Gargiulo[11] and Salvator Rosa,[12] together with others identified as his pupils by De' Dominici, such as Paolo Porpora,[13] Carlo Coppola[14] and Giuseppe Trombatore.[15] Some further artists not mentioned in this connection have also been associated with Falcone's ambience on the basis of documented and/or stylistic links. These include Niccolò de Simone,[16] Luca Forte,[17] Viviano Codazzi,[18] Giuseppe Piscopo,[19] Marzio Masturzo[20] and Bernardo Cavallino, the last of whom was also linked to Falcone on a personal level since he is known to have called on Falcone's assistance for his act of emancipation in late 1636.[21]

It seems ironic that this first impulse towards creating an alternative model to the traditional, closed workshop system of Neapolitan painting was initiated by an individual who was himself deeply embedded in the tribal artisanal and familial traditions he was now seeking, in this respect at least, to bypass. Gilding, in particular, seems to have been a characteristic of the Falcone family. Aniello Falcone's father,

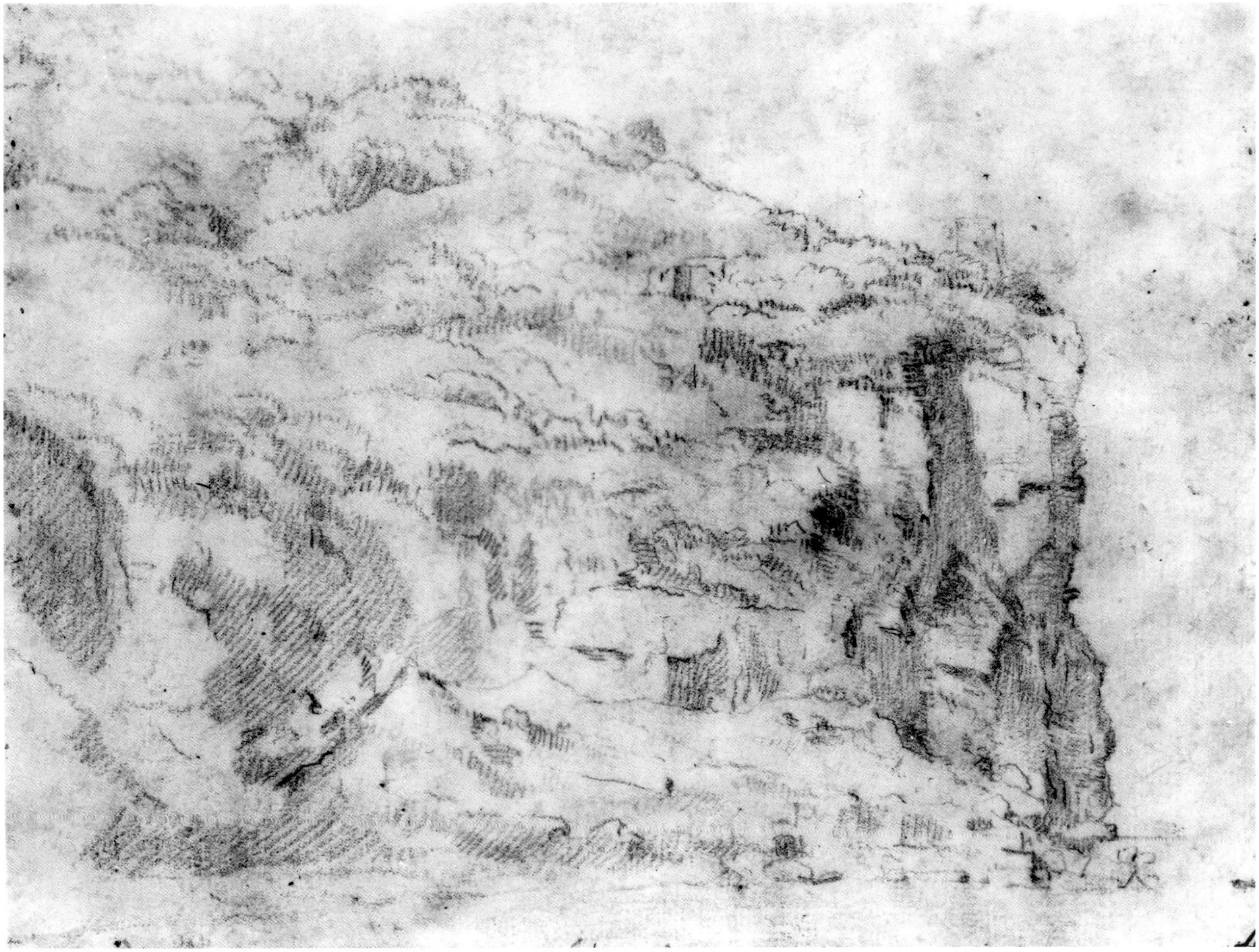

54 Aniello Falcone, *A Landscape with Boats at the Foot of a Craggy Bluff with a Tower and Ruined Buildings Above*, late 1630s. Red chalk, 162 × 211 mm. Sale Christie's, Paris, 22 March 2007, lot 218

Vincenzo, was a successful gilder who served for some time as consul of the Arte delli Indoratori e Mettitori d'Oro.[22] So too were his cousins, Pietro, Diego and Nicola Falcone.[23] Even one of Falcone's partners in the life modelling arrangement described above worked as both a gilder and a painter (although he was evidently a silent partner when it came to the Accademia since, along with the other individuals mentioned in the contract, nothing more is heard of him in this context).[24]

Falcone was equally closely linked to the familial networks running beneath the surface of so much professional practice. In 1639 he married Orsola Vitale, daughter of Filippo and Caterina Vitale, thus bringing him into the fold of the Vitale/De Mauro dynasty (see Chapter One). In addition to his pre-existing professional links, it linked him by blood relations to the workshops of both Stanzione (via his sister- and brothers-in-law, Diana de Rosa, Agostino Beltrano and Pacecco de Rosa) and his former master, Ribera (via Juan Do, who had married Caterina Vitale/De Mauro's daughter some twenty years earlier).

Falcone was certainly prepared to draw on these networks whenever the need arose. Thus Falcone's cousin, Nicola, assisted Aniello on the gilding and stucco accompanying his frescoes at the Firrao chapel in San Paolo Mag-

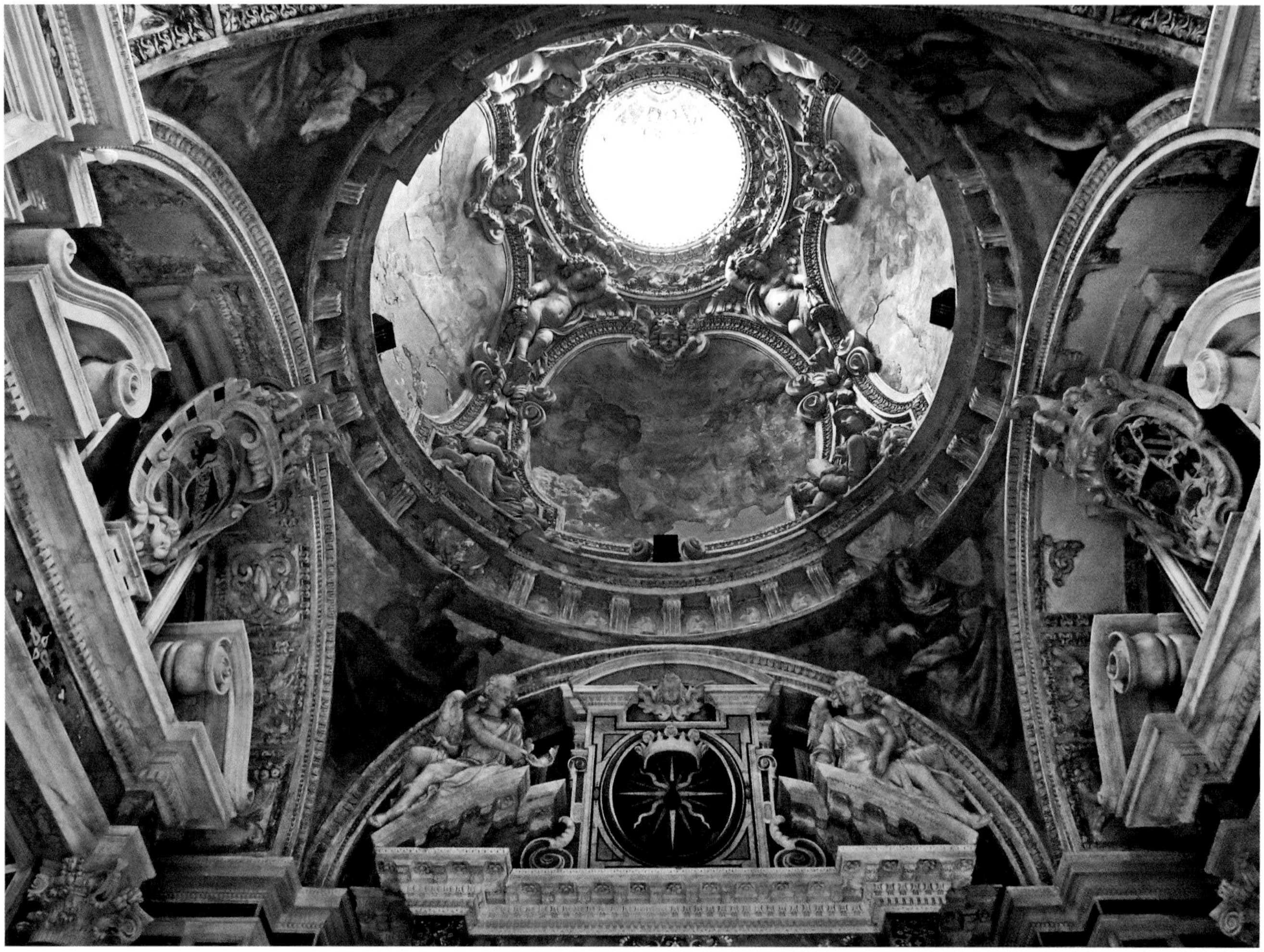

55 Aniello Falcone (frescoes) and Nicola Falcone (gilding and stucco), 1641–2. Cappella Firrao di Sant'Agata, San Paolo Maggiore, Naples

giore in 1641 (fig. 55).[25] Similarly, in 1652 Falcone was aided in his other major church fresco commission – the sacristy of the Gesù Nuovo – by his brother-in-law Onofrio de Leone, who was himself the brother of one of Falcone's most gifted pupils at the Accademia, Andrea de Leone.[26] Yet it would be misleading to read into this any fundamental contradiction between Falcone's continued recourse to these traditional networks and his interest in introducing into Naples a more progressive and open system of artistic training. This was an art world, after all, that allowed for one of the leading painters of the day to be simultaneously both a painter and a modeller in wax, and where it was equally acceptable for another painter – Falcone's brother-in-law no less – to practise as a marginally successful painter in fresco and oil on canvas as well as a better-paid producer of painted fans for export to Spain.

Falcone's contributions to the prestigious export commission of monumental scenes of ancient Roman festivities for the Buen Retiro Palace in Madrid (discussed in Chapter Ten) clearly demonstrate the bravura skill that he was able to apply as a result of his systematic focus on the discipline of life drawing (fig. 56). Yet the real contribution of Falcone's Accademia lay in another direction altogether. As these and other paintings demonstrate, Falcone was capable of producing grand manner history painting on a scale and level of mastery to match anything produced by Ribera or Stanzione. Yet, at the same time, he evidently recognized that the real opportunities for growth and career development in Naples did not lie in these kinds of production.

The traditional career path of seeking periodic commissions for monumental figure painting represented a tried and trusted avenue for public recognition and so would

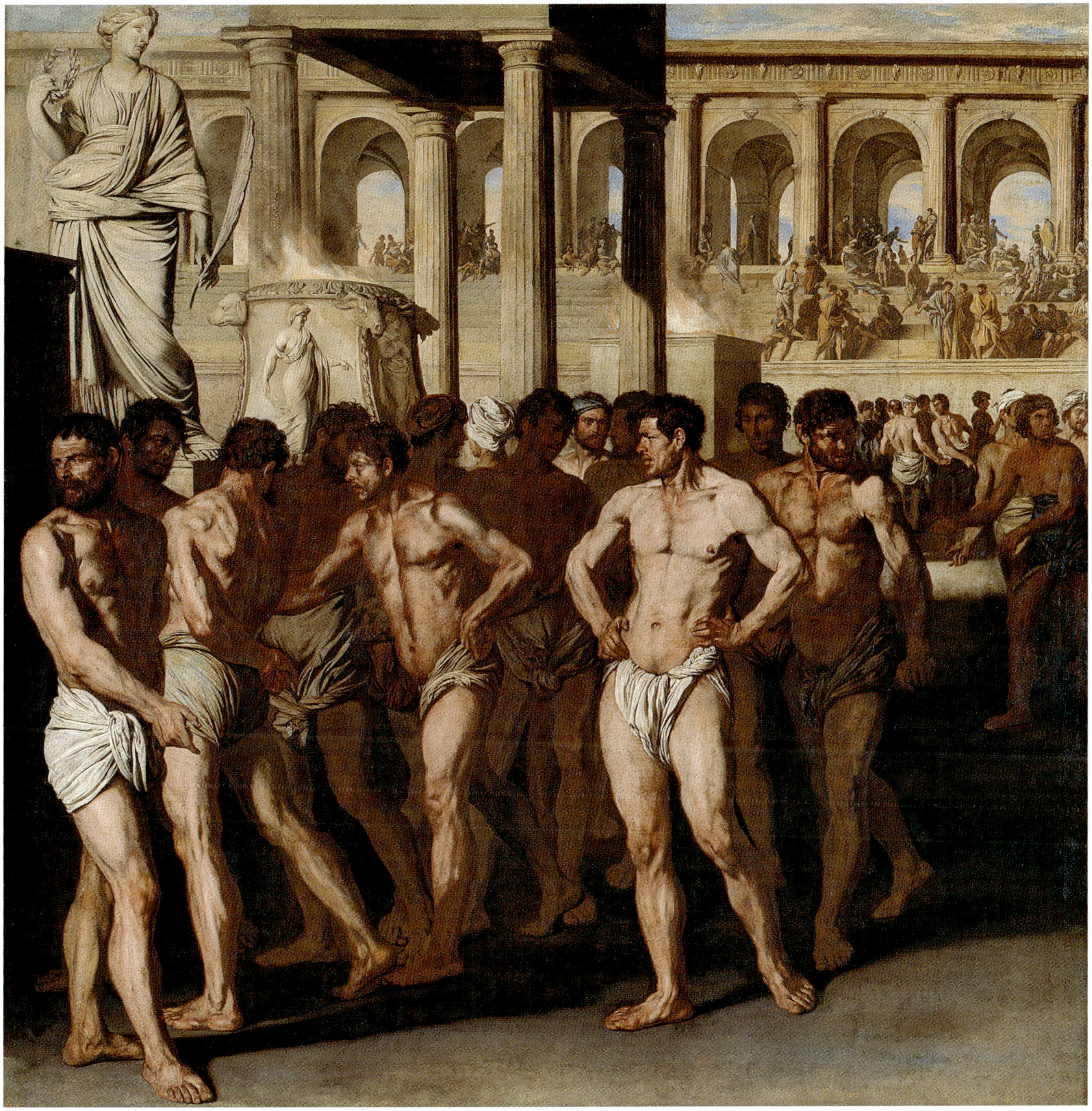

56 Aniello Falcone, *Roman Athletes*, late 1630s. Oil on canvas, 186 × 183 cm. Museo del Prado, Madrid

have been pursued as a matter of course. Yet a strategically minded artist such as Falcone undoubtedly would also have realized that this form of output offered aspiring practitioners only a restricted field. It was constrained first by the inherent limitations of demand at what was, after all, a relatively specialized, high-end level of the market. More immediately, though, its opportunities were lessened to a significant extent because of the overwhelming dominance in this arena as a result of the ascendancy of Ribera and Stanzione and their very productive workshops, together with the more restricted additional contributions of foreign artists such as Lanfranco and Domenichino.

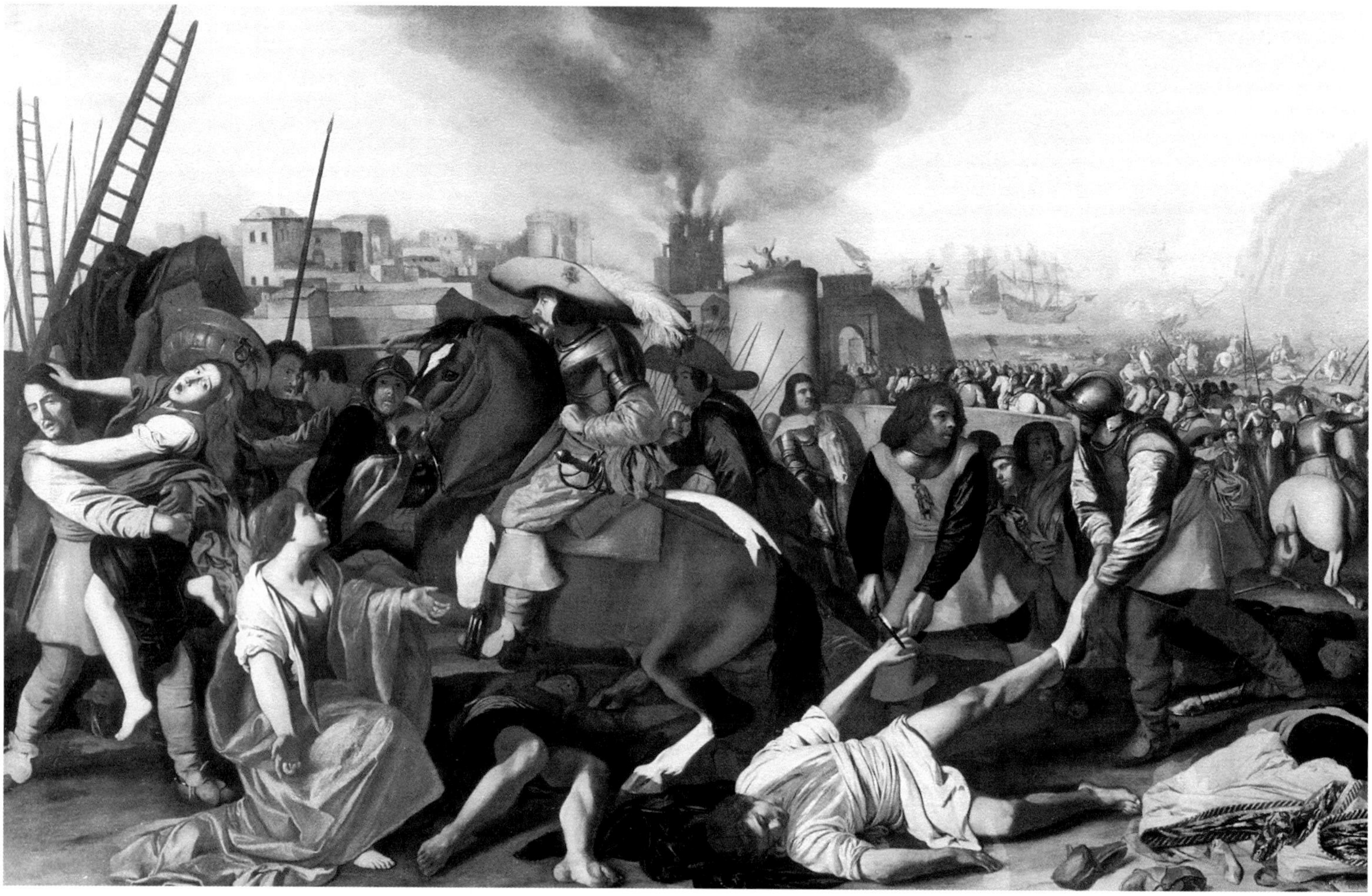

57 Aniello Falcone, *Sack of a City*, 1635–45. Oil on canvas, 101.6 × 156.2 cm. Herbert F. Johnson Museum of Art, Ithaca, New York

NEAPOLITAN CABINET PAINTING

At a certain stage early in his career Falcone evidently came to realize and recognize the importance of diversifying his output into new sub-categories of production. For Falcone, the key to success lay in the new genre of battle painting – a decision that was taken largely as a result of the positive reception enjoyed by his early battle paintings within the framework of the emerging Neapolitan art market – most notably via the early dealerships of Nicola di Martino and Gaspar Roomer (see Chapter Five). Falcone's subsequent work in this category brought him considerable international fame and the sobriquet 'the oracle of the battles' – a title supposedly conferred on him by Luca Giordano, an artist who clearly knew a thing or two himself when it came to the benefits of tailoring one's output to fit popular sub-categories of specialization.[27]

Falcone's essential innovation in the field of battle painting was to combine the classical Italianate tradition represented by the frescoes of the Sala di Costantino in the Vatican Palace with the new emphases found in the scenes of contemporary military engagements just then coming into vogue via the work of Northern artists – as particularly evident in Jacques Callot's immensely popular prints and the paintings of Esaias van de Velde, among other early specialists.[28] The result is a striking hybrid wherein the balance and reserve of grand manner Italian history painting is brought into dynamic alignment with the grit and smaller-scale immediacy of Northern genre imagery. Falcone's *Sack of a City*, for example, confronts the viewer with a strangely poised and slowed-down scene of contemporary rape and pillage following the conclusion of a siege (fig. 57).[29] To the right, two soldiers confront each other over the body of a fallen combatant – one

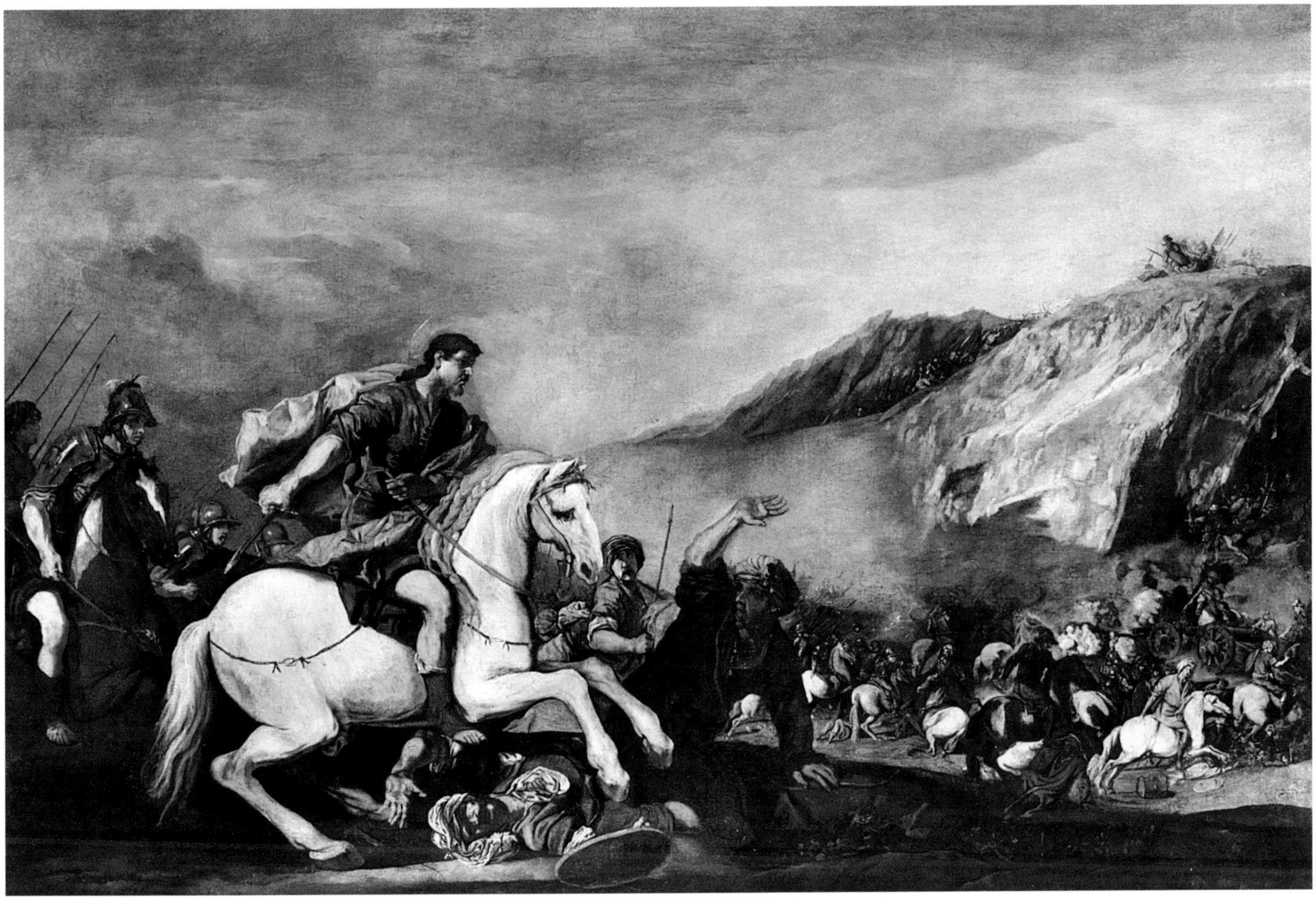

58 Andrea de Leone, *St James at the Battle of Clavijo*, 1640s. Oil on canvas, 87 × 126.5 cm. Formerly Finarte, Milan, 1976

peeling off the corpse's socks, the other severing a finger in order to secure the valuable booty of a ring. Another soldier struggles with a woman who twists away from his grip like a modern-day Sabine – or, more specifically, like a genre version of Bernini's *Pluto and Persephone*, the pose of which the two figures quote directly.

It was a compelling model and one that most of Falcone's pupils attempted to emulate at some stage in their careers. Andrea de Leone (1610–1685), in particular, became renowned for crowded scenes of ferociously battling Christians and Turks and battle scenes from the Old Testament that are in some respects very close to Falcone's compositions (fig. 58).[30] More importantly, though, Falcone appears to have encouraged pupils to move beyond direct emulation in order to find a niche within the expanding field of paintings with smaller figures set amid expansive landscapes that were then becoming fashionable. So, Andrea de Leone developed a yet more distinctive, parallel specialization in small- to medium-sized paintings of bacchanals, mythologies and ancient histories set amid ruins and prominent landscapes (fig. 59).[31] These were produced in response to the contemporary taste for neo-Venetian scenes inspired by Poussin, Castiglione and Titian's Ludovisi *Bacchanals*, the last of which was then creating a sensation in the city after being brought to Naples via the cultural diplomacy of the viceroy, the conde de Monterrey (see Chapter Ten).

The conjoining of Northern and Italian influences was evidently one of the hallmarks of Falcone's curriculum. It did much to ensure that he and his associates played a central role in instituting a native school of Neapolitan landscape, genre and related categories of the so-called minor genres of painting. Prior to the 1630s, in fact, the field for paintings of this kind was almost entirely dominated by the scores of Northern artists resident in the city,

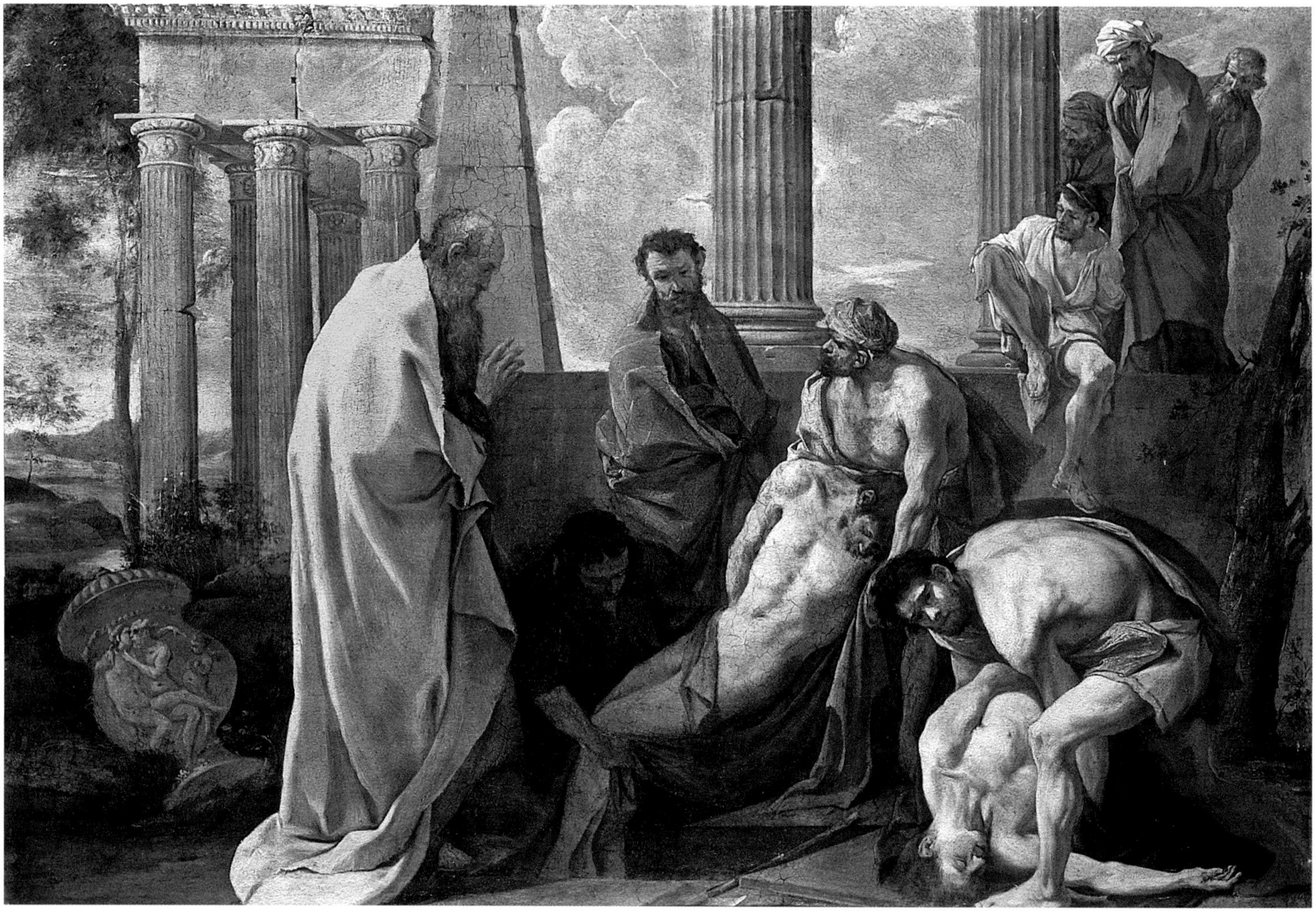

59 Andrea de Leone, *Tobit Burying the Dead*, late 1640s. Oil on copper, 61 × 89 cm. Formerly Sotheby's, New York

who had emigrated there above all as a result of the disturbances created by the religious wars in France and the Netherlands.[32] As early as 1593, for example, Giovanni Battista Ròta, son of the leading patron, poet and academician Berardino Ròta, paid Pietro del Rea, 'pittore fiamengho', for four landscapes.[33] In the same year Pietro Menens, 'pittore fiammengo', was paid for 'two paintings that he has to make of a view of Naples and the entire Gulf' (an early example, therefore, of the architectural view paintings subsequently developed by Viviano Codazzi, discussed below).[34]

In documents from this period the names of certain painters recur whose works are often completely unknown today but who developed profitable specializations of these kinds. In 1612, for example, Loys Croys was commissioned to paint an extensive series of twelve paintings of 'Eremitaggi', presumably hermit saints in landscapes. The following year, the principe di Sansevero commissioned from Croys a series of the *Four Seasons* and 'due altri di paesi'.[35] Commissions are also recorded from these years for the otherwise entirely unknown Northern landscape painters Jacopo Coppola, Giacobo Zoabio, Jacopo Iumiello, and Bartolomeo and Cornelio Ghesenz.[36] The extent to which landscape was then considered the particular domain of Flemish painters is indicated by a commission of 1613, in which Bartolomeo Ghesenz was contracted to paint six hunting scenes that are described generically as 'paintings of the Flemish hunt'.

Falcone would have had numerous opportunities to observe the works of the early Northern specialists during his initial years of activity. It is known, for example, that his early patron and dealer, Gaspar Roomer – himself a Flemish resident of the city – stocked his palace with scores of landscapes by Goffredo Wals, Léonard Bramer (1596–1674)

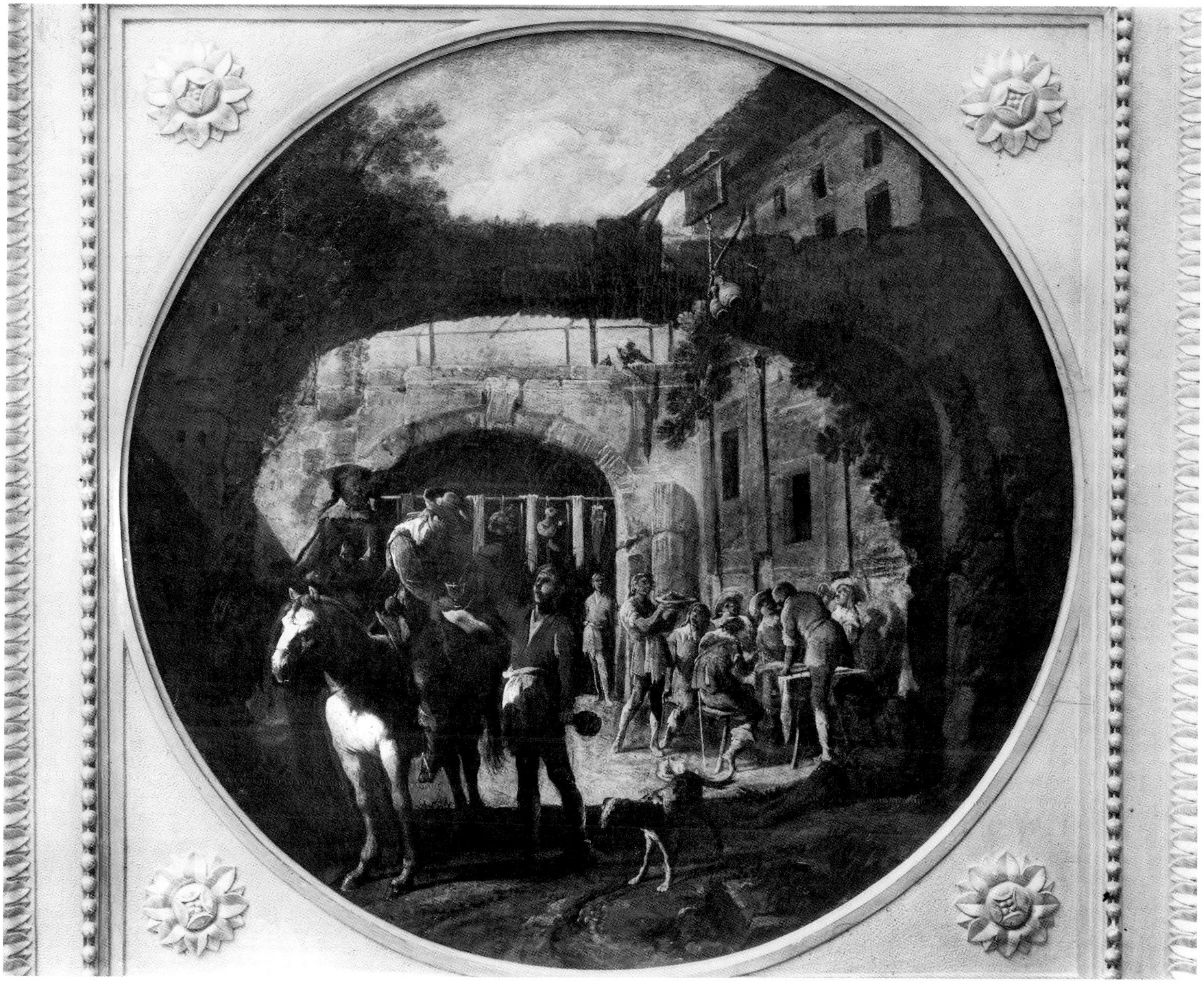

60 Domenico Gargiulo, *The Inn Keeper*, 1636. Oil on canvas, diameter 50 cm. Present whereabouts unknown; formerly principe di Fondi collection

and other Northern specialists (see p. 129). Falcone's interest in the genre paintings of the Dutch and Flemish artists of the Bamboccianti (a school of artists specializing in contemporary scenes of everyday life working in Rome in the 1630s to 1650s) has also been noted since at least the time of Roberto Longhi's observations during the 1950s.[37] Yet the thoroughly Italianate nature of Falcone's interpretations demonstrates a concern to adapt his models to suit his own agenda. This, in essence, was the challenge that he set his pupils. If he could successfully convert the military scenes of Callot and Esaias van de Velde into a distinctively Caravaggesque Neapolitan idiom, the task for his colleagues would be to achieve an analogous conversion for the other emerging genres as well.

Domenico Gargiulo (1609/10–1675) seems to have been Falcone's most gifted and perspicacious pupil in this respect. Gargiulo began his career during the early to mid-1630s producing a Neapolitan version of the genre paintings of the Roman Bamboccianti (fig. 60), the closest the city would come to this manner and strongly suggesting a brief

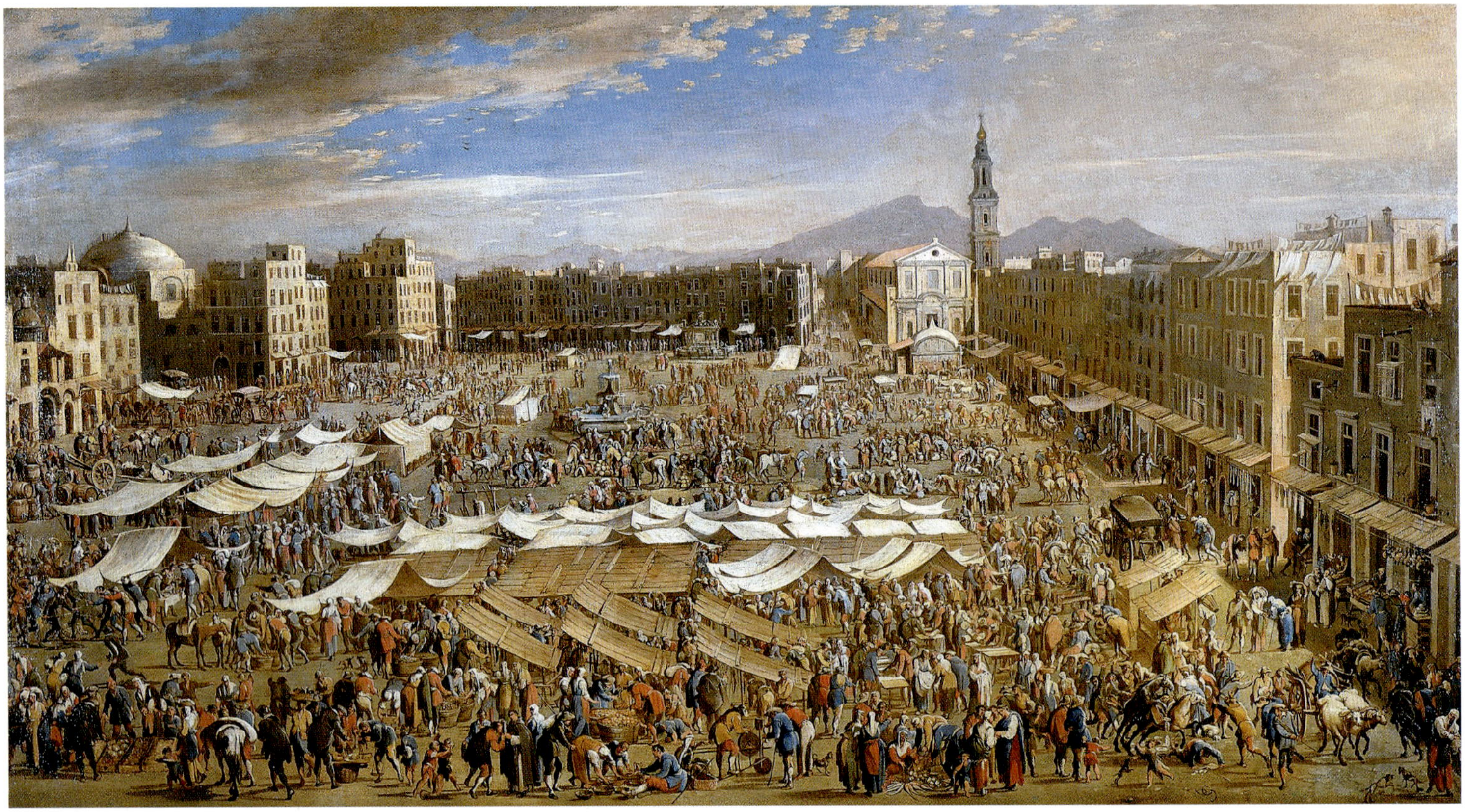

61 Domenico Gargiulo, *Market in the Piazza del Mercato*, mid-1650s. Oil on canvas, 80 × 145 cm. Fundación Casa Ducal de Medinaceli, Palacio Lerma, Toledo

stay in Rome at more or less the same time as Falcone.[38] Within a few years, however, he had progressed under Falcone's tutelage to an increasingly sophisticated synthesis of Northern genre and landscape imagery with the classical landscapes of Poussin and Claude, as well as the prints of Jacques Callot. In a series of closely related drawings from the mid-1630s, Falcone, Gargiulo and his early associate Salvator Rosa attempted to master Callot's unmatched facility in composing hundreds of animated, small-scale *figurine* into panoramic scenes set amid expansive landscapes.[39] The results were soon evident in Gargiulo's paintings of crowded and incident-filled scenes of contemporary fairs and the like (fig. 61).[40]

Gargiulo subsequently progressed to a culminating series of paintings, worked on from the late 1640s, that were produced in response to an urgent need to document the catastrophic events that had befallen Naples: the eruption of Vesuvius in 1631, the Revolt of Masaniello in 1647–8, and, most traumatic of all, the terrible calamity of the plague of 1656 (fig. 62).[41] In these paintings Gargiulo more than fulfilled the challenge to create an innovative picture type: genre, landscape and architectural view painting are successfully blended with history painting and the lessons learned from Falcone's teeming battle scenes seen from an elevated viewpoint.

In between the early genre paintings and the later scenes of contemporary events, in 1638 Gargiulo won a contract for a series of frescoes at the Certosa di San Martino. These and subsequent commissions undertaken at the Certosa throughout the 1640s and beyond cemented his reputation as the pre-eminent landscape painter of the day and, ultimately, as the originator of a rich tradition of idealized views of the Neapolitan *campagna* and Bay of Naples that would stretch from the Baroque to the mid-nineteenth-century *plein-air* landscapes of Giacinto Gigante and the School of Posillipo (fig. 63).[42]

Also painting at the Certosa di San Martino during this same period was Viviano Codazzi (1603–1670), an artist originally from Bergamo, who was then developing a specialization in architectural view painting, a closely related sub-category of the so-called minor genres. Codazzi had arrived in Naples only a few years earlier, sometime around 1634, and, like

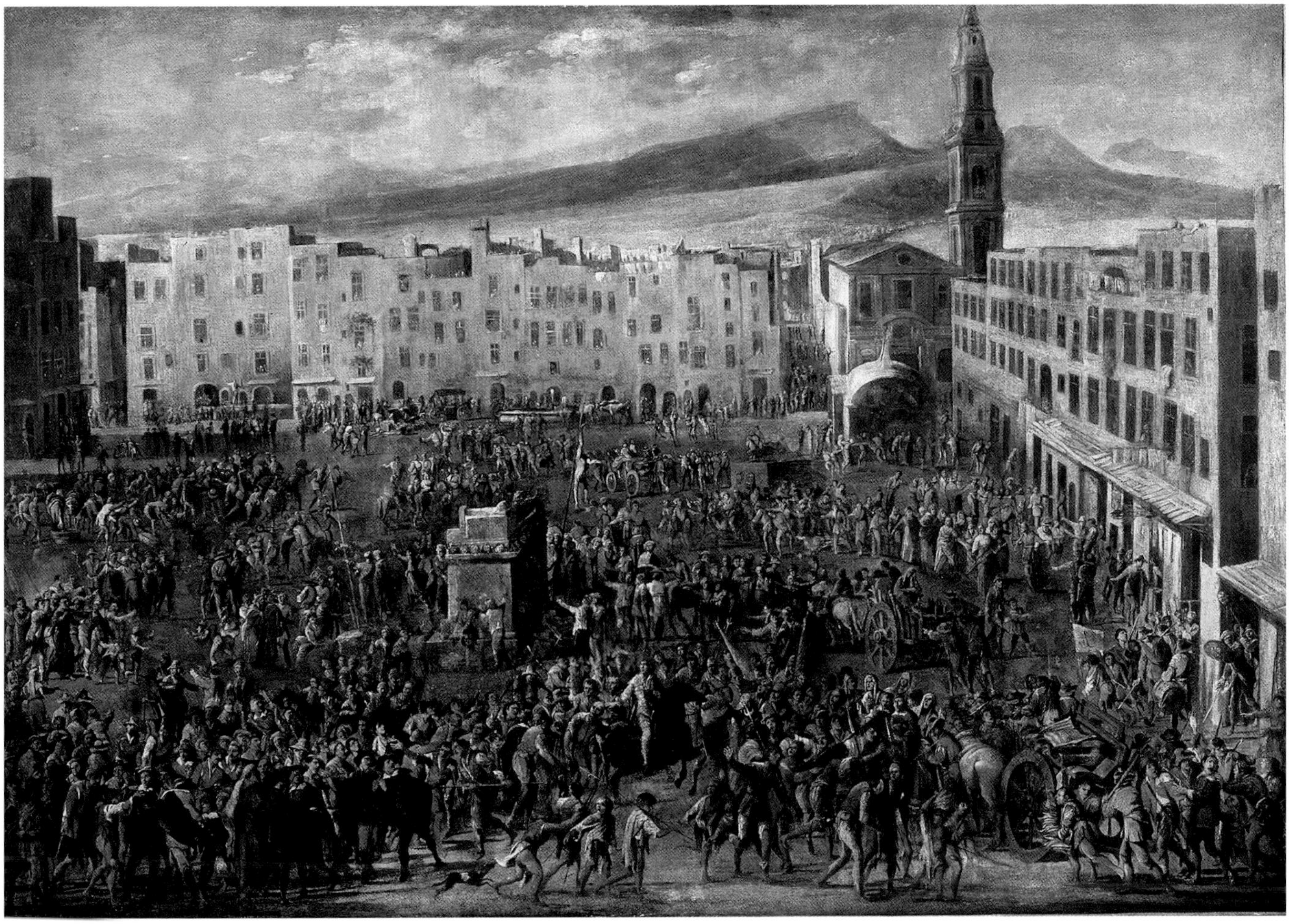

62 Domenico Gargiulo, *Piazza del Mercato during the Revolt of Masaniello*, late 1640s–early 1650s. Oil on canvas, 126 × 177 cm. Museo di San Martino, Naples

63 Domenico Gargiulo, *Landscape with Abraham Conducting Isaac to be Sacrificed*, late 1640s. Oil on canvas, 45 × 117 cm. Museo di San Martino, Naples

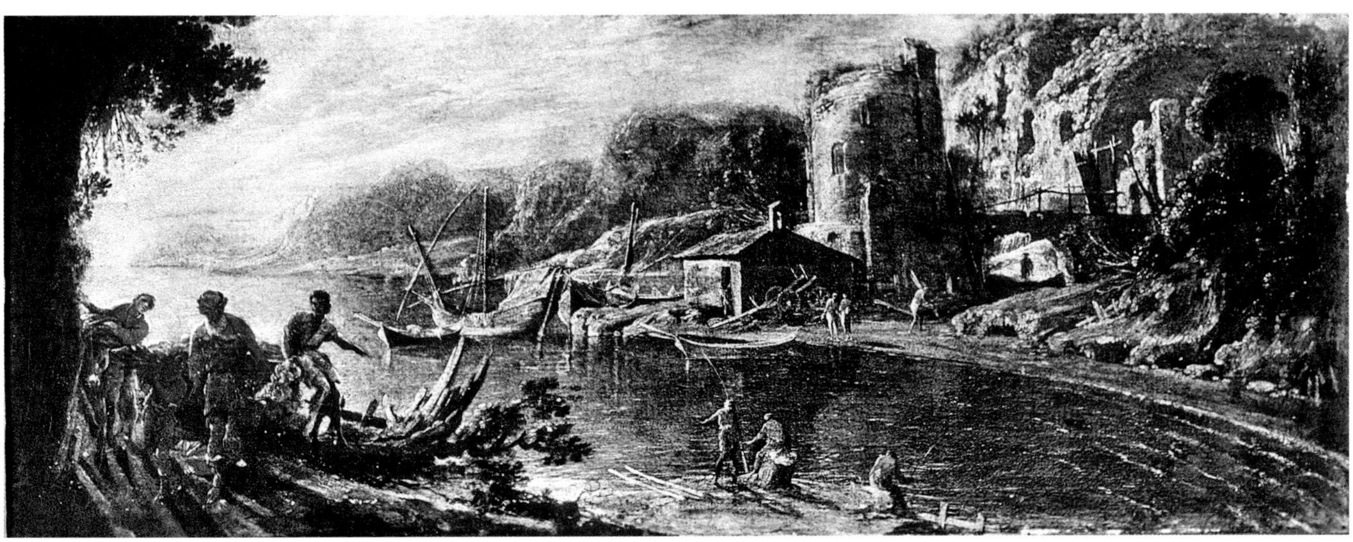

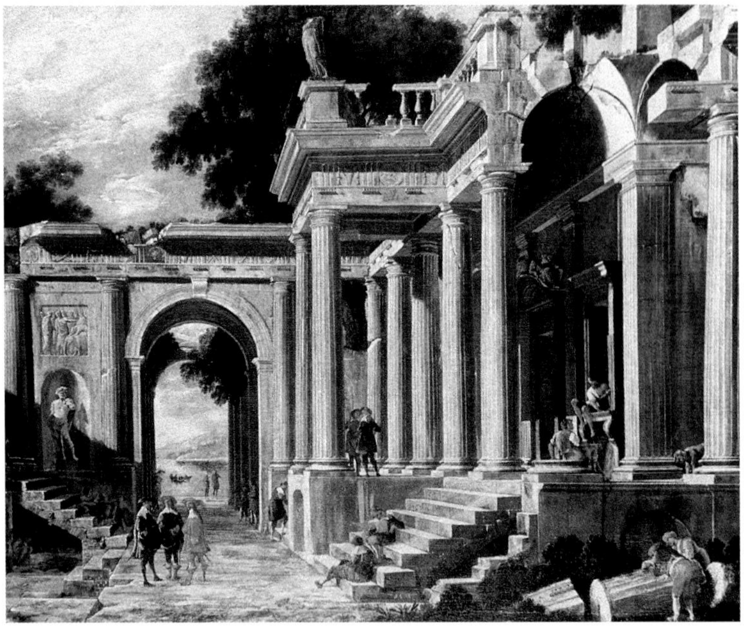

64 Viviano Codazzi and Domenico Gargiulo, *Barrel-vaulted Doric Palace Portico with Steps and an Archway, with Coastal View Beyond*, signed and dated 1641. Oil on canvas, 161 × 190 cm. Formerly Matthiesen Gallery, London

Falcone and so many other painters, recognized the value of drawing on tribal affiliations when it came to establishing himself in a foreign city. A crucial figure was Cosimo Fanzago: he was not only the leading Neapolitan architect of the day, but also came from Codazzi's home region of Bergamo; he offered Codazzi early employment and assisted his introduction to the Certosa and elsewhere.[43]

It seems inevitable that Codazzi would have also gravitated to Falcone's ambience. De' Dominici notes that the two artists were 'stretto in amità' and Falcone seems to have played a central role in encouraging Codazzi to forge a very successful collaboration with Gargiulo, his most gifted pupil in the field of landscape and genre painting. Codazzi was not himself an accomplished figure painter, so it suited him to contract Gargiulo to contribute animated genre *figurine* to his architectural scenes. The result is one of the most distinctive sub-categories of painting found in the Neapolitan Baroque (fig. 64).[44] Its immediate popularity with Neapolitan collectors is attested by the scores of architectural paintings attributed to Codazzi and Gargiulo that appear in early Neapolitan inventories. Their work also inspired a number of imitators, beginning with Ascanio Luciano, Francesco Maglioli and Antonio di Michele, who were active during the later stages of Codazzi's and Gargiulo's collaboration. It then stretched yet further to encompass the proto-Rococo architectural views of Leonardo Coccorante (1680–1750) and his school in the next century.[45] In this way, Gargiulo and Codazzi became the fathers, particularly via their involvement in Falcone's ambience, of Neapolitan landscape and architectural view painting, respectively.

CABINET PAINTING AND THE REQUIREMENTS OF NEAPOLITAN COLLECTORS

Regolia's view of a Neapolitan palace interior dating to the 1670s is useful in assessing the contribution of these emerging categories of painting to the interior design requirements of contemporary Neapolitan collectors (fig. 65). The collection depicted appears old fashioned in certain respects – at least as far as one can determine from the viewpoint selected. It includes no architectural view paintings, for example, nor does it display any still lifes, despite the fact that still-life painting had been flourishing in Naples for many decades (including a still little-understood association between the early still-life specialists and Falcone and his ambience during the 1630s and 1640s).[46]

Alongside the six large history and devotional paintings that dominate the room is a pair of smaller pendant paintings that are matched, in turn, with two embossed leather armchairs directly beneath them. Their proximity to the chairs, incidentally, raises significant conservation issues, at least when viewed from a current and more conservation-conscious, museological perspective. It encourages one of the waiting figures to rest the brim of his hat against one of the frames: a vivid demonstration of the primary function of these collections to serve as items of decor and daily use, rather than as objects of autonomous aesthetic contemplation, as they would no doubt be considered today.

The two small paintings, in fact, are copies after Callot's *Disasters of War* of 1633, one of the direct models for Falcone's battle scenes. Immediately above them there hangs a copy after another of Callot's prints of contemporary military engagements. This group of three paintings thus helps to visualize the function that small-scale battle paintings by Falcone and his associates played in other Neapolitan col-

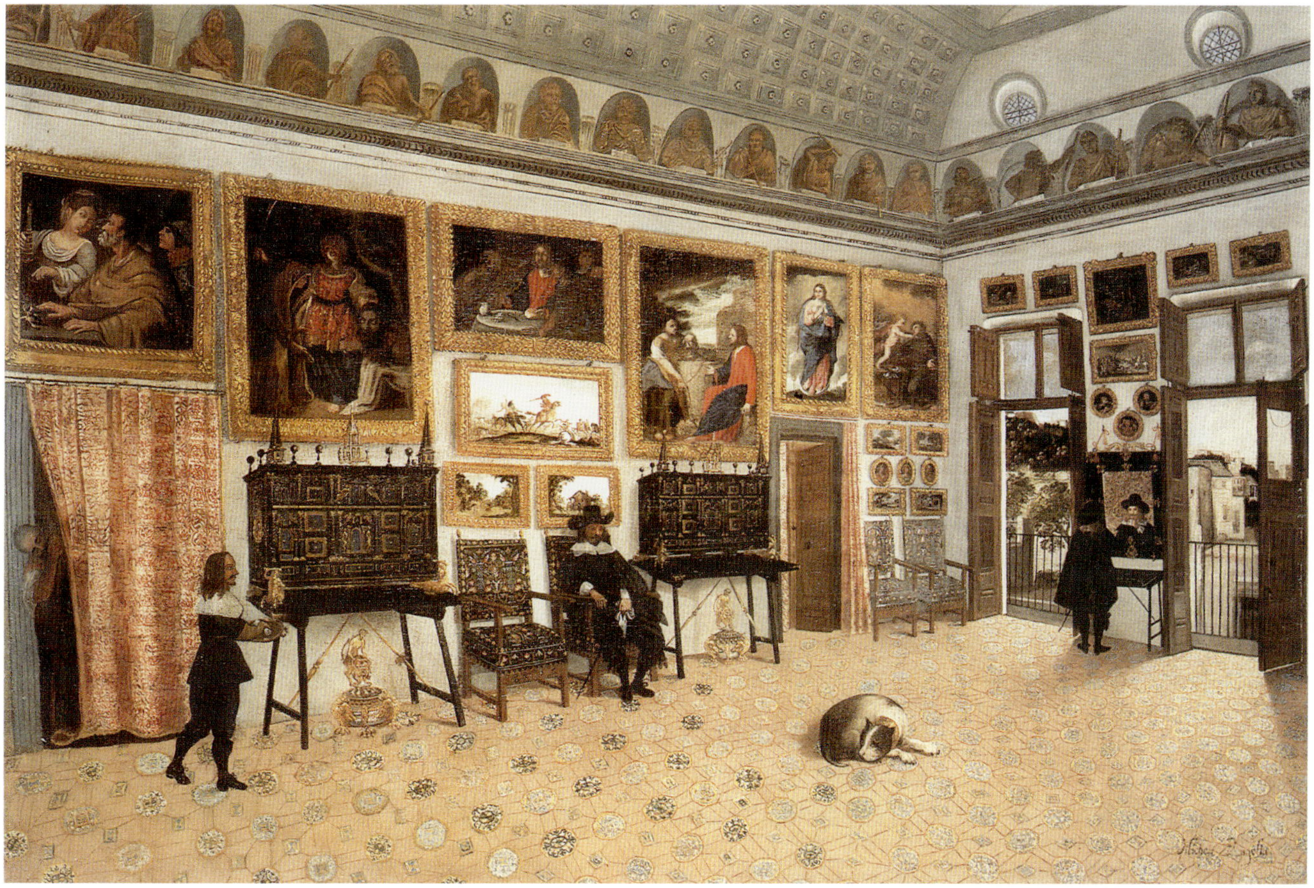

Above 65 Michele Regolia, *Palace Interior, circa* 1675, signed. Oil on canvas, 97 3 × 145.2 cm. Private collection, Naples

Right 66 Massimo Stanzione, *St Agnes, circa* 1640, signed. Oil on canvas, 70 × 52 cm. Quadreria del Pio Monte della Misericordia, Naples

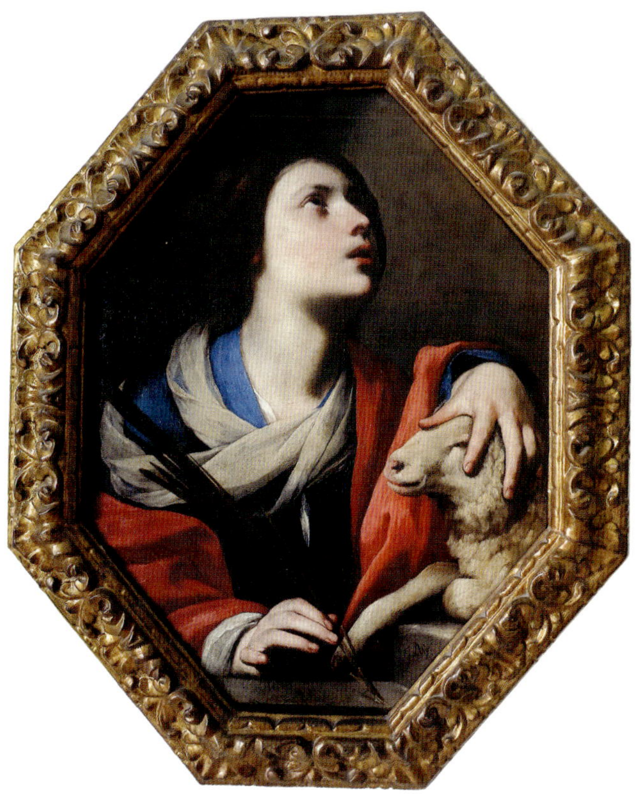

lections: providing points of visual counterpoint to the larger, heavier and darker history paintings hanging alongside them.

On the other side of the door two more embossed leather chairs are matched with a group comprising two twinned pairs of small landscape paintings above and below three small paintings of heads, presumably of virgin saints, in roundel frames. The landscapes are directly analogous to Gargiulo's works, and the heads comparable to bust- and half-length paintings by Stanzione, Cavallino, Guarino and others (fig. 66), introducing into Neapolitan collections a note of intimacy and luxurious feminine beauty to offset both the landscapes and the comparatively static monumentality of the full-length figure paintings above them.

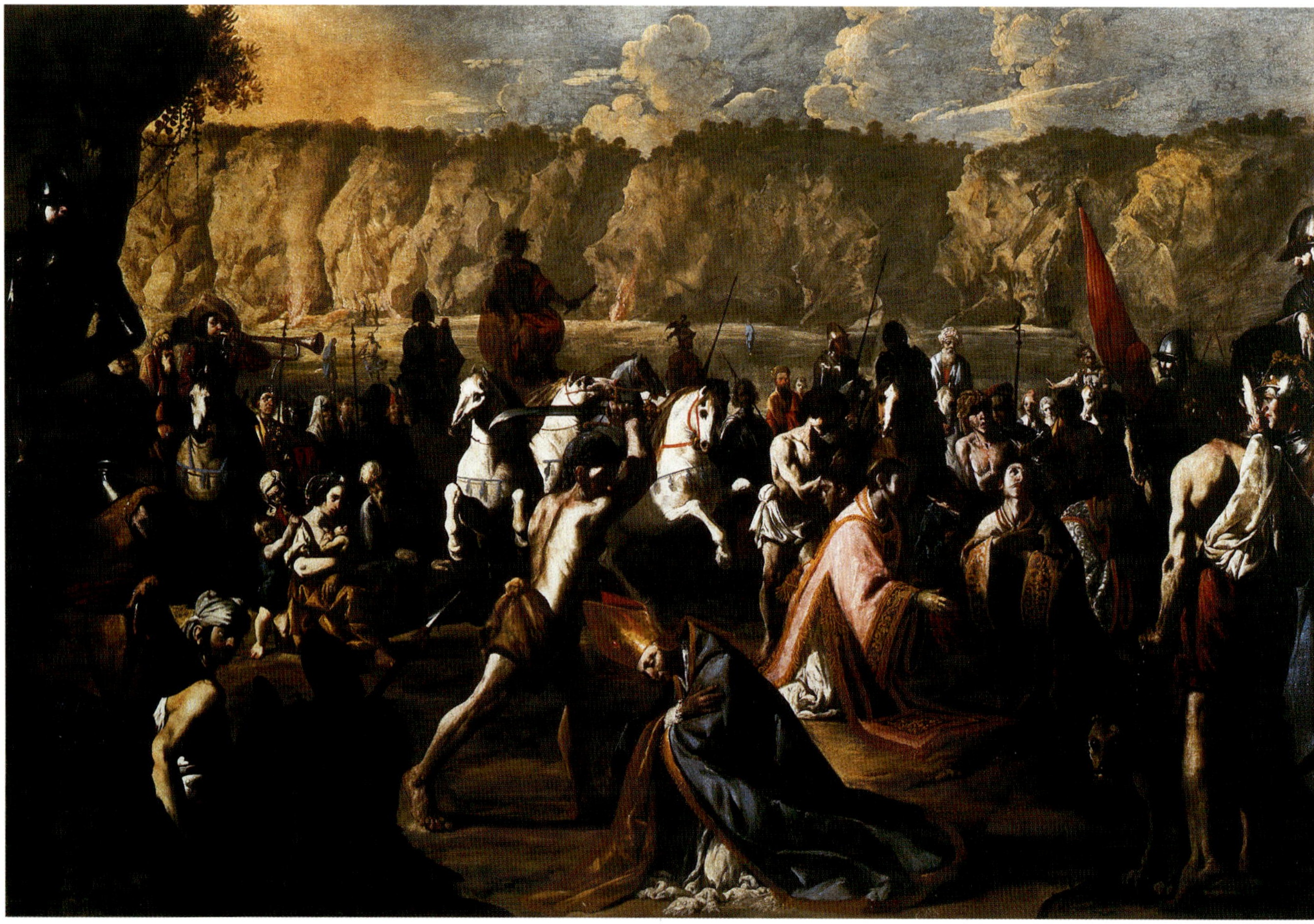

67 Carlo Coppola, *Martyrdom of St Januarius*, late 1630s–1640s. Oil on canvas, 161 × 200 cm. Private collection

On the adjoining wall in Regolia's painting a group of five pictures on black backgrounds – and so probably painted on slate – hangs high up on the wall as *soprapporte*. Their dark backgrounds and clear contours are particularly effective in this location since they help to counteract the glare coming from the balcony. They are probably by one of the early Northern specialists: Léonard Bramer, for example, whose work hung in Roomer's palace and who had a particular reputation for small nocturnal scenes of this type. Directly below them a medium-sized painting can be seen containing a landscape crowded with small figures. This format is directly comparable to the paintings of martyrdoms of saints and biblical narrative scenes set amidst landscapes with small figures that were another of the trademark specialities of Falcone and his colleagues. They derive particularly from a now-lost painting by Falcone of the *Martyrdom of St Januarius* set in the environs of Solfatara that is known today by numerous versions and adaptations by Carlo Coppola and other painters of this group (fig. 67).[47]

Such small- and medium-sized paintings not only played a crucial role in introducing an appropriate sense of variety and visual counterpoint to the larger figure paintings found in contemporary Neapolitan collections, but they also proved very useful to collectors on a financial level. A particularly clear demonstration of this occurs in an inventory of 1659 of the collection of Ettore Capecelatro, the leading Neapolitan aristocratic public administrator.[48] This inventory was compiled with great care and precision by Capecelatro's favourite artist, none other than the landscape painter Domenico Gargiulo, and it includes many paintings by his hand. It contains an unusually detailed series of attributions and valuations for each of the paintings listed (valuations being relatively infrequent in Neapolitan

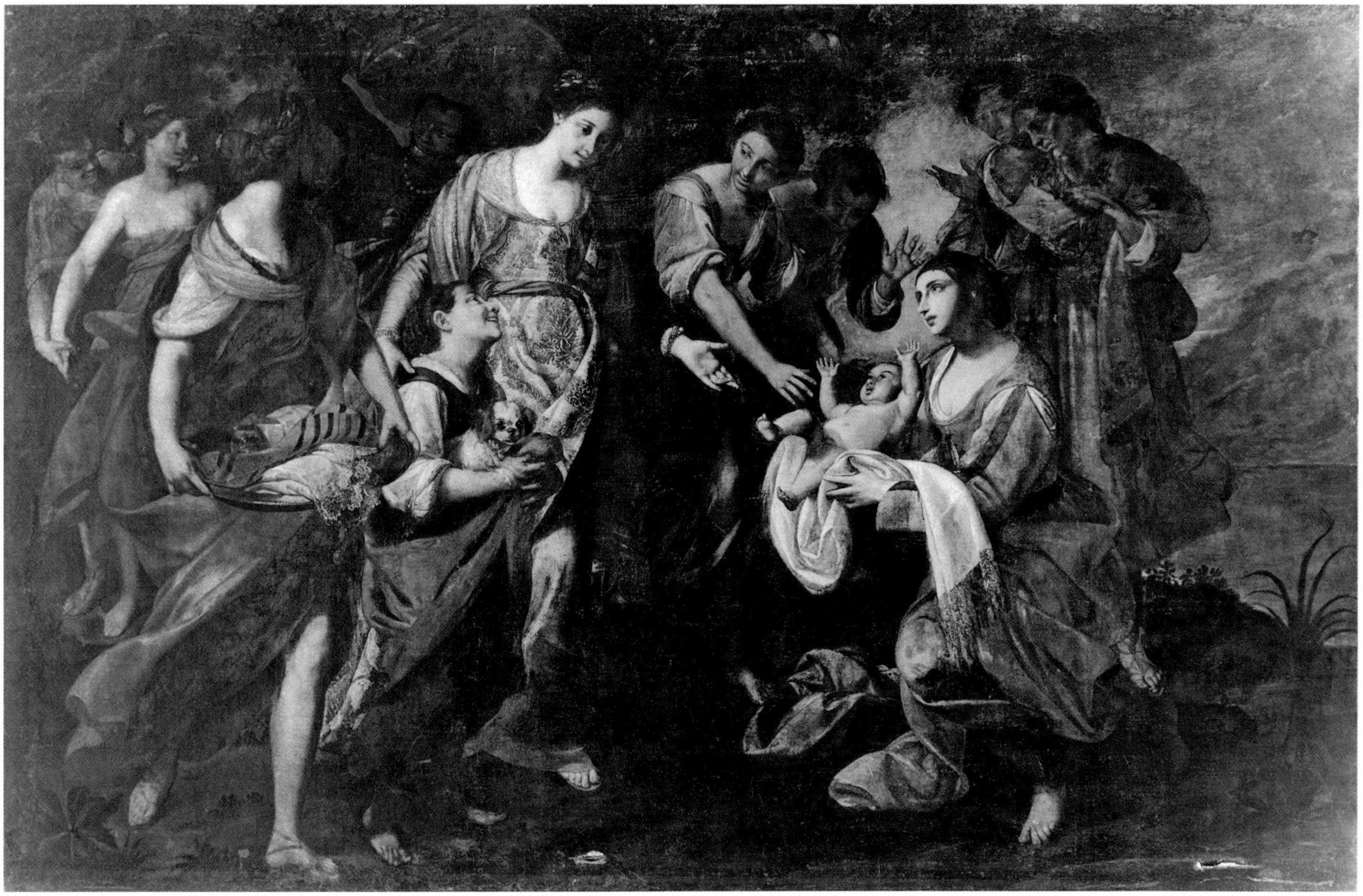

68 Pacecco de Rosa, *Finding of Moses*, mid to late 1640s. Oil on canvas, 200 × 304 cm. Private collection, Naples

inventories). The accuracy of these financial estimations can be confirmed by comparing them to documented prices paid for comparable gallery paintings, ranging from history paintings to more modest landscapes and the like, stretching across the course of the seventeenth century (Table 2).

Only a small number of Capecelatro's paintings were particularly valuable in financial terms. In fact, of the 132 paintings listed only four exceeded 100 ducats in value. At 360 ducats, a large *Fortune* by Van Dyck measuring 8 × 10 *palmi* (approx. 2.11 × 2.63) was by far the most expensive work in the collection. The high valuation reflects both his prestigious reputation in Naples at the time and the scarcity of major works by his hand on the local market. Capecelatro also owned a pair of large gallery paintings – similarly measuring 2.11 × 2.63 metres – by Stanzione and his pupil Pacecco de Rosa.[49] Stanzione's *Rachel* was valued at 280 ducats, making it one of the most expensive gallery paintings of the day. Prices of this magnitude, of 200 ducats or more, occur in the list of bank payments for gallery paintings in only a handful of instances and involve a very small number of major figure paintings by Ribera, Vaccaro, Artemesia Gentileschi, Giordano and Stanzione himself.

At 100 ducats, its pendant, by Pacecco, was much cheaper, but still one of the most highly valued works by this painter then in Naples. Capecelatro evidently appreciated the artist's occasional attempts to emulate the scale and multi-figure complexity of his master's major history paintings (fig. 68).[50] Finally, Capecelatro owned a large and evidently impressive 'prospettiva', or architectural view, by Codazzi that Gargiulo describes as including 'ritratti' by his own hand. The high valuation of 120 ducats and the specific reference to 'ritratti', or portraits of recognizable figures, mean that this painting was to be counted among Gargiulo's and Codazzi's rare scenes of contemporary events – such as a now-lost example of a collaborative work by the two artists depicting the Revolt of Masaniello or some other recent event.[51]

This small group of large and impressive gallery paintings was nonetheless interspersed with scores of smaller and cheaper landscapes, still lifes, devotional paintings and battle pieces. Two battle pieces by Falcone measuring approximately 79 × 105 centimetres, for example, hung next to Codazzi's and Gargiulo's large view painting. These were valued at the much more economical price of 35 ducats each, a valuation that also compares well with the 27 ducats assigned to a slightly larger battle piece by Andrea de Leone. These valuations correspond closely, in turn, to the 15 and 20 ducats paid during the same period by Don Antonio Ruffo of Messina for a small battle piece by Falcone and a slightly larger battle piece by De Leone.[52]

As far as landscapes with small figures depicting martyrdoms or the like, the valuations assigned by Gargiulo to his own paintings are also revealing of the broad range of prices attached to his work in different sizes and formats. These range from the 40 ducats assigned to a large painting of the *Expulsion of the Moneylenders* (measuring around 237 × 185 cm) to the much more economical 8 ducats assigned to a small painting of *Lot and his Daughters* measuring only 53 × 66 centimetres. This last painting would have closely resembled Gargiulo's surviving paintings of this subject in small roundel format (fig. 69).[53]

Finally, the dark *soprapporta* paintings present in Regolia's painting would have been directly comparable to a small painting listed in Capecelatro's collection of *Christ Presented to Pilate* by Gargiulo's pupil, Pietro Pesce. This painting – which is assigned the modest valuation of only 5 ducats – is described by Gargiulo as being painted 'on Genoese stone by Pietro Pesce with a gilt walnut frame'.[54] These valuations and the corresponding list of prices paid for more modestly scaled paintings with smaller figures by Falcone and his associates thus attest to the extent to which their early cabinet paintings helped to diversify the field of Neapolitan Baroque painting, both in terms of the various sizes and formats of the paintings available to collectors and their variation in price: 5–10 ducats for small works by Falcone's associates for example; 15–30 ducats for small- to medium-sized landscapes and battle pieces, and 40 ducats and upwards to 100 and occasionally more for large and imposing, one-off works by these artists. In this way, they enabled collectors such as Capecelatro to counterbalance occasional expensive purchases of monumental figure paintings by Ribera, Stanzione, Vaccaro, Gentileschi and Giordano, with more varied and cheaper options.

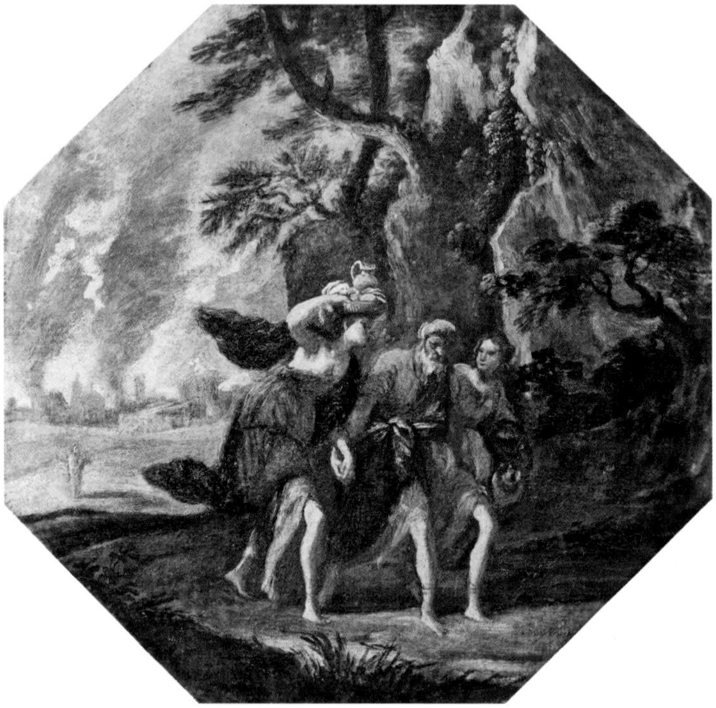

69 Domenico Gargiulo, *Lot Fleeing with his Daughters from Sodom and Gomorrah*, late 1650s–early 1660s. Oil on canvas, 33 × 33 cm. Molinari Pradelli collection, Marano di Castenaso

CONCLUSION

The impact of Falcone's academy is to be noted across a number of different levels of the Neapolitan art world. It was one of the main precedents, on the one hand, for the Accademia del Nudo, instituted in 1665, which constituted the principal training component of the reformed Congregazione dei Pittori. This rebranded version of the professional association of Neapolitan painters was sponsored by the Jesuits and inaugurated in 1664 at the administrative headquarters of the Casa Professa beside their Neapolitan mother church of the Gesù Nuovo.[55] It included an Accademia del Nudo presided over by its first *superiore*, Andrea Vaccaro, 'per giovare a' giovani, e coltivar lo studio del professori' (to benefit the youths and cultivate the study of the masters), as De' Dominici noted.[56]

The Accademia's curriculum was subsequently further strengthened by an additional component of anatomical studies introduced by its next superior, Francesco di Maria. In this way, the Accademia came to stand as the most visible public manifestation of the Congregazione's intention to promote Neapolitan painting as an intellectually based, liberal art, on a par with the painters' associations of Rome and Florence, to which professional and intellectual recognition was already accorded. It formed a central strategy, in other words, of the Congregazione's intention to declare its independence from traditional artisanal practices and to proclaim Neapolitan painting, instead, as 'la professione nobilissima', as De' Dominici put it.

Falcone's Accademia was also significant in offering a new model of workshop practice to the generation of painters reaching maturity following the ascendency of Ribera and Stanzione from the late 1620s onwards. As has been seen, Falcone did not assist these artists in their careers in the traditional ways normally expected of the head of a workshop. He did not teach them to imitate his style to the degree that he was able to sell their work as the product of his own hand, as Ribera did; neither did he teach them how to paint in fresco, unlike Stanzione, who undoubtedly trained his more talented pupils, such as Agostino Beltrano and Pacecco de Rosa, so as to assist him in his numerous public commissions of this kind. Those of Falcone's pupils who were interested in developing an expertise of this kind, in fact, were required to look elsewhere. Both Andrea de Leone and Domenico Gargiulo, for example, were able to develop subsidiary specialities in fresco painting as a result of their earlier training and time spent working under Belisario Corenzio.[57]

What Falcone did teach Gargiulo and the painters associated with him was how to operate as smaller-scale independent specialists capitalizing on the emerging vogue for small- to medium-sized cabinet paintings. His Accademia should thus be seen as functioning less as a workshop in the traditional sense than a kind of open laboratory offering a loose federation of like-minded artists space for experimentation aimed at enabling them to develop their own specializations in the emerging genres of 'minor' painting.

This emphasis also carried with it important implications for the means by which this allied group of painters were able to market and sell their work to the public. Unlike the large, specially commissioned history paintings of Ribera, Stanzione and the like, the cabinet paintings of Falcone and his associates were generally comparatively small and could be painted relatively cheaply and quickly. They did not, moreover, have programmatic subjects and so could be produced independently of any specific contract or need to establish an initial point of contact between patron and painter regarding materials, dimensions and subject matter. They could be painted for the anonymous buyer, in other words – the general public in the modern sense of the term – and then sold independently on the open market. In order to understand this aspect of the industry of Neapolitan Baroque painting, it is now necessary to move from the world of the workshops into the streets. Here are found the enterprising and often innovative activities of a complex array of agents – artists, second-hand traders and the emerging category of the professional art dealer – all seeking to sell their wares and make their way within the dynamic field of the seventeenth-century Neapolitan art market.

Overleaf Carlo Coppola, *Martyrdom of St Januarius*, late 1630s–1640s (detail of fig. 67)

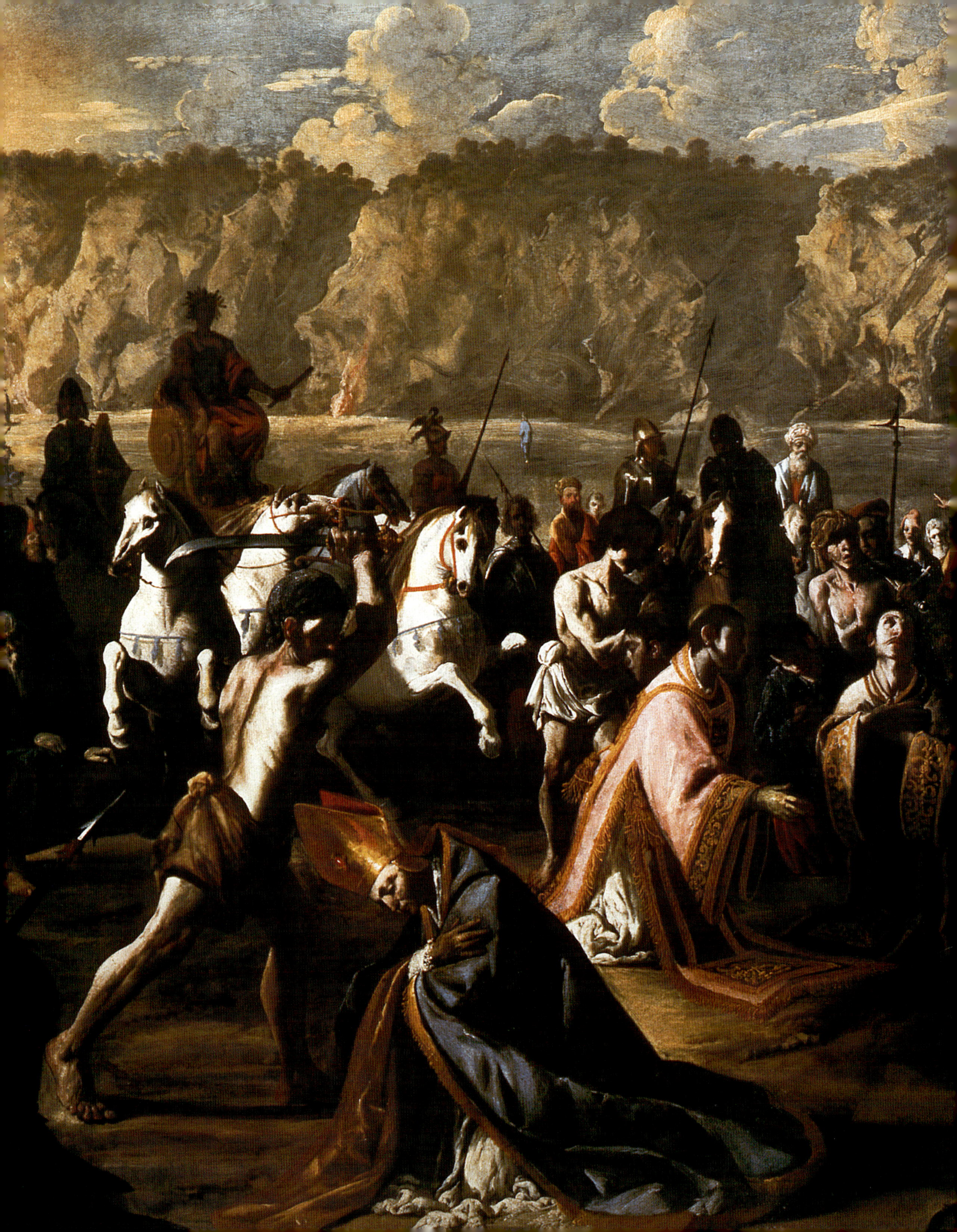

PART II

THE NEAPOLITAN BAROQUE ART MARKET

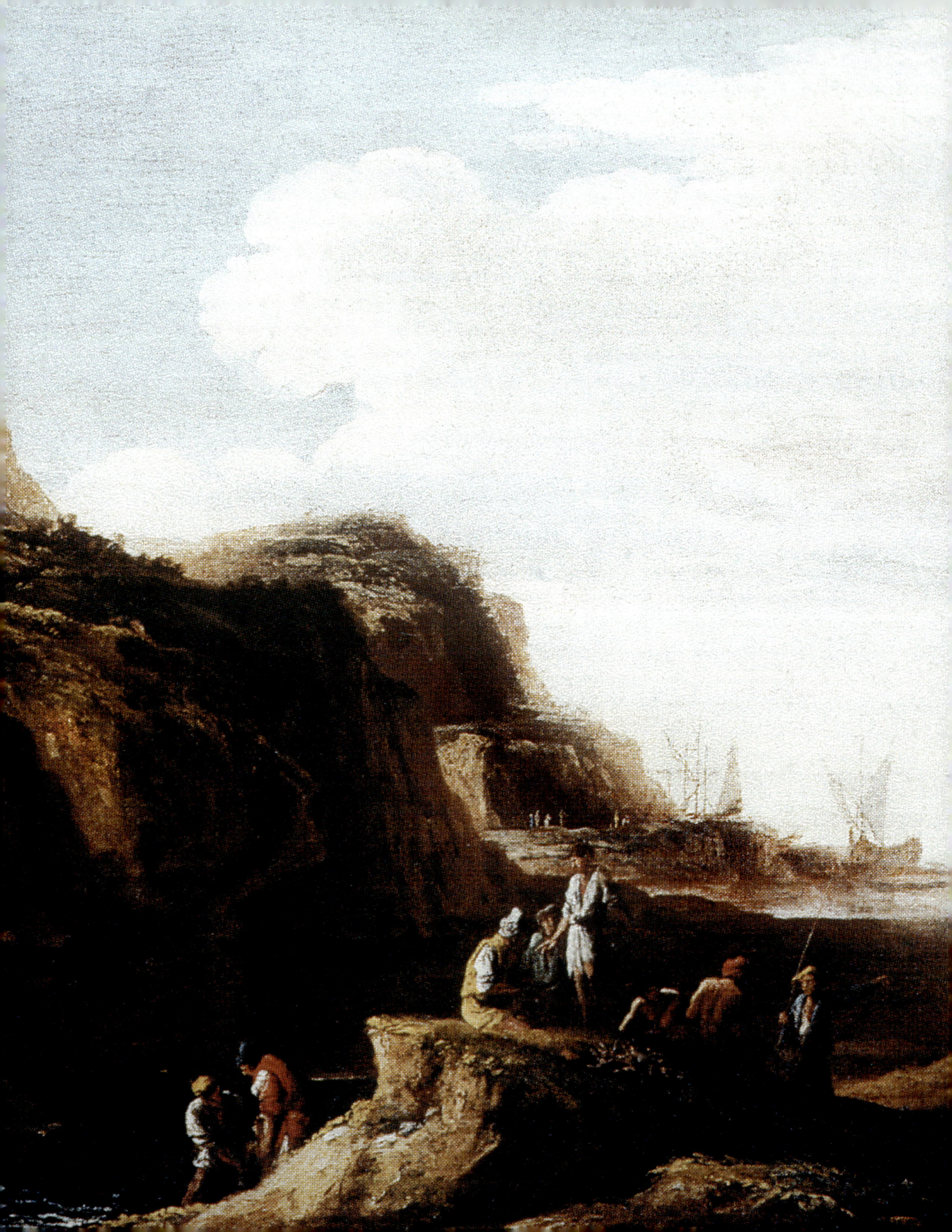

5

Art Dealing at the Lower Levels of the Market

JACOB VAN SWANENBURGH AND THE NEAPOLITAN INQUISITION

In November 1608 a Dutch painter resident in Naples devised a scheme for marketing his work directly to the public that he would soon have cause to regret. Jacob van Swanenburgh (1571–1638) was nearing forty and had lived in Naples for a decade. Until then, he had been operating at the margins of the Neapolitan art world, at least from the point of view of the more established painters of the day. From his own words one learns that he had been working for an art dealer for the better part of a decade before coming into a position of sufficient independence and financial security to be able to open his own workshop selling paintings to the public on his own merit. He had an advantage in this in that the workshop was optimally situated, being close by the church and piazza of Santa Maria della Carità in the heart of the painters' neighbourhood along Via Toledo.

In order to attract the attention of passers-by, Van Swanenburgh decided to exhibit his paintings on the outer wall of his workshop in a manner that is comparable to the second-hand dealer's workshop depicted in the contemporaneous view of the Palazzo Gravina, which was close to his workshop (fig. 70, see also pp. 12–13). But whereas the shop at the Palazzo Gravina displayed blandly conventional fare – half-length paintings of saints and the like – Van Swanenburgh had the idea of exhibiting something distinctive and eye-catching. He displayed what was for him an unusually large and ambitious painting measuring 4 × 7 *palmi* (approx. 105 × 184 cm), depicting a *Witches' Sabbath*. (The painting is now lost, but would have been similar to the subsequently produced *Hell* scenes for which he is better known today: fig. 71.)[1] This unusual choice, whose novelty would have ensured maximum impact on the viewing public, was an early forerunner to the kinds of exhibition strategies devised by Ribera, Rosa and Giordano, to be discussed in Chapter Eleven. The subject of the *stregoneria*, as it came to be known in Italian, was at that stage virtually unknown in Naples, although it would occasionally occur a decade or so later in the work of like-minded artists with a taste for the bizarre, such as Filippo Napoletano, François de Nomé and Salvator Rosa.[2]

Van Swanenburgh exhibited the painting, as he subsequently put it, 'in order to give pleasure to the people who would see it'.[3] But he should perhaps have anticipated the consequences of his decision, since the painting soon began to attract undue attention. 'Crowds of people gathered around examining it closely', one observer noted – evidently a hostile witness, since he denounced the painting as being 'against the Catholic faith'. Even the painter himself was drawn to admit under subsequent cross-examination that 'many members of the clergy visited my workshop to see

Facing page Salvator Rosa, *Coastal Landscape*, 1633–8 (detail of fig. 75)

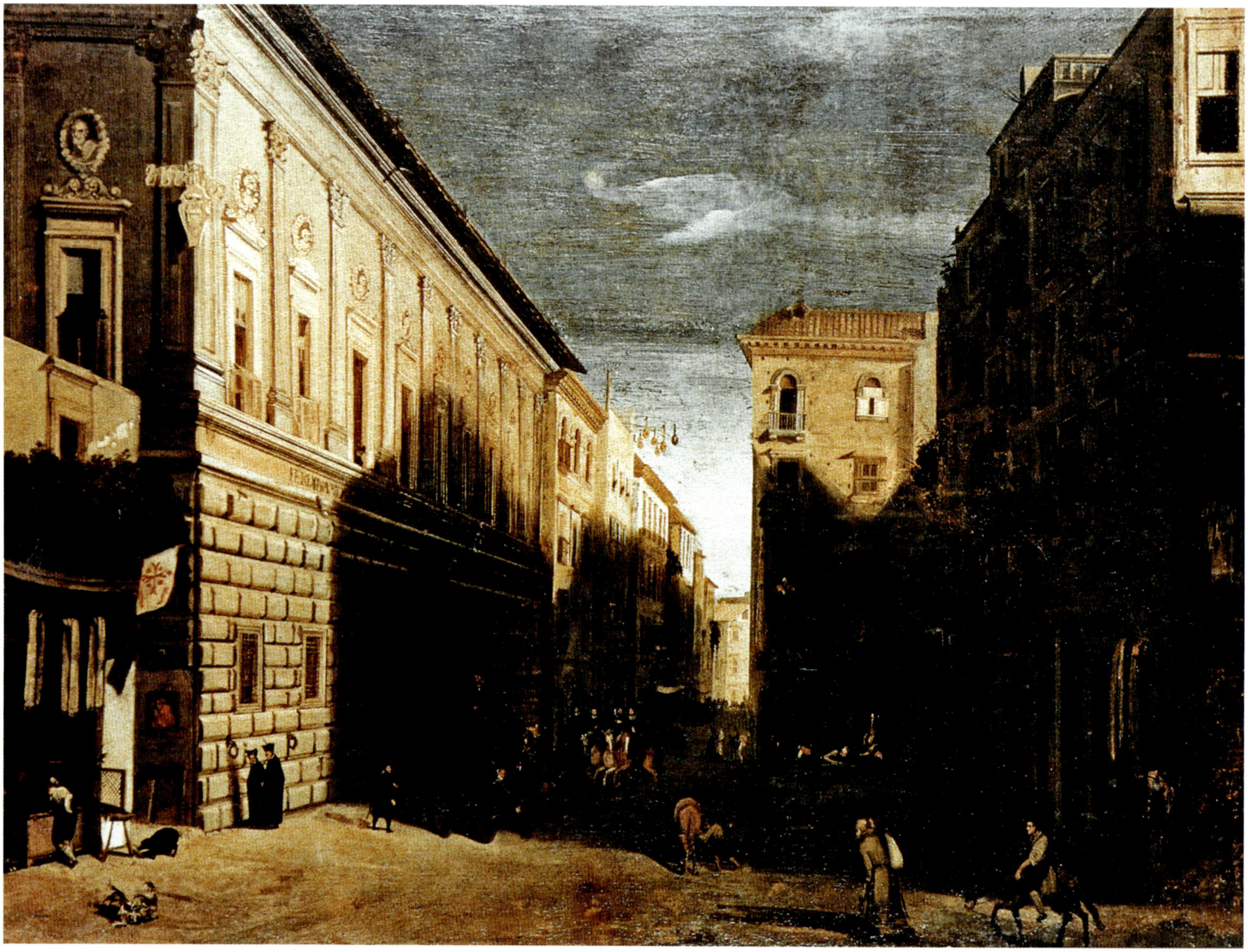

70 Unidentified topographical painter in the circle of François de Nomé and Alessandro Baratta, *View of the Palazzo Gravina, Naples*, 1620s–1630s. Oil on canvas, 98 × 125 cm. Private collection, Rome

it'. This effective strategy of attracting publicity via novelty, and thus reaching new audiences, was all too successful, as it transpired.

The response, in any event, was swift. The Inquisition raided the premises, confiscated the painting (and another smaller variant found inside) and called the painter to account. Although Van Swanenburgh appears to have escaped punishment, the incident evidently soured his relations with his adopted home. Within a few years he had returned to Leiden, the city of his birth. There he would attract a certain amount of posthumous fame as an early teacher of the young Rembrandt.[4]

In attempting to make the transition from a modestly ranked artist working for an art dealer to an independent master in charge of his own workshop, Van Swanenburgh was following a career progression common to painters both before and after him. Yet it took him a full eight years, the better part of the second decade of his post-apprenticeship career, before he was able to contemplate this step, which points to the struggles involved in making this transition for all but the most hard-working, well-connected and perhaps also most talented painters. It is also a reminder of the importance of the art market for artists struggling to advance their careers.

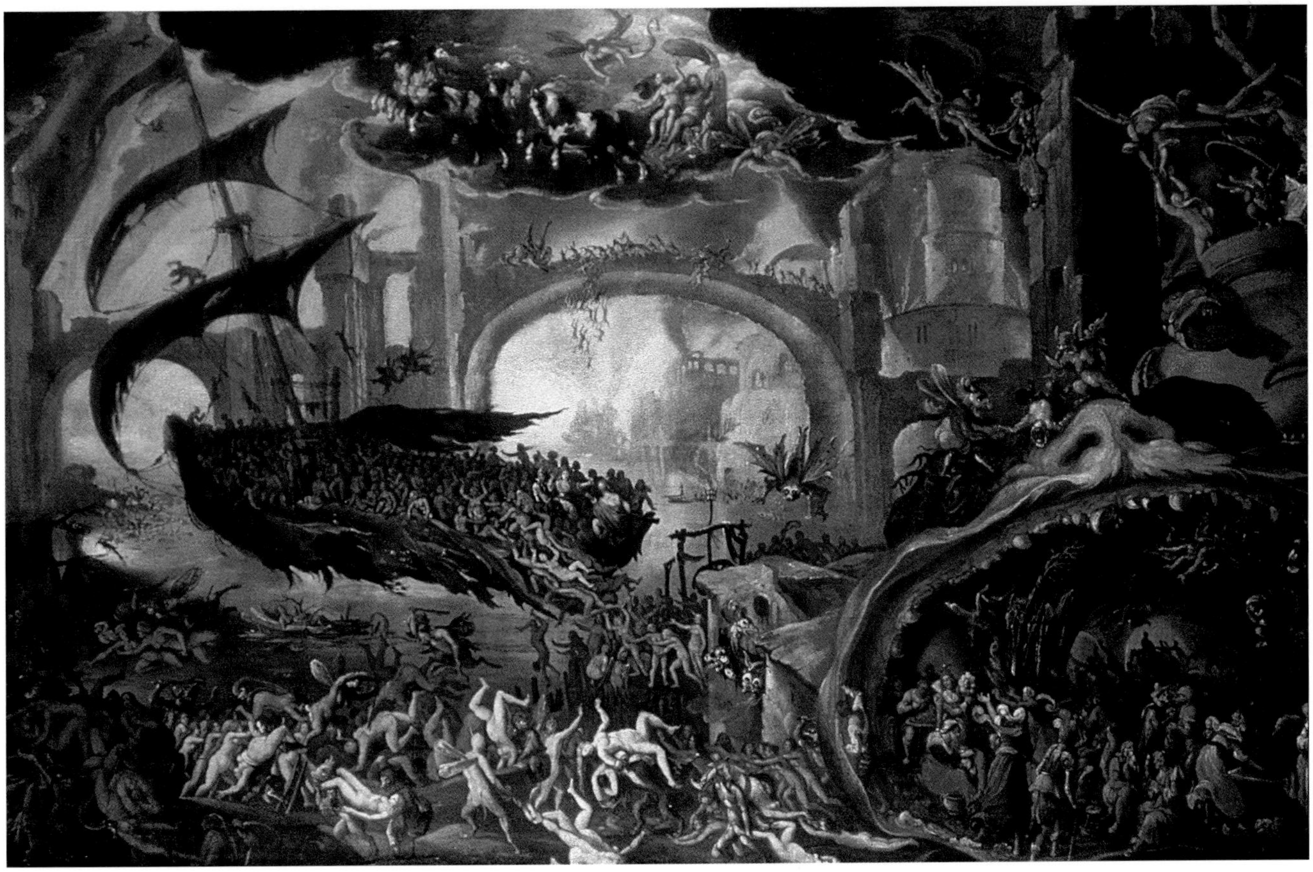

71 Jacob van Swanenburgh, *The Crossing of the River Styx*, *circa* 1625. Oil on canvas, signed with monogram. Muzeum Narodowe w Gdańsku, Gdansk

FROM *BASSO* TO *BOTTEGA*

There were obvious advantages for emerging independent artists who chose to begin their careers working for art dealers. The arrangement not only offered a modicum of relatively steady pay, but it also enabled them to draw on the dealers' previously established commercial networks. It gave them access as well to work spaces and materials, which was particularly important since rent represented one of the highest running costs involved in maintaining an artistic practice during this period.

To rent an artist's workshop in the centre of Naples – such as the neighbourhood of the Carità and the Palazzo Gravina, where so many painters of the day concentrated their work and living quarters – cost between 30 and 40 ducats a year or more, depending on the location or number of extra rooms for living/storage that a painter was able to afford.[5] This level of annual outlay would have been beyond the reach of most modestly ranked manual workers and artisans. It was certainly more, for example, than the *portiere* of the Banco di Napoli could afford in 1637 when he signed on to the job for a salary of 3 ducats a month or 36 ducats a year.[6] A worker of this kind would have had to be content, instead, to lodge with his family in one of the cramped *basso* apartments that are still to be seen in Naples today. These window-less, one-room living quarters opening directly onto the street could be rented at the more affordable rate of approximately 11 ducats a year, attainable not only for the *portiere* but also for Van Swanenburgh, one imagines, during his first decade spent working for the dealer prior to relocating to the workshop on the Piazza della Carità.

The notion that Van Swanenburgh or any other artist would be in a position to purchase a workshop outright when making the transition from the *basso* to the *bottega* would have been out of the question for all but the most successful painters of the day. In 1616–19, for example, the going price for a workshop was between 1,600 and 2,000 ducats.[7] This unattainably high cost for all but the wealthiest practitioners meant that Van Swanenburgh and the vast majority of his peers would pay annual rent on their workshops throughout their lives. Workshops were mostly unavailable for purchase, in any event, since they were generally held as long-term investment properties in the possession of the banks, churches, convents and aristocratic families of the area.[8]

Van Swanenburgh identified his early employer as a 'mercante nella pittura' and when asked to describe what kind of business he undertook, noted that this merchant exported Van Swanenburgh's paintings to Sicily. This reference to art export provides a further indication that he spent his first eight years working at the lowest reaches of the market. The practice of traders employing relatively unknown artists to turn out copies of well-known compositions and cheap versions of conventional devotional subjects or other easily saleable secular picture types that were then sent to the provinces was, of course, unique neither to Naples nor the seventeenth century. Many of the early biographers mention young artists undertaking employment of this kind as a necessary first stage of their careers. In Florence, for example, Baldinucci noted that Bartolomeo Bimbi started his career producing copies after Carlo Dolci's popular devotional compositions that were sent by a merchant by the name of Bettin Francesco Seminati 'to many places over there, beyond the mountains'.[9] The same is true of Gersaint's account of Watteau's early years. The biographer described Watteau's initial involvement in contributing to the production of 'many small portraits and subjects of devotion [that] were wholesaled to merchants in the provinces who bought them by the dozen or even the gross'. Watteau is said to have been known for the great speed with which he was able to paint multiple images of St Nicholas for export, explaining: 'I knew my St Nicholas by heart and had no need of the original to copy.'[10]

How much might Van Swanenburgh and other artists operating at this level of the market have expected to receive for their work? Relatively few documented instances for comparable kinds of production survive (Table 3), but they indicate that the base rate for cheap paintings was between half a ducat to a couple of ducats or slightly more depending on factors such as size, subject, degree of specialization and extent of serial repetition involved in production – of course this was a trifling amount compared to the fees commanded by leading artists, who could obtain 100 ducats for a large church altarpiece, Ribera, for example, receiving this sum in 1618 for a gallery painting of the *Martyrdom of St Bartholomew*.[11] Still, when viewed from the perspective of the street, a ducat or two was a not inconsiderable amount and could make a significant difference in staving off economic hardship during times of need.

A good example of this level of earnings comes in the payment in 1637 of 7.5 ducats to Antonio Giordano, Luca Giordano's father, for five paintings of *St Nicholas* (see p. 58). He was paid 1.5 ducats per painting for what was evidently a serial production contract for five half-length images of a popular devotional saint produced for ready sale.[12] Nothing is known about the dealer who paid Giordano except that his name (Francesco Maria Vaglies) sounds Spanish. This suggests an involvement in the export of Neapolitan painting to Spain or its territories. A particularly detailed documentation of this kind of activity occurs in a contract of 1623 drawn up between the little-known painter Domenico d'Aquino and a Spanish merchant by the name of Jusepe de Torcalina. The terms of this agreement indicate an efficient, semi-industrial scale of serial production. It specified that D'Aquino was to deliver to Torcalina no fewer than 100 small paintings on copper at a rate of twenty-five per week for a month.

The subjects to be painted by D'Aquino again constitute conventionalized devotional figures. He was to produce thirty images of the *Virgin*, followed by twenty of *St Francis* and ten each of *St Jerome*, *St Isidore*, *St John the Baptist*, *St Mary Magdalene* and *St Bernard*. (The reference to St Isidore the Labourer provides a further indication of the contract's intended Spanish destination, given that Isidore was particularly venerated in Madrid and had been canonized only the year before.) D'Aquino was to be paid 5 *carlini* – or half a ducat – for each image, bringing the total to 50 ducats. Torcalina was called back to Spain less than a week after signing the contract. This, together with the quantity and type of paintings involved, make it clear that he intended to export them to Spain in order to participate in the thriving trade in *pinturas ordinarias* then operating out of Madrid and other regional Spanish centres.[13]

A similar arrangement occurs in another document of this kind, dated to June 1618. This records an agreement between the little-known artist Principio de Concilio and a certain 'Capitan Andrea de Sillia'. De Sillia evidently intended to include De Concilio's paintings in his ship's cargo for subsequent sale at their point of disembarkation. On this occasion he agreed to pay the artist 30 ducats for 'thirty figures in copper', costing 1 ducat each. This payment was an instalment towards a larger contract, since the document notes that the artist was yet to complete a further seventy coppers required within six weeks in order to receive the total agreed amount of 100 ducats for one hundred coppers.[14] Assuming a productivity rate of six days a week, this meant that De Concilio would have needed to finish two coppers a day for six weeks in a row in order to complete the order by the deadline.

This trade in serially produced devotional imagery offloaded from the Neapolitan docks could flow in the opposite direction as well. In 1610, for example, a merchant by the name of Francesco Guevara was granted an export licence from the papal chamberlain in charge of granting licences from the Papal States, giving permission to transfer into the kingdom of Naples 'a bale of 100 painted portraits of martyred Jesuits'.[15] Guevara was evidently seeking to capitalize on the emerging market in devotional imagery then being stimulated in Naples following the inauguration of the Neapolitan Jesuit mother church of the Gesù Nuovo a few years earlier.

D'Aquino would have received a weekly wage of 12.5 ducats, almost the same amount as that earned per week by Principio de Concilio for his presumably larger paintings on copper produced for export to the Spanish markets. Both these agreements represented a substantial windfall in comparison to Antonio Giordano's payment of 7.5 ducats, and of course the artists in question earned much more than the 36 ducats per year paid to the *portiere* of the Banco di Napoli. Nevertheless, these agreements constituted short-term business opportunities rather than a fixed, steady wage. D'Aquino's take-home pay would also have been rather less than 50 ducats, since his contract stipulated that he was to provide all the materials at his own expense. This included the copper supports, which constituted a much more expensive material than canvas – albeit one that was more durable and probably therefore one of the reasons why it was stipulated in both Torcalina's and De Sillia's export orders.[16]

DAY WAGES VERSUS WEEKLY SALARIES AND STIPENDS

D'Aquino, De Concilio and Antonio Giordano were paid on consignment for their work – a straightforward arrangement that allowed both the buyer and the producer to remain very clear about what was being paid for. It was possible, nonetheless, for dealers and artists to enter into either simpler or more complex and longer-standing financial arrangements depending on the nature of their working relationship and the degree of specialization required in the transaction. The simplest form of payment was a fixed day wage – in the same way that a day labourer might be paid at the end of each day's work for laying bricks, helping with farm work, cutting marble, etc.

The early sources frequently describe activity of this kind. Mancini, for example, noted that Ribera began his career in Rome 'painting by the day for those who deal in pictures with all the trials such work involves for young men'.[17] The perception that working for day wages was a demanding activity suitable only for struggling young artists grew out of Mancini's wider prejudice against art dealing as antithetical to his understanding of the innate nobility of painting. In Naples, on the other hand, De' Dominici, who was himself the son of an art-dealing artist, did not disparage such work, and provided two especially revealing anecdotes in relation to the early careers of Aniello Falcone and Bernardo Cavallino.

De' Dominici wrote that Aniello Falcone worked early in his career for a certain Nicola di Martino, 'negoziante di quadri', who was most probably related to Salvator Rosa's early dealer, Pietro di Martino, discussed below. Nicola di Martino's workshop, like Pietro di Martino's, was situated in the painter's neighbourhood in the Quartiere della Carità, close to Van Swanenburgh's workshop and the art-dealing workshop at Palazzo Gravina, a further piece of information attesting to the high concentration of art dealing in this area.

Falcone began his career as an independent painter in Nicola di Martino's employ, after serving apprenticeships first to an unknown painter and then to Ribera (this dates the anecdote to the late 1620s).[18] Nicola di Martino was a *rigattiere*, or dealer in second-hand wares. He was one of those traders 'who paid by the day', and for whom young, unestablished artists would work when in need of ready cash.[19] His business included an upstairs workshop where artists worked on paintings that were then exhibited for sale in the shop below. Falcone painted some battle pieces for Di Martino's shop that would have been comparable to his earliest-known works in this field (fig. 72).[20] They were subsequently noticed by the Cavalier d'Arpino, who was then in Naples to work on the Cappella del Tesoro di San Gennaro, as well as by Gaspar Roomer, the most important Neapolitan art collector of the day.

Like many of De' Dominici's anecdotes, the reference cannot be regarded as strictly accurate, at least in a chronological sense. D'Arpino worked on the Tesoro di San Gennaro sometime between 1618 and 1622, and, given that Falcone was born in 1607, and not 1600 as De' Dominici thought, he would have been too young to produce work

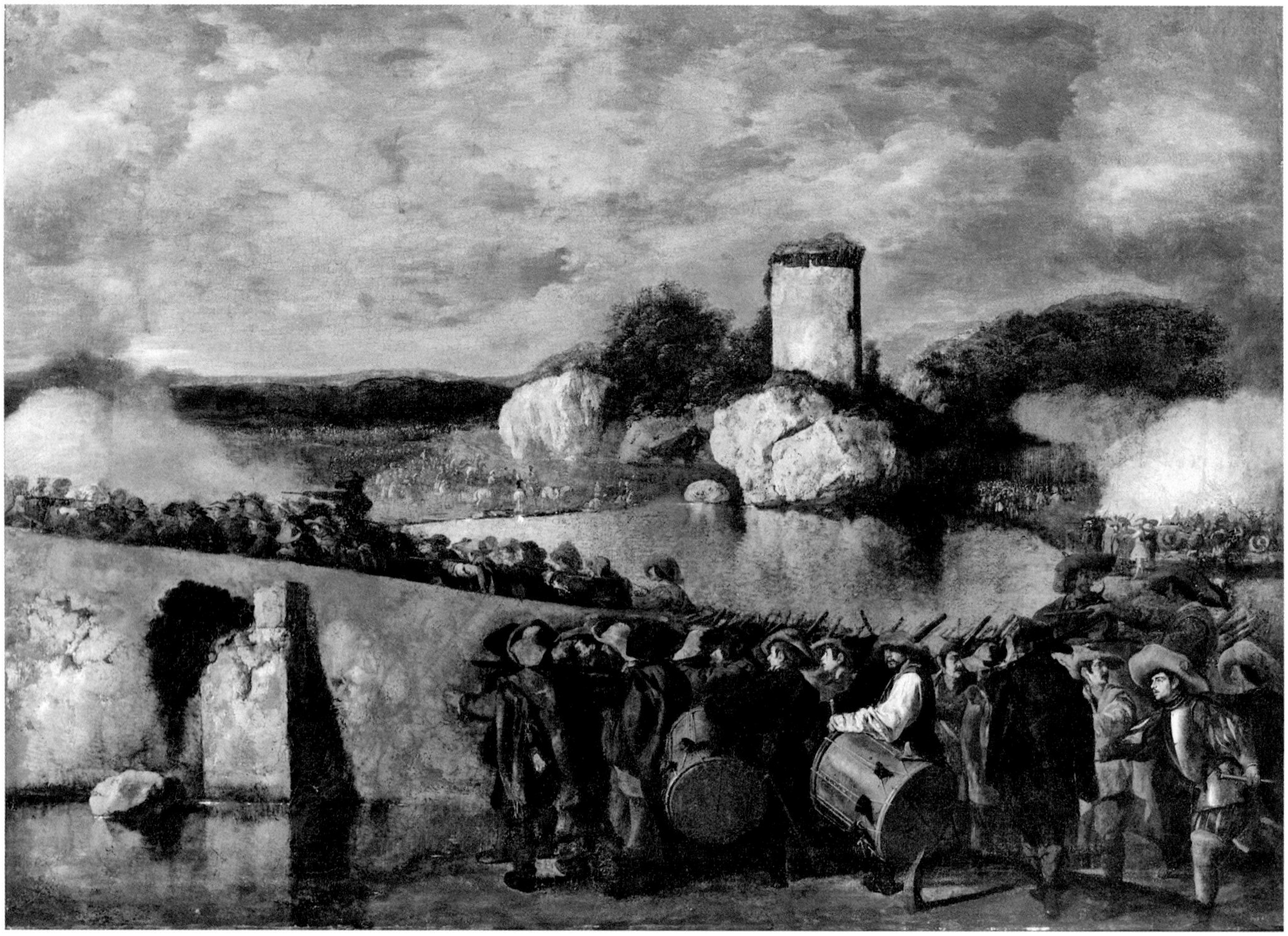

72 Aniello Falcone, *Battle Scene*, late 1620s–early 1630s. Oil on canvas laid down on panel, 64 × 88.5 cm. Formerly art market, London

of this kind in the early 1620s.[21] The essential elements of De' Dominici's account nonetheless ring true. Roomer is known to have owned paintings by Falcone as early as 1630 (see pp. 76–7). Moreover, the working arrangements described by De' Dominici conform closely to the practices outlined in the documents relating to the trial of a Roman picture dealer of the late seventeenth century named Domenico Castiglione. In 1688 Castiglione kept a shop that served both as a workshop for the execution of paintings and a display area for their sale. In 1679 he rented rooms near Piazza Trevi and kept a shop nearby with at least three storerooms of paintings. Much of his stock had been produced by his own establishment, since according to the testimony Castiglione 'kept some young men constantly at work making pictures'.[22]

De' Dominici's account is also corroborated by independent documentation confirming Nicola di Martino's subsequent activities as a dealer. In 1680 his name appears as the principal signatory of the newly redrafted regulations of the professional association of second-hand dealers – the Corporazione di Rivenditori, who maintained a chapel at the now-demolished church of San Tommaso d'Aquino situated on Via Toledo in this same neighbourhood.[23] Di Martino is listed in the statutes as the Corporazione's chief *console* and treasurer, indicating that, by the end of his career at least, he had enjoyed considerable success and risen to a position of high standing in the profession.[24]

The statutes of the Corporazione di Rivenditori are revealing in listing the broad range of items sold by traders of this kind. They claim for the association the right to examine all those applying for a patent to maintain a *rivenditore*'s workshop: 'in the recognition of the quality, value and other circumstances related to all the types of goods maintained by this profession and trade, namely: beds, mattresses, seats, desks, console tables, glassware, paintings, fabrics, either of wool or of silk, and finally every other sort of used furnishing'.[25] As the statutes make clear, the bedrock of a *rivenditore*'s profession lay in the ongoing trade in second-hand furniture and furnishings more generally.[26] Yet as the anecdotes relating to Falcone and other artists indicate, a number of *rivenditori* nevertheless saw the benefits of adding into their business a specialization in primary market sales of new paintings and displaying them alongside their second-hand wares. The statutes of the Rivenditori of 1680 also address this aspect of their business in reserving for themselves the right to 'create new desks, beds, console tables, seats, stands, paintings, mattresses and any other kind of furniture without being impeded by any other person, workforce or trade'.

As the references to Nicola di Martino's and Castiglione's employment of artists indicate, some at least of these *rivenditori* chose to specialize in this field to such an extent that their primary market sales came increasingly to form a major part of their business. They were becoming, in effect, specialized art dealers rather than *rivenditori* who dealt in art on the side. These more enterprising traders with an increasingly full-time involvement in the primary market were then well equipped to make a further transition – as particularly evident in the years after the plague of 1656 – to a new sub-category in the typology of art dealing known from the anecdotes and documents here discussed. This was to move from dealing in cheap to moderately priced paintings and to specialize instead in the trade in paintings by more recognized artists that constituted the more lucrative field of the prestigious art merchant.[27]

As one of the early traders in the emerging field of battle painting and other forms of cabinet paintings, Nicola di Martino was very well placed to make this transition during the later stages of his career. A small number of bank records further corroborate this picture. In 1677 he paid Carlo della Torre the substantial sum of 300 ducats for eleven 'copies of Luca Giordano of various measurements and Saints'.[28] The paintings were for the most part very large. Four measured around 3.16 metres wide, a further four measured 3.69 metres, while two are simply described as 'small'. The individual selling the paintings to Di Martino is elsewhere documented as Luca Giordano's pupil, business agent and sometime art dealer (discussed in Chapter Seven). It seems, therefore, that this acquisition formed part of a more complex, ongoing business arrangement with Della Torre that put Di Martino into the ranks of the more prestigious art merchants that gravitated around Luca Giordano in the years following the plague of 1656. Della Torre's involvement in the transaction also makes it likely that Di Martino was buying not just copies after Giordano, but also more specifically copies issuing directly from Giordano's workshop, hence their substantial size and relatively high value of a little over 27 ducats per copy.

Another *rivenditore* who appears to have developed an increasing specialization in primary market sales features in De' Dominici's biography of Bernardo Cavallino. Speaking of a period datable to the early 1630s by other external information, De' Dominici writes that Cavallino began his career earning a few *carlini* per day (10 *carlini* making up a ducat) painting various works for a succession of second-hand dealers during a period in which he was forced by necessity to provide for his family at a young age following the early death of his father.

Cavallino's talent nonetheless allowed him to be recognized and so to advance his career – in relative terms at least – while working at this level. De' Dominici noted that one merchant who profited by paying Cavallino by the day was a certain Giuseppe di Felice, 'Negoziante Napoletano'. Di Felice was so taken by Cavallino's work that he offered him board and a daily wage of 5 *carlini* in exchange for his work – 3 ducats a week, in other words, for a notional six-day working week. This was a significant break for the young artist, since it enabled him to make the transition from the sporadic day wages of his earliest productions to a slightly more settled and marginally more financially secure position. This amount was nevertheless equal to only about half the earnings of De Concilio and D'Aquino, suggesting that Cavallino still had a long way to go in financial terms before he attained a more secure position in the Neapolitan art world.

According to De' Dominici, Cavallino worked for Di Felice for many months, specializing in small history paintings that would have been similar to his earliest extant works (fig. 73).[29] Di Felice earned a great deal of money trading in Cavallino's pictures to local collectors such as Gaspar Roomer, as well as to other countries, particularly England,[30] although Haskell is probably correct in doubting that Cavallino's work was exported at this early date. Nonetheless, Percy confirms the essential accuracy of the anecdote, since many paintings by Cavallino, widely dispersed today, were misattributed from an early date.[31]

Why would a merchant like Giuseppe di Felice consider it in his best interests to stop paying daily wages to an artist like Cavallino and to move instead to the more complex – and costly – arrangement of paying him board and a fixed wage?

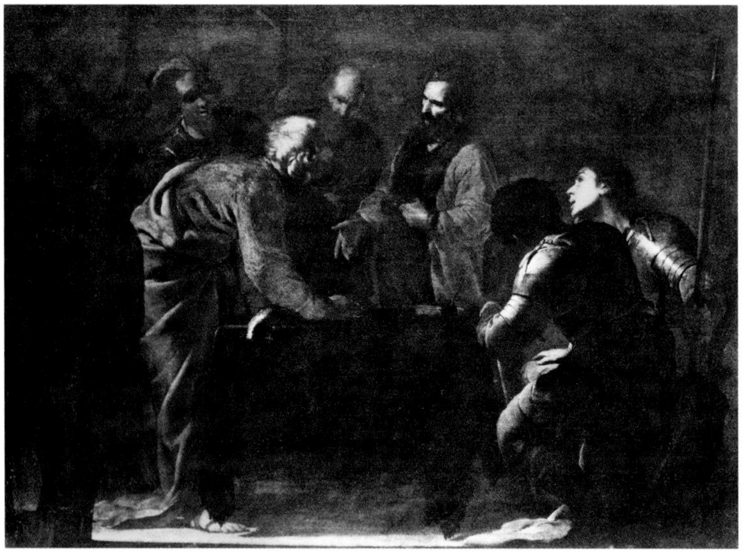

73 Bernardo Cavallino, *Payment of the Tribute Money*, 1635–40. Oil on canvas, 76 × 102 cm. Museo e Gallerie Nazionali di Capodimonte, Naples

Presumably, he did so in order to secure a monopoly on Cavallino's increasingly profitable output. The new arrangement would have also enabled the dealer to formulate a more fully thought-through, longer-term business strategy for the marketing of Cavallino's work.

This seems also to have been the case for the few other instances of documented examples of this kind that have come down to us. One occurs in a contract of 1686 between the painter and art dealer Domenico Oliva and the virtually unknown painter Aniello de Letizia. In the contract, De Letizia agrees to paint for a period of four months history paintings, animal paintings, flower pieces, devotional paintings and 'every other kind and whatsoever item the given Domenico orders from him'.[32] De Letizia is to be paid a fixed monthly wage of 16 ducats – or 4 ducats a week (1 ducat a week more than Cavallino's wage when he was similarly employed). He is to be given workshop space, canvas and pigments. De Letizia's employer was himself a painter. Although hardly known today, Oliva's work appears in some early inventories and he is mentioned in De' Dominici's *Vite* as one of the pupils of the landscape painter Domenico Gargiulo.[33] De Letizia would thus presumably have worked alongside Oliva in his workshop. De Letizia's hours of employment were strictly regulated. He was to work from 10.30 am until 3.00 pm and then again from 7.00 until 11.00 pm every day except Sundays, with a penalty of a ducat for every day of missed work.

The strict hours and penalties for missed work suggest a rather harsh and even exploitative working arrangement. Nonetheless, 16 ducats a month over a period of four months – or 4 ducats a week totalling 64 ducats for the entire period – represents a very respectable short-term wage for an artist operating at this level of the market. It was marginally more than Cavallino earned for his work, and it was more than five times the weekly earnings of the *portiere* of the Banco di Napoli.

The documentation also suggests that De Letizia was no mere apprentice or junior journeyman. Rather, he was a skilled artist being paid a premium for an accomplished and versatile output. He was evidently capable of working across a broad range of genres – from history painting to still lifes and animal paintings, as the document is careful to spell out. This flexibility must have made him very useful to Oliva, as his wages seem to reflect. What was at premium in this sector of the market, therefore, was less the inventiveness and individuality of an independent master's distinctive style than a responsive and adaptable talent capable of responding to market demand and, under the dealer's guidance, to potential openings to be exploited in the future.

That this was indeed the basis of De Letizia's career is corroborated by the only other known document for him. In this reference – from July 1678 – De Letizia agreed to complete two copies, measuring approximately 132 × 211 centimetres, after the *Decollation of the Baptist* and the *Liberation of St Peter* by Mattia Preti. The total agreed price was 13 ducats.[34] Although this sum may appear trifling in comparison to the earnings achieved by such high-ranking artists as Ribera, it was certainly respectable from the street-level perspective. As Table 3 makes clear, it is roughly equivalent, in fact, to the prices paid to second-tier artists for smaller works, and thus comparable to the 6 and 8 ducats paid to Andrea de Leone in 1679 and 1685 for three 'quadretti'. One of these is mentioned as being a small battle painting, and so would have been similar to the many small battle scenes by his hand that are still circulating on the market today (fig. 74).[35]

THE STRUGGLE FOR INDEPENDENCE: THE EXAMPLE OF SALVATOR ROSA'S EARLY CAREER

It goes without saying that these traders would make payments of these amounts only if they felt confidant of generating a profit by setting the retail price for the paintings higher still prior to selling their work to the public.

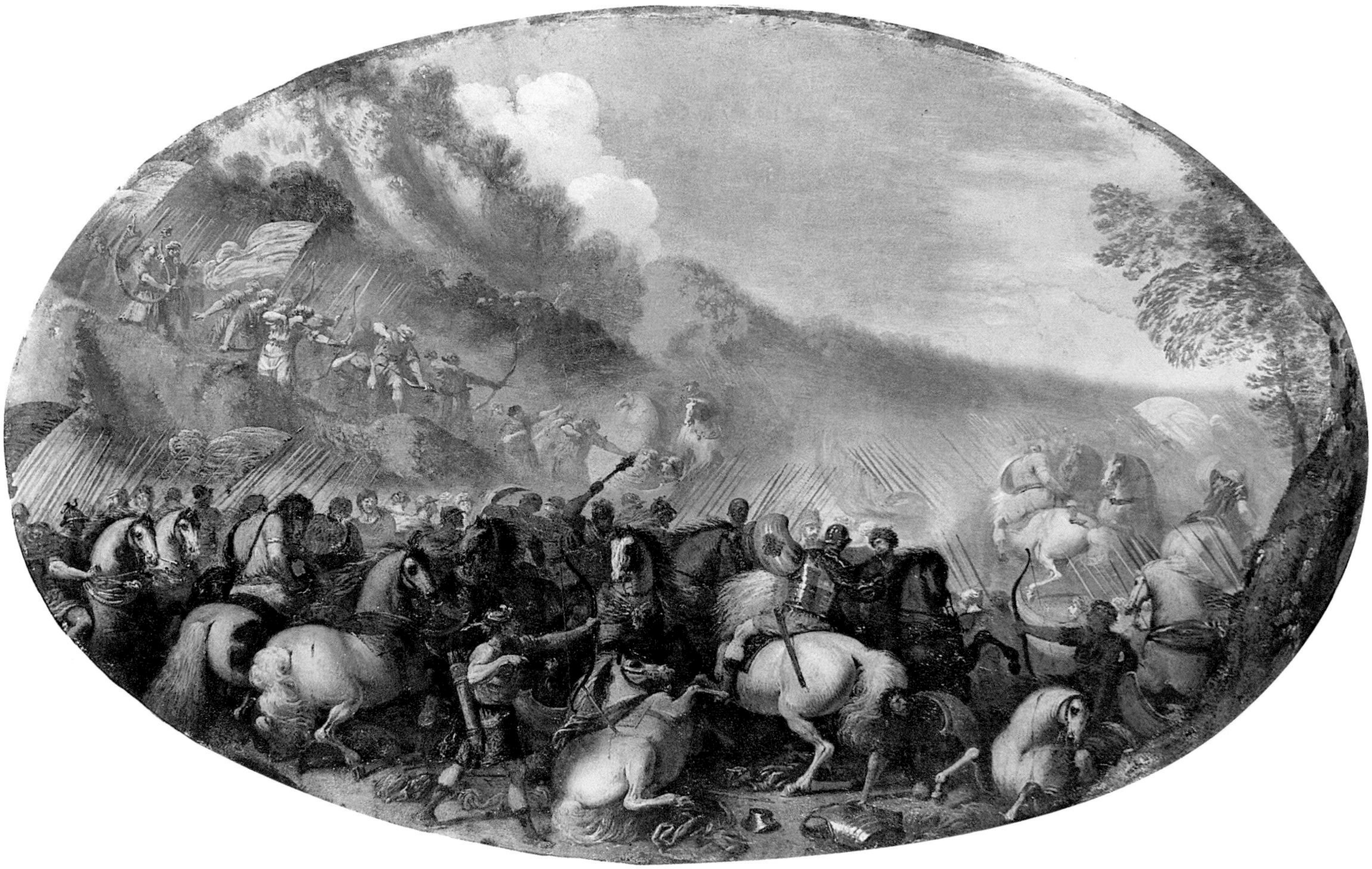

74 Andrea de Leone, *Battle Scene*, 1660s–1670s. Oil on copper, 33 × 52 cm. Formerly art market, Rome

Just how high they raised their prices and how low they negotiated the painters' wages and working conditions, of course, provided considerable scope for a sense of inequity to arise on the part of the artists working for them, particularly those artists such as Van Swanenburgh who were keen to make the transition to a more established independent career. For every painter like Cavallino – who appears to have thrived and consolidated his emerging specialization while working for Giuseppe di Felice – there may have been others who were resentful at being held back or even exploited.

This tension forms a particular focus of an account by De' Dominici of the early career of Salvator Rosa. The anecdote is independently verifiable since it is based on an initial account written by Rosa's friend and early biographer, Giovanni Battista Passeri, in the 1670s, who noted that Rosa's work first came to the attention of Lanfranco while he was in Naples from 1634, working on the frescoes in the Gesù Nuovo. Lanfranco had bought a painting by Rosa when it was displayed anonymously in a *rivenditore*'s workshop, while he was passing along the Via della Carità on his way to work.[36] De' Dominici extended the anecdote, noting that Rosa was forced to provide for his family around 1632, at the age of seventeen or eighteen, after his father died. Reduced to such poverty that he could not even afford canvas and paint, Rosa was compelled to paint landscape sketches on paper that he sold to the *rivenduglioli*, or dealers in cheap second-hand wares, for a few *baiocchi* (10 *baiocchi* equalling a *carlino*).

The *rivenditori*, for their part, marked up Rosa's landscape sketches considerably, managing to sell them for 3 or 4 *carlini* each (0.3–0.4 ducats), equivalent to around ten times the amount they had paid Rosa for them. Lanfranco eventually noticed one of these and paid the second-hand dealer a full ducat more than its asking price. This led the *rivenditori* to press Rosa for more stock. Provided with

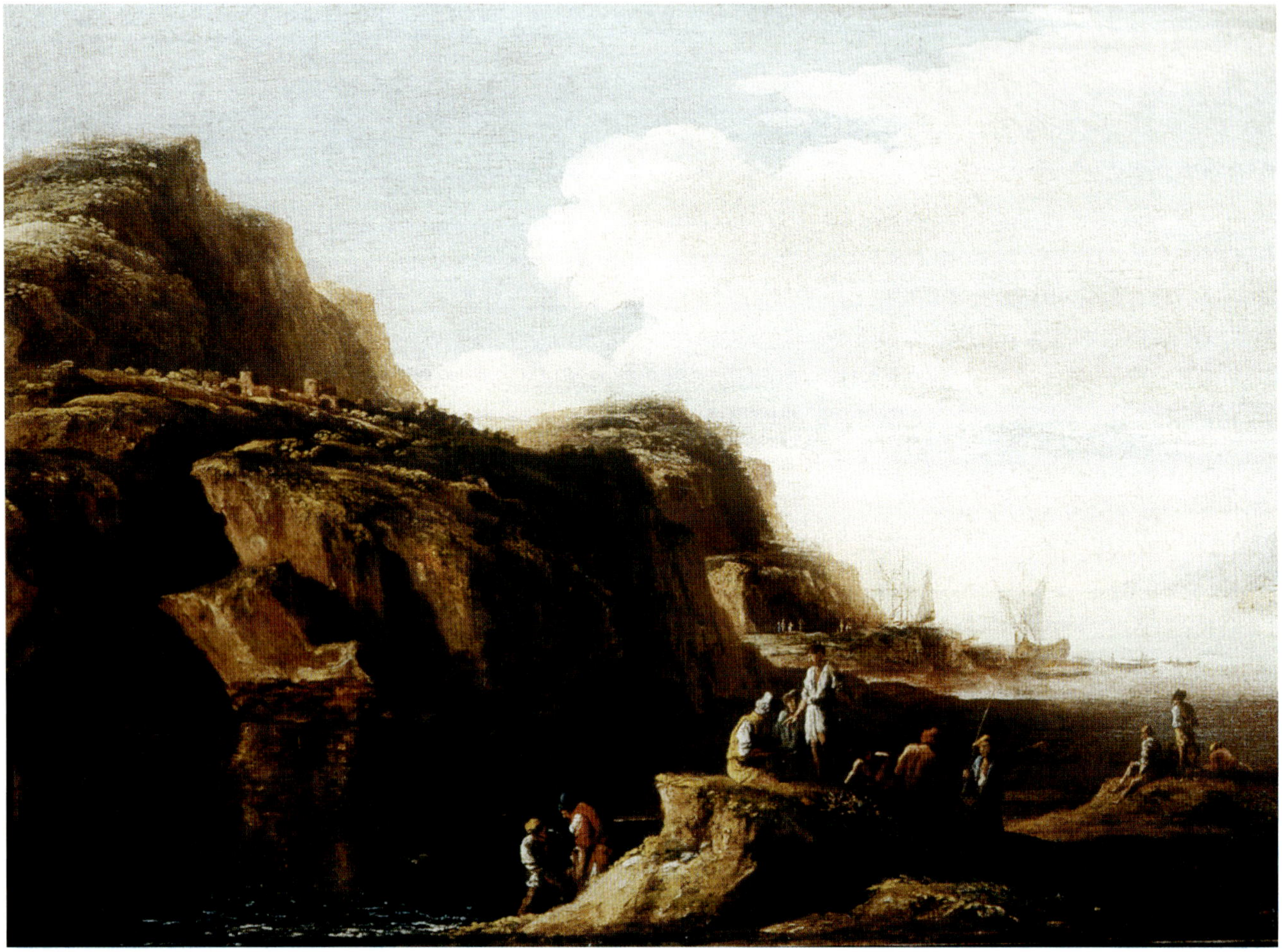

75 Salvator Rosa, *Coastal Landscape*, 1633–8. Oil on canvas, 44 × 62 cm. Museo Nazionale di San Martino, Naples

enough money to buy canvas and materials, and following the advice of his brother-in-law, Francesco Fracanzano, Rosa was encouraged by this recognition of his work to produce some fully fledged landscape paintings on canvas that he also sold to the second-hand dealers, and which would also have compared directly with his earliest-known Neapolitan landscapes and seascapes from around this period (fig. 75).[37]

The *rivenditori*, for their part, seeing that Lanfranco had acquired his work, marked up the prices for Rosa's paintings on canvas further still.[38] A little later, Lanfranco, passing through the area again on his way to the Gesù Nuovo, bought one of these paintings – a landscape with the story of *Hagar and the Angel* – for the still higher price of 10 ducats. Lanfranco met Rosa shortly afterwards and purchased a further two landscapes from him directly, which Passeri subsequently viewed in Lanfranco's workshop following his return to Rome in 1646.[39]

The anecdote is suspiciously reminiscent of the story of D'Arpino's discovery of the young Aniello Falcone, discussed above, so it is quite possible that it has been embellished to a certain extent. Even so, Rosa did come from a humble background and had to provide for his family, so his straitened economic circumstances during the early to mid-1630s cannot be doubted.[40] Moreover, De' Dominici is quite specific about the source of the supplementary information that he was able to gather independently of Passeri's account. His informant was the main dealer who promoted Rosa's early work, Pietro di Martino, who also maintained a workshop in the area of the Carità. De' Dominici identifies him as the father of Falcone's early art dealer, Nicola di Martino, and he also mentions another dealer by the name of Nicolò di Martino as being active in the area. The Di Martino family, therefore, seems to have been one of the most prominent and active local families involved in the art trade in Naples during the period.

WORKING FOR DEALERS, WORKING FOR PATRONS

How much more would the lower-ranked artists here discussed have hoped to receive for their work beyond what they were paid by dealers once they had made the transition into operating as independent masters? A sense of this can be gained from an additional reference contained in Jacob van Swanenburgh's testimony to the Inquisition in 1608. When explaining his earlier career, he noted that he had been fortunate in receiving some commissions from private patrons in the period after he had worked for the dealer and at around the same time as he opened his workshop in the area of the Carità.

Van Swanenburgh identified one of these patrons as the conte di Montemiletto, and this passing reference is helpful in clarifying rates of pay, since another payment from this patron is known for a similar kind of work produced during the same years: in 1606 he and the contessa made a down payment towards a total price of 50 ducats to the early landscape specialist Cornelio Ghesenz 'for six paintings that he has to complete of landscapes with figures'.[41] Like Van Swanenburgh, Ghesenz evidently belonged to the sizeable Neapolitan colony of Dutch and Flemish residents who were known for their expertise in the emerging specializations of landscape and view painting, and his landscapes for the count and countess were probably directly comparable to those Van Swanenburgh painted for them (and thus would have resembled the early landscapes produced in Naples during this period by slightly better-known specialists such as Filippo Napoletano and Goffredo Wals; fig. 76).

One may deduce from this that a price of around 8 ducats per painting is comparable to what Van Swanenburgh would have earned for his work for these patrons. If so, he was evidently hoping to progress from earning around 3–4 ducats per week while in the employ of dealers to receiving 5–8 ducats per painting from private patrons. This shift in earnings corresponds to payments made to Van Swanenburgh's other associates from among the Northern landscape and view specialists of the period. It compares well, for example, with the 8 ducats paid to Jacopo Coppola for a landscape in 1610, and the 5.8 ducats per painting – for a series of the *Four Seasons*, plus two landscapes – paid to Loys Croys in 1613.[42] The painter Principio de Concilio also appears to have belonged to this foreign colony of early landscape specialists. In 1617, the year before his contract with the ship captain Andrea de Sillia, he agreed to paint for an unidentified private patron four large narrative paintings depicting *Noah's Ark*, the *Great Flood*, the *Destruction of Troy* and the *Expulsion of the Rebel Angels*. The total agreed price was 20 ducats, averaging 5 ducats per painting.[43]

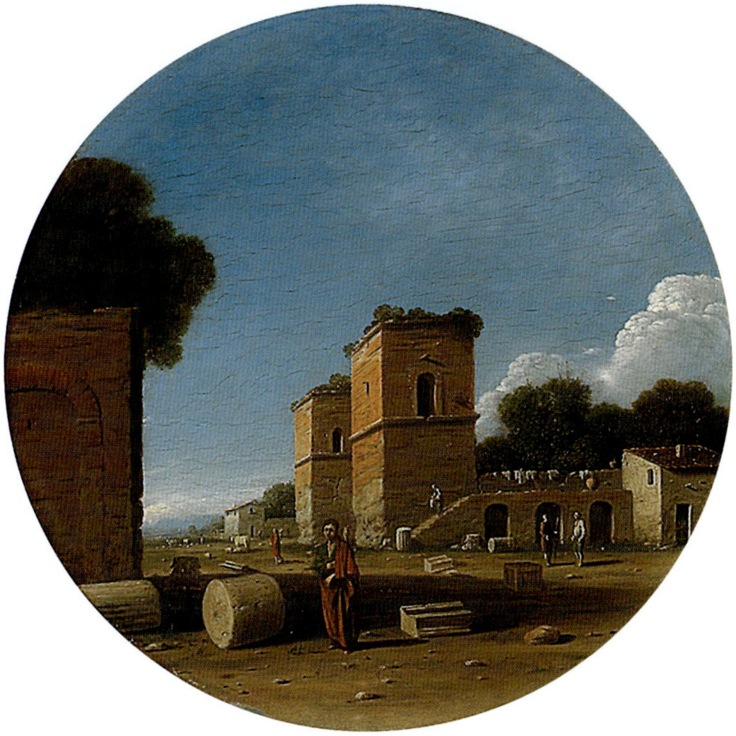

76 Goffredo Wals, *A Roman Landscape with Figures*, 1630s. Oil on copper, diameter 40.6 cm. Metropolitan Museum of Art, New York

This reference is a reminder of the relative facility of painters active at the lower levels of the market. Despite his low rates of pay in comparison to Ribera and his high-ranked colleagues, it seems that De Concilio was no mere hack turning out multiple copies of roughly produced, cheap devotional work. From this document at least, he emerges as an early specialist in the semi-fantastic nocturnal landscapes set amidst ruins animated by vivid incidental scenes of fire that may be recognized today in the work of other slightly better-known early Neapolitan specialists – such as Jacob van Swanenburgh himself, François de Nomé and Cornelio Brusco, whose own *Destruction of Troy* would probably have directly resembled Ghesenz's now-lost work (fig. 77).[44] This can also be further correlated with a known contract for work of this kind. In 1616 François de Nomé was paid 8.1 ducats per painting for a set of eight large paintings with architectural ruins.[45]

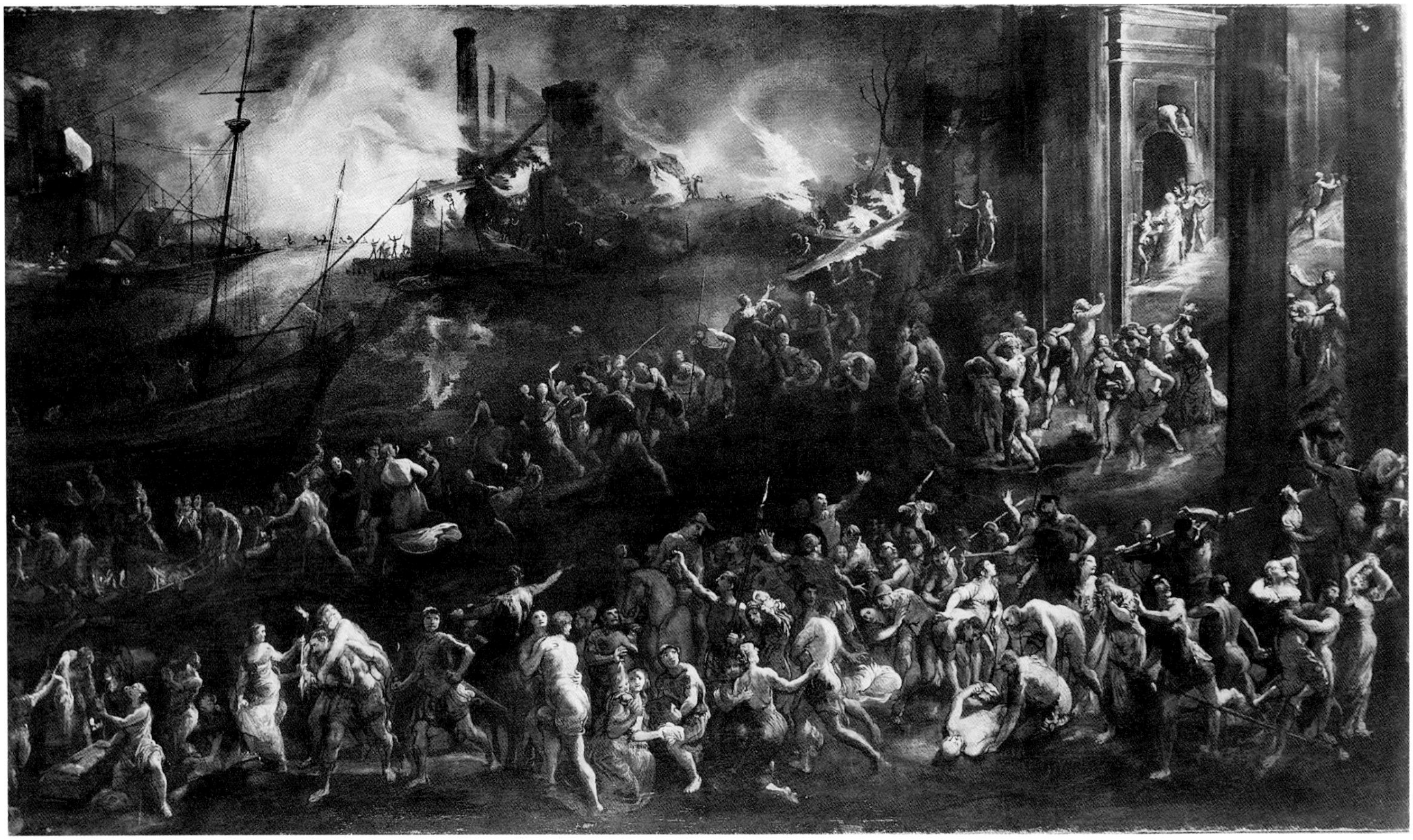

77 Cornelio Brusco, *Destruction of Troy*, 1615–30. Oil on canvas. Private collection, Naples

MOVING UP OR SLIDING DOWN?

Van Swanenburgh's probable shift from 3–4 ducats per week to 5–8 ducats per painting suggests the attainment of a reasonable degree of success and financial security. But the move to a higher wage bracket brought with it the pressure of higher standard of living expectations and increased running costs: 30–40 ducats per year or more for maintaining a workshop to start with. And what of the cost of living itself? This remains a subject that has not been definitively studied for Italian Baroque cities, but some initial conclusions can nonetheless be drawn for seventeenth-century Naples.[46]

Adding up the annual costs incurred for a few staple commodities, it is clear that if Van Swanenburgh and his colleagues were to live reasonably securely in Naples (if not especially comfortably), they would have required 100 ducats or more in annual earnings on top of rent.[47] Wheat, for example, cost around 3.5 *carlini* per kilo (or 0.35 of a ducat), making it only a little cheaper than the 4 or 5 *baiocchi* per kilo needed to buy wheat in Rome.[48] One contemporary report estimated that an individual living at subsistence level needed 6 *tomoli* of wheat to live on per year (or 240 kg, converting to approximately 600 grams of bread a day), thus costing each person around 8.5 ducats per year.[49] If one factors in the need to provide for a family, then this could represent an additional cost of another 40–50 ducats per year. Van Swanenburgh himself had a family, since his testimony mentions that he had married the daughter of a Neapolitan grocer some years earlier, and three children are subsequently listed as living with him and his wife when they moved to Leiden.

Wine, on the other hand, was a less burdensome residual cost, at least for cheap *vino da tavola*. This type of wine could be bought for just under 3 *grana* per litre (or 0.03 of a ducat) and thus again it was only a little cheaper than in Rome.[50] This could still reduce an annual budget to the tune of some 6 ducats or more per year, depending on consumption. Half a kilo of pasta, likewise, cost 8.5 *grani* (0.085 of a ducat), also a small price in isolation but very expensive on an annual basis if used regularly. Cooking 4 kilograms of pasta a week, for example (which would cost approximately 0.7 of a ducat per week), would convert to an annual outlay of more than 35 ducats for this commodity alone.

Beef was in fact quite cheap in seventeenth-century Naples: 8–12 *grana* per *rotolo* (0.08–0.12 of a ducat), for example, although veal would have been prohibitively expensive for most Neapolitans at 25–30 *grana* per *rotolo* (that is to say, nearly a third of a ducat, the *rotolo* being equivalent to just under a kilogram). Fish, on the other hand, varied much more in price, understandably so given Naples' status as one of the great fishing ports of the Mediterranean. Red mullet and other high-quality species could cost up to 29 *grana* (0.29 of a ducat) per *rotolo*.[51] Cheaper and more plentiful varieties like sardines, on the other hand, cost only 18 *grana* per *rotolo*. This again would amount to a little under 9 ducats per year, assuming an average consumption of a kilogram of sardines or their equivalent a week.

Contemporary viewers would certainly have had these cost of living issues in mind while contemplating, for example, the heaps of shiny fish piled high in Neapolitan still-life paintings of the period. The seafood displayed in Recco's *Copper Vessels with Fish and Squid* represents a decidedly modest and readily attainable repast, depicting as it does the common sea mullet with the equally plentiful squid (fig. 78). By contrast, the deep-sea swordfish, up-ended tortoises and other more exotic marine life heaped together in Giordano's and Recco's *Riches of the Sea with Neptune and Two Sea Nymphs* present a contrasting spectacle of extreme luxury that would have placed it well beyond the resources of all but the most princely patron (fig. 79).[52]

The costs noted here were all for basic foodstuffs. If Van Swanenburgh and his colleagues were to aspire towards other, more substantial indicators of wealth and attainment – if they wanted to feast on Recco's swordfish, in other words, rather than his mullet – then they would have to find a way of earning much more. In 1632, for example, at the height of his fame, Ribera paid his father-in-law's widow 210 ducats for a horse and carriage.[53] He even employed an *alfiere* or ensign bearer to run before him as he made his way through the narrow city streets. He is said to have paid this servant around half a ducat per day – the same amount as the day wages that he himself had received at the outset of his career and that were paid to Cavallino, Van Swanenburgh and the other lower-ranked painters working for dealers.[54]

Ribera also owned a residence, which was maintained separately from his workshop – a further indication of his wealth and status. In 1619 he purchased this property outright – constituting a house and garden for his extended family in the Strada di Santo Spirito in the centre of the artists' quarter – all for the large sum of 1,900 ducats.[55] In 1641 Ribera acquired a small villa with adjoining garden on the outskirts of Naples in the much sought-after area of the Borgo di Chiaia, for an even higher asking price of 3,100 ducats. To help recoup the costs he initially rented out this property for 100 ducats per year – more than double the price, that is to say, for the annual rent payable on a painter's workshop and living quarters in the city itself.[56]

Finally, in 1647 Ribera set the seal on his social prestige and exceptional attainment of wealth by outlaying the massive sum of 5,000 ducats as the dowry for his daughter when she married a local administrative functionary, Giovanni Sersale.[57] This far exceeded the financial capabilities of any of his associates, with the possible exception of Stanzione. Ribera's future father-in-law, Giovanni Bernardino Azzolino, for example – who had been one of the leading painters of the previous generation – had been in a position to endow his daughter with only 600 ducats when she married Ribera in 1616.[58] Corenzio was able to afford only half as much on the occasion of his daughter's marriage in 1641, an amount that was more in line with the customary levels for dowries committed by reasonably successful artisans during this period.[59]

Painters such as Cavallino and Van Swanenburgh, on the other hand, would never have been able to come close to these amounts. When Cavallino married, aged eighteen in 1634, his future bride had a dowry of only 100 ducats.[60] These more modestly ranked artists may not have been able to improve much on that level by the time of their own daughters' marriages, and in fact the dowries may have been even less – in some cases not much exceeding the 25 ducats stipulated in the rules and regulations of the Corporazione di Rivenditori as the base-level amount to be given to the daughters of impoverished heads of workshops.[61]

And yet, of course, any perspective on cost of living considerations is relative, depending on one's financial aspirations and sense of what might constitute a basic necessity as opposed to an extravagant luxury. Even Ribera's attainments would have paled into insignificance in relation to

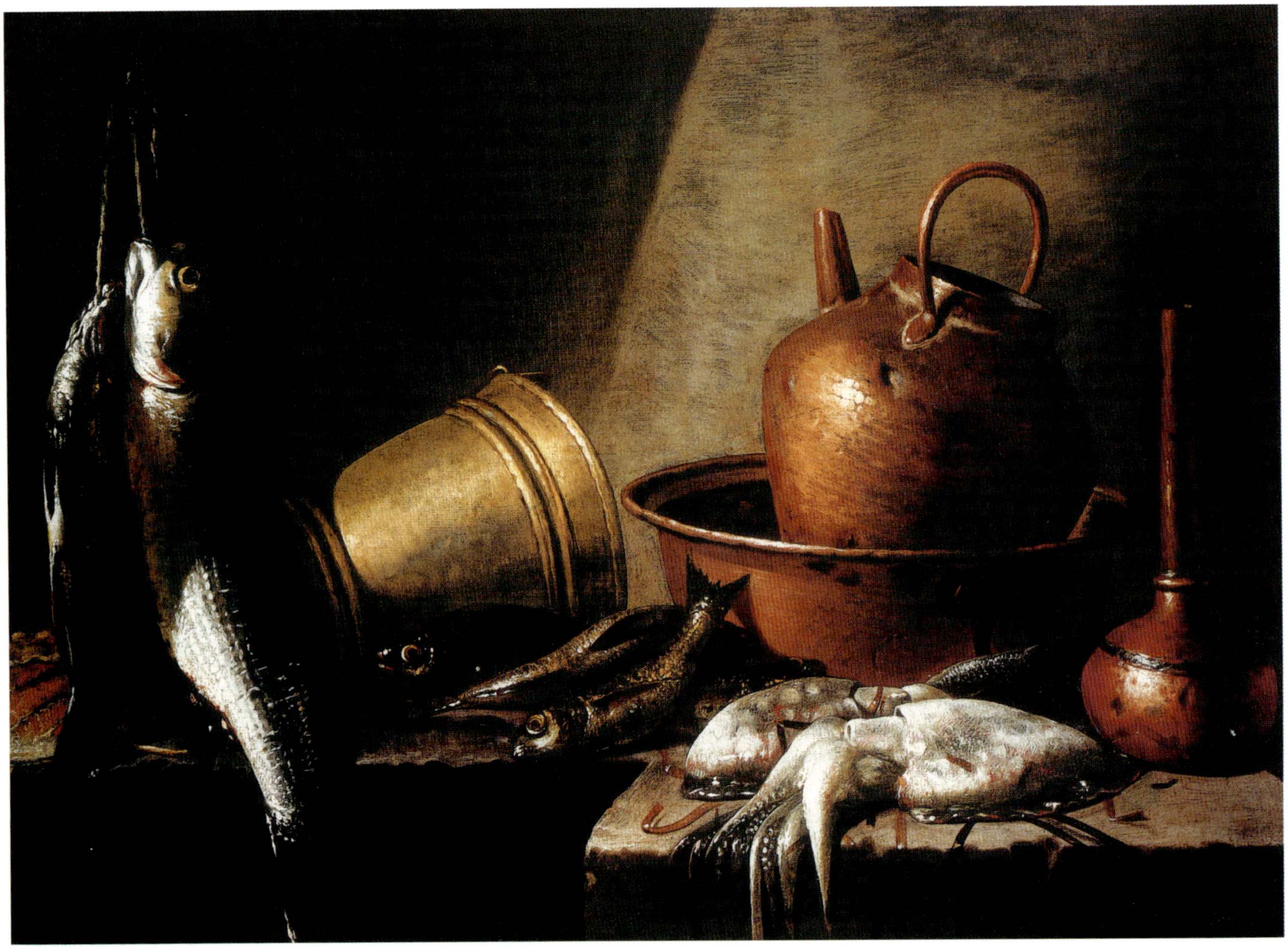

78 Giuseppe Recco, *Copper Vessels with Fish and Squid*, 1660–65. Oil on canvas, 73.5 × 99 cm. Private collection

the economic preoccupations of his aristocratic and high-ranking mercantile patrons, but, of course, if this were not the case they would have been unable to pay him and his senior colleagues the 100 ducats and more required for their paintings. Although Ribera's dowry of 5,000 ducats may seem like an astronomically high amount by comparison to other painters of the day, it represents a trifling sum when compared with the dowry of 20,000 ducats that was brought by Vittoria Albrici to her marriage in 1617 to Francesco Antonio Francone, principe di Pietracupa.[62]

Yet the luxury and fame attendant upon Ribera's considerable economic success could not spare him the indignity of a significantly impoverished and reduced final few years. One can only speculate as to the reasons for this. Perhaps he had been profligate in his desire to enjoy the fruits of success without planning for the uncertainties of tomorrow, particularly the economic downturn that followed the Revolt of Masaniello of 1647–8. Or perhaps he had failed to handle well the complex requirements of a busy workshop. And maybe these and other unknown human factors caught up with him following his long periods of incapacitation from an illness that began in 1642 and increased in intensity in the years thereafter.[63]

What is certain is that Ribera's begging letters sent to the prior of San Martino while he was negotiating with the Carthusians to complete the long-unfinished contract for the *Communion of the Apostles* in 1651 indicate a significant downward slide. In them, the aged artist complains about the state of his health and regales the monks with repeated entreaties for financial assistance:

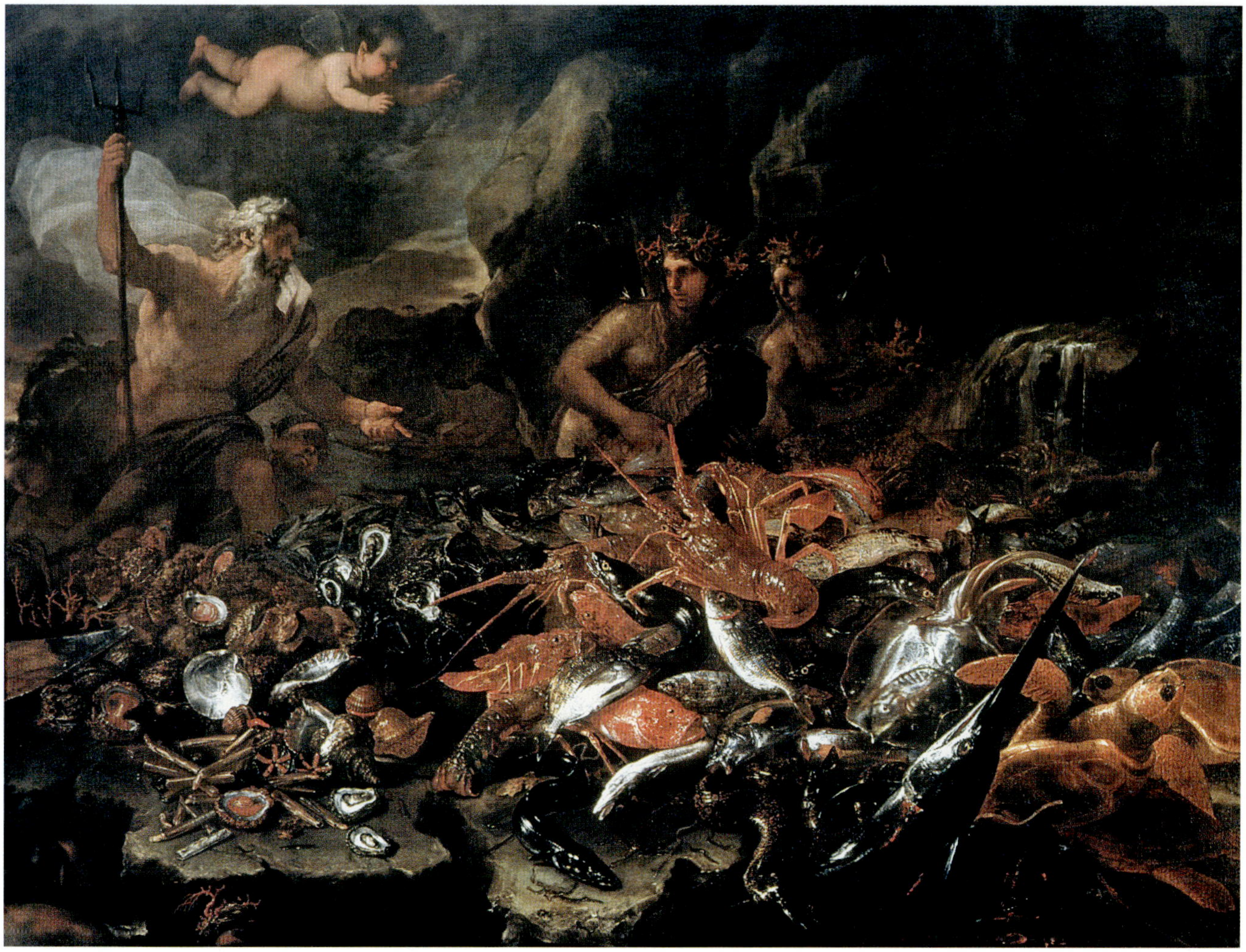

79 Luca Giordano and Giuseppe Recco, *Riches of the Sea with Neptune and Two Sea Nymphs*, *circa* 1683–4. Oil on canvas, 234.5 × 296 cm. Art Gallery of South Australia, Adelaide

> . . . yesterday a father came to bring me the assessment from the Father Vicar of the fifty ducats, without which I cannot and never could conceive of a plan for the care of the household. Would to God that I did not have these anxieties. It would give me great pleasure to receive the whole sum at once, the work continues to progress.[64]

In a subsequent letter Ribera also asked the Carthusians to help pay the costs incurred for his son-in-law's funeral in September 1651 – one year prior to his own death, as it transpired.[65]

If the great Ribera could fall on hard times within a few years of the high watermark of his career, then how much more potentially difficult might it have been at times for the artists traced in these pages. They did not have the insulation of an established career or prestigious reputation to keep high-ranking patrons coming their way. Equally, they could not rely on a steady wage – which at least the *portiere* of the Banco di Napoli was able to enjoy in his modest way. Rather, they were required to operate in the far less secure environment of temporary, transitory employment. They had, in a word, to be much more entrepreneurial in their activities, and their success was at all times contingent on their ability to broadcast their talents to the second-hand dealers and other traders in the area, and maintain the relevance of their work.

This necessity is emphasized in a particularly revealing anecdote in De' Dominici's *Vite*. The story appears in the account of the careers of Cesare and Francesco Fracanzano – two brothers who emigrated from Apulia to Naples in

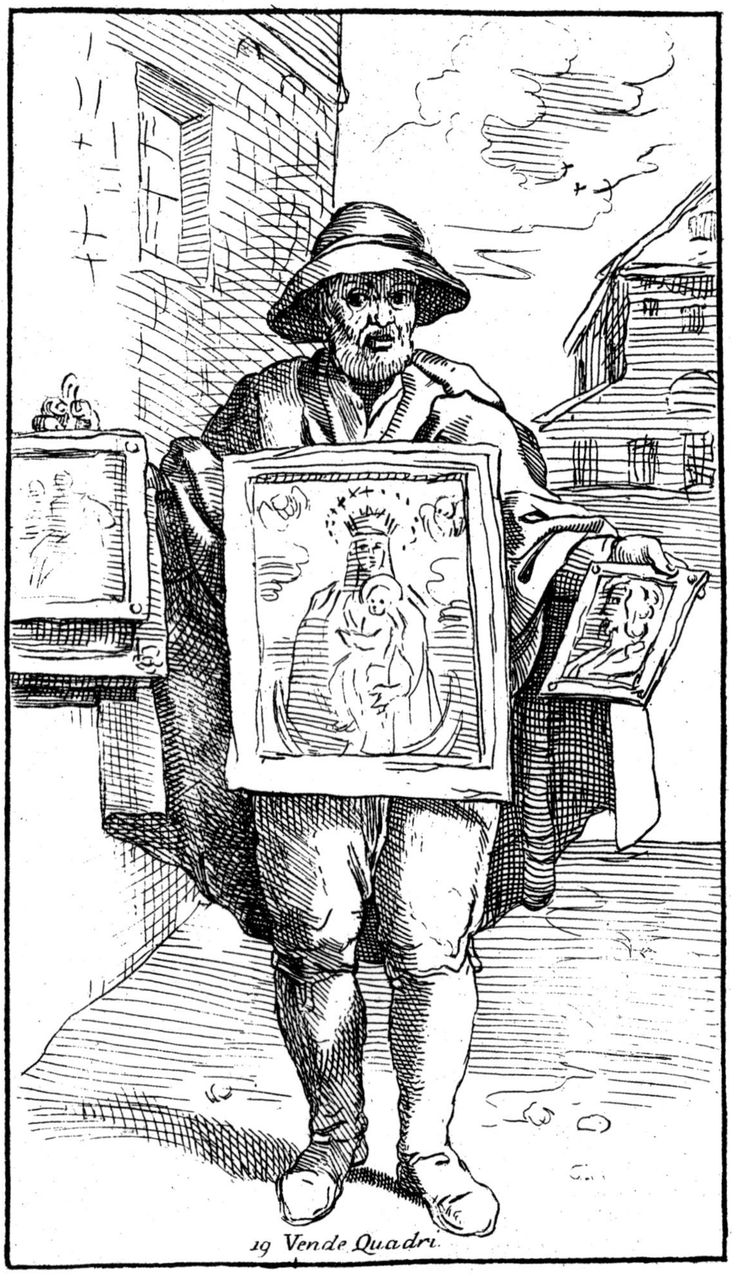

80 Simon Guillain after Annibale Carracci, *Picture Seller*. Etching, plate 19 of *Le arti di Bologna*, 1646

the 1620s and subsequently became workshop assistants to Ribera. The narrative begins with a philosophical meditation on the rarity of success. De' Dominici states that he does not know whether it is because of the high number of painters working at any one time or simply ill fortune that reduces certain painters to a miserable working existence. Only a few reach the ultimate success of a Raphael or a Titian. Cesare and Francesco Fracanzano failed in their ambitions. Although very distinguished painters, they ultimately disgraced themselves as a result of the strains created by economic hardship.[66]

De' Dominici comments frequently on the financial difficulties experienced by the brothers. They could not find work after leaving Ribera's studio (a move that seems to have occurred sometime in the early to mid-1630s), and were accordingly forced to paint devotional paintings for some of their painter acquaintances for little money (a practice that would have found them working for day rates). A small number of commissions improved their prospects marginally, but still not sufficiently to alleviate their difficulties. The situation worsened for Cesare when he married and had to provide for a large family. Cesare and Francesco now found themselves in desperate straits:

> they were without commissions to such an extent that they were forced to paint half-length figures for second-hand dealers, and sometimes not even finding anyone ready to buy their work, they were forced to hawk them through the city selling them at a low price in order to buy their daily food. So, coming to lead an unfortunate and miserable life they were induced once again to paint for the shopkeepers those heads of St Anastasius, which they place at the head of children's cradles in order to preserve them from malignant spells. This misery was such that it somewhat diminished both the goodness and the reputation of their works, since for the sake of speed they painted them heedlessly, and without study ...[67]

De' Dominici clearly wished his readers to share his sense of shame at the idea that distinguished painters of the evident talent and achievements of the Fracanzani could be reduced to the level of pedlars and producers of the cheapest form of devotional imagery. His description of Cesare and Francesco wandering the streets hawking whatever paintings they could carry to catch the interest of passers-by puts them on the same level as the individual represented in Annibale Carracci's late sixteenth-century illustration of an itinerant pedlar of cheap paintings and prints (fig. 80). The rudimentary art dealer represented one manifestation of the many categories of itinerant sellers of sundry goods and services that Carracci observed while walking along the streets of Bologna, from travelling shoe salesmen to knife grinders and street minstrels, and all occupations in between.[68]

Although these hawkers were required to work long and hard to earn a living, they were understood as belonging to the lowest levels of professional activity and were associ-

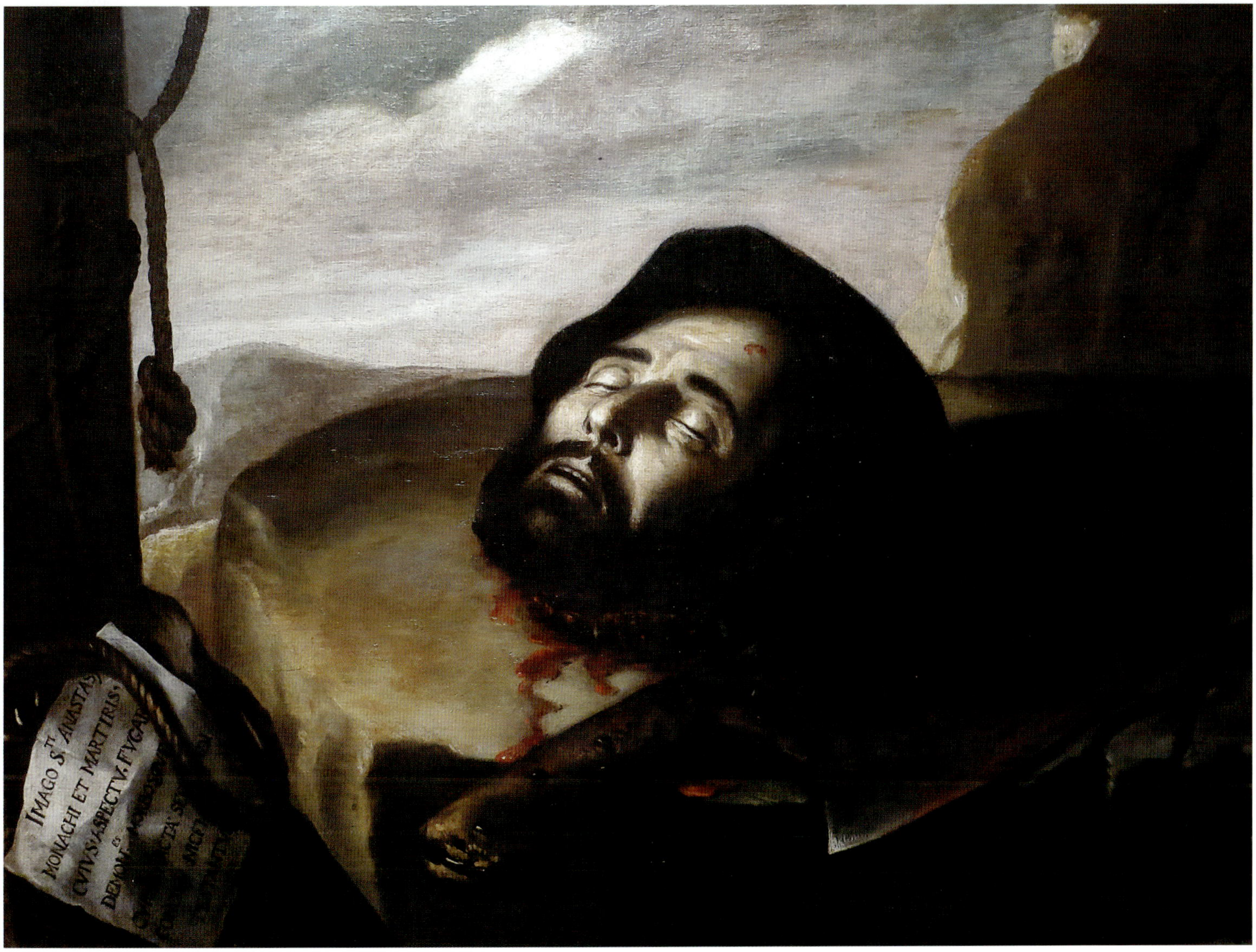

81 Unknown monogrammist 'TR', *Head of St Anastasius*, 1650s. Oil on canvas, 80 × 110 cm. Museo Diocesano Napoli, Santa Maria di Donnaregina Nuova, Naples

ated with popular notions of vagrancy and the hand-to-mouth lives of the urban destitute. The reference to heads of St Anastasius produced for cribs suggests that the Fracanzani participated in the production of the most basic form of devotional imagery created in industrial numbers by predominantly anonymous artists to ward off illness in infants (fig. 81).[69] They were, in a word, back where they had started at the lowest rung of the Neapolitan art world.

This anecdote should be taken with a pinch of salt, since De' Dominici may have been exaggerating in order to tug at the heartstrings of his readers.[70] Yet the essential truth of his narrative is certainly recognizable from the point of view of the considerations here discussed. The Fracanzani may have been highly accomplished graduates of Ribera's workshop, but this would not insulate them from the pressures of the market. Indeed, financial problems such as those described by De' Dominici may well have coincided with their involvement in the more elevated aspects of their careers.

Cesare Fracanzano, for example, is known to have been patronized by Count Giangirolamo II Acquaviva d'Aragona, as will be discussed in Chapter Nine. He also received, at least on occasion, prestigious ecclesiastical commissions (Table 5) and associated with the Neapolitan academies in

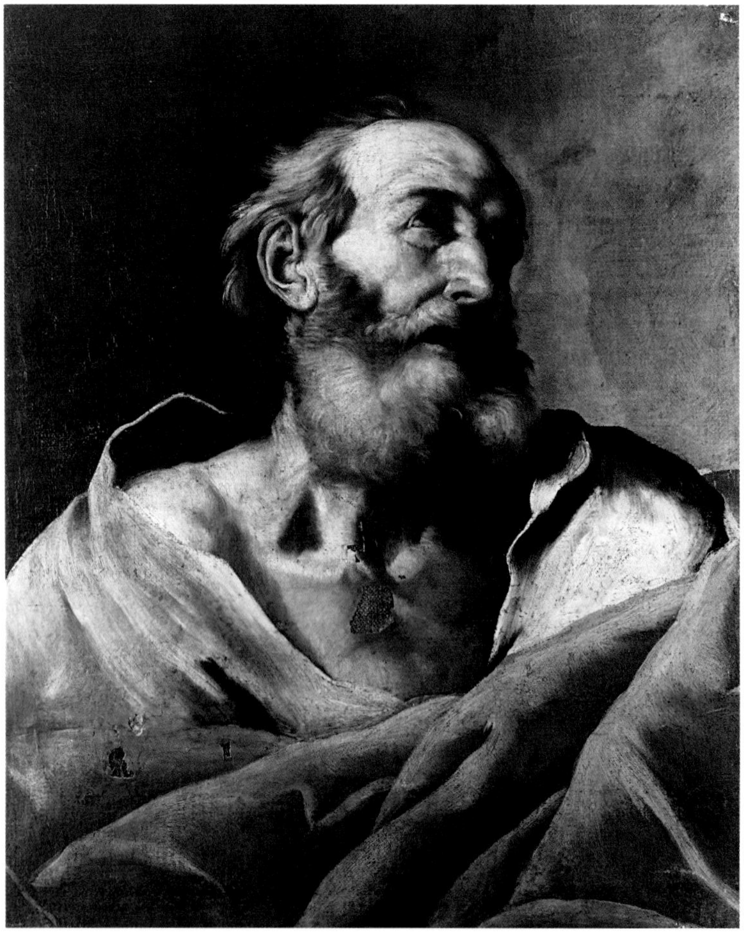

82 Francesco Fracanzano, *Apostle*, *circa* 1640. Oil on canvas, 79 × 63 cm. Museo e Gallerie Nazionali di Capodimonte, Naples

the 1630s. He even went so far as to seek the patronage of Urban VIII by sending the pope an elaborate reconstruction of a famous painting by Aristeides of Thebes of a *Dying Mother* that was known only from the ekphrastic literature, and which was accompanied by an elaborate panegyric poem produced by a poet attached to the entourage of his friend and associate Giambattista Basile.[71] Francesco Fracanzano received an important commission to fresco one of the chapels of San Gregorio Armeno in the mid-1630s, and he was secure enough in his practice in 1638 at least to take on an apprentice for a period of two years.[72]

Yet these career benchmarks and significant personal associations would not in themselves bring food to the table. And this seems precisely the point that De' Dominici wished to underline in order to remind the reader that even talented and distinguished artists could slip easily from a position of relative financial security to one where they had to seek immediate and modest financial returns through dealers and other traders in second-hand wares. Moreover, his account of the kinds of work produced by the brothers at this level of the market does correlate with some of the more modest aspects of their production (fig. 82).[73]

At times, both these levels of output may have occurred in an artist's oeuvre more or less simultaneously. This seems to have been the case for Luca Giordano's father, Antonio, who spent much of his career active in the workshop of Jusepe de Ribera, where he was said to have specialized in half-length pictures of *St Anthony* and other saints, which, following retouches by the master, were then sold as originals by Ribera himself (see p. 58).[74] At the same time, Giordano the elder also developed an interesting specialization that suggests an artist with considerably more potential and individuality than an anonymous workshop assistant to Ribera or a struggling artist toiling away at the bottom of the artistic food chain.

In 1630 Antonio Giordano's name crops up in one of the most interesting texts written on Neapolitan art and culture prior to De' Dominici in the eighteenth century. The reference occurs in Giulio Cesare Capaccio's *Il Forastiero* in the context of a discussion about the most important private collection of the day: that of Gaspar Roomer, the wealthy Flemish merchant and influential patron and collector who would come to be renowned for his holdings of work by Aniello Falcone, Luca Giordano, Rubens and scores of other artists. Capaccio's detailed description of Roomer's collection at this relatively early stage of its development lists paintings by Stanzione, Ribera, Van Dyck, Saraceni, Brueghel, Bril and many others. Yet among this noteworthy list of names mention is also made of battle pieces by none other than Antonio Giordano and Aniello Falcone.[75]

The contemporary battle piece – or battle scene without a hero as characterized by Fritz Saxl in his now-classic account – represented an innovative sub-category of genre painting at this time. In the later 1630s and 1640s Falcone's name would become synonymous with this specialization in a manner that brought him considerable distinction and even a degree of international renown.[76] That Giordano the elder was producing work of the same kind at this very early date suggests that he too might have gone on to become a painter of some renown and not just an almost entirely unknown artistic identity who is chiefly remembered today for the simple fact that he was the father of Luca Giordano.

De' Dominici's anecdote, therefore, rings true on a fundamental level with the examples here discussed. Painters such as Cavallino, Van Swanenburgh, Giordano the elder and the Fracanzani – and many more whose names could be cited in this context – were not so far removed from the struggles of the lowest-ranked painters. This was one of the reasons why so many artists chose to develop sidelines in other areas – as in appraisals or restoration – in order to maximize their earning capabilities. It was also one of the main factors contributing to the common practice – evident at all levels of the Neapolitan art world – of artists involving themselves in the art market by becoming dealers themselves.

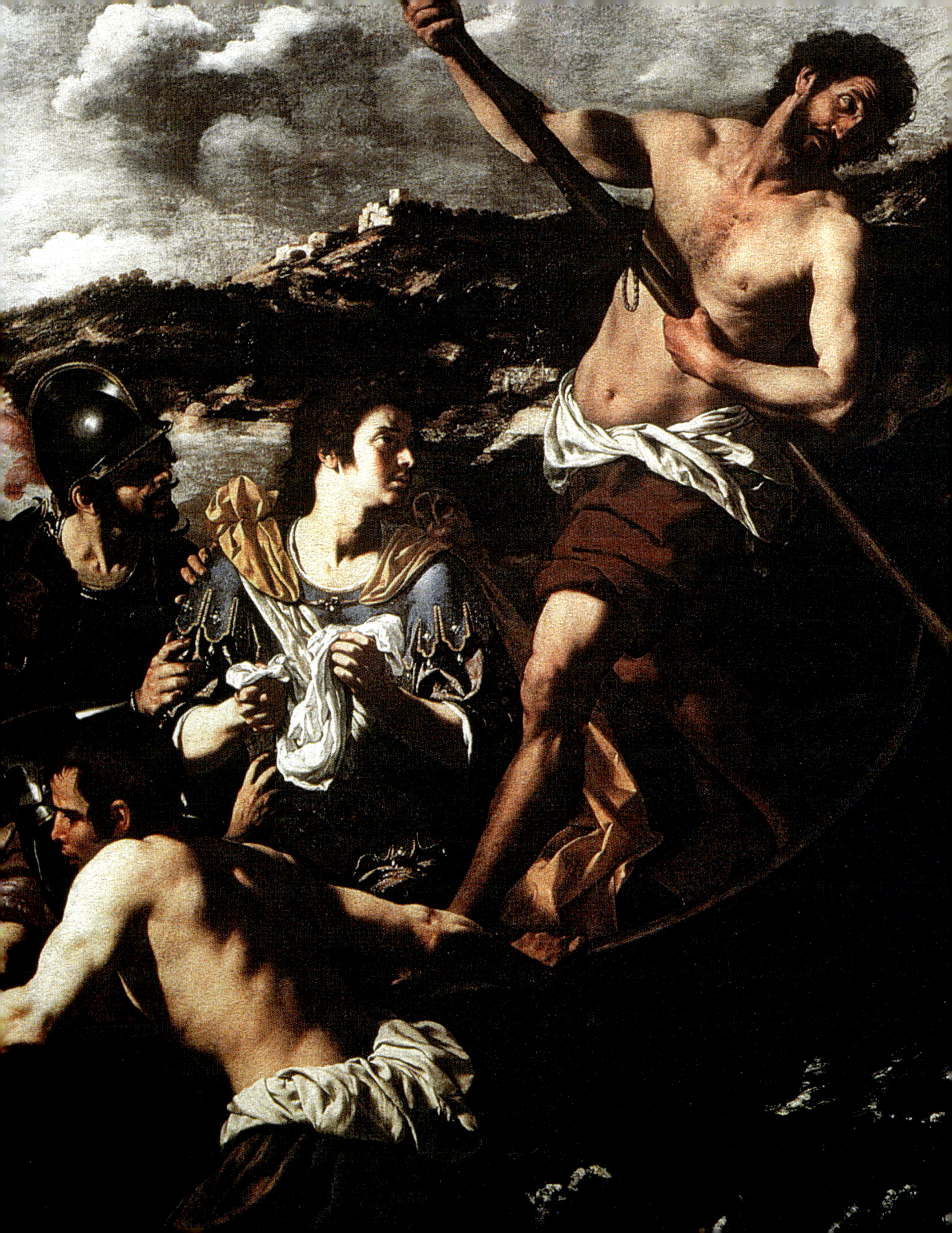

6

Dealing by Artists

Few of the traders in second-hand wares discussed in the previous chapter had any direct connection with the production of goods for sale in their workshops: they were traders pure and simple. Yet, as was seen, the Corporazione di Rivenditori also reserved for themselves the right to produce new work of any kind to supplement their stock of used goods. This made sense, since increased efficiency and supply would have benefitted those workshop heads who were able to produce tailored work themselves in order to create a particular specialization or fill a gap in the supply of used furniture and other items of interior decoration.

Hence it was common in Naples, as in Rome and elsewhere, for art dealing to be combined with related trades involving the production of artisanal goods such as gilding and frame making. Another common combination was for dealing to be combined with servicing the art trade more generally, as evident particularly in traders whose careers combined involved art dealing with the provision of artists' materials.[1] In Rome, the lists of those 'rivenditori di quadri' who paid tax to the Accademia di San Luca during the 1630s to 1660s, for example, frequently cite dealers of both these kinds: as an 'indoratore e rivenditor de quadri' (gilder and reseller of paintings), for instance; or as a dealer who 'vende colori et tele' (seller of colours and canvases), 'imprimitor di tele, Colo raro, e rivenditor di quadri' (preparer of canvases, seller of fine colours and reseller of paintings) or even 'che vende specchi e rivende anco quadri' (seller of mirrors and reseller of paintings). A connection between gilding and art dealing is further suggested by the fact that in some of the lists of tax payments to the Accademia no differentiation is made between art dealers and gilders.[2]

The will of 1703 of Andrea Cautiero, 'Mastro indoratore', provides a good example of this kind of activity in Naples.[3] As a gilder, Cautiero was not considered for a biography in De' Dominici's *Vite*. Nevertheless, he was sufficiently important to appear as the gilder 'Andrea Galtieri' who oversaw the framing and display of the annual loan exhibition of paintings held during the Festa dei Quattro Altari, which formed part of the celebrations of Corpus Christi (see Chapter Eleven). This arrangement would have furthered his business interests, since it brought him into contact with many of the leading painters seeking to include their pictures in the exhibition, as well as collectors. It was also a position of some influence in the highly competitive Neapolitan art world.

Cautiero lived and maintained his workshop, as De' Dominici indicated, close to San Giacomo degli Spagnuoli, off Via Toledo. His inventory lists all the stock-in-trade items to be expected from a gilder and trader in furniture and other items of interior decoration.[4] These include desks,

Facing page Paolo Finoglio, *Rinaldo Departing from the Enchanted Island, circa* 1642–5 (detail of fig. 86)

pedestals, reliquaries, mirrors, frames, wooden statues and candelabra. The inventory also lists fifty-six paintings and two painted mirrors, most of which seem to have been assembled with the lower reaches of the market in mind. Examples of the cheap decorative and devotional work that characterized this end of the market are the two small framed still lifes (measuring approx. 25 cm), valued at 1 ducat, and the four small, framed *tondi* or roundels (measuring approx. 40 cm) of Sts Paul, John, Januarius and John the Baptist, which were valued together at 10 ducats.

Cautiero also owned a smaller number of paintings by identified painters, including pictures by Andrea Belvedere, Onofrio Loth, Pietro Paolo Bonzi, Giuseppe and Nicola Recco, Nicola and Simone Cassisa, and Gaetano Brandi, together with a copy after Farelli.[5] That they were all, besides Farelli, specialists in the so-called minor genres of landscape and still-life painting is significant in itself, since these kinds of pictures lent themselves particularly well to art dealing. Unlike the large, specially commissioned history paintings of Jusepe de Ribera and the like, they were generally relatively small and could be painted cheaply and quickly without any contact between patron and painter about the subject matter.

Cautiero's high standing facilitated his dealing in the work of reasonably successful still-life and landscape painters. But his decision not to deal in paintings systematically and in depth seems typical of artisan dealers. Gilders' workshops did not naturally lend themselves to the exclusivity and prestige of the upper reaches of the market, such as the emerging specialization of the art merchant, to be discussed in the next chapter. They would have generally involved a faster turnover of cheaper stock-in-trade gilded furnishings and second-hand wares. Cautiero's inventory is again characteristic. Hardly any of the items listed exceed 10 ducats in value. By far the most expensive stock in his workshop were two pairs of elaborately framed mirrors. At 100 and 300 ducats respectively, these mirrors were of far higher value than the 30 ducats assigned to a pair of pictures by Giuseppe Recco that were the next most expensive items. Dealing in pictures was thus for Cautiero, as it was for so many other gilders, a necessary adjunct that enabled him to provide his clients with everything necessary for interior furnishings and decorative ensembles.

Nevertheless, it would be misleading to deduce from this that dealing at this level involved only superficial relationships between painters and dealers. Some more enterprising individuals used their contacts to develop important intermediary roles between artists and collectors in a manner directly comparable to the more specialized activities of the Neapolitan *rivenditori*. Such appears to have been the case for Nicola Spasiano, a trader in artists' wares who is documented in 1697 acting as an agent for the architectural painter Angelo Maria Costa.[6] In the document, Spasiano paid Costa for his work partly in money and partly in the form of prepared canvases.[7] He also appears in this capacity in the only other known reference to him, a payment in 1700 by the painter Nicola Vinaccia for twenty prepared canvases (described as 'tele' rather than 'quadri').[8] Spasiano probably sold Costa and Vinaccia stretched canvases, possibly with the ground already painted, a practice that appears to have been established in Naples for some time, since it is probably referred to as early as 1613 in a payment from Carlo Sellitto for 'tele impremite'.[9]

The document of 1697 records seven paintings, all ordered by Spasiano from Costa. Two architectural pictures measuring approximately 1.32 by 1.84 metres had been completed and delivered for a total cost of 40 ducats. Five more were still to come. Two smaller architectural pieces (measuring approx. 80 by 25 cm) and a seascape were to be painted within the month at a cost of 28 ducats. These may have been painted for sale on the open market from Spasiano's workshop, but here Spasiano was more enterprising than many of his colleagues, since he was evidently not content with selling only second-hand pictures. The document also records a small down payment from a total price of 8 ducats for two architectural pictures measuring 53 by 66 centimetres that had been commissioned on behalf of a certain Antonio Pentenato. Spasiano's arrangements for selling Costa's work were thus more sophisticated than the simple display of paintings in his workshop. He helped place Costa's work with collectors and would have stood in relation to Costa as a patron, commanding from him similar respect.

PAINTERS' WORKSHOPS AND THE SALE OF PICTURES ON THE OPEN MARKET

What evidence is there for artists themselves engaging in art dealing? In Rome, only a few individuals stand out in this regard, the art dealing usually forming only a small part of their careers. The Cavalier d'Arpino and Antiveduto Grammatica sold the work of younger artists attached to their workshops, employing painters like the young Caravaggio to turn out still lifes.[10] From the beginning of the seventeenth century, however, it became more difficult to maintain a sideline in dealing as a result of the Accademia di San Luca's well-known professional dispute with the Roman *rivenditori* and the accompanying injunction against their members engaging in dealing on pain of expulsion from the academy.[11]

Exceptions to this were extremely rare. In 1655 the flower painter Mario dei Fiori applied successfully to the Accademia di San Luca for the granting of a patent 'di poter tenere aperta in Roma una Bottega di rivender quadri, e pitture' (to keep a shop in Rome for the resale of canvases and paintings), even though art dealing was technically prohibited for full members of the academy.[12] As a result of the research of Ruffo and Vaes, the two best-known art-dealing painters in Rome are Corneille de Wael and Abraham Brueghel.[13] But their position as relative outsiders to the circuit of Roman patronage is undoubtedly significant. As foreign residents who were not members of the Accademia di San Luca, De Wael and Brueghel were evidently much freer to engage in dealing than most Roman painters.

In Naples, on the other hand, until 1664 there was no painters' academy to legislate against painters acting as art dealers. Even then, once this new version of the Neapolitan Congregazione dei Pittori did re-establish itself, its statutes continued to omit any injunctions against art dealing for the rest of this association's long history. This is not surprising, given that Naples operated, as has been seen, according to a very different notion of the interrelated nature of art and artisanal activity, with a far less pronounced emphasis on the standard special pleading arguments found in other cities in favour of the higher status of painting as a liberal art.

There were, therefore, no intrinsic cultural or professional factors in Naples to impede the idea that painting could be viewed as both a liberal art and a straightforwardly economic activity. The painters of Naples were accordingly free to insist on the higher intellectual dimension of their activities while also seeking to exploit the economic basis of their profession freely and without prejudice. Painting could be, in effect, both an intellectual calling and a trade. As a result, and with none of the inhibitions and prohibitions experienced by their colleagues in Rome and elsewhere, Neapolitan artists tended to deal in art as a matter of course.

One of the most vivid indications of this type of activity occurs in an inventory of 1644 of the workshop of the otherwise unknown painter Onofrio de Anfora. This document offers an unusually revealing snapshot of contemporary workshop practices, since this artist had been wounded in a street brawl the night before the list was made – mortally, it would soon transpire. The inventory was accordingly put together hurriedly to record his assets and clear his debts. As a result, it records the contents of a fully operational Neapolitan Baroque workshop – as opposed to the relatively closed-down and tidied-up legacies recorded at the end of an artist's career, as is usually the case for artists' inventories.[14]

One can sense the paint still drying on many of the 200 canvases listed in De Anfora's inventory: an unfinished head of *St Nicholas*, 'diversi tele picole di diverse mesure sbozati et senza sbozare' (various small canvases of varying dimensions, some roughed out and others still to begin) and three portraits, one finished, the other two only just started. Evidently the artist made his living producing for the most part cheap standardized devotional subjects that he could turn out quickly: there was a head of *St Januarius*, for example, as well as 'due vercenelle una madonella' (two small virgins and a small Madonna). This common reliance on offsetting cheapness against efficiency was also true of his larger canvases. Many were lined up like serially produced merchandise on a store rack: two paintings of *St Nicholas* measuring just over 2 metres, and two of *St Agatha* measuring half as much, and so on.

Most of De Anfora's paintings were left unframed (150 out of 200), including even those completed. This would naturally have made business sense since it would have allowed him to fit a frame from his separately maintained stock, presumably on the spot, if the buyer so desired. He probably did this in order to introduce a certain price differential into the sale. This would have been useful, one suspects, given that the differently graded frames were in many instances just as valuable as the modestly priced paintings themselves.[15] Yet what is perhaps even more revealing is how much of De Anfora's workshop stock was not by his own hand. This challenges any anachronistic assumptions one may have about the abstractly self-contained nature of an artist's production at this period and beyond.

This modest painter included in his workshop stock no fewer than thirty pictures that he had certainly not painted himself. These are described as 'vecchio' (old) or, in one case, 'antico' (antique – very old – presumably therefore marginally more valuable than the others). Their subjects included further instances of the simple devotional works in which De Anfora specialized: 'Una madonella con cornice vechia' (a small framed Madonna, old). They also comprised more complex biblical narratives – an *Adoration of the Magi*, two paintings of *Tobias and the Angel* – as well as examples of more recently developed genres that he would almost certainly not have practised himself: 'Doi battagliole di dui palme con doi quatri di frutti et una montagna di soma di due palmi e mezzo e uno S. genaro e una madona picola uno quatro di fiori di tre palmi scarzo vechi' (Two small battles measuring approx. 53 cm, with two paintings of fruit and a high mountain measuring approx. 66 cm, and a St Januarius and a small Madonna, a painting of flowers measuring approx. 75 cm, [all of them] old). Evidently, then, De Anfora sought to maximize sales by diversifying his output, bringing in old paintings in other styles and formats and thereby acting, in his own modest way, as a secondary dealer on the side.

But he did not just trade in old work. A separate section appended to the end of the list itemizes fifty paintings (a quarter of his stock, in other words) that De Anfora had purchased with money loaned to him by his wife's aunt – and that thus now constituted a debt that needed to be liquidated before any proceeds could accrue to his widow from future sales. None of this group of paintings is described as 'vecchio', so they were all produced relatively recently and thus represented further potential primary market sales. A high proportion of them were also framed (twenty-four out of fifty, as opposed to thirty out of one hundred and fifty for those in the other list). This suggests that they represented the pick of the works not painted by De Anfora himself, the choicest 'new old masters', in other words, among the items for sale in his workshop. De Anfora had presumably picked these works up over the course of his daily activities buying – and no doubt also bartering and trading in his own work wherever possible – from other Neapolitan workshops.

He may have been operating at a modest level of the market, but De Anfora nonetheless had the resources to advance his business by generating sufficient extra capital to diversify his output and buy more stock. It can be assumed, on the basis of the previous discussion regarding the costs of cheap paintings, that these works would have averaged around 1 or 2 ducats per item. If so, this would mean that they would have represented potential earnings for De Anfora of 50–100 ducats. This represents a not inconsiderable increase to his trade, since it would have been worth as much as two or even three years' rent on his workshop. Relatively humble he may have been, yet his inventory documents vividly the enterprising and business-oriented acumen that all successful painters needed to maintain – no matter what their position in the overstocked art world of seventeenth-century Naples.

De Anfora was not, in any event, at the bottom of the heap. Even this supposedly minor artist had yet more minor artists working under him. In fact, no fewer than thirteen of the paintings listed in the inventory (most of them bought with the loaned money) were by the only artist whose name is actually spelled out in the lists of work: Pietro Pesce. All that is known about him is that he was a follower of the leading landscape painter of the day, Domenico Gargiulo. Although his paintings have not yet been identified, he is mentioned briefly in this capacity by De' Dominici, and his landscapes and small biblical scenes with landscape backgrounds appear in a number of early inventories of the period.[16]

De Anfora's workshop included two unfinished works by Pesce, which suggests that De Anfora had been paying him according to the per diem or weekly wage arrangements discussed previously. One of these is described as a coastal landscape 'sbozata', and so would have presumably been similar to the early coastal landscapes produced by Gargiulo from the mid-1630s. Another group of Pesce's works in the workshop are described as 'quatro disegni di chiaro scuri di tela di carino' (four *chiaroscuro* drawings on fine canvas).[17] These sound very similar, in fact, to the early cheap landscape sketches on paper by Salvator Rosa that were sold in the early 1630s by Nicola di Martino and the other *riven-ditori* discussed previously. It seems, therefore, that De Anfora was operating as a painter of modest devotional work while at the same time developing a sideline in the trade in the emerging genres of still life, battle paintings and above all freshly painted landscapes, which he sold direct to the public alongside more traditional devotional images.

That this was a common practice is further suggested by an inventory of 1634 of the assets belonging to an even more obscure and modestly placed painter, Giuseppe Iovine,[18] whose stock comprised a mere thirty-eight paintings as opposed to De Anfora's two hundred. Nonetheless, only twelve of these were by Iovine's own hand. Some of these are described as 'incomenciati, et non finiti' and they were all of standard devotional subjects – *St Catherine*, *St Jerome*, *St Charles Borromeo*, the *Crucifixion*, a *Guardian Angel*, *Our Lady of Mount Carmel*, a *Virgin and Child*, and so on. The authors of the twenty-six other pictures are indicated generically as 'per mano di valente homo' (by the hand of a talented artist) or else more simply as old – 'usato'. Some at least of these pictures were nonetheless by recognized painters. Three were by the recently deceased, late Mannerist painter Avanzino Nucci, while two were attributed to Bassano. These last two canvases were evidently among Iovine's most valuable assets, since he had previously attempted to pawn them to a certain Pietro Antonio de Prisco for the considerable sum (to Iovine at least) of 20 ducats.

Iovine's stock of work by other artists also included a series of the *Four Evangelists* and two small paintings of heads that call to mind the bust- and half-length character studies produced by Ribera and his workshop during the same period. The workshop also included four landscapes. These were evidently among Iovine's more valuable assets since they form part of a group of only eleven framed paintings and are described as 'paijsi fini'. Finally, Iovine owned two paintings 'sopra carta pintati di valente homo' (by a talented artist [painted] on paper) that also recall Salvator Rosa's early landscapes on paper from this period. Once again, then, all this testifies to the formulation of a diversified sales strategy – even at this decidedly modest level of the market. Although operating within significant financial and professional constraints, Iovine had nonetheless developed a targeted plan for maximizing sales that involved supplementing his own traditional devotional works with canvases in the format of Ribera's half-length *Apostles*, as well as with framed landscapes, cheaper works on paper and a handful of other more exclusive works by well-known masters.

This high degree of specialization well demonstrates the potential natural advantages that painters were able to maintain over gilders, second-hand dealers and other artisans when it came to the trade in paintings. Painters were, after all, best informed when it came to their own profession, and their close contacts with other painters, for the most part concentrated conveniently close at hand, gave them the ability to provide clients with a generally more focused selection of contemporary and recent paintings.[19]

The degree to which this enabled enterprising artists to develop an expertise in emerging niche markets is suggested by a partnership contract of 1630 between the still-life painter Giacomo Recco and the little-known painter Antonio Cimino.[20] In 1630 Recco, then aged twenty-seven, formed a partnership with Cimino for an agreed period of one and a half years. The partnership contract mentions an annual rent of 30 ducats on a workshop on Via Santo Spirito and specifies in some detail the partners' joint obligations for the running of the business. Cimino provided the capital for the joint venture, paying for the rent and materials. In addition, he provided 50 ducats (or 100 ducats if he could raise the money, in which case Recco would have to contribute 50 ducats of his own) for acquiring paintings. These were to be purchased by Recco, who was to use the money:

> to purchase from outside the workshop various paintings by various painters and of varying quality, as will appear pleasing to Giacomo, for the common good and benefit of the partnership, and always once having acquired the paintings from outside the workshop and after finishing the transaction, Giacomo must carry them back to the workshop and there they must sell and dispose of them for whatever price they can attain and for the major benefit and usefulness [of the partnership] as will be possible.

Prota Giurleo describes Giacomo Recco, father of the better-known still-life painter Giuseppe Recco, as 'the true founder of the entire school of Neapolitan still-life painters'.[21] The emphasis elsewhere in the contract on paintings of flowers and fruit suggests that the partners hoped in this instance to capitalize on Recco's specialist knowledge by developing a niche market in the emerging genre of still-life painting. Recco's capital lay in his expertise, since he appears to have been given the money by Cimino in order to use his informed judgement to buy other still-life paintings. These were then no doubt hung alongside Recco's own still lifes and gathered conveniently together for prospective clients in the workshop (figs 83–4).[22] The timing of the partnership is also significant in that it occurred at the beginning of a decade of significant growth in the popularity of the genre among collectors. The first well-known Neapolitan still-life painters achieved prominence during this period, such as Giacomo Recco himself, together with his pupil Paolo Porpora and Luca Forte.[23] The partnership document thus provides a further indication that the early development of landscape, still-life and genre painting was as much a product of the market as it was of patronage and artistic talent.

ART DEALING AT THE UPPER LEVELS OF THE MARKET

That Recco and Cimino were able to generate up to 150 ducats start-up capital for their business indicates their aspiration to operate in a more prestigious sector of the market than De Anfora, Iovine and the other more modestly ranked artists discussed hitherto. That some at least of the better-known Neapolitan painters of the day recognized the benefits of combining their careers as heads of leading workshops with varying degrees of sideline ventures in art dealing is further indicated by the case study of Carlo Sellitto.

Sellitto has been previously encountered as the earliest-known Neapolitan follower of Caravaggio, responsible for an important early commission in the church of Sant'Anna

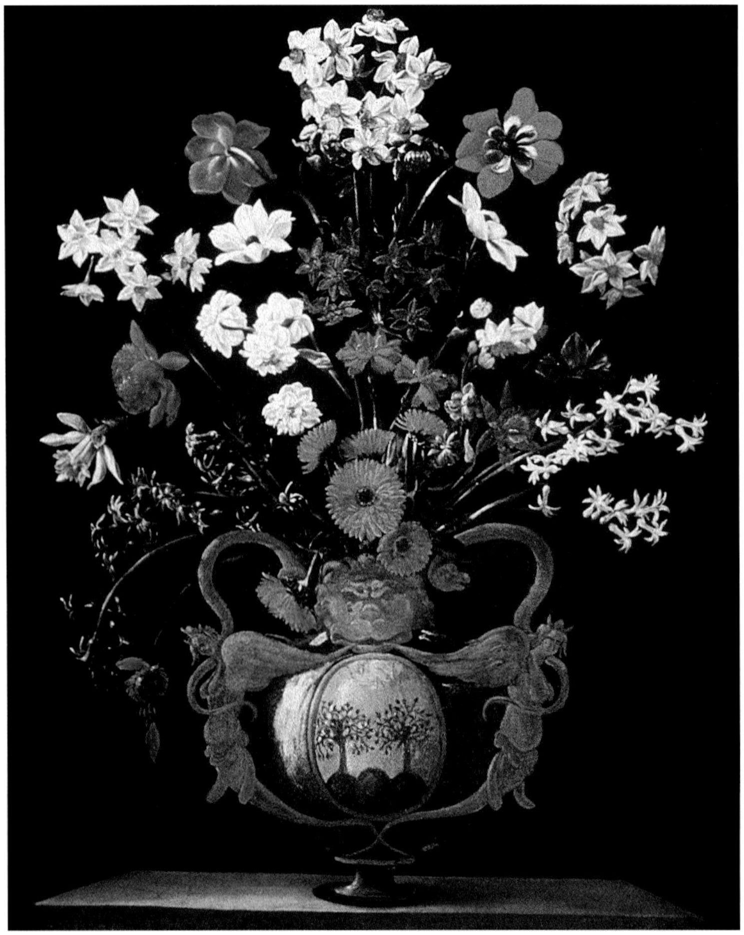

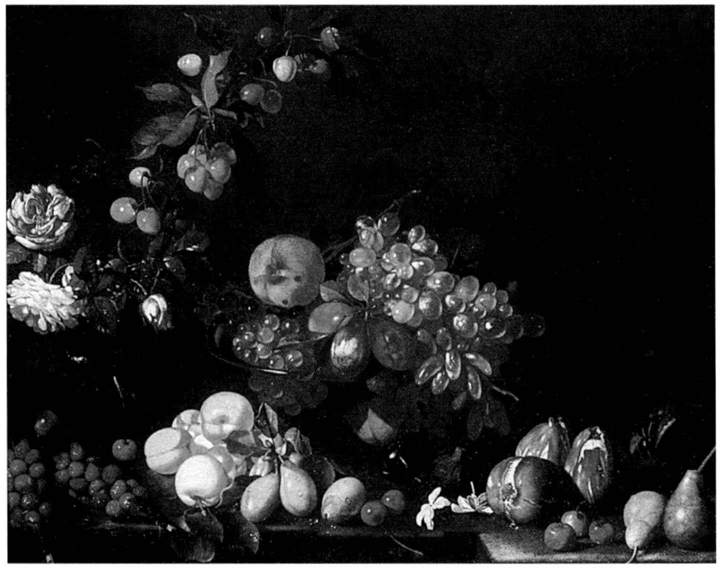

Left 83 Giacomo Recco, *Still Life with the Arms of Cardinal Poli*, 1623–53. Oil on canvas, 76 × 60 cm. Pietro Lorenzelli collection, Bergamo

Above 84 Luca Forte, *Still Life with Apples and Pears*, 1625–35. Oil on canvas, 26 × 35 cm. Museo e Gallerie Nazionali di Capodimonte, Naples, on deposit from the Museo Duca di Martina, Naples

dei Lombardi, as well as the recipient of a commission for one of the first lateral altarpieces to hang alongside Caravaggio's *Seven Works of Mercy* in the Pio Monte della Misericordia. Sellitto was not able enjoy this success for long, however, since he died from an unspecified illness in October 1614, aged thirty-three. From the inventory of his possessions drawn up following his death as well as from payment documents, one learns that Sellitto enjoyed considerable financial success during his lifetime and that consequently his paintings fell into the highest price bracket for work of the period. His altarpieces were priced at between 50 to more than 100 ducats (see fig. 6), while his gallery paintings averaged around 50 ducats, particularly his portraits, which proved especially popular among patrons seeking the novelty of realistic likenesses produced in the new Caravaggesque style.[24]

The inventory of Sellitto's possessions confirms the extent to which the artist capitalized on this success by maintaining a lifestyle of substantial means and considerably elevated social aspirations. The opulence of Sellitto's household in comparison to his artist colleagues – with the possible exception at this stage of Santafede – is indicated first by his possession of such relatively luxurious items as an organ and other musical instruments, costly wall hangings (one part of which was subsequently sold for 71 ducats) and three rooms all decorated lavishly with paintings that were maintained separately from the main section of his workshop.[25] Sellitto's bed alone was valued at 118 ducats – three to four years' rent in itself – while he also owned numerous items of gold and silverware, including a pair of emerald bracelets that were subsequently sold by his brother for 45 ducats.[26] He had clearly managed his earnings more prudently than would Ribera in the following decades so that he was able to leave to his family and friends a sizeable bequest of just under 2,000 ducats – including even his slave, who received no fewer than 200 ducats, presumably the amount needed to buy his freedom following many years of indentured servitude.[27]

The list of paintings left in the workshop situated directly beneath Sellitto's residence conveys vividly the daily struggle maintained by painters to extract full payment from dilatory clients, even those at the upper reaches of the market. Terse annotations accompany eight portraits, for example, noting that, as far as a down payment was concerned, the artist had 'ricevuto niente' (received nothing). Another item, for a portrait of the viceroy's secretary, emphasizes the importance of diplomacy in negotiating payments since it notes, rather more optimistically: 'se se ne possa havere, bene, se no, patienta' (if it can be obtained, good, if not, patience).[28] In the months that followed Sellitto's executors sought to follow up these leads. They nonetheless had to wait two years before receiving final payment for Sellitto's portrait of the viceroy, for example.[29]

The inventory of Sellitto's workshop also lists a number of paintings by other artists.[30] Most of these are by artists who today remain totally unknown, such as the *David* by 'Petrillo', the *Pietà* by 'Mattia', the *Madonna* by 'Carola', the copy after a *Virgin* by Titian and a *St Charles Borromeo* by Giovanni Matteo Arciero, a copy after Zingaro's *Virgin* by Bartolomeo Principe and five paintings, including a copy after a *St Anthony*, by Francesco Abbenante.[31] Many of these paintings, of course, were the products of workshop assistance in the traditional sense of the term. In this regard, the inventory of 1614 provides an unusually clear indication of the standard composition of an especially successful Neapolitan workshop. Of the many portraits listed, one had been copied from Sellitto's portrait of the viceroy – the same presumably as that for which his executors awaited payment. Abbenante's *St Anthony* had also been copied from Sellitto's *St Anthony* commissioned for San Nicola alla Dogana, which also remained in Sellitto's workshop on his death.[32] Carola, Abbenante and the others listed were thus Sellitto's pupils in the same sense in which Agostino Beltrano, Hendrick van Somer and their associates acted as pupils of Stanzione and Ribera (as discussed in Chapter Three). They would thus have been responsible for at least some of the extant pictures in Sellitto's style.[33] Their association with Sellitto may have stretched back some years. In 1614, for instance, Arciero had been working for him for three years.[34]

Not all the paintings can be regarded in this light, however, since many cannot be classed as paintings after Sellitto or in his style. Some, for instance, had been copied from originals after Titian and Zingaro. A framed painting by Zingaro worth 20 ducats, which had been sold earlier to a private collector, may have been the original upon which Principe had based his copy.[35] Sellitto appears to have had a reputation for dealing in copies. In 1603 he sold a painting of *Christ Bearing the Cross* by Bassano to Giovanni Battista Ròta for 20 ducats.[36] Ròta, the son of the leading patron, poet and academician Berardino Ròta, was himself a collector and early admirer of landscape paintings, and is documented as a patron of Loys Croys, Giovanni Maria Bevilacqua, Pietro del Rea and Teodoro d'Errico.[37] In order to ensure the uniqueness of his acquisition, he gained Sellitto's undertaking not to have the painting copied. At the same time, Ròta was also interested in Sellitto's copies. Six years later, he ordered from Sellitto a copy after an unspecified painter.[38]

Sellitto's workshop also included a number of paintings by a 'Sig. Filippo' who has been identified, with some degree of certainty, as the young Filippo Napoletano prior to his removal to Rome and Florence, where he soon established himself as one of the most influential landscape painters of the early seventeenth century (and also one of the crucial early influences on the landscape paintings of Gargiulo and the other early Neapolitan landscape specialists associated with the ambience of Falcone) (fig. 85).[39] Napoletano had left behind in Sellitto's workshop a *St Lucy*, a copy after Titian's *Madonna*, a *St Charles Borromeo* and four large and six small landscapes. Sellitto was not himself a landscape specialist and so he presumably stocked Napoletano's paintings to fill this gap in his production. This would also have been the case for the nine unattributed still lifes listed, five of which were sold in the following year.[40] Sellitto's stock even comprised paintings of animals – including at least one large canvas of this type that was sold in the months thereafter for the respectable sum of 15 ducats.[41] At that stage, animal painting represented an especially rare and little-practised sub-genre of painting in Naples, so Sellitto's possession of these works attests to a high degree of specialization on his part.

Although not painted by Sellitto, these pictures remained his property and after his death passed to his brother, who attempted to sell many of them in the following year. If the painters responsible for them were apprentices in the traditional sense, their output would have belonged to Sellitto by right of his position as master of the workshop, who kept all that they made in exchange for teaching them. It is unlikely, however, that they were apprentices of this kind. Napoletano was twenty-seven in 1614, well beyond the general age for apprenticeship. One would not, moreover, expect a master to pay an apprentice 50 ducats as Sellitto paid Arciero, who was then aged twenty-one, in 1612. It also seems improbable that Sellitto would have been able to offer Napoletano much guidance in his preferred spe-

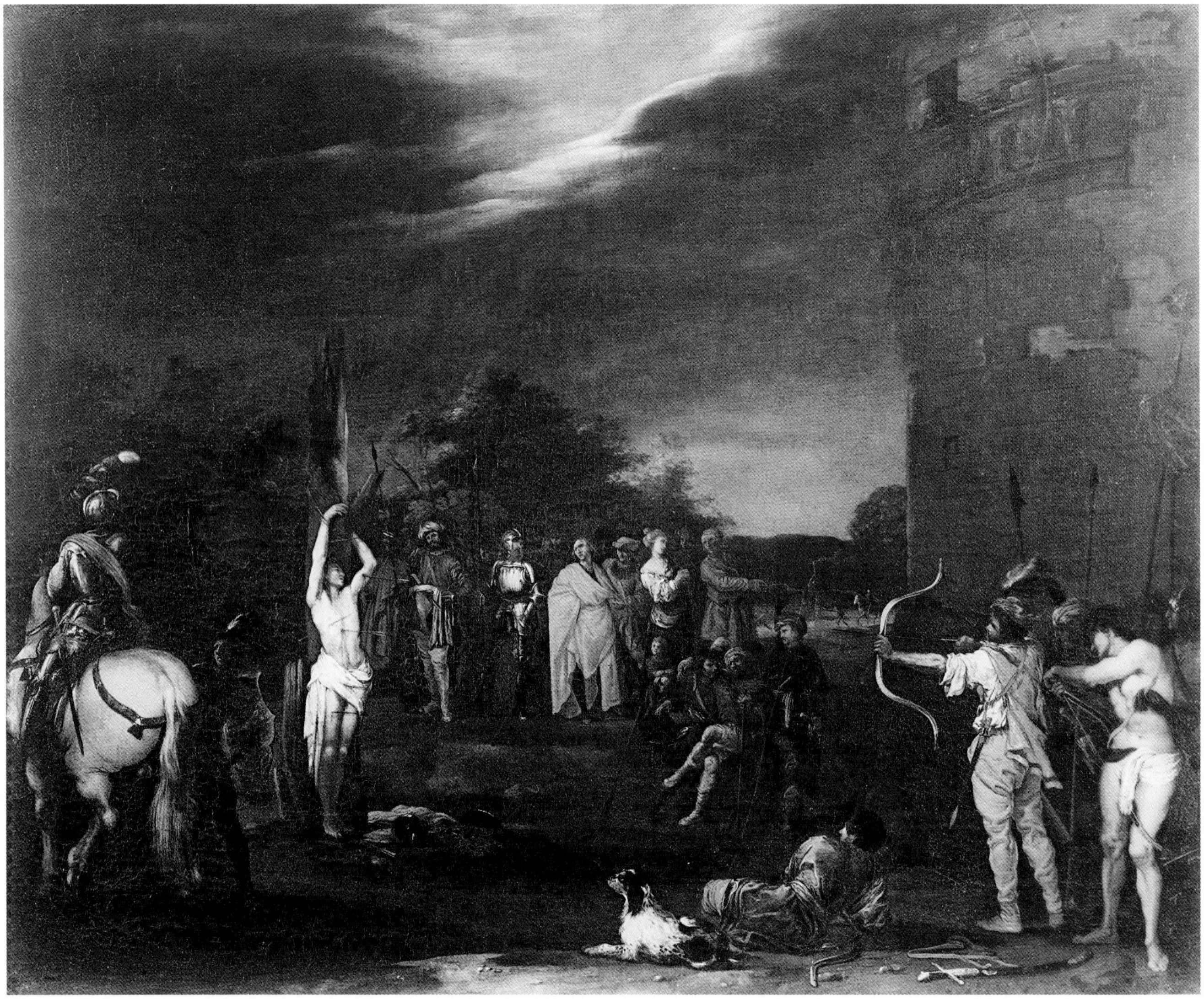

85 Filippo Napoletano, *Martyrdom of St Sebastian*, 1618. Oil on canvas, 72 × 87 cm. Galleria degli Uffizi, Florence

cialization of landscape painting. This is even more the case when it came to the artists responsible for the other still lifes and animal paintings, since these specialities are otherwise unknown in Sellitto's oeuvre.

It seems, therefore, that this documents a similar arrangement to Caravaggio's during the period of his involvement with the Cavalier d'Arpino's workshop in Rome, since D'Arpino's workshop had provided an early point of sale for Caravaggio's still lifes. As with D'Arpino, this arrangement increased Sellitto's marketability, since it included in his workshop not only his own paintings but also pictures by and in the style of respected old masters such as Bassano, Titian and Zingaro, as well as examples of the latest developments in still-life and landscape painting.

PAINTERS AND ART DEALING IN THE SECONDARY MARKET

In the practices discussed thus far artists used art dealing as a means of supplementing their own workshop stock with paintings sourced either from the surrounding local workshops or else by more junior artists employed by them to paint in the workshop pictures in other genres so as to enable them to diversify their output and fill in gaps in production. The idea that these artists might have dealt more systematically instead in secondary market paintings – in the sense of developing a particular expertise in the sale of old master, foreign or otherwise rare works not readily available on the local market – is not something that would have appealed to most Neapolitan painters. Such activities were well beyond the constrained finances and limited networks of De Anfora and Iovine, for example. Neither could a more established artist like Carlo Sellitto have aspired to this level of activity for the simple reason that he was too preoccupied practising in his own right to do more than draw on dealing as a means of supplementing his output with a more diversified product base.

A handful of artists nonetheless do appear to have made the next step and involved themselves to a greater degree in more exclusive and expensive secondary market sales. Paolo Finoglio is one of the few names that has come to light in this regard. As previously noted, he attained a level of some prominence during the 1620s and early 1630s, undertaking important public commissions at the Certosa di San Martino, Pozzuoli Cathedral and elsewhere (see fig. 20). In 1635 he emigrated to the court of Giangirolamo Acquaviva in Conversano, one of the most important political and cultural centres of the kingdom, where he painted, among other works, an important series of scenes from Tasso's *Gerusalemme liberata* (fig. 86).[42] His large gallery paintings were highly prized. In 1718, for example, one was valued at 250 ducats.[43]

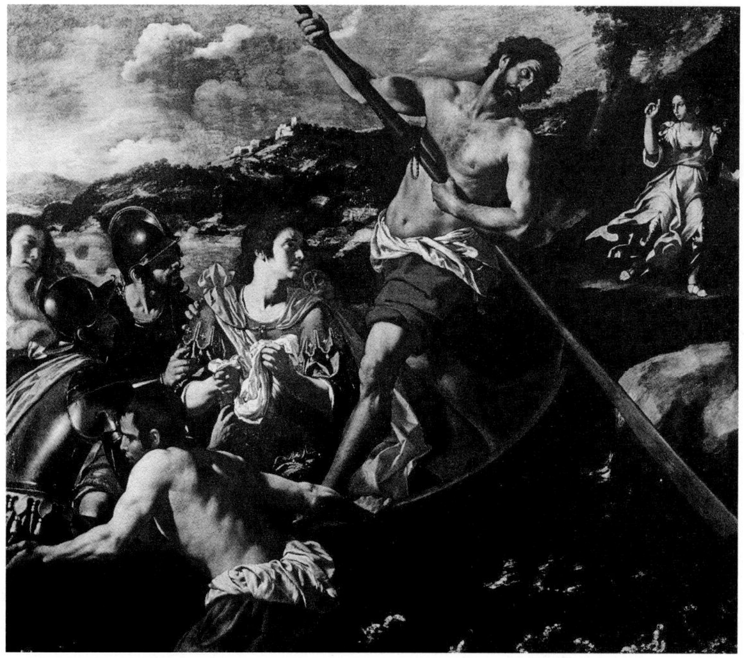

86 Paolo Finoglio, *Rinaldo Departing from the Enchanted Island*, *circa* 1642–5. Oil on canvas, 257 × 312 cm. Pinacoteca del Castello, Conversano

At the same time, though, in Naples in the early 1630s Finoglio also maintained an art dealing partnership with a certain Giovanni Domenico Casolano. A series of notarial contracts record his acquisition, on 15 May 1631, of thirty-four paintings from the estate of Tommaso della Vigna that had passed to Della Vigna's widow, Grazia d'Angelo.[44] Finoglio and Casolano also agreed to pay D'Angelo rent plus interest on a workshop on Via Toledo owned by the Ospedale di San Giacomo, which had probably also belonged to her deceased husband. The terms of the agreement were subsequently modified as a result of D'Angelo's proposed marriage to Tiberio Mazzucco (the paintings and rent forming part of her dowry). The money owed to Grazia and Tiberio was declared to be settled on 5 January 1635, three and a half years after the acquisition of the paintings, when both Casolano and Finoglio were declared absent.[45] This probably occurred when Finoglio's move to Conversano necessitated the dissolution of the partnership and settlement of remaining debts.

The paintings they acquired are described as being of various sizes and both framed and unframed. They cost 300 ducats, making them a considerably higher investment than Giacomo Recco's and Antonio Cimino's contemporary purchase of workshop stock. They averaged just under 9 ducats per painting, suggesting that some, at least, were valued highly. A better indication of the kinds of paintings involved in the sale can be obtained from another transaction involving Della Vigna's widow that had been arranged some months earlier. On 4 January 1630 Grazia D'Angelo sold seven framed paintings from Della Vigna's estate to the merchant, collector and sometime art dealer Gaspar Roomer.[46] Roomer paid D'Angelo the substantial sum of 230 ducats for a large *Crucifixion with Saints* by Vouet, three landscapes by Tassi, a 'prospettiva' by Napoletano, an *Ecce Homo* 'antico', and a large *Christ Ministered to by the Angels* by Jean Ducamps, the Roman Caravaggesque painter and co-founder of the *Schildersbent*.[47] This confirms that Della Vigna dealt in other painters' work, and thus that the paintings acquired by Finoglio and Casolano were by a number of different artists.

At just fewer than 33 ducats per work, the paintings acquired by Roomer were prime examples of their kind: so much so that all except the *Ecce Homo* were included in Capaccio's fulsome description of Roomer's collection compiled the same year.[48] D'Angelo's sale was also of some significance in that it constitutes one of the earliest references to Neapolitan holdings of gallery paintings by Vouet, a painter of some influence during the 1620s and 1630s, and whose work was just then coming into vogue with Neapolitan collectors.[49] Napoletano, who had died the previous year, had probably returned to Naples *circa* 1624–6, while Tassi and Ducamps do not appear to have worked in the city.[50] Tommaso della Vigna thus emerges as a knowledgeable importer of examples of recent developments in Roman painting, particularly of genre and landscape paintings by foreign artists resident in Rome.

As a painter of imposing, Caravaggesque history paintings, altarpieces and the like, Finoglio would have probably seen the sale as a means of diversifying his output in a similar way to that achieved by Sellitto fifteen years earlier. The significant difference between the two, however, is that Finoglio was evidently developing a more specialized expertise in the sale of more prestigious and expensive work by artists from outside Naples.

Only one other artist is known to have specialized in this more rarefied sector of the market. Giacomo de Castro's career combined painting, restoration and art dealing, and he attained a high degree of respectability and success during his lifetime. Francesco di Maria believed him to be one of the two most knowledgeable connoisseurs of earlier Neapolitan painting (the other being Antonio di Simone, a pupil of De Castro, and also an art dealer from later on in the century).[51] A further indication of De Castro's high standing and reputation among Neapolitan connoisseurs was his appointment in the 1660s to the administrative council of the church of San Nicola alla Dogana as the individual in charge of restorations.[52]

De Castro's activities are documented between 1637 and 1673, and he died around 1687.[53] De' Dominici lists him as one of Caracciolo's pupils, and a few of the published documents are for paintings, including two public commissions, by his own hand.[54] But De' Dominici noted that De Castro painted relatively few pictures during his career because of his success as a restorer of old paintings. He appears to have been a particular authority in this little-practised speciality at that time.[55] He restored a painting by Santafede in the Chiesa dell'Annunziata in 1659 and may also be documented in this regard in 1640 working on paintings in the collection of the leading civil administrator and academician Giovan Camillo Cacace.[56]

These skills facilitated the development of related specialities, such as appraising collections and drawing up inventories.[57] It was also natural that De Castro should use his knowledge of other styles of painting to deal in art. In February 1637 the rich merchant collector Pietro d'Amore paid him 40 ducats for a small painting of the *Crucifixion* with a gold frame. Less than a month later D'Amore paid him a further 48 ducats for a painting of *Christ Washing the Feet of his Disciples* by 'Giovanni Castiglietti', who can probably be identified as Giovanni Benedetto Castiglione, an influential Genoese artist painting in the fashionable neo-Venetian style who was in residence in Naples during the period.[58] A few months later Francesco d'Allegria (who is elsewhere documented as a patron of Caracciolo and Stanzione) paid De Castro 18 ducats for an architectural painting by an unidentified painter.[59] D'Amore appears to have been a long-standing client, dealing with De Castro until 1656, when De Castro compiled an inventory of his collection. In 1646 he also paid De Castro 30 ducats for an octagonal painting with a frame.[60]

That De Castro was selling pictures by other artists rather than commissioned work from his own hand is evident from his sale of Castiglione's painting, and it can be confirmed from a close reading of the documents of 1637 and 1646. These payments were made in one lump sum rather than in instalments, as was standard for commissioned work. They are both specified, moreover, as being for paintings that had been sold and delivered rather than for paintings that the artist had made, which was the standard formula for final payments for commissioned works ('vendutoli, et consignatoli' rather than 'che li ha fatto'). They are also indicated as being for the entire price of the paintings ('per il prezzo di'), rather than on account ('in conto di'), which was usual for commissioned paintings. Finally, both specify that the paintings were sold with frames. This occurs very infrequently with privately commissioned pictures. From the beginning of the seventeenth century, as measurements for gallery pictures became increasingly standardized, it became more and more common for collectors to order frames directly from gilders, since this allowed them to rotate paintings, keeping some unframed in storage to exchange periodically with the framed paintings on the walls, while also making it easier for them to unify a gallery's heterogeneous assembly of subjects and styles through a judicious assemblage of frames of similar dimensions and gilding.[61]

This reading of the documents can be further confirmed from an examination of De Castro's inventory of D'Amore's collection, in which only one painting by De Castro, of *St Januarius*, is listed. The *Crucifixion*, which De Castro had earlier sold to D'Amore, remains unattributed but is valued, together with another unattributed painting, at the respectable price of 50 ducats. Castiglione's *Christ Washing the Feet of his Disciples* may possibly have been in the group of paintings that are not itemized. It is difficult to identify the small octagonal painting sold in 1646, but, given the values of the works, it is possibly to be counted among D'Amore's small landscapes by Herman van Swanevelt and Napoletano, such as the 'Due quadri in ottangolo con paesi de Felippo dell'Angeli' (two octagonal paintings with landscapes by Filippo dell'Angeli [Napoletano]), valued at 100 ducats.[62]

The paintings sold by De Castro were by more prestigious painters than the pictures at the lower reaches of the market discussed above. Even allowing for the frames, which were included in the cost, the prices of 40 and 30 ducats for D'Amore's small paintings indicate that they were relatively expensive examples of their kind, compared with, for example, the 1 and 2.5 ducats assigned to Cautiero's anonymous pictures of saints and still lifes, and, closer in time to D'Amore's purchases, the 7.5 ducats paid in 1637 to Luca Giordano's father, Antonio, for five half-length paintings of *St Nicholas*.[63]

Major works by the leading painters of the 1630s to 1650s, by contrast, could fetch up to ten times the amounts paid by D'Amore. Artemisia Gentileschi's commissions for large gallery paintings cost between 150 to 230 ducats, while Ribera demanded 270 ducats for a *Pietà* commissioned in 1649. In the late 1640s Stanzione likewise set 300 ducats as the asking price for two separately commissioned paintings of the *Rape of Persephone* and the *Judgement of Paris*, while Andrea Vaccaro asked for 280 ducats for a commission of 1643 (see Table 2). These prices represent the highest level of the market for privately commissioned pictures and match closely the prices outlaid for major altarpieces and other public commissions. Two characteristic examples, from among the many documented instances of this kind, are the 251 ducats paid in 1631 to Giovanni Battista Caracciolo for the altarpiece of the chapel of the Assumption in the church of the Certosa di San Martino and the 300 ducats paid in 1652 for one of the organs of Naples Cathedral.[64]

But it would be inappropriate to compare D'Amore's collecting activities with work of this kind. A much closer correspondence can be found with the prices paid for the smaller cabinet paintings by the landscape and genre specialists of the 1630s to 1650s. A landscape with small figures measuring approximately 132 by 158 centimetres by the leading landscape painter of the period, Domenico Gargiulo, for example, could cost around 30 ducats, while his smaller paintings might be valued considerably lower, at approximately 6 to 10 ducats including frames.[65] The similar landscapes of Gargiulo's associate Scipione Compagno might likewise reach up to 40 ducats, while Agostino Beltrano's landscapes and Andrea de Leone's battle pieces with small figures cost around 20 ducats.[66] De Castro's prices thus match these examples quite closely and suggest that he was dealing in what might be characterized as the middle to upper reaches of the market.

De Castro moved to more expensive dealings in the 1650s and 1660s. In 1653 Gaspar Roomer, the best-known and most influential collector of Neapolitan art, paid him the considerable sum of 550 ducats 'for all the paintings sold and delivered to his complete satisfaction, including a large *Bacchus* measuring nine by seven *palmi* [approx. 237 by 184 cm] made by the hand of the deceased Jusepe de Ribera, the Spaniard'.[67] The painting referred to in the document has been identified as Ribera's great masterpiece of the 1620s, the *Drunken Silenus*, since it corresponds closely to the measurements given in the document and is not mentioned in a contemporary description of Roomer's collection made in 1630 (fig. 87).[68]

De Castro had acquired this painting from the collection of Giovanni Francesco Salernitano, barone di Frosolone. This is known since De Castro himself included a description of the painting in an inventory he compiled for Salernitano five years earlier. 'Lo Bacco dello Spagnuolo' was one of the jewels in the crown of an unusual and carefully assembled collection that included paintings by Castiglione, Poussin and Guido Reni, all artists not otherwise well represented in Neapolitan collections at that time. It was the second most expensive painting in the collection, worth 150 ducats, and, De Castro noted, would have been worth much more were it to be sold in more economically and politically stable times (Naples was then still recovering from the economic downturn brought about by the Revolt of Masaniello).[69]

That De Castro was able to acquire this painting from Salernitano demonstrates the obvious professional advantage in providing ongoing assistance to clients by appraising their collections and drawing up inventories. Salernitano's inventory was ordered as part of the arrangements surrounding the negotiations for his forthcoming marriage. He was evidently forced to sell the *Drunken Silenus* a few years later, however, for reasons that are still not known. It would have made good sense for him to turn for assistance in this regard to the individual from whom he had been buying work and who had subsequently appraised his collection. The case study of the *Drunken Silenus* provides a clear indication that, in Naples, art dealing could involve the foremost painters and patrons, as well as one of the most significant paintings of the period.

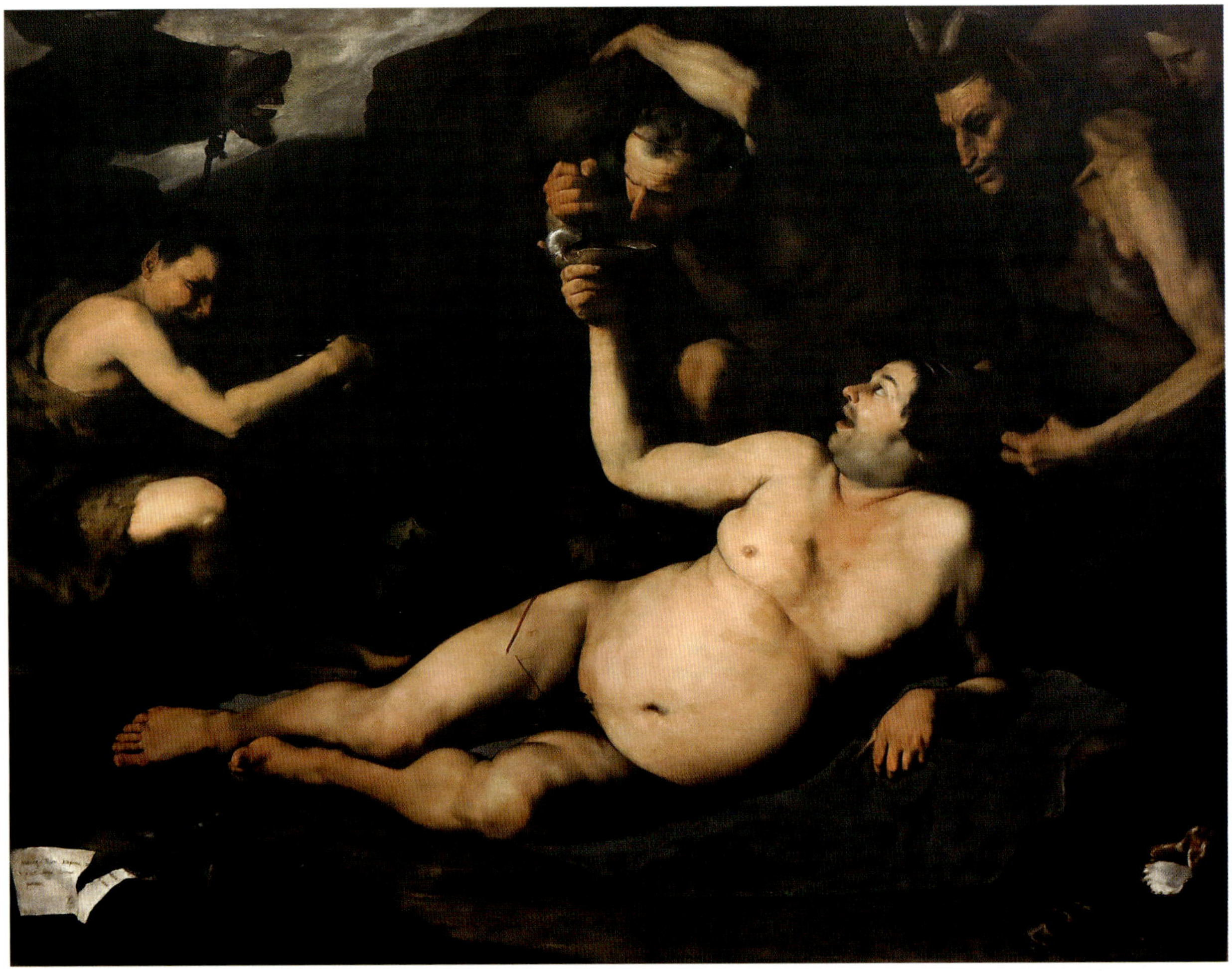

87 Jusepe de Ribera, *Drunken Silenus*, signed and dated 1626. Oil on canvas, 185 × 229 cm. Museo e Gallerie Nazionali di Capodimonte, Naples

De Castro's dealings with prestigious collectors continued over the following decades. Together with Corneille de Wael and Abraham Brueghel in Rome, he remained the principal Neapolitan dealer for the important Messinese collector Don Antonio Ruffo during the 1660s and 1670s.[70] As was the case with Salernitano, Ruffo evidently trusted him, and accordingly employed him in a number of different capacities. Occasionally, De Castro agreed to act as Ruffo's agent. In 1671, for example, he was asked to commission Ruffo's portrait from Cosimo Fanzago. He also searched unsuccessfully on Ruffo's behalf for paintings by Polidoro da Caravaggio, and from time to time sold to Ruffo items from his own stock.

De Castro also worked for the Spanish viceroys during these years, assisting them in their ongoing project of stripping the kingdom of many of its most valuable art works. In 1664 he was charged with selecting and packing the picture gallery of the viceroy, Gaspar de Bracamonte y Guzmán, conde de Peñaranda, which was sent to Spain among a cargo of 1,500 large boxes.[71] According to De' Dominici, he was employed in a similar capacity by the next viceroy, Pedro Antonio de Aragón (viceroy 1666–72). De Aragón commissioned De Castro to compile a list of the most important paintings in Neapolitan churches that could be bought and dispatched to Spain. Among them were altarpieces by Raphael and Titian. Many more would have gone had not De Castro realized the danger to the city's artistic patrimony and lied to the viceroy about their worth, telling him that originals by Raphael and Andrea del Sarto were only copies and not worth buying. De' Dominici also mentions that De Aragón sent four paintings by Bernardo Cavallino to Spain, and, although no name is given, it was presumably De Castro who advised him on the purchase.[72]

De' Dominici's account needs to be qualified. Many of the paintings esteemed in his time as masterpieces by Raphael and other artists have since been de-attributed.[73] But Wethey raises more fundamental doubts about De' Dominici's accuracy, noting that some of the paintings said to have been shipped to Madrid were never, in fact, taken from Naples.[74] De' Dominici may well have made a few factual errors regarding which paintings were sold, but there can be no doubting the fundamental accuracy of his account. De Aragón had a reputation as a ruthlessly acquisitive collector of Neapolitan art, even during his viceregency. Celano describes him in this light, and there is a drawing by Falcone of a statue that bears an old inscription noting that it had been sent to Spain by De Aragón.[75]

SALES NEGOTIATIONS AND THE UPPER-LEVEL ART DEALER

De Castro himself corroborated his role in servicing the extreme acquisitiveness of the viceroy, lamenting in a letter to Ruffo of 1670: 'at the moment we are almost depleted of paintings and marbles as a result of the pleasure of the viceroy, so much so, in fact, that one needs, as they say in the proverb, to search with a lantern at noon, nevertheless, we are diligent'.[76] These pointed yet understated assurances to Ruffo typify the adroit skills of communication to be expected of a dealer operating in this rarefied sector of the market. On the one hand it subtly draws attention to a critical shortage of quality stock, thereby increasing a sense of urgency and demand on the part of the client. On the other, it seeks to assuage the client's fears by highlighting the agent's self-assured command of the market and ability to circumvent these obstacles in order to secure whatever the client desires – all at a premium, no doubt.

Only a small number of artists would have been able to match De Castro in combining financial acumen with the tact, discretion and attentiveness to the elaborate protocols of aristocratic modes of address that were essential to the maintenance of successful relationships with prestigious collectors and patrons. Francesco di Maria (1623–1690) appears to have been one such artist and a particularly accomplished practitioner, as it transpired, of what amounts to an especially rarefied brand of art trade–diplomatic communication skills.

After an early period influenced by Domenichino followed by periods spent in Rome studying Sacchi and other practitioners of Baroque classicism, Di Maria emerged during the years following the plague as one of the leading Neapolitan painters of the second half of the seventeenth century (fig. 88).[77] He has been encountered as Andrea Vaccaro's successor occupying the influential post of *superiore* of the newly reformed Congregazione dei Pittori in the late 1660s, with a particular interest in maintaining an academy based around advanced lessons in anatomy (see p. 84). He will also reappear at a later stage of this study in the context of a high-profile and increasingly rancorous competition during the 1670s for supremacy of the Neapolitan art scene that pitted him against the rapidly ascendant star of Luca Giordano (see pp. 239, 243–4).

Alongside these social ambitions, Di Maria also maintained a profitable sideline in dealing, selling paintings and drawings to the upper echelons of both local and foreign patrons and collectors. One of the most vivid documents of his activity along these lines is, in fact, an elaborately courteous correspondence recorded by De' Dominici between Di Maria and his close friend and associate Giuseppe Valletta, who was a lawyer of considerable renown and one of the leading figures in the scientific and literary academies of the day. De' Dominici records that Valletta once came to admire four canvases in Di Maria's possession by a little-known Roman still-life painter, Andrea Bonnano. He asked to buy two of them, but Di Maria shrewdly suggested that he take all four home to hang on a wall in order to select the two that he preferred.

After a period of indecision, Valletta eventually sent to Di Maria a long and effusive letter – transcribed in full by De' Dominici – in which he complains about the impossibility of choosing only two canvases; he concludes by enclosing a blank cheque, asking Di Maria to fill out for him whatever sum the artist considered appropriate:

> I send therefore to Your Lordship a certificate of credit and request that you indicate the amount to be paid . . . and with it I send my protestations of indelible friendship, constant servitude . . . [and declaration] that I have no other consolation but to savour the sweetness of your presence by way of your paintings . . . [and to enjoy] your fame that spreads so lavishly through every cloud, and I affectionately kiss your hands etc.[78]

Di Maria's ability to blend the elaborate conventions of aristocratic tactfulness and courtesy with the hard-nosed dictates of high-level commerce evidently stood him in good stead. In 1674 a collector paid him 125 ducats for paintings by Mola, Lanfranco and Angelo Caroselli, and three battle

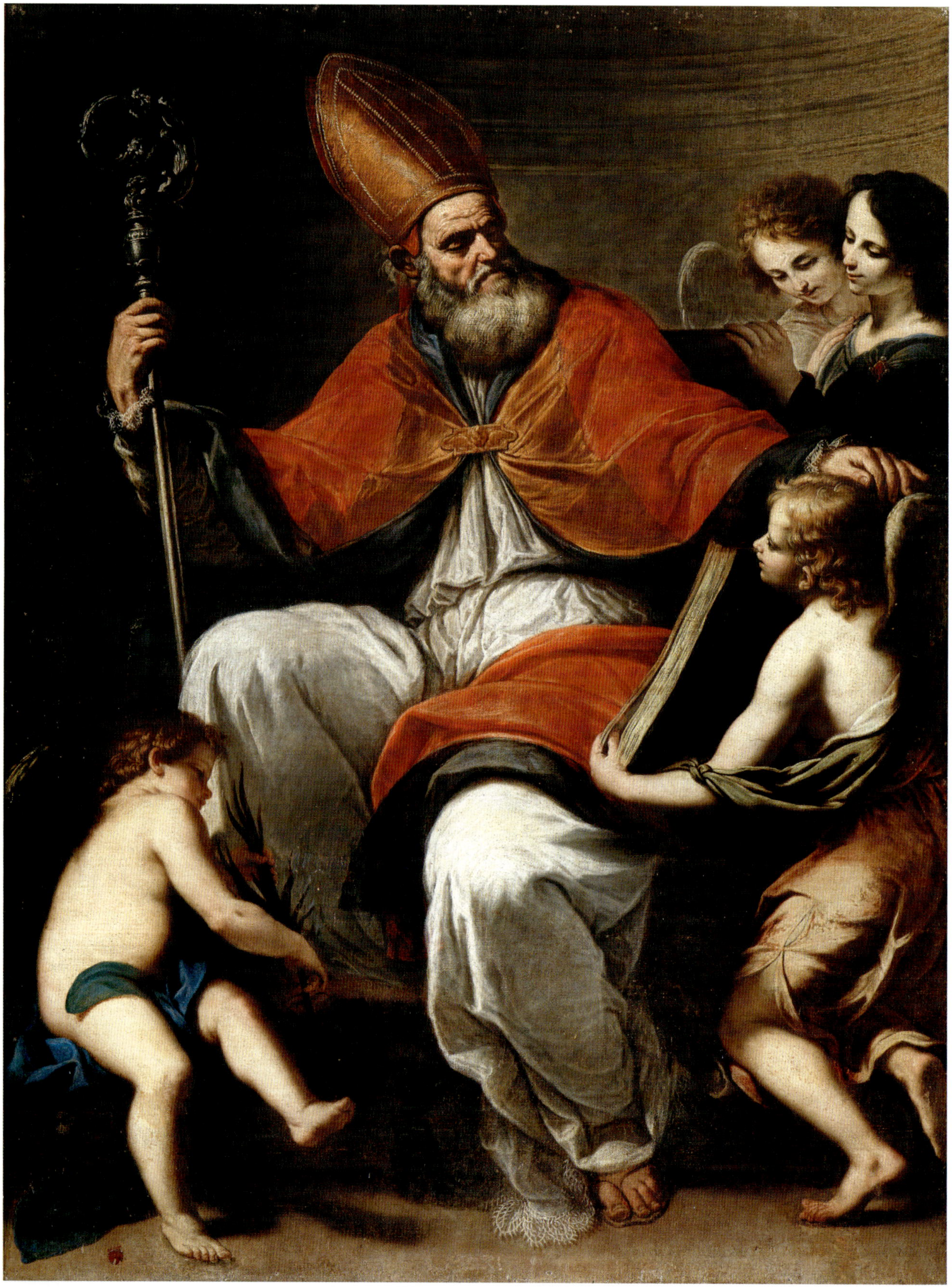

88 Francesco di Maria, *St Gregory the Illuminator*, 1658. Oil on canvas, 230 × 170 cm. San Gregorio Armeno, Naples

pieces by Jacques Courtois and his workshop (these, together with the paintings by Bonnani mentioned above, having been acquired presumably during one of Di Maria's frequent trips to Rome).[79] In 1686 Gaspare Lanzetta, who is elsewhere documented as a patron of Pietro del Po,[80] paid him 25 ducats for two small paintings, one of which was attributed to Reni.[81] Di Maria also sold paintings to the English consul in Naples, George Davies, although their authors are not specified.[82]

Most of all, though, it seems that during these years Di Maria was able to convert to financial advantage his advanced expertise in the finer points of Italian Renaissance and Baroque draughtsmanship, a knowledge that flowed naturally from his status as one of the most accomplished draughtsmen of his generation. This enabled him apparently to corner the market in the newly emerging trade in drawings – a field not especially valued among collectors prior to that date, but coming increasingly into prominence in the 1670s and thereafter.[83]

Di Maria was the source, for example, of many of the Neapolitan drawings purchased in the early 1670s for Cardinal Leopoldo de' Medici that are today preserved among the holdings of the Uffizi in Florence.[84] In 1673 Di Maria sold forty-six drawings to the lawyer Agostino Odoardo (later to attain some prominence in civil law),[85] for 150 ducats.[86] These came with attributions ranging from Raphael, Sebastiano del Piombo retouched by Michelangelo, Federico Zuccaro, Cavalier d'Arpino, the Carracci, Polidoro, Muziano, Titian, Tempesta, Perugino, Guido Reni, Domenichino and a large group by Ribera. Di Maria must have felt secure in his expertise, since he agreed to return the money paid for any attribution found to be incorrect (although Odoardo was only given six months to establish this).[87]

De' Dominici also wrote that Caracciolo's sketchbook, which included drawings after Raphael and others, was sold by his heirs to Di Maria, who in turn sold it to 'alcuni Signori Inglesi' for the massive sum of 2,800 scudi.[88] The brief reference to 'Signori Inglesi' is significant, since it points the way to the increasing significance of foreign collectors of Neapolitan art, as discussed in Chapter Seven. Yet for all his ability to combine the authority of his position as one of the most knowledgeable painters of the day with the elaborate and necessary protocols of aristocratic address, Di Maria nonetheless had an only very limited capacity to extend his reach beyond Naples, particularly when it came to the emerging international trade in Neapolitan art. These expanding new horizons represented yet another reason for him to be resentful, by the way, of his great rival, Luca Giordano, since they involved above all else an increasingly complex international trade in works by Giordano and his workshop, as will be seen.

The individuals given responsibility for exploiting these new commercial ventures, moreover, were not, for the most part, to be counted among the aristocrats and dilettantes cultivated by Di Maria in his habitual association with the academies and salons of the day. Instead, they came from the recently ascendant professional class of internationally oriented merchants active both locally and abroad in the wholesale buying and selling of Neapolitan and foreign art, and with whom Di Maria was also associated through the salons held by one such merchant, Aniello Mele. These individuals would effect a significant transformation of the field of Neapolitan dealing in the years after the plague of 1656. Through their influence, the image of the dealer would change from that of the relatively straightforward workshop trader of the *rivenditori* to the more sophisticated and urbane 'onorato mercante d'arte' characterized by De' Dominici. They would also play a vital role in the ongoing project of internationalizing Neapolitan art, a trend that became increasingly significant in the later decades of the century and that will emerge as an increasingly significant factor in the discussion that follows.

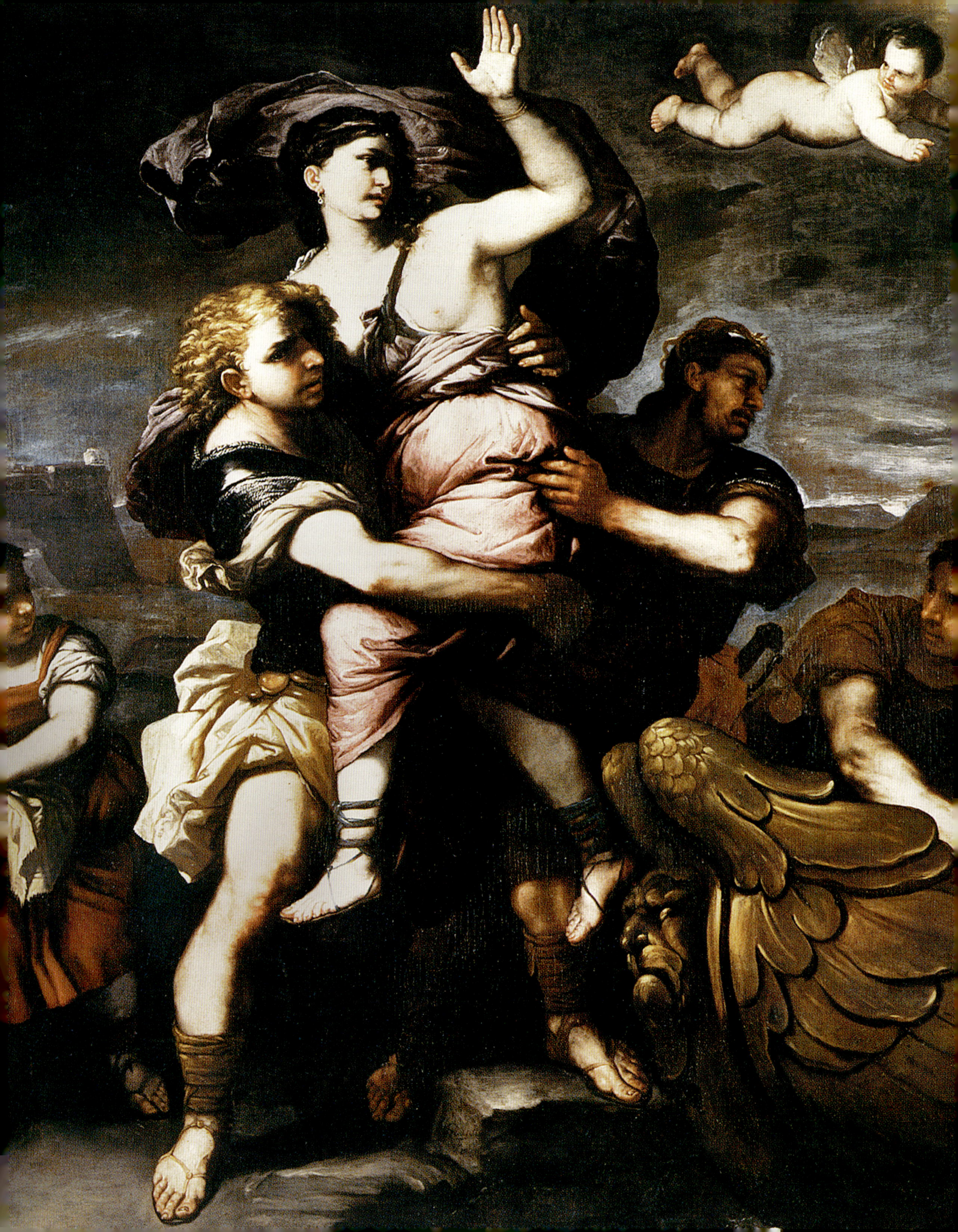

7

The Rise of the Art Merchants

ART FRAUD AND THE ECONOMICS OF CONNOISSEURSHIP

In January 1664 the painter-dealer Giacomo de Castro wrote to his client, Don Antonio Ruffo of Messina, expressing his displeasure at hearing that the Roman-based painter-dealer Abraham Brueghel had recently passed through Naples without paying him a visit. Part of the reason for this lack of professional courtesy, De Castro intimated, was that Brueghel was unwilling to show his face in the city following a recent scandal involving the circulation on the Neapolitan market of a number of purportedly old master paintings. These had been sent from Rome by Brueghel and his colleague Corneille de Wael, but they were, in fact, 'cose del mondo corrente' (things of the current world). Speaking of which, De Castro noted that this was not the time to buy works of this kind because Naples was, in fact, additionally flooded by a group of forgeries by none other than Luca Giordano that had been bankrolled by Gaspar Roomer (*circa* 1596/1606–1674), among other merchant dealers:

> Here there is no occasion to apply or spend because nothing of quality appears, only some pieces that have been counterfeited by a certain Luca Giordano working now in the style of Titian and then Paolo Veronese . . . he has done a good job and then he gives an antique tint which does not appear badly to Signore Gaspar [Roomer] nor to many other merchants; however, it has been discovered and so they won't accept them anymore...[1]

One reading of De Castro's letter would be to view it simply as a slanderous attempt on his part to discredit his competitors for business with Ruffo, an especially desirable client since he was one of the most active and distinguished collectors in southern Italy.[2] This is revealing in itself, since it points to an upper-level market that was as closely interconnected as it was highly competitive. At the same time, however, it is also clear that, no matter how self-interested De Castro's claims may have been, his accusations were at least to some extent true. This is confirmed by the existence of a number of early compositions by Giordano that go well beyond the limits of Renaissance and Baroque conventions of quotation and paraphrasing of earlier artists as to constitute full-blown pastiches or even (if one could be sure of the circumstances of their production) forgeries of Renaissance masters in a variety of styles (fig. 89).

That a small minority at least of these early works by the young Giordano were, in fact, outright forgeries is confirmed by the letter cited above, as well as by anecdotes circulating around the Neapolitan workshops that derived, in part, from the artist himself. One version of the story

Facing page Luca Giordano, *Abduction of Helen*, 1655–60 (detail of fig. 93)

appears in a manuscript of 1681 that was probably composed by Giordano in order to provide information for a planned commentary on Neapolitan art being worked on in Florence by Francesco Saverio Baldinucci. It notes that the young Giordano had created a number of forgeries in the style of earlier masters that his father sold to Roomer as originals, thus bringing considerable profit to the family home. In 1656, aged twenty-two, Giordano was eventually forced to leave the house, however, after his father forbade him from pursuing an intended marriage because of the young woman's meagre dowry. In order to provide the necessary funds, Luca worked on four large canvases that he sold to Roomer himself for the considerable sum of 200 ducats, thus enabling him to marry his intended; this would thus date the forgeries to the period between *circa* 1652 and 1656 prior to his subsequent nuptial agreement and marriage on 10 November 1657 and 17 September 1658, respectively.[3]

The sum of 200 ducats represented a sizeable return for a young and emerging artist. As a contribution to a dowry, it constitutes an amount that is double that provided to the young Cavallino and his bride, and eight times higher than the 25 ducats assigned by the Corporazione di Rivenditori for the daughters of its impoverished workshop heads (see p. 101). It is more in keeping with the standard amounts set aside for dowries by reasonably successful artisans at the later stages of their careers. It seems, therefore, that the young Giordano's strategy was both well planned and highly efficient in a manner that would come to define his subsequent career. Just how successful this would prove to be is indicated by the dowries that Giordano was able to allocate for his own daughters decades later: 4,000 ducats for his first two daughters and 7,000 ducats for his youngest daughter Teresa's marriage in 1704.[4]

A subsequent and presumably further embellished version of the story of Giordano's early forgeries also appears in De' Dominici's *Vite*. De' Dominici's source of information in this instance would have been his father, since Raimondo de' Dominici had been a workshop assistant to Giordano during the later decades of the seventeenth century. It notes that the young Luca Giordano had been working for Roomer for some time via the agency of his father, Antonio Giordano, who sold to Roomer as originals a number of Luca's early works in the style of Titian, Bassano and Tintoretto, among other artists. Luca eventually met Roomer personally in order to interest him in paintings produced in his own style. When Roomer attempted to pay him much less for these than for the earlier forgeries, Giordano pointed out his hidden signature in the pictures that Roomer had acquired earlier and that now had pride of place on the walls of his palace. Roomer was initially outraged at the deception, but soon came to appreciate Giordano's talents, selling more of the same works abroad and going on to become one of Giordano's strongest protectors and an early dealer in his work.[5]

Bernardo de' Dominici's father certainly knew what he was talking about in this instance, since he had himself been involved earlier in his career in perpetuating art fraud deception of a similar kind. Prior to coming to work for Giordano, Raimondo had been trained in his homeland of Malta by Mattia Preti. On a subsequent return trip to Malta, De' Dominici notes, his father took the opportunity to sell secondary market paintings to local collectors. In his life of Vaccaro, De' Dominici expands on this aspect of his father's career when he notes that many of Vaccaro's copies after Caravaggio had been sold as originals. He has clear evidence to attest to this activity, namely the sale orchestrated by Raimondo during a trip to Malta undertaken by the father and son in 1698:

> And the author can attest that his father Raimondo de' Dominici at one stage acquired in lieu of credit from [Vaccaro's pupil] Giuseppe Fatturuso ten academies [e.g., nude studies], painted on canvas and measuring around three *palmi* [approx. 79 cm], that had been created as exercises by Andrea [Vaccaro]. He subsequently sold these in Malta to a French cavalier who was a great dilettante of paintings as originals by Caravaggio. And he did this without the least scruple of conscience since Vaccaro's talent is in no way inferior to Caravaggio's.[6]

This anecdote may well strike a discordant note in the mind of the modern reader, at least when considered from present-day preoccupations with the importance of business ethics. But for De' Dominici and his intended readers the story was understood as an expression of the pre-existing topos of artists deceiving their clients with incorrect attributions in order to reveal the true mastery of their talent.[7] In the case of Raimondo de' Dominici's story, the topos was switched from the more common one of an artist deceiving a client by passing off one of his own works as that of a better-known master to the idea that an artist might be justified in deliberately misattributing a work produced by another artist, since, so the argument goes, Vaccaro was just as good a painter as Caravaggio and thus deserved the same high prices for his work.

Giordano's effortless 'counterfeiting' of other artists' work falls into this same category of a rich tradition of a topos

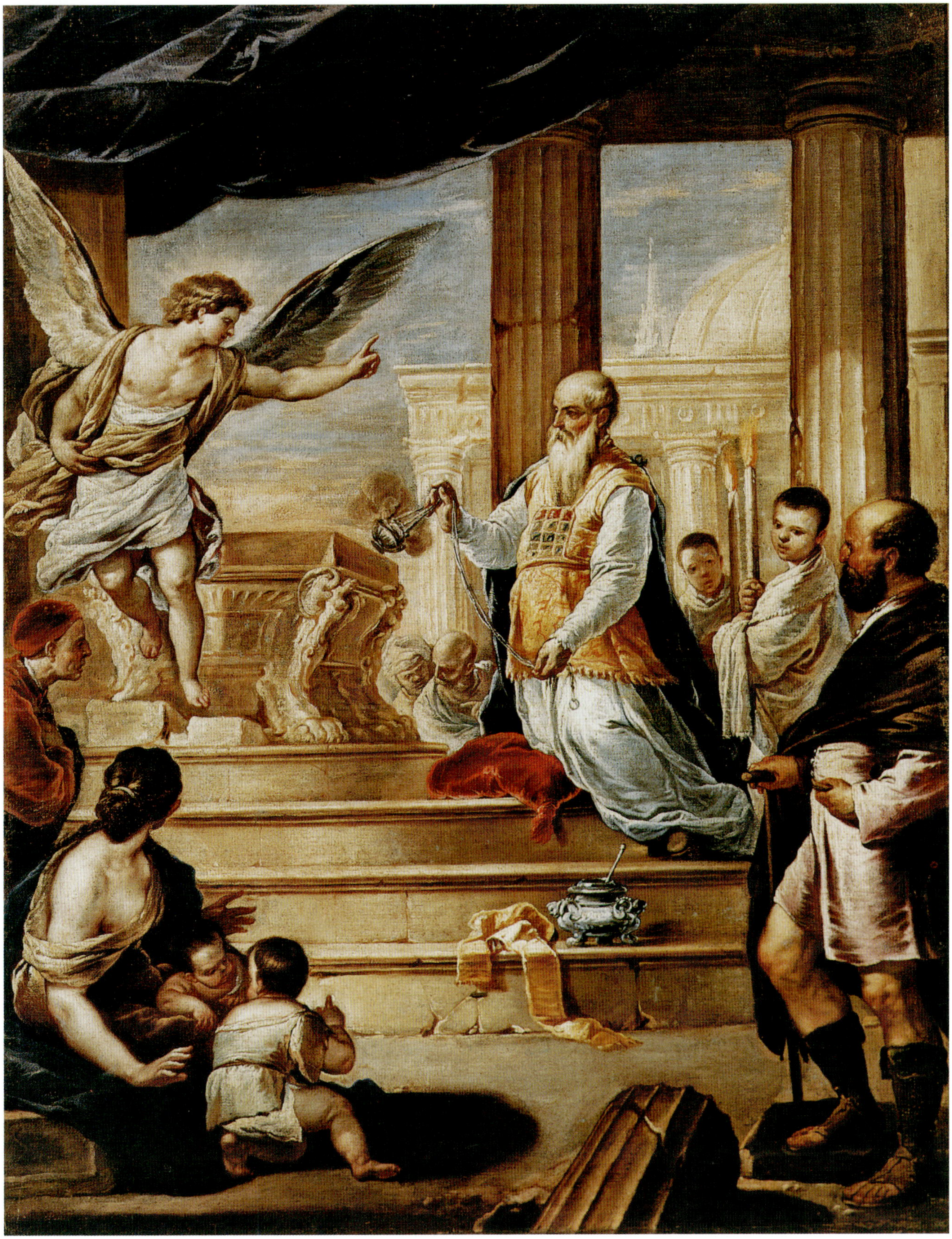

89 Luca Giordano, *Archangel Gabriel Appearing to St Zachary*, *circa* 1653–5. Oil on canvas, 133 × 91 cm. Museo e Gallerie Nazionali di Capodimonte, Naples

that stretches back to Condivi's similar story about the young Michelangelo and beyond.[8] But the point of these other accounts found in contexts outside Naples tends to lie more simply in the revelation that they bring about, in which an initial deception leads to an ultimate disclosure of a worthy artist's true identity, thereby revealing the true value of the artist involved in the deception. What is striking about Raimondo de' Dominici's and Giordano's anecdotes, by contrast, is their emphasis not simply on this part of the topos, but also on the financial profit they were able to gain by way of their deceit. Giordano's story seems especially overt in its acknowledgement of this, since part of its effectiveness clearly hinges on the reader knowing to what extent the artist was able to profit financially from his crooked scheme. Jarring though these accounts may now seem, in their own setting they should be understood as additional indications of the Neapolitan perception that there was no intrinsic contradiction between a growing interest in the status of painting as a liberal art and an ongoing professional concern to view it as a trade that should be exploited for commercial ends as a matter of course.

A further piece of evidence corroborating the essential truth of Giordano's account comes in a payment made by Roomer to Luca Giordano's father in October 1652. On this occasion, Roomer paid Giordano the elder 100 ducats – a substantial amount that must have been for something other than Antonio's own paintings, given their low values, and would have also constituted an unacceptably high amount for Luca's paintings at such an early stage of his career, had they been sold as such (he was then aged only eighteen).[9] Roomer evidently went on to become a strong backer of Giordano's work. Besides De' Dominici's assertions to this effect, there are also comments by Celano made along the same lines at the end of the seventeenth century, as well as a payment from Roomer to Giordano for 60 ducats for unspecified work in 1661.[10]

Roomer evidently appreciated the extraordinary talent presented by Giordano's swift rise to fame during the mid- to late 1650s. It is also not difficult to appreciate why Giordano, for his part, might have sought to associate himself at the outset of his career with the fabulously wealthy Flemish merchant resident in Naples. Roomer combined a heightened refinement of personality with an extensive network of contacts that came with his being the most discerning collector of the period (see Chapter Nine). He also added to this the shrewdly focused sensibility of the most enterprising and resourceful entrepreneur of the day, all making him a perfect mentor for the keenly ambitious young artist.

GASPAR ROOMER: MERCHANT TURNED MAECENAS

Roomer had been active as a dealer since at least the early 1630s. His payment of January 1630 to the widow Grazia d'Angelo for seven works from the workshop of her recently deceased art-dealing husband has been noted (see p. 117), as has Capaccio's fulsome praise of six of these pictures in his description of Roomer's collection in his guide to Naples from the same year. That Roomer subsequently sold a number of these paintings together with many other works from his collection is confirmed by the subsequent reappearance of some twenty of the paintings described by Capaccio in the inventory of the collection of Giovanni Andrea Lumaga in Venice in 1677.[11] Lumaga belonged to a banking family with business interests stretching from Nuremburg to Naples, and presumably it would have been in his capacity as a financier that he would have first made contact with Roomer and, from there, to engage with Roomer's activities as an art dealer.

Art dealing would have represented a relatively minor component within the wider portfolio of Roomer's many and varied business interests, at least when considered from the point of view of immediate financial returns alone. As the city's leading shipping magnate and financier of the Habsburg/vice-regal administrative enterprise more generally, Roomer would no doubt have viewed as quite minor the approximately 30 ducats rising to 200 that were involved in individual transactions at the secondary sector of the upper reaches of the art market (Table 4). He had certainly many more immediately profitable and regular sources of income on which to draw: 9,400 ducats, for example, was the amount paid to him and his partner in May 1637 for a single freight transaction.[12]

Yet art dealing nonetheless offered Roomer a source of return whose value was measurable in more than simply financial terms. Roomer's connoisseurship was an important element contributing to his international reputation (gaining three mentions, for example, in Joachim von Sandrart's *Teutsche Academie*).[13] It accordingly raised his status above the ranks of his fellow merchants to the position – as endorsed wholeheartedly from Celano onwards – of a great Maecenas and promoter of the arts. For the artists employed, it is easy to see his powerful source of attraction. Roomer offered local painters unparalleled international access during a period in which Neapolitan painting held little traction in overseas markets as a generally recognized prestige commodity. He was also, closer to home and perhaps of most rele-

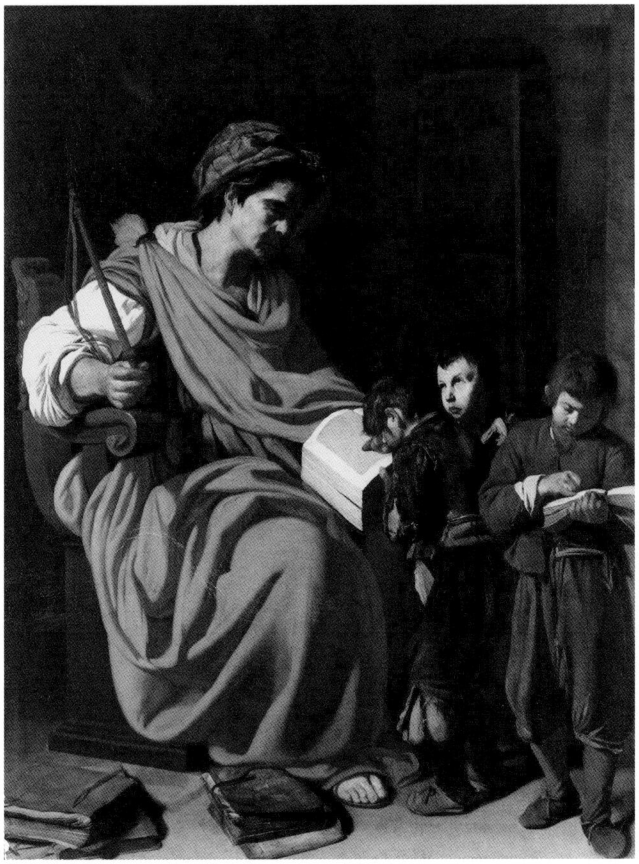

90 Aniello Falcone, *Schoolmistress*, *circa* 1630. Oil on canvas, 101.5 × 75 cm. Museo e Gallerie Nazionali di Capodimonte, Naples

vance as far as Neapolitans were concerned, a reference point to all the local patrons and collectors of the city, since, as De' Dominici noted, 'his opinion was reported to all the lovers of painting in that period'.[14]

Celano and De' Dominici both mention Roomer's involvement in the export of artists' works to Flanders and elsewhere. They note that Roomer sent abroad in this respect work by an otherwise little-known follower of Ribera, Bartolomeo Bassante (possibly identifiable as Bartolomeo Passante, who may be identifiable, in turn, as the Master of the Annunciation to the Shepherds; see p. 57),[15] together with paintings by Bernardo Cavallino, the still-life painter Giovanni Battista Ruoppolo,[16] Aniello Falcone,[17] Mattia Preti[18] and, of course, Giordano himself.[19] A little more information about the nature of these activities can be reconstructed in the case of Aniello Falcone. This artist's innovative reframing within a contemporary Italianate Caravaggesque style of battle paintings and other genre subjects previously associated with Northern specialists must have appealed strongly to Roomer, given his Flemish tastes and extensive contacts with collectors in the Dutch Republic, Flanders and elsewhere. From the information that can be reconstructed, it seems that he lost no time in assuming responsibility for the promotion of Falcone's work both locally and abroad.

De' Dominici recounts that Roomer took over the promotion of Falcone's work after seeing his battle pieces for sale in the workshop of the *rigattiere* Nicola di Martino (thus dating his association with Falcone from *circa* 1630). Roomer became so enthusiastic about Falcone's talent that he came to exert almost a monopoly over his output. He had such a close oversight of Falcone's production, in fact, that Falcone was required to add to his contracts with prospective patrons the proviso that he would deliver his commissioned work 'only if Signor Roomer does not wish it'.[20] The large numbers of Falcone's paintings present in other Neapolitan collections from an early date indicate that De' Dominici's words should not be taken strictly at face value. They would nonetheless appear to ring true in the sense of suggesting a mutually rewarding dealer–painter partnership that went far beyond the relatively modest and simple business transactions outlined in the previous chapter. The anecdote, together with the evidence cited below, suggests, in fact, that Roomer may have entered into a non-exclusive option giving him a right of first refusal on Falcone's work.

It is known that Roomer stockpiled large numbers of his favourite artists' work in his palace situated in the heart of the artist's quarter close to the monastery of Monteoliveto. Capaccio, for example, mentions that Roomer possessed no fewer than 60 paintings by the landscape painter Goffredo Wals, 40 by Léonard Bramer and 168 by the obscure 'Jacobo Sibraut', who is probably to be identified as Jacobus Sibrandi Mancadan.[21] These high figures suggest, as Vaes has indicated, that Roomer monopolized the production of certain artists so that he could act as both their patron and business agent, selling their pictures in Naples and further afield to Flanders, the Dutch Republic, Spain, England and wherever his ships sailed.[22] Roomer's palace was thus both a private collection and a public showroom, a space to promote his image as an enlightened and knowledgeable connoisseur, as well as a stockroom from which to interest prospective clients – fellow merchants and collectors alike.

De' Dominici notes that Roomer exported many of Falcone's paintings to Flanders, an account that is corroborated by the presence of his *Schoolmistress* in a private collection in Antwerp as early as 1673 (fig. 90).[23] Roomer is even said to have exported one of Falcone's greatest works, the *Martyrdom of St Januarius*, despite the fact that it was Roomer's personal favourite. This painting is now lost, but its influence can be discerned in numerous closely related variants of the subject produced by artists associated with his circle during the 1630s and 1640s (see fig. 67).[24]

A final corroboration of De' Dominici's account comes in two recently published payments from Roomer to Falcone, for 80 ducats in June 1640 and 90 ducats in May 1643.[25] The relatively large sums involved, together with the fact that they are described generically as being 'per altritanti' (for other things) rather than for specific paintings, suggests that the payments constituted contributions towards an ongoing stipend rather than amounts for one-off transactions. Similar lump sums paid over time by Roomer are recorded for other artists, indicating that the merchant dealer developed a number of comparable relationships with artists including Andrea Vaccaro, Mattia Preti, Giacomo Farelli and, of course, Luca Giordano himself.[26]

Besides contracting artists to paint works for him to sell locally or abroad, Roomer habitually scoured the city's workshops as well as other private collections for choice secondary market acquisitions. His purchase in 1630 of seven of the best paintings from the legacy of the art dealer Tommaso della Vigna has already been noted, as has his acquisition from De Castro in 1653 of a group of paintings that included Ribera's celebrated *Drunken Silenus* of 1626, for the considerable sum of 550 ducats (see pp. 117, 119). Finally, a further document has more recently come to light recording Roomer's acquisition, in March 1652, of four framed paintings by Cavallino and another painting by the somewhat mysterious Bergamasque painter resident in Naples Giovanni Battista Spinelli. These were acquired from a local collector for 160 ducats, a figure of approximately 30 ducats per painting that accords well with the standard prices paid for pictures by reasonably well-known artists circulating on the secondary market (Table 4).[27]

But perhaps the most famous instance of Roomer's engagement with secondary market sales occurs in the small amount of information that can be gathered together regarding his involvement in the dismantling and selling off of part of the collection of the celebrated poet and academician Berardino Ròta. Ròta was a figure of some significance in sixteenth-century Neapolitan humanist circles. He is best remembered as the author of the *Egloghe pescatorie* (1533) and for an especially influential series of Petrarchan *canzone* dedicated to the memory of his deceased wife, Porzia Capece (1560). Towards the end of his life he sought further to commemorate his importance for the humanist culture of the day by commissioning from Giovanni and Geronimo d'Auria a particularly magnificent tomb to adorn the family chapel in San Domenico Maggiore (fig. 91).

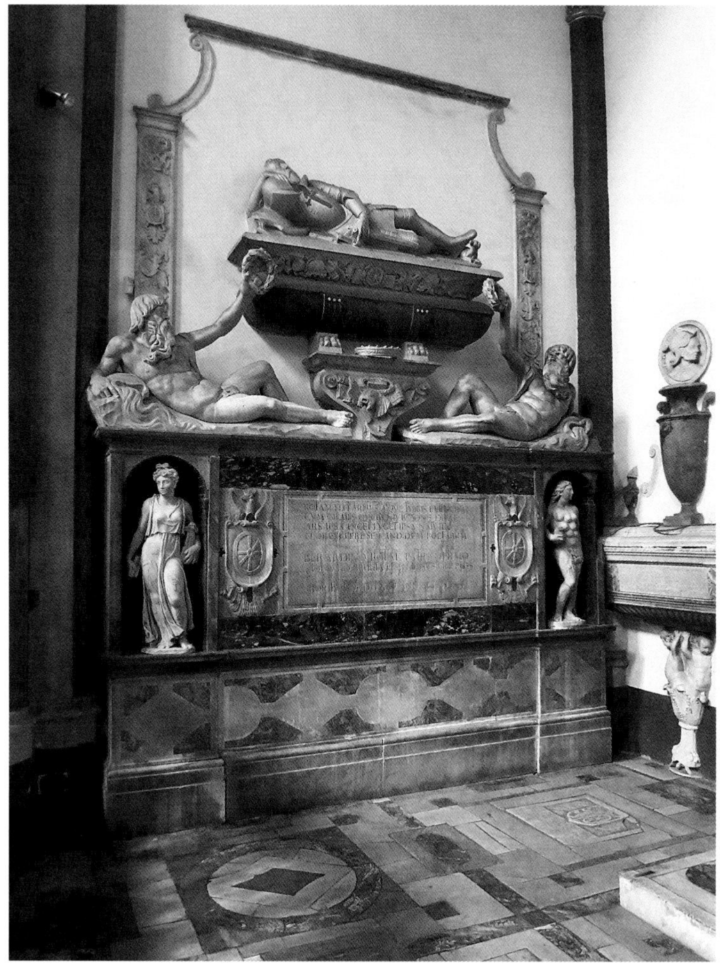

91 Giovanni and Geronimo d'Auria, tomb of Berardino Ròta, 1569–71. Cappella di San Giovanni Battista, San Domenico Maggiore, Naples

Ròta was also one of the leading figures involved in what was at that stage a relatively small circle of significant art collectors in sixteenth-century Naples. His palace in the centre of the city was adorned with a façade painted by Giovanni Bernardo Lama and included antique statuary as well as paintings attributed to Raphael, Salviati, Vasari, Correggio and others. Pride of place within the collection was given to two rooms decorated with a suite of ceiling paintings by Polidoro da Caravaggio (fig. 92).[28]

Celano's guide to Naples of 1692 identifies Roomer as the person responsible for buying up Polidoro's panels following the alteration of the palace by his descendants. Roomer is

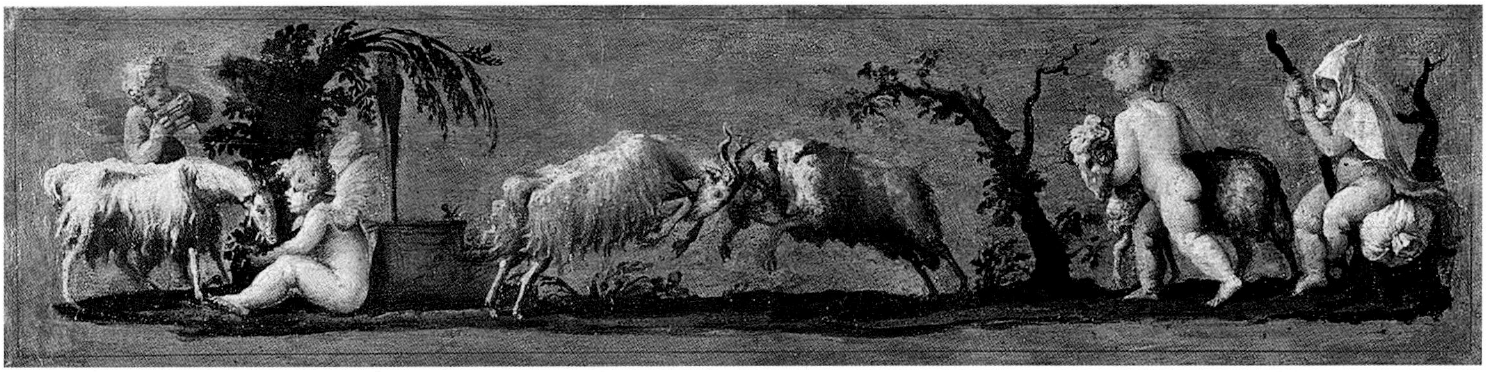

92 Polidoro da Caravaggio, *Putti Playing with Goats*, *circa* 1527–8. Oil on panel, 30.2 × 141.9 cm. Royal Collection, Hampton Court, inv. no. 24

said to have kept the twelve best panels for himself, sending the rest to Flanders.[29] Some further information concerning the date of this acquisition can be determined from the probable entry of a group of these panels into the English royal collection in the late 1630s. From this it appears that nine of the panels were, in fact, acquired directly from Roomer in Naples in 1636 by two visiting English antiquarians/collectors working in the service of the renowned connoisseur Thomas Howard, 21st Earl of Arundel. They were then acquired, in turn, for the collection of Charles I soon after their transfer to England in 1637.[30]

The asking price for these panels would have been considerably higher than that offered for the paintings by Cavallino and Spinelli in 1652. A sense of this can be determined from some other panels, probably deriving from the same series, that were acquired during this period for the palace of Giacomo de Castro's correspondent Don Antonio Ruffo of Messina. Ruffo's paintings by Polidoro – eight in total, although only half were of large format – were acquired for a total cost of 200 Messinese *onzie*. This converts to a sum of 500 ducats, making an average cost of approximately 70 ducats per panel – a high price reflecting the relative scarcity of Polidoro's works of this kind.[31]

The dispersal of Polidoro's soffit paintings from the Palazzo Ròta highlights the growing influence and international reach of certain individuals involved in the upper levels of the Neapolitan art market during this period. The paintings had originally been commissioned from the artist to lend dignity to the activities of a small circle of academicians, poets and dilettante collectors operating in a traditional Renaissance humanist mould. Now, instead, they were dismantled and sold off piecemeal in order to attain maximum profit to a varied group of mostly international collectors by an entrepreneurially minded foreign merchant resident in Naples. The nationality of the purchasers is also significant, since it constitutes one of the very earliest records of the involvement of English collectors in the Neapolitan art market. It accordingly marks the beginning of the growing internationalization of the Neapolitan scene in the decades to come, most particularly during the opening decades of the eighteenth century, when Naples became the culminating point of the European Grand Tour.

ART DEALING AND THE RISE OF THE 'ONORATO MERCANTE D'ARTE'

Roomer and his merchant colleagues played an important role in establishing the foundations for this more prestigious and internationally oriented market for art. They achieved this, in effect, by taking the paintings out of the street-level workshops of individuals like Gaspare de Popolo and other *bottegari/rivenditori* and by placing them, instead, within the more rarefied – and also more profitable – environs of the *piano nobile* of the palace itself. For this to occur, though, two fundamental pre-conditions had first to be met. First, Neapolitan Baroque painting needed to achieve the higher critical validation and status long since accorded to painting in the other major centres. Second, and following from this, it needed to be able to gain traction beyond the confines of its borders so as to achieve broader international recognition – and concomitant luxury exchange value – in centres elsewhere, both in Italy and beyond.

The establishment of a critical infrastructure to support and extend a generally accepted appreciation of the critical and theoretical value of Neapolitan art was still very much an ongoing project during the first half of the seventeenth century. That it was nonetheless reaching fuller recognition in Naples during the decades following the plague of 1656 is indicated, among other factors, by the foundation of the Congregazione dei Pittori at the Casa Professa of the Jesuits in 1664, as previously discussed (see p. 84). It seems that certain individuals also made their contribution to this process, including a number among the merchant dealers of the day.

Foremost among these was Aniello Mele, a still somewhat shadowy individual, documented in 1668 and 1683, who appears to have occupied a transitional status in the development here sketched out. On the one hand, he seems to have operated within the traditional workshop-based model of the *rivenditore*, but at the same time he seems also to have been interested in upgrading his sales by developing a more critically informed customer base among the political and intellectual elites of the day.

De' Dominici recounts that Mele was in the habit of hosting salon-style gatherings at his workshop during the mid- to late 1650s, which the city's leading 'rinomati Professori, ed onorati cittadini dilettanti' (renowned artists and honourable local dilettantes) would attend.[32] The artists frequenting these gatherings are said to have included Francesco di Maria, Giovanni Battista Ruoppolo and the aged Aniello Falcone, together with Luca Giordano and Andrea Vaccaro, who were both at that stage still on a more or less equal footing as the leading artists of Naples.[33]

Mele and the painters were joined at these gatherings by a group of collectors and merchants, including none other than Gaspar Roomer, as well as Giuseppe Valletta, Antonio Ciappa, Carlo Arici and Giacomo Capece Galeota, who were all prominent at various levels of Neapolitan society. Giuseppe Valletta (1636–1714), friend of the sometime art dealer Francesco di Maria, who was also present, was just then starting a brilliant career that would lead to a considerable international reputation as an influential philosopher, lawyer and academician. His importance for the development of later seventeenth-century collecting and patronage has long been recognized. During the later decades of the century he assembled one of the city's finest collections of antiquities, and he also owned works by most of the leading artists, including Giordano, Solimena, Ruoppolo, Caracciolo, Cavallino, Salvator Rosa, Andrea Belvedere and Teresa del Po. He was also an associate of many artists of the day, particularly Giordano, whom he is said to have counselled on the subject matter of his paintings.[34]

A comparable significance would have attached itself in the mind of the reader of the *Vite* to De' Dominici's reference to Giacomo Capece Galeota's presence at Mele's gatherings. Capece Galeota (1617–1680) held the title of duca della Regina and was one of the highest-ranked civil administrators of the day. Among other posts, he maintained the regency of the Neapolitan chancellery, which, as it transpired, he exploited to great personal advantage until his summary dismissal in 1679 on a charge of malfeasance.[35] At the same time, though, he was also a noted and discriminating patron and collector. Like Valletta, he is said to have advised Giordano on the subject matter of his paintings, an association that is further corroborated by documentation from the 1670s.[36] He is elsewhere recorded as an important early patron of Mattia Preti, as well as of Giovanni Battista Recco, Francesco Fracanzano, Lorenzo Vaccaro and Andrea de Leone.[37]

The three other merchant-collectors mentioned by De' Dominici further reinforce the nexus already suggested by the first two individuals in terms of their shared interest in the work of Giordano and his associates. In addition to the involvement of Gaspar Roomer in Mele's gatherings, Antonio Ciappa was a leading figure of the evidently tightly knit circle of merchant backers of Giordano's career. He owed a significant part of his prosperity to his position as *razionale* – or financial agent – for Roomer's long-term business partner, Ferdinand Vandeneynden, another leading Flemish entrepreneur/collector to be discussed elsewhere (see pp. 203–5).[38] Ciappa maintained an unusually close and sustained relationship with Giordano over the course of many years, to the extent that in 1688 Ciappa's son eventually married Giordano's daughter. In the same year he transferred possessions and financial concerns worth a generous 13,000 ducats to his son in order to assist the young couple in setting up an independent household. More than 1,000 ducats of this bequest took the form of a group of paintings that reveal Ciappa as a keen collector of Giordano's work, together with that of Cavallino and Nicola Vaccaro.[39]

Finally, the prosperous Lombard merchant resident in Naples, Carlo Arici, is likewise mentioned in the *Vite* as one of the leading patrons of the period, as well as one of Giordano's first Neapolitan patrons.[40] Although no inventory exists from his lifetime, he must have nonetheless acquired most of the artworks listed in the family collection at the time of its documentation in 1744, shortly after the death of his son, Antonio.[41] At this time, the collection included numerous paintings by and after Luca Giordano, together with an emphasis on still-life paintings by Giuseppe Recco and Abraham Brueghel.

De' Dominici was evidently confident in his sense of the reader's recognition of the calibre of the figures brought together by Mele, noting: 'laonde può immaginarsi il Lettore di quanto piacere e di quanto profitto ella fusse un'erudita, e virtuosa conversazione' (so the reader can but imagine how much pleasure and profit was to be had from this erudite and virtuous conversation). His description of Mele as 'onorato mercante di quadri' (honourable merchant of paintings) is also striking in that it projects a very different model of a more elevated and socially mobile art market professional than that encountered by the workshop traders of the previous chapter. While still not at the level of international reputation and prominence attained by Gaspar Roomer, Mele's activities were nonetheless significant in encouraging the city's developing culture of collectors, the cultivation of which would have helped further his sales as much as it would have helped to consolidate the reputations of his artists. The small amount of surviving documentation for his activities, incidentally, corroborates De' Dominici in all respects. This records him, in 1668 and 1683, selling paintings for 40 and 50 ducats apiece by the then deceased Andrea Vaccaro to a certain Angelo Petagna and to that fellow habitué of Mele's gatherings, Antonio Ciappa.[42]

GIORDANO'S BUSINESS ASSOCIATES AND THE DEVELOPMENT OF AN INTERNATIONAL MARKET FOR NEAPOLITAN ART

If Neapolitan painting was to establish itself at the more prestigious – and lucrative – upper reaches of the market, it had to be able to hold its own as a de luxe tradeable commodity with a broader reputation among distinguished collectors competing for choice works on the international stage. This was, however, not a realistic proposition for most Neapolitan painters active during the first half of the seventeenth century. In effect, a de luxe export trade in Neapolitan painting did not exist prior to the 1660s, because there were no artists of international standing.

The scene was nonetheless gradually changing as, from the 1630s onwards, a small number of leading Neapolitan artists began to make limited inroads into foreign markets. Ribera's Spanish origins and close association with the viceregal administration meant that he was always consistently represented in Spanish aristocratic collections as much as in Neapolitan ones (see pp. 53–4).[43] He and Stanzione, together with Giovanni Battista Caracciolo (albeit the latter to a slightly lesser degree), all began also to find sporadic representation in other near-contemporary collections in Rome, Florence, elsewhere in Italy and Spain.

Roomer's promotion of the 'oracle of the battles', Aniello Falcone, also played an important role in internationalizing this artist's work to an unusual degree at this early stage of its development. As early as 1647, for example, Juan Alfonso Enríquez de Cabrera, duque de Medina de Ríoseco and almirante de Castilla, included in his collection in Madrid nine battle pieces attributed to Falcone, including some with very high valuations.[44] Four years later Don Gaspar de Haro, marqués de Carpio, likewise owned two battle pieces by Falcone (the only other Neapolitan painters in his collection at this stage being Ribera and Stanzione) and in 1682, a year before he reached Naples as viceroy, he owned another two.[45] In Rome, Cardinal Flavio Chigi acquired a battle piece by Falcone in 1663, the same year in which he acquired work by Ribera.[46] Similarly in Mantua in 1661, Carlo Gonzaga II authorized Salvatore Castiglione to acquire two paintings by Falcone in Naples.[47] Battle paintings by Falcone also appear occasionally in the lists of pictures included in the exhibitions mounted in San Salvatore in Lauro, whereas very few by other Neapolitan painters are to be found here.[48] Falcone's reputation extended as far as France as well, where Louis XIV owned one of his battle paintings.[49]

Falcone's international reputation was exceptional for its day and was a source of some family pride, as is attested by the inscription on his now-lost tomb in the church of the Carmine.[50] But these limited inroads pale into insignificance when viewed against the phenomenal success of Luca Giordano from the 1660s onwards. Among his many accomplishments, Giordano distinguished himself as the first Neapolitan painter to achieve a truly international reputation, creating a benchmark in this respect for the subsequent international careers of Francesco Solimena and others. This was partly based on his extensive travels. From the late 1650s, for example, Giordano made a number of trips to Venice.[51] His campaigns of work in Florence – commencing with frescoes in the Corsini chapel in the church of the Carmine (1682–83) and culminating in his decoration of the ceiling of the Palazzo Medici-Riccardi (1682–3 and 1685) – are also well known.[52] He was equally assiduous in cultivating contacts with high-ranking Spanish collectors, a lifelong process that eventually paved the way for a decade's residence in Madrid working at the behest of Charles II (1692–1702). He also executed often extensive series of paintings for many other collectors in Genoa, England and elsewhere.[53]

While Giordano's success in the international arena undoubtedly drew on his tremendous energies and artistic

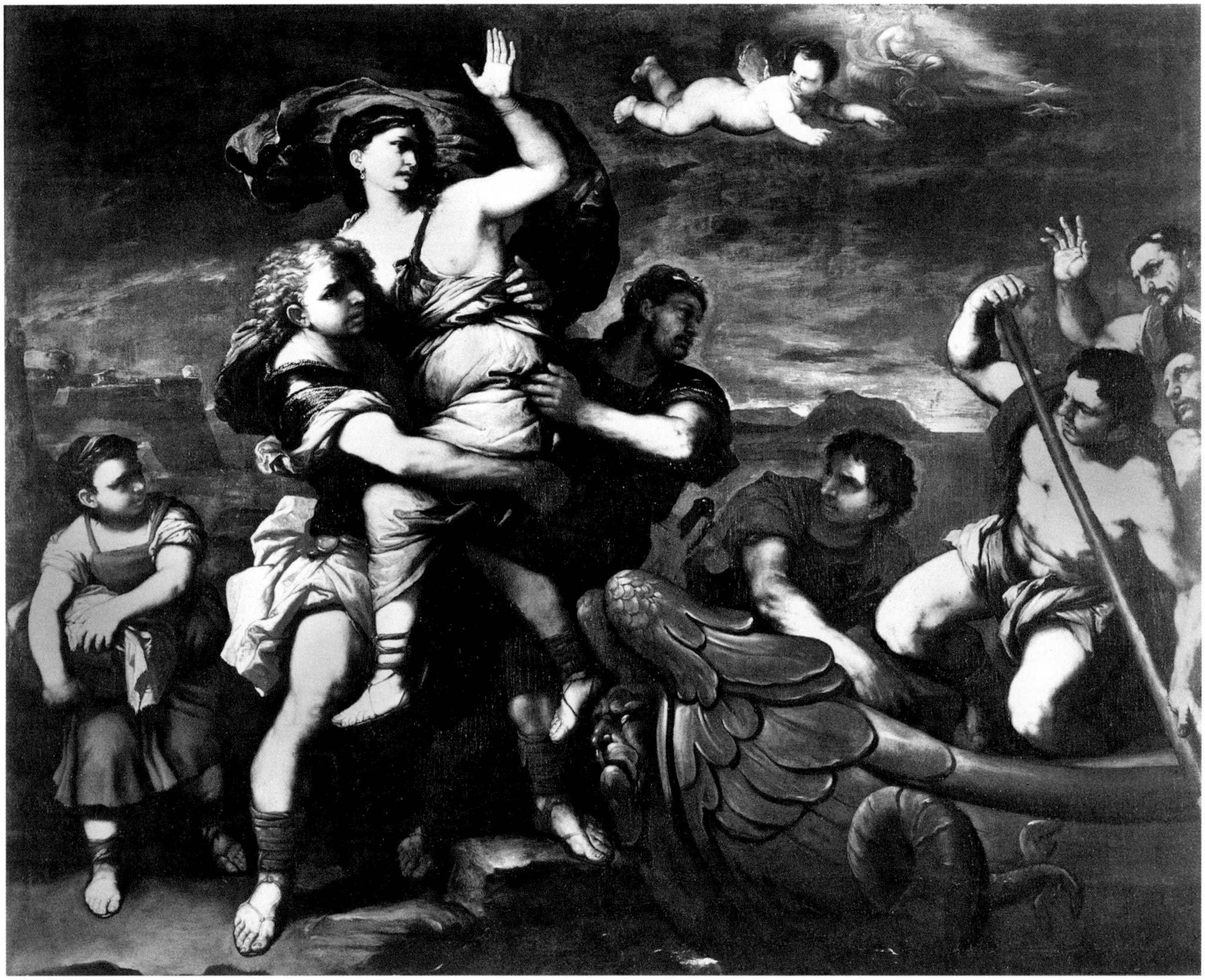

93 Luca Giordano, *Abduction of Helen*, 1655–60. Oil on canvas, 254 × 310 cm. Banco di Napoli collection, Naples

talents, it needs also to be credited to the activities of the closely linked network of merchants mentioned by De' Dominici. As noted, Roomer seems to have been the first of this group to recognize Giordano's potential to cross over internationally to a far greater extent than had previously been achieved by any Neapolitan. Roomer's association with Falcone in the 1630s and 1640s seems to have functioned, in effect, as a dry run for the more systematic breakthrough into foreign markets that he was able to facilitate through his involvement with Giordano.

When it came to business, however, Giordano was evidently too shrewd to allow himself to become monopolized by a single agent – even one as influential as Roomer. Instead, he chose to diversify his business relationships strategically, refusing to allow himself to be drawn into an exclusive contract, as Falcone had done some twenty years earlier, evidently contentedly. Giordano preferred, rather, to develop a number of long-term and increasingly complex business arrangements with a closely interlinked group of merchant entrepreneurs whose combined activities helped to spread his influence far and wide, beyond even the reach of Roomer's network of interests during the 1650s and 1660s.

Crucial to this process was a series of business associations centred upon the merchant collectors identified by De' Dominici – particularly those with a business interest in Venice, given the importance of this city as a starting point to Giordano's broadening international horizons from the early 1660s onwards. The earliest of these seems to have been a wealthy Venetian merchant resident in Naples, Guglielmo Samuele, and his nephew, Vincenzo. De' Dominici mentions Vincenzo Samuele on a number of occasions, noting that he sold Preti's paintings in Naples and Venice, and he is also mentioned, with Carlo Arici, Roomer and others, as one of Giordano's longest-standing Neapolitan patrons and earliest art dealers, particularly in terms of exports of Giordano's work to Venice.[54] He is also said to have exported many paintings by Cavallino to Venice.[55]

De' Dominici also identifies Vincenzo as one of Giordano's earliest employers. Vincenzo is said to have employed Giordano to paint in his house during the early to mid-1650s for 25 scudi per day (the word scudi being used interchangeably with ducats in this context). Giordano once neglected his work because of a game of cards and did not pick up his brush until the end of the day when he painted a 4 *palmi* (approx. 1.05 m) canvas of the *Virgin and Child* within an astonishingly brief space of time. Giordano and Samuele bartered over its price: Giordano wanted 100 scudi but was beaten down to 50, a figure still twice his daily rate.[56] The anecdote is reminiscent of De' Dominici's account of Giuseppe di Felice's early employment of Cavallino, except that the wage paid per day is much higher than Cavallino's half ducat. From the outset, it seems, Giordano never underestimated the market value of his work.

De' Dominici seems, in fact, to have confused Vincenzo Samuele with his uncle, Guglielmo, on this occasion. An inventory of 1677 and a series of bank payments dating to the 1660s and 1670s document Guglielmo's close and long-standing business relationship with Giordano. Vincenzo nonetheless seems to have also played an important role in the family business. In 1677 Guglielmo Samuele took the unusual step of passing over his son in favour of his nephew as his heir, a decision pointing to Vincenzo's important position in the family business for many years prior to that date. At that time, Guglielmo also left to his nephew a significant art collection that included a concentration of works by Giordano and his workshop.[57]

Of the 151 attributed paintings in the Samuele collection (from a total of 257), no fewer than 91 could be directly linked to Giordano. The inventory lists 26 originals by Giordano, 32 copies after Giordano, 9 copies after Giordano retouched by the master, 6 by 'un giovano del Giordano' and 18 by either Carlo or Francesco della Torre, important individuals involved in the trade in Giordano's work (see pp. 136–8).[58] The careful distinctions between attributions to Giordano and his workshop, which reveal a very close knowledge of its working procedures, as well as the sheer number of paintings by and after Giordano, further reinforce the veracity of De' Dominici's information concerning the Samuele family's professional association with the artist during the 1650s to 1670s.

Eduardo Nappi's research into the archives of the banks of Naples has added to this a partial record of Guglielmo Samuele's financial activities from 1669 to 1672. Limited though this information is, it nonetheless sheds further light on the activities of a tightly interconnected network of business associates all engaged in multiple levels of dealings with Giordano and his workshop over the course of many years.

The payments show Guglielmo, in the first instance, to have commissioned work from Giordano regularly and directly. In 1670, for example, he paid Giordano the considerable sum of 500 ducats for unspecified work, along with a further 200 ducats in July 1672.[59] He also acted in partnership with one or more other agents working in league to export Giordano's work to Venice and other centres. In 1669, for example, he paid Giordano 150 ducats for a large painting of the *Abduction of Helen*, said to have been commissioned on behalf of Simon Giogali in Venice, and which would have been similar to Giordano's extant work of this subject (fig. 93).

From this and the other evidence cited below, it is clear that Giogali was a dealer rather than a financially disinterested collector.[60] Guglielmo and Giogali must, therefore, have been entering here into a partnership to place Giordano's works with leading collectors in Venice and elsewhere. This partnership must have lasted many years, since in 1672 Guglielmo paid Giordano for more paintings said to have been ordered on Giogali's behalf. The sums involved in these transactions point to a considerable growth in the amounts of money that Giordano's increasingly prestigious – and also prolific – output was able to command from the later 1660s onwards. Guglielmo paid Giordano on this occasion 790 ducats to make up a total amount received thus far of the substantial sum of 1,290 ducats.[61]

Guglielmo also turned on occasion to other individuals to source work from Giordano. In particular, he commissioned and acquired completed works by Giordano from Carlo della Torre, an important artist/merchant associate of Giordano presently to be discussed. In 1670, for example, he paid Carlo della Torre 600 ducats for various paintings.[62] Guglielmo's nephew Vincenzo would continue this association. On 1 April 1684 Vincenzo would ultimately be required to call in a debt of no fewer than 2,400 ducats said to be owed to him by Carlo della Torre, a point further attesting to the intricate web of deals involving Giordano and his associates, some of which stretched over many decades.

The bank payments published by Nappi finally record Guglielmo entering into complex agreements with Giordano involving lucrative deals that had little – if anything – to do with art. In 1671, for example, he paid Giordano 900 ducats for the profits accruing from the sale of 1,600 *salme* of oil. A *salma* is approximately equivalent to 160 litres of oil, so 1,600 *salme* convert to the massive amount of 250,000 litres, or 215 tonnes of oil: a major business investment then, of considerable scope and complexity that had been brokered, once again, via the agency of Carlo della Torre.[63]

Giordano and Guglielmo reconvened the following week in order to enter into a yet more substantive business agreement. On this occasion Giordano lent Guglielmo the enormous sum of 7,000 ducats – interest-free for a week and then to be set at an annual rate of 5 per cent. Giordano would not, one can only assume, have lent such a substantial investment of funds lightly. This amount was equivalent to the entire legacy set aside at the height of his career for his youngest daughter's dowry. Clearly, therefore, these two individuals were heavily invested in each other's business – Guglielmo in the creative capital presented by Giordano's output, and Giordano in Guglielmo's ability to take care of his business interests involving often very complex transactions centred on the sale of his work in Venice and beyond.

In a way, though, the most interesting and yet at the same time most shadowy figure, in this complex chain of interdependent agents was the merchant/artist Carlo della Torre. Della Torre appears in the *Vite* as one of the leading connoisseurs of the day, working in tandem with the merchant Antonio Ciappa, together with the canon and author Carlo Celano, to advise Giordano on the iconography of his paintings.[64] The true nature of Della Torre's relationship with Giordano is nonetheless much more complex than this: in actuality, he was a long-term business partner of Giordano, both in a general sense as well as in the trade in his work more specifically.

Della Torre first appears in the documents, in fact, in the capacity of a specialist apprentice to Giordano. In 1659 Giordano undertook to teach him how to paint landscapes on glass for 150 ducats, an amount that Carlo was required to settle with Giordano within six months of signing the agreement.[65] This unusual form of contract bore little relationship to the standard terms of a traditional apprenticeship. An apprentice was normally contracted to a master by his parents, the master agreeing to pay the apprentice's food and lodging in return for his labour. This agreement, on the other hand, involved an emancipated adult paying the master to teach him a very particular technique – one that was challenging both in terms of its materials and techniques as well as in artistic terms, since the artist was required to paint on the back of the glass in reverse. No mere apprentice, then, Della Torre had, rather, as Gennaro Borrelli has emphasized, sought Giordano's tutelage on this occasion in order to advance his activities as 'his art dealer and financial adviser on loans and investments'.[66]

The technique of painting on glass – and its variants in painted lead crystal and mirrors – was then little practised in Naples. It would soon become very fashionable, nonetheless, and Carlo della Torre evidently saw an opening in this respect that would grant him an edge over his competitors in what was at that stage an emerging market. He accordingly paid Giordano not only to teach him a specialized technique, but also for the right, in effect, to trade on this specialization once he acquired the inner knowledge of its workings. Della Torre does appear to have practised this skill from time to time. In the 1680s no less a collector than Giuseppe Valletta owned some paintings of fruit on crystal that were said to be 'copie delli quatri granni originali del signor Carlo della Torre', although it is not clear from the wording whether the description refers to his owning copies after originals by Della Torre or copies after originals in Della Torre's possession.[67] Della Torre's brother and sometime business partner, Francesco, on the other hand, did practise as a specialist in this field and seems to have produced much of the work on glass subsequently sold by Della Torre. De' Dominici specifically mentions him as a pupil of Giordano working in this area, and his paintings of this kind are mentioned in a few Neapolitan inventories from the end of the seventeenth century.[68]

Carlo della Torre, on the other hand, did not use his skill primarily for the purpose of producing work by his own hand. Rather, he drew on it in order to advance his early involvement in the specialized trade of the *scrittoriaro*, among other activities. The *scrittoriari* were the purveyors of new and used objects of decorative art and furnishings with a particular emphasis on the elaborate *stipo* or cabinet desks that were a required feature of the gallery arrangements of contemporary collections and which are depicted in Michele Regolia's painting of a Neapolitan palace interior (see fig. 65).[69]

The *stipo* or *scrittoriaro* in its more evolved forms constituted an elaborate and intricate construction, often including extensive detailing of ebony, tortoiseshell, semi-precious stones and gilding.[70] Della Torre was evidently concerned to exploit the market for the new sub-category with inset paintings on glass just then being developed by Giordano and his workshop.[71] In 1666 Giordano himself demonstrated his interest in this area by acquiring two desks from Della Torre for 578 ducats. These are described in the documents as featuring tortoiseshell and gilding and a series of 'christalli con pitture di Paesi mano di Georgicco'.[72] At just under 300 ducats each they were equivalent in price to one or two of the major gallery paintings by Giordano or his upper-ranked colleagues and were thus costly and elaborate luxury items. It was probably for this reason that Della Torre evidently found it useful to introduce a price differential into his sales by offering clients the option of purchasing individual panels. Still quite expensive, but more affordable than the complete desks, these single paintings on glass retailed for around 40–50 ducats each.[73]

For the most part, though, Carlo della Torre specialized in the quicker turnover and more internationally oriented business growth opportunities involved in the lucrative trade in Giordano's paintings on canvas. Like Guglielmo and Vincenzo Samuele, he appears to have acted in a number of different capacities in this respect, varying his arrangements according to the often intricately interconnected nature of the deal being brokered. On occasion, he sold collectors and other merchant dealers already completed works by Giordano and his workshop. So, for example, in 1664 a collector paid him 100 ducats for a painting of the *Nativity* by Giordano measuring approximately 316 × 316 centimetres.[74]

Della Torre also sold work to other merchant dealers who would then have resold the work – no doubt at a profit – at a subsequent date. It was in this capacity that the early employer of Aniello Falcone, Nicola di Martino, paid Della Torre the substantial sum of 300 ducats in 1677 for eleven 'copies of Luca Giordano of various measurements and Saints'.[75] The paintings involved in this sale were for the most part very large. Four measured around 316 centimetres in width, while a further four measured 369 centimetres, and two are simply described as 'small'. As part of the deal, Della Torre agreed to receive from his colleague 100 ducats of the price in kind in the form of a painting. The author of this painting – a very large canvas of *Posillipo* measuring approximately 422 centimetres in width – is not indicated, but it was probably Didier Barra or one of the other early specialists in coastal view paintings. The document thus attests to the diversification of Della Torre's business interests during this period as not only a business agent and trader in luxury furnishings but also a dealer in both primary and secondary market paintings.

Yet more complex, nonetheless, were the numerous instances in which Della Torre served as a commissioning agent working in partnership with other merchants based in Naples and abroad. His dealings with Simon Giogali in Venice and with Guglielmo and Vincenzo Samuele in Naples have already been mentioned in this respect. Carlo Arici, the Lombard merchant resident in Naples, also paid Della Torre from time to time to assist him in commissioning work from Giordano. Thus in 1670 he paid Giordano 70 ducats for two paintings said to have been sold to him through the agency of Della Torre.[76] Finally, Della Torre also acted on occasion as the Neapolitan agent for the Venetian dealer and collector Simon Giogali. Besides Guglielmo Samuele's payment of 1669 to Della Torre for his assistance in commissioning work from Giordano, Giordano is also documented receiving 700 ducats in 1667, said to be for the price of three paintings commissioned by Giogali that were to be delivered to Carlo della Torre.[77]

Cash flow was clearly a constant source of concern when dealing with the multiple and increasingly expensive transactions being undertaken simultaneously by Della Torre and his colleagues. It is readily understandable, therefore, why Della Torre would have preferred to put to good use the money paid to him by Nicola di Martino in 1677 for the workshop paintings of Giordano. No sooner had he received this amount, in fact, than he transferred it into a down payment for another projected commission for two large still-life paintings measuring 12 *palmi* (approx. 316 cm) by Giuseppe Recco, with the requirement that Recco should deliver the works within three months.[78] Della Torre was presumably acting in this instance either as an agent for an already earmarked collector or as a commissioning dealer, intending to sell the paintings at a profit to another collector at a later date.

As Della Torre's multiple transactions with Giordano and his merchant colleagues increased, so too did the increasingly burdensome financial commitments that he was required to keep under control. Between May 1677 and May 1678 alone, Della Torre paid out to Giordano no fewer than 3,000 ducats for unspecified work.[79] All these bills had to be settled sooner or later, and it seems that things ultimately got the better of Della Torre in this respect.

In December 1684 Giordano alluded to the complex and often difficult nature of recouping investments within this increasingly international trade when he elected to make a notarized declaration regarding a debt of 1,500 florins involving Della Torre's dealings with Giogali (the florin being equivalent to just under one ducat, 1,500 florins thus being approximately equivalent to 1,362 ducats). In the document in question, Giordano elected to go on record to state that Carlo della Torre had for some years been selling his work to the Venetian merchant Simon Giogali.[80] Giordano had heard that six of his paintings had been sold on to the elector of Bavaria for the princely sum of 3,000 florins (approximately equivalent to 2,725 ducats, or 454 ducats per painting, making them among the most expensive gallery paintings of the day – for which see Table 2).[81] The payment was to be half in cash and half in kind, in the form of paint pigments. Giordano had been further informed that the 1,500 florins portion of the payment in kind had been transferred as a surety of debt under his own name. He accordingly wished formally to correct this error by declaring that he laid no claim to this amount – and thus also to make it clear that he wished to exempt himself from any future liability for the sum. Instead, Giordano attested, the debt of 1,500 florins should be paid out entirely to Giogali, who, the document also notes, had contracted an agent in Munich to recoup his lost fees.

Della Torre was ultimately unable to handle this complex and long-term accrual of financial obligation. In April 1684 his colleague Vincenzo Samuele called in a long-standing debt that he could no longer wait to receive.[82] In this instance Samuele was operating in partnership with another art dealing merchant resident in Venice – Giovanni Battista Bertocchi.[83] Samuele and Bertocchi had paid out to Della Torre at some time in the past no fewer than 2,400 ducats, but they were now no longer confident of his ability to honour the debt. Accordingly, they elected to settle the amount by taking from Della Torre eight major paintings by Giordano produced in collaboration with the leading still-life specialists of the day. These had been freshly painted in advance of their planned inclusion in the Festa dei Quattro Altari to be held on 25 May that year under the aegis of the viceroy, the marqués del Carpio. As will be discussed, Della Torre had in this instance evidently committed himself to financing this lavish exhibition project in advance of the paintings' completion (see pp. 244–6).

As it transpired, however, Della Torre should not have been confident of his ability to hold onto his investment long enough to realize a return. This was to be achieved instead by Samuele and Bertocchi. Early the following year, the evidently foreign collector or investor – it is often impossible to be certain in these instances – 'Sig. Fausto Wondenheuvel' ordered an appraisal of ten paintings by Giordano in Samuele's and Bertocchi's possession. Wondenheuvel must have ordered the valuation in order to verify the fairness of the extremely high asking price of 2,850 ducats, or 285 ducats per painting.[84] Six of the canvases are described as being by Giordano with still-life elements provided by Brueghel, Recco and Ruoppolo, a reference that therefore makes it clear that these were the bulk of the eight paintings that had been secured from Della Torre the previous year.

CONCLUSION: THE MERCHANT AS PATRON

A significant jump is clearly detectable in the amounts of money involved in the transactions here discussed: the shift from the 50 ducats paid in 1623 to Domenico d'Aquino for 100 small paintings produced on copper for export, to the 300 ducats paid in 1631 by Paolo Finoglio and his partner for thirty-four paintings belonging to the estate of a recently deceased dealer. Now, in the 1670s and 1680s payments of up to ten times as much appear: 2,000 or even 3,000 ducats, sums that would have appeared astronomical from the point of view of all but the most wealthy individuals of the day.

The nature of the transactions entered into by Giordano and the merchants was also far more logistically complex and involved than the simple act of using some start-up capital to purchase desirable works from among the local workshops and then to bring these back for resale at a central point, as in the previously discussed partnership arrangements between Giacomo Recco and Antonio Cimino in 1630. Now, instead, there was found in Naples a true luxury market for art based on a concomitant reach outwards to new international markets for Neapolitan painting.

The merchants responsible for this transformation of the Neapolitan market did more than just help to change the way art was marketed and sold. They also played an active role in changing the image and activities of the art dealer as a professional class. In the process, they created a new form of Neapolitan dealer, the 'onorato mercante di quadri', as De' Dominici expressed it. Their achievement along these lines was, in effect, to elevate the associations of dealing away from the economically pragmatic, second-hand perspective of the *rivenditori* in their workshops to a new and more exclusive image of the art dealer as a knowledgeable and cultivated friend and champion of artists of talent – to take dealing out of the workshop and to conduct it instead in the palace.

It was natural also, as part of this process, that many of these merchants would also undergo transitions in their own wealth and social status so as to become significant patrons and collectors in their own right. As will be seen, besides dealing in Giordano's and Preti's paintings, Gaspar Roomer and the Vandeneynden also commissioned some of these two artists' most significant gallery paintings: indeed, Roomer would become the single most important collector of his generation. This made the leading merchants in many respects indistinguishable from the more traditionally defined collectors and patrons of the day. This was particularly true of the interrelations between merchants and those collectors coming from the emerging professional classes – such as Giuseppe Valletta.

The art merchants thus found it in their own interests increasingly to integrate their marketing initiatives with the more traditional status-creating activities of poets, playwrights, academicians and other 'uomini scienziati', as De' Dominici put it. As will be seen, the increasingly elaborate self-promotional strategies devised by Giordano and his merchant backers in the 1660s and beyond worked simultaneously on a number of levels. They operated as de luxe sales opportunities to be sure, but they were at the same time also powerful expressions of patronal magnificence. This mixing together of commercial and connoisseurial concerns, in turn, would play an important role in binding together the varying agents in the seventeenth-century Neapolitan art world – artists, dealers, patrons, poets, and so on – so as to create a mutually self-supporting culture of refined artistic appreciation. This would go a long way to stimulating the development of Neapolitan collecting and patronage more generally – both private and public – a process that will be examined in the next chapter.

Overleaf Luca Giordano and Giuseppe Recco, *Riches of the Sea with Neptune and Two Sea Nymphs*, *circa* 1683–4 (detail of fig. 79)

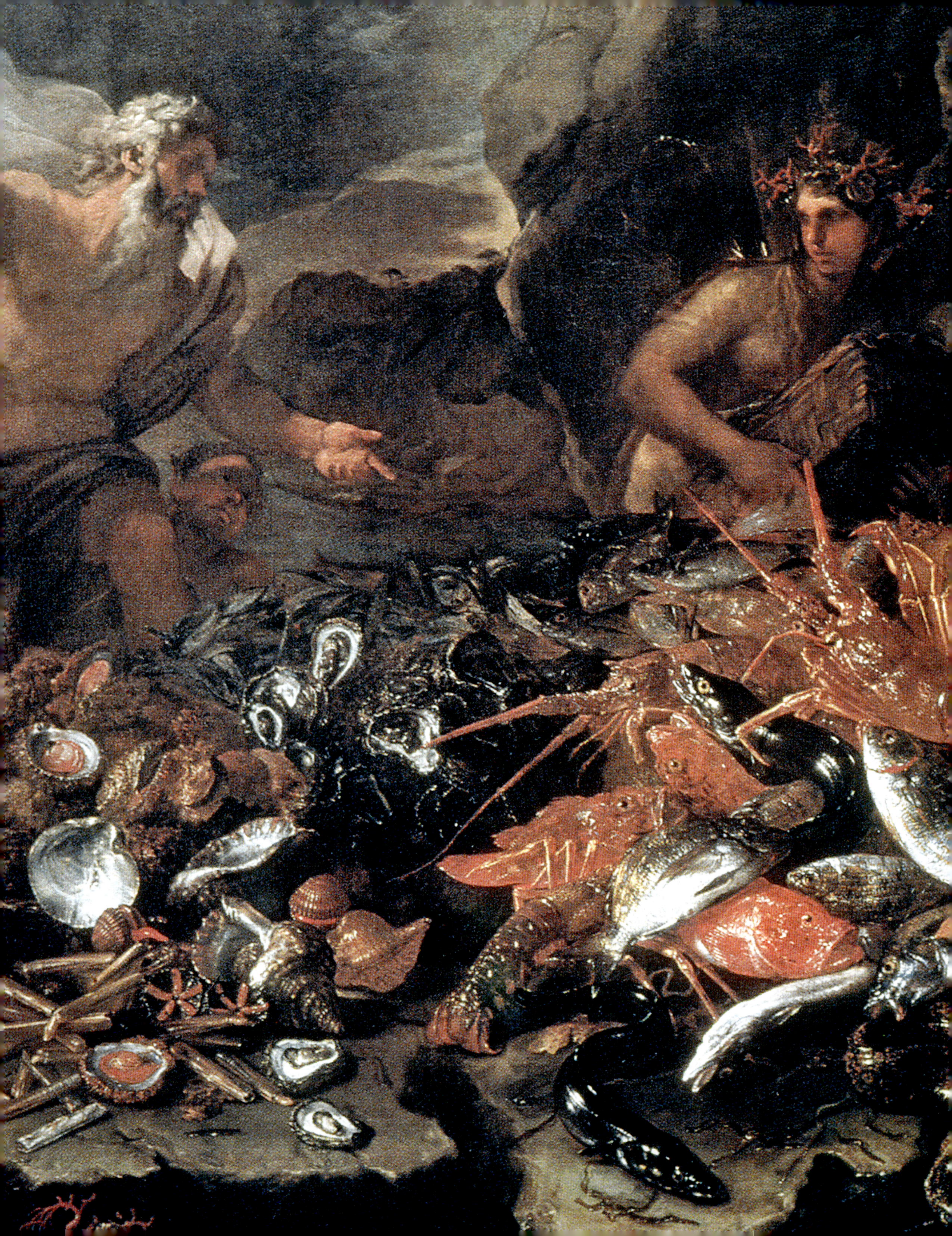

PART III

THE IMPACT OF EXHIBITIONS

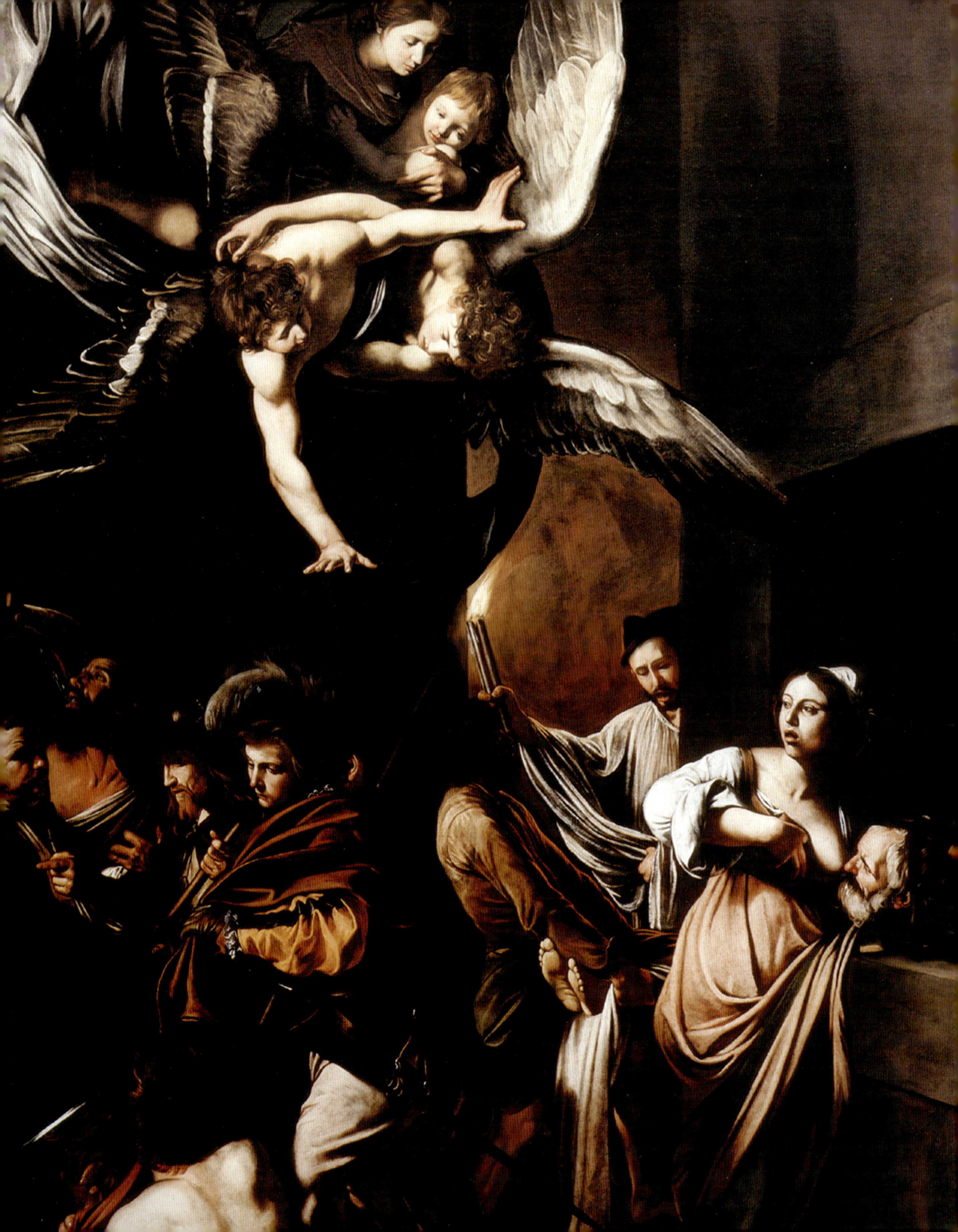

8

Public Commissions

It is impossible today to appreciate the seismic impact exerted on the local scene by Caravaggio's paintings for the church of Sant'Anna dei Lombardi, since they now figure among the lost treasures of Naples.[1] Here, during his second visit to the city in 1609–10, Caravaggio executed three chapel paintings for a certain merchant from Bergamo resident in Naples by the name of Alfonso Fenaroli. This was the only instance outside Rome whereby Caravaggio completed work on an entire chapel – an altarpiece and two laterals – so their cumulative effect must have been comparable to that evident today at the Contarelli chapel in San Luigi dei Francesi, Rome. The early sources convey a palpable sense of marvel tinged with shock in the presence of these late works. Scaramuccia emphasizes the radical iconography of the main altarpiece: the *Resurrection of Christ*, noting that it showed Christ 'non come d'ordinario far si suole, agile e trionfante per l'aria, ma, con quella sua fierissima maniera di colore, con un piede dentro e l'altro fuori del sepolcro posando in terra' (not as He usually appears, agile and triumphant in the air, but rather, in keeping with the artist's tempestuous manner of painting, with one foot in and the other outside of the tomb touching the ground).[2] For De' Dominici this constituted '[un'] idea bassa ed indecente al rappresentato' (a base and indecent representation), since it seemed as if Christ were 'quasi con ispavento esce dal suo sepolcro' (emerging from the tomb almost as if in fear).[3]

Celano's compendious late seventeenth-century survey of Neapolitan art and culture is more even-handed, expressing admiration for the way Christ seemed to 'esca dal quadro' (step out of the painting). Yet even he was moved to qualify this with the observation that 'alcuni intendenti dell'arte dicono che sia mancante nel costume, perché le manca una gloriosa maestà' (some of those knowledgeable in art are of the opinion that this was a disrespectful approach to adopt since He seems to lack an appropriate appearance of glorious majesty).[4] Caravaggio's shrouded and anguished, earthbound Christ must, therefore, have presented itself as a powerful, yet puzzling artistic model standing in stark contrast to the bland conventionality of other renditions of the scene – most notably perhaps Vasari's famous altarpiece of 1545 on prominent display in the adjacent monastery of Santa Maria di Monteoliveto (fig. 94).[5]

Also on view in the Fenaroli chapel was Caravaggio's *Stigmatization of St Francis*, echoes of which are probably discernible in a painting of the same subject by Carlo Sellitto (fig. 95).[6] Caravaggio's second lateral painting depicting *St John the Baptist* must have exerted a particularly powerful pull on local painters, judging by the scores of early Neapolitan Caravaggesque paintings of this subject by Caracciolo, Stanzione, Finoglio, Ribera and others.[7] Its role as a model for the dissemination of Caravaggio's single-figure compositions of austere saints cast out from the world in

Facing page Caravaggio, *Seven Works of Mercy*, 1606–7 (detail of fig. 97)

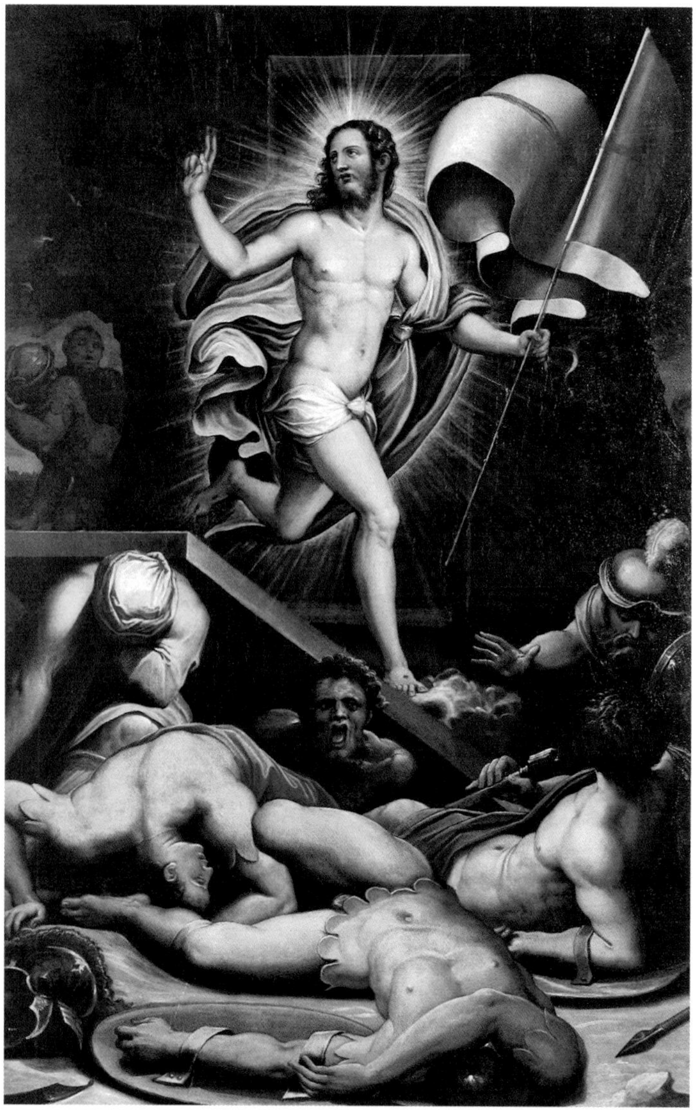

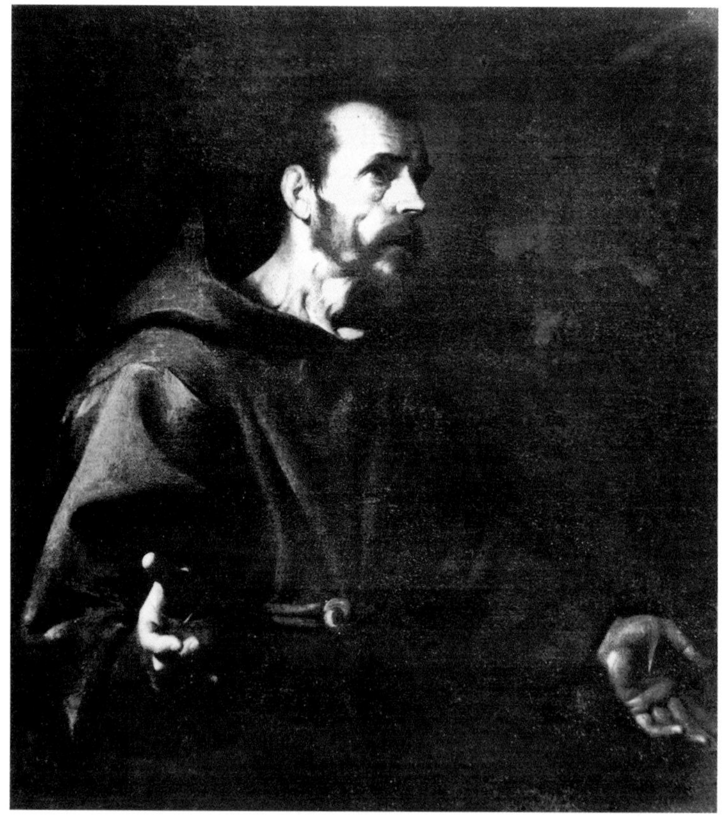

Left 94 Giorgio Vasari and Raffaellino del Colle, *Resurrection*, 1545. Oil on panel, 117 × 73 cm. Museo e Gallerie Nazionali di Capodimonte, Naples, on deposit from the Chiesa di Monteoliveto, Naples

Above 95 Carlo Sellitto, *Stigmatization of Saint Francis*, *circa* 1618. Oil on canvas, 152.5 × 125 cm. Private collection, England

eremitical isolation must have been particularly important given the rarity of his private gallery paintings of this type.

It is known that Caravaggio took out of Naples two other paintings of *St John the Baptist* that he had produced during this last period. These were loaded onto the felucca bound for Rome that he boarded immediately before his death in Port'Ercole on 18 July 1610. One of these paintings subsequently made its way to the collection of Scipione Borghese in Rome and so to the Galleria Borghese, where it remains today. The other was wrested from Borghese's ownership – or so it seems – by the viceroy, the conde de Lemos, who took it with him back to Spain.[8] The importance of the publicly commissioned works, by contrast – placed together on continuous display in a prominent Neapolitan church in the centre of the artists' quarter – cannot be underestimated.

Visitors to Sant'Anna dei Lombardi were also able to study Caravaggio's pictures in relation to other important examples of early Neapolitan painting influenced by his work. Of particular significance were an altarpiece and two scenes from the *Life of St Peter* by Carlo Sellitto that had been begun a full year prior to Caravaggio's second stay in the city in 1609–10, thus making them some of the very earliest appearances of the new style in a public Neapolitan context.[9] A few years later – in 1618 – Filippo Vitale was also paid the substantial sum of 200 ducats for an altarpiece of the *Virgin and Child with St Carlo Borromeo and Franciscan Friars* in another of the side chapels of this church.[10] The

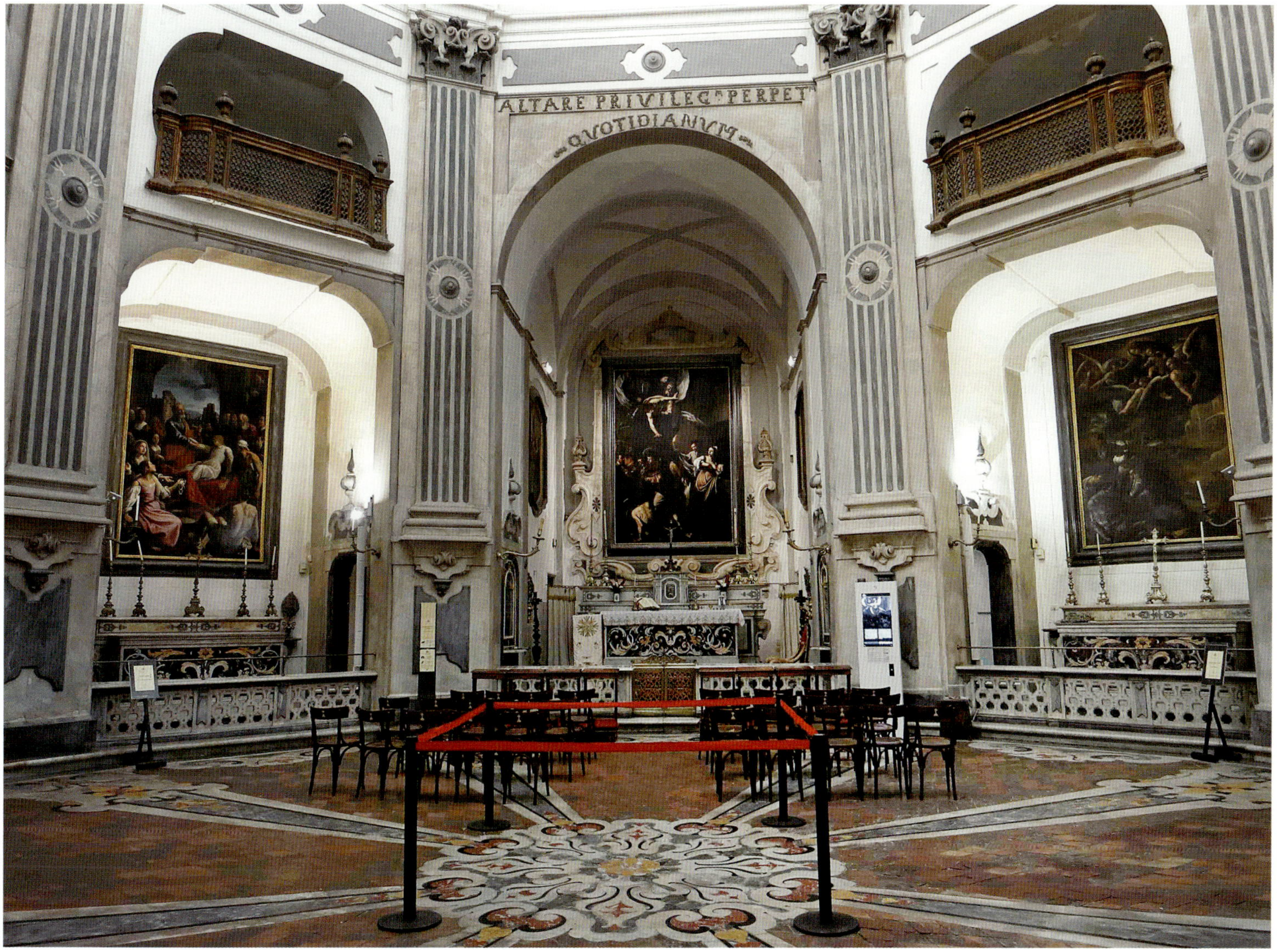

96 Interior view, Chiesa del Pio Monte della Misericordia, Naples

church also housed the altarpiece donated in 1639 by Lanfranco to this – the church of the Lombard nation – after its rejection by the Carthusians of the Certosa di San Martino (see pp. 15, 17). Today all these works have been dispersed or destroyed, and the paintings by Caravaggio were lost as a result of an earthquake in 1805.[11] Accordingly, their influence can be glimpsed only through their reverberations in the words of early commentators and in the compositions of local painters.[12]

A more tangible impression of the dramatic impact exerted by Caravaggio's paintings in a public exhibition context can be gauged in the case of the *Seven Works of Mercy* painted for the church of the Pio Monte della Misericordia. This commission had been the main focus of Caravaggio's first Neapolitan visit in 1606 (fig. 97). This church and its internal decorations have been painstakingly restored, although the sense that this documents the original setting for the *Seven Works of Mercy* is somewhat misleading, since the church that is seen today is, in fact, a second edifice built by Francesco Antonio Pichiatti from 1658 onwards (fig. 96). Even so, the later seventeenth-century ambience that it does project communicates vividly the shockwaves sent out by Caravaggio's high altarpiece in relation to a series of subsidiary altarpieces commissioned in the years following its installation as the centrepiece to the new church. Immediately to the right of the *Seven Works of Mercy* is Giovan Vincenzo Forli's *Good Samaritan*. Completed within a few months of Caravaggio's work,

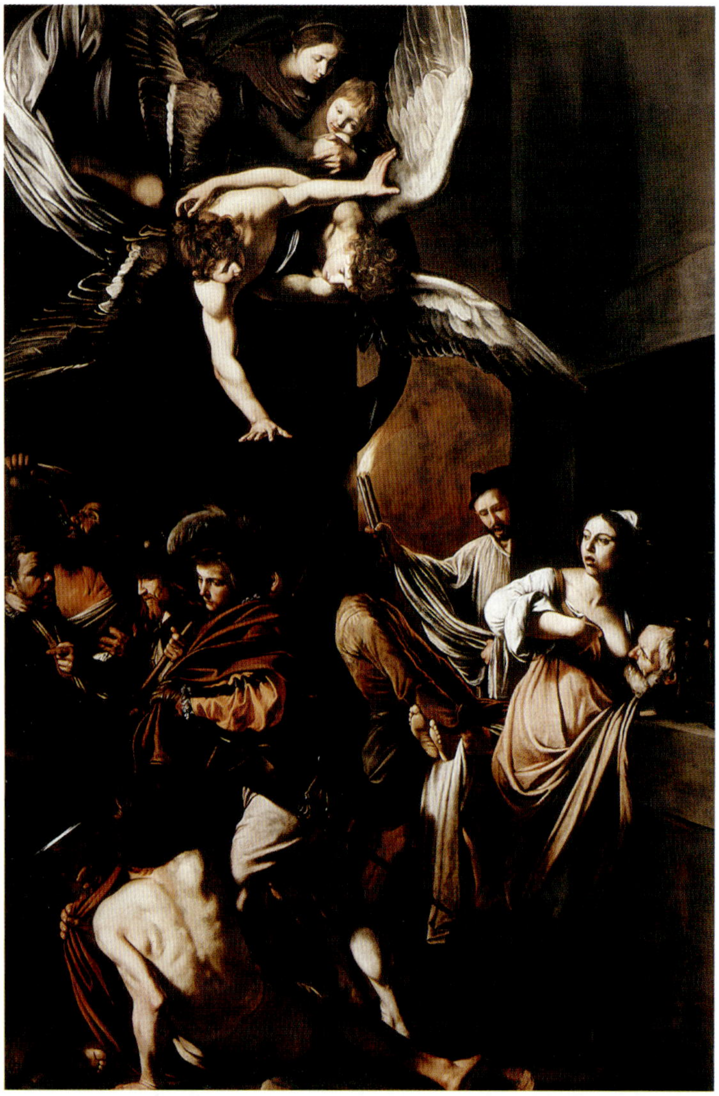

97 Caravaggio, *Seven Works of Mercy*, 1606–7. Oil on canvas, 390 × 260 cm. Chiesa del Pio Monte della Misericordia, Naples

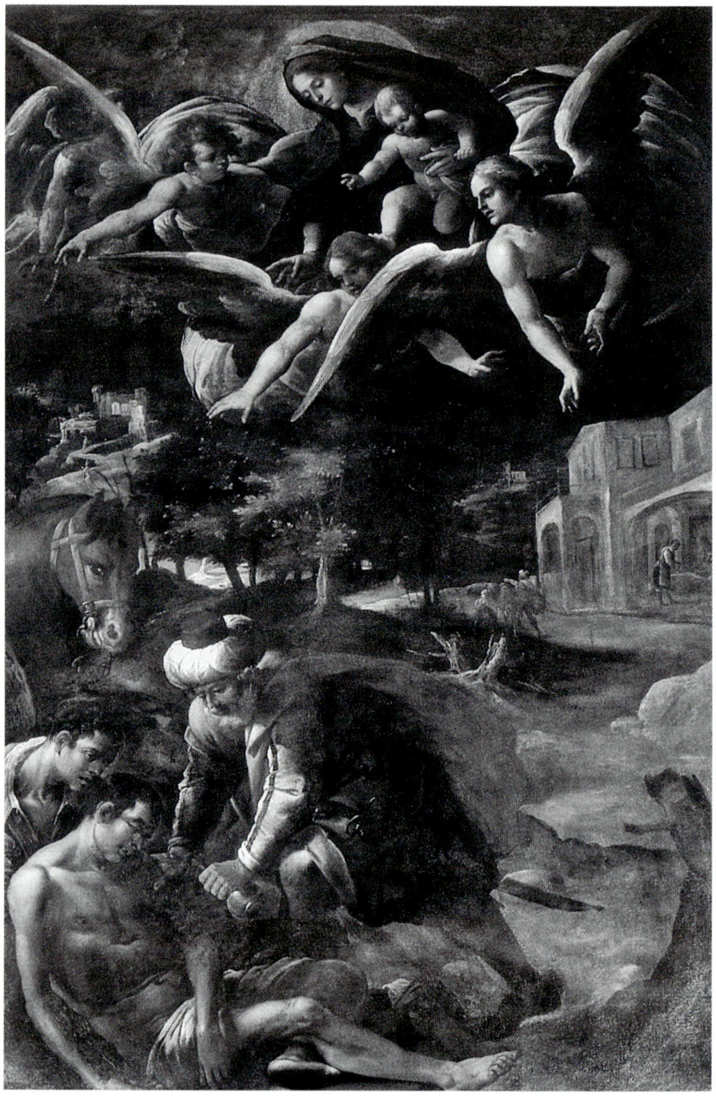

98 Giovan Vincenzo Forli, *The Good Samaritan*, 1608. Oil on canvas, 306 × 205 cm. Chiesa del Pio Monte della Misericordia, Naples

the altarpiece remains firmly rooted within Forli's references in late Mannerist Romano-Neapolitan painting and accordingly bears only superficial similarities to Caravaggio's canvas (fig. 98).

Flanking the other side of Caravaggio's altarpiece, Fabrizio Santafede's *The Raising of Tabitha* of 1611 demonstrates a greater attentiveness to Caravaggio's model – most notably in the motif of the beggar, which has been lifted directly from the comparable figure in the left foreground of Caravaggio's painting (fig. 99). This figure remains nonetheless at odds with the rest of the composition, which builds, in other respects, on the bedrock of Santafede's background in the late sixteenth-century Florentine Reform style. In fact, it would be four more years – until Caracciolo's *Liberation of St Peter* of 1615 (fig. 100) – positioned diagonally across from the *Seven Works of Mercy* – before one could witness the work of a younger artist capable of absorbing the lessons of Caravaggio and projecting them into a new, vernacular style: the birth of a new Neapolitan Caravaggesque naturalism, in fact.

At the other end of the spectrum – from the time, that is, of the opening of the new church in the late 1660s – these, at times, faltering early responses to Caravaggio can be compared with Luca Giordano's much more assured *Entombment*

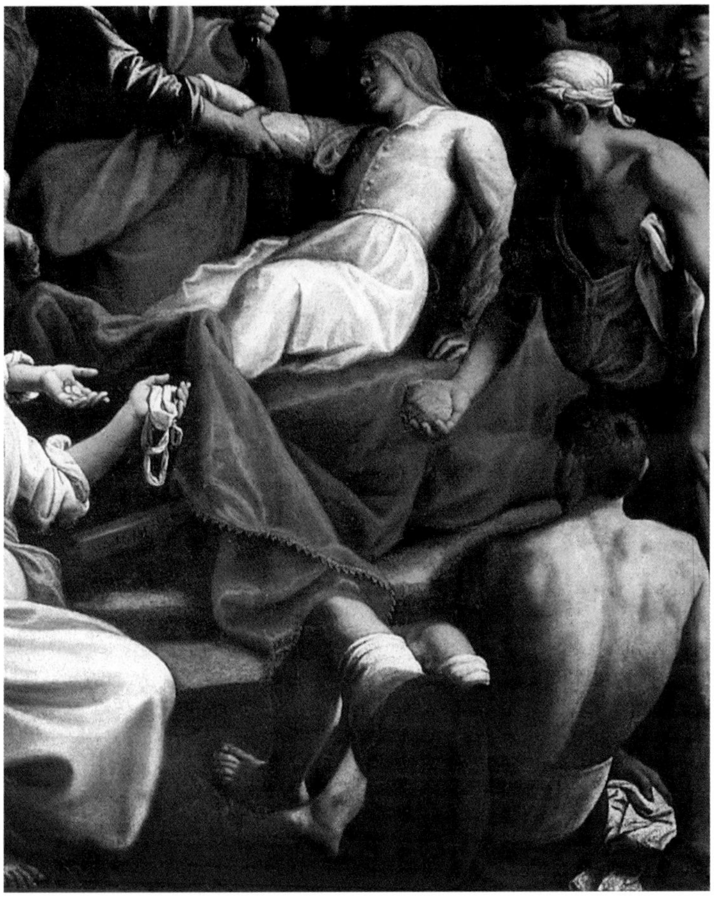

99 Fabrizio Santafede, *The Raising of Tabitha*, 1611. Oil on canvas, 306 × 205 cm. Chiesa del Pio Monte della Misericordia, Naples (detail)

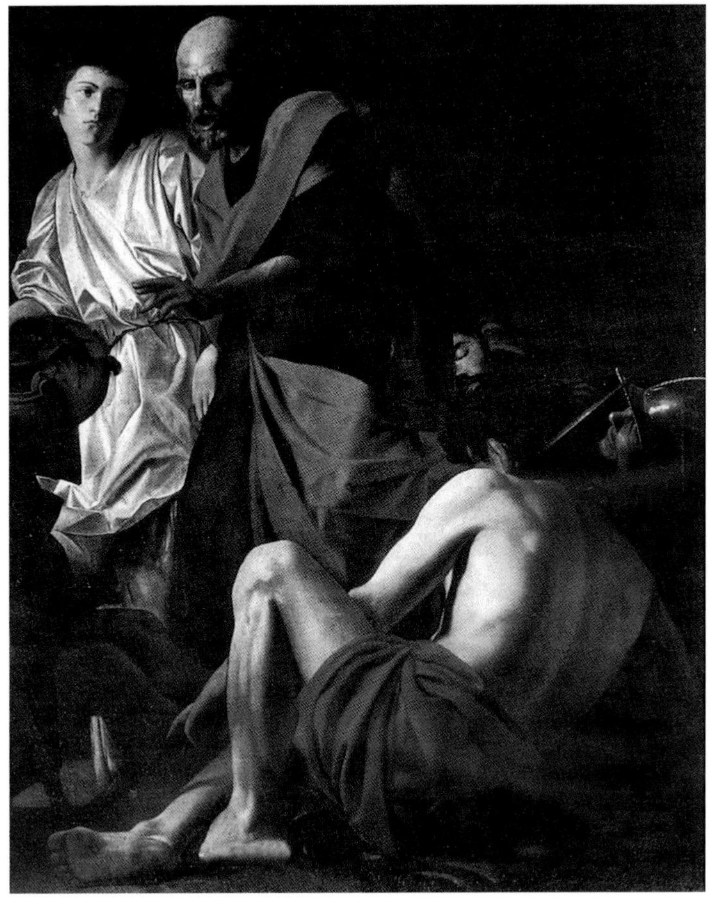

100 Giovanni Battista Caracciolo, *Liberation of St Peter*, 1615. Oil on canvas, 310 × 207 cm. Chiesa del Pio Monte della Misericordia, Naples (detail)

of 1671 (fig. 101). This altarpiece – which was installed two altars along from Caravaggio's – was commissioned as a replacement for an earlier painting of the same subject that had been sent from Rome by Giovanni Baglione during the period of Caravaggio's initial commission. *The Entombment* exudes Giordano's suave blend of the bedrock of Neapolitan Caravaggism combined with neo-Venetian style, the high Baroque of Pietro da Cortona and much more besides. It speaks eloquently, therefore, of the great distance travelled by Neapolitan Caravaggism in the intervening decades between Caravaggio's arrival in Naples and Giordano's rise to international fame following the plague of 1656.

The display settings of Sant'Anna dei Lombardi and the Pio Monte della Misericordia testify to the instantaneous impact arising from the installation of a leading artist's work in a public religious commission. Hundreds of years prior to the establishment of a public museum culture in Naples, these and other examples of significant works by Neapolitan and foreign painters placed on continuous display in public religious settings functioned as fundamental points of reference for the spread of knowledge about current trends in painting throughout the city and beyond. During a time in which the notion of travelling to Rome or elsewhere to update one's professional training was beyond all but a few artists, these public display contexts provided precious opportunities to study the work of painters from other Italian centres and beyond.

Neapolitan churches accordingly provided local artists and collectors with examples of significant works to study by Raphael and Titian (Raphael's *Madonna of the Fish* and Titian's *Annunciation*, both in San Domenico Maggiore), together with more recent work by Guido Reni (at the Quadreria dei Girolamini and the Certosa di San Martino), Simon Vouet (at the Certosa di San Martino and the church of the Arciconfraternita di Sant'Angelo a Segno) and Pietro da Cortona (in the Chiesa dei Girolamini), as well as, of course,

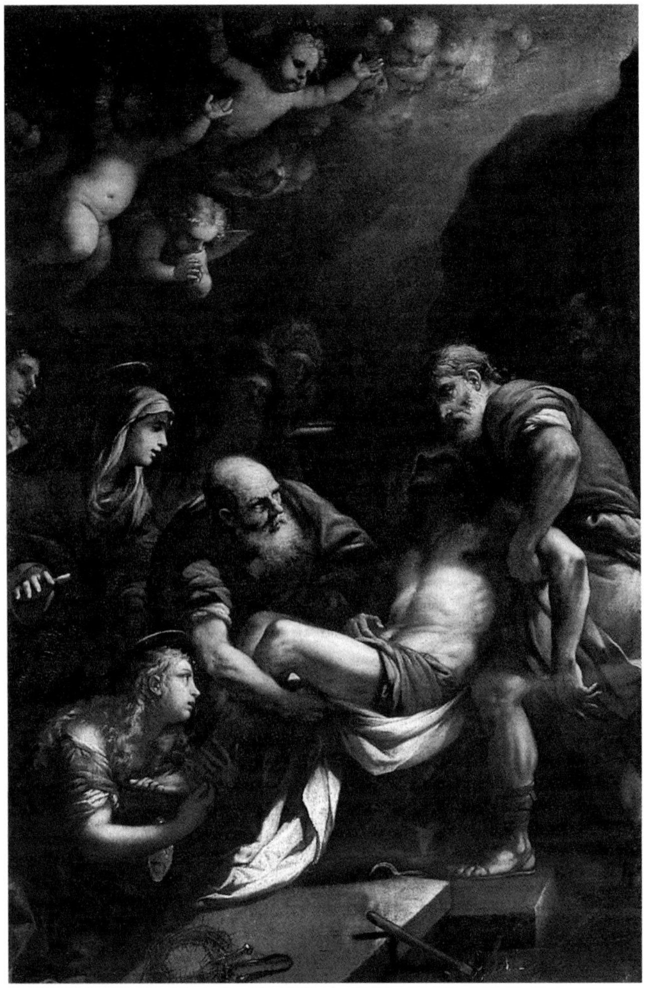

101 Luca Giordano, *Entombment*, 1671. Oil on canvas, 310 × 210 cm. Chiesa del Pio Monte della Misericordia, Naples

more extensive displays of paintings by those foreign artists who had resided in Naples for more or less extended periods, including the Cavalier d'Arpino, Domenichino, Artemisia Gentileschi, Charles Mellin, Lanfranco and Preti.

Neapolitan public commissions could thus rapidly transmit to a wide public messages of taste, power, authority and prestige emanating from patron to patron, as well as among artists themselves. As Giordano is said to have observed in the context of the unveiling in 1659 of Mattia Preti's monumental series of canvases for the ceiling of the nave and transept of San Pietro a Maiella (see figs 17–18), a prominent public commission could act as an effective proclamation of its patron's religious agenda while at the same time also becoming a 'school of studious youth'.[13] Giordano certainly knew what he was talking about since he was himself a master in the art of exploiting the self-promotional opportunities provided by public exhibitions of paintings, as patrons and painters alike turned commissions into competitive arenas, playing off one talent against another – Ribera against Stanzione at the Certosa di San Martino, for example, and Giordano against Vaccaro at Santa Maria del Pianto, as will be seen.

Timing and chronology are also fundamental to any consideration of Neapolitan patronage, since these factors determined the possibilities – as well as the limitations – placed on patrons at any particular time. The patrons of the Pio Monte della Misericordia were certainly blessed by good timing in being able to draw on the services of the just-arrived Caravaggio at precisely the moment that they began to turn their attention from the construction of their church to the decoration of its interior. Conversely, though, they were also impeded to a certain degree by this chronology. Caravaggio's revolutionary style took some years to be assimilated into a native Neapolitan idiom, which is one of the reasons why the completed altarpieces in the church lack the greater sense of Baroque unity found in other comparable ambiences constructed after this date – as in the Cappella del Tesoro di San Gennaro in Naples Cathedral decorated by Domenichino, Stanzione, Ribera and Lanfranco during the 1630s and 1640s (see pp. 37, 39). Of course, patrons would not necessarily have seen the issue in these terms. Their more immediate objective, rather, was to commission the most effective expression of their communications agenda from the most worthy painters of the day – and artistic unity is something that becomes fully apparent only after the fact. That these patrons chose to replace Baglione's *Entombment* of 1608 with a more up-to-date work by Giordano is nonetheless surely significant, and points to the difficulties that patrons faced in seeking to project a consistent and convincing image of their collective identity via the diverse talents and backgrounds of a broad range of artists, often working over a number of decades.

The importance of personal networks in deliberations of this type should not be underestimated. It has been plausibly suggested, for example, that one of the most prominent individuals responsible for commissioning Caravaggio at the Pio Monte della Misericordia was Giovan Battista Manso, marchese di Villa.[14] Besides being one of the seven founders of the Misericordia, Manso was also a leading figure in the Neapolitan cultural circles of the day. He was an early advocate for the new sciences – counting among his associates both Galileo and Giovan Battista della Porta, for example – and he went on to found the most important Neapolitan academy of the period, the Accademia degli

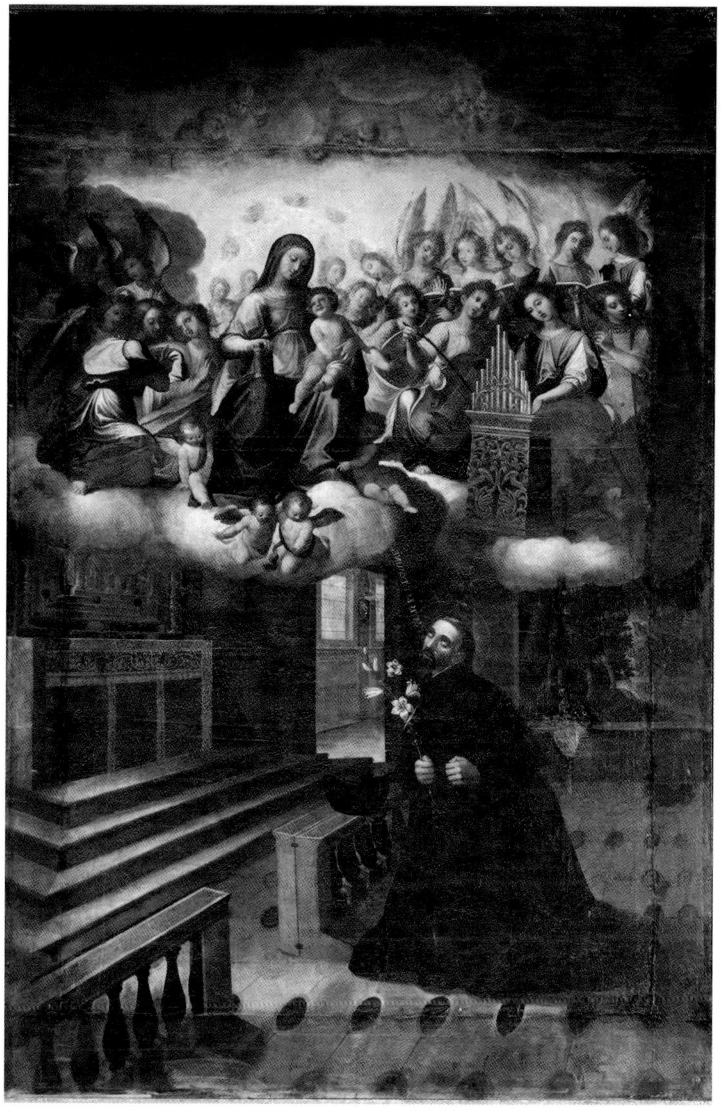

102 Giovanni Bernardino Azzolino, *St Francis Xavier Adoring the Virgin and Child*, 1622–8. Oil on canvas. Cappella di San Francesco Saverio, Chiesa del Gesù Nuovo, Naples

Oziosi, in 1611. This involved him in acting as a leading patron and supporter of both Torquato Tasso and Giambattista Marino.[15] He probably received advance notice of Caravaggio's talents prior to the artist's arrival in Naples from Marino, since, as is well known, Marino had previously acted as an important early champion of Caravaggio and had even commissioned from him a now-lost portrait.

Manso was probably also instrumental in recommending to the Pio Monte della Misericordia the young Caracciolo for the commission of the *Liberation of St Peter* following the death of Carlo Sellitto, to whom the contract had been entrusted originally. The early sources emphasize Manso's importance to Caracciolo as a private patron and also, at least according to De' Dominici, as a recommender to Caracciolo of the worth of Annibale Carracci in the face of Neapolitan hostility to this otherwise not very well-represented foreign artist.[16] Although little is known about the background of Caravaggio's patron at Sant'Anna dei Lombardi, it is at least clear that these kinds of associations must have been fundamental to his thinking as well, given that Fenaroli came from Bergamo and was therefore motivated to secure work from a famous visiting compatriot for the Neapolitan church of the Lombard nation to which he belonged. In the following discussion there are frequent reminders of the continued importance of association – be it personal, regional, ecclesiastical or familial – as a crucial factor underlying the commissioning of much of the art of Baroque Naples.

A PUBLIC COMMISSION INCITES DEVOTION

The extent to which public commissions were motivated by considerations extending far beyond the artistic issues that are often of prime interest today is exemplified by the case of a miraculous image still on display at the Jesuit church of the Gesù Nuovo (fig. 102). Here, on 18 May 1653, witnesses attested to seeing a painting of *St Francis Xavier Adoring the Virgin and Child* undergoing 'prodigiosi cambiamenti' (miraculous transformations) during the celebration of Mass. As initially observed by a 'simple peasant woman' and thereafter by a swelling crowd of hundreds of awestruck observers, the face of St Francis in this painting was seen to grow pale and sweaty – as if it were suffering from some kind of fever. The eyes of the figure were then observed to close – as if in prayer – before opening and changing direction – sometimes looking up in the direction of the Virgin and Child, at other times looking down towards the congregation. It was as if this painting of St Francis Xavier was miraculously coming to life in order to recommend the Neapolitan populace to the care of the Virgin and Child.

Eventually the Jesuits covered the face of this figure with a veil – presumably in order to regulate the intensity of the spontaneous outpouring of popular devotion precipitated by the event. And yet, so the testimonies assert, the animated face of St Francis Xavier continued to remain visible, shining through the veil. The miracle lasted for a number of weeks, until the Neapolitan archbishop, Cardinal Ascanio Filomarino, ordered a report into the phenomenon, which forms the basis of knowledge about it today.[17]

What is so extraordinary about this event for the present purposes is less the fact that nearly 100 signatories representing all ranks of Neapolitan society attested to it than the inclusion in this group of seven painters. Their testimony added an important level of specialist corroboration of the miracle's veracity, since, as the report notes, 'many famous painters asserted that it would not be possible for any human hand to equal this [effect] with a brush'.[18]

And yet the painting had been painted by a human hand – by Giovanni Bernardino Azzolino, in fact, around thirty years previously. And this was a fact that all the painters would have known. Azzolino had died only a few years earlier and in their varying ways all the artists – including the three best-known signatories – Luca Forte, Francesco Fracanzano and Agostino Beltrano – would have had close associations with him over the course of many years. Francesco Fracanzano, for example, had been trained by Ribera – Azzolino's son-in-law – while Beltrano had lived all his life in the same artists' quarter – the Quartiere della Carità – as did Azzolino. It seems especially striking, therefore, to observe these painters attesting to the miraculous transformation of a painting that had been created within living memory by one of their own colleagues.

Be this as it may, the transformation of Azzolino's painting into a miraculous image was timely and proved extremely beneficial to his patrons, since it enabled the Jesuits to present their recently canonized co-founder as one of the great defenders of the city – even though St Francis Xavier had established no direct link with Naples during his lifetime. This would assist them significantly in their quest to have him formally recognized as one of the patron saints of the city: a privilege that was granted only to a select few – thereby representing a significant vindication of the Jesuits' Neapolitan mission in a way that many of their rivals had not been able to achieve.

THE BOOM IN BAROQUE RELIGIOUS WORKS

In 1645 the English diarist and traveller John Evelyn declared that, save for St Peter's in Rome, the city of Naples 'exceeds all cittys for stately Churches & Monasteries'. Elsewhere he exclaimed that its '3000 churches and monasteries . . . [are] the best built and adorned of any in Italy'.[19] His estimation of numbers was exaggerated, but this in itself conveys the powerful impression that this super-abundance of newly built or freshly redecorated religious edifices made on him, as they did on so many other visitors to the city.[20] During a time in which Neapolitan private patronage was only beginning to advance beyond the early seventeenth-century perception of its being somewhat conservative and retardataire, Naples was, by contrast, fully established as the most outwardly confident manifestation of the post-Tridentine reform in all Italy.

The statistics, such as they are, clearly confirm this picture. A late sixteenth-century census counted a population of some 4,000 monks and nuns resident in Naples.[21] By the time of Enrico Bacco's *Descritione del regno di Napoli* of 1671 this figure had doubled to 8,152.[22] This represents an extraordinary increase that could be added to yet further if one were to include in it those associated with the forty parish churches or those working for such new organizations as the Oratorians or the Pio Monte della Misericordia. All these individuals had, of course, to be spiritually and administratively maintained, and to be housed appropriately in the rapidly expanding metropolis. So it was that the orders followed a process of establishment that was repeated many times throughout the seventeenth century. First they gained a foothold in the city by securing a palace – either through direct purchase or via the donation of a well-disposed patron. Next they acquired properties on either side and thence initiated expanding and building until – sometimes sooner, at other times later – they were able to carve out an island of monastic seclusion from amid the dense urban fabric of the city.

These substantial complexes of buildings were centred on a large courtyard (or even courtyards), offering oases of calm in a densely built-up urban landscape where such an ideal presented an otherwise impossibly rare commodity (fig. 103). When this was not possible, green-field sites were sought in the newly opened neighbourhoods created by the viceroys during their periodic extension of the city walls. *Fare insula* (to make an island), the process was termed, and it was repeated so often during the Neapolitan Baroque that Giannone was moved to lament at the beginning of the eighteenth century that 'per tal mezzo i monaci a lungo andare giungere a comprarsi l'intera città' (as a result of this, before too long the monks will have bought up for themselves the entire city).[23]

Some examples can be cited to demonstrate the speed and efficiency with which the new orders and confraternities established themselves and then expanded their operations during this period. The Pio Monte della Misericordia was initiated by a lay association of seven aristocrats in 1601. Moving from the drawing up of statutes to the granting of royal and papal approbation in the short space of two years, this group was then able to levy donations received in order to acquire two contiguous properties on which to build a church in 1604. A mere three years later – and only six years after their initial meetings – their administrative and ecclesiastical base was complete and ready to receive Caravaggio's *Seven Works of Mercy* and the other altarpieces mentioned above. This church was then found wanting, and some forty-five years later the rapidly expanding confraternity was required to build a new church.[24]

This continuous expansion kept the small number of architects and engineers operating in Naples extremely busy. Giovan Giacomo di Conforto (*circa* 1569–1631), for example, who created the Pio Monte's first church, was also at work during these years supervising constructions for the Discalced Carmelites, an order that had arrived in Naples from Spain soon after its foundation in 1593. In 1602 the Carmelites acquired a palace on the flank of Capodimonte overlooking the Porta di Costantinopoli, which they used to build a new church dedicated to Santa Teresa degli Studi (1612), followed shortly thereafter by a monastery (1622) and then the completion of further ecclesiastical buildings and grounds, including an extensive garden (1628). The Franciscans also commissioned Conforto during this period to build a nearby church and convent – this one dedicated to the Trinità delle Monache – which was likewise completed within the space of a decade (1610–21).[25]

Speaking in the middle of the seventeenth century, the Oratorian Carlo de Lellis betrayed perhaps a hint of envy in his assessment of the achievements of the Neapolitan Carmelites. He noted that the nuns were 'poveri nel vitto, poveri nelle celle, poveri nel vestire . . . solamente sono ricchi nel mostrarsi prodichi per dir così negli abbigliamenti di un'altare' (paupers at the table, paupers in their cells, paupers in their clothing . . . the only place in which they are rich, nevertheless, is in showing themselves to be unrestrained when it comes to ornamenting their altars).[26] His words perfectly express the seventeenth-century attitude towards what might seem an otherwise apparent contradiction between the eremitical austerity of an order such as the Carmelites and the opulence of their artistic commissions.

The chapel of St Teresa of Ávila, for example, which was the devotional focus of the new church of Santa Teresa degli Studi, is a case in point. It was commissioned from Cosimo Fanzago for 30,000 ducats, while the subsequent commissioning of a tabernacle cost an additional 15,000 ducats. Added to this were a major series of frescoes by Massimo Stanzione and a life-size silver statue of St Teresa said by De Lellis to be worth 'many thousands' of ducats.

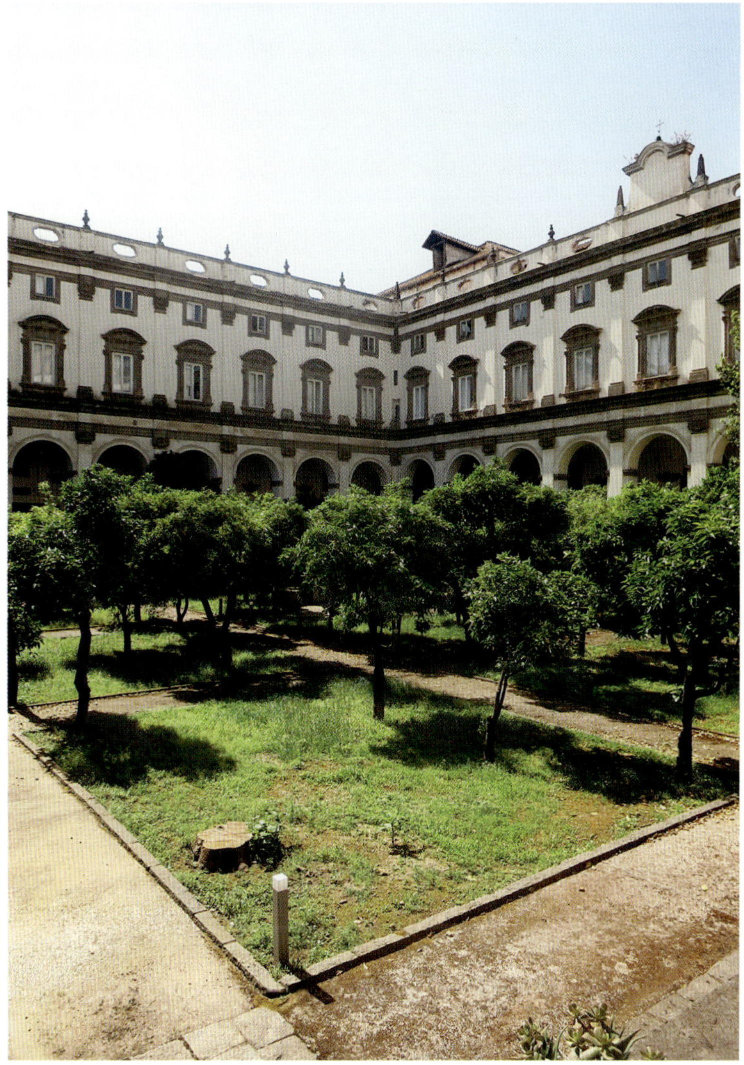

103 Cloister of the Girolamini, Monumento Nazionale dei Girolamini, Naples

The resulting richness and distinction of this chapel was such that it was prominently featured in Sarnelli's *Guida de' forestieri* of 1685 as one of the spectacular sights of the city, and it was fulsomely praised by De Lellis as 'celebrata per un Teatro di meraviglie, e per una delle fabbriche più bella d'Europa' (celebrated as a theatre of marvels and as one of the most beautiful edifices in all Europe).[27] It was for the greater good after all, and, in this respect religious patrons often proceeded with far greater diligence than the often dilatory artists in their employ. Ribera, for example, took five years to complete an altarpiece for the Franciscan church of the Trinità delle Monache, which is to say that he took half as long to complete a single altarpiece as the friars took to arrange for the building of the entire church.

DONATIONS, COMMISSIONS AND RIVALRY BETWEEN ORDERS AND ARTISTS

All this expansion and building followed shortly thereafter by extensive projects of internal decoration required the leveraging of prodigious amounts of money – far more than was required for individual altarpieces, which seem very minor considerations by comparison. The newly arrived Counter-Reformation orders and congregations had a particular advantage in this regard, being able to draw on the sense of urgency, prestige and novelty created by their missionary presence in the city. Chief among these were the Jesuits, Theatines and Oratorians, all of which developed significant presences in Naples, yet did so in ways that reveal their very different vocational and organizational emphases.

The Jesuits arrived in Naples in 1552 with the strong backing of the Spanish vice-regency and spent their first thirty years attempting to establish themselves in various locations throughout the city.[28] By 1582 they were in a position to expand their operations and to build a consolidated base that comprised a substantial church flanked on either side by a residential/administrative building – or Casa Professa – and an oratory, or Palazzo delle Congregazioni, for Jesuit-supervised lay congregations (including the Neapolitan painters' organization, as previously noted). In that year they accordingly paid 46,000 ducats to acquire the fifteenth-century fortified palace of the principe di Salerno situated favourably on the Decumanus Inferiore – or southern, east–west orientation of the ancient Graeco-Roman city. The site also had the advantage of offering a wide, open piazza in which to create an imposing urban presence for the complex, an opportunity that was in other respects rarely possible, given the densely built-up nature of the urban environment (fig. 104).

Diagonally across from this new base there stood the massive hulk of the Franciscan convent of Santa Chiara that had been built some three centuries earlier through the support of Robert of Anjou.[29] The venerable historical, regal allegiances of the old religious orders were thus now flanked across the crowded city by the rapidly proliferating, vice-regal affiliations of the new orders in a manner that was increasingly characteristic of the city. The Jesuits' newly acquired palace was soon converted into one of the largest churches in the Kingdom of Naples and was consecrated in 1597. The internal decoration of the church then proceeded apace over the next several decades – alongside simultaneous work on the flanking Casa Professa and Palazzo delle Congregazioni – thanks to significant ongoing support from the viceroys and the leading aristocratic families of the day (fig. 105).

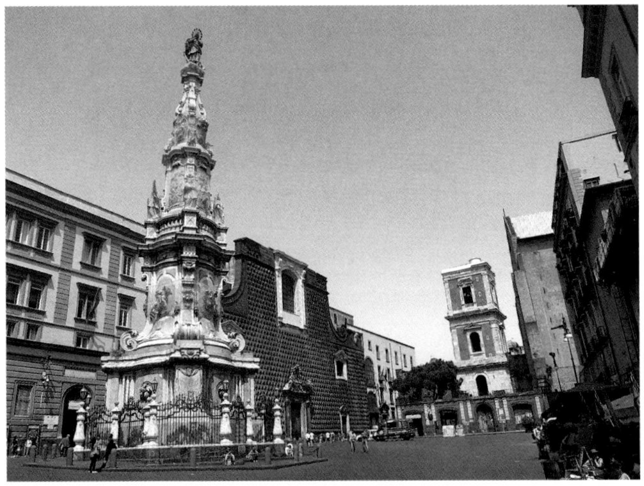

104 Exterior view, Chiesa del Gesù Nuovo, Naples

Perhaps the most extraordinary instance of the extensive patronage network that the Jesuits were able to draw on in this regard is the chapel of St Ignatius in the left transept of the church of the Gesù Nuovo. This – one of the most costly and prestigious commissions in one of the city's most lavish churches – was initiated with the assistance of an endowment from Don Carlo Gesualdo, principe di Venosa and conte di Consa (1566–1613).[30] One can only hope that the 900 ducats paid to Belisario Corenzio for frescoes (1633–7), followed thereafter by 17,000 ducats paid to Cosimo Fanzago and Costantino Marasi for the altar itself (1637–42), helped to offset the penance due for the mortal sins of this benefactor, since he had a great deal to expiate.

In addition to his career as a significant late Renaissance composer and supporter of the local musical culture, Don Carlo was also one of the most notorious individuals of the period, having murdered his wife – Donna Maria d'Avalos, daughter of the marchese di Pescara – and her lover, Don Fabrizio Carafa, duca di Andria, in a fit of jealous rage in 1590 (and according to some accounts adding to this infamy by killing his infant son due to his suspicions regarding the child's paternity). Don Carlo belonged, nonetheless, to a pre-eminent aristocratic family (his uncles being the archbishop of Naples and the future saint Carlo Borromeo, archbishop of Milan, respectively). He was thus accorded protection in a manner that would have been unthinkable for a lower-ranked miscreant. His substantial donation to the Jesuits also helped him to avoid the full strictures of punishment for a crime that would otherwise have led straight to

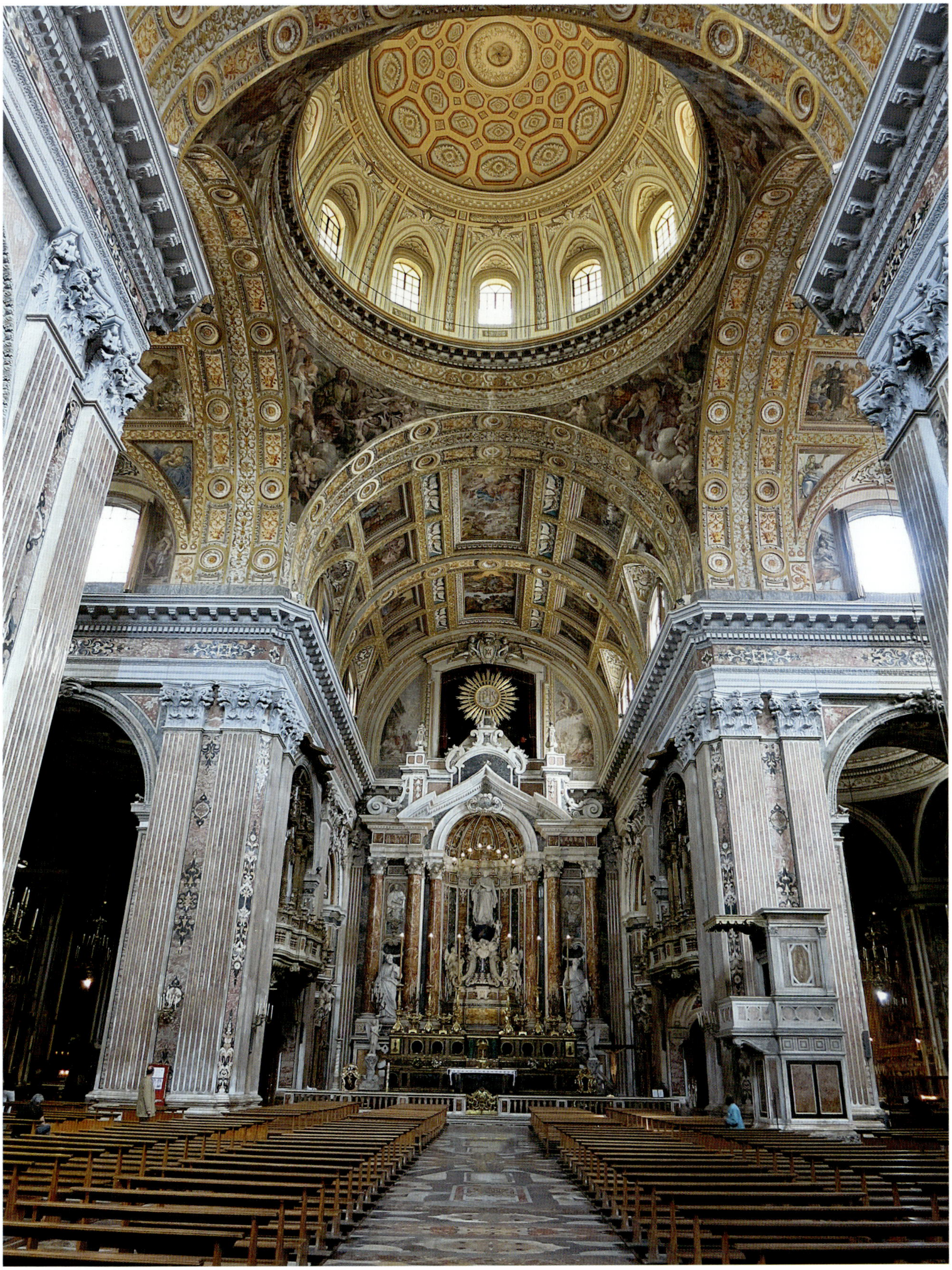

105 Interior view, Chiesa del Gesù Nuovo, Naples

the scaffold. Don Carlo was instead required to retire to his country estate, leaving behind his donation to the Jesuits as a public declaration of his Christian public-spiritedness and desire for expiation.[31]

This lavish – even extravagant – support was characteristic of the Jesuits and is one of the reasons why a certain degree of enmity is detectable among the other orders from time to time. Another characteristic example of high-profile and rapidly effective patronage of this kind came in the Jesuits' decision taken in the early 1620s to open a third training college for novices, together with a new, accompanying church dedicated to the recently canonized St Francis Xavier, which was to be situated close to the vice-regal centre of operations on Palazzo Reale. This project was made possible through a donation of 30,000 ducats that was raised on their behalf in the 1620s by Catalina de la Cerda Sandoval, widow of the conde de Lemos, who had been viceroy from 1610 to 1616. The 'ex Viceregina' levied this sum via an extraordinary tax enacted for this purpose across all the feudal estates of the kingdom.[32] The continued influence of the contessa – at that stage long since departed from Naples and living in seclusion in a convent in Madrid, yet still working on the Neapolitan Jesuits' behalf while making donations of her own – points also to the significant international networks that these orders were able to draw on.[33]

This international flavour applied to their leadership as well as to the artists whom they commissioned. In this respect the Jesuits and other Counter-Reformation orders should be seen as acting akin to international corporations presiding over local headquarters. This was an important factor when it came to the importation of new artistic talent from other cities into Naples. The Jesuit-architect Giuseppe Valeriano was brought down from Rome to Naples, for example, to design the Gesù Nuovo, and it was the Superior General of the Jesuits in Rome, Muzio Vitelleschi, who was subsequently successful in securing Lanfranco's passage to Naples in 1634 to fresco the cupola and spandrels of the newly completed church (fig. 106). Vitelleschi's letters to Lanfranco and the local Neapolitan Jesuits reveal clearly the extent to which the cordial, yet prolonged and complex negotiations surrounding this commission were at all times dictated from Rome, no matter how careful the Superior General was to consult the Neapolitans and keep them abreast of developments.

This is made clear as early as Vitelleschi's first letter on the matter – a full four years prior to Lanfranco's start of work. At this stage Vitelleschi cautioned the Neapolitan *preposito*: 'non faccia niente senza me perche potrò provedere con persona eminente' (don't do anything without referring it to me since I am able to provide for it with an eminent person).[34] He evidently wanted to maintain control over every aspect of the commission, and he accordingly solicited plans from the Neapolitans containing precise measurements of the dimensions of the cupola to aid him in his consultations in Rome. In early 1633, when he had gained Lanfranco's initial agreement to undertake the commission, he also made sure to authorize personally Lanfranco's initial *bozzetto* before informing the Neapolitan Provincial: 'Ha fatto l'abozzo con bellissimi scompartimenti, et io gli ho veduti e sono d'opinione, che sarà una cosa esquisita' (he has produced a *bozzetto* with most beautiful compartments that he has shown to me and I am accordingly of the opinion that it will be an exquisite thing when completed). When Lanfranco did at last travel to Naples to start work in early 1634, Vitelleschi dispatched a letter reminding the Provincial of the need to pay the artist promptly: 'non mendicato, ma pronto con qualche liberalità' (not in a beggarly way, but promptly and with a certain degree of liberality). In general, thereafter, he continued to adopt an attentive and proprietary interest in all aspects of the commission.

With the smooth, though, must come the rough. So Vitelleschi was also drawn into the numerous complications and controversies arising from the commission that were regularly forwarded to his desk for arbitration. First, Lanfranco agitated to remove the stuccoed ribs from the cupola so as to create a freer and more extensive visual field on which to paint (another instance of the old-fashioned Neapolitan liking for *soffitti cassettonati* and heavily gilt and stuccoed chapel decorations that was commented upon previously). The cost and delay involved in converting the cupola at such a late date – not to mention the structural issues that it would have created – would have been prohibitive, so it is no surprise that Vitelleschi politely yet firmly overruled Lanfranco on this point.

When work was nearly complete, some of the Neapolitan Jesuits were next heard to complain about the supposedly excessive nudity of some of the angels in the spandrels. Resolving this controversy required all Vitelleschi's considerable diplomatic skills. His patronal instincts inclined him to side with Lanfranco, and yet his Jesuit brethren could not be so easily brushed aside. So he was required to pacify Lanfranco by, on the one hand, complimenting him on the 'eccelenza' of the figures while noting that anybody who criticized them 'parlava poco bene della pittura' (spoke

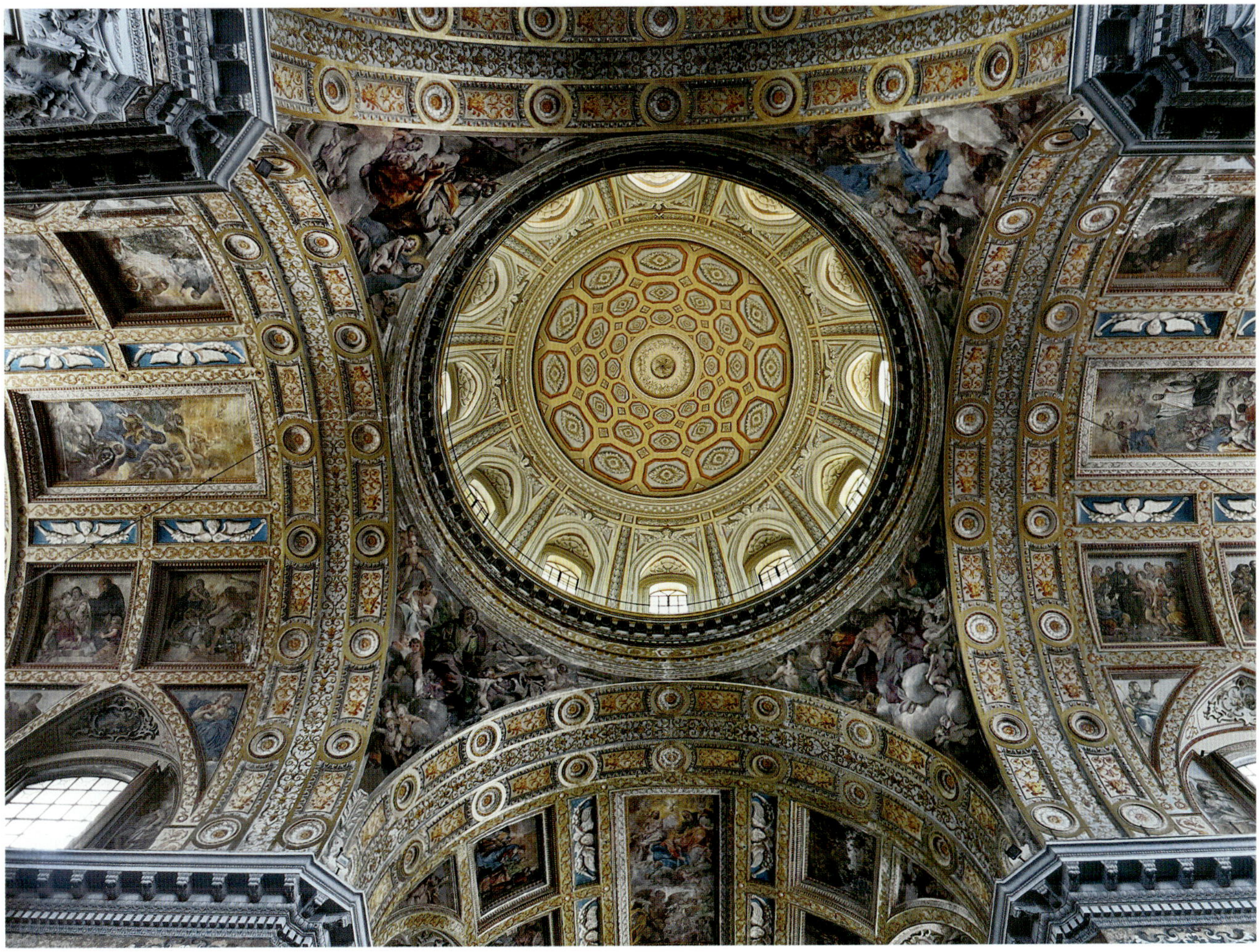

106 Giovanni Lanfranco, *Four Evangelists*, spandrel frescoes, 1634–6. Chiesa del Gesù Nuovo, Naples

poorly of painting). But on the other hand, as he put it: 'Non é possibile il dar sodisfattione a tutti' (it is not possible to satisfy everybody), and so it was perhaps best to 'velare qualche soverchia nudita degli angioli' (cover up some of the excessive nudity of the angels).

This, in combination with the dragging out of the negotiations for a final agreed price for the work, caused Lanfranco to threaten to leave Naples in early 1636 before applying the revisions and finishing touches on the commission. This would have jeopardized the plans to unveil the frescoes on the occasion of that year's feast of St Ignatius (31 July), and so created another issue requiring Vitelleschi's immediate attention. In the end a certain degree of repainting was undertaken and Lanfranco was paid 10,000 ducats for the work – less than he wanted but equivalent, the Jesuits pointed out, to the sum paid by the Theatines for his comparable work at Sant'Andrea della Valle.

One might have expected that Vitelleschi's involvement in Lanfranco's Neapolitan quarrels would have been over by this date. Yet such was not to be the case. In 1639 Lanfranco wrote to Vitelleschi complaining that he had been passed over for the contract for the next major portion of painting required for the church: the choir frescoes. These had been awarded to Massimo Stanzione, despite having been promised to him – or so he maintained – by the Neapolitan Jesuit procurator, Flaminio Magnati. This roused Vitelleschi to write his strongest letter yet to the Neapolitan Jesuits, opening with an unusually direct expression of displeasure: 'Il Signor Giovanni Lanfranco pittore è rimasto molto mortificato, et io con lui' (Signor Giovanni Lanfranco the painter remains extremely mortified, and I with him). Yet time had passed and not even the all-powerful Superior General in Rome, it seems, was able to micro-manage every aspect of the no doubt complex and constantly shifting power relations surrounding the prime artistic commissions at the Gesù Nuovo. Stanzione kept his contract – the Neapolitans presumably considering him a safer and more reliable bet than the quarrelsome and – to some at least – artistically suspect painter of the cupola frescoes. A face-saving compromise was arrived at to appease Lanfranco – no doubt negotiated as much for the Superior General's benefit as for the artist's. Lanfranco was given a subsidiary commission for work in the adjacent Palazzo delle Congregazioni.[35]

Yet for all his protestations there is something of the ambit claim about Lanfranco's complaints to his powerful Roman protector. He must have known that the choir frescoes were no longer his for the asking. He had, in any event, demonstrated this tacitly by moving on to other work – having completed his frescoes for the Neapolitan Carthusians (1637–9) and having already, in fact, begun work on his next and yet more ambitious suite of frescoes for the rival order of the Theatines at Santi Apostoli (1638–46).

Lanfranco no doubt felt justified in agitating for greater recompense for his work. The fact remains, however, that the price paid for the Gesù Nuovo frescoes represents one of the highest sums paid for a public commission in Naples at that date, a point that can be confirmed with reference to a list of the known payments for altarpieces and frescoes in seventeenth-century Naples (Table 5). A comparison between the budget for the Gesù Nuovo and the sums expended on a similar church decoration campaign during the same period can also be cited to clarify further the lavishness of Jesuit patronage relative to the other orders.

Late nineteenth-century archival discoveries – supplemented by further documentation unearthed in the 1980s – allow one to document in unusually rich detail the funds expended by the Dominican nuns of Santa Maria della Sapienza during the 1630s and 1640s for the internal decorations of their recently completed church (the church being another of the many projects realized by Giovan Giacomo di Conforto).[36] These nuns were by no means a minor or impoverished order. They had been established in the city in the previous century – initially as Clarissans, but later as Dominicans under the religious direction of the Theatines. It was through this connection that their activities had come under the patronage of the powerful Carafa family. Their first prioress was Maria Carafa, whose brother was none other than Gian Pietro Carafa – archbishop of Naples, co-founder of the Theatines and subsequently Pope Paul IV (their dual significance to the order being accordingly memorialized by the inclusion of stucco portraits of both Maria and Gian Pietro Carafa above the entrance to the church) (fig. 107).[37] Nevertheless, their expenditures pale into insignificance in comparison to the Jesuits.

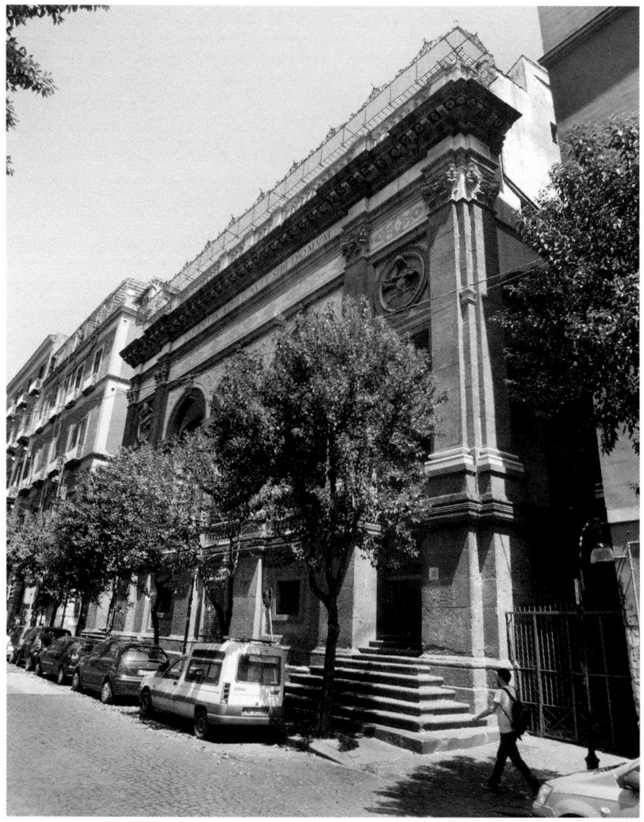

107 Exterior view, Santa Maria della Sapienza, Naples

The total outlay expended during the 1630s and 1640s on the internal decoration of the church of Santa Maria della Sapienza was around 19,000 ducats. This included some 3,000 ducats spent on paintings, including 2,142 for an extensive series of frescoes by Corenzio and a series of nave paintings depicting *Scenes from the Life of Christ* that cost between 50 to 120 ducats each and which were all commissioned simultaneously from Domenico Gargiulo, Enrico de Somer, Carlo Rosa and a number of other pupils and followers of Massimo Stanzione and Jusepe de Ribera. Yet Lanfranco received five times as much as Corenzio for his frescoes, and the altarpieces and the like commissioned by the Jesuits added a further 7,000 ducats to their costs on painting. In fact, the Jesuits and their aristocratic/vice-regal backers spent almost as much on the single chapel of St Francis Xavier (18,300 ducats) as the nuns of Santa Maria della Sapienza expended on the entire internal decoration of their church – that is to say for the stucco, marble, paintings, metalwork and all.

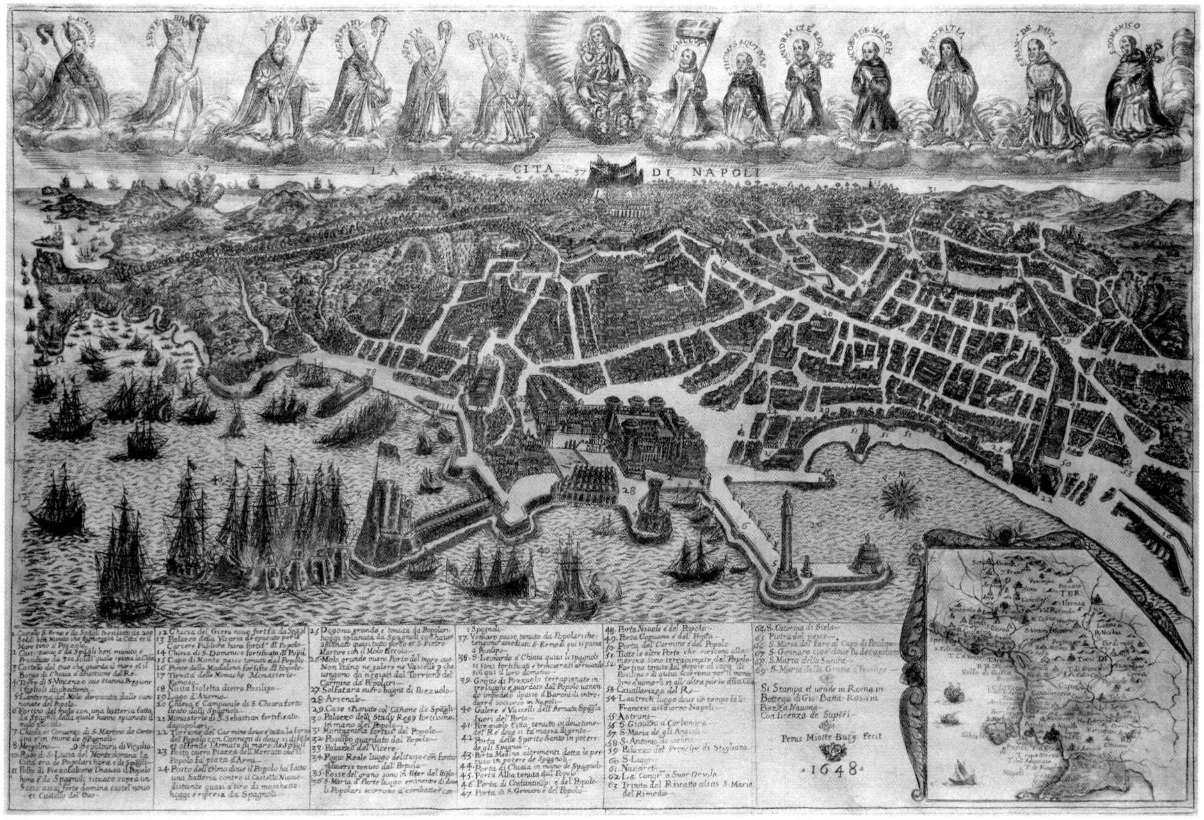

108 Pietro Miotte, *La città di Napoli*, 1648. Etching, 36.5 × 54.2 cm

HOLY CORPSES: INTER-ORDER RIVALRY AND THE NOMINATION OF PATRON PROTECTORS

The Gesù Nuovo as completed proclaims the pre-eminence of the Neapolitan Jesuits: it is one of the most impressive and richly decorated ambiences of the Neapolitan Baroque, notwithstanding the losses it sustained following various regional calamities – most notably an earthquake in 1688 that destroyed the cupola, leaving only Lanfranco's spandrel frescoes intact. Yet the Jesuits could assert themselves on this level for all they liked: still they remained deficient in one fundamental respect. As a recently imported order with a largely foreign history, they were singularly lacking when it came to having any significant local tradition of saints' bodies or other relics that would generate local cults.

The strategic benefits accruing to religious orders in possession of assets of this kind should not be underestimated. They proved particularly useful during the periodically intense competition among the orders for the distinction of adding an especially venerated individual to the ranks of the patron saints of Naples. Patrons of the city were selected on the basis of their devotional popularity and effectiveness as intercessors at times of particular crisis. This supreme honour was accordingly exercised only rarely, and was marked by the addition of a lavish reliquary dedicated to the saint in question that was installed with great fanfare in the central collection of patronal relics maintained in the Tesoro di San Gennaro in Naples Cathedral (see fig. 23).[38]

In the 1620s and 1630s, for example, the nuns of Santa Patrizia carried out a particularly rancorous and protracted dispute with the Neapolitan Theatines concerning the placement in the Tesoro of the relics of their respective patron protectors. The claims and counter-claims for this case were forwarded for adjudication both to Cardinal Giovanni Battista Pamphili, the future pope Innocent X, and to the Sacra Congregazioni dei Riti in Rome.[39] There was much at stake, therefore, in gaining such an exalted status and those orders with venerated saintly relics had a distinct advantage in this regard.

Pietro Miotte's panoramic view of the city of 1648 records the state of play as regards the Neapolitan patron protectors in the middle of the seventeenth century (fig. 108). First in rank, kneeling at the right hand of the Virgin and Child, is

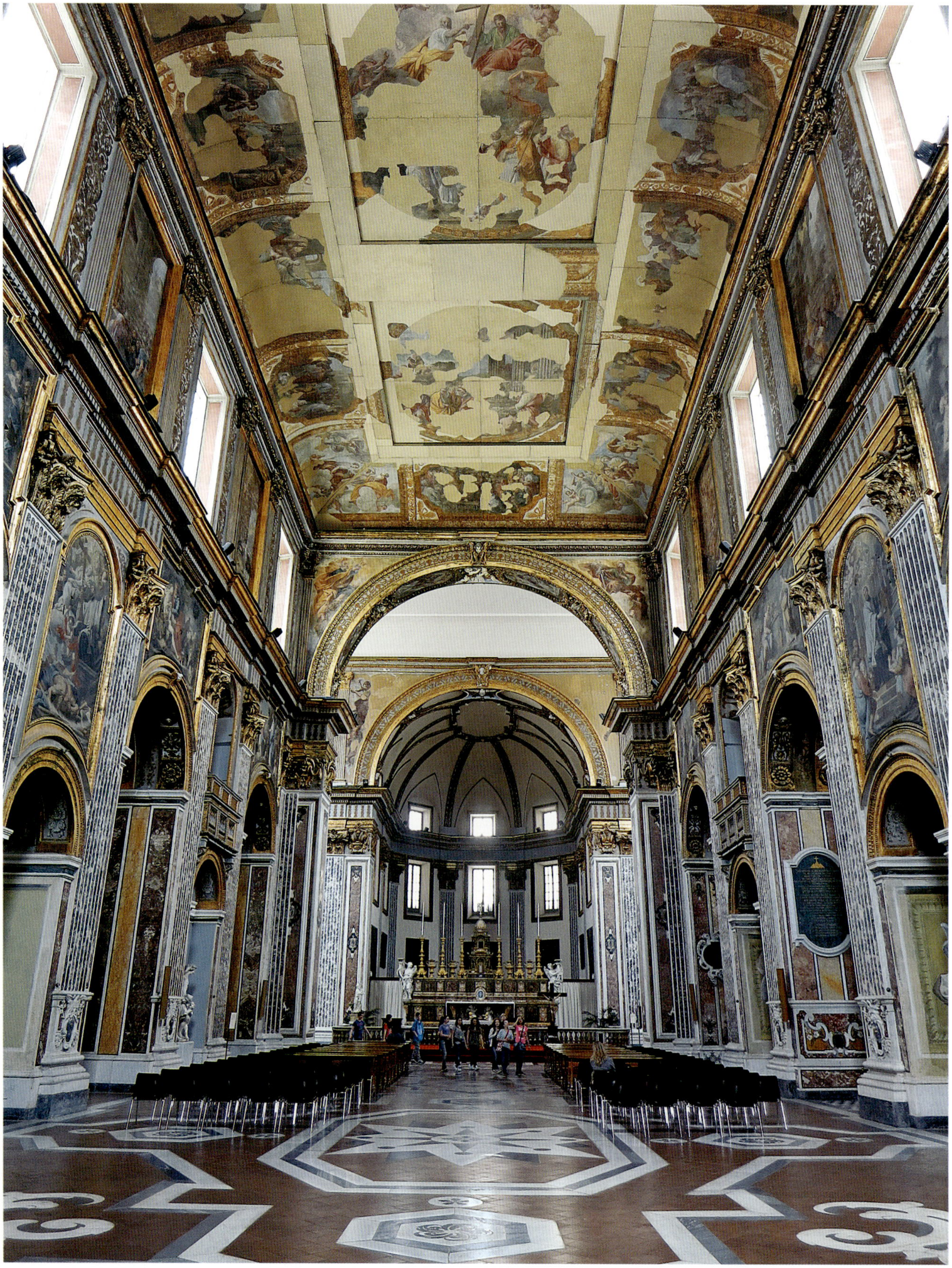

109 Interior view, San Paolo Maggiore, Naples

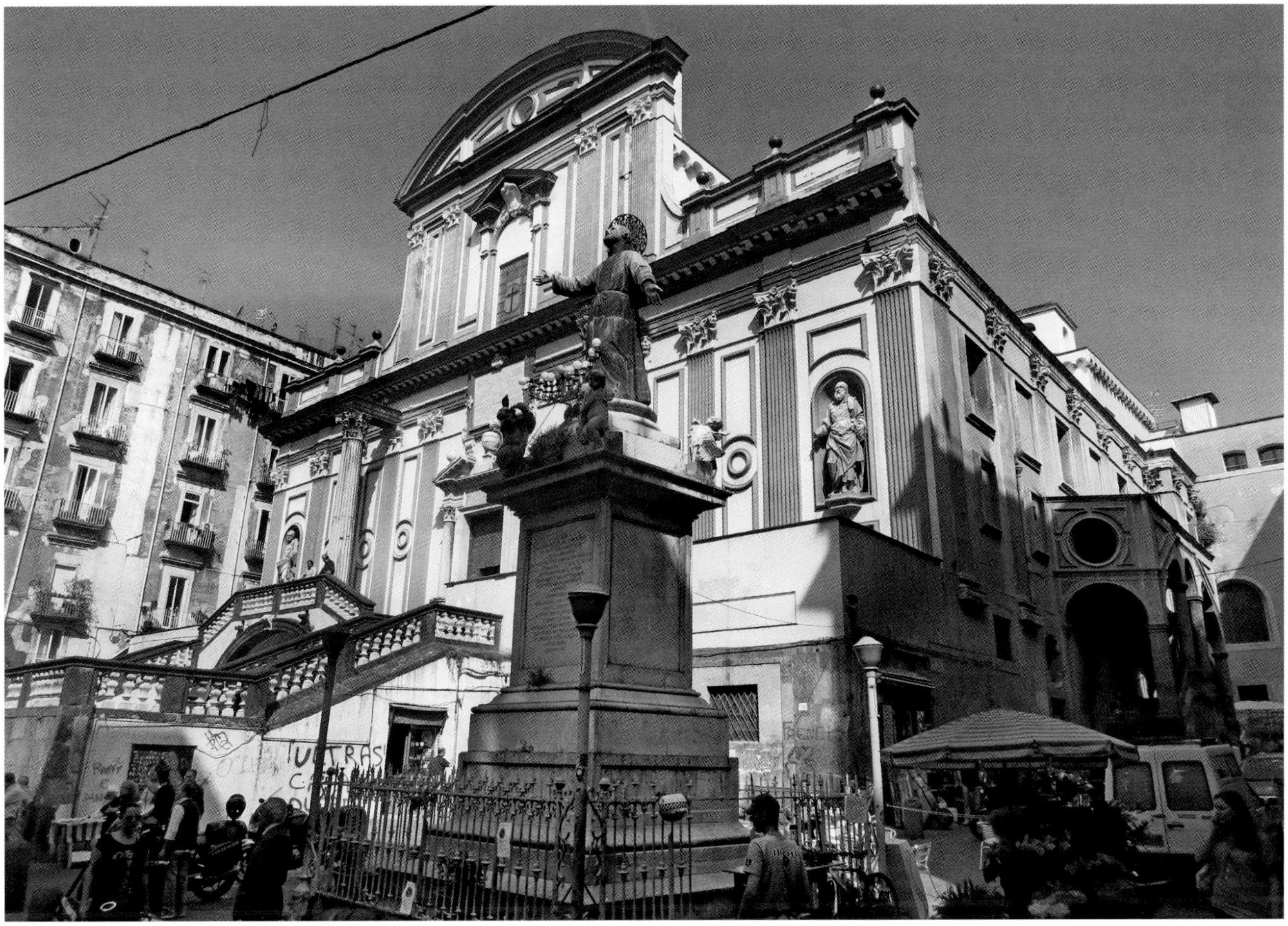

110 Exterior view, San Paolo Maggiore, Naples

the venerable company of St Januarius and five other early Christian/medieval southern Italian bishop patron saints. On the Virgin's other side are arrayed seven more recently added saints, drawn from among the older and more established orders: two Dominicans (Dominic and Thomas Aquinas), two early Christian saints (Patricia and Agnellus) and two Franciscans (Francesco di Paola and Giacomo della Marca), together with, interestingly enough, one Theatine (Andrea Avellino). No other saint of a Counter-Reformation order or congregation is present.

It was, ironically, the physical failing of the body of the Theatine priest Andrea Avellino (1521–1608) that led to the cult surrounding his remains and subsequent rapid promotion to the ranks of the city's *padroni*. Avellino died of a stroke in 1608 while beginning Mass in the Neapolitan Theatines' mother church of San Paolo Maggiore. This church (figs 109–10) – on the site of a former Roman temple situated in the Decumanus Superiore or middle section of the old city – had been granted in 1538 to the founder of the Theatines, St Cajetan (1480–1547), to be used as the base from which to begin the congregation's Neapolitan mission.

Although they had more than a decade's head start on the Jesuits, the Theatines were nonetheless unable to match the Jesuits' rapid advances of building and patronage in the Kingdom of Naples. To be sure, the Jesuits' pro-Spanish affiliations with successive viceroys helped them in this respect. But it is also true that the Theatines' finances were always more constrained with respect to those of the Society of Jesus. When Lanfranco moved on from the Jesuits and Carthusians to fresco the nave and crossing of the Theatine church of Santi Apostoli, for example, he was not given the contract for the cupola, as might be expected, for the simple reason that the Theatines were not yet in a position to finance its construction (it was not finished until 1664 and not frescoed until 1680, when the commission was eventu-

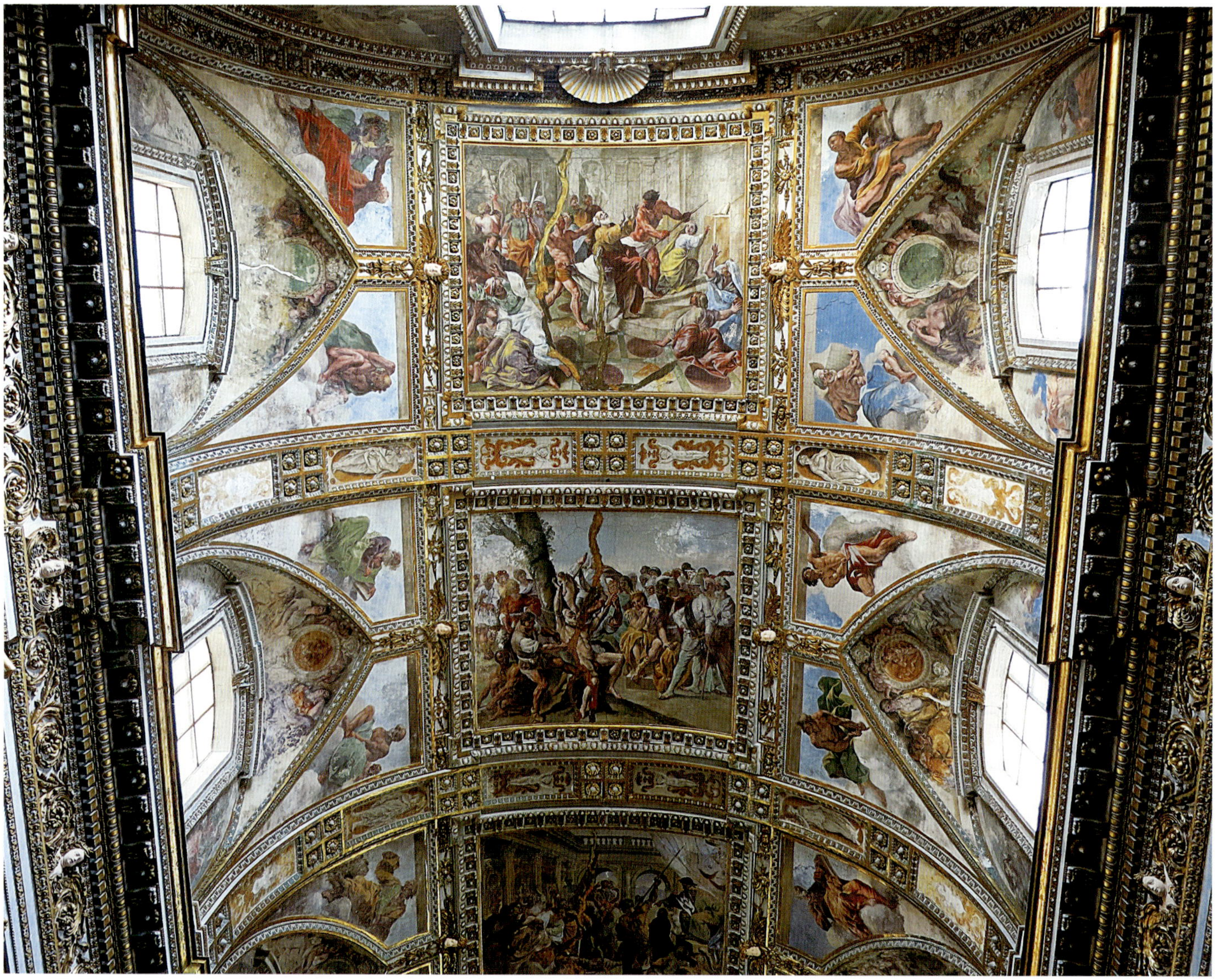

111 Giovanni Lanfranco, nave frescoes, 1638–41. Santi Apostoli, Naples

ally completed by Lanfranco's pupil Giovanni Battista Beinaschi) (figs 111–12).

In the mid-1640s, when Lanfranco was nearing completion of his work at Santi Apostoli, the Theatines ran into difficulties settling the bill to conclude the 10,000 ducats promised to him (the same amount as that paid for his work at the Gesù Nuovo). The Theatines sought to bridge the shortfall in their finances by ceding to Lanfranco a large house in their possession, the benefits of which the artist was to enjoy 'in conto del credito che tiene con questa Casa per la pittura della Chiesa' (on account of the credit owed to him by this religious house for his painting of the church).[40] Comparable cash-flow problems are also evident in the slow construction work on the other Theatine churches, such as Santa Maria degli Angeli.[41]

It is even evident at the mother church of San Paolo Maggiore. The Theatines' major seventeenth-century patronage initiative here was to commission an extensive series of frescoes in the nave from Massimo Stanzione, produced for 3,500 ducats between 1642 and 1644 (although these were badly damaged during the Second World War) (fig. 109).[42] In other respects, though, the church remained a work in progress for the rest of the seventeenth century and was not fully decorated or finished off until well into the eighteenth.[43]

Yet even if they did not have the lavish finances or efficient patronage networks of the Jesuits, the Theatines were still

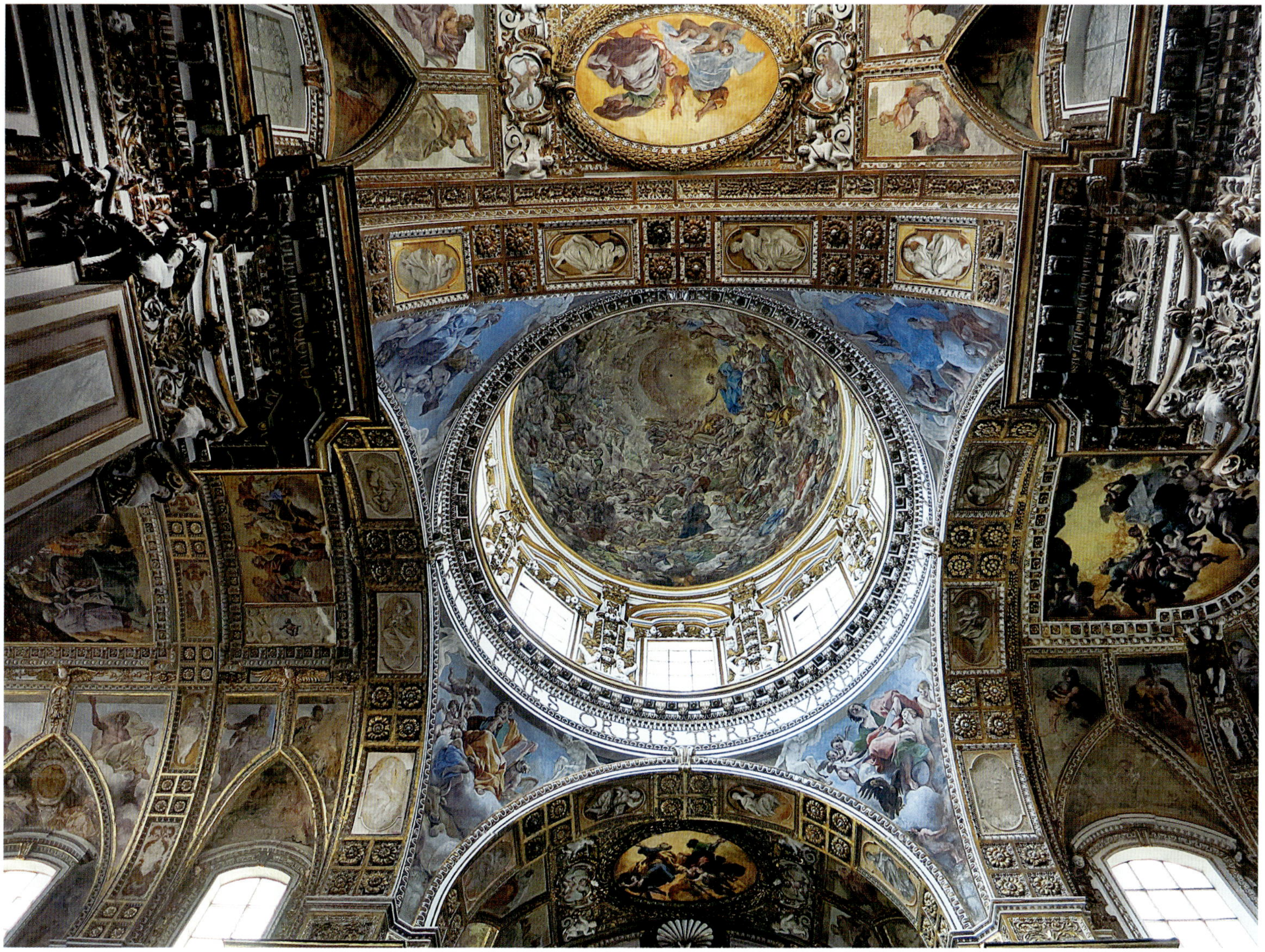

112 Giovanni Lanfranco (spandrel and crossing) and Giovanni Battista Beinaschi (cupola), frescoes, 1638–41, 1680. Santi Apostoli, Naples

ahead of their rivals when it came to their ability to prosecute successfully the case for one of their own to become a patron of the city. Their achievement in this respect is all the more remarkable given that it occurred long before Avellino was even made a saint (he was canonized in 1712). The reason for this rapid escalation of status – beatified in 1624, declared patron of Naples the following year – was simple. Avellino's tomb in San Paolo Maggiore had become a major focus of popular devotion, with numerous votive offerings arrayed on the walls of his chapel given in thanks for his intercession. A painting by Paolo Finoglio accordingly shows him in characteristic stance, still a *beato* rather than a saint, but gesturing to heaven in an attitude of intercessionary zeal (fig. 113).[44]

A similarly rapid promotion is evident in the parallel case of the cult surrounding the Blessed Giacomo della Marca. This fifteenth-century Franciscan Inquisitor was beatified in the same year as Andrea Avellino but was not canonized until even later in the eighteenth century (1726). Yet he too became an early patron of the city, a year after Avellino in 1626, thanks also to the powerful devotional cult that had grown around his tomb in the old Gothic church of Santa Maria la Nova, site of the first Franciscan community in Naples.[45] The Franciscans encouraged this cult further in the 1630s by contracting Cosimo Fanzago to convert the old medieval chapel into something much grander and more appropriately Baroque, and then by capping this off

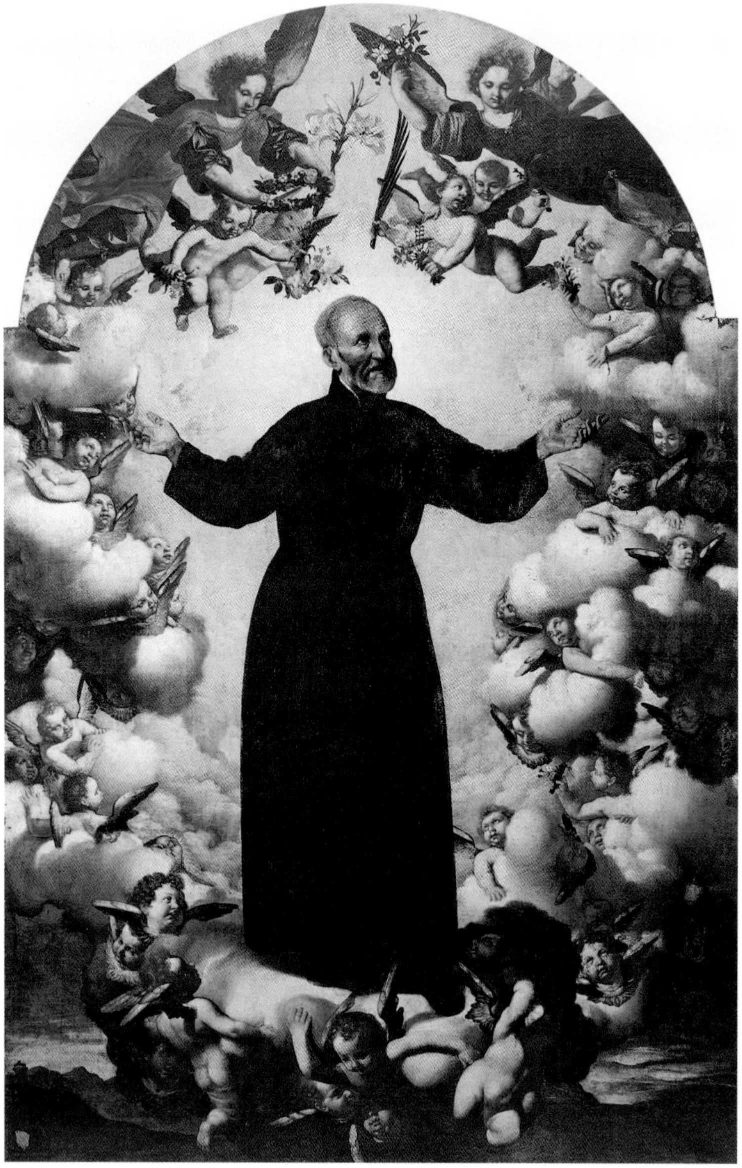

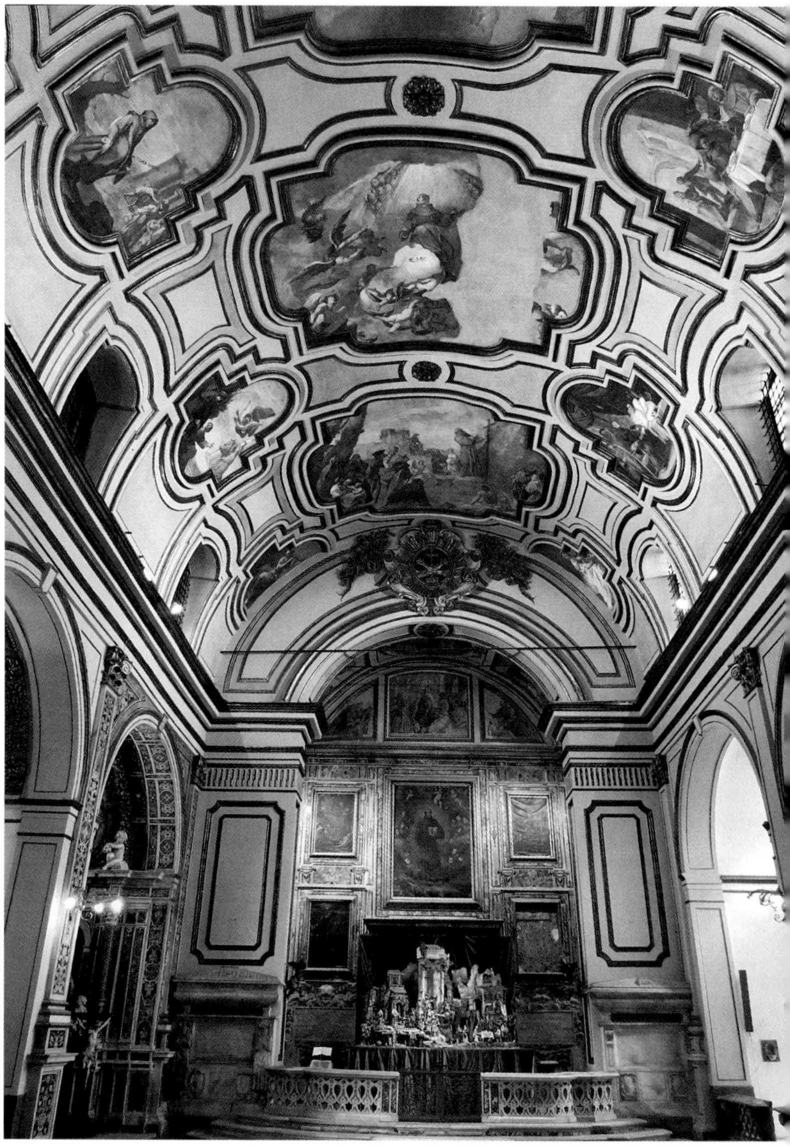

with a major series of frescoes produced once again by Massimo Stanzione (1644–6). This new development projected a massive Baroque annex onto the old medieval church that still to this day proudly emphasizes Giacomo della Marca's status as a saintly protector directly comparable to the city's pre-eminent patron protector, St Januarius himself (figs 114–15).[46]

In the absence of a holy body, then, how were the Neapolitan Jesuits to achieve a similar elevation for one of their own? The miraculous animation of Azzolino's painting of St Francis Xavier in the Gesù Nuovo in 1653 was timely in this context. The Jesuits were also facilitated by St Francis Xavier's growing devotional prominence in other cities, where the saint was already associated with protection against illness and plague. In 1630, for example, he had been named as a patron protector of Bologna in recognition of his prominent role as an intercessor during an outbreak of plague.[47] His significance as an intercessor in Naples during the troubled years between the Revolt of Masaniello of 1647–8 and the plague in 1656 was also increasing – aided by the growing cult around Azzolino's painting.

This momentum came to a head during the plague itself. As far as the Neapolitan populace was concerned, Azzolino's miraculous painting had demonstrated St Francis Xavier's prediction of the plague and commitment to protecting the city years before it struck. Little wonder, then, that the saint now took pride of place as one of the city's chief intercessors

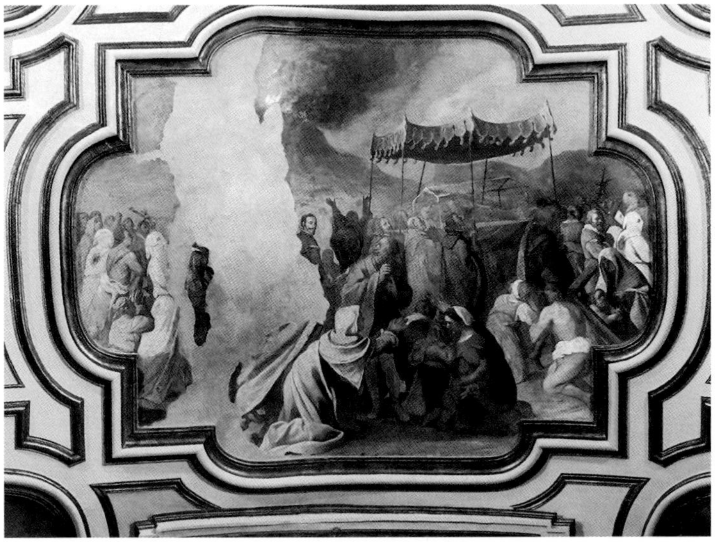

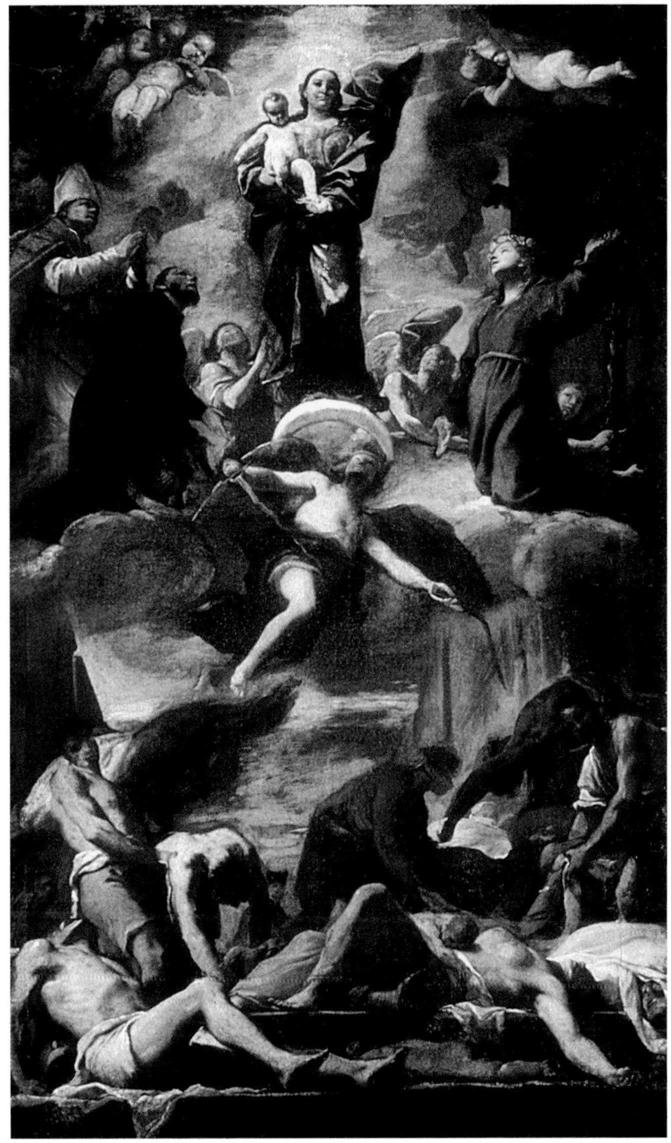

Facing page, left 113 Paolo Finoglio, *Blessed Andrea Avellino in Glory*, 1622–7. Oil on canvas, 296 × 190 cm. Cappella di Sant'Andrea Avellino, San Paolo Maggiore, Naples

114 (*facing page, right*) and 115 (*above*) Massimo Stanzione, *Scenes from the Life of St Giacomo della Marca*; *The Four Cardinal Virtues*, 1644–6. Fresco. Cappellone di San Giacomo della Marca, Santa Maria la Nova, Naples

Right 116 Mattia Preti, *Virgin of the Immaculate Conception with Sts Januarius, Rosalia and Francis Xavier*, *bozzetto* for the city-gate frescoes, 1656–8. Oil on canvas, 125 × 75 cm. Museo e Gallerie Nazionali di Capodimonte, Naples

during its darkest hour. The *deputati delle salute* – or Deputies of Health, who represented the medical response directed by the different neighbourhoods of the city – together with the city's *eletti* – or Syndics – accordingly made a number of public vows to honour St Francis Xavier and to contribute to his cult in exchange for his protection.

One such vow was to commission a series of frescoes depicting the *Virgin of the Immaculate Conception with Sts Januarius, Rosalia and Francis Xavier* to be positioned above the seven gateways to the city to express its desire for heavenly protection. This commission – one of Mattia Preti's first and most important undertakings in the city – was initiated at the height of the plague in June 1656 but not completed until early 1659 (fig. 116). The city also promised to formalize its recognition of St Francis Xavier and to elevate him to the ranks of the *padroni della Città*. It made good on this promise once the plague had abated, hosting a lavish festival in his honour lasting ten days from 1 December 1657.[48] It may have taken the Jesuits longer than the Theatines then: fifty-five years for St Francis Xavier to become *padrone* as opposed to one year for Andrea Avellino. But in the long run they had been able to achieve comparable recognition for one of their own.

But had the Jesuits gone too far? Had they placed themselves above the other orders to an extent that was perhaps audacious – even scandalous maybe – in this instance? This became a topic of some debate once the programme of Mattia Preti's frescoes became known. St Januarius's inclusion in this cycle was inevitable given his special status as *primus inter pares* in relation to the other patron saints of the city. St Rosalia's presence is likewise understandable given her significance as a pre-eminent southern Italian patron protector who had been called upon for intercession during the recent plague of Palermo in 1624.[49] But why was St Francis Xavier singled out above all the other Neapolitan patrons for inclusion in this series? To a certain extent his selection seems to have reflected his particular popularity among the Neapolitan populace during this calamitous period. At the same time, though, it undoubtedly represented a major public relations coup for the Jesuits, and it did not take long to attract complaints from the other orders.

The Theatines in particular felt especially slighted since they had promoted their own founder – the Blessed Cajetan – as a major protector against the plague and since their priests had also willingly placed themselves at the front line of ministry to the afflicted. Of the 250 Theatines who assisted the city, for example, only seventy were said to have survived following the cessation of the plague.[50] They accordingly extracted from the *eletti* of the city a promise to donate 500 ducats to finance the construction of a series of seven busts and full-length statues of Cajetan to be added to the city gates alongside Preti's frescoes. In this way, they were able to redress the balance and to install Cajetan on the city gates in a similar position of prominence to Sts Francis Xavier, Rosalia and Januarius. They also pushed for a more formal recognition of Cajetan as *padrone* – a status that was eventually granted in 1671, the year of his canonization. In the long run, then, perhaps the Theatines should be judged the winners of what today might be seen as an aggressive, even unseemly, ecclesiastical competition for saintly recognition. By the later decades of the century, at least, Naples had two Theatine patron protectors, whereas the Jesuits had only one.

SAINTS IN THE SACRISTY: THE ORATORIANS AND THE IMPORTANCE OF DONATIONS

Standing somewhat apart from this ecclesiastical one-upmanship was the third major Counter-Reformation congregation in Naples. Although they had arrived in the city some decades after the Jesuits and the Theatines, the Oratorians nonetheless went on to achieve a certain prominence and leading status as one of the prime post-Tridentine orders of the city. Their founder – St Philip Neri – for example, was added to the list of patron protectors of the city in 1668, seventy-three years after his death and forty-six after his canonization.[51] The Oratorians had also been fortunate in establishing a strategically advantageous base in Naples early on, via an outlay of 5,500 ducats in 1585 to acquire a well-situated palace opposite the cathedral.[52] From here would grow a significant complex comprising the expansive, barn-like church of the Girolamini (1592–1619), together with an accompanying community residence, meeting house and administrative offices (figs 117–18).

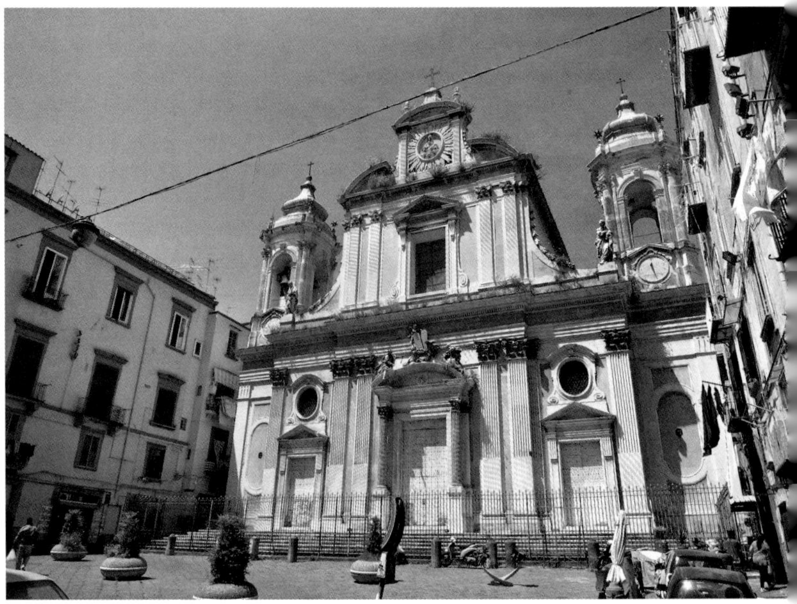

117 Exterior view, Chiesa dei Girolamini, Naples

The Naples Oratory also played a leading role in relation to the congregation as a whole, since it was the first and largest Oratorian foundation outside Rome. Yet the appeal of the Neapolitan Oratorians was based on a much less overtly prominent and, by contrast, much more low-key sense of institutional authority than either the Jesuits or the Theatines. This was characteristic of the Oratorians' mission more generally. As an initially conceived organization of secular priests, the Oratorians were worlds removed from the institutional and militant tone of other Counter-Reformation orders. The Roman Oratory had been founded, rather, on a deliberately non-hierarchical and unsystematic vision for maintaining a communal vocational life with an avowedly informal and non-monastic agenda. St Philip Neri had furthermore voluntarily resigned from the leadership of the congregation, while also strongly opposing the consolidation of institutional power and control via the Oratory's spread into other communities outside Rome.

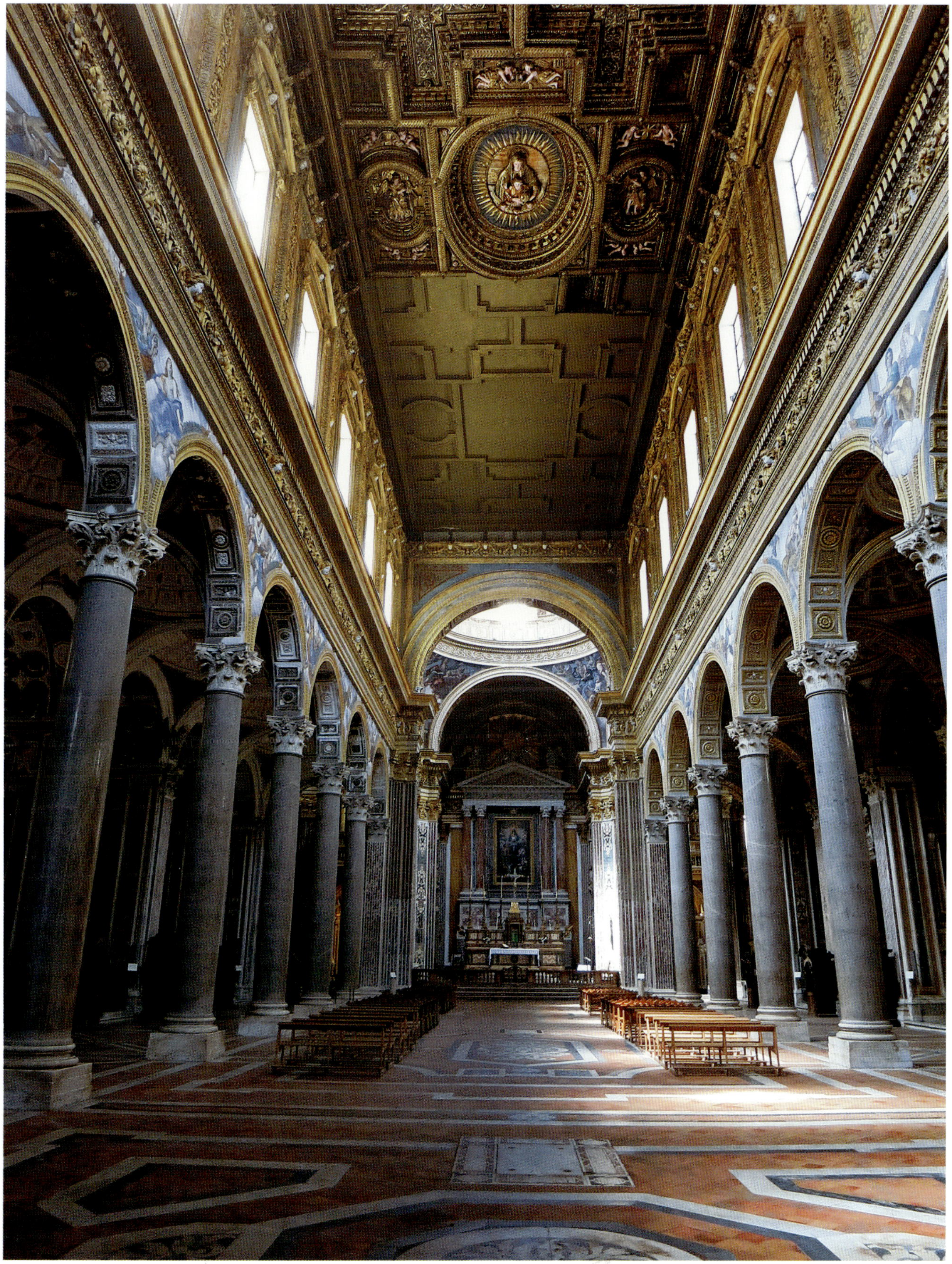

118 Interior view, Chiesa dei Girolamini, Naples

As is so often the case with political or religious movements that outgrow the austerity of their founders' original vision, Neri was ultimately overruled on this last wish by his early followers. The Neapolitan Oratory was accordingly founded in the 1580s, during the last years of Neri's life, by three of his early associates, Francesco Maria Tarugi, Antonio Talpa and Giovenale Ancina. Besides their missionary and evangelizing activities, the Oratorians were renowned in Naples as much as in Rome for their regular musical gatherings and associated cultural activities. In Naples musical recitals at the Oratory came to play a particularly prominent role in the cultural life of the city, with most of the leading musicians of the period being associated in one way or another with the Neapolitan Oratory throughout the seventeenth and early eighteenth centuries.[53] The library of the Girolamini was likewise an important feature and soon became one of the city's most significant bibliographic collections, comparable in this respect to the Roman Oratory's Biblioteca Vallicelliana.

The Oratorians in both Rome and Naples relied on a disparate yet influential community of like-minded individuals who were all drawn to the charismatic model of Neri's blend of Counter-Reformation piety and humility. These supporters included artists as much as they did influential aristocratic and ecclesiastical patrons. Much has been written, for example, concerning the potential affinities between Neri and the down-to-earth religiosity of Caravaggio's paintings, while other authors have likewise sought to identify Oratorian elements in the work of other artists associated with the Roman Oratory, such as Federico Barocci, Cristoforo Roncalli and Francesco Borromini.

Borromini, of course, was particularly important in that he designed the Roman Oratory before ultimately falling out with the Oratorians in the early 1650s.[54] Domenichino was also strongly drawn to the Oratorians from as early as 1614 during the period in which he was working on the altarpiece of the *Last Communion of St Jerome* for the site of Neri's first Roman residence in San Girolamo della Carità. When the deputies of the Tesoro di San Gennaro subsequently decided to request Domenichino's relocation to Naples to decorate the treasury it is surely significant to note that they first approached the head of the Neapolitan Oratory, Muzio Capece, to make the initial contact on their behalf.[55] While lying on his deathbed in 1641, Domenichino then chose to reconfirm the centrality of his association with the Oratorians by bequeathing an artwork to the subsequent head of the Neapolitan Oratory, Padre Rituggi, and expressing his desire to be buried in the Neapolitan church of the Girolamini.[56]

This then was the source of the Oratorians' very particular contribution to Neapolitan ecclesiastical patronage. Even more than the Theatines, they had neither the funds nor the extensive, powerful patronage networks to hasten the construction of resplendent monuments of Baroque magnificence akin to the Gesù Nuovo. The decoration of the Girolamini accordingly dragged on throughout the seventeenth century and beyond. Even the decoration of the chapel dedicated to their founder was still being worked on as late as the early eighteenth century: something that would be hard to imagine in the case of the Jesuits.[57] The Oratorians' significance as patrons lay instead in a different direction, evident above all in the tradition that they developed of encouraging individual donations, which grew out of the early Oratorian practice of displaying donations in the rooms of St Philip Neri in the Chiesa Nuova in Rome.[58]

Over time these donations came to constitute a distinctive and influential artistic legacy. Foremost among the additions to the local culture of Naples that were contributed in this way was a major painting by Guido Reni that was part of a bequest granted to the Oratorians in 1622 by an Oratorian lay brother, Domenico Lercaro (or Larcaro), a tailor based in Naples who came originally from Monopoli in the province of Bari (fig. 119).[59] Lercaro bequeathed his entire art collection to the Oratorians, including another painting of *St Jerome* by Reni's Bolognese pupil, Francesco Gessi. Lercaro most probably commissioned these paintings directly from Reni and Gessi during their ill-fated visit to Naples in 1620 to begin work on the Tesoro di San Gennaro.

Lercaro did not live to see the paintings delivered. Reni's seems to have arrived in Naples between 1628 and 1633, while Gessi's was delivered as late as 1646–8. When they did arrive, the works were framed prominently in the church and immediately constituted a major point of reference for the Neapolitan understanding of contemporary Bolognese classicism. Reni's *Meeting of Christ with St John the Baptist*, in particular, became a Neapolitan benchmark for an understanding of the work of this influential artist, second only to Reni's *Adoration of the Shepherds* that was sent to the Carthusians of Naples a few years later in the early 1640s.

A yet more distinctive group of donations was made to the Neapolitan Oratorians in the 1630s by Princess Anna Colonna Barberini. Anna Colonna belonged to one of the most venerable Roman aristocratic families and had at that stage risen to a position of particular influence via her marriage in 1627 to Taddeo Barberini, nephew to the pope and

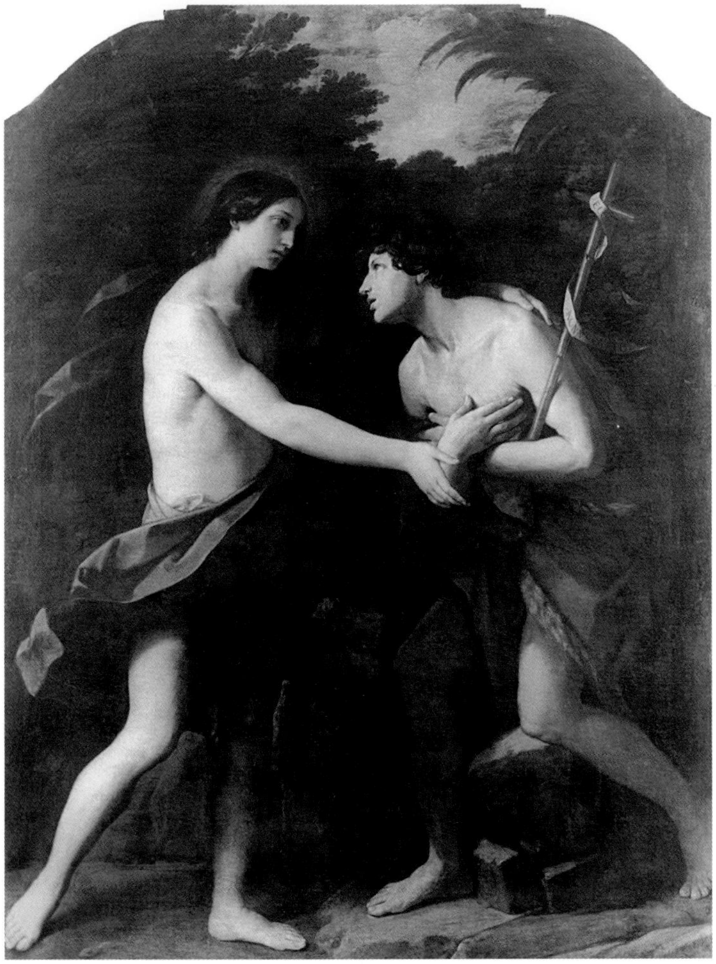

119 Guido Reni, *Meeting of Christ with St John the Baptist*, 1628–33. Oil on canvas, 198 × 148 cm. Chiesa dei Girolamini, Naples

lay head of the Barberini family. She had, at the same time, deep Neapolitan associations, her father having been Grand Constable of the Kingdom of Naples, and having herself been educated by the Discalced Carmelites of San Giuseppe dei Ruffi (this being another of the rapidly founded convents of this order after their arrival in Naples at the beginning of the seventeenth century).[60]

So it was that in the late 1630s she conceived the idea of making some lavish donations to the Neapolitan Oratorians. Her most extravagant – and also controversial – gift was a major cache of relics taken from the body of St Philip Neri that she had managed to obtain through direct papal intervention, over the clamorous opposition of the Roman Oratory itself. So concerned were the Roman Oratorians by the news of her schemes, in fact, that they attempted to move Neri's body from its original resting place to a new, secret location. Yet Anna Colonna Barberini persisted and in the end managed to get her way: an extraordinary public exhumation of Neri's body was carried out on 15 March 1638, presided over by Cardinal Francesco Barberini in the presence of the generals of both the Dominican and Franciscan orders, as well as other high-ranking prelates and aristocrats.[61]

Through this, and by also requiring the Oratorians to cede to her certain additional relics maintained in their collection, Anna Colonna Barberini was able to secure a veritable treasure trove of Nerian relics. These included some strands of the saint's hair, a nerve, a tooth, a section of his heart and a rib (these last being of particular significance, since a belief in the enlarged heart of St Philip Neri formed an important component of his cult and iconography).[62] To present them in an appropriate manner, she then commissioned none other than Algardi to create an especially lavish reliquary set – reportedly for the considerable sum of either 3,000 or 4,000 scudi – that was sent to Naples with all due pomp and ceremony in May 1639.[63]

The relics immediately became one of the main sights of the city and certainly assisted the cause of promoting Neri as a protector of Naples, helped by a dedicatory print produced in celebration of the transfer that shows Neri standing as protector of the city in the presence of his Neapolitan relics. Although the print itself has disappeared, an elaborate preparatory drawing has survived, indicating that it was worked on by the Oratorians' old friend and supporter, Domenichino, as one of his last Neapolitan commissions, with assistance from his Neapolitan heir and assistant, Francesco Raspantino (fig. 120).[64]

Anna Colonna Barberini had at the same time another prominent donation in mind. In May 1638 she arranged for the leading Barberini-aligned artist, Pietro da Cortona, to be paid 100 scudi for an altarpiece of the *Death of St Alexis* that was sent down to Naples to become the centrepiece of the chapel of that name in the Girolamini (fig. 122).[65] Da Cortona was the perfect choice for the Neapolitan Oratorians since he had already completed two major fresco cycles for the order's Roman mother church, the Chiesa Nuova (in the sacristy, 1633–4, and in the rooms of St Philip Neri, 1636), and would go on to produce an extensive series of frescoes in its nave and crossing.[66] The altarpiece was the only publicly accessible painting by Da Cortona to be seen in Naples and it accordingly constituted a precious documentation of the new High Baroque style that was otherwise almost unknown in public Neapolitan contexts prior to the arrival in the city of Mattia Preti in the early 1650s. Its influence is evident, for example, in Giordano's painting of the same subject in the church of Santa Maria delle Anime del Purgatorio ad Arco (fig. 121).[67]

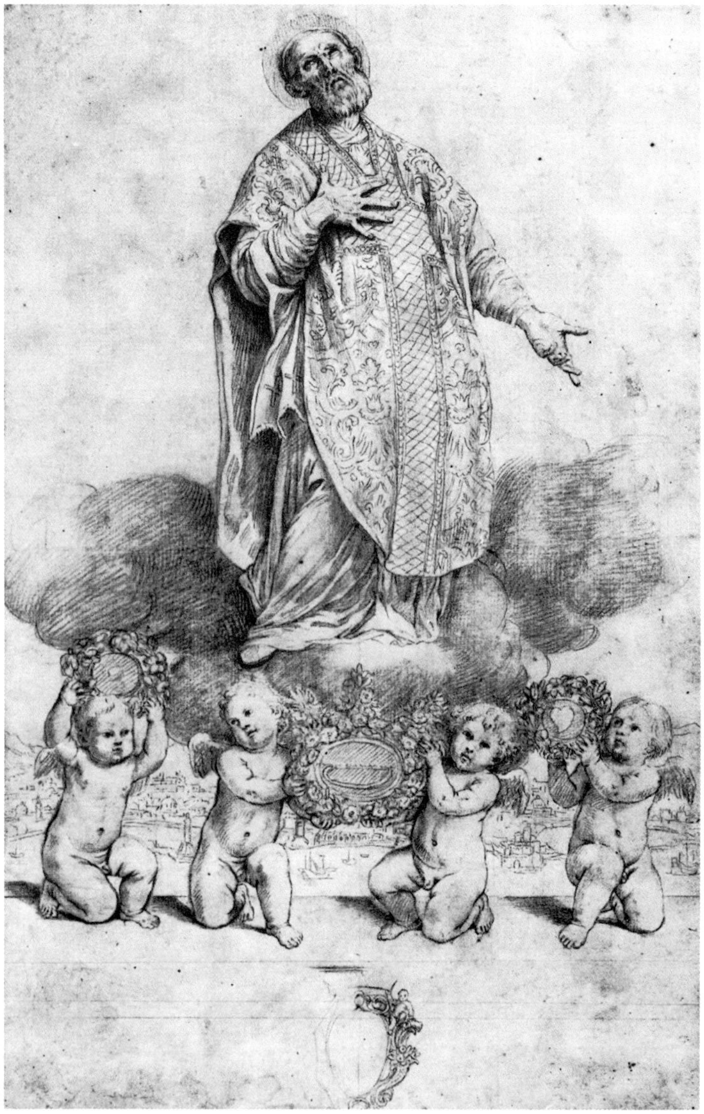

120 Francesco Raspantino after a drawing by Domenichino, *St Philip Neri in Glory*, *circa* 1638–9. Windsor Castle, P.H. no. 1253

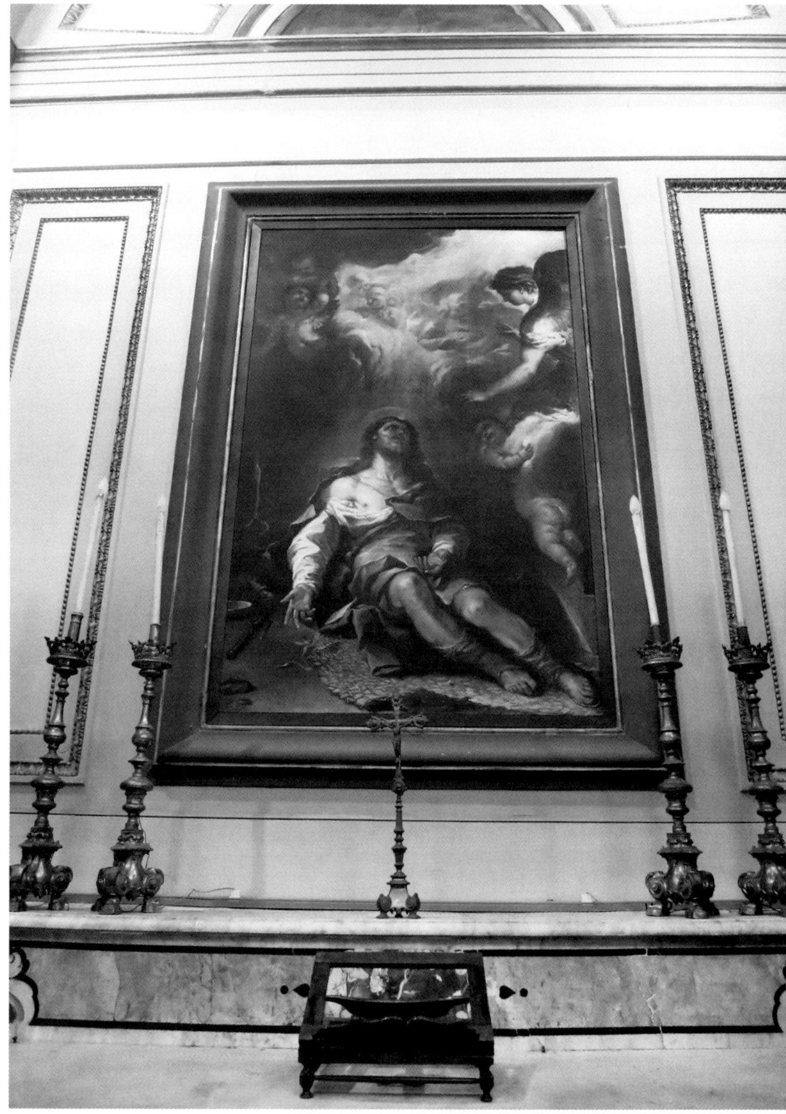

121 Luca Giordano, *Death of St Alexis*, signed and dated 1661. Oil on canvas, 214 × 138 cm. Santa Maria delle Anime del Purgatorio ad Arco, Naples

The choice of subject is very unusual and seems to have reflected the personal concerns of Anna Colonna Barberini. Alexis was a young Roman aristocrat who, according to tradition, had turned his back on worldly possessions in order to live as a beggar, sheltering under his family's palace and going unrecognized by his parents until after his death. The story had experienced a recent revival in Rome via a sacred opera of the subject that had been premiered at the Palazzo Barberini in 1632 and then repeated during the Roman *carnevale* of 1634.[68] The story had resonances with the circumstances of Anna Colonna Barberini's own life – her early ambitions to enter religious life had been thwarted by her family's desire to arrange her marriage as a means of creating a favourable dynastic alliance. From that time onwards, though, she had sought to channel her piety, tenacity and ongoing desire to associate with the purity of cloistered life into significant patronage initiatives, above all through her plans for founding the Discalced Carmelite convent of Santa Maria Regina Coeli in Rome, which she eventually instituted at the end of her life against significant opposition.[69] Her funerary monument from the church of this convent captures perfectly the combination of intense piety and fierce determination that so characterizes the Neapolitan bequests of this most remarkable donor (fig. 123).[70]

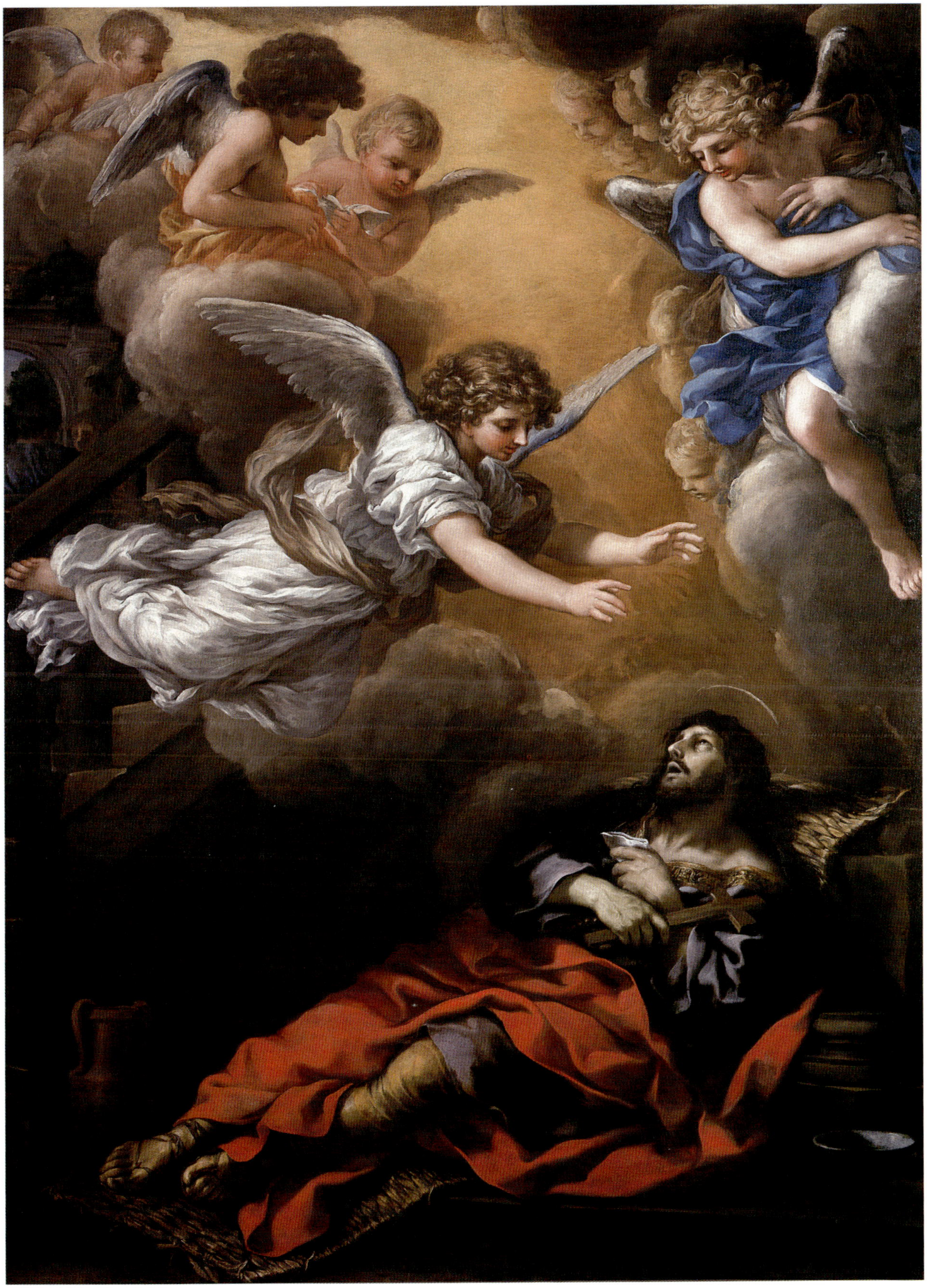

122 Pietro da Cortona, *Death of St Alexis*, 1638. Oil on canvas, 242 × 176 cm. Chiesa dei Girolamini, Naples

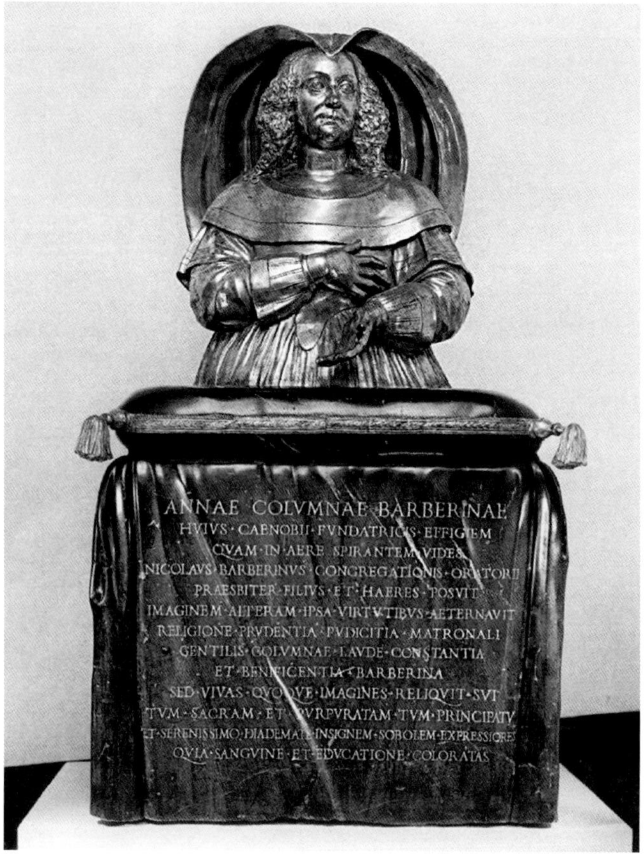

123 Gabriele Renzi, *Princess Anna Colonna Barberini*, 1655–9. Gilt bronze and black marble, 259 × 91 × 58 cm. Albright-Knox Art Gallery, Buffalo (formerly church of the convent of Carmelitane Scalze di Regina Coeli, Rome)

Pietro da Cortona's presence at the Neapolitan Oratory marks another of its striking emphases – namely, its focus on artists who had either pre-existing links with the Oratorians in Rome and/or who came from Neri's home region of Tuscany. The Florentine basis of the Neapolitan Oratory was, in fact, literally written into the stones of the church. The Girolamini had been designed by the Tuscan architect and antiquarian Giovanni Antonio Dosio, following the precedent of his earlier work at the order's mother church of the Chiesa Nuova in Rome in 1580 and as based on Brunelleschi's design for San Lorenzo in Florence.[71] Central to the design was a series of monumental Corinthian columns running the length of the nave that had been donated by the grand duke, Ferdinando de' Medici, reportedly at a cost of 1,000 scudi per column (see fig. 118).[72] Likewise the Florentine sculptor Pietro Bernini was commissioned to produce a series of six statues for the Girolamini (1601–7),[73] and the Neapolitan Oratorians even had a collection of four paintings by the Florentine Reformist painter Francesco Curradi, who is otherwise almost unknown in Naples.[74]

A number of the paintings described above were dispersed in various locations within the church of the Girolamini. Most, however, were kept together and displayed to the public as a coordinated ensemble in the sacristy and an adjoining room. This followed the precedent of the decoration of St Philip Neri's private rooms at the Roman Oratory that were (and still are) maintained as a precious space for the preservation of his memory. These rooms include public attestations of his followers' devotion in the form of donated artworks hanging on the walls.[75] In the case of the Naples collection, on the other hand, the emphasis was less on Nerian relics and other memorabilia associated with the early Oratorians (since these were restricted to the reliquaries in the chapel of St Filippo Neri in the church itself), and more on the display of paintings in their own right. Thus, the *quadreria* – as it is referred to in early documents – stands as one of the first documented public picture galleries in Naples.[76]

The uniqueness of this picture gallery of sacred images donated to the congregation from at least the early seventeenth century and made freely accessible to the general public should not be underestimated. The practices of several other pious institutions and religious orders bear similarities in certain respects. The Pio Monte della Misericordia, for example, is documented receiving bequests of painting collections from as early as the 1640s, and its *quadreria* today displays important early bequests from the likes of Francesco de Mura among other artists and collectors.[77] Yet it does not appear to have focused on developing a gallery in anything like as systematic a manner as the Oratorians; instead, it appears to have sold off bequests of paintings as a means of raising funds to support its charitable activities.[78]

In fact, there are only two other directly comparable examples of ecclesiastical *quadrerie* in Naples during this period. The first occurs in the collection of the Neapolitan archbishop Ascanio Filomarino in the 1640s and 1650s, but this functioned more as a continuation of his earlier private collecting activities carried out in Rome and will be accordingly discussed in that context in the next chapter. The only other example comes in the extraordinary collection of contemporary Neapolitan painting put together by the priors of the Certosa di San Martino – another indication of the remarkable significance of the patronage and collecting practices of this order.

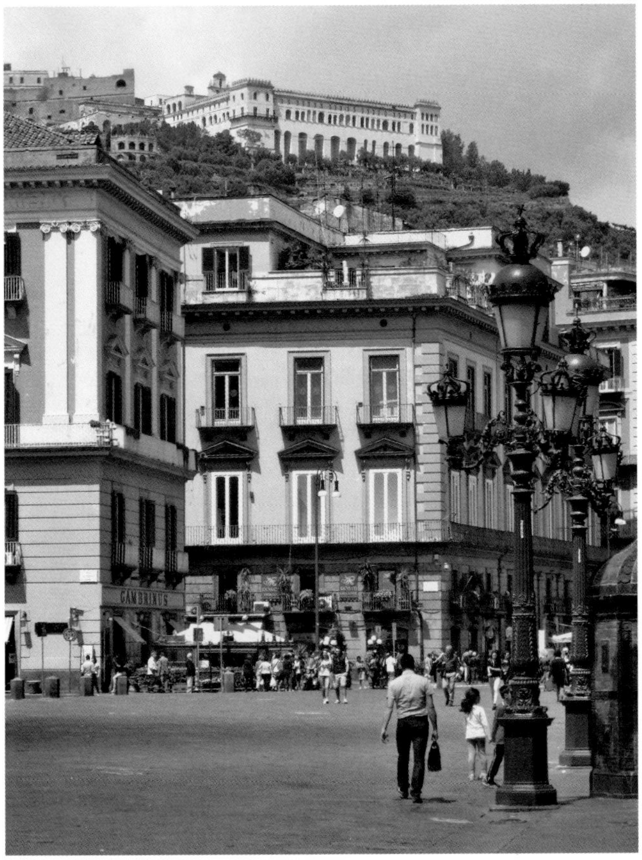

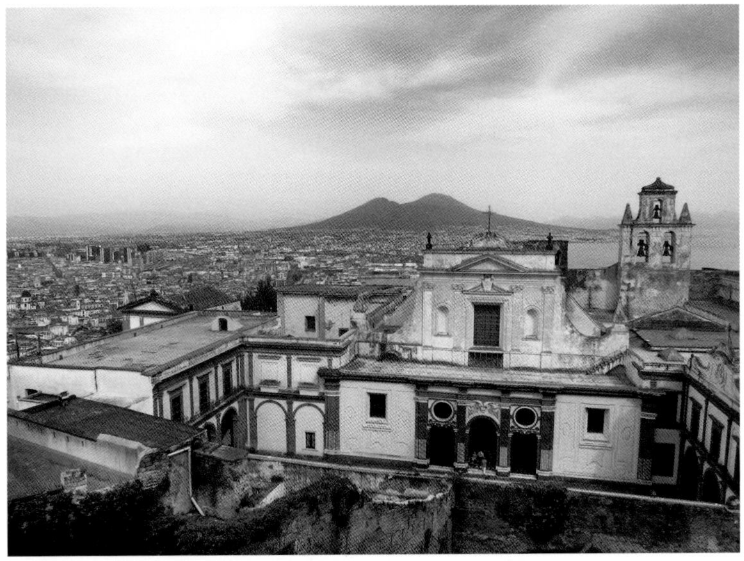

Left 124 View from the Piazza del Plebiscito and Palazzo Reale towards the Vomero hill and the Certosa di San Martino, Naples

Above 125 View from the Castel Sant'Elmo towards the Certosa di San Martino, Naples

THE CARTHUSIANS OF SAN MARTINO

Perched dramatically above Naples on the heights of the Vomero hill and thus offering some of the most spectacular views of the city (figs 124–5), the charterhouse of San Martino has for centuries elicited superlatives. Domenico Antonio Parrino's guide of 1700 describes it 'as beautiful as it is rich', while noting that: 'all that is there, is to be considered as stupendous and magnificent'.[79] In his guide of 1685, Sarnelli declared that it surpassed his powers of description, noting: 'di questa célèbre chiesa e monisterio per gli curiosi, li quali, havendone la comodità, possono con gli occhi propri soddisfare a se stessi, superando la nobilità e maestà delle cose la debolezza della mia penna' (regarding this church and monastery I must advise the curious that, if they get the chance, they should satisfy themselves by seeing it with their own eyes so as to surpass the weakness of my pen with the nobility and majesty of the sights themselves).[80] A yet more vivid account of its visual impact is provided by the commentary of two Tuscan Carthusian priors who recorded their first impressions of San Martino during a formal visitation of 1674:

> We entered to see this temple, or royal basilica, and before us appeared that New Jerusalem descended from heaven ... it was just as an ornamented bride appears to her husband. The vaulted covering with sculpted works all around sublimely catches the gazing eyes, dazzles tired and covered ears with the splendor of sacred likenesses, which portrayed by the most famous brush, in a similar fashion vibrantly impresses with majesty.[81]

At the time of these comments, the Certosa di San Martino stood as one of the most ancient and venerated monastic foundations of southern Italy, having been instituted by Angevin royal decree in 1325 and then reconfirmed and expanded upon in 1347. The Carthusians' vocational orientation was far removed from the evangelizing and missionary emphases of the new Counter-Reformation orders active in the city below. As practitioners of one of the city's most stringent versions of enclosed contemplative monasticism, the Carthusians preferred to remain at all times separate and aloof from the quotidian reality of Neapolitan urban life.

This undoubtedly saved them from the ravages of the plague of 1656, when they remained closed to the outside

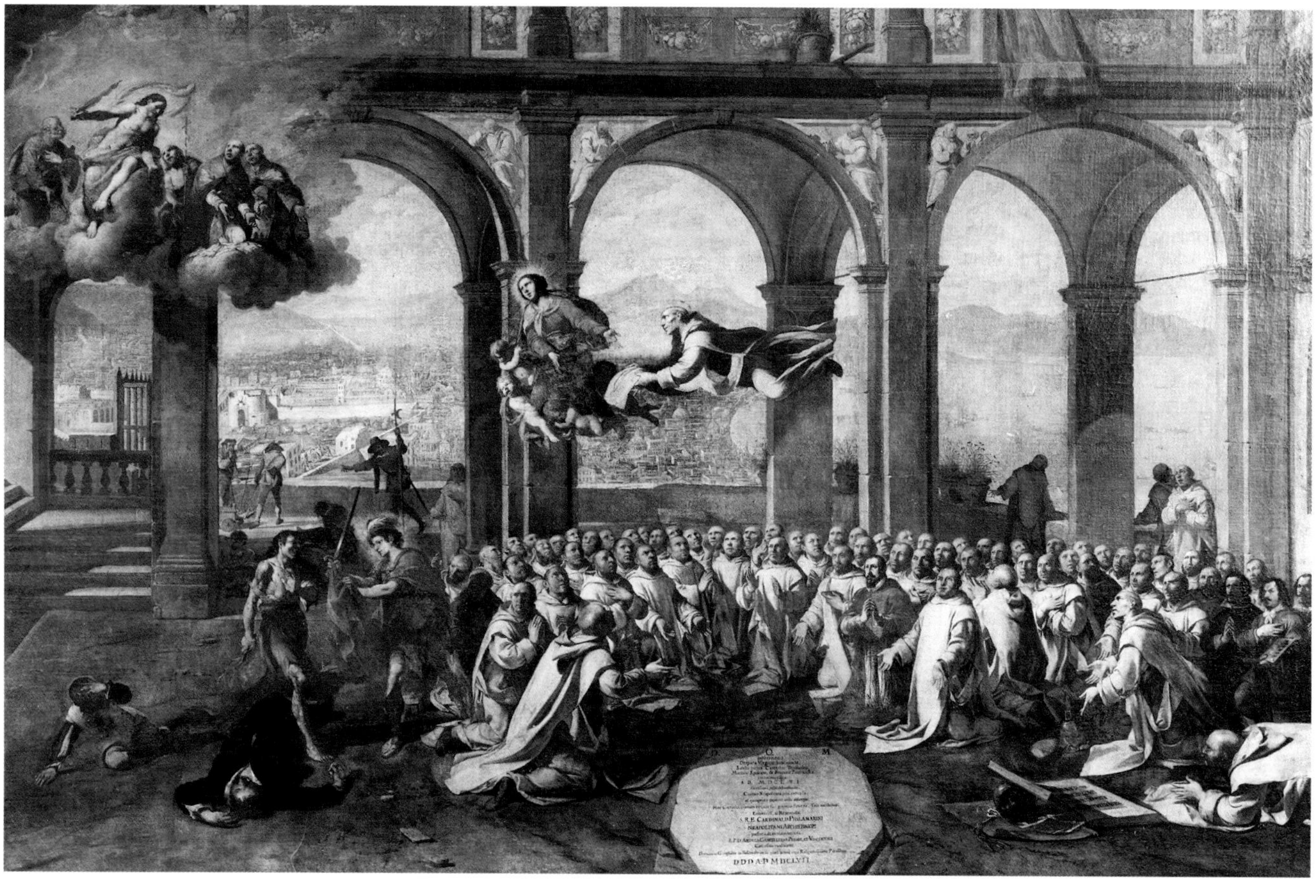

126 Domenico Gargiulo, *Thanksgiving after the Plague of 1656*, signed and dated 1657. Oil on canvas, 207 × 305 cm. Museo Nazionale di San Martino, Naples

world apart from a small number of favoured outsiders to whom they granted sanctuary within their walls. Those seeking refuge in this manner included the archbishop, Cardinal Filomarino, who was nonetheless criticized for fleeing the city during its darkest hour, together with their most trusted painter, Domenico Gargiulo, who recorded his thanks by producing an ex voto painting showing himself and the cardinal praying for deliverance in the presence of the prior, Andrea Cancelliere, and the rest of the Carthusian community (fig. 126).[82]

The *Thanksgiving after the Plague of 1656* evokes many of the unique qualities of the Carthusians' patronage. It emphasizes the inward, single-minded focus that enabled them to put together the city's most impressive and complete ensemble of Neapolitan Baroque ecclesiastical decoration. It also highlights their continued devotion to the eremitical ideals of austerity, solitude and penance (indicated by the monk in the right foreground praying before a book, skull and flail). At the same time, though, it simultaneously recognizes the usefulness of counter-balancing this hermetic inwardness by encouraging the painter's own contribution of a more outwardly focused and urbane contemporary artistic perspective. This is conveyed above all by the innovative aspects of Gargiulo's painting as it reconciles in a single image the otherwise conflicting traditions of informal genre realism and the hieratic formality and idealization required of the grand devotional painting.

Gargiulo's painting also refers to the Carthusians' recent patronage initiatives in a more direct way by situating the scene in an idealized version of Cosimo Fanzago's recently completed loggia for the prior's quarters that still to this day offers unrivalled panoramic views of the city and the bay of Naples (fig. 127). It also quotes the recently completed series of *Prophets* and *Patriarchs* painted by Ribera for the arches above the nave of the church of the Certosa (fig. 128). It was a fitting tribute, then, to a concerted cycle of modernization that was at that stage nearing completion.

In fact, the Certosa had been undergoing a continuous process of renovation since the end of the sixteenth century. The first of its two main phases of decoration and building works was directed during the 1590s to 1609 by Giovanni Antonio Dosio, architect of the Neapolitan church of the Oratorians; and the second was led from the 1620s to the 1650s by the inventive and productive capabilities of Dosio's former assistant, the sculptor and architect from Bergamo resident in Naples, Cosimo Fanzago.

It was Carlo Celano writing in 1692 who first noted the importance of the Certosa di San Martino for introducing into Naples the revetted marble inlay technique that creates such a strong impression of a lavishly coordinated decorative opulence and which constitutes a defining feature of Neapolitan Baroque church decoration more generally (figs 129–30). He noted:

> And beginning with the Church [of the Certosa] . . . it cedes nothing to the richest churches in Italy because of the preciousness of its ornamentation. Present on the pilasters and in the chapels, this vestment of most refined inlaid marble is work that can be called original because it was devised by Cavalier Cosimo Fansaga [*sic*], and it was here that such inlay was first seen in Italy.[83]

More recent analysis has tempered Celano's emphasis by underlining the importance of Dosio's earlier work at the Girolamini and the influence on Dosio, in turn, of broader developments in late Renaissance polychrome marble decoration deriving particularly from the Medicean ambience of Vasari's design for the Cappella dei Principi in San Lorenzo, Florence, and Domenico Fontana's scheme for the Sistine chapel in Santa Maria Maggiore, Rome.[84] The point to note here, though – and Celano was surely correct in pointing out the Certosa's significance in this respect – is that Dosio and the Oratorians were not able to realize fully their initial designs for the Girolamini because of their relative lack of funds. The Carthusians, by contrast, were blessed with a lavish and ongoing regal inheritance that had been supplemented with significant papal, vice-regal and aristocratic support. They were also able to draw on an extensive portfolio of financial resources, including tax farms, rental properties and essential agricultural commodities, to fund a vast array of payments to artists over the space of many decades (Table 6).[85]

Cosimo Fanzago's recommendation appears to have carried considerable weight at the Certosa, so much so that it seems appropriate to credit him with a major part of the consistently high-quality and distinctive nature of the commissions

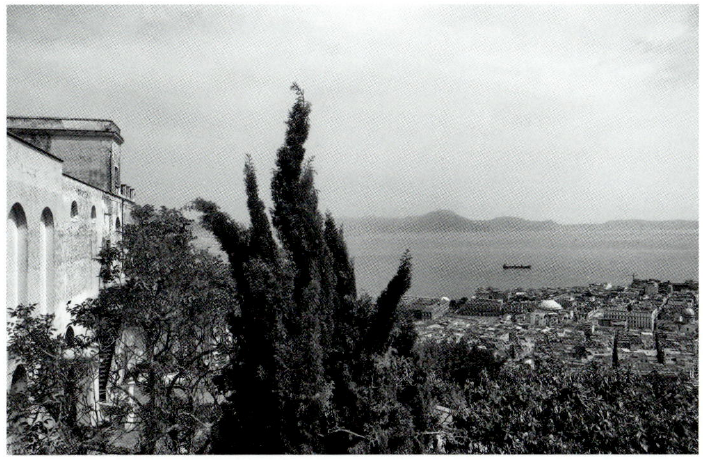

Above 127 View from the Loggia del Priore, Quarto del Priore, Certosa di San Martino, Naples

Below 128 Nave of the church of the Certosa di San Martino showing Jusepe de Ribera, *Joel*, signed, and *Amos*, signed and dated 1640, from the *Prophets* and *Patriarchs* series. Oil on canvas, 252 × 270 cm and 256 × 272 cm, and with the Cappella di San Bruno beyond, Museo Nazionale di San Martino, Naples

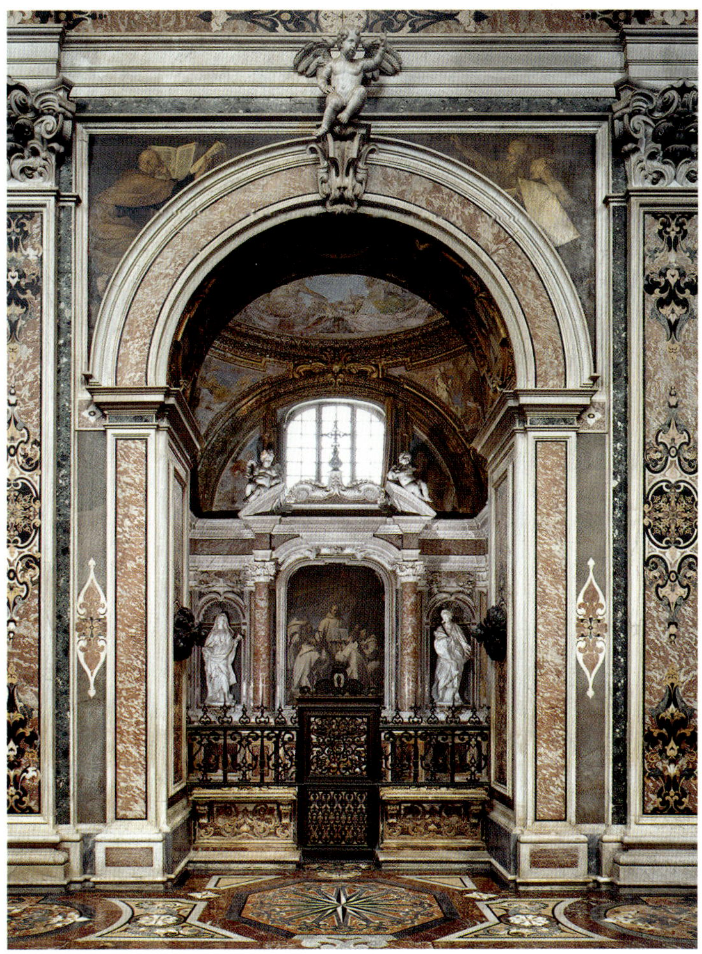

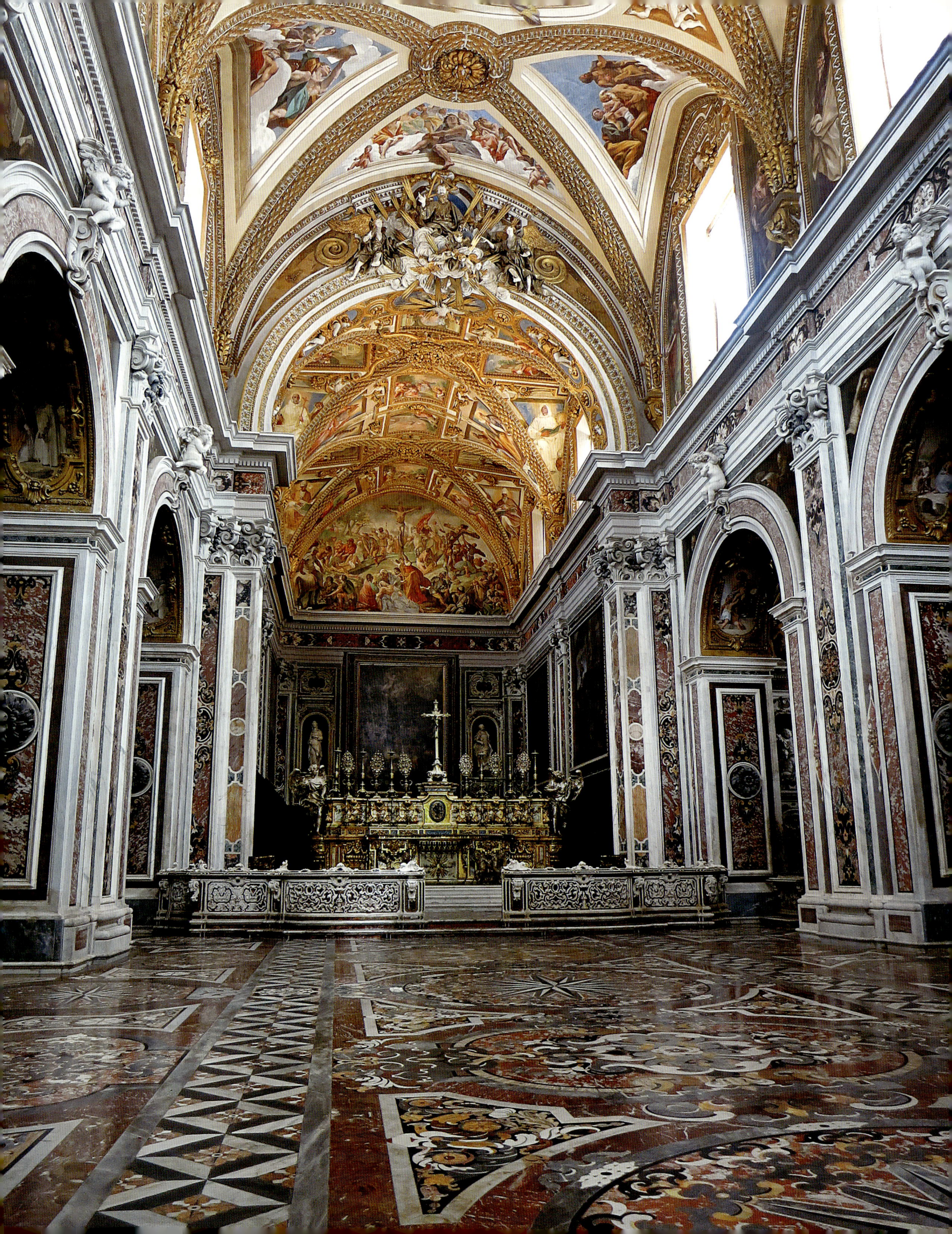

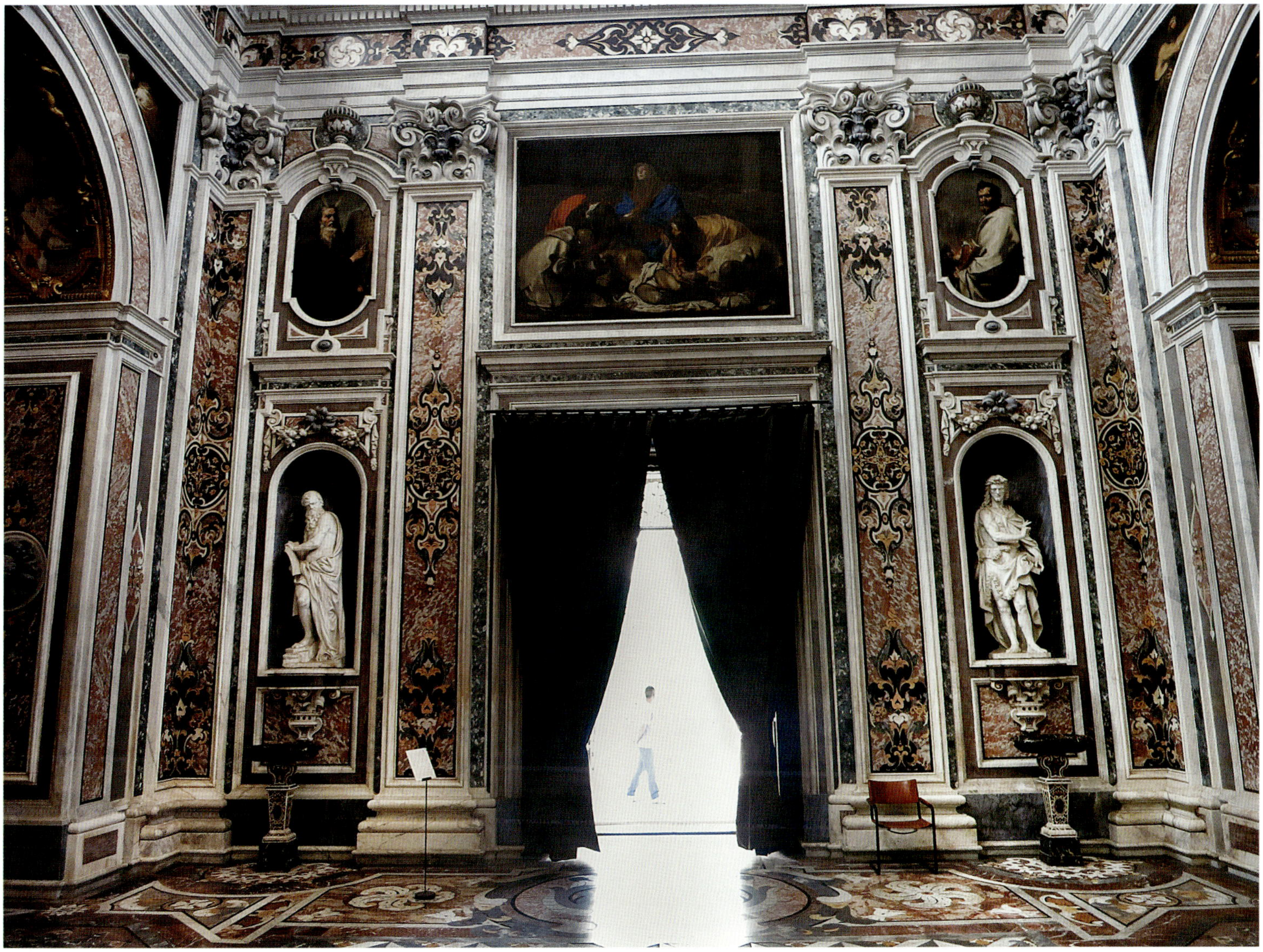

130 Interior façade, church of the Certosa di San Martino, Naples, showing Jusepe de Ribera, *Moses* and *Elijah* (1638) and Massimo Stanzione, *Pietà* (1638)

carried out there from the 1620s to the 1650s. The frescoes of the landscape painter Domenico Gargiulo, produced in the lay brothers' choir in the late 1630s, for example, were almost certainly painted following the model of drawings provided by Fanzago.[86] Likewise, the specialist architectural painter Viviano Codazzi (who also came from Fanzago's home region of Bergamo) was undoubtedly recommended to the Carthusians by Fanzago and then required to follow Fanzago's drawings for his two oil-on-canvas paintings of architectural settings that were produced for the sacristy in 1644–5.[87] Fanzago seems also to have acted more broadly as a trusted artistic adviser to the Carthusians. He appears to have taken on the role of artistic talent scout, acting as their eyes and ears, attentive to the latest artistic developments in the city below in a manner barred to them.

Fanzago is documented in this regard selling to the Carthusians altar frontals and paintings that were attributed to Caravaggio and Ribera.[88] Lanfranco's complaint to his Roman protector Ferrante Carlo concerning the strong influence that Fanzago exerted over the Carthusians in a negative as well as a positive sense should also be recalled. Lanfranco felt that Fanzago had turned the Carthusians against him as a result of his rejecting Fanzago's proposal that his son should marry Lanfranco's daughter. The Carthusians

Facing page 129 Interior view, church of the Certosa di San Martino, Naples

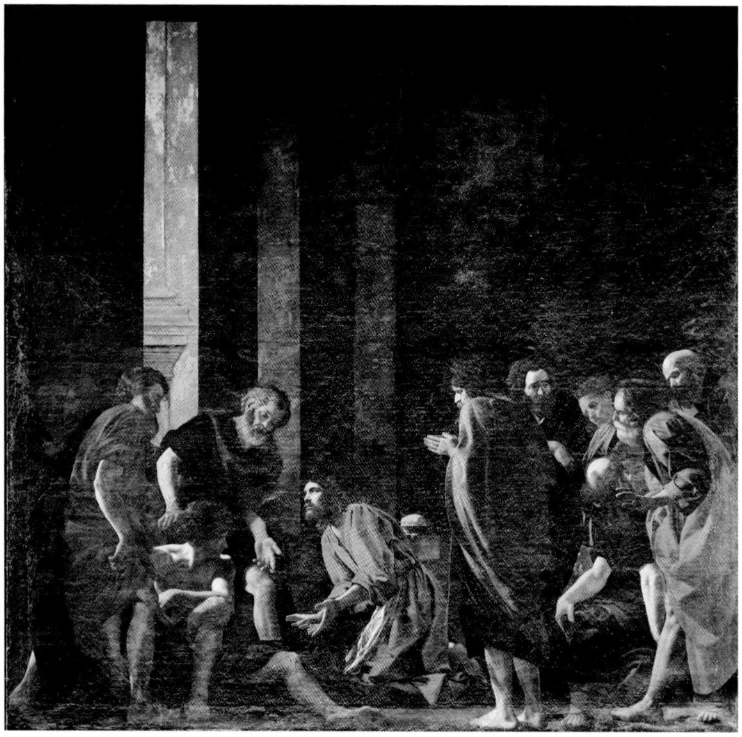

131 Giovanni Battista Caracciolo, *Christ Washing the Feet of the Disciples*, 1622. Oil on canvas, 393 × 390 cm. Choir of the church of the Certosa di San Martino, Naples

had initially got on well with Lanfranco and endorsed his work as a result of Fanzago's support ('nel principio del lavoro ero amato assai dall'architetto ... per il medesimo capo i monaci amavano me' – to begin with I was liked by the architect ... and for this reason the monks also liked me), but after Lanfranco had rebuffed Fanzago relations soon soured. The Carthusians, 'li quali non fanno né più innanzi, né più indietro se non quello che dice il detto architetto' (who go neither forwards nor backwards without the architect's say so), now turned against him, rejecting his altarpiece for the chapel of Sts Hugh and Anselm; Lanfranco donated it instead to the church of his Lombard compatriots at Sant'Anna dei Lombardi (see fig. 9).[89]

Yet while Fanzago may have played a major role, it is also clear that the Carthusians equally knew their own minds as connoisseurs of painting. The priors and procurators of the Certosa were tough and exacting patrons who were not afraid to set rigorous stipulations on their commissions and who were quite prepared to change their minds when not satisfied with initial results. Besides Lanfranco's rejected altarpiece of 1639, they rejected an altarpiece of *St Martin* by Paolo Finoglio in 1631 on the grounds that 'non essendo riuscito a soddisfazione delli padri' (it did not succeed in pleasing the fathers).[90] De' Dominici also heard that they had rejected a major painting by Ribera. He may have been misled in this, but, even so, the story reinforces the prevailing impression of the Carthusians' reputation as severe taskmasters when it came to their standards of patronage.[91]

The Carthusians included unusually detailed requirements in their commission of 1622 to Giovanni Battista Caracciolo for a large painting of *Christ Washing the Feet of the Disciples* to be installed in the choir (fig. 131). The contract was explicitly framed as a trial piece, or *quadro di prova*. Caracciolo was to be given a down payment of 100 ducats that would nonetheless be fully refundable 'che detto quadro non piacessa a detti R.di padri' (in the event that the above-mentioned painting is not pleasing to the said Reverend Fathers).[92] If, on the other hand, the Carthusians were pleased with the results, then the contract included the stipulation that 'promette de piu detto Priore D. Bernardino farli far a detto Gio: battista tucta la pittura della Cappela difora a frisco' (the above-mentioned prior Don Bernardino moreover promises to award to the said Giovanni Battista all the painting of the chapel beyond in fresco).

The Carthusians were evidently satisfied with Caracciolo's work, since it initiated a long association between them. He went on to fresco two chapels – the chapel of the Assumption (1631; fig. 132) and the chapel of St Januarius (1632). He also executed a number of additional altarpieces, including one of *St Martin* that the Carthusians kept as a replacement for the rejected altarpiece by Finoglio (fig. 133).[93] Caracciolo's *Washing of the Feet of the Disciples* also seems to have suggested to the Carthusians the need to revise their earlier plans concerning the programming of paintings in the choir more generally. This, the most sacred space in the church, had initially been decorated with two recently commissioned paintings by Belisario Corenzio that were installed beneath a painting of the *Crucified Christ* by Cavalier d'Arpino hanging above the high altar. This last painting had been commissioned all the way back in 1589.[94] Soon after installing Caracciolo's painting, however, the Carthusians apparently had cause to revise their thinking and so began a process of updating this area with more modern work. Corenzio's paintings were removed altogether and D'Arpino's *Crucified Christ* was transferred to the sacristy, to be replaced by Lanfranco's more modern and visually impressive fresco of the *Crucifixion*.

At the same time, the Carthusians also ordered a suite of unusually large oil paintings to be installed alongside

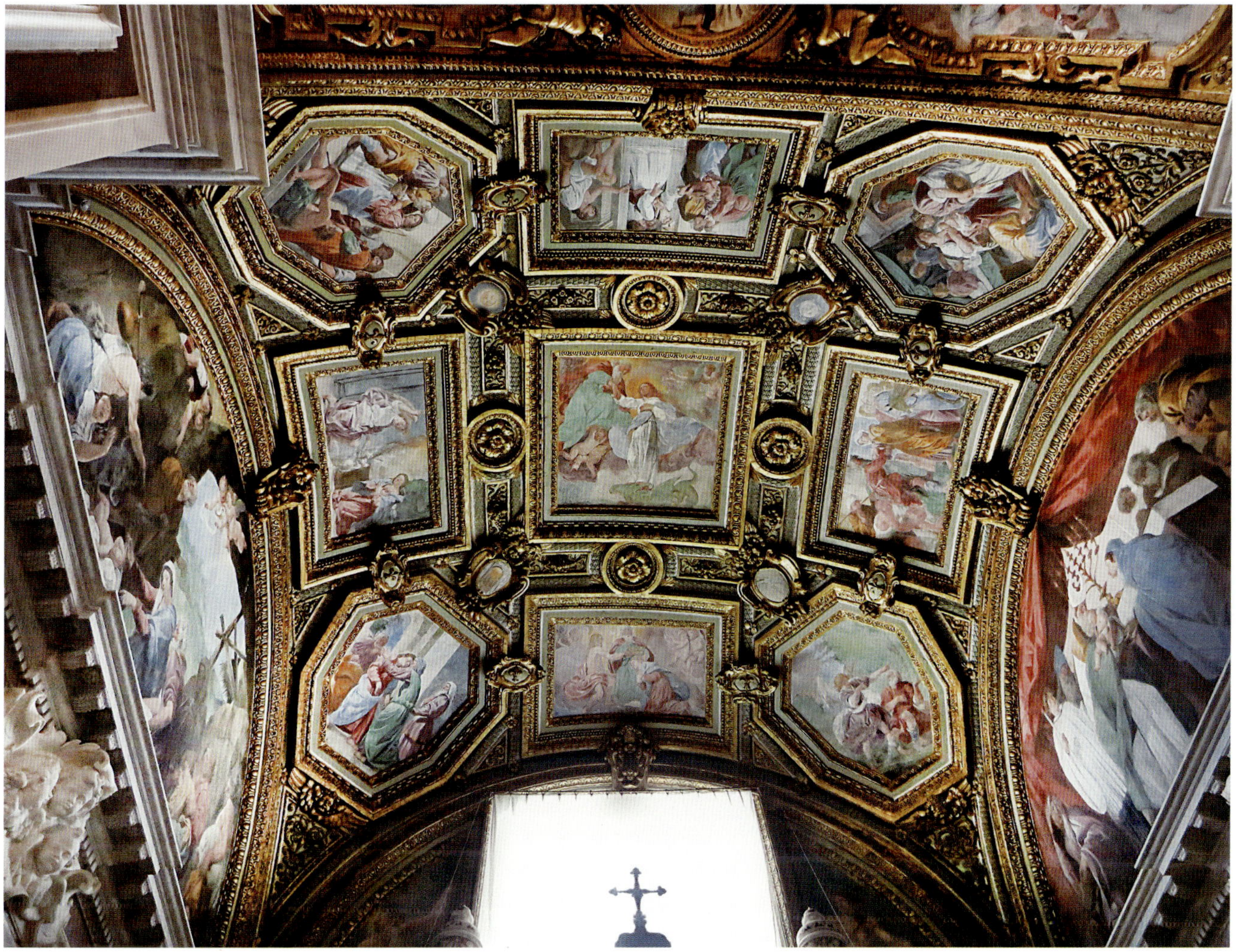

132 Giovanni Battista Caracciolo, *Scenes from the Life of the Virgin*, Cappella dell'Assunta, 1631. Fresco. Church of the Certosa di San Martino, Naples

Caracciolo's *Washing of the Feet of the Disciples*. These included Massimo Stanzione's *Preparations for the Last Supper*, commissioned for 1,000 ducats in 1639, and Ribera's *Communion of the Apostles*, commissioned for approximately the same amount in 1638 but not completed until 1651. They also ordered an *Adoration of the Shepherds* from none other than Guido Reni, which was not delivered until the early 1640s. The cost for this work – or so at least Malvasia would have us believe – was 3,000 scudi 'and a princely gift', making it one of the most expensive oil paintings in Naples.[95]

The Carthusians of San Martino, then, were exacting when it came to quality control yet at the same time flexible and open to changing their plans as it suited them. They evidently needed this latter quality, since they set themselves the demanding task of keeping track of an unprecedented rate of activity all demanding their attention at the same time. In the single year of 1638, for example, they were required to supervise major projects by Lanfranco, Stanzione and Ribera, all painting concurrently in the nave, together with Gargiulo's frescoes in the Tesoro Vecchio, not to mention numerous additional building works, commissions for sculpture and marble decorative schemes for the prior's quarters and elsewhere in the church and monastery grounds.

It is perhaps not surprising that the Carthusians evidently found it difficult to keep abreast of all the finer details of these parallel commissions, particularly when it came to settling accounts for finished work that related back to contracts that had often been devised a number of years earlier. Changed plans and the regular turnover of priors

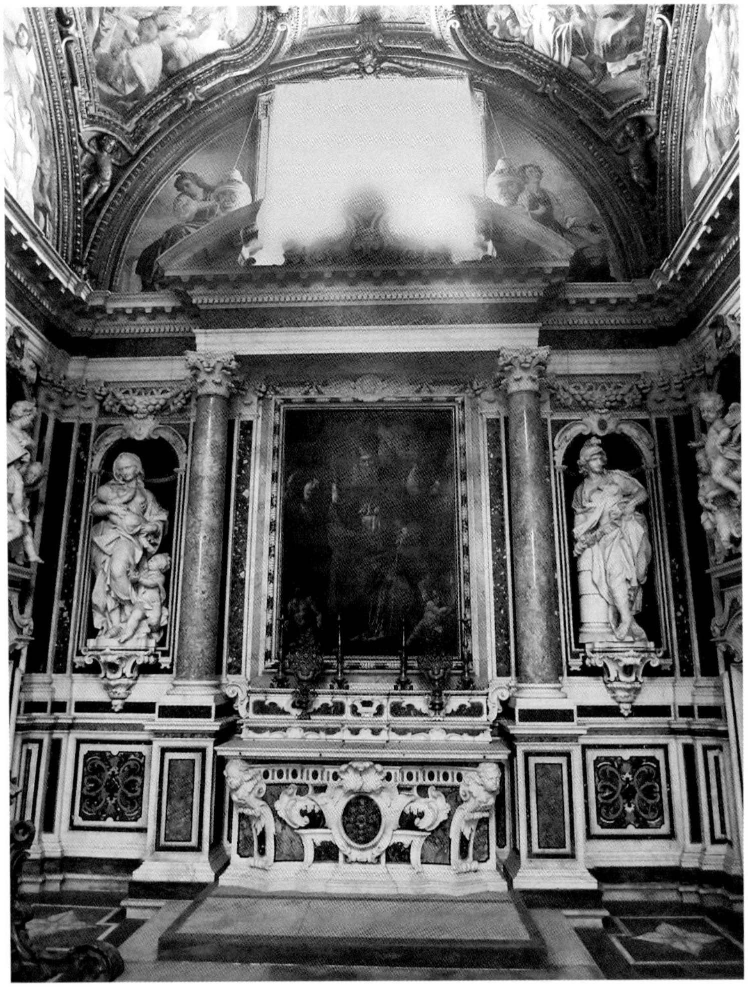

133 Cappella di San Martino, church of the Certosa di San Martino, Naples. Giovanni Battista Caracciolo, *St Martin and Four Angels*, 1631. Oil on canvas, 230 × 160 cm

and other senior members of the community during these years only added to the problems. So, for example, in 1644 the prior, Giovanni Battista Pisante, apparently promised Viviano Codazzi a commission for a large painting in the choir. But when he died the following year, his successor Lorenzo Candela lost interest in the project and Codazzi accordingly felt short-changed for his work. Codazzi subsequently sought redress from the Carthusians,[96] in tandem, it transpired, with most of the artists who had worked at the Certosa during this period – including Lanfranco,[97] Ribera[98] and Cosimo Fanzago himself.[99]

This might justify a suspicion that the Carthusians drove a hard bargain in their contracts and then maintained a less-than-perfect system of bookkeeping for their extensive and complex financial outlays over long periods. It is all the more remarkable then to note that none of this appears to have had any negative impact on the quality of work produced. On the contrary, in fact, the Certosa represents an unparalleled achievement in bringing together a consistently impressive sequence of paintings commissioned concurrently from the leading painters of the day – Caracciolo, Finoglio, Ribera, Stanzione – together with a number of their most talented followers – Gargiulo, Vaccaro, Pacecco de Rosa – and some of the prominent figures of Roman and central Italian painting.

As Table 6 makes clear, this intense programme of artistic upgrading and remodelling of the interior of the church and related spaces resulted in a lavish and systematic commitment of time and money on the part of the Carthusians relative to the other orders. The Carthusians may not have been operating on quite the massive scale of the Jesuits, yet what they managed to create was in its own way just as impressive as the Jesuits at the Gesù Nuovo. From the 1620s to early 1650s, for example, they are recorded as spending no fewer than 23,500 ducats on painting, an extraordinary sum in relation to the 3,000 ducats noted above as the outlay paid by the nuns of Santa Maria della Sapienza for the entire sequence of frescoes and altarpieces in their recently completed church. It is no wonder, therefore, that the finished interior of the church of the Certosa has accordingly been justly characterized in the modern literature as both 'a precious anthology of fine and applied Neapolitan art' and 'a gallery comprised of masterpieces by the most eminent Neapolitan and foreign painters'.[100]

What comes through most clearly, perhaps, amid the range and complexity of the decorative projects undertaken at San Martino, is the Carthusians' evident confidence – even boldness one might say – in commissioning works that represented either a major step up for emerging artists or a considerable extension of the capabilities of more established painters. The year 1622, to take one example, represented a watershed for Caracciolo. At this date, he was seeking to re-establish himself in the city following a long period of travel abroad, working in Florence and Genoa (1618–19). The commission for *Christ Washing the Feet of the Disciples* in one of the most prestigious areas of the Certosa represented a major boost to his somewhat stop-start career up to that point, and his subsequent frescoes and altarpieces at the Certosa represent his largest body of work for a single ecclesiastical patron.[101] The same applies to the breakthrough commission awarded to Stanzione in 1630 for the decoration of the chapel of St Bruno (see pp. 42–3). In entrusting this artist with the contract for the entire chapel dedicated to the Carthusians' patron saint – altarpiece, lateral paintings, lunettes, entrance arch, dome and pendentives – the monks were presenting him with a great opportunity, and its success would pave the way for the pre-eminence of his subsequent career.

Perhaps yet more extraordinary, though, were the opportunities afforded by the Carthusians to Ribera. As a committed Caravaggesque painter of oil on canvas, Ribera was never able to compete with Domenichino, Lanfranco, Stanzione or the other fresco painters of the day in working on large-scale, architectural decorative schemes. And yet, this is precisely what the Carthusians allowed him to attempt when they awarded him the major contract in 1638 for a series of twelve oil-on-canvas paintings of *Prophets* and *Patriarchs* to be installed above the arches of the nave (1638–43). It was a signal moment in Ribera's career and one that he was never able to repeat – being restricted in other respects to altarpieces and gallery paintings.

The Carthusians were similarly innovative when it came to their patronage of emerging artists. They effectively launched the career of the previously unknown Andrea Vaccaro with a commission in 1636 for a painting of the *Penitent Magdalene* that was justly renowned in its day as one of his most influential compositions and that Vaccaro perhaps never bettered throughout the remainder of his long and productive career (fig. 134).[102] The Carthusians appear to have been especially trusting and supportive, moreover, in patronizing the work of Domenico Gargiulo. This hitherto promising yet not especially prominent painter of small-scale landscape cabinet paintings was awarded from the end of the 1630s onwards a series of progressively more important commissions for frescoes in the treasury (1638), lay brothers' choir (1639–40) and prior's quarters at the Certosa (1642–7), together with numerous canvas paintings noted above.

The shift from small easel paintings to extensive frescoes marks an especially dramatic elevation for Gargiulo, since his previous career had not shown any signs of a particular expertise as an independent master of fresco painting.[103] The Carthusians were evidently aware of this when they first contracted Gargiulo and they characteristically displayed a certain amount of initial caution in their dealings with him. First they devised a limited contract for a trial piece to be painted in the old treasury, which they then used as a basis for awarding him further work in the following years. For his part, Gargiulo evidently paid off the Carthusians' growing trust. He went on to become one of the Certosa's most trusted and longest-standing artists (as his assessment of Ribera's ability to complete the *Communion of the Apostles* in 1651 further indicates: see pp. 64–6). In his work at the Certosa, Gargiulo was given the opportunity to project a monumental version of what constituted, in effect, the birth of a new school of Neapolitan painting. This focused on idealized, picturesque landscape vistas of the Bay of Naples and its surrounds that would exert a strong influence on the local scene for hundreds of years, leading up to and including the work of Giacinto Gigante and the so-called School of Posillipo in the nineteenth century.[104]

The culminating point of this unrivalled sequence of work occurred in Gargiulo's frescoes for the prior's quarters (fig. 135). Here he introduced into the city a Neapolitan equivalent of the popular Roman ecclesiastical tradition of landscape frescoes with hermit monks and other incidental religious scenes such as had been introduced at the end of the sixteenth century by Paul and Mathew Bril, among others, and which was also evident in more recent com-

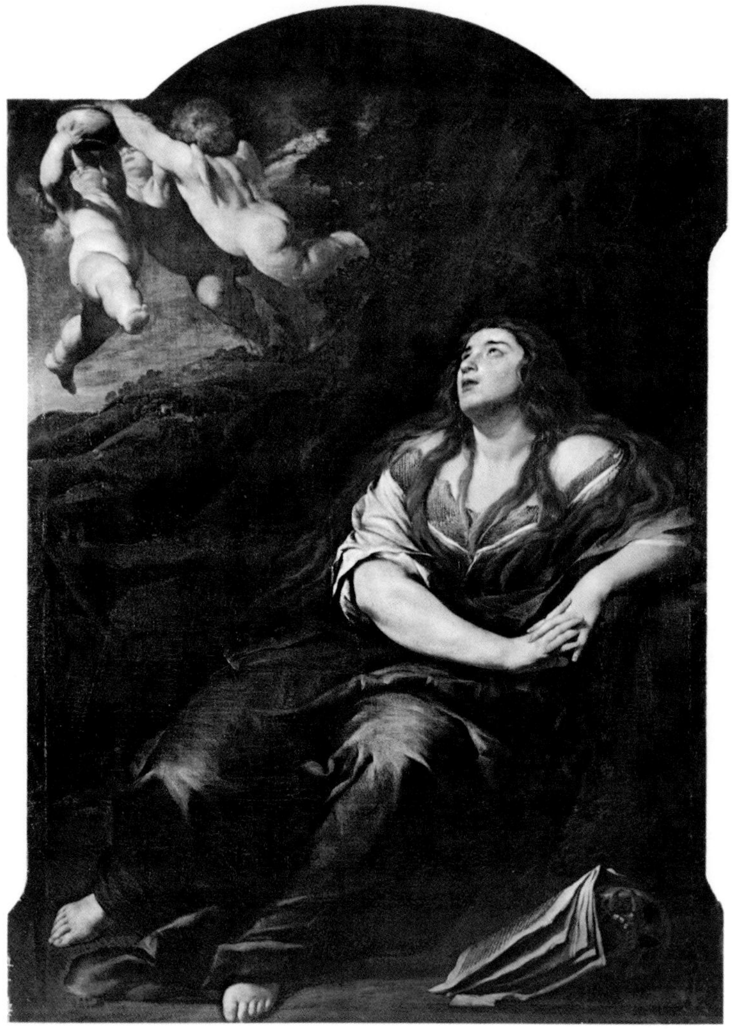

134 Andrea Vaccaro, *Penitent Magdalene*, 1636. Oil on canvas, 180 × 125 cm. Museo Nazionale di San Martino, Naples, chapel of Mary Magdalene

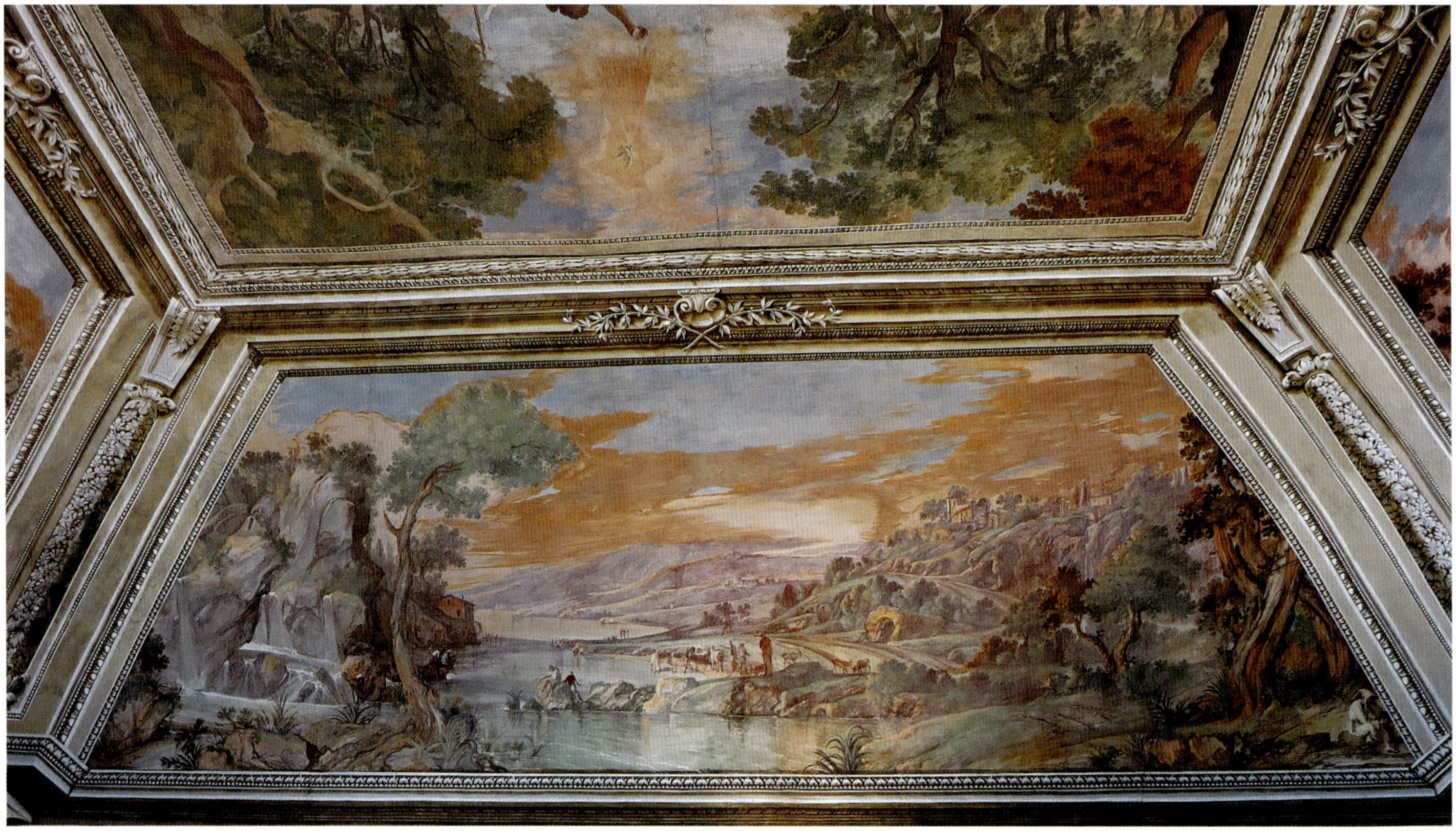

Above 135 Domenico Gargiulo, *Landscape with Penitent Saint and the Bay of Naples*, 1642–7. Fresco. Quarto del Priore, Certosa di San Martino, Naples

Below 136 View from the Loggia del Priore, Quarto del Priore, Certosa di San Martino, Naples

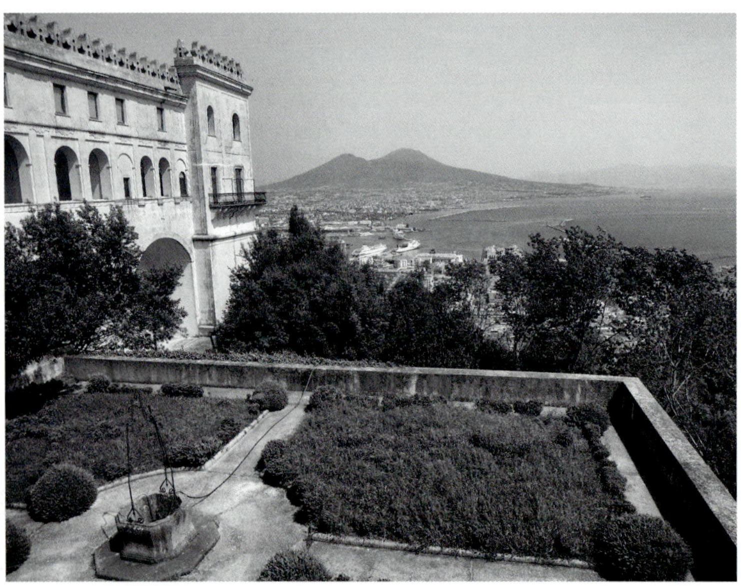

missions such as the work of Tassi and his workshop in the Appartamento Nobile Pontificio of the Vatican Palace and the similar frescoes painted for Urban VIII in 1635.[105] The urbane and sophisticated emphasis in these frescoes on current trends in contemporary landscape painting, combined, in turn, with Carthusian elements of eremitical austerity, played an important role in registering the significance of the prior's quarters as a transitional space providing a ceremonial meeting point between the Carthusians' status as a rigorously enclosed order and the outside world.

The rooms functioned in this respect as *stanze di rappresentanza* that would be shown to important visitors, giving them an impression of the sophistication of the order as a whole. They culminated in a loggia and hanging garden offering views onto the city below that were the equivalent in real terms to Gargiulo's painted vistas in the rooms next door (fig. 136). Thus when the French traveller Mabillon visited the city in 1685 he stressed the palatial appearance of the prior's rooms.[106] Likewise, Thomas Salmon, writing in the early eighteenth century, noted that 'l'abitazione del Priore può infatti gareggiare coll'appartamento di un principe' (the prior's residence could, in fact, compete with the apartment of a prince).[107]

Fundamental to the impression that visitors were meant to gain from these quarters was the inclusion of an extensive library and a significant collection of contemporary religious paintings that the priors had built up over the years as a parallel activity to the commissioned work in the church itself. The *quadreria* of the prior's quarters included significant paintings by most of the artists associated with the Certosa – including Ribera, Stanzione, Gargiulo, Vaccaro, De Rosa – as well as many other often surprisingly diverse artists, such as Aniello Falcone, Aniello de Leone, François de Nomé and Giacomo Farelli.[108] Even more than the gallery of the oratory of the Girolamini, therefore, the *quadreria* of the prior's quarters of the Certosa di San Martino stands as a further early example of the developing trend towards independently conceived picture galleries. Their full flowering will nonetheless need to be traced in the private commissions and collections of art put together over the decades in the gilded palaces crammed together in the tumultuous, crowded streets of the city below.

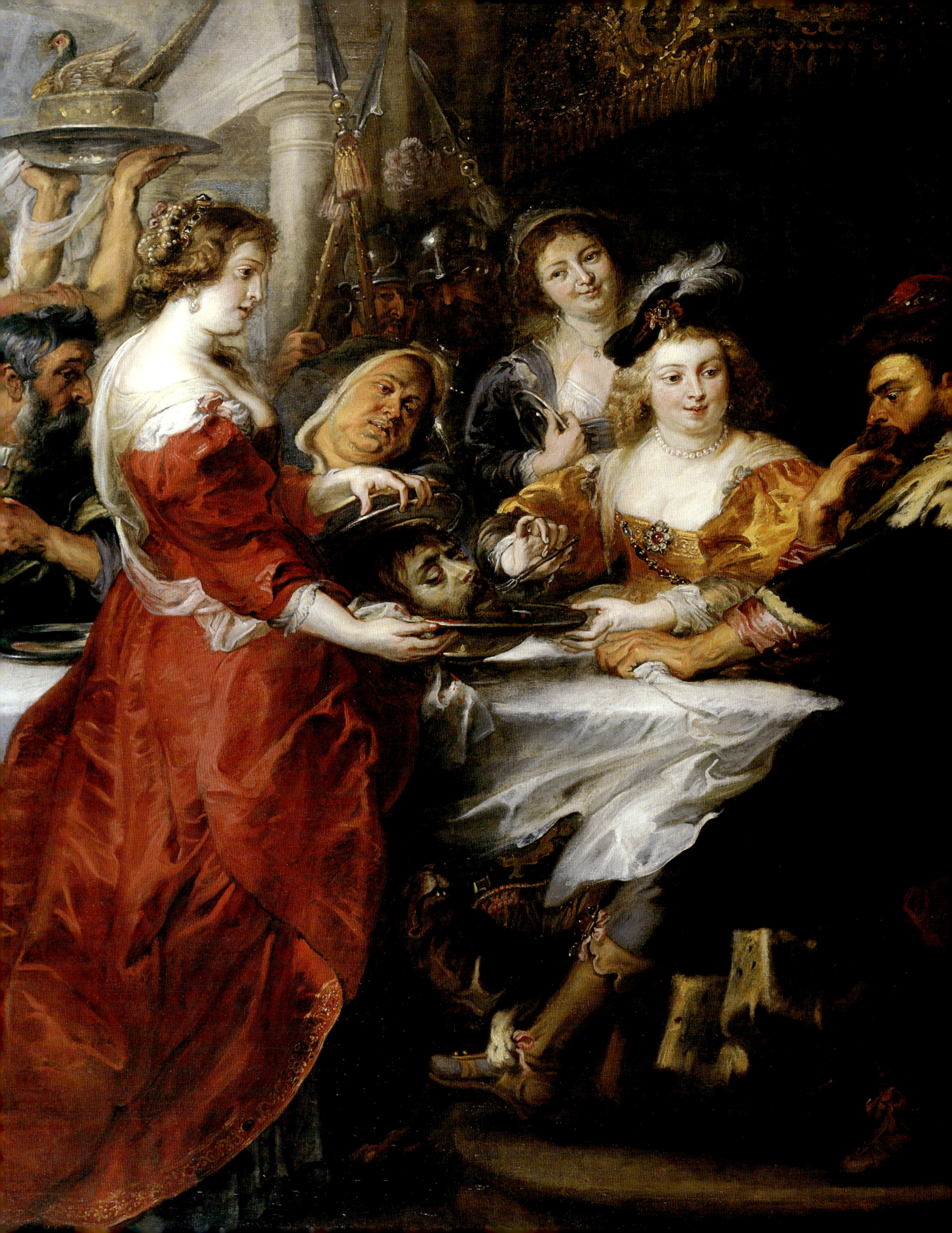

9

Private Collections of Painting

DEATH OF A POET AND BIRTH OF AN IDEAL

In April 1624 Giambattista Marino returned to his birthplace of Naples following more than two decades spent at the forefront of the academic circles of Rome, Turin and Paris. His writings – particularly the *Rime*, *Galeria* and *Adone* – had brought him both adulation and controversy. Now, however, he wished to retire to a quieter and more settled life among the supportive embrace of his countrymen, most notably his friend and protector, the marchese di Villa, Giovan Battista Manso, a co-founder of the Pio Monte della Misericordia, noted academician and patron of Tasso, Caravaggio and Caracciolo, among others.

But Marino was tired: worn down by a restless and dissipated life and by the countless battles that he had been required to play out under the harsh glare of the European literary scene and the baleful gaze of the papal censors. Manso did his best to celebrate the great man's return. He feted Marino among the Neapolitan academies, most notably the Accademia degli Oziosi, that he had founded with vice-regal support in 1611 and which constituted an important gathering point for discussions of new trends in artistic and literary theory.[1] The Theatines of Santi Apostoli attended to the poet's spiritual needs. But Marino had not much time remaining to him. He took up lodgings in a relatively modest apartment on Via Toledo. There he attended to his affairs, continued work on some unfinished projects, then caught a fever and died, aged fifty-six, on 25 March 1625.[2]

An international celebrity he may have been, but this peripatetic poet had little to leave to his homeland in material terms. His small but important library and manuscripts were fought over by Manso and rival claimants, the remainder going to the Theatines, where they were lost in an eighteenth-century eruption of Vesuvius. Marino had also harboured an aspiration to assemble in Naples a distinguished gallery of paintings by the leading artists of the day.[3] This also remained a chimera: a casualty as much of Marino's innate restlessness as it was of his lack of the requisite finances or a sufficiently palatial residence in which to house such a collection. Even the matter of erecting a fitting memorial to Marino's memory following his death remained unsatisfactorily resolved for centuries to come. After interring his remains in the crypt of Santi Apostoli, the Theatines baulked at the prospect of installing in the church a monument to so contentious an individual. Manso was forced, instead, to commission one for his private chapel, situated alongside his palace. When this was demolished, in turn, to make way for planned extensions by the Oratorians later in the century, Marino's memorial was shunted to a lesser-known church on the

Facing page Sir Peter Paul Rubens, *Feast of Herod*, *circa* 1633–8 (detail of fig. 152)

city's periphery. There it languished until the early nineteenth century, when none other than Gioacchino Murat ordered its relocation to its current position in the more appropriately central and prominent setting of San Domenico Maggiore (fig. 137).[4]

Marino's most vital legacy, nevertheless, were his words, and none would prove more influential than those of the *Galeria*. Published in 1619–20, but known in manuscript form before then, the *Galeria* comprises a series of ekphrastic poems about paintings and sculptures that were to be grouped together in the reader's mind to form an ideal gallery – or *musée imaginaire*, as it would be known today. The poems of the *Galeria* covered a wide range of subjects ordered according to the traditional genres of mythologies and history paintings, together with a miscellany of *capricci* (still-life, literary and topographical/view paintings). This was followed by a large group of portraits, reserved particularly for this notional gallery's collection of sculptures.

Besides outlining for potential collectors a full typology and anthology of potential subjects and artists from which to choose, the *Galeria* also demonstrated Marino's up-to-date knowledge of the leading collections of the day, specifically mentioning in this regard the Medici collection in Florence, the Aldobrandini in Rome, the Doria in Genoa, the Savoy in Turin and that of Bartolomeo della Nave in Venice. In so doing, Marino gave early Neapolitan collectors the opportunity to place their activities within a contemporary international context, while reinforcing the essential point that distinction in this field was available not only to the established nobility, but also to merchants and other members of the rising professional classes.

These ideas held powerful sway in Naples during a period in which its inhabitants were just beginning to take advantage of the expanded possibilities created by the continuing processes of social redefinition and urban redevelopment that had been transforming the city from the later sixteenth century. Don Pedro de Toledo, viceroy in 1532–3, had set this in motion with his brilliantly conceived policy of administrative centralization and major infrastructure projects aimed at inducing the Neapolitan aristocracy to quit their feudal estates and to participate in a new vice-regal court culture.[5] Toledo and his successors achieved this above all else by encouraging the *baroni* to share in the benefits of vice-regal administration, most notably by allowing them to acquire public utilities, such as water, bread, salt and oil taxes and monopolies, together with other public revenue sources throughout the length and breadth of the kingdom. These inducements progressively transformed the Neapolitan aristocracy from potentially fractious, colonized subjects dispersed among their feudal holdings to enthusiastic, urbanized participants in the broader Habsburg project. At the same time, the systematic expansion and centralization of vice-regal economic and administrative processes opened up the city to a rapid escalation in the ranks of artisanal, middle-class and professional groups, not to mention the numerous ecclesiastical organizations, which all converged on the city in search of opportunities.

Toledo and his successors were careful to match these ambitious social policies to equally vigorous urban development. Chief among these was the construction of Via Toledo: a long, wide, straight street leading down from the old Aragonese city walls at the present-day Piazza Dante to a new vice-regal administrative centre close to the port. This in turn necessitated a westward expansion of the city walls – thereby extending the city by almost a third, or 150 hectares, and encompassing rapidly built-up residential areas in the newly defined Spanish quarters (reserved particularly for the garrison and Spanish residents of the city), together with the hillside environs of Pizzofalcone and Pignasecca and the first section of the district encompassing the old fishing village of Chiaia. Many of the palaces containing the great collections of the period would spring up in these new neighbourhoods – including those of the Carafa di Maddaloni, the D'Avalos di Montesarchio, the Spinelli di Tarsia and the Vandeneynden, to name a few.[6]

THE COST AND LOCALIZATION OF PAINTINGS IN BAROQUE PALACES

Building up a seigneurial collection of art was a long and drawn-out process. The organic and ongoing accretion of Neapolitan collections over time is accordingly to be contrasted with the more purposeful and focused, short-term patronage projects initiated for particularly prestigious sites of public display and commemoration. The patronage of Cesare Firrao, principe di Sant'Agata, during the 1630s and 1640s is a case in point. This head of one of the most venerable and established aristocratic families of the kingdom spared no expense in commissioning Cosimo Fanzago and the leading sculptors, stuccoists, stone workers and painters of the day to decorate his recently acquired family chapel in the prominent location of the left transept of the Theatine church of San Paolo Maggiore.[7]

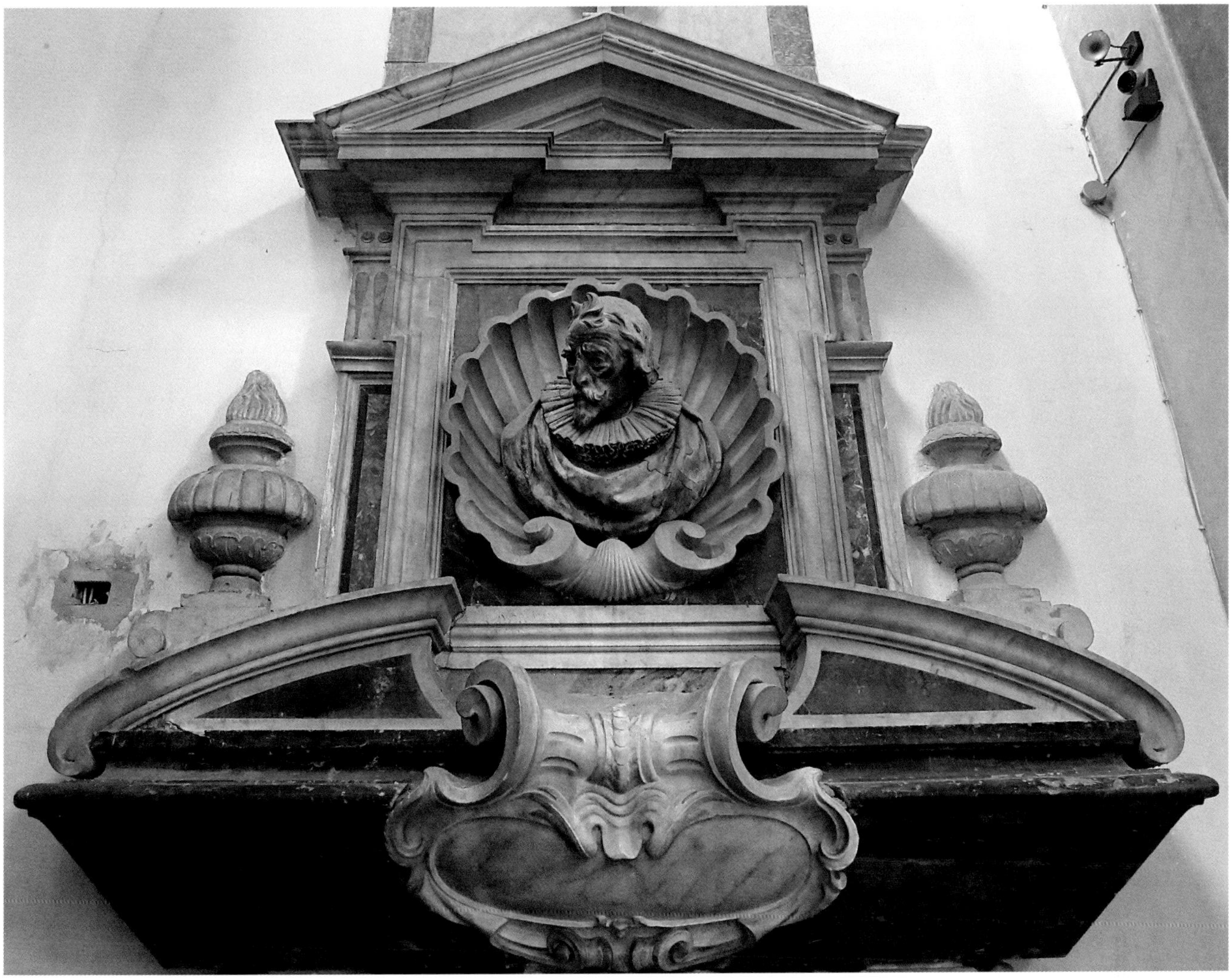

137 Attributed to Bartolomeo Viscontini, *Tomb of Giambattista Marino*, *circa* 1625–8. San Domenico Maggiore, Naples

The Firrao chapel constitutes one of the most impressive and cohesive Neapolitan Baroque ensembles. It converts the chapel space into a scenographic environment with a statue by Fanzago of Cesare Firrao placed in a niche in the left lateral wall (fig. 138). The patron gestures in rapt devotion towards a statue of the *Madonna della Grazie* on the high altar by the Carrarese sculptor Giulio Mencaglia, and is flanked on the chapel's other side by a statue of his father, Antonino. The existing documentation also covers secondary frescoes by Aniello Falcone and an altarpiece by Stanzione, although Stanzione's painting was subsequently removed to make way for Mencaglia's statue, probably in order to compensate Mencaglia following the installation of Fanzago's belated statue of Cesare in 1642. A sum of 3,214 ducats is known to have been expended on this project, but this would have represented only a portion of its total cost (which was complicated, in any event, by a further, prolonged litigation between Firrao and Fanzago in the years that followed).[8] This may be compared with the 8,000 ducats paid for marble-work alone in the Merlino chapel at the Gesù Nuovo during the 1650s, which is probably closer to the total cost of this chapel.[9]

Firrao was also hard at work renovating his palace as the central element of his broader project during this period to consolidate his family's position of power and authority in Naples (fig. 139). The Palazzo Firrao was situated close to the church and convent of Santa Maria della Sapienza along the Via di Santa Maria di Costantinopoli in the northern sector of the old city. In this he was fortunate, since the palace faced onto an open space that enabled him to develop

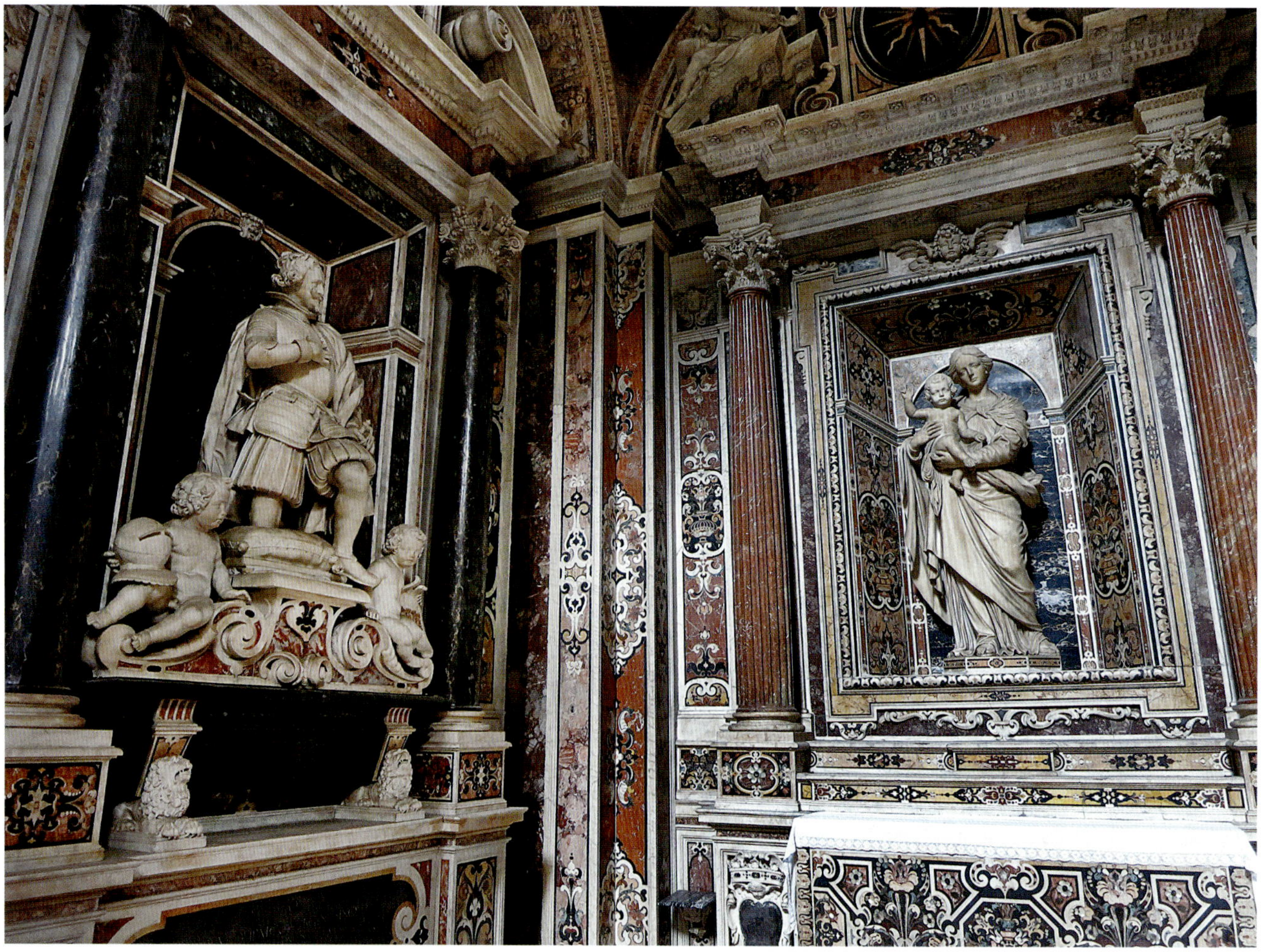

138 Cappella Firrao di Sant'Agata, 1640–42. San Paolo Maggiore, Naples

a project for a fully unified façade: something that is otherwise only rarely encountered in the generally compressed, tightly packed space that is so characteristic of Naples.[10] The resulting statues along the Palazzo Firrao's façade juxtapose symbols of the family's pre-eminence as royal squires to the Spanish crown with statements of their political allegiances via a series of seven prominently displayed portraits of the Spanish kings, beginning with the emperor Charles v and ending with the future Charles ii.[11]

These two projects are to be counted among the major patronage initiatives of Cesare Firrao's life and would almost certainly have cost him much more than all the paintings in his collection combined. This is made clear if these amounts are compared with those associated with the small number of early Neapolitan inventories whose financial value was recorded at the time of their compilation. The inventory of 1659 of the collection of Ettore Capecelatro, marchese di Torella, is a case in point. Capecelatro was a figure of considerable importance within the vice-regal administration. He belonged to a pre-eminent aristocratic family *di seggio*: meaning that his family held hereditary membership in one of the five governing councils of the city, whose ranks had been progressively closed to newcomers and restricted to the old aristocratic families between the late fifteenth century and the early sixteenth.[12] Somewhat unusually for a member of the old nobility, though, Capecelatro pursued a career in law, rising to the position of *prorregente* of the Supremo Collaterale Consiglio, among numerous other important posts held at the Sacro Regio Consiglio, the Collaterale and the Regia Camera della Sommaria.

Capecelatro's inventory also has the advantage of being one of the most accurate and carefully compiled of its kind, having been drawn up by his favourite painter, Domenico Gargiulo, following many years of faithful service. It lists in

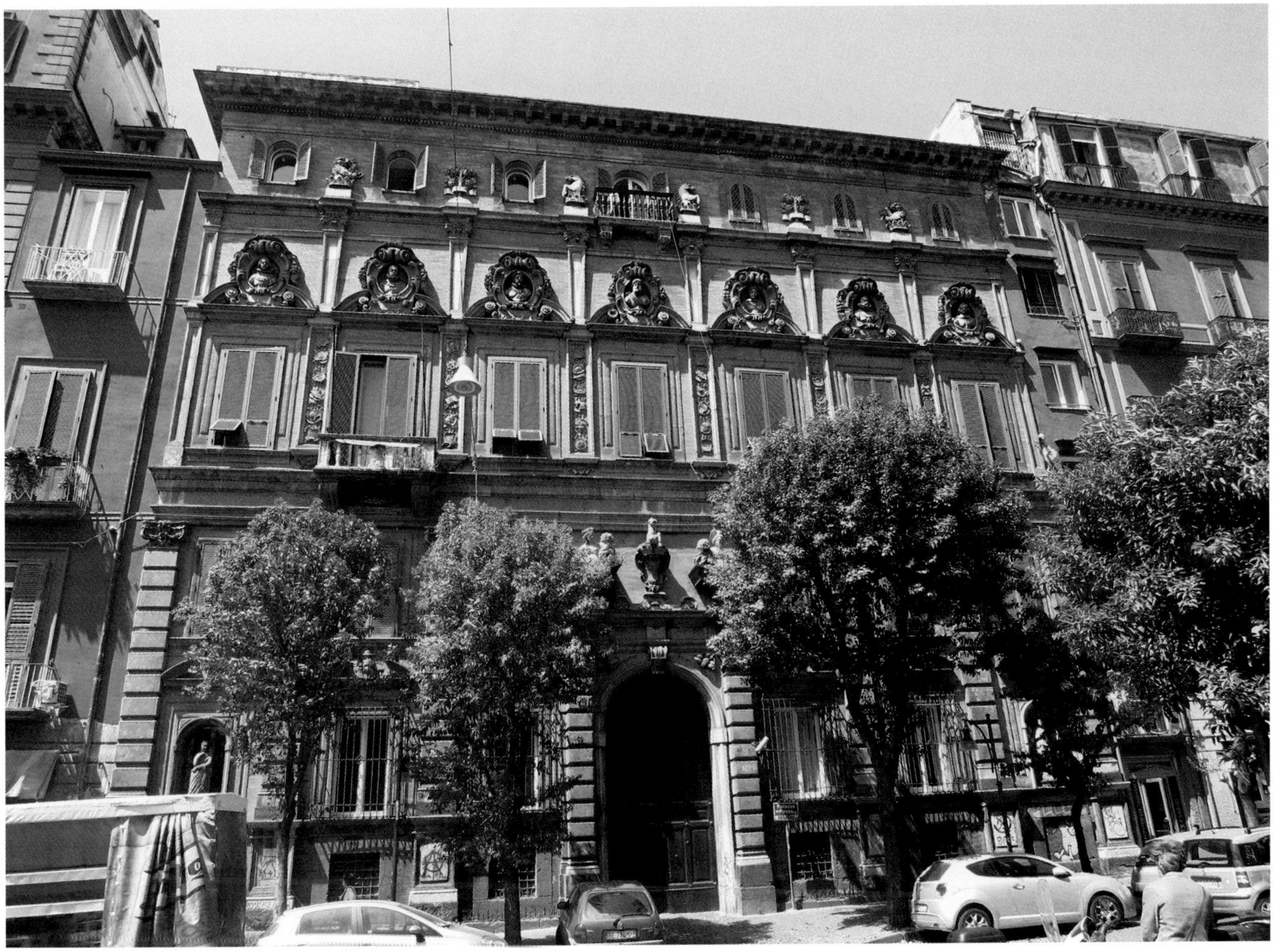

139 Palazzo Firrao, Naples

his palace eighty-five paintings, with attributions ranging across most of the contemporary artists of the day, such as Ribera, Stanzione, Artemisia Gentileschi, Gargiulo and Pacecco de Rosa. The combined value of this core group of works is registered at 2,180 ducats – or just over 25.5 ducats per painting. Added to this is a secondary list of a further forty-eight paintings that are identified as coming from his 'casa della montagnola' in the country. These are valued at 457 ducats, or 9.5 ducats per painting.[13] At the time of his death, Capecelatro's paintings, therefore, represented a patrimony of approximately 2,500 ducats.

Another appraised inventory from the same period occurs in the collection of Don Cesare di Gennaro, principe di San Martino.[14] This can also be regarded as a particularly reliable record of the financial value of contemporary paintings, since it was drawn up in 1646 for the Pio Monte della Misericordia by the painters Filippo Vitale and Andrea Abate in order to assist the Pio Monte in determining the worth of Di Gennaro's estate prior to selling the paintings at public auction.[15] Di Gennaro had a much larger collection than Capecelelatro – 355 paintings as opposed to Capecelatro's 85. Yet many of these were evidently anonymous, unattributed *quadri ordinari* and cheap, serial sets of paintings, such as the unattributed group of 'sixty small, circular paintings of virgins and other subjects' valued at around one-third of a ducat each, and so comparable to the kinds of cheap open market productions discussed previously.

Di Gennaro's collection was nonetheless distinguished in a number of areas, holding one or two works by most of the major painters of the first half of the seventeenth century. These included Santafede, Sellitto, Caracciolo, Ribera, Stanzione, Vaccaro, Van Somer, Gargiulo and De Rosa. Di Gennaro even owned two paintings by Lanfranco, a figure seldom encountered in the early Neapolitan inventories since his heavy workload at the Gesù Nuovo, Certosa di San Martino and Santi Apostoli left him little time to execute independent work for private collectors. The cumulative value of Di Gennaro's collection is given as either 2,192 or 1,919 ducats (the differences being attributable to slight divergences in the valuations that were drawn up by each painter independently of the other). The value of Di Gennaro's picture collection thus averaged between 5.5 and 6 ducats per painting.

This modest financial appraisal of his collection's net worth is a reminder of the relatively low economic ranking of paintings in the overall portfolio of an aristocrat's luxury possessions, this at least being the case at this early stage in the development of Neapolitan collecting. It is important to bear in mind, in this respect, that Di Gennaro's other luxury goods were worth much more than his paintings. His silverware, for example, was appraised at 5,890 ducats, while his 'jewellery and objects of gold' were valued at 7,347 ducats, each category accordingly being worth around three to four times as much as his paintings.

Indicative of this very different understanding of Baroque Neapolitan paintings as items of familial embellishment is a statement by the important later seventeenth-century collector Giacomo Capece Zurlo, that he was passing on his picture collection to the next generation of his family in the hope that it would serve 'per ostentatione e commodità' (for the comfort and ostentation) of his household.[16] This is not to say, of course, that Zurlo and the other collectors cited here did not appreciate their collections in aesthetic terms. Zurlo, for example, possessed a distinguished art collection that included a choice selection of works by locals and foreigners, including paintings attributed to Vasari, Polidoro and Poussin, together with most of the contemporary Neapolitan painters of the day.[17] Yet his and his fellow collectors' aesthetic enjoyment was tempered by an equal concern for their collections to function as part of the daily backdrop to their lives – as a necessary adjunct to the primary function of their palaces as sites for the projection of an appropriately rich and dignified sequence of interior spaces *per rappresentanza*.

Paintings in Neapolitan Baroque collections, therefore, were first and foremost prosaic items of use that were accordingly often liable to the indignity of significant wear and tear over the years. A clear instance of this comes in the listing of paintings belonging to Scipione Porzio, a rich financier who derived much of his wealth from his business dealings with the leading families of the day. His inventory of 1620 concludes with a group of seventeen paintings that were kept in his garden – presumably a small pavilion maintained separately from his residence. Among this group is a painting of the *Crucifixion with Sts Francis of Assisi and Catherine of Siena*, which had apparently reached the end of its life, since it is described, tersely yet with a certain lingering poignancy, as being both 'usato e rotto' (used and broken).[18]

Neapolitan collections from the 1630s to 1650s tended to restrict the display of paintings to a limited number of formal reception rooms that together made up an aristocratic apartment suite or *quartiere*. So, most paintings are found in the *sala* (the drawing or audience room), together with the *anticamera* (the antechamber or waiting room) and one or two generally contiguous and smaller *stanze*. Occasionally, other spaces are identified, such as a private chapel and a studio.[19] The presence of paintings in other more personalized, private spaces, such as the *gabinetto*, would not become common in Neapolitan collections until later in the century.

A further customary subdivision of paintings within this scheme was to place the most valuable canvases (in other words, those attributed to known masters) in the *sala*. This primary space for formal reception and artistic display would increasingly come to be described in the inventories as the palace's *galleria*. But this more international, Marinesque understanding of a *galleria* as denoting a purpose-defined space for displaying artworks comparable to other famous *gallerie* of the day (such as the Uffizi in Florence and the Galleria Farnese in Rome) would not come into common parlance in Naples until the later years of the century. In fact, the inventory of 1646 of the collection of the principe di San Martino contains one of the earliest mentions of a dedicated Neapolitan *galleria* of this kind. Other references include documentation surrounding a donation in 1631 to the Neapolitan Oratorians and the inventory of 1654 of Ferrante Spinelli, principe di Tarsia, the latter being readily understandable given this individual's status as one of the most advanced and discerning collectors of the century.[20] The more widespread, earlier seventeenth-century Neapolitan predilection for describing these display spaces in more generic terms as either *stanze* or *sale* should thus be interpreted as further evidence of the initial Neapolitan belatedness in developing a specialized culture of collecting.[21]

The other impression that emerges clearly from the Di Gennaro inventory of 1646 is the degree to which the *principe*'s paintings were installed so as to coordinate visually with an array of related items of furniture and applied art. So, for example, a list of 'silver objects above the desks within the *galleria*' in his collection records the presence of such diverse items on the top of the cabinets lining the room as

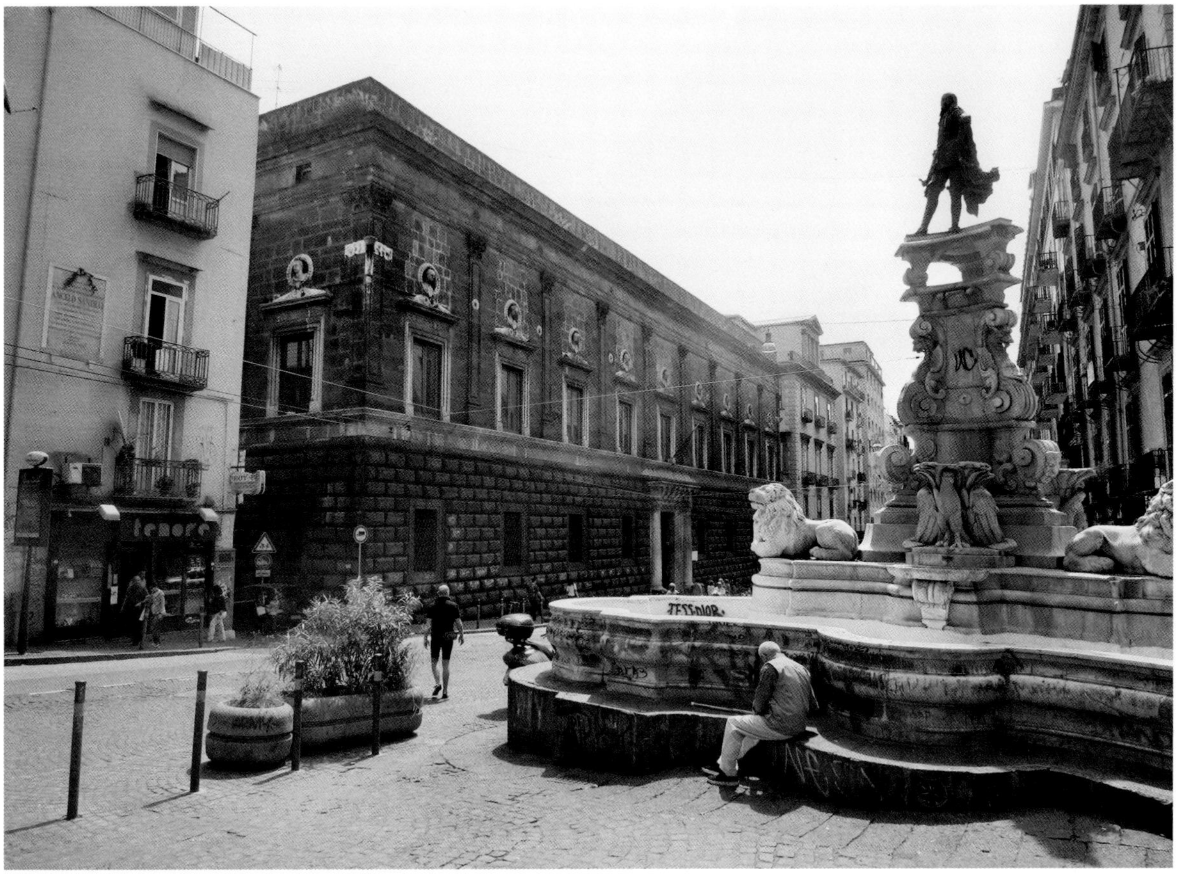

140 Palazzo Gravina and the Largo di Monteoliveto, Naples

figured candelabra, silver flasks, two vases of mother of pearl, two more of coral, four reliquaries, a large goblet 'alla tedesca' and numerous statuettes, including *putti*, *St John the Baptist*, *Sts Peter and Paul*, *Christ at the Column*, a *Crucifix* and *Our Lady of the Rosary*. The richness of the overall effect was augmented by patterned wall hangings, twelve red velvet chairs, numerous console tables and two door coverings of 'false damask'.[22] The descriptions recall, in fact, the appearance of the room depicted in Michele Regolia's representation of a Neapolitan palace interior, but with an even greater emphasis, it seems, on an overall impression of lavish and varied richness (see fig. 65).

THE GRAND ARISTOCRATIC COLLECTIONS AND PROVINCIAL ESTATES

Like the Palazzo Firrao, the Palazzo Gravina's advantageous location adjoining a square proclaimed the family's pre-eminence in the city. This Tuscan-style, later Renaissance palace has an unusually expansive series of bays along the street frontage with a particularly prominent, unified façade. (The ceremonial importance of this prominent open space was further recognized in the eighteenth century with the addition of a fountain dedicated to King Charles II of Spain; fig. 140). The Palazzo Gravina was begun in 1513 following an initial purchase of land from the nearby monastery of Monteoliveto, and the extra space needed for it was acquired gradually over the years until the Orsini di Gravina were able to *fare insula* in a manner similar to the process for the convents and monasteries of Naples.[23]

The Orsini di Gravina represented the southern branch of one of the most venerable, feudal aristocratic families of central and southern Italy. The central line counted two medieval popes among its ranks, while the Orsini di Gravina had contributed a Grand Chancellor and Grand Constable of the Kingdom of Naples among numerous prominent forebears. The southern Orsini's eminence culminated in the eighteenth century with the election in 1724 of the Dominican friar Francesco Orsini (1650–1730), bishop of

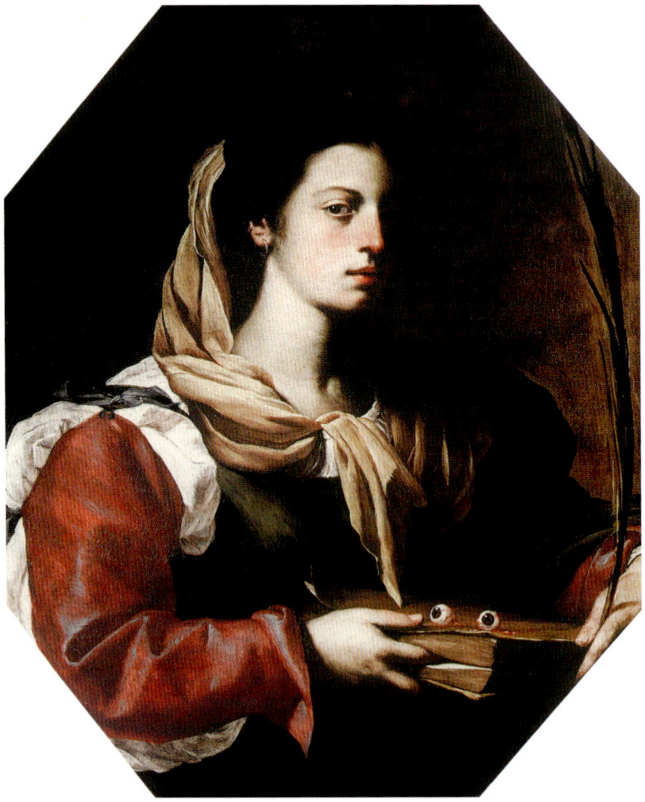

141 Francesco Guarino, *St Lucy*, *circa* 1645. Oil on canvas, 85 × 71 cm. Cassa di Risparmio di Calabria e Lucania, Cosenza

Benevento, as Pope Benedict XIII. Although urbanized following the pattern outlined above, the Orsini di Gravina maintained close links with their feudal territories, particularly their ancestral seat at Gravina in Apulia and their other principal estate some 133 kilometres to the west in Solofra in the province of Avellino.

The forested hills of Solofra, in fact, gave birth to one of the greatest talents of the Neapolitan Baroque. Francesco Guarino (1611–1651) was first active in his home town and then in Naples in the early to mid-1630s, developing a complex synthesis of the realism of Ribera and the classicism of Stanzione, together with Bernardo Cavallino's lyrical naturalism. Although his life is only sketchily documented, it seems clear that the patronage of the Orsini di Gravina was fundamental to his career and movements between Solofra and Naples until his early death in 1651, aged forty. The greatest evidence of this, in fact, comes in the inventory of the Palazzo Gravina's holdings compiled in 1707. This document lists no fewer than thirty-eight paintings by Guarino – almost all devotional subjects, with a small number of portraits and allegories – while a subsequent inventory of 1744 adds a further fourteen canvases.[24]

Guarino, therefore, must have functioned as a kind of 'court painter' to the Orsini di Gravina household, particularly during his early stays in Naples, when the status and material support provided by the presence of his feudal lords in the city must have proved extremely helpful to a young provincial artist trying to make his way in the capital. For their part, the Orsini di Gravina evidently valued his work a great deal, since essentially they seem to have monopolized his production during certain crucial periods of his career. They were presumably drawn to the extraordinary blend found in his canvases of refinement and idealization combined with a quotidian realism and vivid detail.

This approach resulted in some of the most memorable visualizations of southern Baroque Counter-Reformation devotion, an emphasis that would have appealed strongly to this family's collecting practices, given that their inventories contain hundreds of religious paintings but hardly any mythologies, histories or secular subjects. One is struck, for example, by the way that the virgin martyr St Lucy meets the viewer's gaze in a painting originally hanging in a small room in the Palazzo Gravina that was dominated by rows of intimate, devotional paintings of virgin saints and other religious figures (fig. 141).[25] Lucy's direct eye contact, together with her humble peasant attire, lend the painting a grounded, almost portrait-like specificity. This is offset by the striking vision of her severed eyeballs sliding across the Bible that she holds, trailing blood and capillaries onto its curling vellum cover. This almost visionary intensity is counterbalanced by the delicately brushed in, aqua-blue highlights on the saint's red sleeves, which discreetly evoke the noble poise and unassailable virtue that earned this early Christian heroine an eternal place among the elect.

In addition to their dozens of religious and devotional paintings, the Orsini di Gravina also owned a number of Guarino's portraits of family members, a specialization not otherwise known in his oeuvre and one that attests further to their high regard for his abilities and long-term recourse to his services. In the mid-to-late 1640s, for example, a prominent portrait of the family's widowed matriarch, the duchessa Dorotea Orsini, was included as a donor presented by St Dominic to Our Lady of the Rosary in an altarpiece commissioned to commemorate the culmination of her long-term dream to found a Dominican friary in Guarino's home town of Solofra (fig. 142).[26] (This family had traditionally strong ties to the Dominicans, and it was Dorotea's

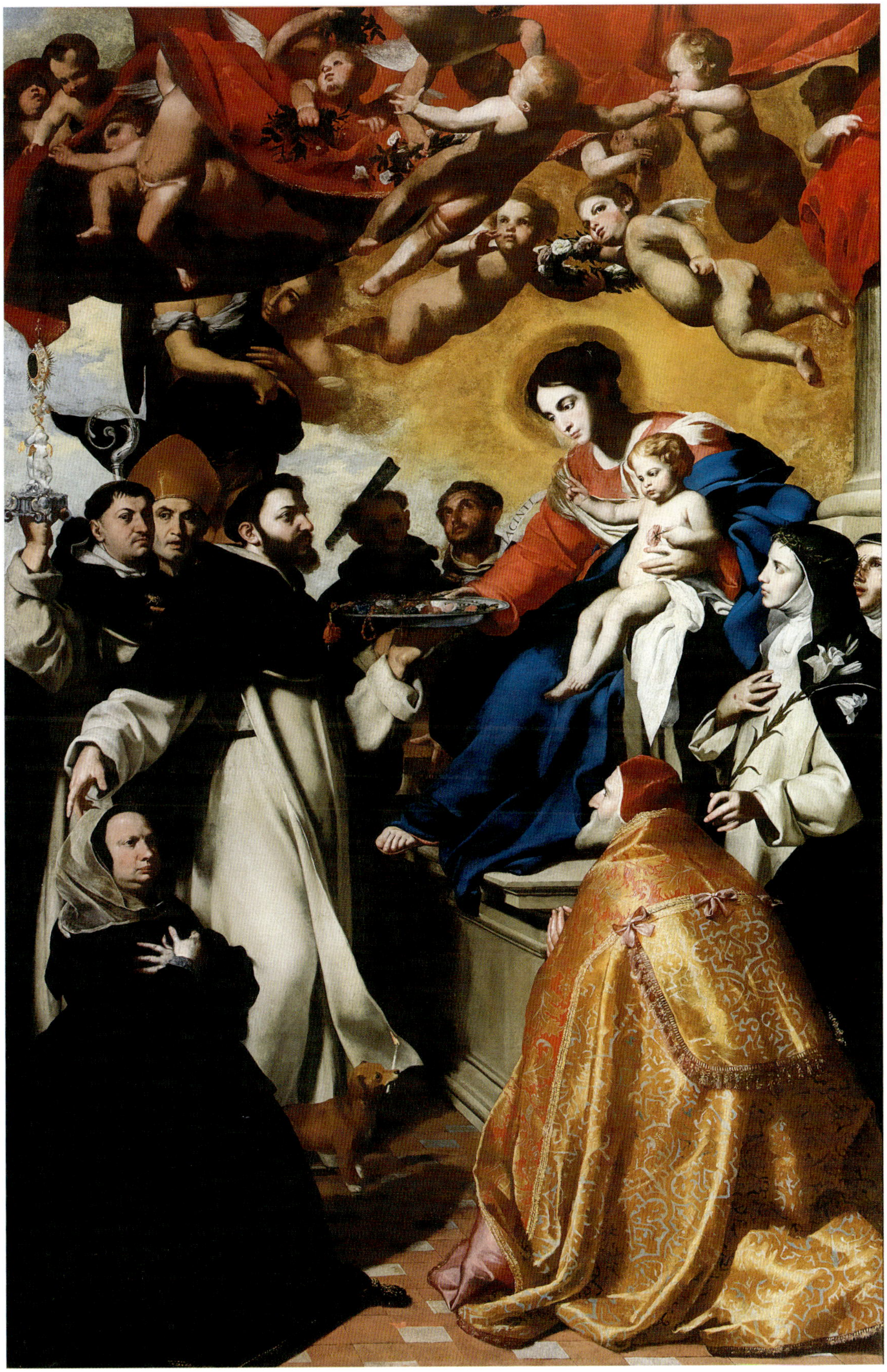

142 Francesco Guarino, *Our Lady of the Rosary with Sts Dominic, Catherine, Thomas Aquinas, Hyacinth, Peter of Verona and Pius V, together with Cardinal Fabrizio Savelli and Duchessa Dorotea Orsini*, 1644–9. Oil on canvas, 351 × 225 cm. Church of the convent of San Domenico, Solofra

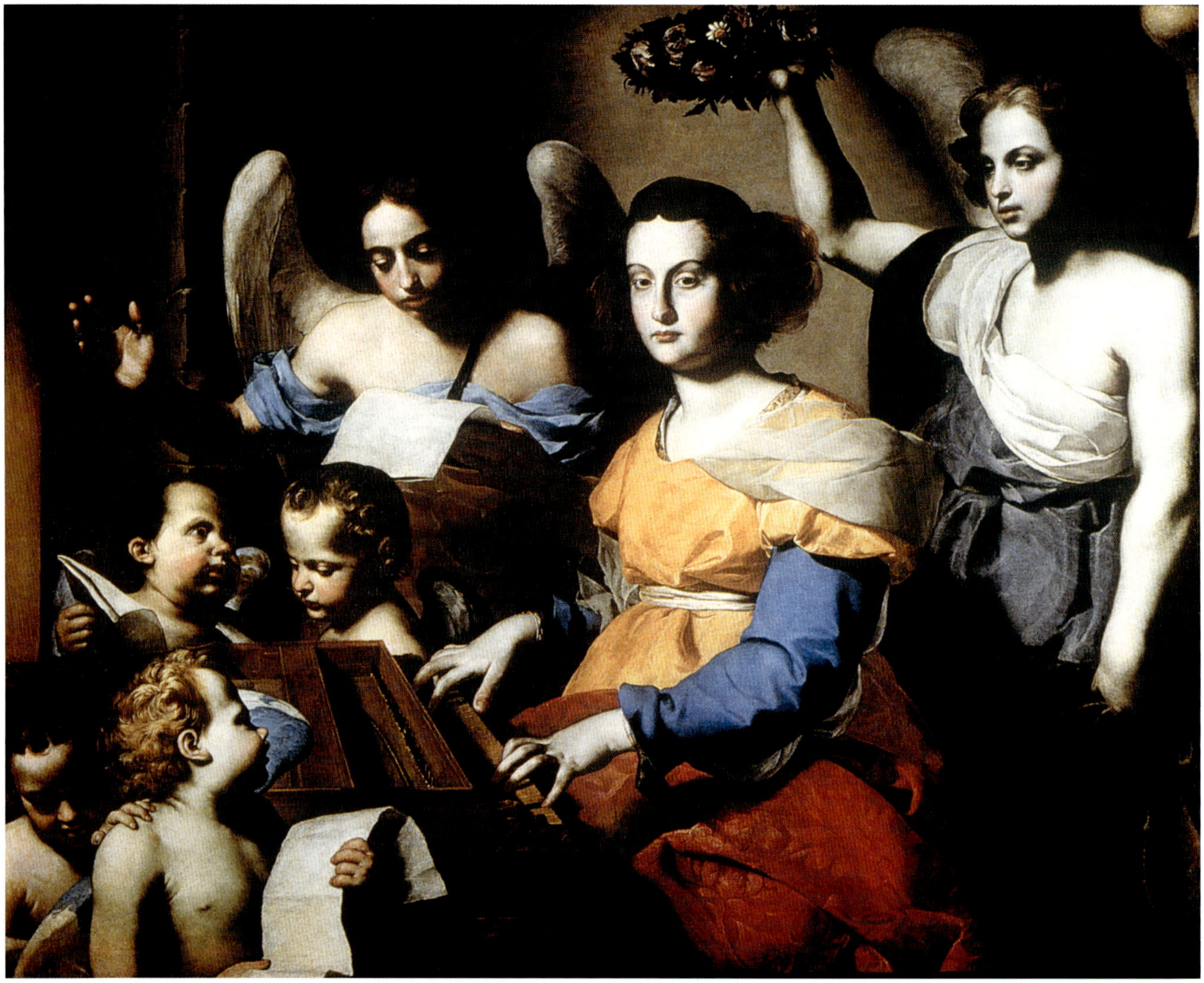

143 Francesco Guarino, *St Cecilia*, *circa* 1647. Oil on canvas, 124 × 152 cm. Museo e Gallerie Nazionali di Capodimonte, Naples

grandson Francesco who entered the order and eventually became pope in 1724.)

Interspersed among the images of *St Lucy* and the other virgin saints in the room of saints in the Palazzo Gravina were Guarino's three touching portraits of family members. On entering this small chamber, the visitor was first greeted by a large painting of Dorotea Orsini's daughter-in-law, the new duchess, Giovanna Frangipane della Tolfa, depicted as *St Cecilia* crowned with a garland and attended by angels (fig. 143). Giovanna married the twenty-four-year-old duke, Ferdinando III, in 1647, so Guarino's canvas was in all likelihood commissioned to commemorate the impending wedding.[27] Another of the Orsini's portraits celebrated a birth, since it showed one of the family's female babies, the radiant innocence of which was further enhanced by its being hung several paintings along from the canvas of *St Lucy* and the other virgin martyr saints in this same room. Finally, the Orsini di Gravina also drew on Guarino to commemorate the family from the grave as well as the cradle, since this room contained a now-lost deathbed portrait of the late duke Pietro Orsini – Dorotea's husband and Ferdinando's father – depicted 'Morto cogli occhi chiusi' (dead with his eyes closed).[28]

Guarino's career challenges many modern preconceptions about a 'provincial' talent working at the so-called margins of a major urban centre. Paolo Finoglio's later output does so as well, albeit in reverse, since this artist emigrated from Naples to the provinces following a reasonably successful career working at the forefront of developments in early Neapolitan Caravaggesque painting. Finoglio has been mentioned as one of the earliest Neapolitan painters selected by the Carthusians for work at San Martino from 1626 onwards, while his parallel specialization in art dealing was developing (see pp. 54–5). Eventually, though, Finoglio tired of competing for prestigious work with the rapidly ascending reputations of Stanzione and Ribera. By early 1635 he had made his way some 300 kilometres to the south-east, to Conversano, in the province of Bari. There he spent the last decade of his life serving Conte Giangirolamo II Acquaviva d'Aragona in a flourishing court culture focused on the family's recently renovated castle, which dominated the centre of the town.

Conte Giangirolomo represented something of an anachronism in the political landscape of the period. He epitomized, in fact, everything about the earlier practices of the Neapolitan feudal barons that the viceroys wished to eradicate. He was, to be sure, periodically of use to them: particularly via his forceful subjugation of rebels in the province of Nardò during the Revolt of Masaniello in 1647–8. Yet his ingrained feudalism, recourse to a private militia whose activities included banditry and the occasional murder of the count's enemies all contributed to a growing reputation of wilful prodigality. More dangerous still were his negotiations with the French party in opposition to the Spanish during the late 1630s and 1640s. This more than anything else brought him many enemies and resulted in his ultimate arrest and transport to Madrid in 1650 to face charges of treason; there he remained, disgraced and imprisoned, until his death in 1665.[29] For all this, though, he was an enlightened and enthusiastic patron of Finoglio, commissioning some of the most distinguished works of this artist's career. In this he seems to have been assisted significantly by his wife, Isabella Filomarino, niece of the similarly pro-French Ascanio Filomarino, one of the leading patrons and collectors of the period.

The patronage of Giangirolamo and Isabella Acquaviva continues the strain of staunchly southern Italian, Counter-Reformation piety that was noted in the case of the Orsini di Gravina. It was this aspect of Finoglio's art, in fact, that seems initially to have recommended the painter to the family. He is in this way first documented working for Giangirolamo's father, Conte Giulio Acquaviva, in Lecce in 1627–8, where he painted two altarpieces of ancient and modern Christian martyrs.[30] These include prominent references to another Acquaviva family member, Rodolfo, who had pursued a brief career as a Jesuit missionary prior to being martyred in Goa in 1583. (The Acquaviva family's close association with the Jesuits was further strengthened during this period by the entrance of Claudio Acquaviva into the order and subsequent rise to positions of leadership as first Superior of Naples and then General of the Society of Jesus itself, from 1581 to 1615). Giangirolamo's and Isabella's patronage of the devotional aspects of Finoglio's art seems to have focused on their foundation in Conversano of a church and enclosed Franciscan Tertiary convent dedicated to the early Christian saints Cosmas and Damian.[31] Finoglio was given charge of almost the entire decoration of this church, including a lavishly stuccoed and frescoed ceiling and no fewer than five altarpieces.[32]

But perhaps most distinctive among Giangirolamo's and Isabella's patronage was their involvement in a late flourishing of neo-Renaissance courtly pastoralism focused above all on a revival of interest in the poems of Torquato Tasso (1544–1595). Born in Salerno, Tasso went on to pursue an early career in Naples, and was revered more highly in the Kingdom of Naples than elsewhere in Italy.[33] The Acquaviva d'Aragona had been early supporters of the poet, and some family members had even distinguished themselves in the literary field (particularly Andrea Matteo III [1458–1529], friend to Sannazaro and translator of Plutarch).[34] Giangirolamo and Isabella accordingly revived and expanded on this tradition in order to place alongside their previously established emphasis on devotional imagery an ongoing claim to distinction in the emerging field of cultural patronage.

Finoglio contributed to this project in a number of ways. In particular, he executed a series of ten very large canvases (each measuring 2.5 × 3 m) dedicated to the knightly epic *Gerusalemme liberata* of 1581, on which Tasso's reputation is principally based (fig. 144, and see further fig. 86). These served as the centrepiece to Giangirolamo's and Isabella's *galleria*, knowledge of which is based today on an unfortunately only summarily compiled inventory of 1666. This inventory reveals the virtual absence in the *galleria* at Conversano of the religious and devotional paintings that one would otherwise expect to dominate a seigneurial collection in this period. True, the gallery did contain canvases of *Susanna* and *Lot and his Daughters*, but it is clear from the other pictures hanging on the walls that these would have been appreciated more for their qualities of sophisticated eroticism and veiled violence than for any ostensible devotional qualities. This is made clear from the other subjects hanging alongside them in the Acquaviva *galleria*: *Cleopatra*, *Lucretia*, *Leda and the Swan*, *Venus with a Satyr*, the *Judgement of Paris*, *Venus and Vulcan*,

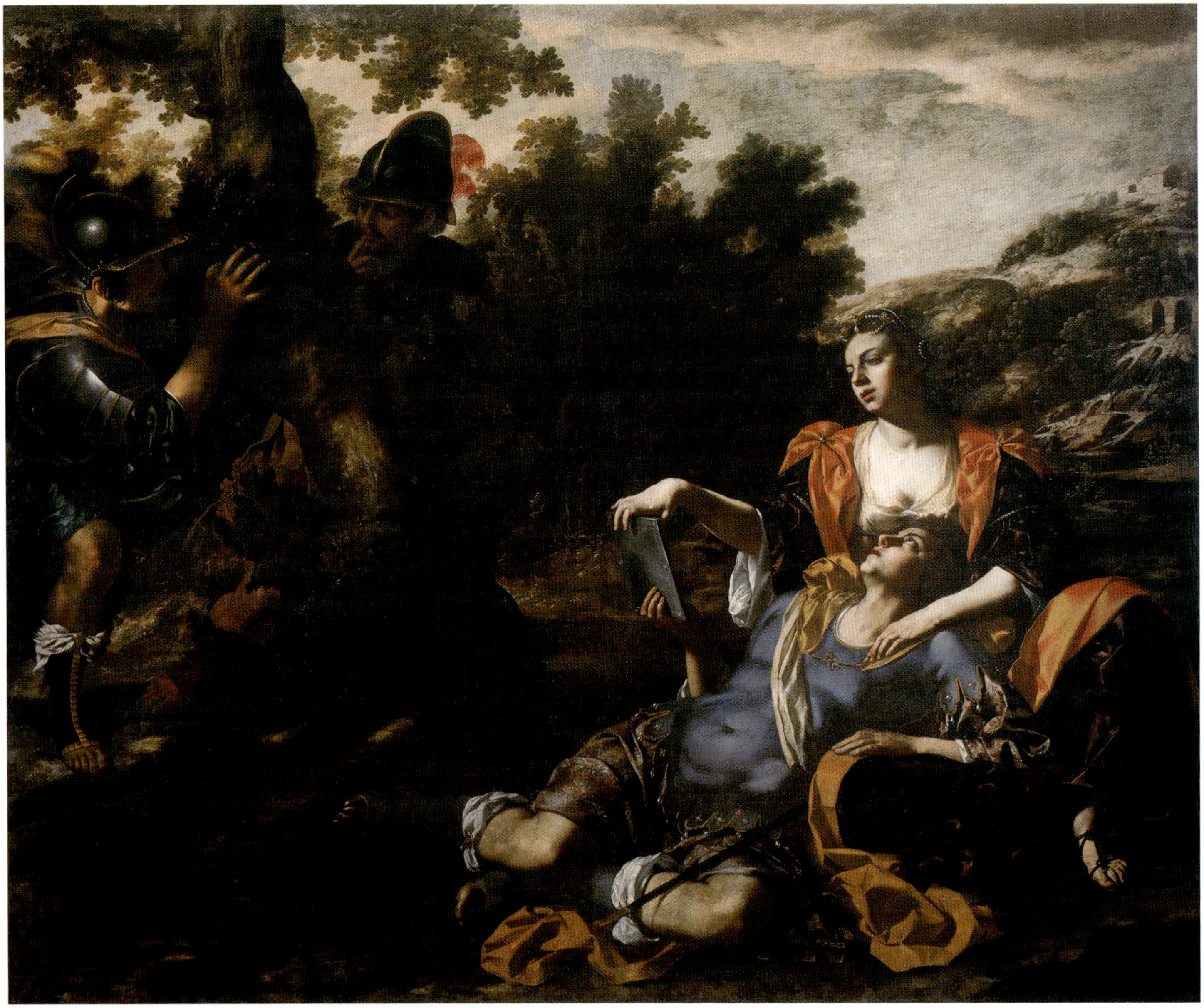

144 Paolo Finoglio, *Rinaldo and Armida in the Enchanted Garden*, *circa* 1642–5. Oil on canvas, 255 × 308 cm. Pinacoteca del Castello, Conversano

Venus Admiring Herself in a Mirror, *Diana at the Hunt* and no fewer than three paintings of *Venus and Adonis*.[35]

Thus it seems that Giangirolamo and Isabella had sought to introduce into their recently renovated castle a belated southern Italian flowering of the classic Renaissance courtly *poesie* of the Este of Ferrara or the Gonzaga of Mantua. As further evidence of this, one need look no further than the lavish frescoes commissioned by Giangirolamo from Finoglio for the grand-ducal bedchamber. This constitutes a southern Baroque version of a *camera degli sposi* along the lines of Mantegna's famous example in Mantua. Finoglio's cycle depicts scenes from the *Story of Jacob* and has also been interpreted in terms of its indebtedness to Tasso and other pastoral poets.[36]

This endeavour might be considered anachronistic in certain respects. Yet the striking independence and even originality of its conception shines through in Finoglio's paintings of the *Gerusalemme liberata* (figs 86, 144). Here Tasso's refined lyricism is transposed into grandiose canvases that combine the classical poise and archaic chivalric associations of the

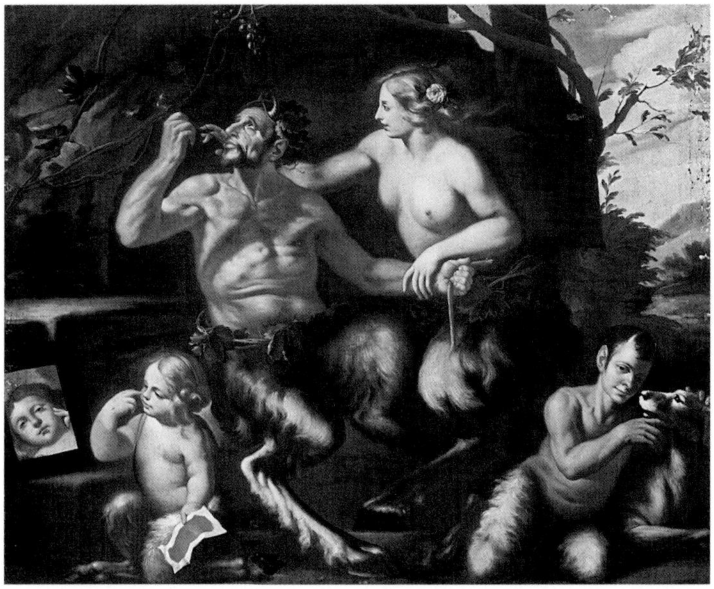

145 Cesare Fracanzano, *Family of Satyrs*, 1640s. Oil on canvas, 170 × 207 cm. Private collection, Naples

original narrative with all the contemporary grit and physicality of Neapolitan Baroque naturalism.[37] Finoglio added a particular attentiveness to the armorial and knightly dimensions of the epic, an emphasis that must have appealed to Giangirolamo's well-known martial inclinations. Finally, the paintings also demonstrate Finoglio's close knowledge of the early battle, landscape and cabinet painting just then being developed in Naples by Aniello Falcone and his associates. These confirm his continued contacts with Neapolitan artistic circles during this period, which must have proved particularly useful to Giangirolamo and Isabella in their desire to source suitable paintings by Ribera, Stanzione and their schools to make up the pictures hanging on the walls of the *galleria* and elsewhere in the Castello.

While the authors of these paintings are rarely mentioned in the inventory of 1666 of the paintings at Conversano, the unusual reference that it contains to a 'quatro grande con satiro che prende tabacco' (a large painting of a satyr smoking tobacco) has led to the identification of Cesare Fracanzano's *Family of Satyrs* (fig. 145) as belonging to the original commissions for Conversano.[38] This undeniably strange and enigmatic painting forms part of the small group of burlesque mythological paintings created by Ribera and his workshop following the model of his famous *Drunken Silenus* of 1626, a painting once owned by the dilettante painter Giovanni Francesco Salernitano, prior to its being acquired by Gaspar Roomer (see p. 119). It functions on one level as an allegory of the senses, but presumably contains other, more personalized meanings that point further to the idiosyncratic quality of the regional patronage programmes undertaken by the Acquavivas of Conversano.

A similar use of Renaissance revival imagery to evoke a family's illustrious traditions is found back in the urban centre of the Palazzo d'Avalos in Naples. This collection is known from inventories of 1739 and 1776 that list the substantial holdings of the family's palace in the recently instituted residential zone of Chiaia on the more salubrious outskirts of Naples close to the bay. This served as the basis for the subsequent family donation of paintings, tapestries and decorative art works to the newly formed Italian state in 1862 that remains one of the most distinguished bequests in the history of the Museo di Capodimonte.[39]

The D'Avalos were another of the leading families of southern Italy. Their greatest period came during the time of Ferdinando Francesco d'Avalos (1489–1525), marchese di Pescara, who led the victorious imperial troops at the Battle of Pavia in 1525 and personally took charge of the captured French king, Francis I. According to family tradition, a magnificent series of seven tapestries of the campaign, woven in Brussels after designs by Bernard van Orley (1528–31), was donated to the family by none other than Charles V in recognition of this achievement.[40]

Ferdinando's cousin and heir, Alfonso d'Avalos (1502–1546), first marchese del Vasto e di Pescara, continued this distinguished association by serving as commander of the imperial troops and governor of Milan during the critical period of the Franco-Italian war of 1536–8. He was also a noteworthy patron, commissioning a number of paintings from Titian, including a version of the *Penitent Magdalene* that he ordered as a gift for his aunt, Ferdinando's widow, Vittoria Colonna, the renowned poet and close friend of Michelangelo. He also commissioned an innovative full-length portrait from Titian that commemorated his speech to the imperial troops in Lombardy convincing them not to mutiny but rather to remain loyal to Charles V, despite their dissatisfaction caused by an ongoing lack of food and wages.[41]

The seventeenth-century heir to this exalted legacy, Andrea d'Avalos (*circa* 1616–1709), principe di Montesarchio, should be identified as the individual responsible for bringing together most of the art works subsequently documented in the eighteenth-century inventories of Palazzo d'Avalos. He patterned himself on the model of his forebears, yet his career was more tumultuous and, at times, also more politically ambiguous than theirs.[42] He first came to prominence as one of the leaders of the campaign pursued

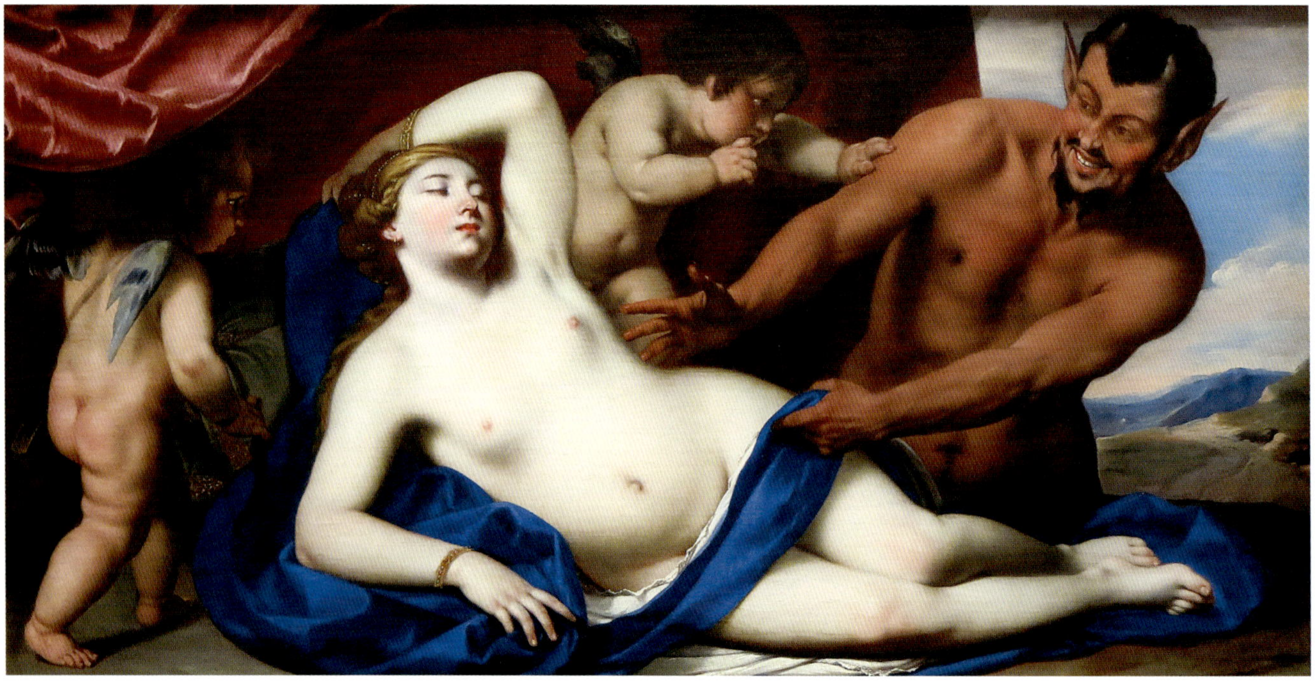

146 Pacecco de Rosa, *Sleeping Venus Discovered by a Satyr, circa* 1645. Oil on canvas, 69 × 132 cm. Museo e Gallerie Nazionali di Capodimonte, Naples

throughout the kingdom to crush the rebels during the later stages of the Revolt of Masaniello. But the chaotic tenor and constantly shifting political allegiances of this period encouraged him to pursue a series of dangerous negotiations, first with those opposed to the reintroduction of the continued power of the viceroys following the conclusion of the revolt, and then – for a time at least – with the pro-French supporters of the duc de Guise.

From here, D'Avalos seems to have progressed to the ill-conceived notion that it might be possible to install Philip IV's illegitimate son, Don Juan of Austria, as independent ruler of the kingdom, following the crushing of the rebellion. The viceroy, the conde de Oñate, accordingly remained very suspicious of him, and at the conclusion of the revolt had him imprisoned in the Castel dell'Ovo in Naples before sending him to Madrid, together with Giangirolamo Acquaviva and others suspected of sedition. Here he languished for a year before being released, probably thanks to the intercession of his powerful friend, Don Juan of Austria. He then sought to rehabilitate his career via a series of senior military postings in the service of the Spanish crown. These eventuated in his appointment in 1660 as admiral of the vice-regal fleet and then, in 1675, as 'capitano generale dell'armata del Mare Oceano', in charge of the imperial fleet sent against the French forces acting in league with the rebellious province of Messina. His leadership of this long and difficult campaign nonetheless also had its moments of controversy, resulting in yet another temporary setback and imprisonment in Spain prior to his reinstatement and eventual participation in the retaking of Messina in 1678.

In setting up his gallery, Andrea d'Avalos seems to have been concerned primarily to draw upon the image of his illustrious forebears in order to work against this somewhat chequered past and to present himself, instead, as the last in a long line of unimpeachable, feudal Neapolitan defenders of the Spanish crown. The legacy of Francesco and Alfonso d'Avalos was accordingly brought to the fore in the form of portraits that were prominently displayed in the company of likenesses of the Spanish monarchs, together with genealogical tables of the family. Two additional large canvases hung as pendants on opposite walls of the *galleria*, where they functioned as memorials to the family's two defining moments, of Ferdinando taking Francis I prisoner and Alfonso addressing the imperial troops in Milan.

Images alluding to significant moments of Andrea's own career were then hung in alignment with these paintings. Thus a portrait of Masaniello was placed opposite a pendant that is identified in the inventory of 1776 as Charles V but which seems more likely to have been a depiction of Masaniello's ultimately victorious opponent, Andrea's friend and

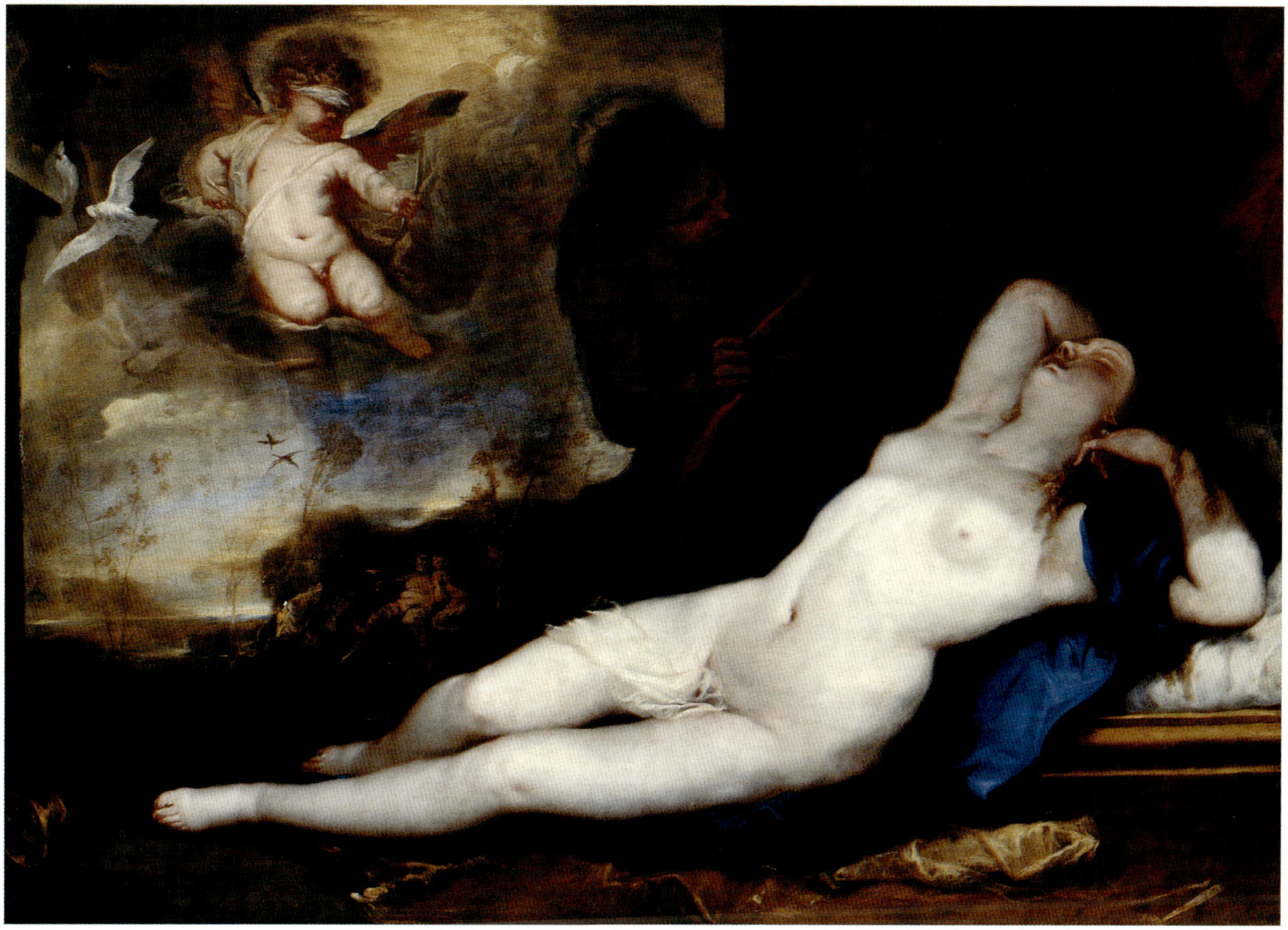

147 Luca Giordano, *Sleeping Venus with Cupid and Satyr*, signed and dated 1663. Oil on canvas, 137 × 190 cm. Museo e Gallerie Nazionali di Capodimonte, Naples

supporter, Don Juan of Austria.[43] Other paintings commemorated Andrea's involvement in the Siege of Messina,[44] together with two portraits (including one placed above the entrance to the *galleria*) that proclaimed his status as 'Generale delle Galee dell'Imperadore' (General of the Imperial Galleys).[45]

Andrea's earliest mythological paintings represent a continuation of the neo-Renaissance imagery found at the Palazzo Acquaviva in Conversano. Chief among these was a version of Ribera's masterpiece *Apollo and Marsyas* of 1637 (see fig. 48). This may have been commissioned by D'Avalos's father, Giovanni, since he is elsewhere documented as a patron of Caracciolo in the 1620s as well as a prospective patron of Ribera in the early 1630s.[46] But if so Andrea nonetheless built on this initial collecting tradition in the 1660s and 1670s by gathering together an innovative series of paintings commissioned from the leading artists of the next generation.

Luca Giordano, in particular, seems to have been a favourite. He painted for Andrea a group of mythologies and classical history paintings that, most unusually for the period, function as quotations and updates of some of the earlier paintings in the collection. Thus a painting of *Sleeping Venus Discovered by a Satyr* by Pacecco de Rosa from the 1640s was matched with a more recent painting of the same subject by Giordano, which De' Dominici described enthusiastically but with nonetheless a tinge of disapproval on the grounds that the figure of Venus was modelled on Giordano's wife, 'who was tall, well proportioned and very beautiful, without looking for others [i.e., other models], and perhaps he did this scandalously' (figs 146–7).[47] Finally, Andrea added a series of spectacular still-life paintings by Giuseppe Recco and others that represent the most lavish and up-to-date manifestations of the new taste in still-life gallery paintings to be discussed further in Chapter Eleven (fig. 148).

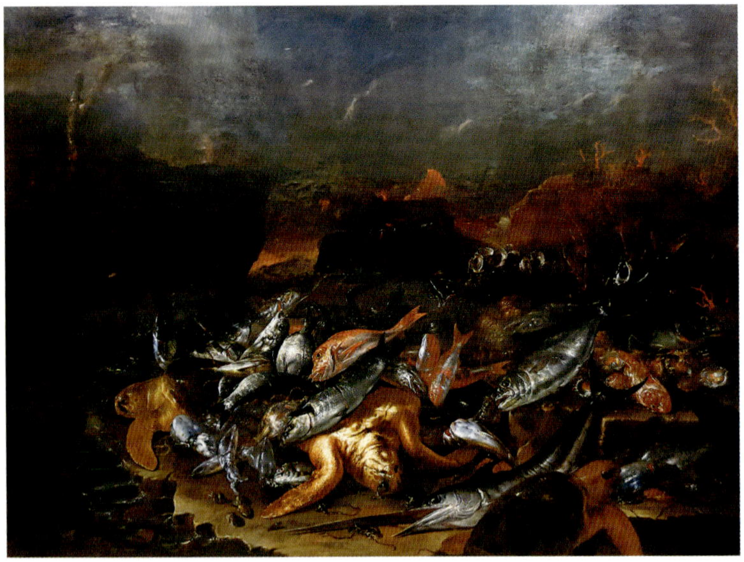

148 Giuseppe Recco, *Still Life with Fish and Other Sea Creatures*, 1671. Oil on canvas, 260 × 340 cm. Museo e Gallerie Nazionali di Capodimonte, Naples

FROM THE PORT TO THE PALACE: FOREIGN RESIDENTS IN NAPLES

Naples benefitted in many ways from the expanded horizons and increased international perspectives that were brought to the city by successive migrations of foreign residents. Foremost among these in influence and reach were the colonies of merchants drawn to the port city's status as one of the chief western Mediterranean points of supply and defence for the entire Habsburg chain of empire stretching from Seville to Santiago. Didier Barra's bird's-eye view of the city of 1647 proudly proclaims the city's maritime importance by focusing on the teeming industry of the metropolis converging on the bay (fig. 149).[48] Its sweeping, panoramic perspective allows the viewer to take in the vast infrastructure of the port: the causeway, quays, shipyard for building and repairs, docks for mooring and the arsenal for storing munitions, all either created or upgraded significantly during the recent period of the vice-regency. Numerous ships make their way out into the bay – from the smaller transport vessels to the more ponderously tacking merchantmen, to the low-slung galleys with their rhythmically beating oars.

Many of the trading vessels would have been owned by the Genoese merchants resident in Naples as part of their dominance of Neapolitan international trade and in financing the increasingly complex loans and exchanges required by the vice-regal administration and the Spanish crown more generally. The merchant-financiers received substantial profits in return, together with an increasing number of fiefs, land revenues and other tax privileges ceded to them by the continuously cash-deprived Spanish monarchs.[49] The Doria were particularly important. The victories of Andrea Doria (1466–1560) as commander of the imperial fleet during the first half of the sixteenth century had set the scene for this process. He had been awarded a series of important fiefs and posts in the kingdom that further encouraged the transfer to the city of many leading Genoese families in the decades that followed.[50]

So it is that one hears of a number of Genoese merchants building up significant collections of art in early seventeenth-century Naples. The Genoese consul, Cornelio Spinola, for example, is known to have commissioned paintings from Azzolino, Tommaso de Rosa and the painter-dealer Giacomo de Castro.[51] He is also documented in the 1640s paying for the decoration of a family chapel in the Neapolitan church of the Genoese nation, San Giorgio dei Genovesi.[52] Spinola was related by marriage to another Ligurian merchant resident in Naples, Lanfranco Massa, who is similarly documented commissioning work from Ippolito Borghese, Azzolino, Corenzio and François de Nomé, among others.[53] Massa's inventory of 1630 of the pictures included in his palace perched on the flanks of the Sant'Elmo hill includes a number of paintings by his compatriot Luca Cambiaso, together with work by Azzolino, Ribera and Caracciolo.[54]

Most of Massa's commissions were nonetheless carried out in his capacity as the Neapolitan agent of Andrea Doria's descendent, Prince Marcantonio Doria of Genoa. Between 1610 and 1620 Massa commissioned on Doria's behalf a series of important pictures by Ippolito Borghese, Caracciolo, Azzolino, François de Nomé and Ribera, all of which he carefully negotiated for, settled with the artists and then shipped off to Doria in Genoa. Massa also managed to commission for Doria a late work from Caravaggio in 1610 of the *Martyrdom of St Ursula*.[55] His example accordingly represents one of the first instances of a truly international interest in placing some of the latest Neapolitan Baroque paintings alongside that of Caravaggio and his contemporaries. (Nevertheless, it should be remembered that Doria was hardly a stranger to Naples, having had a decades-long association with the city as a result of his financial activities there and through his marriage to a local aristocratic noblewoman, whose daughter he continued to support during her later years spent as a nun in a Neapolitan convent.)[56]

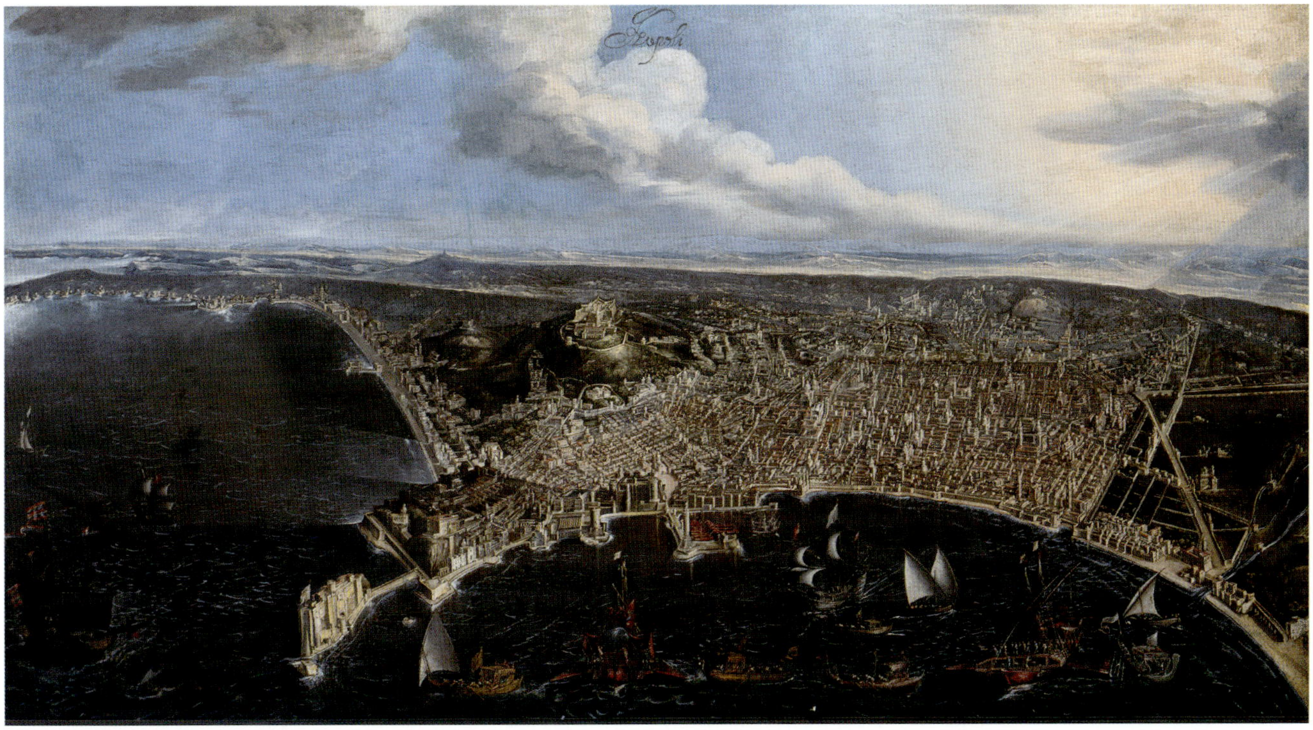

149 Didier Barra, *Bird's-Eye View of Naples*, signed and dated 1647. Oil on canvas, 69 × 129 cm. Museo di San Martino, Naples

The artists selected by these three individuals – first-wave Neapolitan Caravaggesques together with their immediate contemporaries – form a tight group that reinforces the prevailing picture of a closely linked circle of business associates all following converging interests and cultural predilections during the same period. From within this ambience, though, there would emerge the single most important collector of Neapolitan and international painting in the entire kingdom of Naples, Gaspar Roomer, who came from Antwerp but nonetheless maintained close associations with the Genoese and other merchant residents of the city. He was a regular business partner of Spinola, for example, and also subsequently acquired Massa's palace following the latter's death in 1630.[57]

Roomer went well beyond these and other individuals in the kingdom in the extent of his business dealings maintained over the course of a long and prodigiously successful career. From 1616 until his death in 1674 he worked assiduously with two long-term fellow Flemish business partners resident in Naples – Iacomo van Rey and Jan Vandeneynden, the latter becoming his partner following Van Rey's death in 1627. Roomer and his partners maintained a fleet of ships out of the port that enabled them to operate as arms dealers and naval outfitters, international import/export agents and maritime insurers/loan agents and international financiers more generally. The scale and complexity of their dealings went well beyond that of any other private commercial enterprise in the city. Eduardo Nappi's research into the archives of the eight public banks of Baroque Naples has revealed that between 1616 and 1674 Roomer and his partners were paid the staggering sum of 30.5 million ducats for a vast range of commercial activities – a figure that averages around half a million ducats per year. Nappi's published records moreover account for only part of Roomer's financial empire.[58]

The first reference to Roomer's collecting activities occurs, characteristically, in a record of 230 ducats that he paid in 1630 to the widow of a recently deceased painter-dealer for the important pieces of his workshop stock. In this way, Roomer acquired a large *Crucifixion* by Vouet, three landscapes by Agostino Tassi, an architectural scene by Napoletano, an *Ecce Homo* 'antico' and a large *Christ Ministered to by the Angels* by Jean Ducamps, the Flemish Caravaggesque painter and co-founder of the *Schildersbent* in Rome (see p. 117).[59] Here as always Roomer appears to have had a knack for being very well informed about artworks circulating on the market. This, together with his predilection for acquiring collections en bloc – or at least securing a number of impor-

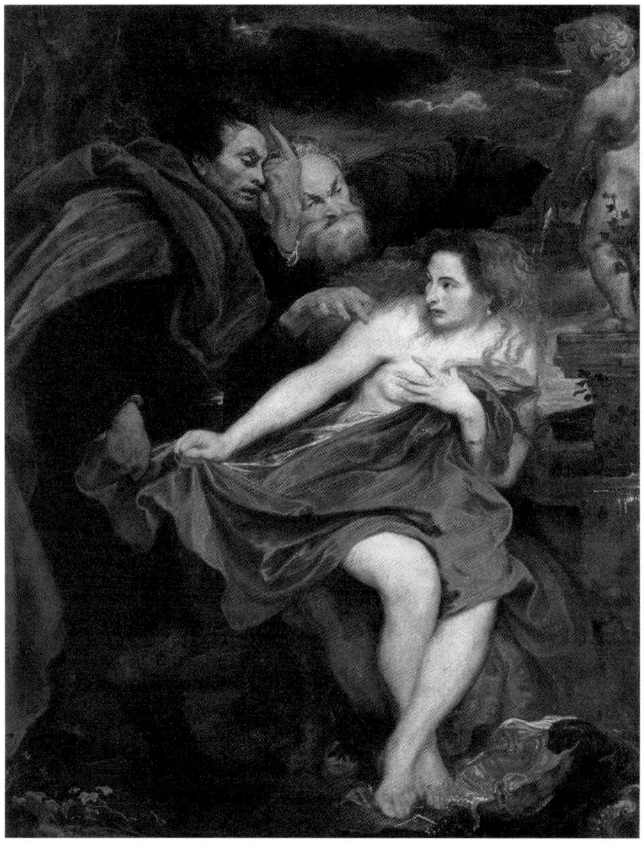

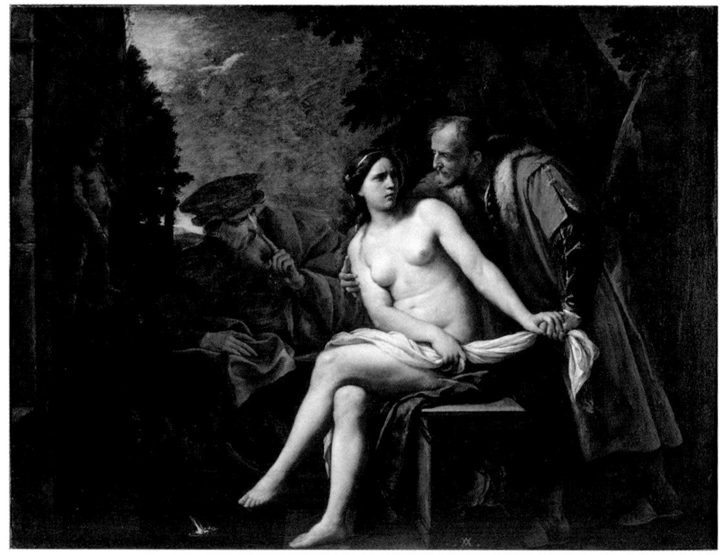

Left 150 Anthony van Dyck, *Susanna and the Elders*, *circa* 1621–6. Oil on canvas, 194 × 144 cm. Alte Pinakothek, Bayerische Staatsgemäldesammlungen, Munich

Above 151 Andrea Vaccaro, *Susanna and the Elders*, 1650s. Oil on canvas, 198 × 257 cm. Museo e Gallerie Nazionali di Capodimonte, Naples

tant works from a collection in a single transaction – forms one of many indications of his activities as an art dealer that were conducted in tandem with his undertakings as a collector in the more traditional sense of the term. So, in 1652 he acquired paintings by Cavallino and Spinelli from a certain Giuseppe Labruto.[60] In the following year he is also documented paying 550 ducats to the painter-dealer Giacomo de Castro for a number of paintings that included Ribera's masterpiece, the *Drunken Silenus* of 1626 (see p. 119).[61]

The fullest surviving account of Roomer's collection comes in a fulsome description contained in Capaccio's early guide to the city, *Il Forastiero*, written in 1630 but not published until 1634.[62] Capaccio notes that Roomer's collection was spread across twelve rooms of his palace, located close to the Palazzo Gravina in Monteoliveto. A subsequent, brief reference by Celano of 1692 reveals that at the time of his death his collection comprised some 1,500 paintings and was said to be worth the huge amount of 80,000 ducats.[63] Capaccio describes seven works by Ribera, including the renowned *Apollo and Marsyas* (evidently an earlier version than the example of 1637 commissioned by the d'Avalos family). He also notes the presence of three large and three smaller canvases by Stanzione, five by Caracciolo, an unspecified number of battle paintings by Falcone and a host of other works by foreign artists.

Roomer hung his Neapolitan Caravaggesques alongside canvases by a broad range of painters working in Caravaggio's style active in other Italian cities and beyond. Besides the work by Vouet, his collection thus contained paintings by Renier, Saraceni, Valentin, Stomer, Francesco Rustici, Spadarino and the Flemish associate of Dirck van Baburen in Rome, David de Haen. No other Neapolitan collection of the day could boast such an up-to-the-moment presentation of the latest developments in Caravaggesque painting, both locally and internationally. Roomer nonetheless added to this other paintings of further significance for the dissemination in Naples of wider international trends.

Foremost among these were two paintings by Van Dyck – *St Sebastian* and *Susanna and the Elders* – that are both mentioned as present in Roomer's collection by 1630 (fig. 150).[64] Van Dyck's model has been frequently emphasized in the literature for its significance in encouraging the Neapolitans to move away from the dark tenebrism of the 1610s and 1620s towards the richer and more painterly chromatic values that came increasingly to the fore in the work of artists like Ribera, Cavallino and Guarino in the

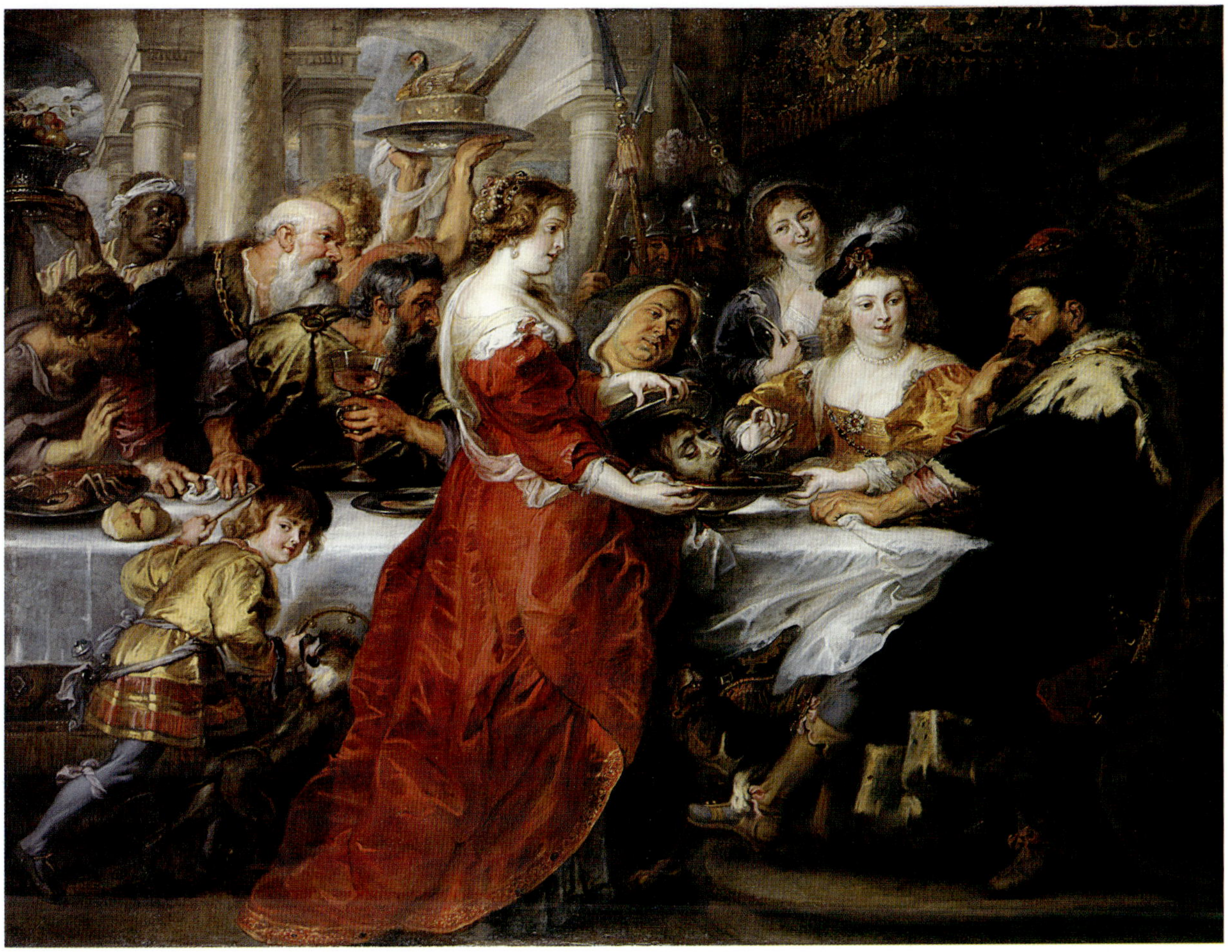

152 Sir Peter Paul Rubens, *Feast of Herod, circa* 1633–8. Oil on canvas, 208 × 264 cm. Scottish National Gallery, Edinburgh

1630s and beyond.[65] Van Dyck never seems to have resided in Naples for any length of time during the period he spent moving between Genoa, Rome and Palermo from 1621 to 1626.[66] So Roomer's early possession of two major works from his early career stands as an especially important point of reference for the transmission of his influence in Naples, an influence that can be seen in a number of artists, including Vaccaro, whose version of *Susanna and the Elders* seems especially indebted to Van Dyck's composition (fig. 151).[67]

Roomer's extensive Flemish and Genoese networks make it almost inevitable that he would have become aware of the work of the brilliant young Fleming, since Van Dyck was in touch with many of his associates during this period. Roomer's Genoese contacts would probably have been of most use to him here, since, in the absence of any specific documentation, he may well have reached out to the Flemish painter-dealer Corneille de Wael for further information. De Wael was at that stage acting as Van Dyck's Genoese host, protector and agent.[68] Roomer was in regular communication with De Wael over the course of many decades, while his partner, Jan Vandeneynden, was distantly related to both De Wael and to another of De Wael's contacts, the renowned Flemish landscape and still-life specialist Jan Brueghel the Elder.

Roomer probably turned directly, on the other hand, to his Antwerp network when it came to sourcing important works by Rubens, Van Dyck's master and the presiding genius of the Antwerp school. There would have been many possible points of contact with Rubens, beginning with Roomer's brother Louis, who is documented as a friend and business partner of Rubens in the late 1620s.[69] Rubens is encountered in Neapolitan seventeenth- and eighteenth-century collections only very rarely. The arrival of his major canvas of the *Feast of Herod* in Roomer's collection around 1640 accordingly appears to have constituted an important cultural event in Naples (fig. 152): De' Dominici noted, in particular, that Cavallino 'came to see this much talked-of work, and he found it so beautiful that, captivated by the magic of brilliant and life-like colouring laid on with such consummate skill, he determined to imitate it himself'.[70] The essential accuracy of De' Dominici's statement is reinforced by the influence of Rubens's dramatic composition in a number of Cavallino's canvases from the early to late 1640s.[71] Roomer's *Feast of Herod* also exerted a strong hold over the next generation of artists, including Giordano and Preti (see pp. 203–5).

Capaccio's description also includes reference to hundreds of paintings by the early Northern landscape specialists of the first decades of the seventeenth century. Besides paintings by Brill, Tassi, Poelenburgh and Jan Brueghel (a relative of Roomer's business partner), Capaccio also mentions no fewer than 60 pictures by Goffredo Wals, 40 paintings by Léonard Bramer and 168 landscapes by a painter by the name of Jacobo Sibraut. This artist may be the landscape painter known only as 'Giacobbe' whose work appears in a number of early Neapolitan inventories.[72] The huge quantities of paintings by these artists suggest strongly that Roomer stockpiled their output in his palace in his capacity as a dealer, a reference that ties in further with his activities in the trade and export of Neapolitan paintings.

Roomer died without male heirs in 1674, thus setting in train the rapid dispersal of one of the most substantial legacies in Neapolitan history. Circumspect and devout in his private affairs, Roomer had been careful to plan the future spread of his assets among a series of religious and charitable institutions, most notably the Ospedale degli Incurabili and the Carmelite convent of Santa Maria Maddalena de' Pazzi, which his daughter had entered. These fortunate recipients quickly sold off Roomer's properties and belongings in the months that followed. As a result, no carefully compiled inventory of his possessions was drawn up at the time of his death to give a full understanding of his collecting in the forty-four years following Capaccio's description. This is unfortunate, since it has encouraged a rather restricted characterization of Roomer in the literature as a single-minded devotee of early seventeenth-century Dutch and Flemish landscape, still life and early Caravaggesque naturalism developed in keeping with a supposedly intrinsically Flemish 'taste for the grotesque, the dark and the cruel'.[73]

The reality seems to have been more complex, although this is based on admittedly sketchy information. In particular, it seems that Roomer's later patronage and collecting demonstrate a flexibility that would be familiar to all successful art dealers and collectors operating over a number of decades. Like them, Roomer was able to sustain his enthusiasm by supporting generations of artists and by evolving his tastes. He is thus heard of subsequently collecting work by Pietro da Cortona, Poussin and Claude Lorrain, the last of whose landscapes would have offered a particularly attractive update on the earlier style of Roomer's previously favoured landscape specialist, Goffredo Wals.[74] It should also be remembered that during the 1640s Roomer took pleasure in encouraging the most neo-Poussinesque manifestations of Falcone's talents in the innovative series of frescoes that he commissioned from the artist, following a distinctly Roman model, for his villa at Barra on the outskirts of Naples.[75] Roomer also went on to act as an enthusiastic supporter of the leading figures of the next generation, including Ruoppolo, Preti, Vaccaro and of course Luca Giordano, whose close association with Roomer from his earliest years is emphasized in all the early sources, from Giordano himself to De' Dominici in the eighteenth century.

De' Dominici reiterated Roomer's importance as an arbiter of taste among Neapolitan artistic circles, noting his crucial role in promoting Mattia Preti's gallery paintings to other Neapolitan collectors of the 1650s, since 'his opinion was reported to all the lovers of painting in that period'.[76] As the above examples indicate, Roomer was equally influential as an important cultural go-between introducing local Neapolitan painters to broader international trends, with a particular emphasis on Dutch and Flemish Caravaggesque, landscape and history painting from the first half of the seventeenth century. It is unfortunate, therefore, that the lack of a detailed inventory of his collection at the end of his career renders it impossible to determine with any certainty Roomer's role in introducing into Naples an awareness of Flemish still-life paintings produced after 1630. In particular, it would be of some significance to learn of Roomer's interest in the monumental still-life paintings by Frans Snyders and his contemporaries, since these provide the direct precedent for the shift towards larger, more High Baroque, still-life paintings with monumental figures by Giordano and his associates that became very fashionable in Naples from the 1660s onwards (see pp. 245–6).

Roomer's liking for still life and his close association with Giordano make him an ideal candidate for understanding these artistic developments. His possession of earlier still lifes was made clear already by Capaccio's reference in 1630 to six paintings of fruit and animals by a certain Gerardo van den Bos. This artist is identifiable with the Dutch animal painter Gerrit van den Bosch who resided in Rome in the second decade of the seventeenth century and whose work was also collected by the Medici during the same period.[77] In the later stages of Roomer's life, in the 1660s, Jan Baptist

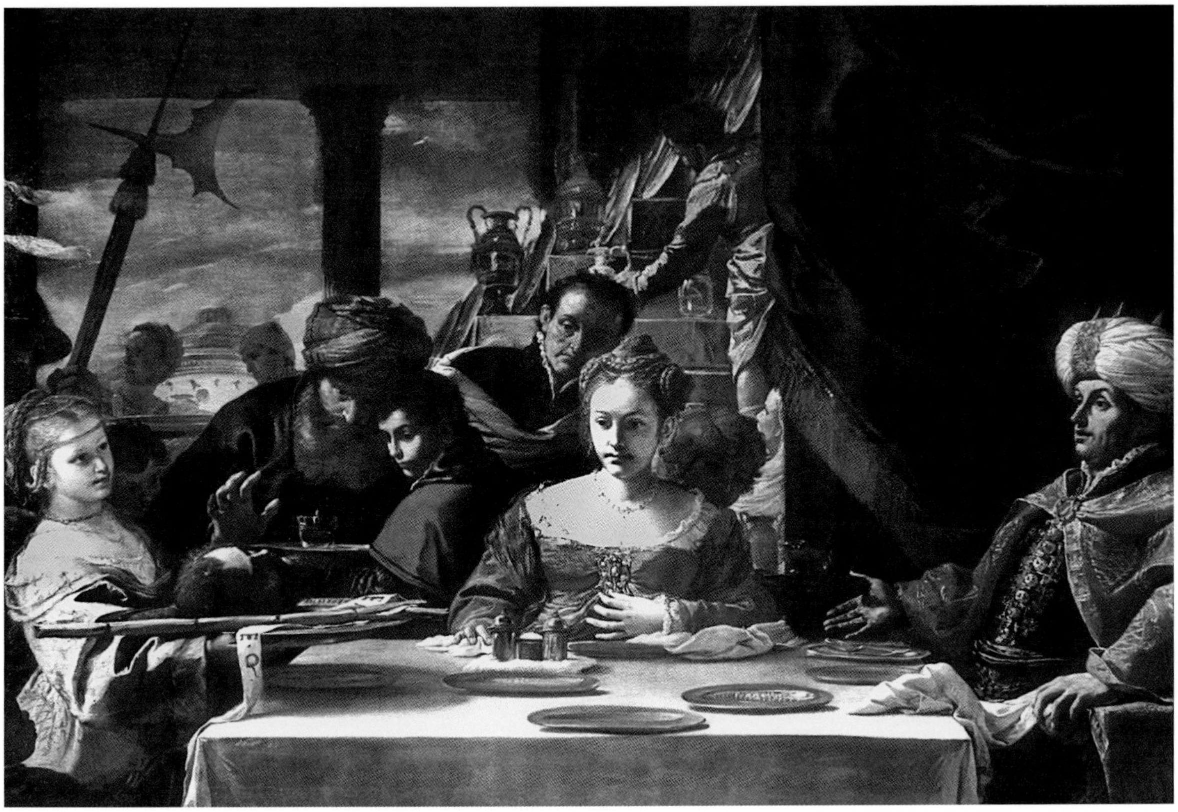

153 Mattia Preti, *Feast of Herod, circa* 1653–5. Oil on canvas, 177.8 × 252.1 cm. Toledo Museum of Art, Toledo, Ohio

de Wael II dedicated to him a series of prints with figures and animals that are very close in mood and composition to Giordano's large paintings of pastoral scenes with shepherds from around the same period.[78]

Roomer may have become aware of Frans Snyders's paintings via his contacts in Genoa or Antwerp, since it is known that this artist's work had reached Genoa from as early as 1625,[79] while a more certain Neapolitan link may be traced for the work of Snyders's ablest pupil, Jan Fyt (1611–1661). Four of Fyt's paintings, in fact, appear in a Neapolitan inventory of 1688 that lists the pictures to be passed via inheritance by Roomer's partner's son, Ferdinand Vandeneynden.[80] Ferdinand may have come into possession of these paintings through Roomer, since in 1674 Roomer bequeathed seventy of his best paintings to Vandeneynden (although for the most part their identity is unknown).

Vandeneynden owned both Fyt's game pieces as well as a marine still life, one of which measured around 233 × 185 centimetres. In Vandeneynden's collection, moreover, the link between Fyt and Neapolitan still life was made explicit, since Fyt's work hung alongside contemporary Neapolitan still lifes by Paolo Porpora and Giovanni Battista Ruoppolo, together with a particularly large and impressive painting by Giordano (measuring around 316 × 185 cm) that is described as 'la favola della Terra, e l'Acqua con diversi figure, e tritoni' (an allegory of the earth and sea with various figures and tritons). This last painting would have resembled the extant gallery paintings of this kind produced by Giordano in partnership with Giuseppe Recco, who contributed impressive displays of fish, shells, crustaceans, turtles and the like (see fig. 79).[81]

From the inventory of 1688 and other sources it is known that Ferdinand was a major collector in his own right, albeit following directly the precedent set by Roomer, who seems to have acted as a mentor to him in an artistic as well as in a business capacity. The inventory of his collection of 1688 lists hundreds of paintings, and De' Dominici also noted that Vandeneynden was a major early patron of Mattia Preti, his commissions including three of Preti's most important early scenes of martyrdom.[82] De' Dominici also singled out for praise Preti's *Feast of Herod*, noting that this was commissioned by Ferdinand in direct homage to Rubens's celebrated painting of the *Feast of Herod*, at that stage still in Roomer's collection (fig. 153).[83] The idea of commissioning a more contemporary response to an earlier

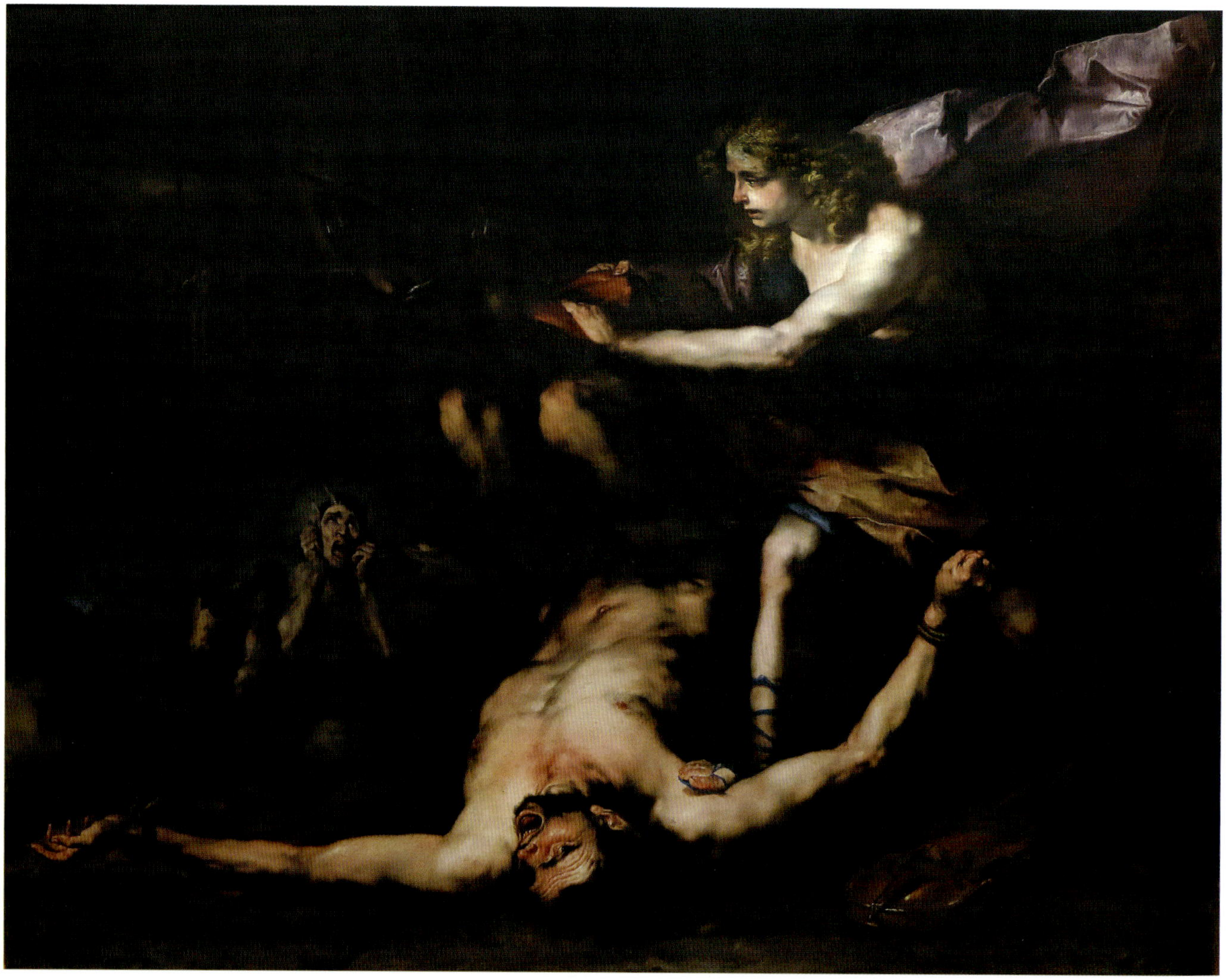

154 Luca Giordano, *Apollo and Marsyas*, *circa* 1655–60. Oil on canvas, 205 × 259 cm. Museo e Gallerie Nazionali di Capodimonte, Naples

work of significance in a distinguished collection (as seen in the case of the collection of Andrea d'Avalos) is something that Roomer himself enjoyed pursuing from time to time. Chief among Vandeneynden's paintings of this kind was an audacious variant on Ribera's *Apollo and Marsyas* in Roomer's collection by Giordano; it is listed in his inventory in 1688 and so appears to have been passed on to him via Roomer (fig. 154).[84]

So it seems that Vandeneynden built on this practice of commissioning works in reference to earlier paintings when he ordered from Mattia Preti in the mid-1650s a version of the *Feast of Herod* that was designed to act as a counterpoint to Rubens's famous canvas in Roomer's collection. Preti's *Feast* constitutes a respectful yet critical reworking of its model. In place of Rubens's relatively frivolous and exuberant treatment, with a multitude of servants and guests all craning forward to witness the gruesome spectacle of the Baptist's severed head, Preti produced a stripped-back composition. This retains all the scale and drama of Rubens's work, but adds a more austere devotional quality in the sombre contemplation of the infamy of Herod's command.

This is particularly evident in the gesture made by the turbaned courtier in the middle of the composition. His hand hovers over the Baptist's head in a manner suggestive of awe-filled reverence, thereby focusing attention on the Baptist's head as an apotropeic form of holy relic. In so doing, Preti shows himself to have been closely attentive to the strong Neapolitan tradition of devotional paintings that focus with an almost visionary intensity on the severed heads of especially venerated martyr saints: be they the Baptist, St

Januarius or St Anastasius (for example, in the context of the Fracanzani's cheap paintings of the head of St Anastasius produced for sale on the open market; see pp. 104–5) (see fig. 81).[85] The result is a composition that effortlessly combines the exotic sophistication of Rubens's original (mixed with an advanced knowledge of the sixteenth-century Venetian influences to which Rubens's painting also refers) with reference to the centuries-old local traditions of viscerally experienced popular devotion.

Preti thus provided Vandeneynden with a suave combination of local and international influences, a cross-cultural synthesis that matched the personal qualities that Roomer and the Vandeneynden, both father and son, had sought to embody in the trajectory of their lives. The two interlinked families had, after all, travelled a great distance in their passage from the docks of Antwerp to the palaces of Naples. Ferdinand, in particular, had set the seal on Roomer's and his father's decades of hard work by marrying into the local nobility and acquiring the title of marchese. He had thus achieved the migrant's dream of social acceptability and advancement, and must have taken great pleasure in enjoying the fruits of this intergenerational enterprise in the cultivated sophistication of Preti's paintings and the other lavish decorations maintained in the family palace on Via Toledo. The palace itself further reflected this trajectory, since it had been acquired by Ferdinand's father from another nouveau riche administrator, after having been designed some decades earlier by Cosimo Fanzago to take advantage of the new development opportunities created by Don Pedro de Toledo's extension of Via Toledo (see p. 184).[86] From such acquisitions, then, Roomer, Vandeneynden and the other foreign residents of Naples were able to proclaim their arrival to the rest of society as fully fledged citizens of wealth and distinction in a city that had offered them shelter and the means to advance themselves to respectability and the heights of splendour.

CARDINAL ASCANIO FILOMARINO: ART AS CULTURAL DISTINCTION

The patronage and collecting activities of Cardinal Ascanio Filomarino (1584–1666) follow a markedly different direction from the cross-cultural emphasis that characterized the collections of Roomer and the Vandeneynden. Although born into an illustrious Neapolitan aristocratic family, Filomarino used art collecting as a mechanism for declaring his cultural independence of local traditions and to present himself, rather, as a sophisticated expatriate.[87] The turning point in this long process of cultural distancing appears to have been his decision, taken in 1616, to leave behind an initial frustrated career searching for opportunities among the crowded ranks of Neapolitan canon and civil lawyers and to move to Rome, where he served initially as master of ceremonies for his uncle, the recently promoted Cardinal Ladislao d'Aquino.[88] Rome, it seems, offered the young Filomarino the chance of a fresh start away from the pressures and restrictions caused by familial financial difficulties that were exacerbated by the early death of his father in 1611 and which are alluded to in some of the primary sources (Fuidoro, for example, goes so far as to say that Ascanio left Naples for Rome 'quasi nudo').[89]

The move proved propitious in many ways, since Filomarino was able during this period to forge deep and longstanding associations with Maffeo and Francesco Barberini, who would go on to become his main protectors in the ensuing years. Following Maffeo Barberini's accession to the papacy as Urban VIII in 1623, Filomarino was rapidly promoted to the role of the pope's *cameriere segreto*, as well as *maestro di camera* to Cardinal Francesco. He thus became a central figure of the Barberini entourage, accompanying them on their diplomatic missions to France and Spain in 1625 and 1626, and more generally sharing both their political alliances and their cultural orientations. As a result, he acquired a strong Francophile taste that inclined him away from the habitual Spanish allegiances favoured by Urban VIII's predecessors, and which would become especially problematic to him following his return to Spanish Naples in 1641.

Building on this background, Filomarino seems to have played a crucial role in encouraging a Neapolitan awareness of the work of many of the French painters associated with the Barberini during the 1620s and 1630s. As early as 1620, in fact, he is recorded paying Simon Vouet for a major painting, and this has been plausibly identified as a down payment for Vouet's otherwise undocumented *Circumcision* of 1622, now in the Museo di Capodimonte but originally hanging in the church of the Arciconfraternita di Sant'Angelo a Segno in Naples (fig. 155).[90] If this is so, then Filomarino's intervention was of major importance to the development of Neapolitan painting, given the primary significance of Vouet's *Circumcision* as one of the first examples to be introduced into Naples of the new 'ennobled Caravaggesque' style that would become very influential during the 1630s and 1640s. The down payment of 1620 to Vouet was nonetheless made by Filomarino on behalf of a relative of his back in Naples, Marcantonio Filomarino, duca della Rocca,

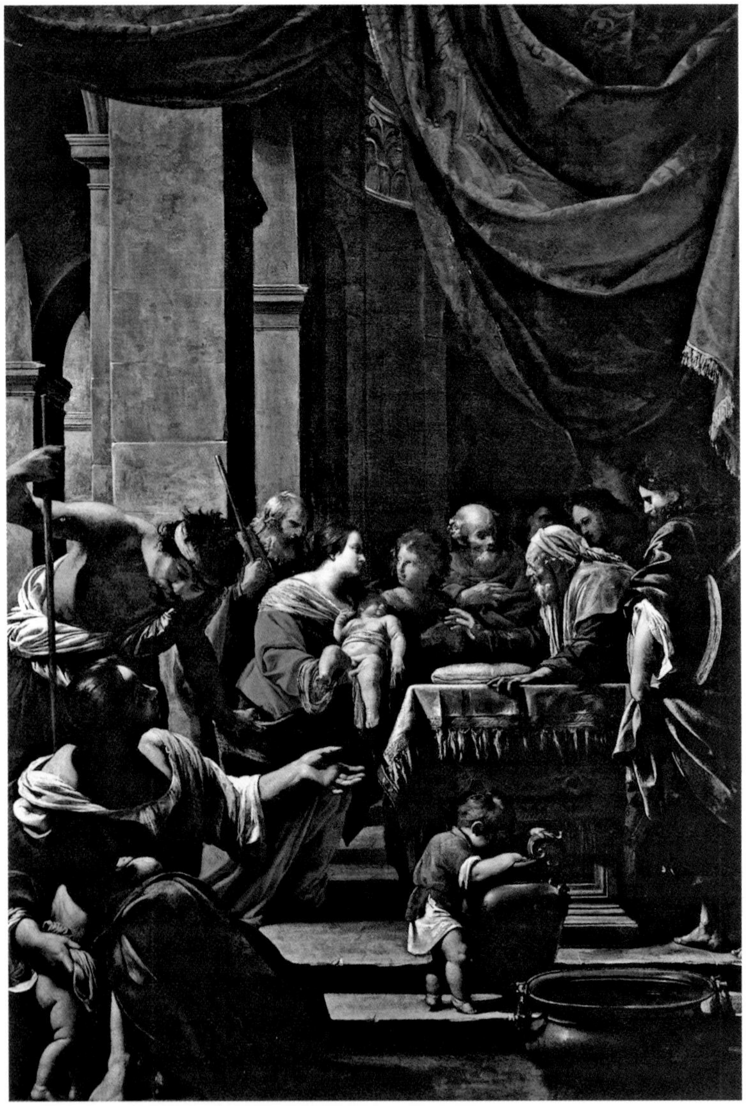

155 Simon Vouet, *Circumcision*, signed and dated 1622. Oil on canvas, 290 × 193 cm. Museo e Gallerie Nazionali di Capodimonte, Naples, on deposit from the Arciconfraternita di Sant'Arcangelo a Segno

who must therefore also be given major credit for introducing this artist's work to Naples. Marcantonio seems to have acted as a mentor to Filomarino following the early death of Ascanio's father. He was also a significant collector in his own right and clearly a major influence on the young Ascanio, since, in 1623, he authorized Ascanio to pay Vouet for a series of now-lost paintings of the *Apostles*, *Christ*, *John the Baptist* and the *Virgin* that were subsequently described in Marcantonio's inventory of 1634.[91]

This commission evidently encouraged Ascanio to commission Vouet to produce work for his own collection. In 1627 he paid Vouet for a series of twelve paintings of angels with the symbols of the Passion, two of which are today in the Museo di Capodimonte (fig. 156).[92] The presence in Naples during this period of these important early works by Vouet and his workshop seems to have encouraged the Carthusians, in turn, to commission a major work from this artist in 1626 for the prominent location of the chapter house of the Certosa di San Martino. Vouet thus emerges, via the agency of the Filomarino family, as a crucial early reference point for the transmission of an elegant and more internationally flavoured form of Caravaggism that would become increasingly popular in Naples in the years to come.

Filomarino progressed from this to commission work from a number of the other French artists then enjoying the patronage of the Barberini. Valentin seems to have been a particular favourite. The Neapolitan inventory of 1685 of the collection of Filomarino's nephew and namesake lists seven paintings by Valentin, many of them also documented by payments from Ascanio dating to 1627. These include two portraits of Ascanio and his brother, Scipione, which were used as the models for the mosaic portraits commissioned for the Filomarino altar in Santi Apostoli to be discussed presently (see pp. 209–10).[93] Filomarino also patronized the work of Charles Mellin, who was at that stage enjoying the particular attention in Rome of Cassiano dal Pozzo and Cardinal Francesco Barberini.[94] The Filomarino inventory of 1685 includes a canvas of the *Liberation of St Peter* by Mellin, and it has been plausibly suggested that Filomarino might have subsequently facilitated Mellin's transfer to Naples in the early 1640s to paint a series of major altarpieces, returning to Rome as a result of the disturbances in the city during the lead up to the Revolt of Masaniello in 1647.[95]

For all this Neapolitan interest in the work of Vouet, Valentin and Mellin, the French painter under Barberini protection who was of greatest influence on the Neapolitan scene during the 1630s and 1640s was without a doubt Nicolas Poussin. Poussin had been active in Rome since 1624 following his move there from Paris on the basis of the initial encouragement offered to him by Giambattista Marino, prior to Marino's relocation to Naples shortly thereafter. In Naples, Marino may well have recommended Poussin's paintings to his friend and protector, Giovan Battista Manso, marchese di Villa, as well as to the other early Neapolitan collectors with whom Manso associated. Poussin's paintings are, in any event, known to have circulated on the Neapolitan art market from a very early date. Accord-

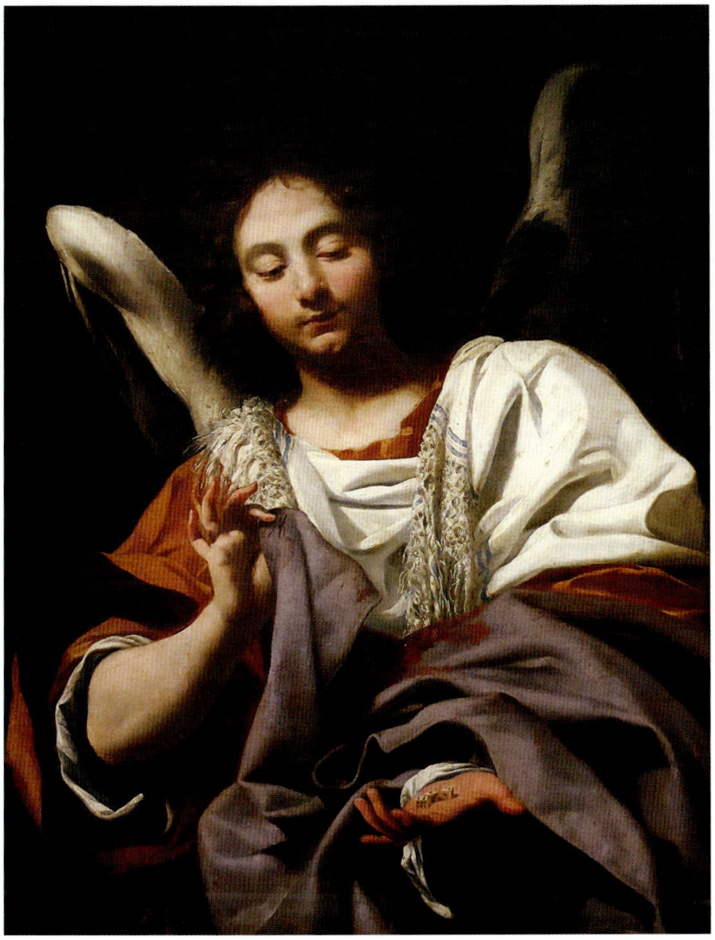

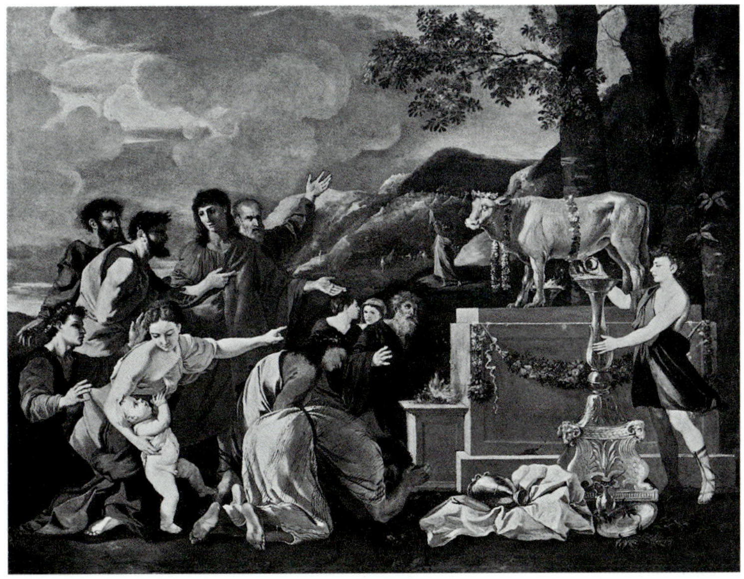

Left 156 Workshop of Simon Vouet (Charles Mellin?), *Angel with Dice and a Tunic*, 1626–7. Oil on canvas, 102 × 78 cm. Museo e Gallerie Nazionali di Capodimonte, Naples

Above 157 Neapolitan follower of Nicolas Poussin (Andrea de Leone?), *Adoration of the Golden Calf*, 1640s. Oil on canvas, 100 × 129 cm. Californian Palace of the Legion of Honor, San Francisco

ing to Sandrart, Poussin's *Plague of Ashdod*, now in the Louvre, was acquired around 1631 by an unidentified 'nobleman of Pozzuoli' following the disgrace and transfer to a Roman jail of its initial owner, the Sicilian art dealer cum diamond thief Fabrizio Valguarnera.[96] The veracity of this account is reinforced by the inclusion of visual references to motifs taken from Poussin's composition in the works of Falcone and other Neapolitan artists in his circle from the 1630s and early 1640s.[97]

Another work by Poussin known to have been in Naples from an early date is a version of the *Adoration of the Golden Calf* dating from the late 1620s. Félibien stated that this canvas was owned by an unspecified Neapolitan collector before being almost completely destroyed by the ransacking populace during the Revolt of Masaniello in 1647.[98] Prior to this, however, the painting's composition was preserved for posterity in a copy which is probably to be attributed to Aniello Falcone's closest follower, Andrea de Leone, which further attests to the importance for local artists of works by foreign artists in Neapolitan collections more generally (fig. 157).[99]

The Neapolitans were especially attentive to the model of Poussin, then, and Ascanio Filomarino seems to have played a crucial role in cementing this popularity. The inventory of 1685 of his nephew and namesake (which remains the most direct documentation for the contents of Ascanio's collection) lists three paintings by Poussin. Two of these – *Christ Healing the Blind Man of Bethesda* and the *Holy Family with St John the Baptist and Angels* – are also documented by payments made by Filomarino to Poussin in Rome in October 1627.[100] The third painting, the *Annunciation*, is otherwise undocumented but presumably dates to the same period. The subsequent fame of the three paintings is attested to by their being singled out for enthusiastic description by Charles Nicolas Cochin in his influential *Voyage d'Italie* of 1756. They were also copied shortly thereafter by Fragonard and Jean Robert Ango during their stay in Naples in 1761 in the entourage of the abbé de Saint-Non. All three paintings were nonetheless destroyed (together with almost the entirety of the Filomarino collection) during the violent disturbances that

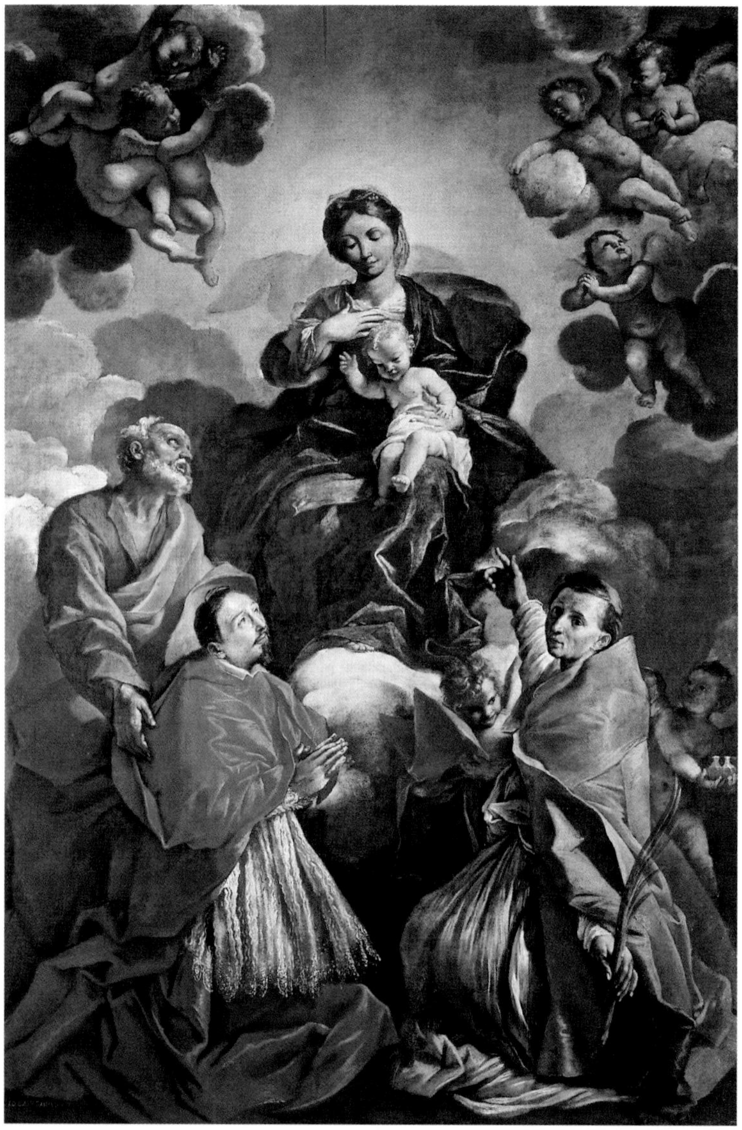

158 Giovanni Lanfranco, *Sts Peter and Januarius Presenting Cardinal Ascanio Filomarino to the Virgin and Child*, *circa* 1645, signed. Oil on panel, 300 × 210 cm. Palazzo Arcivescovile, Naples

accompanied the fall of the Parthenopean Republic of 1799. Earlier, though, the paintings offered artists and collectors the fullest Neapolitan overview then available of Poussin's early style, a style much more in accord with local tastes than the increasingly abstract and intellectualizing style of Poussin's later years.[101]

In 1641 Filomarino ultimately set the seal on his career by securing from Pope Urban VIII the post of archbishop of Naples and cardinal of Santa Maria in Aracoeli, Rome. In so doing, he was fortunate in being able to move back to his home city just before the backlash launched against the Barberini family and its supporters following the pope's death in July 1644. This should, therefore, have represented the culmination of a long and illustrious career. Yet something in Filomarino's character denied both him and Naples the possibility of enjoying such a straightforwardly positive final act of reconciliation. In his classic account of mid-seventeenth-century Neapolitan culture, De Reumont suggests that the reasons for this lay in the degree to which Filomarino harboured 'an inveterate spite against the Spaniards' that was at the same time further complicated by his wish to 'quarrel with the Neapolitan nobility still more on every occasion than with the foreign rulers and against them he waged the fiercest opposition even though he was descended from them'.[102]

Loredana Lorizzo sought to temper this assessment by placing greater emphasis on Filomarino's desire to restore to the position of the archbishop of Naples the traditional dignity and authority that had been progressively eroded over the decades by increased civic, vice-regal and aristocratic incursion into its jurisdiction.[103] Yet even she was forced to concede that 'Ascanio fu sopratutto un nobile volitivo' (Ascanio was above all else a volatile member of the aristocracy).[104] There can be no doubting, therefore, that the reintroduction of Filomarino's imperious personality into the complex political landscape of Naples during the 1640s and 1650s gave rise to a fractious relationship characterized by confrontations over precedence and authority.

These tensions reached a pitch during the Revolt of Masaniello of 1647, when Filomarino assumed the role of intermediary negotiating terms between the rebellious Neapolitan populace and the directly threatened vice-regency and Neapolitan aristocracy.[105] Filomarino's anti-Spanish sympathies combined with his strong pastoral identification with the spiritual needs of the people afforded him a certain degree of sympathy for the rebels' aims. In the weeks that followed the insurrection's outbreak he accordingly sought to negotiate a fraught middle path between the revolt's opposing factions, becoming a rallying point for the people's aspirations to the extent that it was at one stage proposed that Cosimo Fanzago should erect a permanent memorial to the accord supposedly struck between the viceroy and the Neapolitan populace that would include statues of the king, the viceroy and Filomarino himself.[106] This did nothing to dispel the Habsburgs' fundamental mistrust of the archbishop. Since even before the revolt, in fact, Spanish diplomatic channels in Rome and elsewhere had regarded Filomarino as an enemy affiliate of the Barberini and member of the 'partito filof-rancese' that had been seeking to destabilize the kingdom for years and that became a particular threat during the increasingly chaotic later stages of the revolt, when Naples temporarily came close to coming under the control of a French republican faction led by the duc de Guise.[107]

Yet at the decisive moment Filomarino knew where his allegiances lay. As a member of the ecclesiastical and aristocratic hierarchy he was as threatened as they were by the primal challenge to the established order signalled by Masaniello and his followers. In the end he retreated from identifying too closely with the rebels or with any of the other anti-Spanish sentiments that came to the surface during these years. He thus managed to escape the accusations and recriminations that accompanied the inevitable suppression of the revolt and return to order that ensued in 1648.

What remained, then, was for Filomarino to reapply himself during his final years to the ongoing project of reinforcing the dignity and authority of the position of the archbishop of Naples and on elevating and consolidating his own status and that of his family more generally. For the first task, he further embellished the cathedral and renovated the archiepiscopal palace, in the process commissioning frescoes and an altarpiece by Lanfranco that depicted him in the presence of Saints Peter and Januarius, thereby reinforcing his dual authority as both archbishop of Naples and cardinal (fig. 158).[108]

For the second, he acquired in 1645 the sixteenth-century palace of Marchese Alfonso Sanchez di Grottola, advantageously situated in the centre of the old city in Piazza San Domenico Maggiore. In the years that followed he substantially modernized and amplified the palace. He also transferred to it his distinguished collection of paintings formed primarily in Rome that included not only the canvases by the French artists favoured by the Barberini, but also some significant works by prominent Roman and Bolognese artists including paintings by Guido Reni and Domenichino and a renowned painting by Annibale Carracci, of the *Three Maries at the Sepulchre*, at one stage owned by Giovan Battista Agucchi and today in the Hermitage in St Petersburg. Filomarino had also managed to acquire a version of Caravaggio's *St Francis in Ecstasy* from the Barberini-endorsed sale of the estate of Cardinal Francesco dal Monte that had been held in Rome in 1628.[109]

During this period, Filomarino commissioned the young Francesco di Maria to paint his portrait standing proudly in front of the Palazzo Filomarino in his dual role as cardinal archbishop of Naples and returned family head responsible for restoring the family name to its former glory (fig. 159). Yet what was conspicuously absent from the Filomarino collection was precisely a connection with the local Neapolitan artistic culture that made up the bulk of almost all other collections of the period. During his twenty-five years spent resident in Naples, in fact, Filomarino almost entirely ignored the Neapolitans, save for a smattering of works by the young Luca Giordano and a conspicuous group of eight paintings by the Fracanzani, which might to some degree corroborate the shadowy story recounted by De' Dominici concerning the Filomarino family's protection of the Fracanzani after they had come under suspicion for fomenting anti-Spanish activities during the revolt.[110] It seems therefore that here as elsewhere Filomarino wished to promulgate an image of himself as a cultivated outsider, insisting on his higher status as a Barberini-affiliated, Romano-Bolognese and determinedly Francophile collector of considerable significance, standing well apart from the Hispanic and southern Caravaggesque emphases of his fellow Neapolitans.

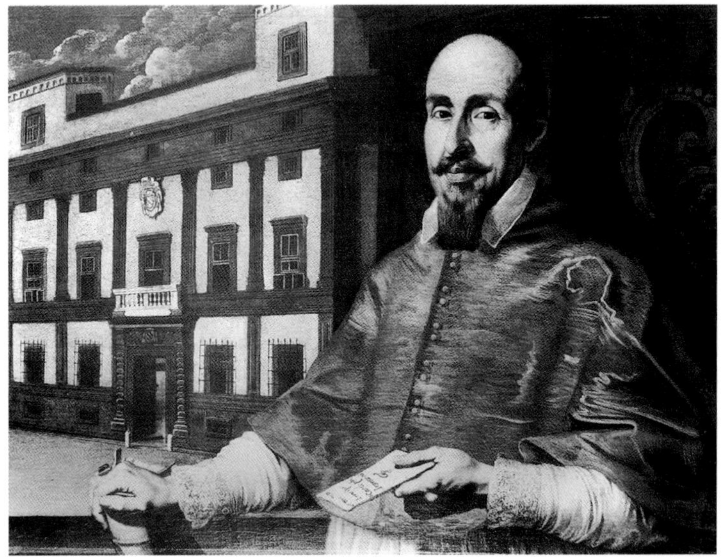

159 Francesco di Maria, *Portrait of Cardinal Ascanio Filomarino*, after 1645. Oil on canvas, 72 × 95 cm. Palazzo Corsini, Florence

By far the most grandiose expression of this projected sense of cultural superiority – and the most lasting legacy of Filomarino's patronage more generally – is the Filomarino chapel that he commissioned for the Theatine church of Santi Apostoli during the 1630s and 1640s (fig. 160).[111] The chapel was conceived and initially directed while he was still resident in Rome, and its genesis preceded by at least seven years his elevation to the cardinalate and archbishopric. Yet everything about its scale and positioning belies this by proclaiming Filomarino's ability to project his family's memorial on the imposing level of the grandest prince of the Church.

The chapel fills the entire left transept of Santi Apostoli and complements Lanfranco's contemporaneous frescoes with a costly and elaborate Carrara marble altar designed by Borromini himself and decorated with seven mosaic inserts by the papal mosaicist Giovanni Battista Calandra. This element alone cost 700 scudi out of a total commission price of more than 5,000 scudi, convertible to more than 6,000 Neapolitan ducats following the unfavourable Roman–Neapolitan rate of exchange.[112] Calandra's mosaics reproduce the altarpiece and four of the flanking *Virtues* from Guido Reni's commission of 1610 for the pope's private chapel in the Quirinal Palace. Around the mosaics were added an elaborate series of statues and decorative reliefs by Andrea Bolgi, François du Quesnoy, Giuliano Finelli and Giulio Mencaglia. The whole was capped by two mosaic roundels by Calandra depicting the two heads of the family – Filomarino, representing the ecclesiastical side, and his younger brother Scipione, who distinguished himself as a military commander working in the service of the Spanish crown.[113]

The presence of a work by Borromini in Naples would be extraordinary enough (there being only one other such work – significantly, also a Barberini commission – undertaken during this time).[114] But the addition to this of all the other overtly Francophile and Roman elements results in a work that is unique within the Neapolitan scene. It acts, in the final analysis, proudly to reinforce the fact that Filomarino – and his family by extension – had successfully elevated himself above the other Neapolitan elites by attaining the status of a Roman-Vatican insider par excellence.

NEW GENRES MEET NEW AUDIENCES

In 1696 Francesco d'Andrea (1625–1698) wrote some words of advice to those considering a career in law. Writing from the perspective of a long and successful career in civil law and jurisprudence, he observed that Naples offered an especially fertile field in which to practise the profession, 'because the Kingdom is full to bursting with lawsuits, major estates and magnificently opulent inheritances, so the lawyers of Naples could be said accordingly to govern the entire kingdom'.[115] Francesco had certainly himself profited greatly from this decision. During his lifetime he had accrued such prestigious governmental appointments as *consigliere* of the Sacro Regio Consiglio and *consigliere fiscale* of the Sommaria. His standing on legal matters, moreover, was such that he had been called on during the late 1660s by the viceroy, Pietro d'Aragona, to compose a Neapolitan legal response to dispatch to Madrid to act as a constitutional bulwark against Louis XIV's claims to Flanders and the Spanish succession.[116]

More fundamentally, though, a lifetime spent at the forefront of the Neapolitan legal profession had helped both Francesco and his younger brother Gennaro (1637–1710) to exert a major influence on the Neapolitan intellectual reformation of the second half of the seventeenth century more generally,[117] acted out primarily in the fervid environment of the Neapolitan intellectual academies. These academies thrived during the second half of the century, particularly as a result of the climate of reform set in motion by the viceroy, the conde de Oñate, as part of a broader policy of Neapolitan cultural renovation following the Revolt of Masaniello of 1647–8.

In the first instance their contributions helped to revitalize the deliberations of the oldest and most important of the Neapolitan academies, the Accademia degli Oziosi, previously mentioned as the forum for Giovan Battista Manso's celebration of Marino's return to Naples in the mid-1620s. On a more modernizing note, nevertheless, Francesco was also a co-founder in 1650 of the Accademia degli Investiganti, which had a particular brief to promulgate awareness of the new sciences following the model of the Royal Society in London and the Accademia del Cimento in Florence.[118]

But the D'Andreas' commitment to scrutinizing Neapolitan laws and customs according to the emerging findings of the rationalist, natural philosophy of Boyle and his contemporaries inevitably attracted its share of opprobrium, as well as praise. To the early eighteenth-century Neapolitan lawyer and historian Pietro Giannone, Francesco was one of the principal architects of the cultural reform of the previous decades. The Neapolitan chronicler Fuidoro, on the other hand, suspected both brothers of atheism, a charge that was later brought against the Accademia degli Investiganti by the Roman Curia and the Neapolitan Inquisition.[119]

Francesco and Gennaro also sought distinction in the fields of art and architecture. Francesco was said to have designed the family palace himself, an extraordinary feat of advanced dilettantism, if true. Celano was certainly impressed, praising the Palazzo d'Andrea as: 'exhibit[ing] an architecture that one could not imagine as being any more

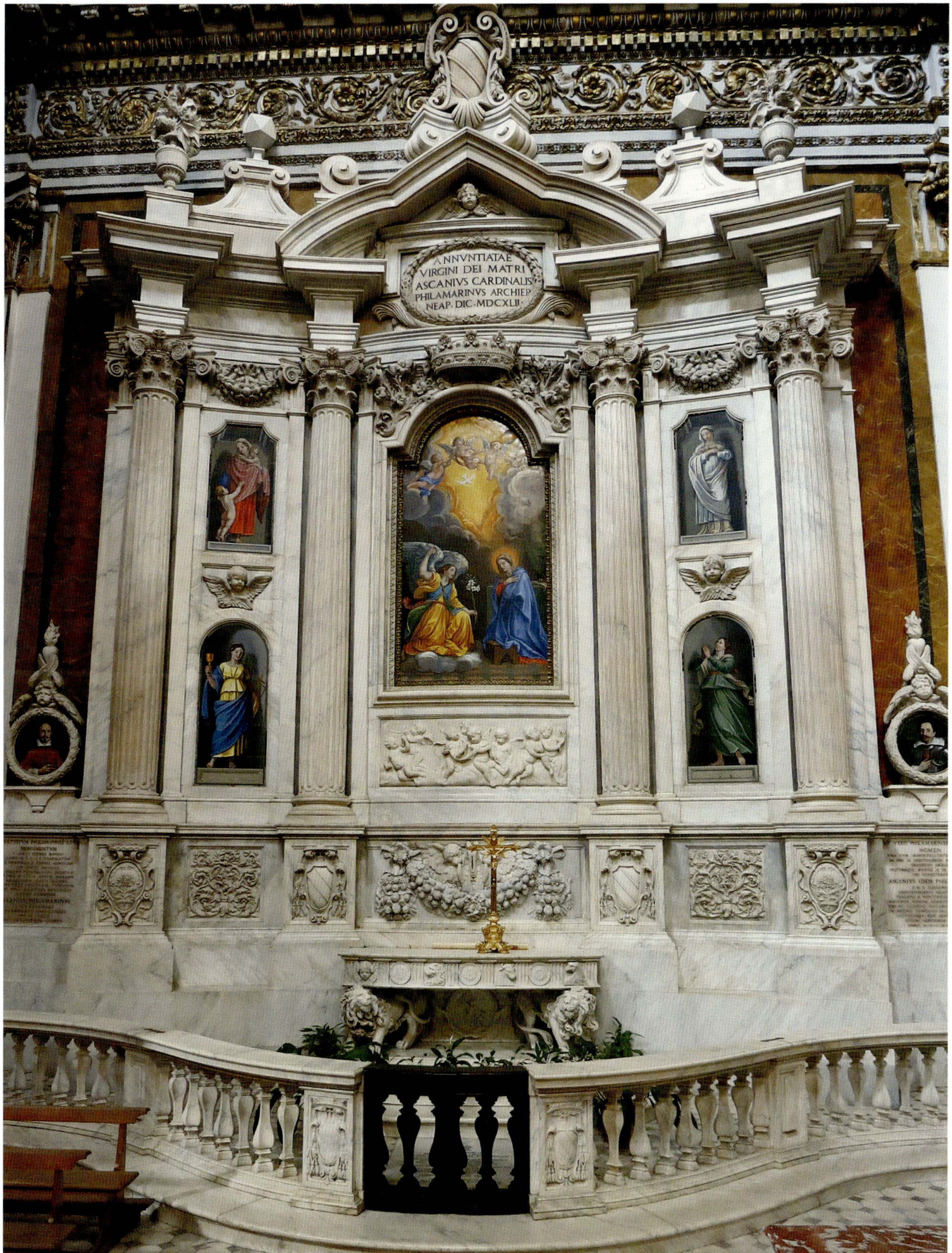

160 Cappella Filomarino, 1634–47. Santi Apostoli, Naples

noble and inventive (*bizzarra*) in form'.[120] Although by no means grandiose in comparison to the other leading seigneurial collections of the day, the brothers' art collection was nonetheless distinguished in bringing together a judicious spread of retrospectively acquired paintings by artists of the 1630s and 1640s – Stanzione, Ribera, Pacecco de Rosa, Falcone, Lanfranco, Artemisia Gentileschi, Fracanzano and Gargiulo – as well as some representative works by practitioners of the next generation, including canvases by Preti, Vaccaro, Beinaschi and Giordano.

A particular predilection for still-life painting stands out as one of the most distinctive features of the D'Andrea collection. The brothers owned a number of works by Abraham Brueghel (1646–1697), the art-dealing artist disparaged by Giacomo de Castro (see p. 125), but nonetheless a distinguished still-life specialist in his own right who eventually migrated to Naples during the later stages of his career. They also owned no fewer than nine paintings by Giuseppe Recco, including some of his largest and evidently most impressive marine still-life compositions that measured as much as 9 × 8 *palmi* (approx. 2.37 × 2.11 m). Most of these were concentrated, moreover, in a single room devoted to a dazzling display of contemporary still-life, genre and animal paintings.

The D'Andrea brothers were joined in this interest by one of their close colleagues in the legal fraternity, Giuseppe Valletta (1636–1714). Valletta's equal significance for the intellectual reform of the later seventeenth century has been underlined from the time of Giannone to Galasso, who describes him as 'without doubt the most important figure of the Neapolitan philosophical culture of the late seventeenth to early eighteenth century'.[121] Valletta shared many of the interests of the D'Andrea brothers. He was a member of the Accademia degli Investiganti and he also founded an academy, attended by Vico among others, which he convened in his own residence.[122] Valletta, moreover, owned one of the most famous libraries in Europe and wrote, among other books, an important *Historia filosofica* towards the end of his life.[123] He was also an antiquarian, with a world-famous collection of antique statues, Etruscan vases, epigraphs and inscriptions.[124]

Valletta also shared Francesco and Gennaro d'Andrea's liking for contemporary still life. His correspondence with Francesco di Maria concerning the acquisition of four still-life kitchen paintings by Andrea Bonnano has already been mentioned (see p. 121). He also commissioned a suite of no fewer than twenty-one still lifes in 1681–2 by Abraham Brueghel and his workshop that are described as 'Pitture in cristalli' and which are thus to be understood as instances of the new taste for paintings on mirrors that was discussed as an early specialization of Carlo della Torre during the 1660s and 1670s (see pp. 136–7).[125]

Four of these works are identified as overdoors, so the commission would have presumably comprised a coordinated decorative scheme with still-life elements produced for a single room. Valletta's room of painted mirrors must have constituted one of the most innovative and striking ambiences of the period. It represents an early Neapolitan manifestation of the taste for painted mirrors in decorative ensembles that had been initiated in Rome, in the renowned commission for four large still-life paintings on mirrors produced for the Galleria Colonna from 1660 to 1670 by Mario dei Fiori and his pupil Giovanni Stanchi, with figures painted by Carlo Maratta.[126]

The D'Andrea and Valletta collections speak powerfully of the growing influence of the collecting and patronage activities of the increasingly prominent Neapolitan mercantile and professional classes during the later stages of the seventeenth century. One should be careful, however, not to overstate the innovativeness or distinctiveness of their aesthetic choices relative to the more established collecting and patronage activities of the Neapolitan aristocrats.[127] A pronounced taste for still-life paintings was not, in any event, a particular hallmark or 'discovery' of middle-class collectors during this period. As early as the 1630s and 1640s, for example, Ferrante Spinelli, principe di Tarsia, distinguished himself as one of the most advanced collectors of the first wave of still-life painting during the years before the plague.

The principe di Tarsia's collection – in its way as significant as Roomer's, although less well known and publicized in its day – contained no fewer than nineteen still-life paintings by Luca Forte, together with four by Giovanni Battista Recco (brother of the better-known Giacomo Recco, previously encountered via his workshop arrangements of 1630 – see p. 113). The Tarsia Spinelli collection also included scores of still lifes by other early specialists that are known today only from inventory descriptions, such as Ambrosiello, Giuseppe Andonino and Pietro Fiammingo, the last of whom contributed numerous animal paintings that were gathered together in a single room similar to that of the D'Andrea brothers.[128] At the same time as Valletta and the D'Andrea brothers, the collection of Andrea d'Avalos, principe di Montesarchio, also contained one of the most dazzling displays of still-life paintings, by Giuseppe Recco and his contemporaries (see pp. 195–7).

The activities of Valletta and the D'Andrea brothers should be recognized as forming part of a growing confluence of shared cultural interests that enabled otherwise disparate social and cultural groupings to form powerful alliances of taste. These shared interests would help to stimulate, in turn, a broader public interest in certain artists' work so that it quickly became fashionable and in demand. This process can be seen in the phenomenal rise of interest in Giordano's paintings from the late 1650s onwards, and also in the apotheosis of taste for High Baroque-styled still-life paintings during the 1670s and 1680s, to be discussed.

For all their effectiveness in working behind the scenes to develop new tastes, dealers and artists alike recognized the need to associate themselves with the most elevated sections of the Neapolitan elites in order to advance their agendas. In this respect, the viceroys were crucial. Their patronage not only conferred on artists a lustre of prestige that no amount of championing by merchant entrepreneurs or legal dilettantes could hope to match, but they also played a fundamental role in internationalizing Neapolitan art. As influential intermediaries moving between the Italian mainland and the far-off territories under Habsburg control, they helped to stimulate the demand for Neapolitan art in a way that also broadened the parameters of patronage in seventeenth-century Naples. Under their influence patronage could be understood not simply as the direct act of commissioning art, but also as a more indirect process, of promoting art via cultural diplomacy. Artists – as well as dilettantes, intellectuals, collectors and their merchant backers – soon recognized that this process provided great opportunities for publicity and promotion. In considering this component of the Neapolitan Baroque art world, then, the focus will shift to the dissemination of the reputation of Neapolitan painting through commissions, exhibitions and other channels of communication open to the viceroys throughout the period under examination.

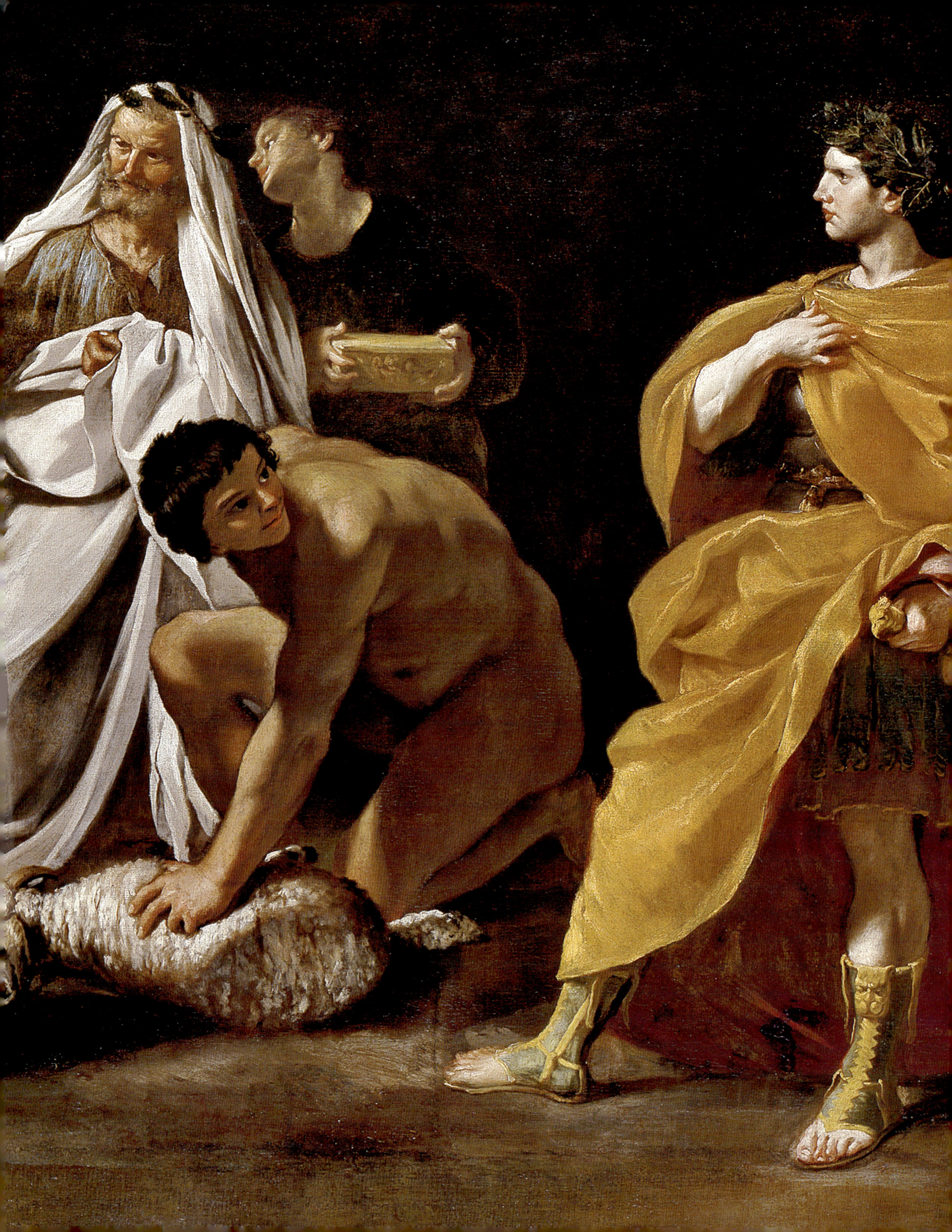

10

The Viceroys

In 1631 a diplomatic request for financial assistance resulted in the transfer to Naples of two of the most celebrated masterpieces of the Italian Renaissance. The Spanish crown had recently come into possession of the small but strategically important territory of Piombino in southern Tuscany. An outlay of 800,000 florins was nonetheless required to maintain its ownership. So the decision was taken to convert this potential drain on the royal coffers into a profit by seeking another buyer from among the high-ranking Italian aristocracy. The diplomatic channels of Rome, Milan, Genoa and Naples were pressed into service, but the only individual able to provide a solution, as it transpired, was the newly appointed viceroy of Naples, Don Manuel de Acevedo y Zúñiga, the 6th conde de Monterrey.

Monterrey put forward the name of Niccolò Ludovisi, a shrewd choice since Ludovisi belonged to one of the most staunchly pro-Hispanic families of the realm and would subsequently rise to the post of viceroy of Aragon and Sardinia.[1] He was, moreover, a man of substantial means, having been one of the chief beneficiaries of the accession to the papacy of his uncle, Alessandro Ludovisi, Pope Gregory XV (1621–3). Monterrey assured Madrid that Ludovisi would accordingly be able to pay 'el dinero, que la tiene pronto' (the money that he holds promptly).[2] This proved to be an overly optimistic estimation of Ludovisi's financial circumstances, however, and the negotiations dragged on for a further decade before reaching a satisfactory conclusion. Yet what Monterrey and Ludovisi added to the negotiations to help bring them to a conclusion was a series of dazzling diplomatic sweeteners – in this case artworks to be presented as 'gifts' to the Spanish crown.

Chief among these were Titian's *Bacchanal of the Andrians* and *Worship of Venus* painted for Alfonso I d'Este's legendary 'Alabaster Chamber' in Ferrara a century earlier (fig. 161). These were dispatched from the Villa Ludovisi in Rome to Naples in the summer of 1634 and remained on display in the Palazzo Reale for three years, until Monterrey took them to Madrid to present to the king following the conclusion of his tenure as viceroy on 2 November 1637. It would be difficult to overestimate their dramatic impact on the local Neapolitan artistic scene during a time in which the so-called neo-Venetian influence was reaching its apex. This was a new and fashionable revitalizing trend that touched everybody from Falcone and his associates through to Ribera, Stanzione and many of the other leading Caravaggesque painters of the preceding decade.[3] It was at that stage being followed eagerly by Neapolitans through the works of other contemporary neo-Venetian painters accessible to them in Naples, most notably holdings of the work of Poussin, as well as through the presence of a Genoese painter temporarily resident in Naples, Giovanni Benedetto Castiglione. Here, though, for the first time the Neapolitans were given the

Facing page Giovanni Lanfranco, *An Augur Sacrificing for a Roman Emperor, circa* 1635 (see fig. 172)

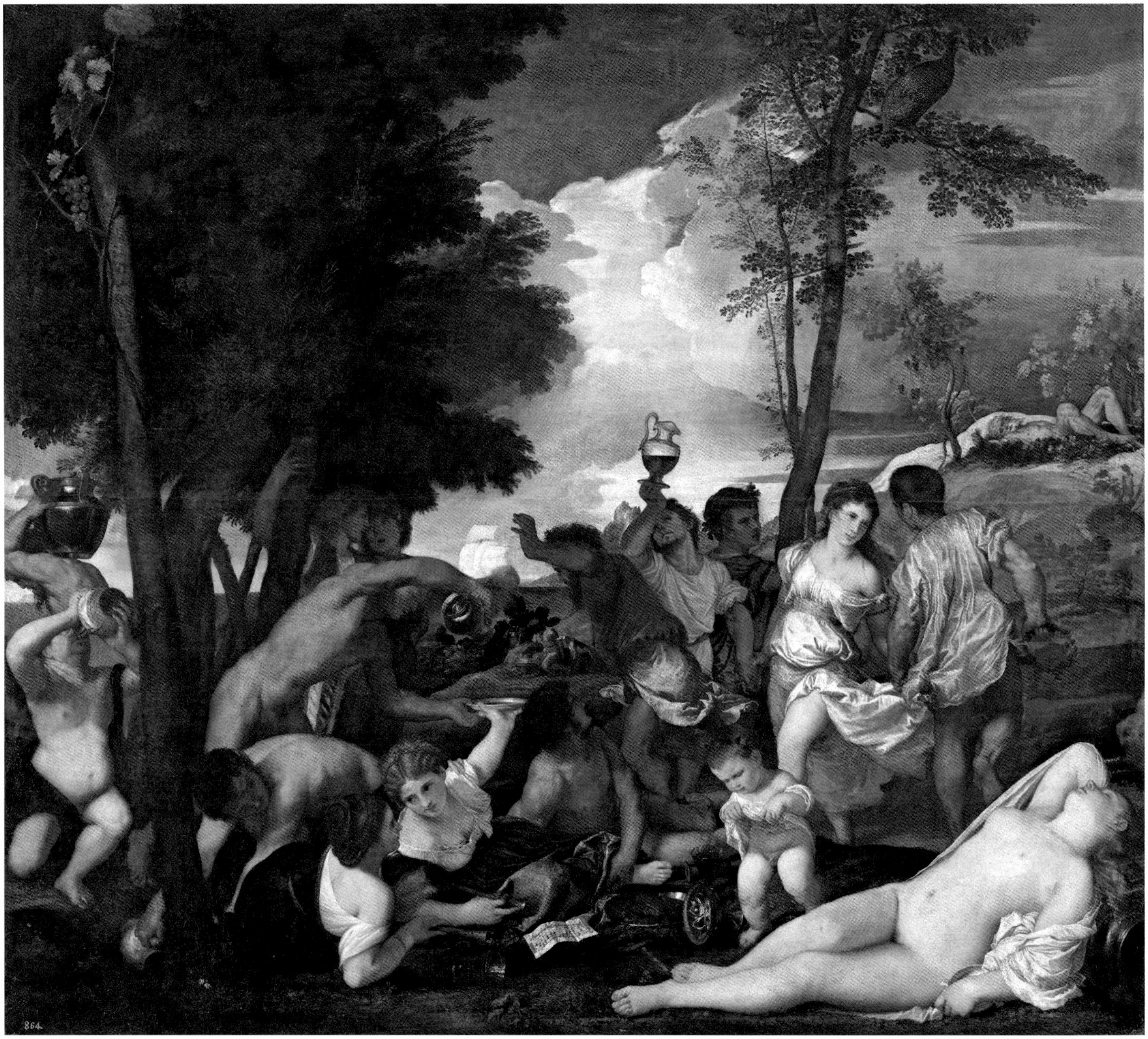

161 Titian, *Bacchanal of the Andrians*, *circa* 1523–6. Oil on canvas, 175 × 193 cm. Museo Nacional del Prado, Madrid

opportunity to study two of the foundational masterworks of this tradition. It is clear from the many canvases inspired by these compositions that the Neapolitans considered the paintings very closely indeed (fig. 162).

The foreign artists resident in Naples were also greatly taken by the appearance in their midst of these masterworks. Boschini's *La carta del navegar pitoresco* of 1660 includes a long account of their transfer and sensational reception in Naples. Among those wishing to pay tribute, Boschini recounts, was none other than Domenichino, at that stage hard at work on the commission for the Cappella del Tesoro di San Gennaro in Naples Cathedral. Domenichino would have had an earlier opportunity to study the *Bacchanals* while he was working on frescoes at the Villa Ludovisi in the 1620s, but here he is said to have wept copiously at their appearance in Naples. Describing them as the 'breasts and milk that nourished my genius in painting', he went on to exclaim: 'Can it really be that Rome has sent these treasures into exile?'[4]

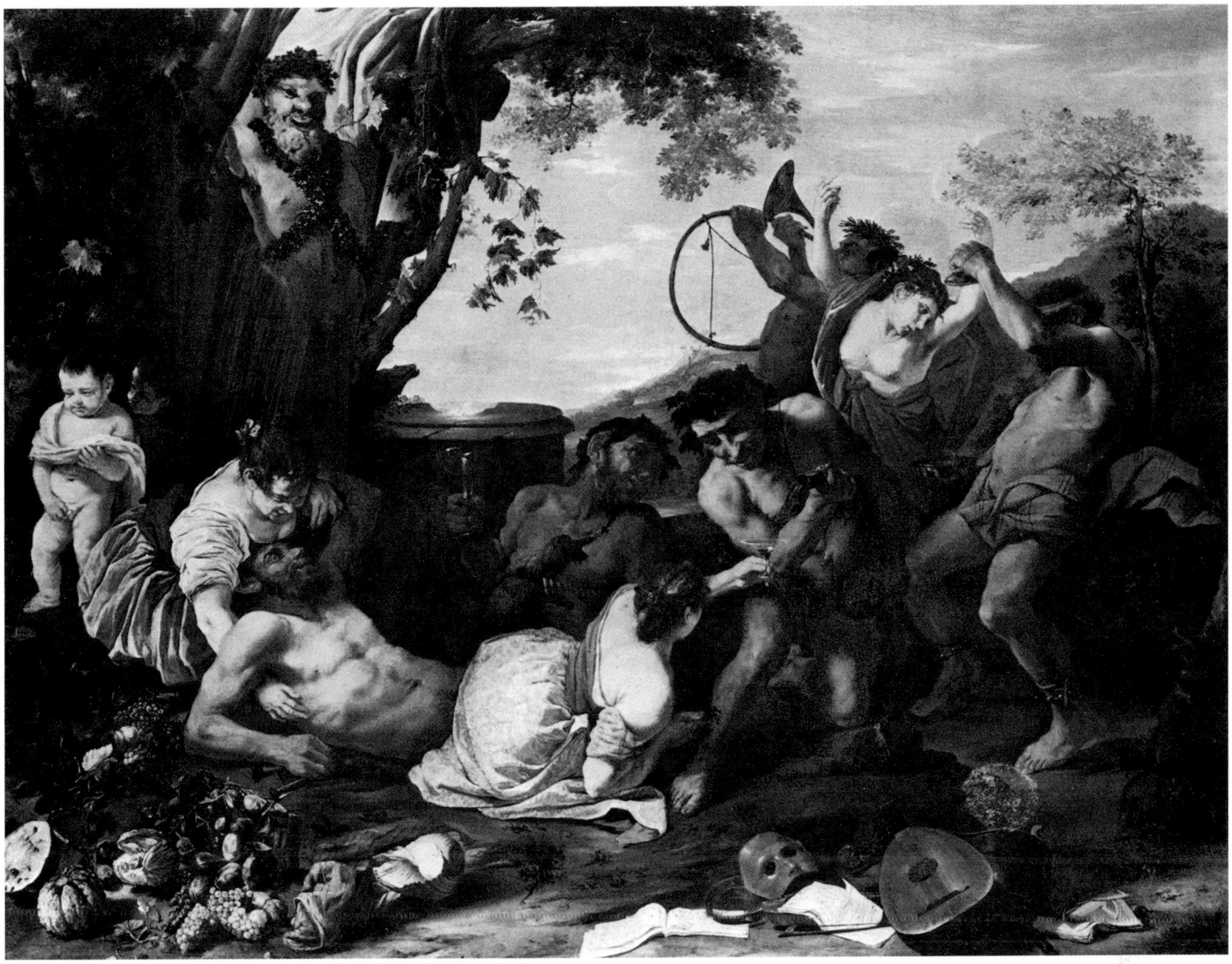

162 Andrea de Leone, *Bacchanal*, 1640s. Oil on canvas, 100 × 128.5 cm. Formerly Matthiesen Gallery, London

THE VICEROYS AND NEAPOLITAN CULTURAL PATRIMONY

Domenichino's perception of the paintings as tragic exiles cast adrift from the nourishing ambience of their homeland is a reminder of the relativity of notions of cultural patrimony – and its loss – down through the ages. The paintings had, in fact, resided in Rome only for several decades, having arrived there following their confiscation from the Este collections of Ferrara by Cardinal Pietro Aldobrandini in 1598. Nevertheless, the story reinforces the importance of the Neapolitan viceroys as conduits for the transmission into Naples of international artistic and cultural cross-currents of taste. This is opposed to the more commonly held view, expressed vociferously since at least the time of De' Dominici in the early eighteenth century, that the viceroys had only a limited impact on Neapolitan culture and that they should be remembered more for their ability to denude the city of its treasures than for their contributions to it.[5]

The viceroys' readiness to strip Naples of particularly renowned artworks in order to gain favour at the royal court was true enough. For example, they worked assiduously to remove from the territories under their control all of Raphael's major works that remained in ecclesiastical settings. So it was that Raphael's *Madonna of the Fish* was extracted from the Neapolitan church of San Domenico Maggiore in the 1640s to serve as a diplomatic gift for Philip IV by Monterrey's successor, the duque de Medina de las Torres. Similarly, in 1655 a subsequent viceroy, the conde de Castrillo, removed from the regional church of San Silvestro in Aquila Raphael's renowned altarpiece of the

Visitation.[6] Finally, in the 1650s to early 1660s, the conde de Peñaranda was able after much effort to wrest Raphael's late, great masterpiece, the *Wonder of Sicily*, from the monastery of Santa Maria dello Spasimo in Palermo.[7]

But exceptional works of this kind constituted a limited resource that could be tapped only from time to time. Much more readily available was the plentiful supply of contemporary painting being produced in the city, which the viceroys also exported avidly in a manner that benefitted the Neapolitans materially much more than any sporadic confiscation of their cultural patrimony might have done. As the example of the Ludovisi *Bacchanals* indicates, the viceroys were, moreover, equally significant for what they helped bring into Naples. This, then, was their major contribution – as significant conduits for the import and export of foreign art and ideas flowing in and out of the port of Naples, rather than as patrons in the more traditional sense of the term.

At least in relative terms, the viceroys' patronage was invariably disappointing. This was understandable, given that the circumstances of their appointment inclined them towards political and economic preoccupations that were ruled above all by their often fraught dealings with their subjects and the demands of Madrid to find additional means of levying financial contributions to fill the royal coffers. Naples generally represented, moreover, the last leg of a diplomatic circuit that sent the viceroys back to Spain after a period of only four or five years – or even less, depending on their often volatile political fortunes in Madrid and their attempts to make headway in the often crushing mix of responsibilities and political pressures that came with the post.

Little wonder, then, that the viceroys did not contribute a great deal when it came to major artistic projects commissioned for the city. The viceroys of the first half of the seventeenth century were preoccupied above all in completing the Palazzo Reale, commissioned from Domenico Fontana by the conde de Lemos in 1599 on a vast scale so as to proclaim the pre-eminence of the Kingdom of Naples among all the Habsburgs' vice-regal possessions (fig. 163).[8] In terms of painting, their main consideration during this period was accordingly a suite of large audience rooms in the Palazzo Reale, which were given over to an extensive series of impressive – though hardly innovative – panegyric frescoes recording the military *faste* of the early viceroys, and other significant events in the history of the Aragonese and Spanish monarchy (fig. 164). These were painted from 1611 onwards by the dependable rather than exceptional Belisario Corenzio, with Giovanni Balducci and Giovanni Battista Caracciolo.[9]

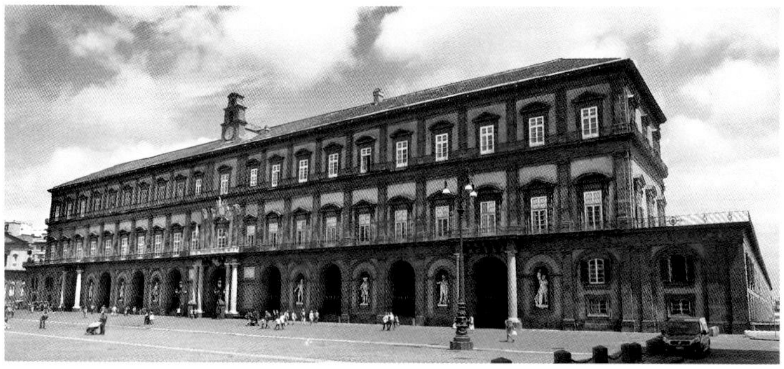

163 View of the Palazzo Reale, Naples

Towards the middle of the seventeenth century the viceroys also commissioned a series of altarpieces and frescoes for the recently completed chapel in the Palazzo Reale. Their choices for this project – ranging from Ribera and Lanfranco to Mellin – indicate the greater dynamism and diversity that characterized the artistic scene during this period.[10] From time to time the viceroys also commissioned works for especially important Neapolitan religious settings. Chief among these were the high altarpiece and two lateral altarpieces commissioned in 1660–61 by the conde de Peñaranda from Andrea Vaccaro and Luca Giordano as one of the viceroy's major dedicatory offerings following the cessation of the plague in 1656 (see pp. 233–4).

Yet while these commissions may have afforded periodic opportunities for the leading painters to work on a grand ceremonial scale, they were far from being the viceroys' most important engagement with Neapolitan art. Of much greater significance were their acquisitions of the work of local artists as an initial stage in the growing interest in placing Neapolitan painting within an international arena.

RIBERA AND THE VICEROYS: DIPLOMACY, EXPORT, RENOWN

As a Valencian émigré resident in Italy, Ribera was best placed to receive the lion's share of the viceroys' attention. Even prior to his transfer to Naples, he had sought their support, a factor already noted by Mancini in Rome at the end of the second decade of the seventeenth century.[11] On his arrival in Naples, Ribera lost no time in developing close and sustained working relationships with each of the viceroys in turn, up to the time of his prolonged illness and decreasing productivity during the later 1640s. De' Domin-

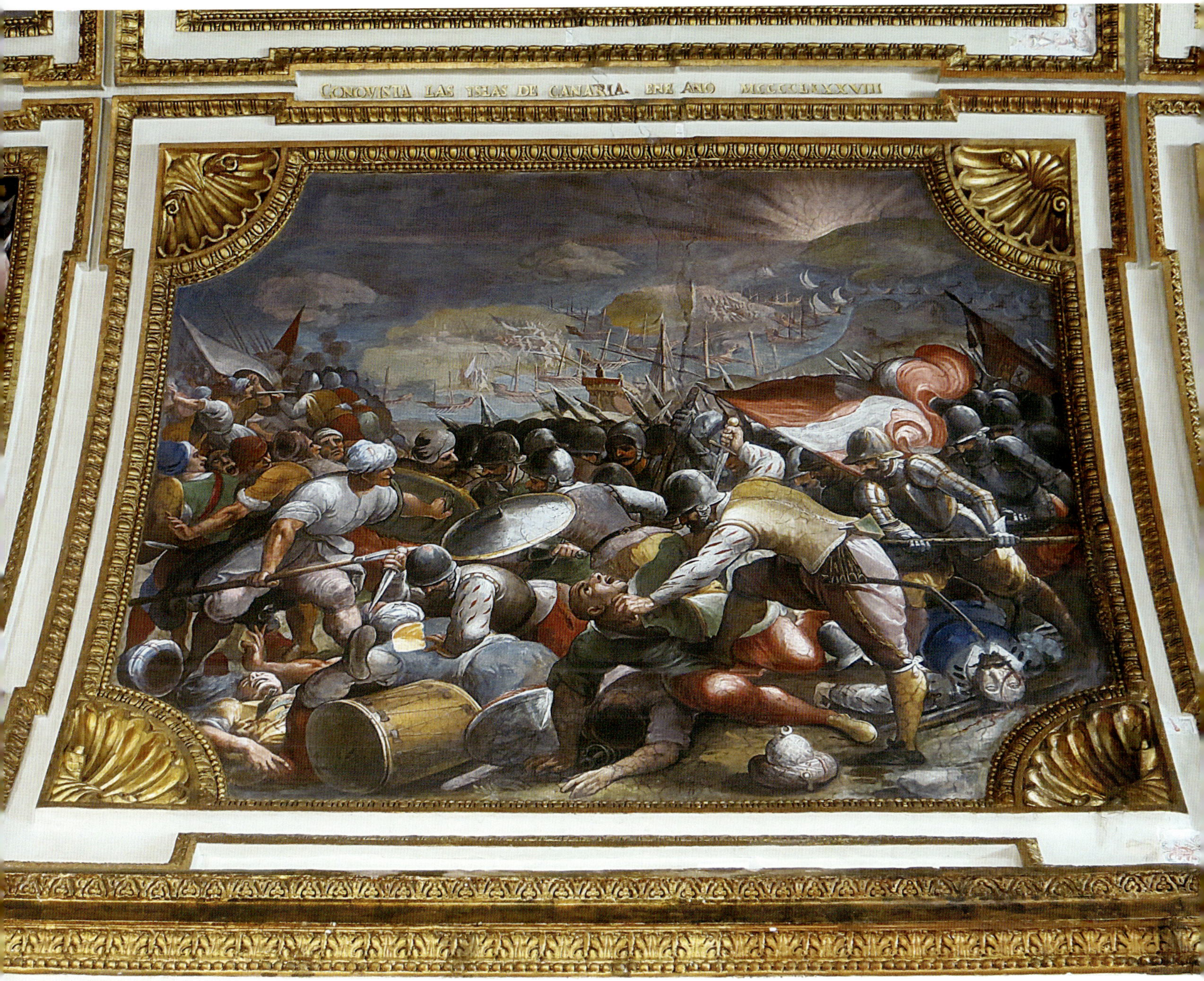

164 Belisario Corenzio and workshop, *The Conquest of the Canary Islands in 1488*, early 1630s. Fresco, Sala degli Ambasciatori [Sala VIII], Palazzo Reale, Naples

ici recounts that following his arrival in the city Ribera exhibited a *Martyrdom of St Bartholomew* close to the Palazzo Reale during a religious festival and that this attracted the attention of the duque de Osuna (viceroy 1616–20). This facilitated Ribera's entrance as painter to the vice-regal court soon thereafter (an anecdote that was represented in embellished form by the French painter Antoine Gibert in the nineteenth century).[12] This would have occurred in 1616, since already by the middle of the following year Ribera is described as 'pittore di sua Eccellenza' and is documented receiving payments for a painting of *St Sebastian* that would form one of the centrepieces of the duke's and duchess's donation of four important early paintings by Ribera (including another version of *St Bartholomew*) to the

Colegiata de Osuna in their home town of Seville in 1617–19.[13] The duchess also commissioned a *Calvary* from Ribera during the same period, which she donated to the Colegiata in 1627.[14]

Osuna's successor, Antonio Álvarez de Toledo, duque de Alba (viceroy 1622–9), was also an important collector of Ribera's work.[15] In certain respects, in fact, his influence was even greater than the Osunas, since it was he who first introduced Ribera's work to Philip IV. In the mid-1620s he sent to the Spanish court three now-lost paintings by Ribera of *Jael and Sisera*, *Samson and Delilah* and *David and Goliath*. The first two of these appear to have formed part of the initial group of paintings commissioned for the Alcázar between 1624 and 1637, thus linking Ribera with one of the earliest Spanish commissions of work for the royal palaces by the leading international painters of the day. This included canvases by Rubens and Van Dyck, Domenichino, Guido Reni, Procaccini and Orazio and Artemisia Gentileschi, the last of whom sent to the Alcázar a large *Hercules and Omphale* from Venice, shortly before her move to Naples in late 1629 or early 1630.[16] This set in train a steady flow of paintings by Ribera to the Spanish court, most of which are now among the Museo del Prado's substantial holdings of his work. In 1626 Alba also facilitated Ribera's admission into the military and religious Order of Christ of Portugal.[17] This signal distinction recognized Ribera's aspirations for higher status as an artist, and the same order was subsequently conferred on his colleagues Stanzione (1627) and Caracciolo (around 1629).[18]

Toledo's successor, from 1629 to 1631, was Fernando Enríquez Afán de Ribera, duque de Alcalá. He was not a greatly successful viceroy, and in fact was suspended from the post and recalled to Spain after only two years following a series of bitter clashes with his predecessor. Alcalá was, nevertheless, to be counted among the Spanish aristocracy's most sophisticated connoisseurs. Building on family traditions, he maintained in his palace in Seville an exceptional collection of paintings and antiquities (the latter being particularly unusual in Spain at that time). He also owned an extensive library that was described by a contemporary as 'compet[ing] with the most illustrious [libraries] in the world'.[19] It was decorated with a complex allegorical cycle devised by his friend and fellow academician Francisco Pacheco. All this set him apart from the customary interests of his fellow grandees and marked him out as a scholar of unusual erudition. A series of diplomatic postings in Rome, Naples and Sicily from the mid-1620s onwards subsequently offered Alcalá the opportunity to indulge his interests fully, as indicated by the fact that he eventually sent twenty-four cases of artworks back to Seville at the conclusion of his Italian sojourn in 1631.[20]

Among these was a series of paintings that confirm him as one of the earliest Neapolitan patrons of Artemisia Gentileschi. In fact, his knowledge of Gentileschi's work predated his Neapolitan tenure by a few years, since he is known to have acquired several canvases by her during his initial stay in Rome in 1625–6, while serving as Spanish ambassador to the Holy See. Gentileschi and Alcalá evidently struck up cordial relations during this time since she subsequently sent him advice on what paintings to buy in Venice.[21] He probably helped secure for Artemisia the commission of *Hercules and Omphale* for the Alcázar, and it has been reasonably suggested that Alcalá's arrival in Naples to serve as viceroy in June 1629 was a strong motivating factor encouraging Gentileschi to relocate to Naples from Venice either later that year or early in 1630.[22]

Of yet greater significance, nonetheless, was a series of works by Ribera that testify to Alcalá's influence in encouraging him to produce some of the most distinctive and innovative creations of his career. Foremost among these is Ribera's portrait of Magdalena Ventura and her family that was painted at the Palazzo Reale in early 1631 (fig. 165).[23] This canvas still retains its astonishing power to confront the viewer with a deeply unsettling image of the seventeenth century's fascination with mental and physical abnormality.

The long inscription in Latin included in the painting identifies the work as depicting 'the great wonder of nature' and goes on to document its circumstances as representing a bearded woman from the Abruzzi who had been brought to the vice-regal court at the express command of the duke. Her presence at the Palazzo Reale would have served as a diversion in a manner that is comparable to other contemporaneous instances of the courtly interest in retaining dwarves, 'fools' and other 'monstrosities', as evident in Velázquez's paintings, as well as in works by Agostino Carracci and Sanchez Cotan. Cotan's precedent is probably the most relevant. In the 1590s he had painted a portrait of a famous Spanish bearded woman, which entered the Spanish royal collections shortly afterwards.[24] His painting, nonetheless, is far surpassed by Ribera's in its evocation of the resigned, tragic dignity of its subject and the stunned befuddlement of her husband, who looks out from the shadows where he has been placed as a mere corroborating footnote to his wife's notoriety.

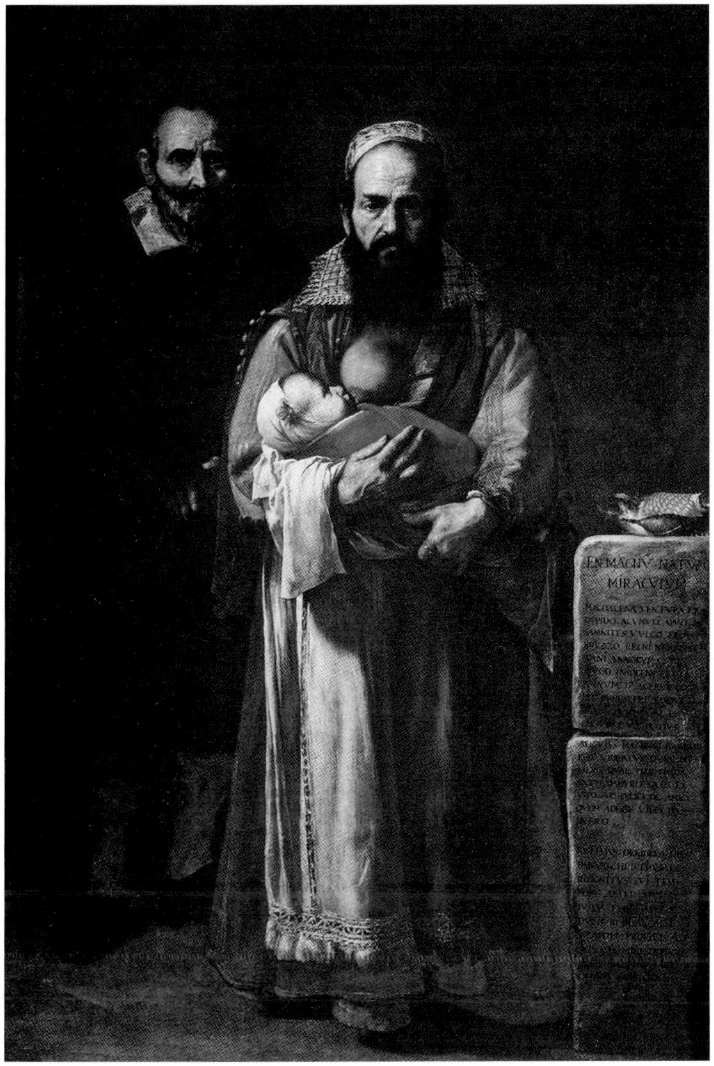

165 Jusepe de Ribera, *Magdalena Ventura with her Husband*, signed and dated 1631. Oil on canvas, 196 × 127 cm. Fundación Casa Ducal de Medinaceli, Palacio Lerma, Toledo

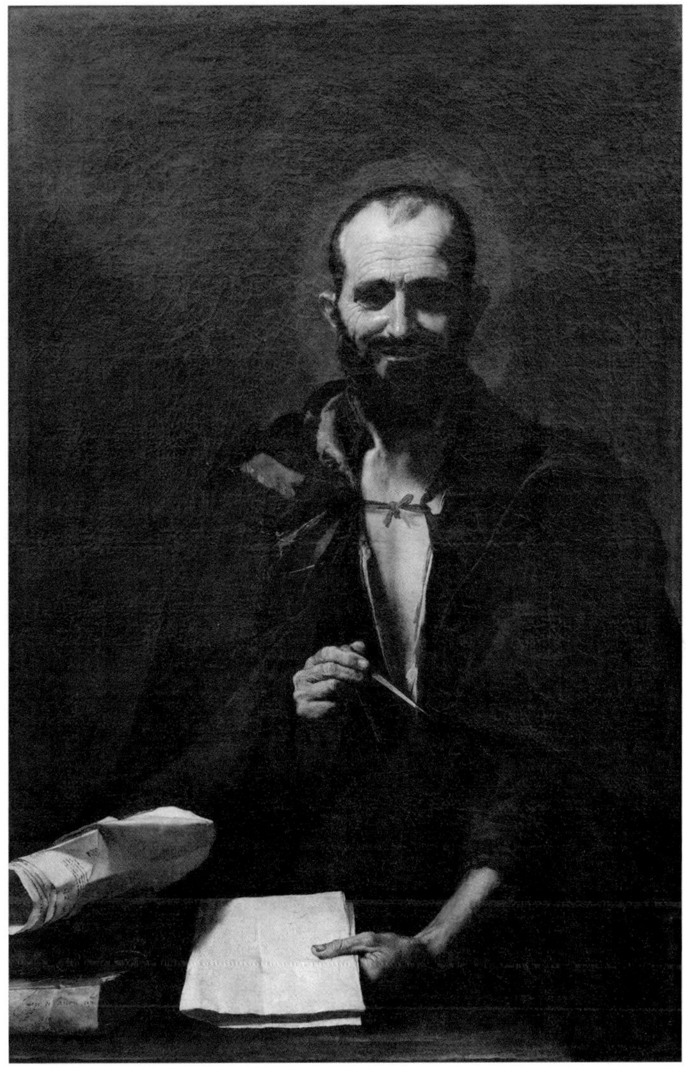

166 Jusepe de Ribera, *Democritus* (?), signed and dated 1630. Oil on canvas, 125 × 81 cm. Museo Nacional del Prado, Madrid

Alcalá also owned a group of *Four Philosophers* by Ribera, one of which can be identified with a painting now in the Prado in Madrid (fig. 166).[25] In these works Ribera effected a paradigm shift in the traditional iconography of the ancient philosopher. Leaving aside the customary ideal of the august and dignified, toga-clad worthies of Raphael's *School of Athens* and the like, he presented instead an image of the ancient thinkers as pungently down-to-earth 'beggar philosophers', who, by virtue of the striking poverty of their unkempt appearance, are able directly to confront the viewer with the transience and vanity of earthly preoccupations.

The development of this novel iconography forms a continuum with Ribera's parallel emphasis on the 'holy poverty' of his numerous prophets, apostles and hermit saints, as well as with the series of the *Five Senses* painted in Rome some years earlier. He had, moreover, already created a handful of philosophers, including one of *Democritus* in the same shaggy and unkempt guise for the Giustiniani, during his early stay in Rome. It would be over-stating the case, therefore, if one were to ascribe the innovation of these images entirely to Alcalá.[26] That they chime closely with Alcalá's particular interests is without doubt – with his sustained study of philosophy most of all, as well as with the other pictures of philosophers already in his collection. It seems reasonable, therefore, to concur with the conclusions originally advanced by Delphine Fitz Darby in the 1960s that these striking and innovative paintings must have been 'created at his behest, even that they were his brain-children'.[27]

Whatever the case concerning Alcalá's input into the works, his decision to order them in groups was to have far-reaching consequences for Ribera's career and for the transmission of his influence more broadly. Ribera's updating of the traditional series of paintings of philosophers immediately became popular well beyond Naples and it was one of the crucial factors cementing his international reputation during this period. Within six years of Alcalá's commission, for example, he was asked to produce no fewer than twelve pictures of philosophers for the residence of Prince Karl Eusebius von Liechtenstein in what is today the Czech Republic (although Ribera characteristically seems only to have completed half the works before giving up on the remainder of the commission).[28] There are also numerous instances of subsequent archival inventory references to works of this kind by Ribera and his workshop in later seventeenth-century international collections. His *Philosophers* are in this way recorded during the 1650s and 1670s in locations as far afield as Madrid,[29] Amsterdam[30] and Venice.[31]

The impact of Ribera's beggar philosophers accordingly also stretched beyond Naples. They are vital for the later Roman output of Salvator Rosa, for example, as well as in the early paintings of Giordano and certain canvases by Velázquez. The down-to-earth verisimilitude of Velázquez, in fact, bears deep resonances with Ribera's approach. It is probably significant in this respect that Velázquez seems to have met Ribera in Naples in 1630 while he was visiting the city as part of the retinue of the Spanish Infanta, Doña Maria of Hungary, en route from Spain to Vienna to meet her husband, the Holy Roman Emperor. This meeting may also have been facilitated through Alcalá, since he had been one of the earliest collectors of Velázquez's *bodegones* (still lifes) in Seville during the 1620s, and Velázquez's paintings of this type have long been noted as bearing significant parallels with the work of Ribera.[32]

Alcalá and his contemporaries should, therefore, be understood as having played important roles in encouraging Ribera to envisage himself as a truly international artist, but they were exceeded in this by the conde de Monterrey, Alcalá's successor as viceroy from 1631 to 1637 and one of the most powerful and influential figures at the Spanish court. He owed his status to the pre-eminence of Philip IV's principal adviser, the all-powerful Don Gaspar de Guzmán, to whom he was connected via a double alliance: he was married to Don Gaspar's sister, and his sister was married to Don Gaspar.[33] As a result, it was only to be expected that Monterrey was given the prime position of ambassador to the Holy See from 1628 to 1631, following an earlier diplomatic posting in Rome in 1622. By the time of his arrival in Naples, therefore, he had already had ample time to forge associations with the principal artists and collectors of the day and to amass a significant collection that reflected the latest artistic developments.

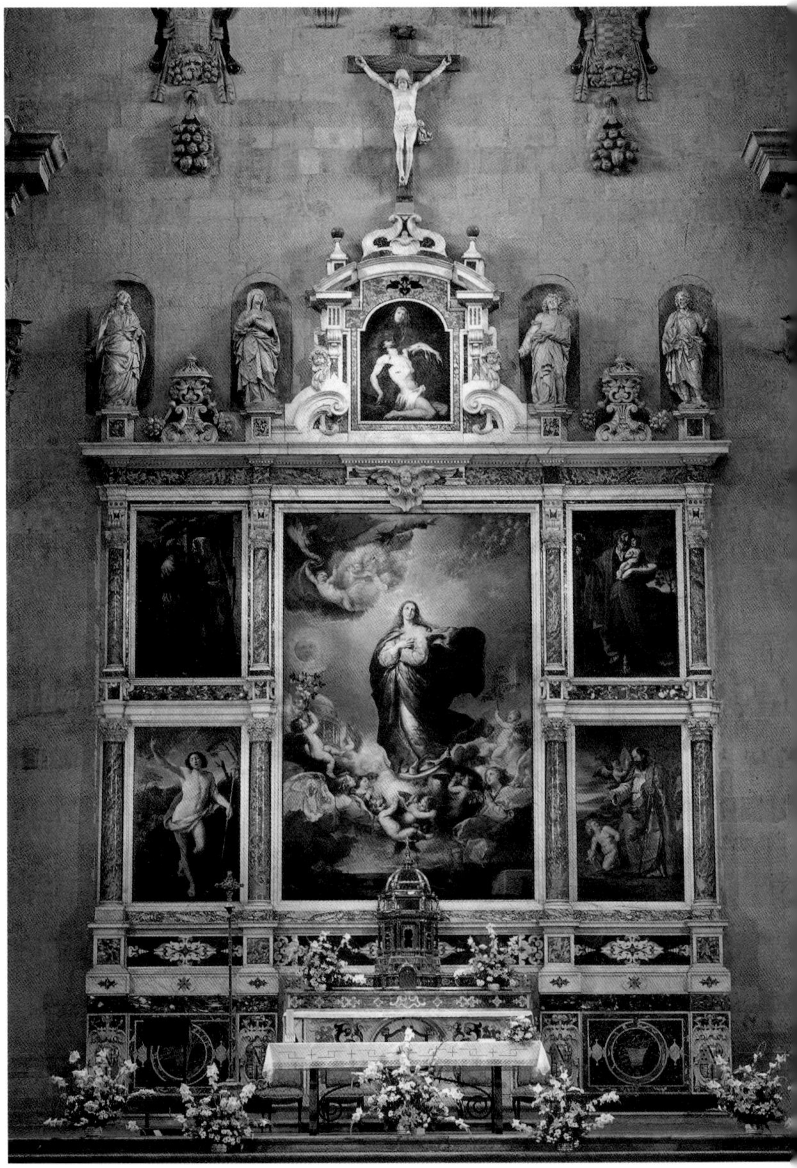

167 View of the high altar, Iglesia de la Purísima, Convento de las Agustinas, Salamanca

Monterrey continued to add to this collection in Naples, and at the end of his tenure shipped his acquisitions back to

Spain among no fewer than forty shiploads of possessions. At his death in 1653 (although the inventory is more summary than would be preferred), he owned a choice collection including works attributed to Michelangelo, Raphael, Giovanni Bellini, Titian, Veronese, Bassano, the Cavalier d'Arpino, Tempesta, Guido Reni, Albani, Baglione, Lanfranco, Brueghel, Van Dyck and Stanzione, as well as no fewer than seventeen paintings by his favourite artist, Ribera.[34]

Ribera received the lion's share of the painting component of the count and countess's major patronage project during this period. In 1633 the Monterreys conceived the idea of constructing a sepulchral monument in the church of Santa Ursula near the family palace in Salamanca. In the years that followed, this commission grew to such an extent that it came to encompass the building of an entire new church and attached convent, designed by the Neapolitan architect and vice-regal engineer Bartolomeo Picchiatti. Its centrepiece was a massive retable and altar by Cosimo Fanzago alongside subsidiary altars and accompanying statues by Giuliano Finelli, which framed, in turn, paintings by Stanzione, Lanfranco, the workshop of Guido Reni and once again Ribera (fig. 167).[35] Made in Naples and then shipped to Salamanca, the completed project constitutes one of the most impressive Baroque ensembles of the period, demonstrating the significant shift in scale and ambition from the commissions of the duke and duchess of Osuna for the Colegiata in Seville some twenty years earlier.

All this distinguishes Monterrey and his consort as among the most significant patrons and collectors of Spain's golden age,[36] but his inclusion of local painters in the often very ambitious schemes of cultural diplomacy in which he was involved was probably of even greater significance for the Neapolitans. One of his most important schemes again involved Ribera, although the documentation is sketchy. In the early 1630s Monterrey's brother-in-law, the conde de Olivares, initiated plans for a new royal palace to be built on the outskirts of Madrid. Construction was rapid. Inaugurated in December 1633, the Buen Retiro urgently required a vast array of paintings, tapestries and other decorative items to furnish its apartments, galleries and public ceremonial spaces.

One of the first of these commissions appears to have been a group of paintings ordered by Monterrey from Ribera in 1631–2 to represent the *Furias*, the Spanish name given to the four Titans of Greek mythology who were made to endure eternal torment for challenging the authority of the gods.[37]

Ribera's *Tityus* and *Ixion* (the other two works in the series apparently being lost)[38] would have constituted an apposite gift to commemorate the Buen Retiro's inauguration. In commissioning them Monterrey was clearly seeking to associate himself with distinguished Habsburg traditions of patronage, since they function as a homage to one of the most celebrated groups of paintings by Titian depicting the same subjects, which had been hanging at the Alcázar Palace in Madrid since 1558 (figs 168–9).

From the time of their installation in Mary of Hungary's palace on the outskirts of Brussels in 1549, Titian's paintings had been regarded as political allegories demonstrating the terrible punishments that would be meted out to all those seeking to oppose the divinely appointed authority of the Habsburgs.[39] Here, however, Ribera reinterpreted Titian's august prototype in a daring – even shocking – manner. Basing the composition on prints rather than the originals, which he was unable to see in Naples, he transformed the Hellenistic-inspired, muscle-bound idealization of Titian's *Tityus* into a scrawny peasant undergoing extreme torture, complete with mud-caked palms and heavily wrinkled, sun-bleached skin. He also radically redefined the depiction of pain.

Titian's *Tityus* communicates pain indirectly, through the flinching twist of his body rather than his expression, which remains inwardly focused and stoically detached. Ribera's *Tityus*, on the other hand, howls out of the composition in unalloyed agony, his gestures amplifying his torment. In particular, his left hand is chained to a rock in the very act – now rendered brutally comic and impotent – of attempting to fend off his tormentor. A pitch-black eagle perches atop him, seemingly grinning at the viewer through its beak, which reinforces the overriding impression of violently burlesque humour. As it does so, the eagle slowly pulls from a gaping hole in Tityus's chest a long piece of intestine with all the insouciance of a strand of spaghetti being plucked from a bowl.

The novelty of this lurid painting proved very popular, requiring Ribera and his workshop to produce a number of versions for other collectors. These included a further workshop series in the Prado that is sometimes attributed to Ribera's assistant, Antonio Giordano, working in collaboration with his son, the young Luca.[40] Sandrart also describes a series painted for the rich Flemish merchant and collector Lucas van Uffel, who was a distinguished patron of Van Dyck and one-time owner of Raphael's *Portrait of Baldassare Castiglione*.[41] He shipped the works to Amsterdam in 1632, where

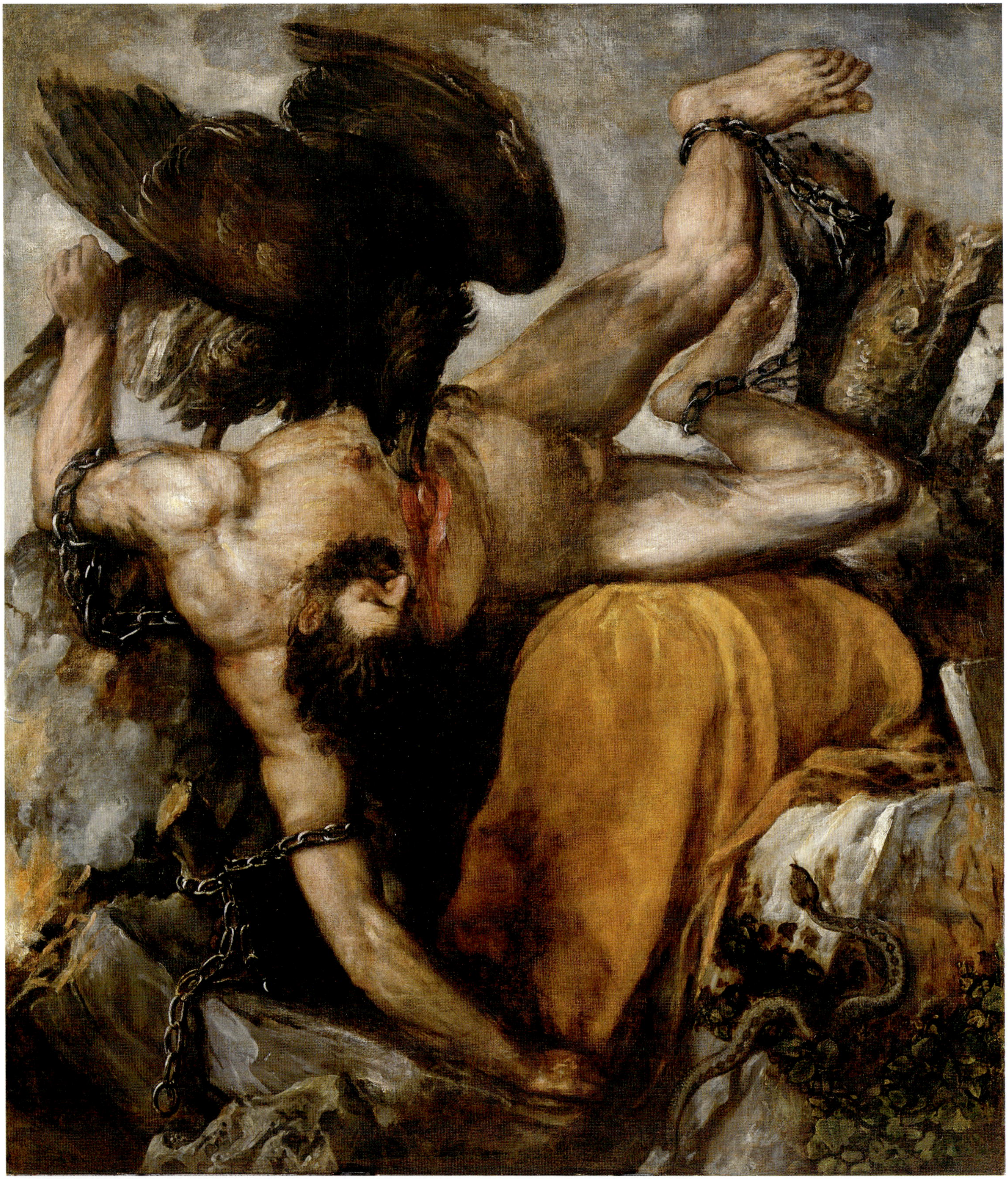

168 Titian, *Tityus*, 1560–65. Oil on canvas, 253 × 217 cm. Museo Nacional del Prado, Madrid

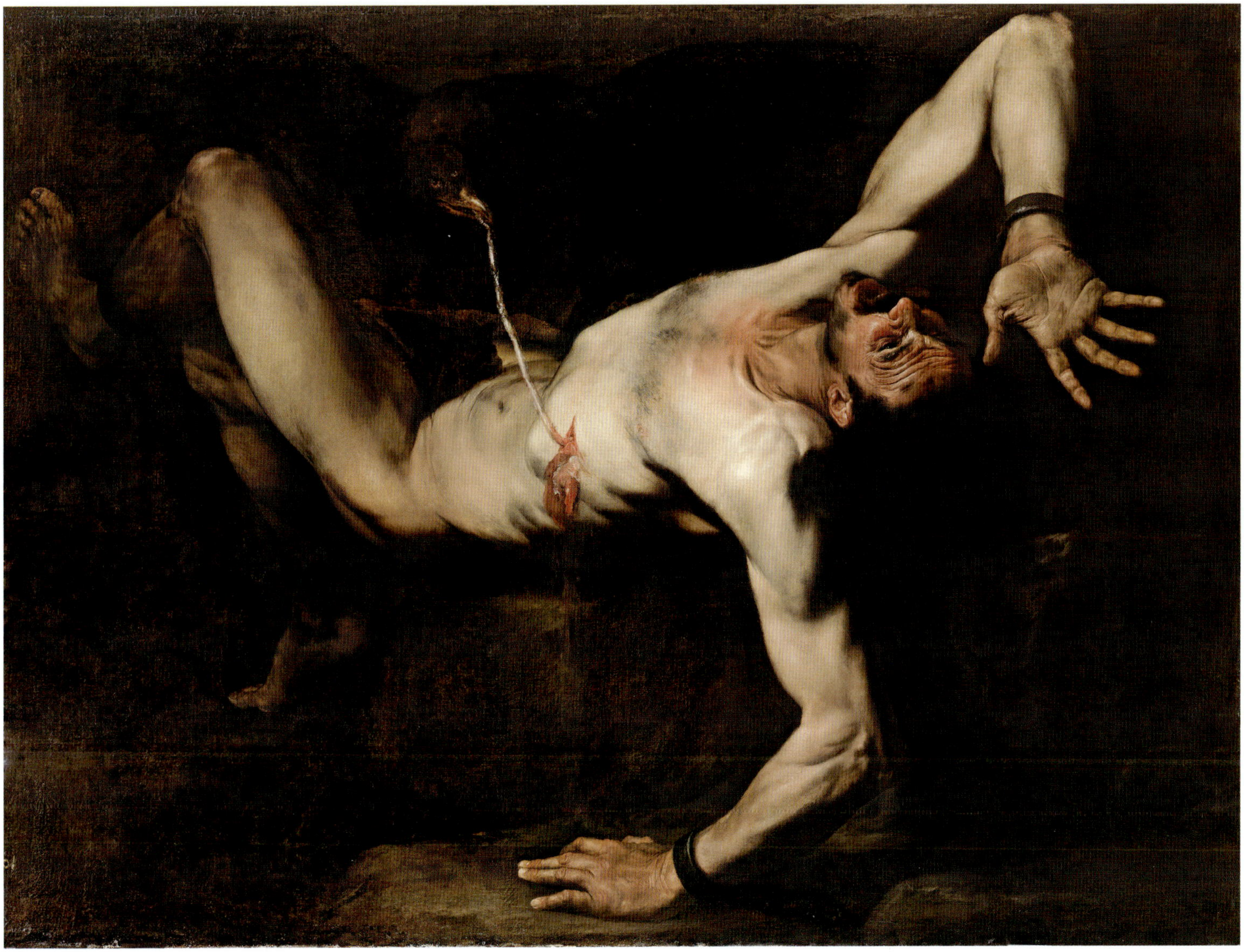

169 Jusepe de Ribera, *Tityus*, signed and dated 1632. Oil on canvas, 229 × 301 cm. Museo Nacional del Prado, Madrid

their terrifying appearance is said to have frightened his wife into giving birth to a deformed child.[42] One trusts that Sandrart was in this instance speaking rhetorically. His comments nonetheless evoke the works' significance in helping to establish Ribera's international reputation as a celebrated inventor of sensational images of extreme violence. Their continued role in promulgating this perception remained to the fore some two hundred years later, in fact, when they were cited by the Romantic artist and critic Théophile Gautier in his florid characterization of Ribera: 'You, cruel Ribera, harsher than Jupiter, from his hollow sides you make flow in streams of blood, by way of horrible cuts, cascades of intestines.'[43]

THE *LIFE OF ST JOHN THE BAPTIST* AND THE SCENES OF ANCIENT ROMAN LIFE

Seeking to advance his reputation at the Spanish court, Monterrey commissioned two additional series of paintings for the Buen Retiro. The first was a group of six large canvases dedicated to the *Life of St John the Baptist* that are generally identified as having been commissioned for the official residence at the palace that was reserved for the use of Monterrey's brother-in-law, the powerful conde-duque Olivares.[44] The series was appropriate for the residence, which was designed as a small hermitage – or Ermita – given

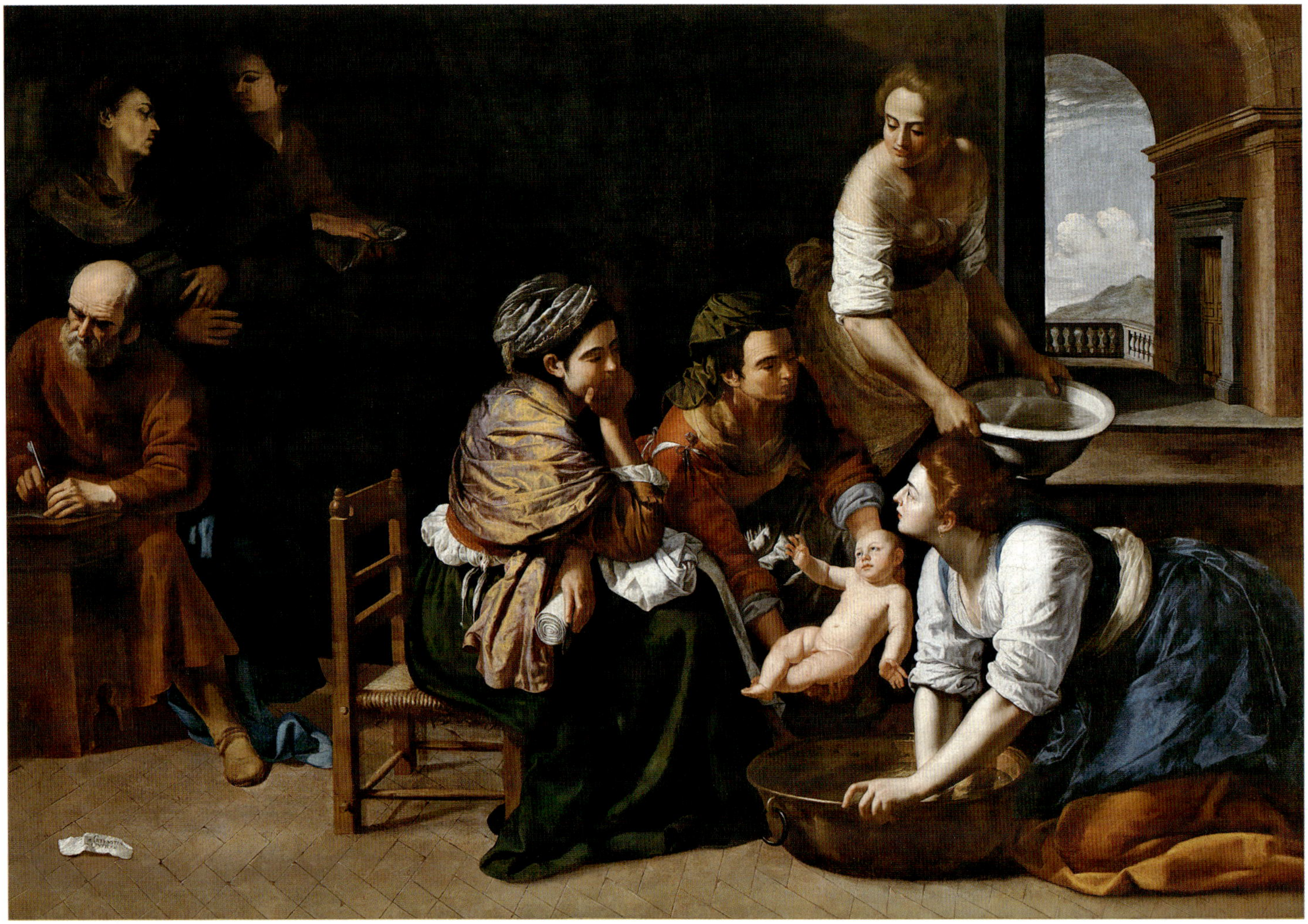

170 Artemisia Gentileschi, *Birth of the Baptist*, *circa* 1633–4. Oil on canvas, 184 × 258 cm. Museo Nacional del Prado, Madrid

over to prayer and meditation. Stanzione, it seems, acted as project manager for the commission and executed four of the scenes himself. The *Birth of the Baptist* was commissioned from the recently arrived Artemisia Gentileschi, while Paolo Finoglio was assigned *St John the Baptist in Prison*, now lost.

Measuring between approximately 2.5 and 3.5 metres in length, the five remaining canvases rank among the most ambitious Baroque biblical history paintings produced in Naples. Carefully coordinated by Stanzione so as to flow together harmoniously as a sequence, they have long been regarded as watershed works in the evolution of Neapolitan Caravaggism, from the dark tenebrism of the 1620s to the more chromatic and classicizing emphases of the 1630s and beyond. Stanzione's contributions combine native Caravaggesque traditions with a complex synthesis of references taken from his recent Roman immersion in the work of Carracci, Domenichino, Vouet and others.[45] Artemisia's canvas also shows a close knowledge of grand manner Roman history painting, but adds a particular facility in the rendition of rich coloured fabrics, as encountered during her previous engagement with contemporary trends in Venetian painting (fig. 170).

This innovative blend of elements exerted a powerful influence on a number of emerging artists, despite the fact that the paintings remained in Naples for only a brief period prior to being shipped to Madrid. Francesco Guarino's *Birth of the Virgin*, for example, is unthinkable without the model of the rich garments and meditative solemnity of the female figures in Gentileschi's *Birth of the Baptist* (fig. 171).[46] The young Bernardo Cavallino was also struck by the series, as was Aniello Falcone.[47] Their impact in Madrid should also not be underestimated, since, when

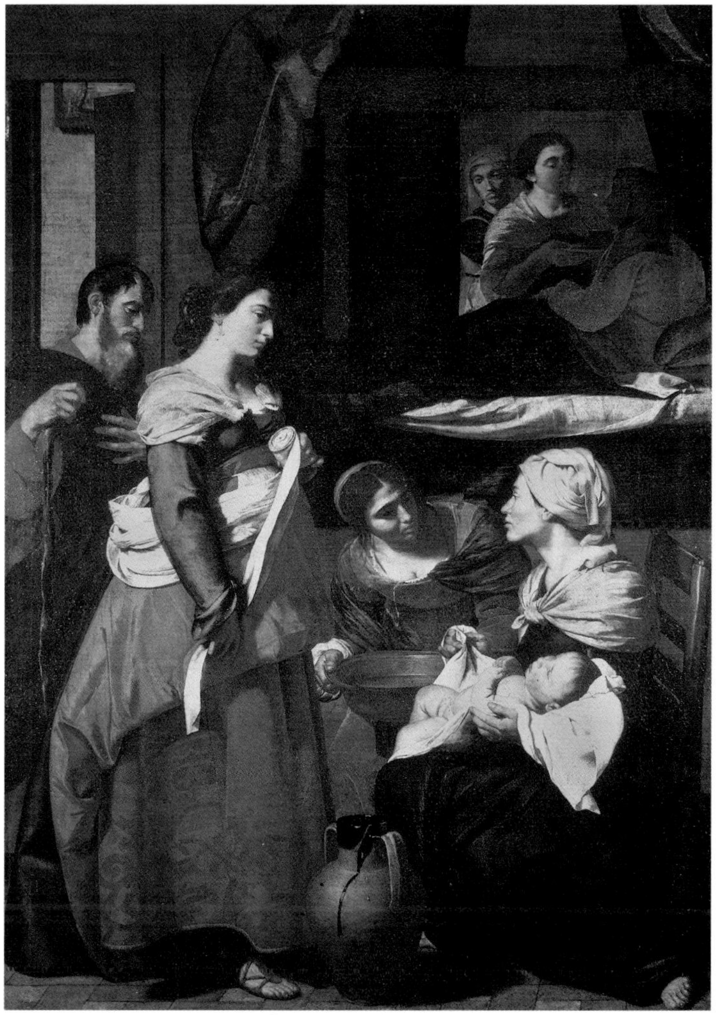

171 Francesco Guarino, *Birth of the Virgin, circa* 1645. Oil on canvas, 170 × 118 cm. Catello collection, Naples

viewed together in their original context, they would have presented one of the first ensembles of contemporary Neapolitan painting then to be seen outside Naples.

Monterrey's and Olivares' next decorative scheme for the Buen Retiro was on an even more ambitious scale. This involved some three dozen large canvases depicting scenes of ancient Roman life and mythological subjects that rank among the largest and most significant group commissions of Italian Baroque painting produced for foreign export during the course of the seventeenth century.

As with so many other aspects of the Buen Retiro commissions, the documentation for this project remains frustratingly incomplete. It is clear from its vast scale and the extensive number of artists working on it, however, that other individuals besides Monterrey must have been involved in its supervision. It is known, for example, that a small but important group of paintings were produced in Rome – including contributions by Poussin, Romanelli and Camassei. These were probably ordered through the agency of Monterrey's successor as Spanish ambassador to the Holy See, the marqués de Castel-Rodrigo. Castel-Rodrigo was also at work during this period on an equally large group commission of landscape paintings for the Buen Retiro that was commissioned from Poussin, Dughet, Claude Lorrain, Van Swanevelt and others.[48] Another point made clear by the paintings themselves is that the production of the Neapolitan scenes of ancient Roman life evidently dragged on until well after Monterrey's departure from Naples. So, too, Monterrey's successor, the duque de Medina de las Torres (viceroy 1637–44), should also be identified as having played an important role in supervising the later stages of the series.[49]

For all this, though, the dominant role that Monterrey played in conceiving the commission and orchestrating all its sprawling, complex details has been recognized since his own time. Both Passeri and Bellori, for example, specifically identify him as the person responsible for Lanfranco's contribution to the series, and Lanfranco himself boasted, in a letter to Rome, that Monterrey had favoured him by assigning to him the largest number of works given to any of the contributing artists (six paintings in total).[50]

That Monterrey did this is a testament to his skills as both a diplomat and connoisseur. It is noteworthy that he was able to secure for Naples most of the works for this commission, rather than the figure painters of Rome. He then demonstrated additional discernment in his ability to apportion the works in a manner that best matched the expertise of the painters available to him, and in relation to the other commissions in which he was involved.

Monterrey evidently recognized Lanfranco to be the most experienced master then resident in Naples when it came to producing grand manner figure scenes of ancient history (see fig. 172). (He apparently also considered Domenichino for this role, but Domenichino was then preoccupied with the commission for the Tesoro di San Gennaro in Naples Cathedral, and so completed only one work for the series.) Monterrey also perceived that Stanzione was the best artist to oversee the biblical history painting commission for the Ermita, since he was then emerging as the painter par excellence of monumental religious narrative paintings. When it came to producing the violent *terribilità* required of the Titans, on the other hand, Ribera would have been the most obvious candidate.

The scale of the commission created considerable challenges of timing and selection, necessitating a hurried, if not

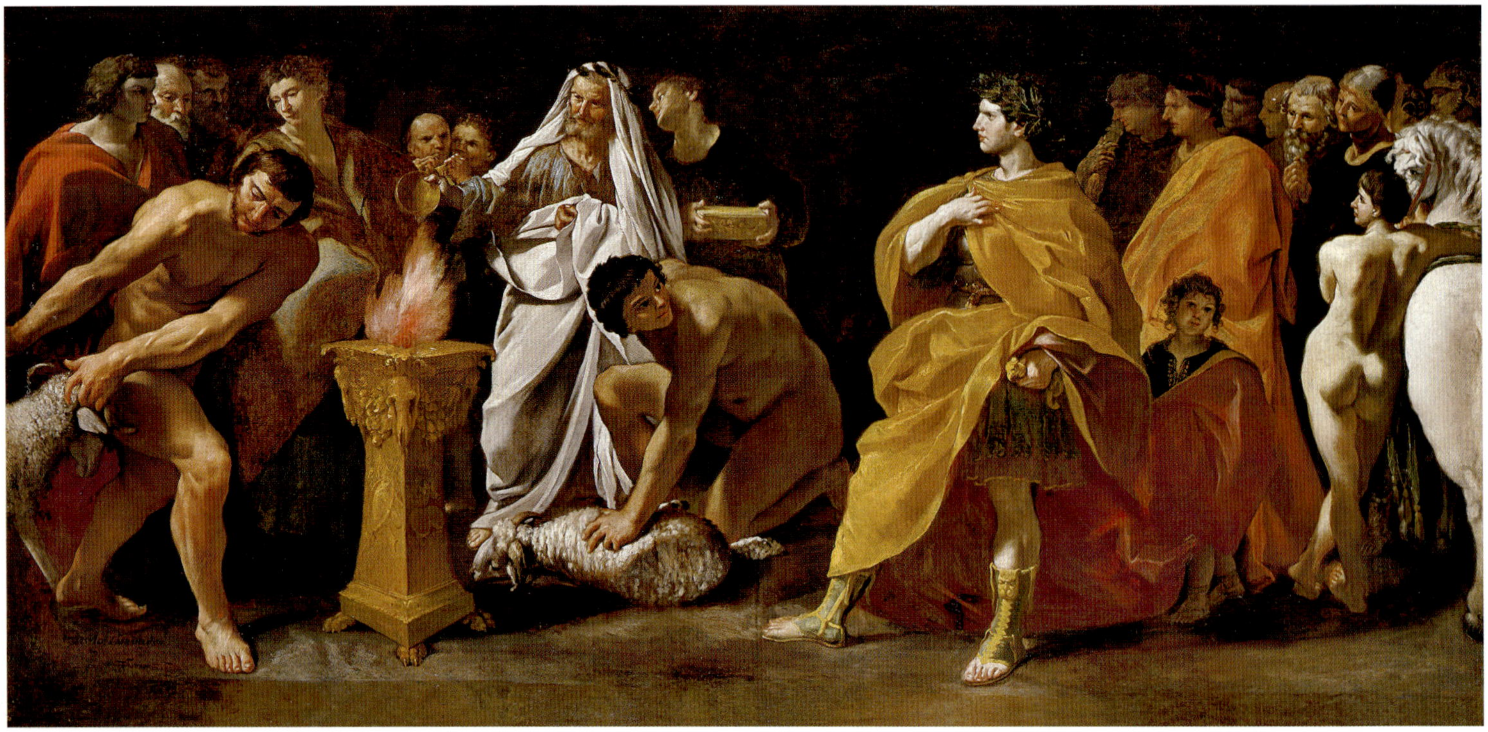

172 Giovanni Lanfranco, *An Augur Sacrificing for a Roman Emperor, circa* 1635. Oil on canvas, 181 × 362 cm. Museo Nacional del Prado, Madrid

chaotic production schedule. As a result, Monterrey clearly had to exercise considerable latitude in the selection of painters. This proved beneficial to a number of emerging artists not previously known for work of this kind, and Falcone's circle, in particular, benefitted significantly. Andrea de Leone's *Elephants in a Circus*, for example, represents an extraordinary step up in scale and ambition from the small, *petit-maître* landscapes and battle scenes for which this artist was otherwise known during this period. The same is true of Domenico Gargiulo. His two paintings of the *Triumphs of Constantine and Vespasian*, produced in collaboration with the architectural painter Viviano Codazzi, measure more than 3.5 metres in width, and would have represented an unparalleled opportunity for an artist otherwise known for much smaller, Northern-inspired landscapes with small-scale figures painted mostly for private collectors. The large number of extant drawings relating to these commissions shows just how keenly Falcone and his associates felt the need to produce their very best work for such a high-profile international commission.

Like the series of the *Life of St John the Baptist*, this commission included some of the most ambitious and innovative paintings of the period. Domenico Gargiulo, for example, teamed up with Codazzi to produce a series of views of ancient buildings animated with figures performing various ceremonies and pastimes. The *Perspectival View of a Roman Amphitheatre* takes the meticulously detailed, sectional view of the Colosseum found in the printed reconstructions of Giacomo Lauro's *Meraviglie della Roma antica* – among other antiquarian publications popular during the period – and then blows it up to the colossal scale of 3.5 metres in width (fig. 173). The result is a unique, even strange creation that combines a monumental reconstruction of accurately rendered ancient buildings with a distinctly unreal and fantastic treatment of a gigantically scaled cut-away diagram, swarming with a multitude of ant-like figures all enjoying the spectacle of a day out at the Roman games.

Conversely, Falcone's *Roman Athletes* emphasizes a prominent group of monumental male nudes placed hard up against the foreground (see fig. 56). These display a muscularity and emphatic naturalism that, to one modern commentator at least, seemed 'worthy of Courbet'.[51] At the same time, though, this continuation of the most forthright aspects of Caravaggesque realism is tempered with an equally prominent blend of references taken not only from early sources

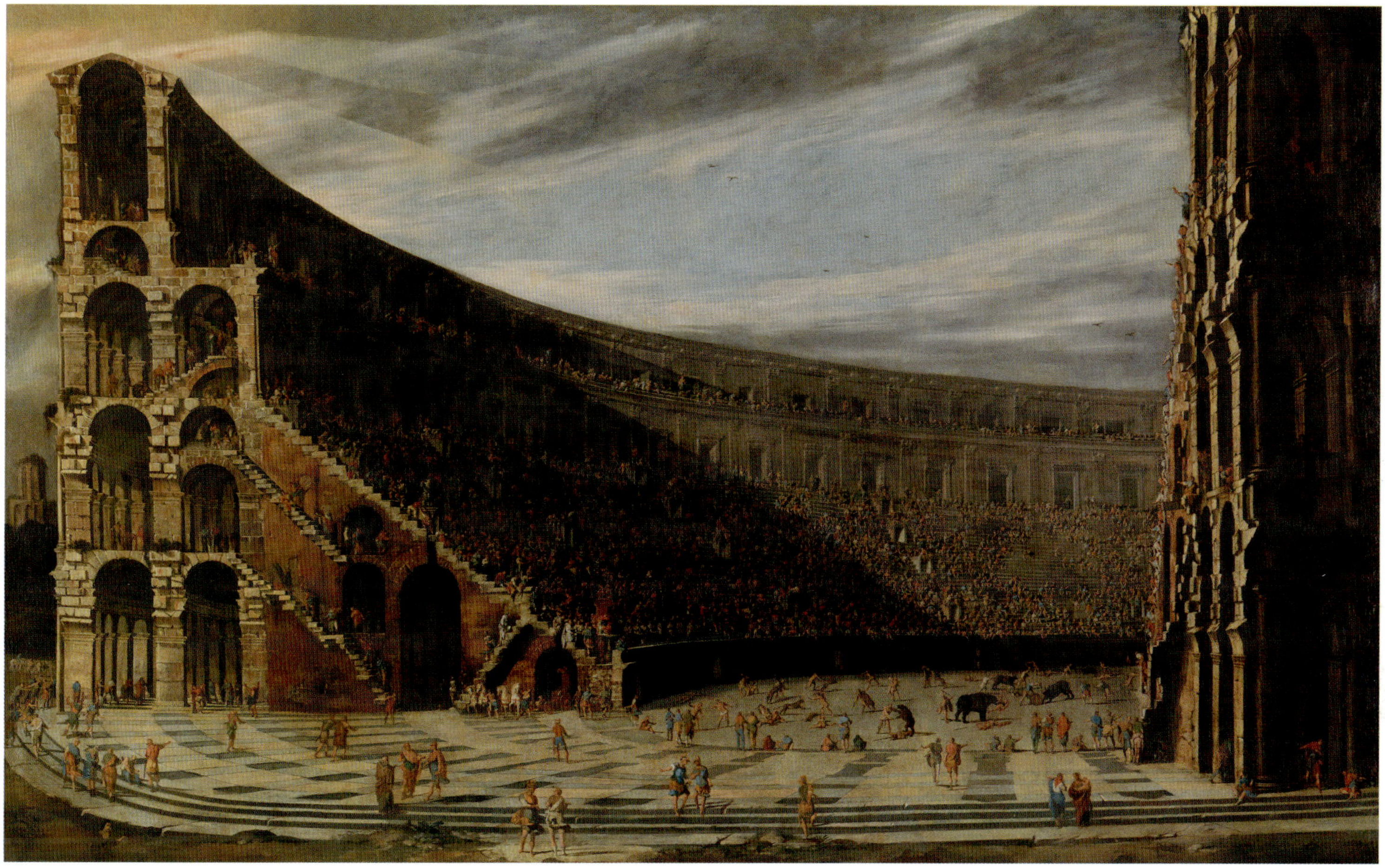

173 Vivano Codazzi and Domenico Gargiulo, *Perspectival View of a Roman Amphitheatre*, *circa* 1636–8. Oil on canvas, 220.5 × 352.7 cm. Museo Nacional del Prado, Madrid

on Roman festivities but also from contemporary Roman classical painting and sculpture of the 1620s and 1630s. These more contemporary influences range from Poussin and Sacchi to a prominent quotation of Duquesnoy's much-admired statue of 1629 of *St Susanna* at Santa Maria di Loreto in Rome.[52] The resulting work, therefore, represents a signal achievement in combining the fastidiousness of the learned antiquarian tradition with all the verve and swagger of the contemporary Caravaggesque realist.

NAPLES: BETWEEN DEVOTION AND DEFIANCE

The studies undertaken at Falcone's private academy during the late 1630s clearly equipped him and his colleagues with the flexibility needed to adapt their skills to meet the significant challenges presented by the vice-regal commissions. Once successfully negotiated, these commissions opened up new possibilities for an increased, international exposure of their art. As has been seen, the Neapolitans' success in this regard hinged, in part, on their ability to combine an ongoing commitment to the bedrock of Neapolitan Caravaggism with an interest in exploring new and more modish artistic influences, such as the classicizing and neo-Venetian trends that the viceroys themselves had helped to introduce into the city, above all via the towering precedent of Monterrey's Ludovisi *Bacchanals*.

The Buen Retiro commissions thus make manifest the processes of mutual benefit to which patron–artist relations can give rise. Once installed in the palace, the paintings helped the Spanish monarchs and their courtiers to feel closer to the Italian cultural epicentre. Here, gazing upon the ancient circuses, funerals and battles that the Neapolitans had sent them, they could feel that they were on a par with the greatest of Roman emperors, as well as with the most discerning of contemporary Roman connoisseurs. Conversely, they also assisted the Neapolitan painters to look beyond their local context so as to feel part of the most august traditions of Roman history painting stretching from Raphael to Pietro da Cortona. It was a mutually reinforcing relationship for these two sets of individuals, therefore, who were, in other respects, separated by cultural and social distinction as well as by the expanse of the Mediterranean itself. This relationship would continue to flourish in the decades to come, as will be seen.

And yet cultural exchanges of these kinds could only go so far in seventeenth-century Naples. Just how tenuous – and how fraught – was the Habsburgs' hold over their ostensibly faithful Neapolitan subjects was brought home ten years after Monterrey's departure from Naples. On 7 July 1647 – the Feast of Our Lady of Mount Carmel – a spontaneous outbreak of civil disobedience against the levying of yet another unpopular tax by the viceroys spread like wildfire to become a full-scale popular insurrection. It was led initially by a humble fisherman turned revolutionary – Masaniello, a name that would grip the European imagination for the rest of the century and beyond.[53]

In the weeks and months that followed first Naples and then the entire kingdom were drawn into an increasingly destabilizing and threatening internecine rebellion. These destructive impulses would then turn in on themselves, so as to encompass a faction-led tumult between pro-Spanish and pro-French forces that would begin to settle only in April 1648 with the arrival of an expeditionary force sent to subjugate the rebellion led by the king's illegitimate son, Don Juan of Austria.

The long road back to the status quo – or what would pass for such during the brief interregnum before the traumatic disruption of the plague in 1656 – was painful and slow. And perhaps no one was more mindful of this than the man sent to reinstate Habsburg authority, Iñigo Vélez de Guevara, conde de Oñate, viceroy from 1648 to 1653.[54] Oñate's main contribution to the position of the viceregency was that he well understood the need to give with one hand while taking with the other. So his efforts to reinstate the king's authority and to punish the scores of perceived traitors among his subjects (including a number of the most distinguished collectors of the day) were balanced against a commitment to foster a climate of growth and optimism throughout the city via a vigorously prosecuted policy of cultural renewal.

To be sure, this policy served Oñate's broader concern to promulgate his authority and limit the power of the aristocracy following the revolt. Thus, while obliging feudal aristocrats to travel to Naples to attend court, Oñate also encouraged a resurgence of interest in the Neapolitan academies (see pp. 210–212), together with the university, all of which further encouraged the advancement of the intelligentsia and bourgeoisie. At the same time, it is also clear that Oñate was committed to these cultural activities on a personal level. In particular, he initiated a flurry of activity in the fields of music and theatre. The first Neapolitan melodramas were performed in his presence in specially adapted spaces in the Palazzo Reale, thus stimulating a local tradition of musical excellence that would go on to encompass the operas of Provenzale and Scarlatti, the performances at the Teatro di San Bartolomeo and, ultimately, the foundation of the Teatro di San Carlo under the Neapolitan Bourbons in 1737.[55]

Oñate was equally mindful of the need to project a strong image of Habsburg power and magnificence at the most popular level of the often spectacular ephemeral public displays created to accompany religious feast days and the like. In particular, he commissioned grandiose temporary exhibitions of eulogistic propaganda to celebrate crucial dates in the Habsburg calendar, such as the marriage of Philip IV to Mariana of Austria on 7 October 1649; the birth of the Infanta Margarita Teresa on 12 July 1651; and the capture of Barcelona in November 1652. A contemporary description of one such display, erected outside the Palazzo Reale on the occasion of the Feast of the Baptist on 28 June 1652, provides a vivid impression of the not-so-subtle symbolism that these occasions were intended to convey:

> two statues were installed beneath two arches, on the right a statue of Love was placed wearing a crown and holding a cornucopia overflowing with riches, and this signifies the love with which the Spanish Monarchy governs us. To the left there stood a statue of Faithfulness holding a shield on which was painted the *impresa* of the People while at her feet there was a dog and this denotes the loyalty that the Neapolitans maintain towards the Catholic Monarchs.[56]

So the bread and circuses of Oñate's festivals helped assuage the Neapolitans' restiveness. Clearly, however, such initiatives could create only a temporary impression of civic unity and concord in the absence of any more longer-term social and economic policies. Policies of these kinds would have been, in any event, well beyond the viceroys' mandate and capabilities. That they did, nonetheless, at least provide additional stimulus for local artists – as well as entertainment for the populace – would have been recognized as a much more immediately felt benefit by all those involved in their design and construction. The viceroys, moreover, were significant during this period in encouraging a number of temporary exhibitions to which all the local painters contributed enthusiastically. Many of the contributing artists further recognized the potential of these temporary public displays to provide high-profile platforms for the development of increasingly sensational self-promotional strategies, the consideration of which will necessitate redirecting attention towards the crowded city streets along which the analysis here first ran.

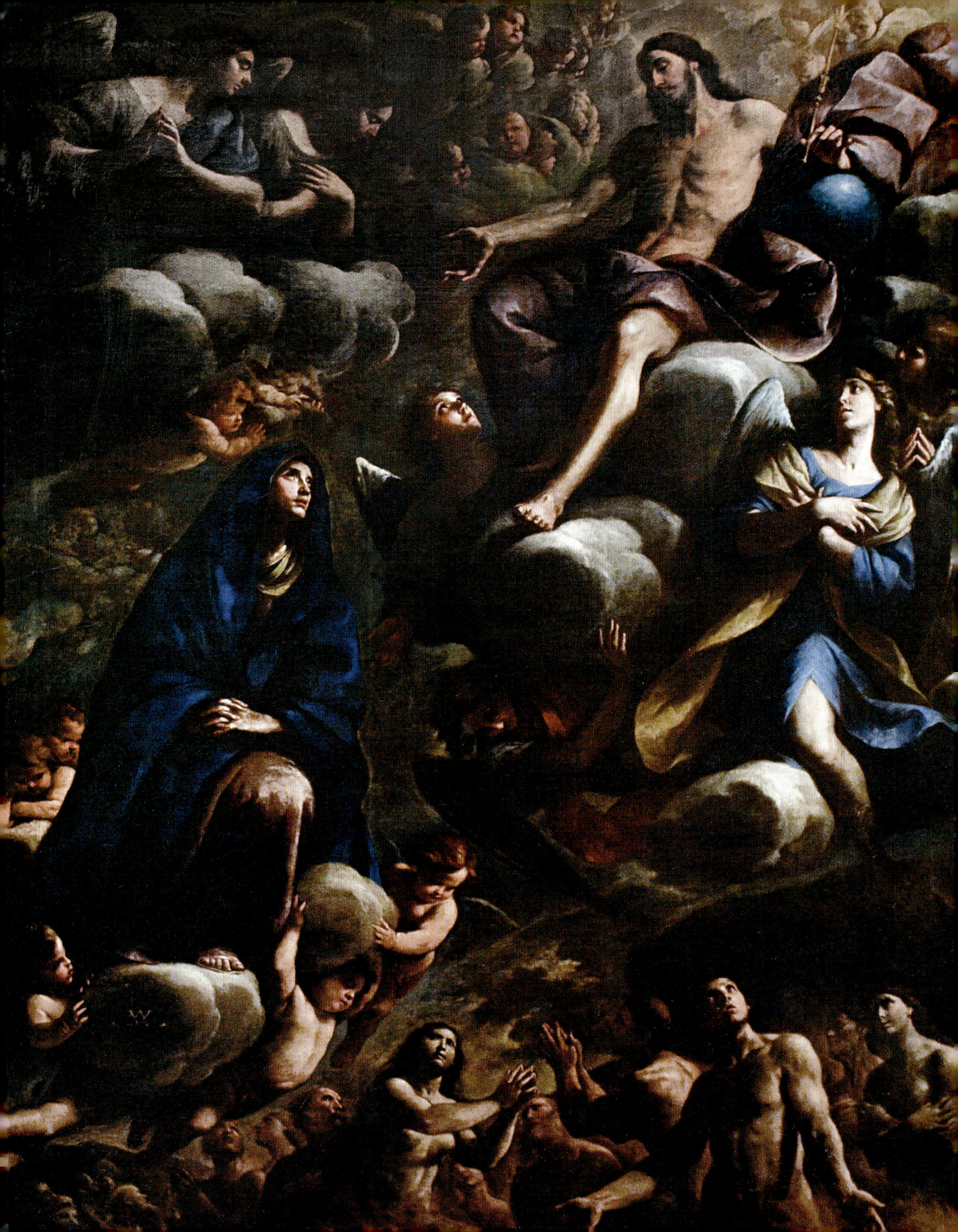

11

Public Exhibitions, Artistic Rivalry and the Internationalization of Neapolitan Baroque Painting

In 1662 the viceroy, Gaspar de Bracamonte, conde de Peñaranda, joined the people of Naples in celebrating a Mass of Dedication for a new church dedicated to Santa Maria del Pianto – Our Lady of the Tears.[1] This commemorative church had been built rapidly and with great zeal in the space of five years thanks to the support of the viceroy, together with a host of other private and public benefactors. It was located on a raised site outside the city walls that was situated close to the so-called Grotta degli Sportiglioni or Grotto of the Bats – a massive, ancient cave that had been converted out of necessity into a mass grave for some 50,000 victims of the plague of 1656.

In pride of place above the church's high altar there hung Andrea Vaccaro's recently completed *Intercession of the Virgin for the Souls in Purgatory* (fig. 174).[2] This altarpiece proclaims the Neapolitan populace's overpowering sense of grief mixed with a fervent commitment to pray for the souls of the plague victims – most of whom had died without receiving the Last Rites of the Church. In the two lateral altars there also hung a pair of subsidiary altarpieces by Luca Giordano – one depicting the city's patron saints in adoration of the Crucifixion, the other showing the cessation of the plague following the intercession of St Januarius and the Virgin (fig. 175).[3] The church and its altarpieces were thus designed to function as a ritually consoling gesture of resolution and memorialization following the devastation wrought by the plague itself: a devastation unforgettably documented in its immediate aftermath by Domenico Gargiulo, in another of his extraordinary paintings of contemporary Neapolitan events (fig. 176).[4]

Behind the scenes of this high-profile public commission there nonetheless ran a fierce undercurrent of artistic rivalry. De' Dominici characterizes this as a set-piece confrontation between the audacity of youth and the experience of old age. Vaccaro was then in his mid-fifties and was beginning, in De' Dominici's estimation, 'rallentarsi il primiero vigore degli spiriti, e per conseguenza viene a mancare il fervore dell'immaginazione, e quella perfezione de' sensi esterni, ch'è tanto necessario all'operante' (to slow down from the first vigour of his spirits and as a result to begin to lack the fervour of the imagination and that perfection of the external senses that is necessary for an artist).[5] Giordano, on the other hand, was some thirty years younger and was moving meteorically in an opposing trajectory. In the space of a few years he had gone from working for day rates for Gaspar Roomer and his other early merchant employers (see pp. 126-8, 135), to a series of increasingly important private and public commissions, culminating in a recent contract to decorate the organ doors of Naples Cathedral that had been awarded by Cardinal Ascanio Filomarino.

Facing page Andrea Vaccaro, *Intercession of the Virgin for the Souls in Purgatory*, 1660 (detail of fig. 174)

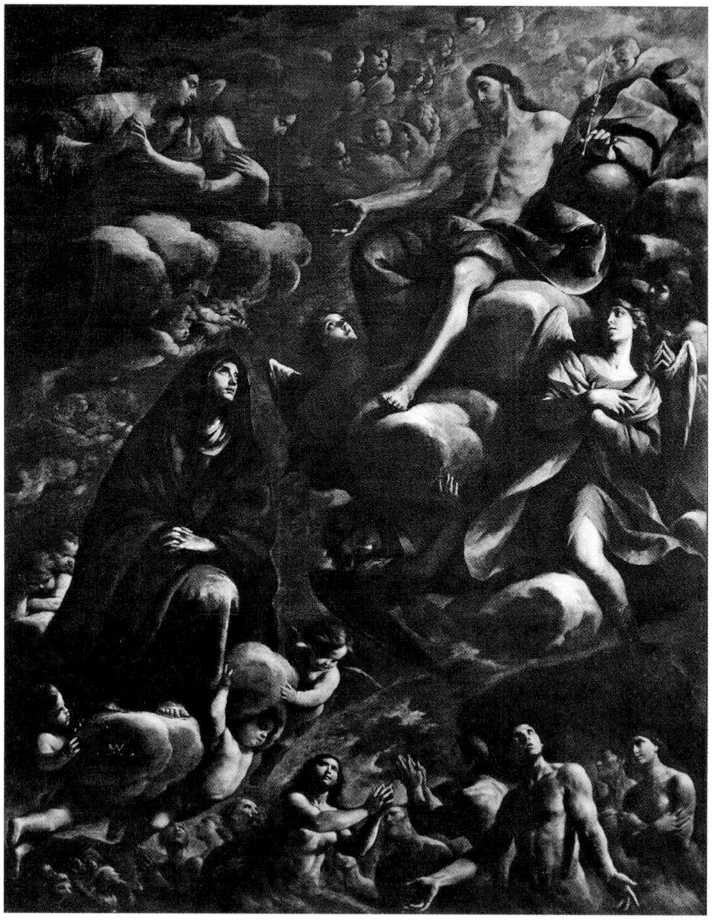

174 Andrea Vaccaro, *Intercession of the Virgin for the Souls in Purgatory*, 1660. Oil on canvas, 407 × 310 cm. Museo Diocesano Napoli, Santa Maria di Donnaregina Nuova, Naples, on deposit from Santa Maria del Pianto, Naples

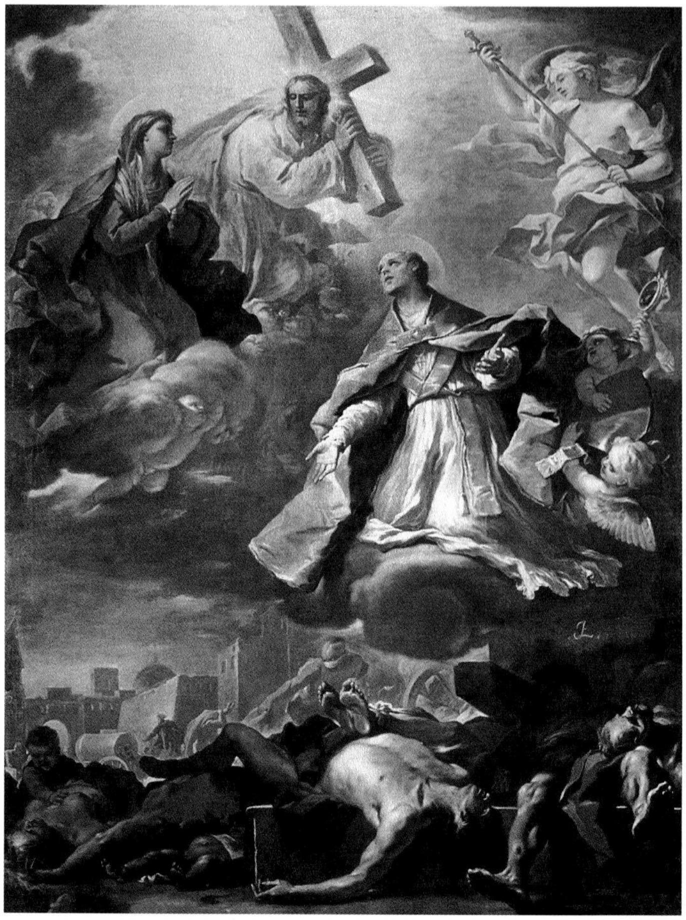

175 Luca Giordano, *St Januarius Intercedes with the Virgin, Christ and the Eternal Father during the Plague of 1656*, 1660–61. Oil on canvas, 400 × 315 cm. Museo e Gallerie Nazionali di Capodimonte, Naples, on deposit from Santa Maria del Pianto, Naples

Giordano ardently desired the honour of being assigned the church's high altar. He was backed by a vociferous band of supporters, all of whom believed, according to De' Dominici, that the outcome of this pitting of ascendant talent against the old guard could only be considered a 'cosa certa'. And yet the viceroy, bearing as he did the greater burden of patronal authority and diplomatic responsibility, was not so certain. According to one of De' Dominici's slightly varying accounts of the story, he decided to order a second altarpiece from Giordano so as to give the older and slower Vaccaro more time to finish his work before reaching a decision. At some stage during his deliberations, the viceroy had the inspired idea of referring the matter to a higher artistic authority for arbitration. He accordingly sent the two artists' *bozzetti* to a panel of eminent judges in Rome. These were said to include Sacchi, Brandi, Baccicio and Pietro da Cortona. Perhaps predictably, given the combined authority and experience contained within this group, the panel concluded in favour of the 'merito ed alla età del Vaccaro' (merit and age of Vaccaro). Giordano was forced to act magnanimously in the face of defeat, and the two artists were soon thereafter supposedly fast friends and mutual supporters of each other's work.[6]

A happy resolution of this kind was not to be the case for most of the other instances of artistic rivalry that were so often a part of high-profile public commissions during this period. The debacle of the battle in 1620 over the contract for the decoration of the Cappella del Tesoro di San Gennaro and Lanfranco's displeasure at being passed over in favour of Stanzione for the contract for the choir frescoes of the Gesù Nuovo in 1639 have already been noted. Another prominent rivalry – and one that attained

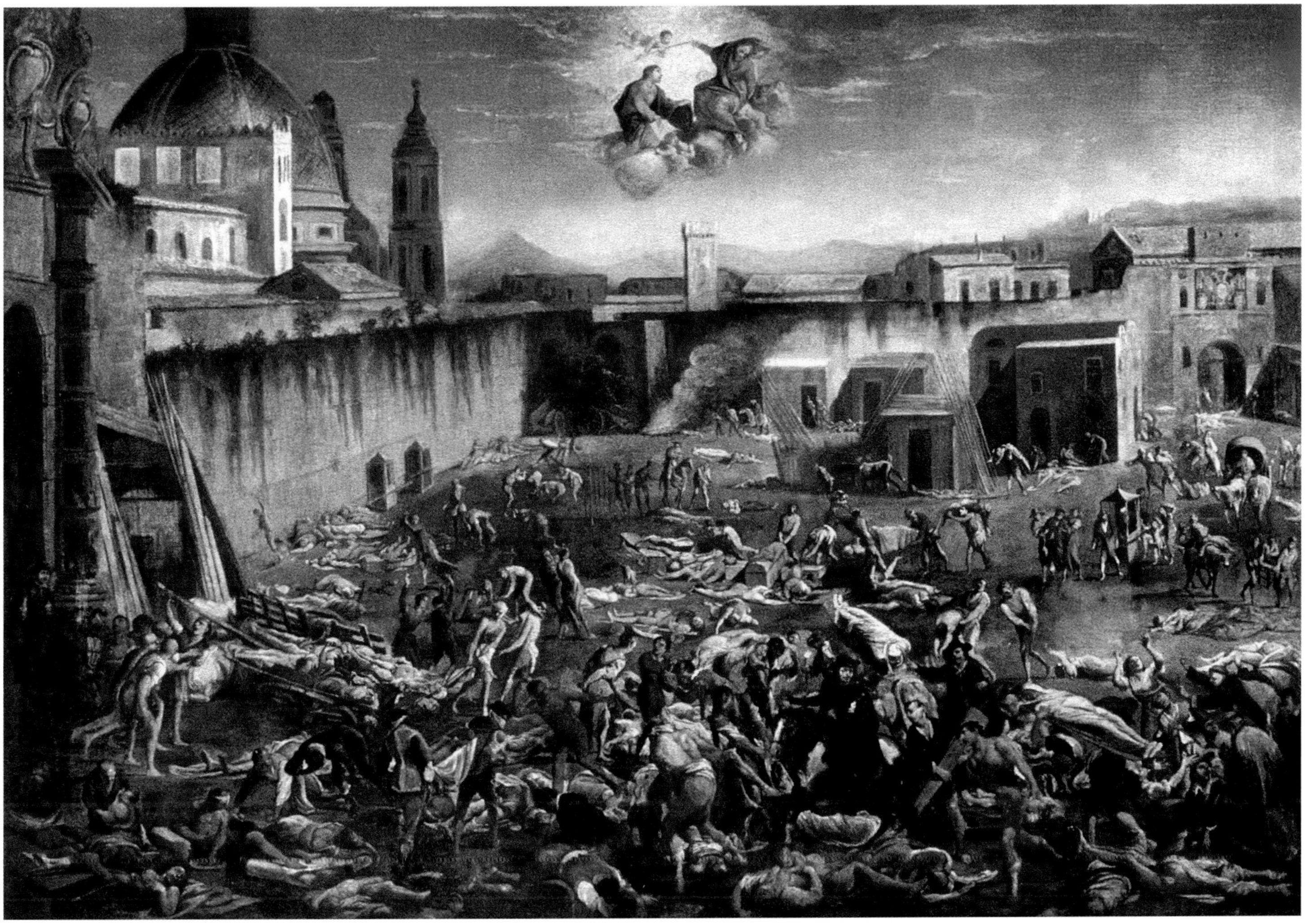

176 Domenico Gargiulo, *Piazza Mercatello during the Plague of 1656, circa* 1657–60, signed. Oil on canvas, 125 × 177 cm. Museo Nazionale di San Martino, Naples

semi-legendary status through its elaboration in the course of numerous retellings – was that between Stanzione and Ribera at the Certosa di San Martino. References to Stanzione's and Ribera's professional competitiveness stretch back to the artists' own time.[7] De' Dominici's *Vite* nonetheless contains an elaborately spun-out version of the story that has clearly been expanded upon to the extent of its becoming a paradigmatic fable revealing the two artists' divergent characters and underlying approaches to art.

De' Dominici notes that during the mid-1630s the priors of the Certosa had initially led Stanzione to believe that he would be given the important commission for the series of *Prophets* and *Patriarchs* along the walls of the nave. Instead, Ribera was awarded the contract, thanks to the intercession of the viceroy (Monterrey's successor, the duque de Medina de las Torres, and another instance of the pro-Spanish bias enjoyed by Ribera during this period). Stanzione and his supporters subsequently expressed their dissatisfaction at the presence in the Certosa of Ribera's darkened Caravaggesque canvases filling the position of honour, since they believed it would have been more appropriately occupied by the brighter keyed and more decorously idealized, classicizing frescoes of Stanzione and his studio. They complained that Ribera's *Prophets* were too dark and 'more akin to paintings produced in grottoes than in sacred edifices', while also noting that the arm of one of the prophets was too long for its body.[8] Ribera naturally thought otherwise, and in a manner consistent with De' Dominici's characterization of him as a haughty and disdainful individual, he signed his name beneath the contentious figure as a matter of pride (fig. 177).[9]

The two artists then increased their rivalry by competing for the honour of a contract for the altarpiece for the prestigious site of the Certosa's sacristy (figs 178–9). Ribera won the competition with his *Pietà* in 1637 (the canvas was soon moved to the Certosa's new treasury). He then rubbed salt into the wound by recommending to the priors that they clean Stanzione's prematurely darkening competition piece with a corrosive mixture of water and cleaning agents that he knew would accelerate the inherent instability already present within the canvas.

RIVALRY AND SELF-PROMOTION AT THE FESTA DEI QUATTRO ALTARI

Leaving aside the issue of how to separate historical fact from such an elaborately mythologized narrative,[10] both this and the previous anecdote are nonetheless insightful in addressing the behind-the-scenes politicking and jockeying for position that so often accompanied prestigious public commissions but which are commented on in the literature only rarely.[11] The Neapolitan painters had at their disposal one other vehicle for self-promotion that also lent itself to an overt manifestation of artistic competitiveness. This was the Festa dei Quattro Altari that took place in the middle of each year as part of the broader festivities associated with the Feast of Corpus Christi.

177 Jusepe de Ribera, *Noah*, signed and dated 1638. Oil on canvas, 254 × 271 cm. Museo Nazionale di San Martino, Naples

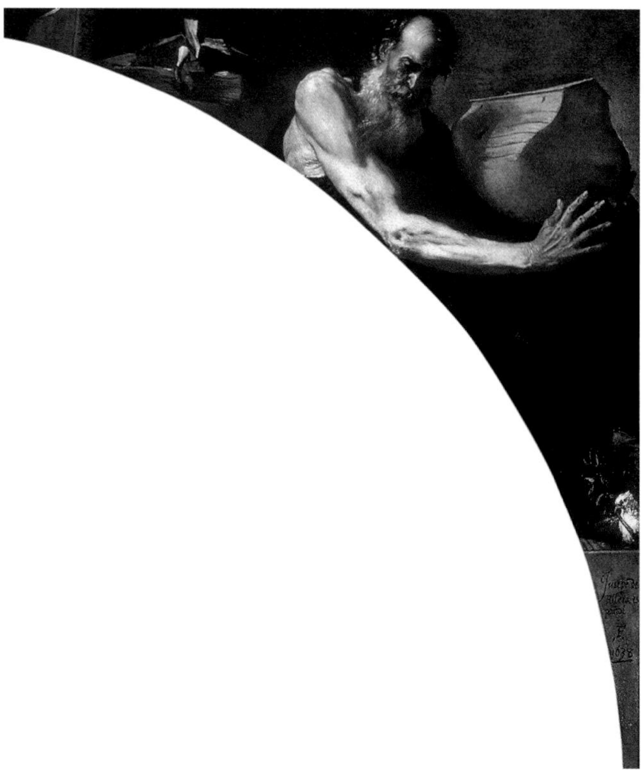

While Corpus Christi had been celebrated in Naples for centuries (the feast had been recognized formally by Urban IV in 1264), the Festa dei Quattro Altari dated only as recently as the vice-regency of Don Pietro Fernandez de Castro, conde de Lemos (1610–16). De Lemos had instituted the feast on the occasion of the dedication of San Giacomo degli Spagnoli, the church of the Spanish residents of the area. He did this in order to reinforce, both ceremonially and religiously, the emphasis on the new *centro cittadino* around the newly constructed Palazzo Reale that had been such a prominent feature of vice-regal policy since the time of Don Pedro de Toledo's institution of the Via Toledo stretching from the old city walls towards the port (see p. 184). The Festa culminated in a procession of the Blessed Sacrament (consecrated Host) from San Giacomo degli Spagnoli and proceeding to four elaborately constructed temporary altars – and also including a ceremonial blessing of the Palazzo Reale – which was attended by the viceroy, his retinue and magistrates.[12]

An understanding of the temporary art exhibition that was held during this festival is constrained by a lack of independently verifiable archival information, as is the case for the Roman art exhibitions.[13] From the information available, it seems that Naples differed from Rome in certain significant respects. The Roman exhibitions – most notably those held at the Pantheon and San Giovanni Decollato – seem to have included a high proportion of old master paintings loaned by collectors for the duration of the exhibition. The Neapolitan exhibition coinciding with the Festa dei Quattro Altari, on the other hand, appears to have been organized by the painters themselves and to have included a correspondingly higher proportion of contemporary art.

Among the many aspects of this exhibition still awaiting further clarification is the matter of its precise location. One suggestion is that the paintings may have been included in an area set up with stalls and other temporary activities along Via Santa Brigida close to the intersection with Via Toledo.[14] Another possibility, and one that has the advantage of affording greater cover and security while conforming to the model of Roman and Venetian exhibitions, is that

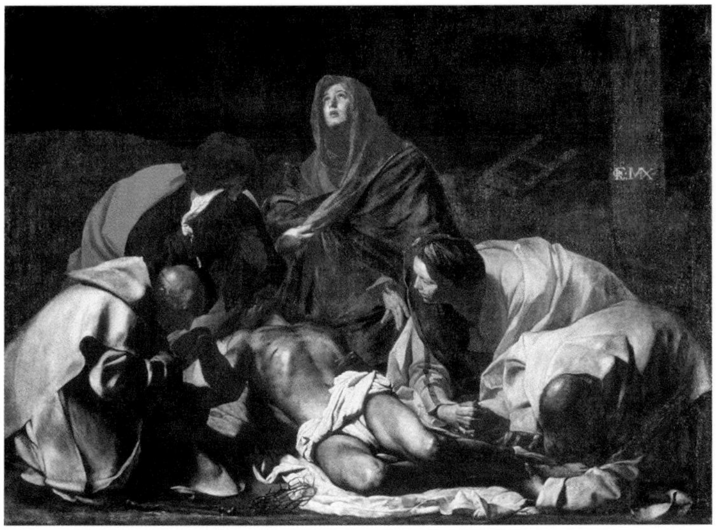

Above 178 Massimo Stanzione, *Pietà*, 1637–8. Oil on canvas, 240 × 320 cm. Certosa di San Martino, Naples

Right 179 Jusepe de Ribera, *Pietà*, 1637. Oil on canvas, 240 × 320 cm. Certosa di San Martino, Naples

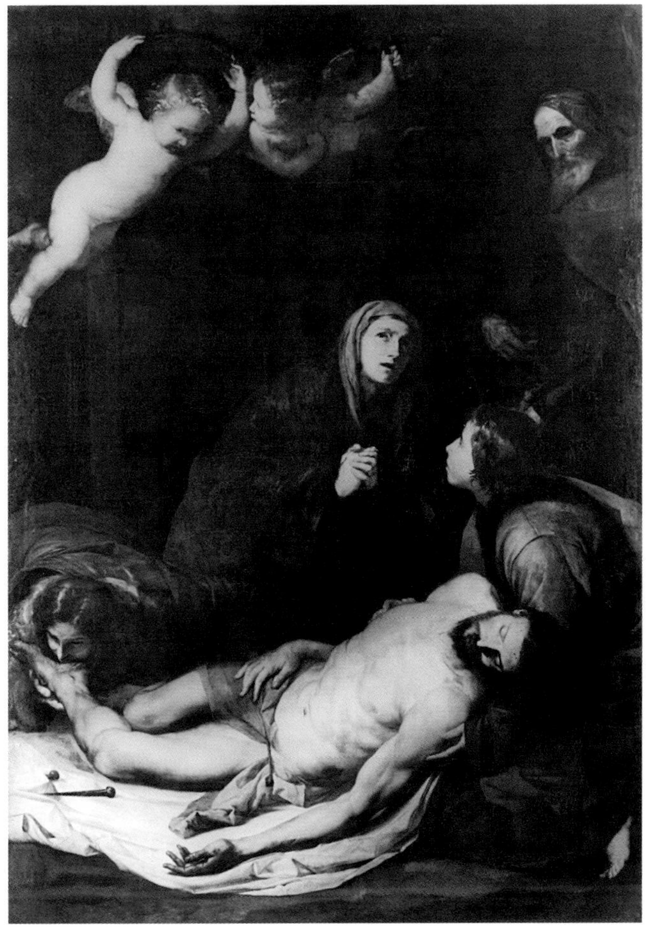

the paintings might have been displayed in either the cloister or the narthex of San Giacomo degli Spagnoli. This church, which marked the start of the ceremonial procession of the Festa dei Quattro Altari, was situated a block to the north-east of Santa Brigida.[15] Another factor in favour of this location is that it was situated conveniently close at hand to the workshop belonging to the gilder described below, who was put in charge of framing and installing the paintings for each year's exhibition.

According to De' Dominici's *Vite*, the paintings exhibited during the Festa included both canvases produced on speculation and privately commissioned work that artists evidently wished to exhibit before they were removed from public circulation. Thus De' Dominici notes that Domenico Gargiulo helped to launch his career in the mid- to late 1630s by exhibiting an independently produced treatment of the *Massacre of the Innocents* that was acquired soon afterwards by a high-ranking Neapolitan councillor.[16] He also notes that Gargiulo received a commission later in his career for a large and impressive *Triumph of Caesar* that was intended as a diplomatic gift to be sent to the Spanish court. Gargiulo was so pleased with this painting that he opted to exhibit it temporarily prior to its dispatch to Madrid. This was evidently a sound move, since it generated a commission for another version that De' Dominici saw hanging in a Neapolitan collection, an assertion subsequently corroborated by its inclusion in the late seventeenth- and early eighteenth-century inventory of the individual identified as its owner by De' Dominici.[17]

The exhibition's emphasis on independent self-promotion meant that it also became a frequent focus of artistic competition and rivalry on a par with that documented between Giovanni Baglione and Orazio Gentileschi at the annual exhibition of San Giovanni Decollato, Rome, in 1602.[18] De' Dominici cites in this manner the example of a rash decision taken by the aristocratic collector and would-be dilettante painter Don Francesco Salernitano (the original owner of Ribera's *Drunken Silenus*). Salernitano decided to include a painting in the Festa one year 'di gareggiare col celebre Luca Giordano' (to compete with the celebrated Luca Giordano). Notwithstanding Salernitano's high opinion of himself, his contribution was judged by the other paint-

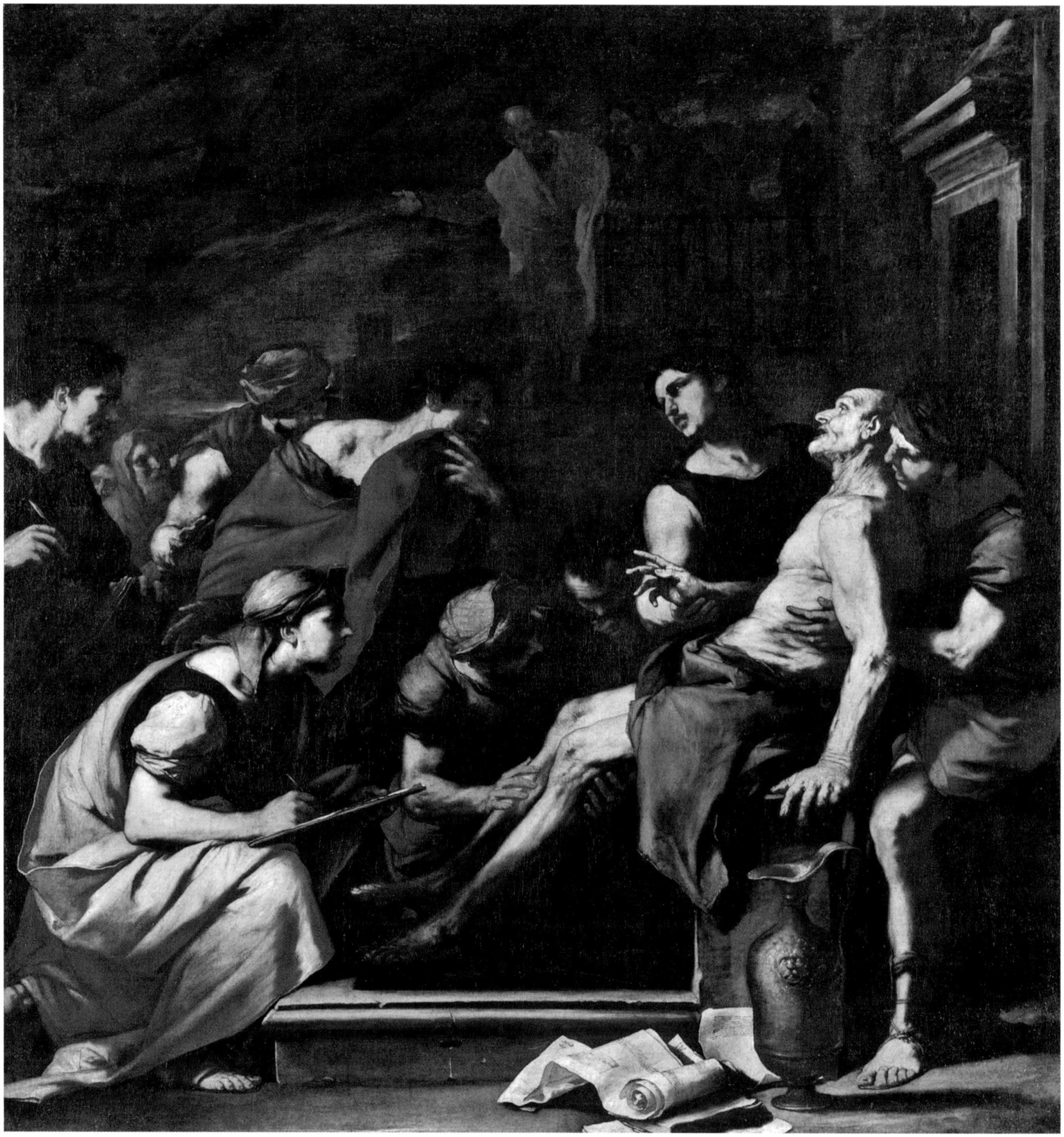

180 Luca Giordano, *Death of Seneca*, 1660s. Oil on canvas, 259 × 241 cm. Bayerische Staatsgemäldesammlungen, Munich

ers as being well below the level of Giordano's and so, as De' Dominici put it, 'sicché per molto tempo non comparve in pubblico' (his work did not appear in public for a long time thereafter).[19]

Salernitano should have anticipated the risks involved in taking on Giordano in such a public context, particularly given that Giordano was himself the undisputed master of high-profile strategies of this kind. One of the most notable instances of Giordano using the Festa as a vehicle for upstaging his competitors is said to have occurred sometime around 1678. During this period, De' Dominici notes, Francesco di Maria had hoped to make a strong impression by exhibiting at the Festa a large painting of the *Death of Seneca* to which he had devoted a great deal of time planning and executing. Di Maria and Giordano were at that stage locked in a battle for ascendency on the local scene that pitted the more academic and *disegno*-based approach of Di Maria against the more rapid and *colorito*-oriented, 'pronta abilità' of the younger Giordano and his followers.[20]

In order to demonstrate his supremacy over Di Maria, Giordano is said to have gained access to the workshop of the gilder/dealer placed in charge of the exhibition's installation, Andrea Cautiero, on a day prior to the opening. This enabled him to view Di Maria's *Seneca* while it was waiting to receive one of the temporary frames that Cautiero had responsibility for placing on the paintings before installing them in the exhibition. Giordano then returned to his workshop, and, with the characteristic speed and facility that had earned him the nickname *Luca fa' presto*, he produced his own version of the *Death of Seneca*, arranging for Cautiero to hang it alongside Di Maria's painting so as to make a comparison between the two works unavoidable. Giordano's *Seneca* (a variant of which is known from the same period, fig. 180) is said to have been praised over Di Maria's, to such an extent that Di Maria 'ebbe a morirne per tale affronto' (felt like dying of rage for receiving such an insult).[21]

INDEPENDENTLY ARRANGED EXHIBITIONS OF PAINTINGS

From this and the other information available, it is clear that the exhibition associated with the Festa dei Quattro Altari offered considerable scope to those more entrepreneurially minded artists who sought a means of promoting themselves in a manner that would cause their work to become talking points – to generate, in other words, that ineffable yet magical quality that is known today as 'hype'. Salvator Rosa has long been recognized as the Italian Baroque artist most associated with this approach. Haskell's pioneering studies highlighted the single-mindedness with which this artist, following his transfer from Naples to Rome in the mid- to late 1630s and then again during the 1650s and 1660s, sought to produce a succession of arresting subject paintings to include in the Roman exhibitions each year. Haskell concluded by emphasizing Rosa's exceptional status in this regard, noting that no other artist seems to have used the Roman exhibitions in this way, save perhaps for Velázquez and the inclusion of his striking and innovative portrait of *Juan de Pareja* at the Pantheon exhibition of 1650.[22]

While this may be true of Rome, Haskell's comments should nonetheless be qualified here, since Rosa's strategy of using temporary exhibitions as a vehicle for independent self-promotion can be seen to have drawn, in fact, upon a rich Neapolitan tradition. This certainly appears to have been the case for Ribera, since his influence can also be traced directly to one of Rosa's early exhibitions. De' Dominici cites the example of a sensational painting exhibited by Ribera following his transfer from Rome to Naples in 1616. Seeking to promote his new style of Caravaggesque naturalism to the Neapolitan public, Ribera exhibited a large and impressive painting of the *Martyrdom of St Bartholomew* close to the Palazzo Reale.[23] De' Dominici notes that this occurred during 'non so qual festa', but it seems likely, given the location and the context, that it was at the exhibition associated with the Festa dei Quattro Altari.

Ribera's strategy evidently paid off, since the painting is said to have elicited a clamorous response from the public – both negative and positive – that soon attracted the attention of the viceroy, the duque de Osuna. Osuna was apparently so taken with the painting that he employed Ribera as painter to the vice-regal court. This anecdote is based, at least in part, on independently verifiable fact, since Ribera is described as 'pittore di sua Eccellenza' in the following year and is known to have produced a number of works for the duke and duchess of Osuna during this period – including another version of the *Martyrdom of St Bartholomew* (see pp. 219–220).

One of the most striking features of De' Dominici's account is its description of the sensational reception accorded by the Neapolitan *cognoscenti* to the 'nuova maniera' of Ribera's *St Bartholomew*, particularly the intense depiction of the 'perfidia e crudeltà' of the executioners. This specialization in lurid images of sadistic and violent acts would soon become acknowledged as one of the hallmarks of Ribera's approach (see pp. 223–5). It seems that Rosa also recognized the benefits to be gained by drawing upon 'perfidia e crudeltà' when he came to consider how best to publicize his talent in a new city and in a manner that would make maximum public impact.

Rosa's friend and associate Giovanni Battista Passeri includes in his life of the artist a long anecdote concerning

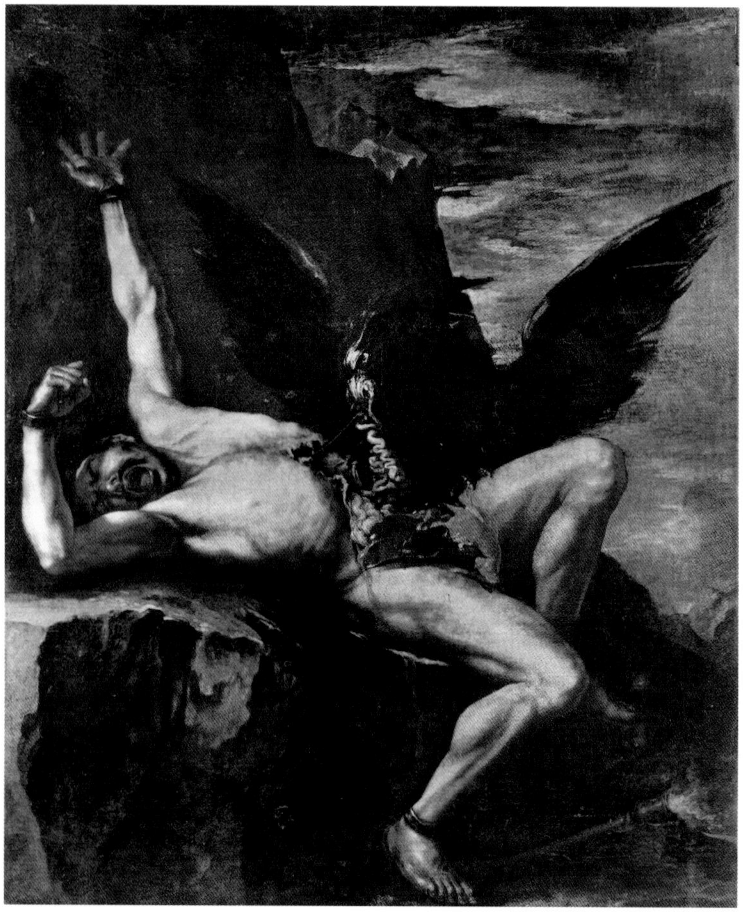

181 Salvator Rosa, *Prometheus,* 1638. Oil on canvas, 220 × 176 cm. Galleria Nazionale d'Arte Antica, Palazzo Corsini, Rome

the launching of Rosa's career in Rome in the late 1630s. Rosa had, in fact, first attempted to establish himself in Rome in 1635 when he was aged twenty, but this does not appear to have borne immediate results since he seems to have spent the next several years shuttling back and forth between Naples and Rome – returning home now and then for work, health and family reasons – while still attempting to make his mark in the Roman art world via the cultivation of useful contacts.[24] In particular, he forged an important friendship with the influential Roman connoisseur and sometime art dealer Nicolò Simonelli, who, Passeri informs us, would subsequently prove instrumental in promoting Rosa's work to the wider Roman public.[25]

The breakthrough eventually came in 1638 when Rosa decided to contribute a painting to the Pantheon exhibition of 19 March. At that stage based in Naples, he worked on the canvas at home before dispatching it to Simonelli to arrange for its installation in the Pantheon. In a gesture that would prove characteristic of his entire career, Rosa did everything he could to attract attention. He produced an over-life-size canvas of *Tityus* that, Passeri recounts, 'il suo tormento mostrando le viscere fuori dal suo squarciato, e lacerato petto' (demonstrated his torment in showing his guts hanging out of his crushed and lacerated torso). The painting reportedly made a dramatic impression on the public, particularly thanks to its association with Simonelli, who wrote a now-lost laudatory poem in its honour. As Passeri put it: 'since Simonelli was considered to be a connoisseur and was given credit for his views, he won universal renown and tumultuous applause for the name of Salvator Rosa'.[26]

A painting now in the Palazzo Corsini (fig. 181) is probably identifiable with this canvas (it represents *Prometheus* rather than *Tityus*, but Passeri may have confused the subject in his recollection).[27] All modern commentators have noted its Riberesque character, many pointing as well to the obvious precedent provided by Ribera's *Tityus* of 1632 – a painting that Rosa could easily have seen while it was being worked on, since Rosa's sister was married to Ribera's pupil Francesco Fracanzano (see fig. 169).

What needs to be stressed in this context is Rosa's more specific use of the marketing strategy contained within Ribera's earlier focus on the most sensational aspects of his art to promote himself abroad. The extreme violence of Ribera's *Martyrdom of St Bartholomew* and *Tityus* had announced the arrival of a great new talent from afar on not one but two occasions – from Játiva to Naples via Rome in the first instance and from Naples to Madrid in the second. Rosa now sought to repackage what might be called the Ribera shock effect so as to reach another new audience. In fact, with characteristic bravado, he aspired to beat the master at his own game. The result is one of the most lurid and grotesque compositions of the seventeenth century – a painting that exchanges the spaghetti-like strand of intestine depicted by Ribera for a figure who has had his entire stomach ripped open and splattered across his body so that it now begins to ooze down his thighs.

Giordano would have appreciated the audacity of Rosa's self-promotional strategy, but his approach to artistic promotion was inherently sociable, and he was always client-driven. He eschewed Rosa's path of caustic provocation and deliberate shock tactics, and sought instead the most effective means of producing in his audience a powerful yet genial state of bedazzlement.

Seeking to break into a foreign market, Giordano employed a bold strategy of this kind in the context of a disputed commission in 1668 for the Venetian church of Santa Maria della Salute. This initiative is known largely through the correspondence of Paolo del Sera, a long-time Neapolitan resident in Venice who acted as an agent for Cardinal Leopoldo de' Medici in Florence. By the mid-1660s Giordano had already travelled to Venice and cultivated fruitful associations with a number of collectors and merchants, as previously noted (see pp. 133–4).[28] Back in Naples in 1668, however, he raised his profile much more aggressively by intervening in a disputed public commission between the procurators of Santa Maria della Salute and the dilatory Florentine artist Baldassare Franceschini (also known as Il Volterrano), who had failed to complete the commission on schedule.

Hearing of the procurators' dissatisfaction, Giordano lost no time in producing his own version of the commission. He then arranged to have this sent independently to the Salute and installed in the place reserved for Franceschini's *Assumption of the Virgin* – all of which must clearly have been done with the advanced logistical support of a number of influential associates based both in Naples and Venice (fig. 182). Giordano asked for no money for his work, Del Sera informed the cardinal, but only for the honour of being judged capable of the commission. Clearly it was an inspired strategy, albeit a risky one, since apart from anything else Del Sera had to reopen negotiations with Franceschini and to inform Cardinal de' Medici in Florence of the situation, since the cardinal had been one of Franceschini's supporters.

Yet the gamble paid off because, as Del Sera explained in his letter, both the procurators and the public at large responded enthusiastically to Giordano's action. Certainly this strategic placement of his work helped advance his cause in a spectacular manner. It promoted his talent to the Venetian public in a manner that can only be described as high impact. For their part, the procurators ordered two additional lateral altarpieces in the following years. By 1675, therefore, Giordano had managed to place three of his altarpieces along the entire right-hand side of the church – an extraordinary achievement that constituted the most prominent display then to be seen of Neapolitan painting in an Italian ecclesiastical context outside southern Italy.[29]

Del Sera's letter further reveals that the project was the outcome not solely of Giordano's shrewd marketing, but also of the advice and assistance offered by the 'corrispondenti

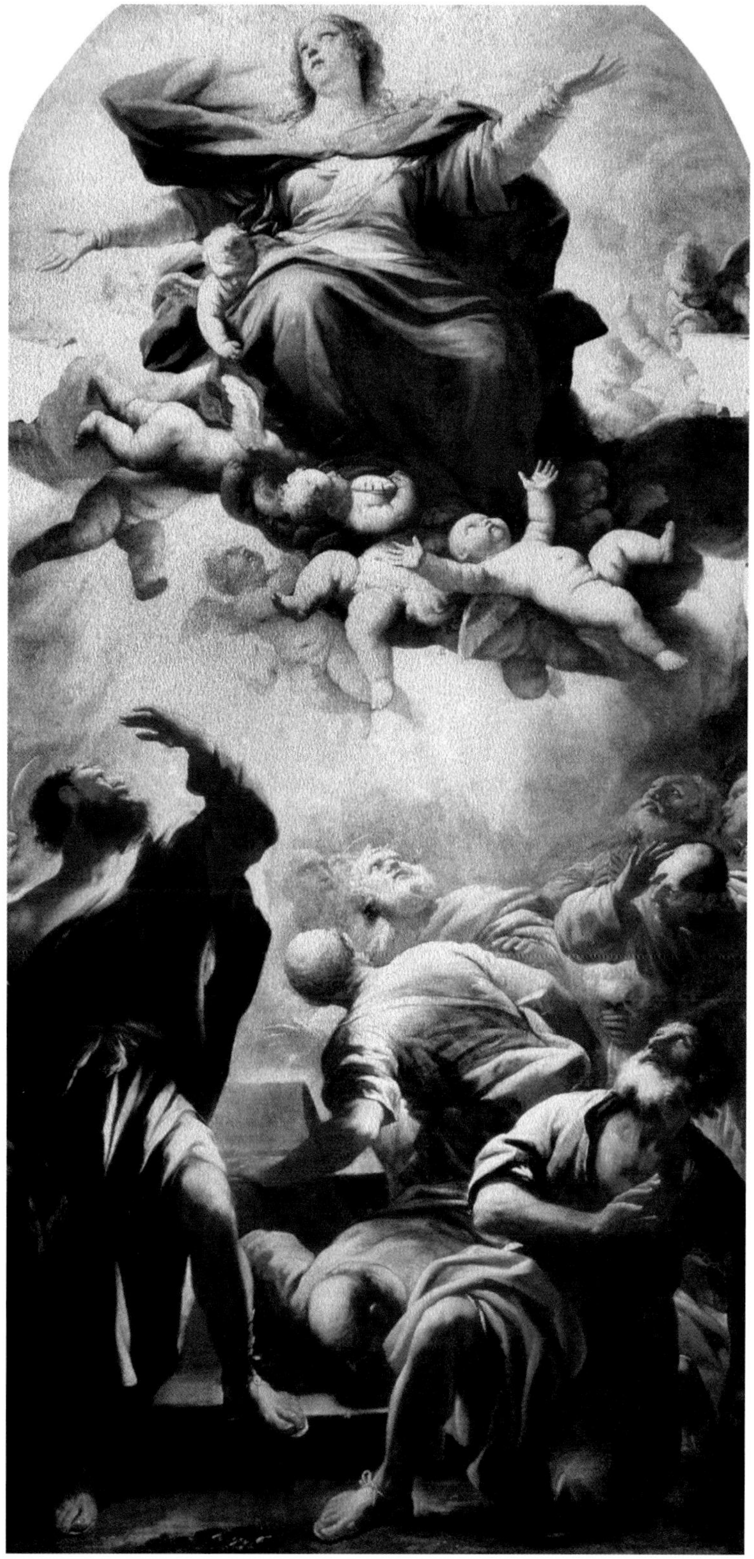

182 Luca Giordano, *Assumption of the Virgin*, 1668. Oil on canvas, 438 × 188 cm. Santa Maria della Salute, Venice

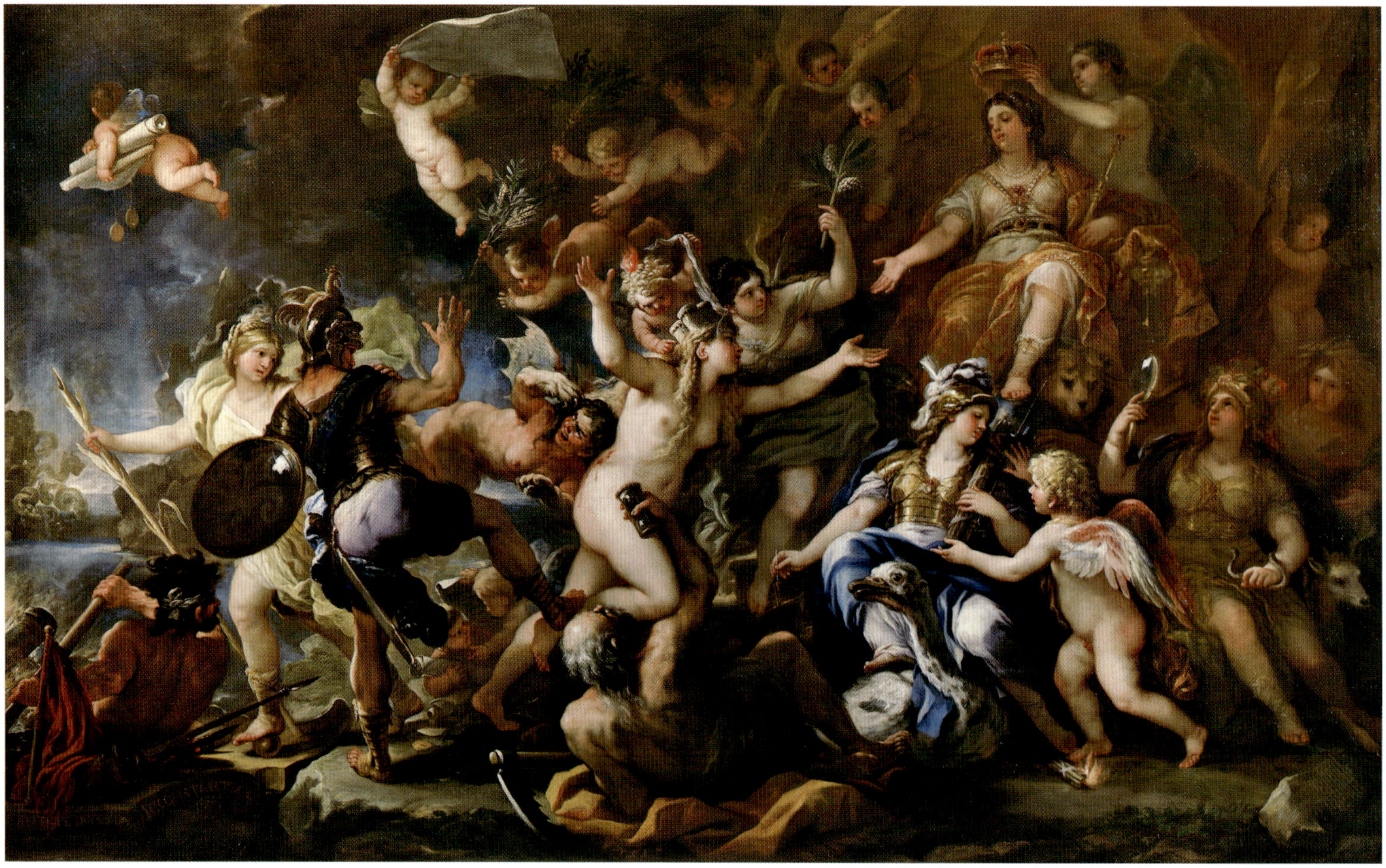

183 Luca Giordano, *Allegory of the Reintegration of Messina into Spain*, 1678. Oil on canvas, 272 × 443 cm. Museo Nacional del Prado, Madrid

del detto Giordano, che sono mercanti principalissmi di qui (per quanto mi è stato refferto)' (associates of the above-mentioned Giordano, mostly merchants from this city [or so I have been informed]).[30] Although he does not identify the individuals responsible, they were clearly from among the merchant advisers and dealers in Giordano's work, such as Carlo Arici (whom Oreste Ferrari has suggested as the possible consultant for this project)[31] and Simon Giogali, or even Guglielmo Samuele, whose association with Giordano stretched from the 1660s to the 1680s (see pp. 135–6).

A final strand to Giordano's nuanced Venetian publicity initiative is its reference to exalted Venetian artistic and literary traditions. Besides translating the precedent of Titian's *Assumption* in Santa Maria dei Frari into a distinctive Baroque idiom, Giordano's *Assumption* also quotes the promotional strategies of Tintoretto. In 1564 Tintoretto (as recounted shortly afterwards by Vasari, among others) had won a commission for the Scuola di San Rocco in the face of stiff competition by installing completed work there when all the procurators had asked for were small-scale *disegni*.[32] Del Sera cited this precedent in explaining Giordano's actions to Cardinal de' Medici, and it forms another instance of Giordano's and his advisers' shrewd manipulation of the marketing dimension of traditional benchmarks of artistic worth.

Giordano drew upon the support of the same circle of merchant backers when planning his next independent exhibition. This took place on the occasion of the reversion of Messina to the Spanish crown in 1678 following a period of tumultuous unrest that had left it briefly in the possession of France.[33] To celebrate this reintegration of such an important component of southern Italy into the continuity of Spanish rule, Giordano produced a massive political allegory of the peace that is said to have measured no fewer than 40 *palmi* in width (approx. 10.5 m). This was flanked by two larger-than-life allegorical portraits of the

Spanish king and queen that were accompanied by personifications of *Honour* and *Majesty* and of *Dominion* and *Magnificence*, respectively. Although the paintings are now lost, a canvas in the Prado has been identified as a reduced variant of the allegory's central component (fig. 183).[34]

The massive scale, temporary display format and eulogistic political orientation of this exhibition are comparable to the spectacular ephemeral festival decorations that have been noted as an especially prominent feature of the vice-regency of the conde de Oñate (1648–53) (see pp. 230–31).[35] Giordano would have been familiar with these triumphal arches, catafalques and other forms of elaborate temporary decoration. Not only would he have witnessed them regularly as part of the many civic and religious festivals held in Naples throughout the year, but he is also known to have worked on a number of decorative cycles of this kind at various stages throughout his career.[36]

As the venue for this spectacular manifestation of Neapolitan loyalty to the Spanish crown, Giordano chose the Pio Monte dei Poveri Vergognosi, a charitable institution maintained by the Jesuits that was located at the Palazzo De Curtis on Via Toledo.[37] These grandly scaled works hung along the façade or were placed in the entrance to the Pio Monte in a manner similar to today's billboards, which would have made them appear dramatically larger than life and at the same time instantly accessible to the public passing along this major thoroughfare. They would probably have resembled, in fact, the dramatic emphasis found in contemporary illustrations showing the integration of paintings within similarly grandiose Neapolitan ephemeral displays (fig. 184).[38]

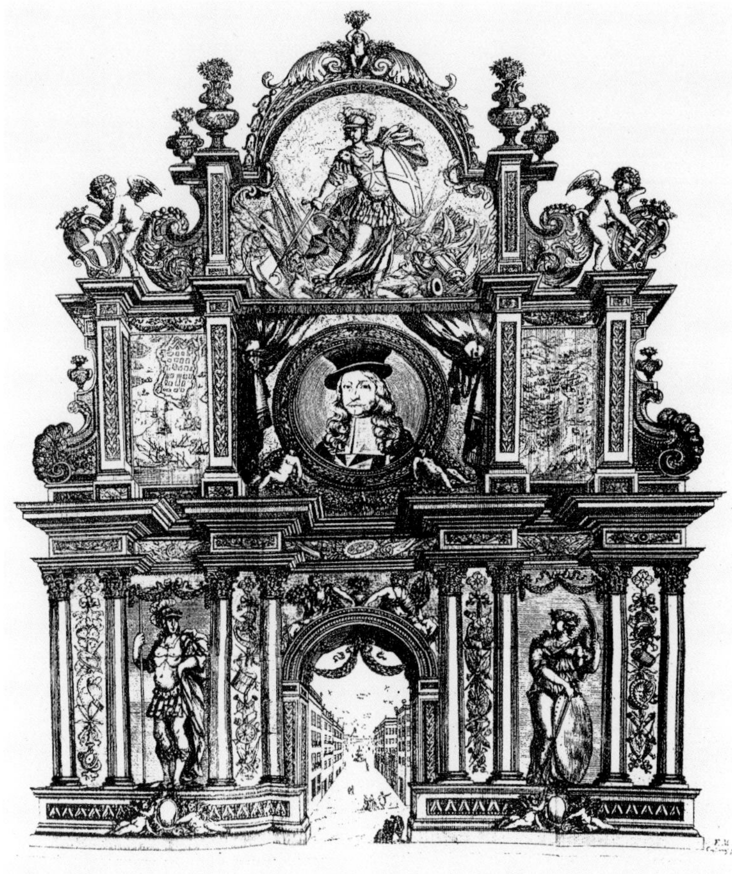

184 F. M. Cassineses, *Triumphal Arch Erected in Honour of the Election of Gregorio Carafa as Grand Master of the Knights of Malta* (from Tommaso Strozzi, *Il tempio della virtu e dell'onore eretto . . . a festeggiare le glorie dell'Eminentissimo Principe F. D. Gregorio Carafa*), Naples, 1681

De' Dominici was careful to assign credit for this inspired piece of self-promotion not solely to Giordano himself but also to a close circle of advisers. Two of these – Antonio Ciappa and Carlo della Torre – are to be counted as coming from the group of merchant dealers associated with Giordano during this period. The third is identified as the canon Carlo Celano, who was one of the most active Neapolitan playwrights and commentators of the day, and author of a comprehensive, multi-volume guide to the city published in 1692.[39] The painting's complex iconography, meanwhile, was devised by the leading Mannerist poet Giuseppe Artale.[40] What is striking about this grouping, therefore, is the nexus that it created in bringing together the effective marketing awareness of Giordano's merchant advisers and the specialized iconographical knowledge and cultural prestige of some of the city's most distinguished *uomini letterati*, a convergence of mutually beneficial self-advancing agendas as was noted in the context of the salons convened by the merchant/dealer Aniello Mele (see pp. 132–3).

The effectiveness of such temporary displays lay partly in their ability to function on a number of different levels simultaneously. The *Allegory* and its accompanying portraits would have stressed Giordano's suitability as an artist for the highest echelons of the Habsburg administration. In fact, he was well on the way to achieving that goal. Besides receiving numerous official commissions from high-ranking members of the civil administration and successive viceroys, including the current incumbent, the marqués de los Vélez, Giordano would eventually, towards the end of his career, work for the Spanish crown.

At the same time, the exhibition was effective in manifesting Giordano's absolute ascendency of the Neapolitan artistic scene. For his competitors, this audacity could only have constituted a major provocation. It was in this context that De' Dominici returned to his earlier narrative concerning Giordano's ongoing rivalry with Francesco di Maria at the exhibition of 1678. He noted that the entire city of Naples came to see the display and that 'Furono infinite le laudi date a quest'opera . . . e alla fama che se ne sparse concorse infinito popolo a vederla, che rimaneva quasi estatico' (the work attracted infinite praise . . . and as a result of its fame infinite crowds of people competed among themselves to hasten to see it, so that they remained almost ecstatic).[41]

Di Maria evidently felt that such a challenge could not go unanswered. He launched a series of bitter invectives that he relayed to his followers for them to communicate to a wider public. He proclaimed Giordano and his school to be against the best manners of the established painters. The centrepiece of this attack was the epigrammatic assertion that they were to be identified as 'la Scuola Ereticale, che traviava da diritto cammino con la dannata libertà di coscienza' (The school of heretics, led astray from the true path by an infernal liberty of conscience).

This was a loaded and provocative statement to make, aimed at asserting the primacy of tradition against the growing forces of artistic innovation. Its particular offensiveness lay in the way that it insinuated a correlation between the progressive approach of Giordano and his school and the current 'heretical' proposals of the emerging proponents of the new sciences from among the Neapolitan *letterati* who were just then beginning to attract debate for their contentious new ideas.[42] Clearly such an accusation – if it could be shown to be to any extent true – would significantly undermine the credibility of Giordano's attempt to curry favour with the Habsburg authorities by glorifying their military and political achievements.

Giordano was, moreover, an associate of some of the leading advocates of the new sciences – most notably the famous lawyer, Giuseppe Valletta. And yet, in a manner typical of the Byzantine complexities of the underlying politics of the period, so too was Francesco di Maria. Be that as it may, Di Maria was clearly aiming to cause maximum offence to Giordano, particularly given the artist's fundamentally devout public persona and unswerving loyalty to ecclesiastical and political authority.

Such a scandalous denunciation required a powerful rejoinder. Giordano sought to defuse the accusation by turning his rival's words against him in a similarly epigrammatic form, which he relayed to his pupils to broadcast to the public. If they were to be classed as heretics, Giordano proclaimed, then Di Maria and his school were to be classed, for their part, as the 'Ebrei ostinati, fissi ne' rancidumi di loro legge' (Obstinate Hebrews, fixed in the rancidness of their laws). This cutting riposte was said to have won the day, and Di Maria and his followers were forced to beat a temporary retreat.

THE APOTHEOSIS OF SPECTACLE: THE STILL-LIFE EXHIBITION OF 1684

The publicity surrounding the exhibition of the *Allegory of the Reintegration of Messina into Spain* in 1678 certainly helped spread notice of Giordano's exceptional abilities beyond Naples, and particularly towards Madrid to which the strategy had clearly been oriented in the first place. According to Baldinucci, the *Allegory* was acquired soon afterwards by the viceroy, who sent it as a diplomatic gift to Madrid, from whence it was said to have been presented, in turn, to King Peter II of Portugal. Baldinucci also noted the presence of a variant composition that had been ordered for an unidentified Venetian collector.[43] But all this publicity paled in comparison to the reputation that soon became attached to Giordano's involvement in the exhibition associated with the Festa dei Quattro Altari of 1684.

It is easy to appreciate how the buzz surrounding an especially successful exhibition can take on a life of its own and grow to the point that it causes longer-term distortions to the historical record, created by an insistent and self-mythologizing creation of outright hyperbole. Such was the case, for example, for the exhibition of paintings held on 10 June 1631 at the church of Santa Maria di Costantinopoli in Rome. Sandrart's fulsome account of this event describes twelve history paintings included in the exhibition as originally forming a set that had been purportedly commissioned from the leading figure painters of the day by none other than the King of Spain. The truth behind this grand claim, however, has been subsequently proved to be rather less glamorous than the account suggests. The paintings (which included one of Sandrart's own) had not been jointly commissioned by the king; they did not form part of a series; and they featured copies as well as originals. They did, however, include two major works by Guido Reni and Guercino that, when viewed together, seem to have represented the kernel out of which grew the legend regarding the King of Spain's commission.[44]

A similar process of aggrandizement and exaggeration appears to have occurred in the case of the Neapolitan still-life exhibition of 1684.[45] De' Dominici noted of this event that Giordano outdid all his previous efforts in including in the Festa of that year a colossal display of no fewer than fourteen monumental still-life paintings with figures added by himself.[46] The still-life components of the paintings were said to be provided by the leading specialists of the day, including Giuseppe Recco, Francesco della Quosta, Abraham Brueghel (recently arrived from Rome) and Giovanni Battista Ruoppolo. As patron of the project, De' Dominici asserted that the series had been produced according to the wishes of the viceroy himself – the marqués del Carpio (1629–1687, viceroy 1683–7), just arrived from Rome as successor to the marqués de los Vélez, and also one of the leading collectors of the day.[47] Finally, and in terms of the impact of the series, De' Dominici noted that the paintings 'furono lo stupore e 'l diletto universale di tutti' (they prompted astonishment and universal delight among all who saw them) and that their splendour was said to eclipse even the procession of the Blessed Sacrament that formed the centrepiece of the festivities on that day.[48]

Although some of De' Dominici's observations need to be qualified in light of subsequent information, it is at least clear that the exhibition must have constituted an unparalleled event in the Neapolitan artistic calendar. The exhibition of 1684 constituted the grandest statement hitherto made of the status and significance of Neapolitan still-life imagery, asserting that still life could now project itself on an equal footing with monumental history painting, and thus to present itself as being much more than a mere 'lesser' category of painting.

There can be also no doubt that the paintings made an extraordinary visual impact when gathered together for public viewing. De' Dominici provides various indications of their width – ranging from 10 to 14 to 18 *palmi* and so from around 2.63 to 3.69 metres to a monumental 4.75 metres in width. The paintings that have been associated with the exhibition correspond quite well with these estimations in measuring 2.5 metres high and between 3 and 3.5 metres in width (with a further two recently identified canvases measuring 3.64 × 4.68 m).[49] As a result, the gilder Andrea Cautiero would have needed to find more than 50 metres of wall space to exhibit the group from end to end – a prodigious expanse of exhibition space that indicates the extent to which Giordano's still lifes must have dominated that year's exhibition.

Other aspects of De' Dominici's account, on the other hand, appear to have become somewhat exaggerated and obscured in the re-telling. In particular, it seems that the viceroy should not be identified as the patron of the series in the immediate sense of the term. Del Carpio can be identified as its 'patron' in the broader social-clientage meaning, since he was the highest representative of the Spanish administration presiding over the celebrations accompanying the Festa as a whole. But it does not follow from this that he actually commissioned the series as a group.

In fact, only two of the extant still lifes can be traced back to Del Carpio's collection. These pictures, depicting *Autumn* and *Summer* and painted with the assistance of Giovanni Battista Ruoppolo, Abraham Brueghel and probably also the young Paolo de Matteis, must have originally belonged to Del Carpio since they are recorded as having carried his monogram on their reverse.[50] A further two paintings from the series may possibly be accounted for as diplomatic gifts sent by Del Carpio to the Spanish court, since the inventory of the royal collection of 1700 describes two further pictures by Giordano and Giuseppe Recco, one of which has been identified with a painting by these artists now in the Art Gallery of South Australia (see fig. 79).[51] None of the other paintings of 1684 can be identified from among the many pictures by Giordano listed in Del Carpio's inventories of 1687 to 1689.[52]

As previous studies have highlighted, most of the other paintings were produced independently of Del Carpio's involvement and had, in fact, already been accounted for by other individuals prior to the exhibition's installation.[53] The bulk of the paintings appear to have been pre-financed and secured in the months leading up to the exhibition as a joint investment under the control of the merchant associates of Giordano. Carlo della Torre seems to have led the preliminary stages of this venture until an over-commitment of financial obligations forced him to transfer ownership of eight of the paintings to Vincenzo Samuele and his Venetian associate, Giovanni Battista Bertocchi, in April 1684 (see p. 138).

Samuele's and Bertocchi's eight paintings were valued at 2,400 ducats or the very high price of 300 ducats per painting, thus suggesting a total investment of approximately 4,200 ducats for the fourteen paintings. The two merchants were no doubt intending to sell on the paintings individually or as smaller sub-sets to local and foreign collectors (particularly in Venice, one assumes, but presumably also elsewhere, given their international connections). In so doing, they no doubt hoped to capitalize on the positive publicity attendant on the exhibition. In the event, the publicity surrounding the still-life exhibition of 1684 was so laudatory that it achieved perhaps even more than Giordano and his associates had anticipated. It magnified the prestige attached to the viceroy's name to the extent that he became identified as the originator of the idea to create the series itself.

This process of patronage by association – or virtual patronage, it might be termed – is comparable to the way in which the King of Spain had come to be identified with the paintings exhibited at Santa Maria di Costantinopoli in Rome in 1631. The less glamorous reality behind this account was that most of them had been acquired as a speculative scheme that had been foiled following the arrest of the scheme's true author – a Sicilian art dealer cum diamond smuggler – and death in custody shortly thereafter.[54] In both instances, the prosaic reality of the exhibitions' planning and execution had become obscured by the aura of the exalted reputation of some of those associated with the exhibitions, however tangentially. In the case of the Roman exhibition, this helped to add a sense of glamour and prestige to an otherwise criminally compromised undertaking. It was also beneficial in Giordano's instance, since it meant that the still-life exhibition of 1684 would be interpreted thereafter in terms of its artistic significance and basis in traditional patronage, rather than through the more forthrightly promotional and entrepreneurial motivations that had driven it to an equal extent. So it was that in Baroque Naples, on this occasion at least, the perception of events could end up becoming reality.

CONCLUSION: THE WORLD COMES TO NAPLES, NAPLES MAKES ITS WAY IN THE WORLD

In 1675 George Davies, the English consul in Naples, was asked to report to the English Government on the current state of trade in the region. His response was bullishly optimistic about its scope and potential for future expansion:

> As touching the trade of this Kingdome . . . it consumes as much English Woollen goods, fish of all sorts, Pepper, Tin and Lead nigh as Italy does besides, and our Shippes make returnes in Silk and Oyle chiefly for England, and in Corne and Wine for other parts, whereof this Kingdom is very abundant. I believe 60 ships a year, one year with another, lade for England, and as many more for other Parts . . . There is no nation drives one quarter of the trade here that our Nation doth, which makes these people love them beyond others . . .[55]

Although a formally recognized diplomatic agreement between the two nations was still lacking, the English mercantile presence in Naples had nonetheless been steadily increasing since the peace between England and Spain in 1604 and the initial thawing of relations between the two powers. Increasingly hostile French incursions into the Mediterranean had further strengthened the position of the English relative to the Genoese and other previously dominant mercantile groups. This had occurred, most notably, as a result of the disruptions to trade created by the Revolt of Messina, a Sicilian rebellion against Habsburg authority that had been fomented and supported by the French, and which was alluded to in Giordano's independent public exhibition of a painting celebrating its conclusion in 1678.[56]

Recently, however, the consul had been charged with sourcing from Naples a number of more prestigious, one-off luxury items to add to his usual range of business dealings. In the previous year of 1674 he had paid Francesco di Maria 110 ducats for five canvases by an unspecified artist and on behalf of an unspecified client, presumably an English visitor whom he had been accompanying throughout the city. He paid Di Maria in this instance partly in cash and partly in kind, in the form of the costly pigment of ultramarine to which Davies had ready access via his connection to the main centre of English trade in Italy at the port of Livorno.[57]

In this he was not alone. Davies's sometime partner, John Smith, is also documented in 1669 paying this same artist a little more than 600 ducats for a series of unspecified paintings that were commissioned on behalf of Heneage Finch, second Earl of Winchelsea, a high-ranking diplomat just then passing through Naples on his way home from a posting in Constantinople.[58] Evidently, therefore, at least some of the more enterprising English diplomats and tourists were beginning to trickle down to Naples, part of the stream of foreign visitors who would increasingly make their way there from this time onwards on the Grand Tour.

The most prominent – and for the Neapolitans no doubt most auspicious – precursor to this future flood of wealthy foreign tourists was John Cecil, fifth Earl of Exeter (1648–1700). Cecil arrived in Naples in early 1684 in the midst of a year-long buying spree while travelling throughout Italy. He acquired scores of mostly contemporary paintings to decorate his recently renovated Jacobean seat of Burghley House in Lincolnshire. In fact, the earl had already become acquainted with the attractions of Neapolitan painting even before reaching the city. In particular, he had been struck by two very large paintings by Giordano that he had seen hanging in the palace of Giordano's Florentine hosts, Andrea, Lorenzo and Ottavio del Rosso (themselves keen collectors of Neapolitan painting), following the artist's return to Naples only a few months earlier.[59] The earl lost no time in snapping up these canvases and then ordered thirteen additional works by this artist, most of them still to be found as originally installed in Burghley House.[60]

On reaching Naples, Cecil began to acquire works on both the primary and secondary markets. He purchased a large allegory by Mattia Preti and four small paintings on slate by the recently deceased Domenico Gargiulo, these having been quite probably sold to him by Francesco di Maria, whose specialization in secondary sales to foreigners has been noted.[61] The earl also appreciated Di Maria's own talents. He commissioned no fewer than eleven paintings from him – with subjects covering the full extent of Di Maria's specializations – all for the substantial amount of 1,250 ducats, or 113 ducats per painting.[62]

The earl was equally munificent in his patronage of Giuseppe Recco. He commissioned eight still lifes from Recco, including two large and impressive flowerpieces that are still to be seen at Burghley House. These were commissioned for the generous price of 200 ducats each – as much as the most prestigious gallery paintings of the day and double the fee, it seems, as received by Recco for a comparable commission from a local Neapolitan aristocrat a few years earlier.[63] Recco had finished only one of these canvases at the time of the earl's departure so it was left to Davies to finalize payments on his behalf and to arrange for the transport of the finished works to England (fig. 185).[64]

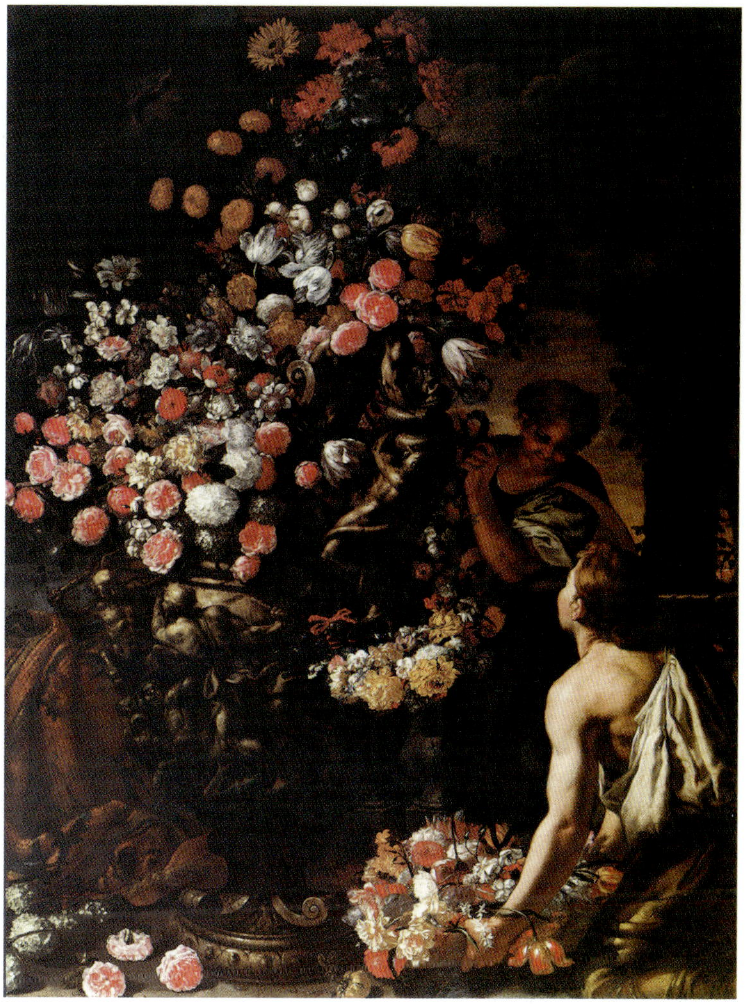

185 Giuseppe Recco, *Flowerpiece*, 1683–4. Oil on canvas, 265.5 × 201 cm. Burghley House, Stamford, Lincs

The Earl of Exeter must have seemed too good to be true to the Neapolitans. Here was a foreigner who paid handsomely, bought in bulk and was equally enthusiastic about the full spectrum of Neapolitan painting – from Di Maria's classicizing canvases to Giordano's exuberant High Baroque style and Recco's still lifes all at the same time. Clearly, with prices like this it was in the Neapolitans' best interests to produce work for this new and emerging market as efficiently and to the highest standard that they could. And in fact, just how handsomely the English could pay in return was confirmed several years later, in 1688, when the 'Signor Conte di Kingston Inglese' authorized George Davies to pay Giordano the massive sum of 600 ducats for an admittedly grandiose and complex multi-figure painting of the *Battle of the Lapiths and Centaurs.* As indicated by the list of payments in Table 2, this painting, measuring nearly 4 metres in width and now in the Hermitage, ranks as the single most expensive privately commissioned painting in all seventeenth-century Naples.[65]

At the same time, the Neapolitans were flexible enough to see the advantages of adapting themselves to suit the most stringent of specialized foreign tastes. Among the most intriguing and idiosyncratic creations of the late Neapolitan Baroque is a pair of canvases by Giacomo del Po (1652–1726). These depict scenes from *Paradise Lost* and appear to have formed part of a larger series based on Milton's great poem that was commissioned by an unidentified English patron

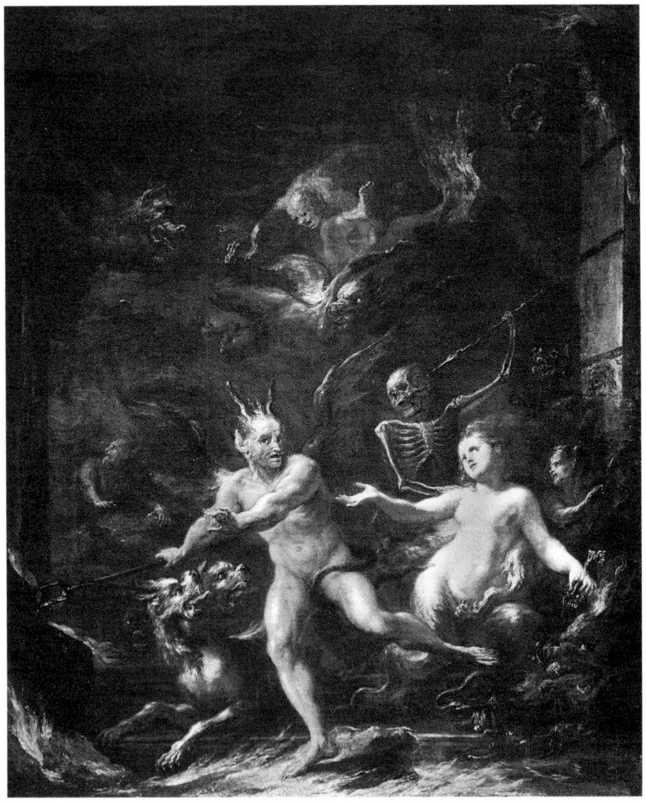

186 Giacomo del Po, *Gates of Hell*, 1705–12. Oil on canvas, 126 × 101 cm. Mr and Mrs Paul H. Ganz collection, New York

(fig. 186).[66] Del Po almost certainly would have lacked knowledge of the poem's content besides the most basic of synopses since it was not translated into French or Italian until some years after his death.[67] And yet, basing himself solely on the illustrations to an edition of 1705, it seems, the artist was nonetheless able to enter into the mysterious and enigmatic mood of the original via his dark and flickering evocations of the dramatic encounter between Satan, Sin and Death: a subject otherwise without parallel in Neapolitan Baroque and Rococo art.

Another abstruse and idiosyncratic foreign commission came about as a result of the retirement to Naples of one of Britain's most influential public thinkers. On 15 November 1711 Anthony Ashley Cooper, third Earl of Shaftesbury (1671–1713), arrived in the city literally, as it transpired, to see Naples and die. In a manner reminiscent of Marino's return to the city a century earlier, the bowed-down and prematurely aged Whig politician cum philosopher had come to seek relief amid the mild Parthenopean climate from a chronic respiratory illness, an illness to which he succumbed a little more than a year later.

Before dying, however, Shaftesbury embarked on a feverish study of aesthetic theory that involved his commissioning from Paolo de Matteis a complex and ambitious allegory of the *Judgement of Hercules* that he conceived as a summary and illustration of his ideas (fig. 187).[68] De Matteis worked for several months on the project and was paid the princely sum of 360 ducats for the completed painting, and an additional 120 ducats for a reduced copy.[69]

These payments might initially appear extremely high, given that they were for a canvas with only three figures measuring 2.5 metres in width and for a copy measuring only 77 centimetres across. Yet, there can be no doubting that De Matteis earned his money. As Edgar Wind noted, Shaftesbury 'did not conceive of the artist as a genius responsible only to his own inspiration, but he treated him as a manual executant who carries out in visible material the ideas dictated to him by the philosopher'.[70] He accordingly bombarded the evidently flexible and diplomatic painter with reams of instructions, corrections and qualifications concerning every aspect of the composition to the extent that the finished work cannot help but appear somewhat stilted and constrained by the process.

Be this as it may, the substantial benefits to be gained by De Matteis from persevering with the commission must have appeared obvious. Shaftesbury was a major international figure and he had great ambitions for the project. He saw the finished painting as exerting a powerful moralizing influence back in England, informing his cousin that it should serve as 'a present not only worthy of a Prime Minister but even of the reigning Prince or of some Prince of the Royal Family to whom the piece itself may be a council and instruction'.[71]

In the event, none of these grand schemes came to fruition and the work was instead shipped along with Shaftesbury's other possessions to the family estate in Dorset. Yet prior to his death the earl did manage to commission an engraving after the painting, to which he referred portentously as 'the great Plate'.[72] This served as the frontispiece to the accompanying publication outlining his aesthetic theories, *A Notion of the Historical Draught of Tablature of the Judgment of Hercules*, which was included, in turn, in a subsequent republication of his most famous treatise, *Characteristicks of Men, Manners, Opinions, Times*, in 1714. Thus it was that De Matteis's name and reputation came to be circulated widely throughout the European republic of letters as a fundamental component of one of the most influential texts of eighteenth-century moral philosophy and aesthetic theory.

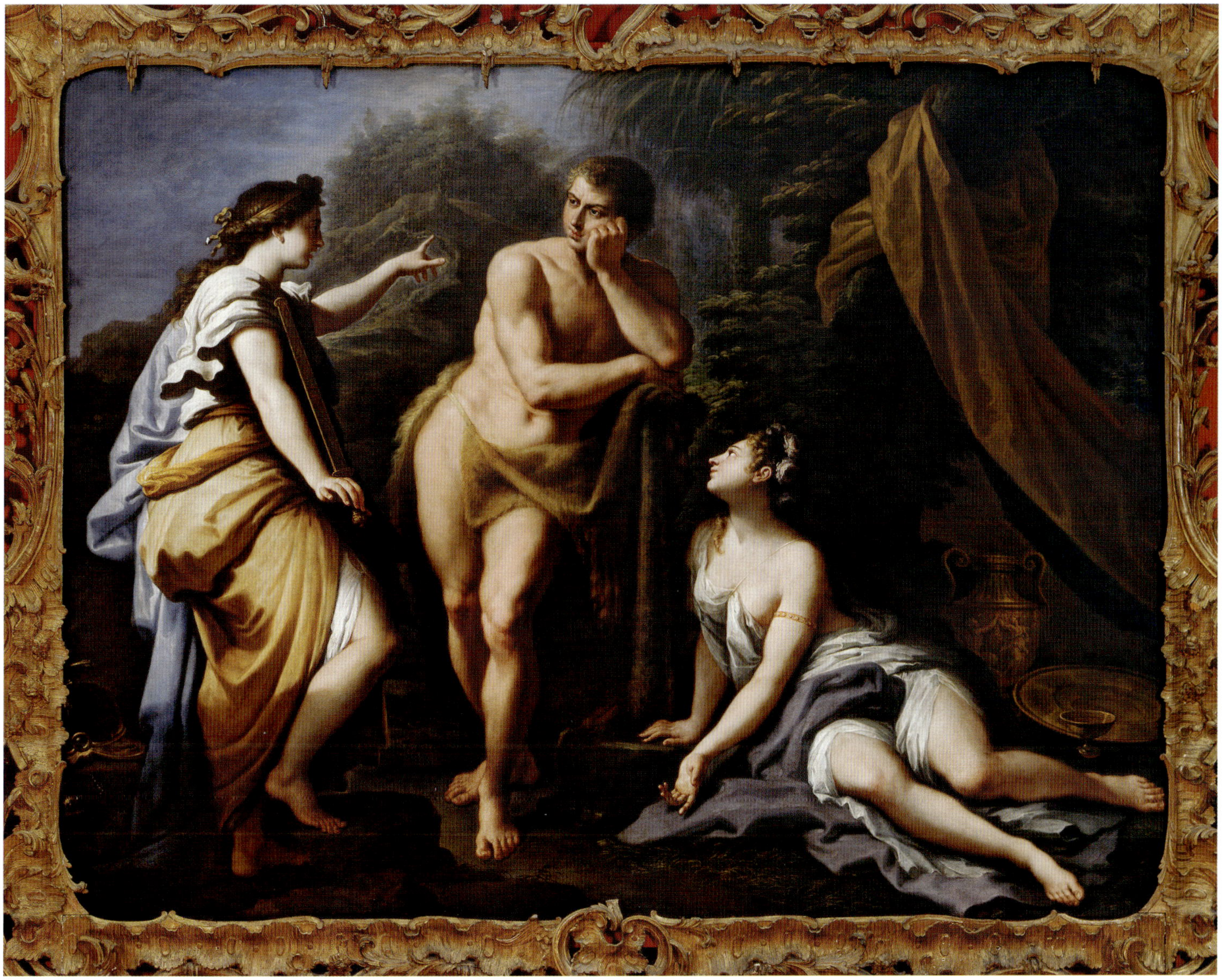

187 Paolo de Matteis, *Judgement of Hercules*, 1712. Oil on canvas, 198.2 × 256.5 cm. Ashmolean Museum, University of Oxford

The world, it seemed, was at last coming to Naples. And as these examples all attest, this process was significantly increased by the throng of newly ascendant foreign powers all seeking to fill the vacuum created by the progressive decline of Spanish hegemony in the region. The conclusion to this long and drawn-out process finally came about as a result of the death of Charles II in 1700. At that moment, the Spanish crown passed from the extinct Spanish Habsburgs to a seventeen-year-old French Bourbon grandson of Louis XIV: Philip, duke of Anjou.

The ensuing War of Spanish Succession caused havoc and destruction throughout Europe, and included what was the relatively minor sideshow campaign of the invasion of Naples by Austrian troops on 7 July 1707. In the years that followed, the war nonetheless dragged on, before finally reaching an exhausted conclusion with the signing of the treaties of Utrecht and Rastatt on 11 April 1713 and 7 March 1714, respectively. From this point onwards, the European powers recognized Philip's title to the Spanish throne in exchange for his renunciation of all future claims to the Spanish Habsburg possessions in Italy. So it was that from 1707 to 1734 Naples passed from being part of Spain to becoming an outpost of the Holy Roman Emperor in Vienna.

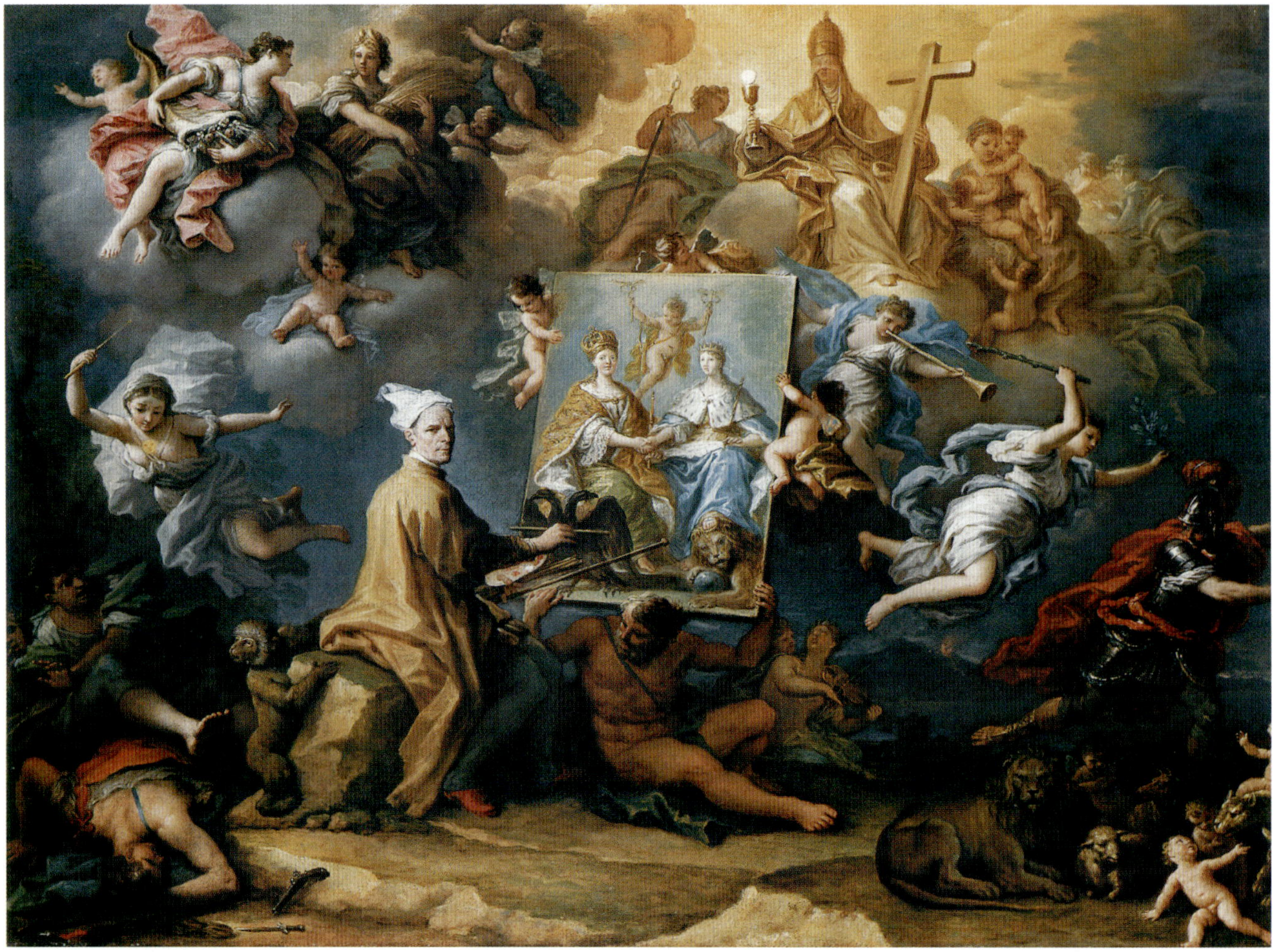

188 Paolo de Matteis, *Allegory of the Peace of Rastatt and Utrecht*, *circa* 1714. Oil on canvas, 77.2 × 106.6 cm. Sarah Campbell Blaffer Foundation, Houston

Unsettling as this constantly shifting geo-political background undoubtedly was, it nonetheless added significant additional stimulus to the ability of successive generations of Neapolitan artists to look beyond Naples so as to produce work on a wider European stage. It was Giordano, once again, who acted as the forerunner to this process. In 1692 he accepted an offer to travel to Spain to serve as court artist in Madrid during what turned out to be the final years of the reign of Charles II.[73] It was a signal honour, yet a daunting challenge for an artist reaching what might otherwise have represented the most settled and secure stages of his career.

As an addendum to this, De' Dominici also recorded that Charles II had become aware of Neapolitan still-life painting as a result of the international renown accorded to the exhibition of 1684. Giordano accordingly recommended Giuseppe Recco's services to the king and, as a result, Recco was asked to follow Giordano to Spain. In the event, however, Recco's desire to serve the Spanish court proved disastrous. The rigours of the passage across the Mediterranean seem to have been too much for him, and he died soon after landing in Spain, a sad end to an otherwise flourishing career.[74]

Yet Vienna was also now calling the Neapolitans. Francesco Solimena (1657–1747) responded to this new market for painting in a manner that was fully in keeping with the ability of the Neapolitans to adapt themselves to suit the differing needs of various masters. In so doing he demonstrated remarkable flexibility – both political and artistic. By 1707 he had already distinguished himself as an effective producer of grandiose pro-Spanish propaganda, as well as by serving as official portraitist to the young pretender to the

Spanish throne, Philip of Anjou, during Philip's official visit of 1702 to his soon-to-be relinquished royal possession of Naples.[75] Following the fall of Naples to the Austrians, Solimena nonetheless happily switched allegiances and painted instead a grandiose state portrait of the rival claimant to the Spanish throne, Archduke Charles of Austria.[76]

When Charles subsequently became Holy Roman Emperor and ruler of Naples, instead of Spain, Solimena was quick to capitalize on the possibilities that this opened up for the reception of Neapolitan art north of the Alps. He travelled to Vienna, where his paintings soon became an ubiquitous presence in the imperial capital, and went on to contribute scores of important works for the newly constructed ambiences of the Belvedere, the palace of the Austrian viceroy, as well as numerous altarpieces and gallery paintings for private and public patrons alike.[77] He also built on the recognition received in Vienna to leverage additional commissions further afield until, as Spinosa noted: 'there was not in Europe a prince or monarch, refined collector, or leading patron, who did not wish to own a composition ... by the celebrated master for either his private collection or family chapel'.[78] Giacomo del Po also made his way to Vienna during this period. His airy proto-Rococo style found significant favour with the Viennese so that he also received a number of major commissions for work in the Upper Belvedere Palace, among other locations.[79]

This account of the enthusiastic European response to the now increasingly migratory Neapolitan school could be extended if it were to include a consideration of the artists active from the 1730s onwards. But perhaps Paolo de Matteis, former associate of Giordano and youthful contributor to the still-life exhibition of 1684, should be given the final word here. As has been seen, he was quick to tap into the growing British presence in Naples. Besides his work for Shaftesbury, De' Dominici also mentions his painting in 1719 for the visiting British Admiral, Sir George Byng (1668–1733), commander of the British Mediterranean fleet, who was then stationed in Naples as a guest of the Austrians during another allied military engagement against the Spanish forces off the coast of Sicily.[80]

This was the second time, in fact, that De Matteis had caught the attention of a visiting foreign admiral. In 1702 he had met the commander of the French fleet in the Mediterranean, the duc d'Estrées, during the admiral's residence in Naples as part of the official delegation of Philip of Anjou. De' Dominici notes that De Matteis returned with Estrées to Paris, where he spent the next three years working for both private and public patrons. Although most of his Parisian commissions have been destroyed, they were evidently of some significance and included frescoes for various Parisian mansions, the decoration of a library for the Augustinians and the high altarpiece of the church of the Celestines.[81] They also provided De Matteis with an exceptional degree of first-hand insight into the latest trends of French and European classicism. He subsequently put this knowledge to good effect when, following his return to Naples, he was able to use it as the basis for the creation of an increasingly sophisticated and stylish contemporary synthesis of proto-Rococo, Baroque classicism.[82]

De Matteis, finally, well understood the significant self-promotional advantages to be gained from continuing in the footsteps of the flourishing traditions of Neapolitan public exhibitions. The most sensational instance of this was his independent exhibition to the public in 1714 of one of his largest and most ambitious compositions, the *Allegory of the Peace of Rastatt and Utrecht*, which is known today from a preserved fragment taken from the original canvas and a reduced-scale *bozzetto* of the complete composition now in Houston (fig. 188).[83]

De Matteis's allegory draws directly on the model provided by two earlier paintings by Giordano. In the first place, it takes the central motif of the artist shown painting an allegory from Giordano's innovative painting of *Rubens Paints the Allegory of Peace* that De Matteis had been able to study in the collection of his former patron and protector, the viceroy of Naples, the marqués del Carpio.[84] The *Allegory* also draws heavily on Giordano's *Allegory of the Reintegration of Messina into Spain*, the exhibition of which had provided the setting for the clash between Giordano and Francesco di Maria in 1678. In fact, viewers would have made the connection between these two paintings readily, since De Matteis chose as the venue for his exhibition the same setting as that used by Giordano in 1678: the Pio Monte dei Poveri Vergognosi on Via Toledo.

In linking himself to the precedent of Giordano's *Allegory* of 1678, De Matteis was aiming to create a parallel between the two paintings that would add to the political message of his work. In particular, it helped to strengthen the impression of political continuity and thus stability that characterized the progression from the Spanish dominance glorified by Giordano in 1678 to the transfer to Austrian possession celebrated by De Matteis some thirty-seven years later. It was all part of the glorious continuity of Habsburg rule in the Kingdom of Naples, De Matteis suggested, as symbolized by the peaceful reconciliation between the two nations taking part in the centre of the composition.

Perhaps the most unusual and compelling aspect of the painting for its contemporary audiences, however, was the depiction of the artist himself, magnificently attired in a flowing golden robe and cap finishing off the work. This was a daring reinterpretation of a traditional theme, particularly when one takes into account its placement in the centre of the composition. Its effect is to create a startling contrast between the quotidian reality of a focused depiction of an artist at work and a grandiose allegorical representation of the world of European diplomacy.

Artists have always been at liberty to play with the boundaries of convention and invention in the relative privacy of their workspace, but here De Matteis decided to take this composition out of the workshop and subject it to the harsh glare of the public gaze in a temporary exhibition on a major public thoroughfare. This would have magnified and intensified the painting's startling strangeness, and a number of contemporary viewers found it challenging – even shocking. De' Dominici certainly felt as much. He was quick to censure the wilfulness of De Matteis's decision to include himself: 'in the middle of the canvas in front of an easel, in the act of painting, but wearing a cap and housecoat. [This was] certainly a base concept and he was criticized for it by everyone when the painting was exhibited at the Monte de' Poveri Vergognosi.'[85]

So this consideration of the interlinked dimensions of the Neapolitan Baroque art world – from the humblest workshop to the most grandiose palatial and ecclesiastical exhibition setting – concludes with the contentious spectacle of a painter dressed in his housecoat displaying himself to all and sundry in one of the busiest thoroughfares of the city. This seems a very great distance from the kinds of concerns highlighted at the beginning of the study. The self-conscious complexity and international ambitions of De Matteis's composition are far removed from Van Swanenburgh's decision, for example, to hang one of his most unusual and innovative works on the outside wall of his workshop in order to catch the attention of passers-by (see pp. 89–90).

There is a similar contrast between De Matteis's depiction of himself at work within a grandiose allegory oriented towards the diplomatic and political worlds of Naples, Paris, Madrid and Vienna and the kinds of relatively straightforward workshop practices encountered earlier in the book. This cosmopolitan framing bears little relationship to the humble daily toil registered in the inventory of the workshop of Onofrio de Anfora, for example, with its mix of cheap devotional canvases and freshly painted landscapes produced by a modest painter who was rewarded for his efforts according to cheap daily rates of pay (see pp. 111–12).

And yet, De Matteis was not so elevated from the interlinked jungle of professional, geographical and personal associations that characterized the Neapolitan Baroque art world. He was connected, after all, to the long line of dynastically aligned Neapolitan artistic intermarriages stretching back to the union in 1597 between Tommaso de Rosa and Caterina de Mauro (so that his grandfather, for example, was none other than Ribera's assistant, Juan Do) (see p. 13).

So it is that De Matteis and all the artists here discussed were linked together by the common struggle to succeed and prosper in a complex and challenging, constantly evolving working environment. They all had in common a fundamental concern to optimize their position through an attentive and proactive attitude of industriousness and ingenuity, constantly recognizing and anticipating the interests of their audience. In fact, the effectiveness with which they achieved this last goal could be viewed as the ultimate source of all their varying degrees of success – however they were able to define that vital yet elusive term and according to whatever level they were able to attain in the teeming and overstocked art world of the Neapolitan Baroque.

De' Dominici in fact recorded a statement of just this kind made by Giordano during the exhibition of the *Allegory of the Reintegration of Messina into Spain* in 1678, in response to his rival Francesco di Maria's incessant criticisms of the painting. Giordano ultimately silenced him, stating that the best painter knows more than the others how to please the public ('il migliore Pittore . . . sapea più degli altri appagare il Pubblico'), thus expressing in epigrammatic form the ongoing preoccupation of generations of Neapolitan painters.[86]

Table 1

SIGNIFICANT MOMENTS IN THE PUBLIC RECEPTION OF PAINTING IN BAROQUE NAPLES

Date	Artwork	Political and Historical Context
1597	Cavalier d'Arpino completes an extensive series of frescoes for the Neapolitan Charterhouse, the Certosa di San Martino (choir frescoes, 1588–91; chapter house and sacristy frescoes, 1595–7)	
1599–1603		The viceroy, Fernando Ruiz de Castro, conde de Lemos, orders the construction of the Palazzo Reale, designed by Domenico Fontana
1602	Dirck Hendricksz (aka Teodoro d'Errico) completes work on the *soffitto cassettonato* decoration of the nave of the Franciscan church of Santa Maria la Nova	
1606–7	Caravaggio arrives in Naples, the first of two visits to the city. In 1607 his *Seven Works of Mercy* is installed on the high altar of the Pio Monte della Misericordia with the *Flagellation* delivered to the Dominican church of San Domenico Maggiore either later that year or shortly thereafter	
1607	One of the very first manifestations of Neapolitan Caravaggism, Giovanni Battista Caracciolo's *Immaculate Conception*, is commissioned by Domenico Barile for the church of Santa Maria della Stella	
1608–11	Carlo Sellitto paints an altarpiece and two scenes from the *Life of St Peter* for the Cortoni chapel in Sant'Anna dei Lombardi	

Date	Artwork	Political and Historical Context
1609–10	Caravaggio's second stay in Naples, where he paints a large *Resurrection of Christ* and two lateral altarpieces commissioned by the Lombard merchant Alfonso Fenaroli for Sant'Anna dei Lombardi (the paintings were subsequently destroyed in an earthquake in the nineteenth century)	
1610–16		Vice-regency of Pedro Fernández de Castro y Andrade, Conde de Lemos
1610–23	Lanfranco Massa, acting as Neapolitan procurator for the Genoese collector Prince Marcantonio Doria, commissions work from Caravaggio (*Martyrdom of St Ursula*), followed by paintings by Azzolino, Caracciolo, Ribera, the landscape painter Ferrante Maccario and others	
***circa* 1612–13**	Filippo Vitale paints an altarpiece of the *Guardian Angel* for the church attached to the orphanage of Santa Maria della Pietà dei Turchini	
1615	Giovanni Battista Caracciolo's *Liberation of St Peter* installed at the Pio Monte della Misericordia	
1616	Jusepe de Ribera arrives in Naples from Rome. He launches his Neapolitan career by exhibiting to the public a large painting of the *Martyrdom of St Lawrence*	
1617	Giovanni Battista Caracciolo travels to Genoa, where he paints unspecified work for Prince Marcantonio Doria	
1617–18	Massimo Stanzione travels to Rome	
1618	Cosimo del Sera, Neapolitan agent to the Grand Duke of Tuscany, commissions work on his master's behalf from Ribera and Santafede Cavalier d'Arpino returns briefly to Naples to begin work on the Cappella del Tesoro in Naples Cathedral, but returns to Rome shortly afterwards	
1620–21	Guido Reni arrives in Naples from Rome to work at the Cappella del Tesoro in Naples Cathedral, but flees the city five months later following intimidation by local painters	
1620–22		Economic crisis in the Kingdom of Naples precipitated by devaluation of Neapolitan currency, leading to social unrest and financial insecurity

Date	Artwork	Political and Historical Context
1622–6	Simon Vouet's *Circumcision* (1622) is sent from Rome to be installed in the church of the Arciconfraternita di Sant'Angelo a Segno. He also subsequently sends a painting of *St Bruno Receiving the Rule of the Carthusian Order* for the chapter house of the Certosa di San Martino (1626). Vouet may have come to the attention of the Neapolitans around this time via the agency of Ascanio Filomarino, since Filomarino is known to have commissioned a series of fifteen paintings from Vouet in 1623 of the *Apostles*, *Christ* and the *Virgin Mary* to be sent to Naples for the collection of his relative Marcantonio Filomarino, principe di Rocca.	
***circa* 1622–9**	Belisario Corenzio and Giovanni Battista Caracciolo commissioned to execute an extensive series of frescoes in the Palazzo Reale by the viceroy, Antonio Álvarez de Toledo, duque de Alba	
1623	Juan Do emigrates to Naples from Játiva and becomes a close associate of Ribera	
1624	The renowned poet Giambattista Marino returns to Naples from Rome, bringing his collection with him, including paintings by Sinobaldo Scorza, Claude Vignon, Lionello Spada, Raffaello Vanni and Giacomo Palma. He dies in early 1625, when his collection passes to his Neapolitan protector, Giovan Battista Manso, founder of the Accademia degli Oziosi (*circa* 1611) and earlier co-commissioner of Caravaggio at the Pio Monte della Misericordia	
***circa* 1624–5**	Paolo Finoglio wins the contract for a series of ten lunettes depicting the founder saints of the Carthusian Order for the chapter house of San Martino	
1626	Ribera produces two of his most celebrated compositions: *St Jerome and the Angel of Judgement* (Trinità delle Monache) and *Drunken Silenus* (Salernitano collection, subsequently sold in 1648 to Gaspar Roomer)	
1626–9	Ribera is admitted to the military and religious Order of Christ of Portugal (1626). This order is also conferred on Stanzione (1627) and Caracciolo (*circa* 1629)	
***circa* 1628–33**	Guido Reni's *Meeting of Christ and St John the Baptist* is completed and dispatched from Rome to be sent to the Chiesa dei Girolamini following its commission by a local Oratorian benefactor in 1621	
1629–30	Artemisia Gentileschi emigrates to Naples following a brief period of residence in Venice. In 1630 she signs and dates an altarpiece of the *Annunciation* for an unidentified Neapolitan church	

Date	Artwork	Political and Historical Context
late 1620s–mid-1640s	Stanzione wins the contract for the chapel of St Bruno in the church of the Certosa di San Martino (1630–37). During this period the Certosa becomes the focus for the most intense and sustained commissioning sequence of the period involving commissions for major work by Domenico Gargiulo, Lanfranco, Caracciolo, Ribera, Francesco de Rosa, Andrea Vaccaro and others	
1630	Visit to Naples of the Spanish Infanta, Doña María of Hungary, who also commissions work from Artemisia Gentileschi. Accompanying the Infanta is the painter Diego Velázquez, who is travelling between Sicily and Rome on the first of two trips to Italy	
early 1630s	Francesco Guarino travels to Naples from his home town of Solofra in the Campania. In Naples he spends extended periods of time in residence at the Palazzo Gravina, the Neapolitan seat of his protectors, the Orsini di Gravina. Returning home, he paints an extensive series of canvases for the Collegiata di San Michele Arcangelo, Solofra (1636–7), and the church of Sant'Antonio Abate di Campobasso (1642–3) Stanzione paints the *Massacre of the Innocents* in emulation of Marino's poem of the same name (published posthumously in 1632) and two famous earlier treatments of the subject by Reni and Poussin	
1631	Domenichino arrives in Naples to work on frescoes and altarpieces in the Cappella del Tesoro, Naples Cathedral Ribera is in residence in the Palazzo Reale, Naples, where he paints a portrait of *Magdalena Ventura* for the viceroy, Fernando Afán de Ribera, duque de Alcalá	Eruption of Mt Vesuvius
1631–7		Vice-regency of Manuel de Guzmán, conde de Monterrey
1633–5	The Neapolitan viceroy commissions a series of six paintings depicting scenes from the *Life of John the Baptist* for the Buen Retiro Palace in Madrid – four from Stanzione, one from Artemisia Gentileschi and one from Paolo Finoglio	
1634	Publication of Giulio Cesare Capaccio's *Forastiero*, an important early account of Neapolitan society and culture that includes a detailed description of the collection of Gaspar Roomer Giovanni Lanfranco arrives in Naples to work on frescoes for the Jesuit church of the Gesù Nuovo, followed thereafter by frescoes at the Certosa di San Martino (1637–9), Pozzuoli Cathedral (1638–46) and for the Theatine church of Santi Apostoli (1639–46), the last of which will become one of the most extensive Baroque ensembles in Naples and builds on the precedent set by his frescoes produced earlier for the Roman mother church of the Theatine Order at Sant'Andrea della Valle (1625–8)	

Date	Artwork	Political and Historical Context
***circa* 1634–46**	The viceroy commissions an extensive series of paintings of scenes of ancient Rome for the Buen Retiro Palace in Madrid from Lanfranco, Domenichino, Falcone, De Leone, Finoglio, Cesare Fracanzano, Gargiulo, Codazzi and others	
1634–7	Titian's *Bacchanal of the Andrians* and *Worship of Venus* are exhibited in the Palazzo Reale, Naples, en route from Rome to Madrid, where they arc to be presented to Philip IV as a gift from Prince Niccolò Ludovisi. Monterrey will take them back with him to Spain when he returns there following the end of his tenure as viceroy of Naples	
1635	Finoglio emigrates to Conversano to work for the court of Giangirolamo Acquaviva The Genoese painter Giovanni Benedetto Castiglione is in Naples, where he associates with the circle of Aniello Falcone	
1636	Artemisia Gentileschi and Ribera are commissioned to paint a series of three paintings of *Lucretia*, *Susanna* and *Bathsheba* (Gentileschi) and a series of twelve half-length figures of philosophers (Ribera) for Prince Karl Eusebius von Liechtenstein for his residence in Lower Austria Aniello Falcone convenes an 'accademia del nudo' and spearheads a local Neapolitan interest in developing new specializations in *petits maîtres* painting types previously monopolized by Dutch and Flemish painters resident in Naples	
1637	Installation of eleven altarpieces (worked on between 1635 and 1637) at the recently remodelled Pozzuoli Cathedral by Artemisia Gentileschi, Lanfranco, Stanzione, Cesare Fracanzano, Finoglio and Agostino Beltrano Ribera paints an *Apollo and Marsyas* for the principe di Montesarchio	
1638	*Pietà* by Stanzione installed at the Certosa di San Martino	
1638	Salvator Rosa sends a painting of either *Prometheus* or *Tityus* to be included in the annual exhibition at the Pantheon in Rome on 19 March Rosa leaves Naples to emigrate to Rome definitively, following a series of temporary stays there Pietro da Cortona sends a painting of *St Alexis* from Rome to the church of the Neapolitan Oratorians, the Chiesa dei Girolamini	
***circa* 1639–40**	Artemisia Gentileschi leaves Naples temporarily to travel to London to assist her father, Orazio Gentileschi, on work for the court of King Charles I and Queen Henrietta Maria; she stays there to settle her father's accounts following his death in early 1639	
1640	Unveiling of Stanzione's choir ceiling frescoes at the Gesù Nuovo (1639–40)	

Date	Artwork	Political and Historical Context
circa 1640	Rubens's *Feast of Herod* (*circa* 1633–8) enters the collection of Gaspar Roomer: the only major work by this influential artist available for study in Naples	
1641	Death of Domenichino; subsequent completion of his unfinished work in the Cappella del Tesoro in Naples Cathedral by Stanzione (1641–3), Lanfranco (1643) and Ribera (1647)	
1642	Arrival in Naples of the new Neapolitan archbishop, Cardinal Ascanio Filomarino (1583–1666), from Rome. Filomarino had previously been sending paintings to Naples (see Vouet, 1622). In 1642 he definitively transferred to Naples, bringing with him his important collection – including work by Caravaggio, Vouet, Valentin, Poussin and other artists associated with the Barberini entourage in Rome Installation of Guido Reni's *Adoration of the Shepherds* in the choir of the church of the Certosa di San Martino following the artist's death earlier that year	
1642–8	Giovanni Battista Pisante, prior of the Certosa di San Martino, commissions an extensive series of landscapes with hermit saints from Domenico Gargiulo (1642-47). A similar series of frescoes is commissioned from Lanfranco during the same period by Cardinal Ascanio Filomarino for the Palazzo Arcivescovile (1642–8)	
1643	Completion of Ribera's series of *Prophets* and *Apostles* for the nave of the church of the Certosa di San Martino (1638–43)	
1643–6	Charles Mellin resides in Naples – possibly following an invitation sent by Cardinal Ascanio Filomarino – prior to returning to Rome during the lead-up to the Revolt of Masaniello. In Naples he paints a now-lost altarpiece of the *Purification of the Virgin* for the high altar of the Chiesa dell'Annunziata (1643–5), cupola frescoes for the chapel of the Palazzo Reale (1646, subsequently destroyed) and altarpieces of the *Immaculate Conception* (1646) and *Annunciation* (1647) for the church of the Clarissan convent of Santa Maria Donnaregina that were commissioned by the abbess, Dianora Caracciolo	
1643–56	Construction of the Cacace chapel, San Lorenzo Maggiore (unveiled in 1656), commissioned by the high-ranking magistrate and civil administrator Giovan Camillo Cacace, and designed by Cosimo Fanzago with sculpture by Andrea Bolgi and paintings by Stanzione and his workshop	
1644	Stanzione completes an extensive series of nave frescoes at the Theatine church of San Paolo Maggiore (1642–4)	

Date	Artwork	Political and Historical Context
1646	Lanfranco completes an extensive series of frescoes and oil paintings at Santi Apostoli (1638–46) Ribera delivers a monumental *Immaculate Conception* to the Cappella Reale, Palazzo Reale, Naples Lanfranco leaves Naples to return to Rome, where he dies in 1647	
1646–53	Don Antonio Ruffo, principe della Scaletta orders numerous paintings for his palace in Messina from Artemisia Gentileschi, Stanzione, Ribera, Andrea Vaccaro, Luca Forte and other foreign artists, including Guercino and Rembrandt	
1647–8		Revolt of Masaniello
1648	Sale and dispersal of the remainder of the collection of Don Giuseppe Carafa di Maddaloni (following the sacking of his palace during the Revolt of Masaniello). His collection includes important works by Luca Forte, Stanzione, Artemisia Gentileschi, Annella de Rosa, Cesare and Francesco Fracanzano, Ribera, etc.	
1648–53		Iñigo Vélez de Guevara y Tassis, conde de Oñate, viceroy of Naples, institutes an important programme of cultural reformation
1651	Ribera delivers the monumental *Communion of the Apostles* for the choir of the church of the Certosa di San Martino (commissioned in 1638). The artist dies the following year after a long illness	
1653	Arrival in Naples of Mattia Preti following periods spent in Rome and northern Italy	
1654	Death of Ferrante Spinelli, principe di Tarsia, one of the main collectors of Neapolitan contemporary painting during the 1630s and 1640s. His collection spearheads a particular predilection for still-life and landscape paintings and includes numerous battle paintings by Aniello Falcone	
1656	Death from the plague of Stanzione, Falcone, Francesco de Rosa, Beltrano, De Bellis, Cavallino and De Simone The important patron and collector Diomede Carafa, duca di Maddaloni acquires the Palazzo Carafa di Maddaloni allo Spirito Santo from Gaspar Roomer. He dies two years later, but his widow and son go on to amass one of the most significant Neapolitan collections of the later seventeenth century, and the palace will be subsequently remodelled into one of the most advanced manifestations of the emerging Rococo style	Plague of Naples
1656–7	The *eletti* of Naples commission Mattia Preti to paint a series of votive frescoes depicting the *Virgin and Child with the Patron Saints of Naples* over the entrances to the city	

Date	Artwork	Political and Historical Context
1658	Luca Giordano signs and dates the *Ecstasy of St Nicholas of Tolentino*, painted for the Discalced Augustinian church of Sant'Agostino degli Scalzi, together with the *Charity of St Thomas of Villanova* for the same church	
1659	Mattia Preti completes an extensive series of canvases for the nave and transept of the Celestine church of San Pietro a Maiella	
1660–61	The viceroy, Gaspar de Bracamonte, conde de Peñaranda, commissions a high altarpiece from Andrea Vaccaro and two lateral altarpieces from Giordano as one of his major dedicatory offerings following the cessation of the plague. The paintings are commissioned for the church of Santa Maria del Pianto, a votive church built over a site used as a mass grave during the plague	
1661	Preti leaves Naples and emigrates to Malta	
1664	Foundation of the Congregazione di Sant'Anna e San Luca following the dissolution of the Corporazione dei Pittori in 1650. Andrea Vaccaro is elected the Congregazione's first *principe*	
1667	Giordano sends altarpieces to the Venetian church of Santa Maria della Salute	
1674	Death of Gaspar Roomer. Seventy of the most important paintings in his collection pass to the son of his business associate, Jan Vandeneynden, while the rest are dispersed through sale	
1678	Giordano independently exhibits to the public an *Allegory of the Peace of Messina* at the Pio Monte dei Poveri Vergognosi on Via Toledo. The painting is subsequently presented to the Spanish king	
1682–5	Giordano in Florence (in between return visits to Naples) to paint frescoes in the Corsini chapel in the Chiesa del Carmine together with an extensive series of frescoes for the Palazzo Medici Riccardi	
1683–7	Gaspar de Haro, marqués del Carpio, becomes viceroy of Naples following a period as Spanish ambassador to the Holy See (1677–82). One of the major Spanish collectors of the period, he acquires many works by Giordano and other contemporary Neapolitans, together with drawings by Falcone, antiquities, old master paintings, etc.	

Date	Artwork	Political and Historical Context
1684	Francesco Solimena (who had arrived in Naples in 1674) completes a major fresco commission for the church of the Clarissan convent of Santa Maria Donnaregina Nuova The Festa dei Quattro Altari of this year includes an unusually ambitious series of monumental still-life paintings with figures by Giordano and his workshop and still-life elements by Giuseppe Recco, Giovanni Battista Ruoppolo and other leading specialists of the day John Cecil, fifth Earl of Exeter, visits Naples as part of an extended tour of Italy, and commissions and acquires work by Giordano, Giuseppe Recco, Domenico Gargiulo and others	
1690	Solimena completes a monumental commission for frescoes in the sacristy of San Paolo Maggiore	
1692	Giordano called to Spain to work as court painter to Charles II Publication of Carlo Celano's *Notizie del bello, dell'antico e del curioso della città di Napoli*	
1695–1700		Luis de la Cerda, duque de Medinaceli, viceroy of Naples, institutes a major urban development programme at the Riviera di Chiaia on the outskirts of the city. It becomes a favourite site for new palace construction
1697	Death of Stefano Carrillo y Salsedo, a high-ranking civil administrator, and one of the leading Neapolitan collectors of the later seventeenth century	
1698	Death of the senior civil administrator and academician Francesco d'Andrea, who together with his brother Gennaro d'Andrea (1637–1710) formed one of the most progressive collections of the later seventeenth century housed in a palace designed by Francesco himself	
1702–5	Following the death of Charles II, Giordano returns to Naples and paints his final works, including frescoes for the Cappella del Tesoro in the Certosa di San Martino, prior to his death, aged seventy, on 3 January 1705	

Table 2

PRICES FOR PRIVATELY ACQUIRED PAINTINGS, I: PAINTINGS COSTING 10 DUCATS OR MORE

Artist	**Date**	**Subject**	**Dimensions (converted into cm from Neapolitan *palmi* where known)**	**Price in ducats**	**Purchaser**
Tommaso de Rosa	1606	*Betrayal of Christ*		10	Claudio Blanditio
Jusepe de Ribera	1620	Heads of *St Paul* and another *Apostle*		10 × two	Pier Capponi
Jusepe de Ribera	1616	Half-length *St Mark*		15	Lanfranco Massa on behalf of Marcantonio Doria
Aniello Falcone	1646–9	Small battle painting	79 × 53	15	Don Flavio Ruffo, abate di San Bartolomeo, on behalf of Don Antonio Ruffo of Messina
Carlo Coppola	1665	*Martyrdom of St Stephen*	132 × 105	15	Agostino Siribello
Giovanni Battista Ruoppolo	1686	Two paintings of fruit	79 × 105	15 × two	Giovanni Battista Mele
Domenico Viola	1698	Four paintings: two of *Susanna and the Elders* and *Toilet of Bathsheba*, two of *Joseph and Potiphar's Wife* and *Lot and his Daughters*	211 × 158 (*Susanna/ Bathsheba*), 211 × 263 (*Joseph/Lot*)	15 × four, total price 60	Domenico Giannattasio

Artist	Date	Subject	Dimensions (converted into cm from Neapolitan *palmi* where known)	Price in ducats	Purchaser
Teodoro d'Errico	1603	*Decollation of the Baptist, Martyrdom of St Ursula*		20 × two	Sebastiano Longo
François de Nomé	1617	Four paintings of the *Martyrdom of Virgin Saints: St Lucy, St Catherine, St Agnes, St Barbara*	Each 185 wide	20 × four (price includes frames)	Pietro Carafa
Artemisia Gentileschi	1631	*St Sebastian*	211 × 158	20	Giovanni Francesco di Afflito, conte di Loreto
Giuseppe Marullo	1644	*Venus and Adonis*	185 × 263	20	Domenico Mazzarotta
Scipione Compagno	1647	*Martyrdom of St Stephen, Martyrdom of St Lawrence*	132 wide each	20 × two (price includes frames)	Michele Angelo dello Mastro
Agostino Beltrano	1646–9	*Landscape with the Story of Jacob and Rachel* and small figures	105 × 158	20	Don Flavio Ruffo, abate di San Bartolomeo, on behalf of Don Antonio Ruffo of Messina
Andrea de Leone	1646–9	*Battle of Joshua*	105 × 79	20	Don Flavio Ruffo, abate di San Bartolomeo, on behalf of Don Antonio Ruffo of Messina
Domenico Gargiulo	1670	*St Januarius*	118 × 132	30	Giuseppe Pandolfo
Jusepe de Ribera	1620	*St Jerome in the Desert*		30	Cosimo del Sera
Bernardo Cavallino	1646	*Annunciation, Immaculate Conception*	237 × 184 each	35 × two	Carlo Cioli
Giovanni Battista Caracciolo	1607	*David*		35	Francesco Antonio Ametrano
Viviano Codazzi	1634	*View of Jerusalem*		37	Giovanni Battista Muscettola
Carlo Sellitto	1613	Two portraits of the *Children of the Duchessa di Mondragone*		40 × two	Orazio d'Aprano

Artist	Date	Subject	Dimensions (converted into cm from Neapolitan *palmi* where known)	Price in ducats	Purchaser
Massimo Stanzione	1621	Two portraits: *Don Fabio Carafa, Principe di Colobrano* and his wife, *Signora Gironima Carafa*		40 × two	Don Fabio Carafa, principe di Colobrano
Giuseppe Piscopo	1645	*Adoration of the Golden Calf*	79 × 92	40	Onofrio d'Alessio
Didier Barra	1656	*View of Naples*, showing outlying hills, the port and ships; *View of Venice*, showing the sea and ships	158 × 210 each	40 × two	Don Camillo Sanfelice
Jusepe de Ribera	1636	Twelve paintings of *Philosophers*	105 × 132 each	41.67 × twelve (500 total), only six completed	Lorenzo Cambi and Simone Verzone on behalf of the Prince of Liechtenstein, Karl Eusebius III (1611–1684)
Carlo Sellitto	1610	Portrait of the *Duca di Nocera*		50	Giovan Francesco Guercio on behalf of the duca di Nocera
Filippo Vitale	1618	*Adoration of the Magi*	Large	50	Santi Francucci
Massimo Stanzione	1648–9	*Lucretia*	105 × 132	50	Don Flavio Ruffo, abate di San Bartolomeo, on behalf of Don Antonio Ruffo of Messina
Mattia Preti	1656	*Decollation of the Baptist*		50	Prudenza della Bella
Artemisia Gentileschi	1651	*Diana and Actaeon*, *Venus and Adonis*, *'A Nude Female Figure with Accompaniment'*	316 (*Diana and Actaeon*), 263 (*Venus and Adonis*), 237 (*Nude*)	50 × three	Fabio Gentile on behalf of 'Sua Maestà Cesarea dell'Imperatore' (Ferdinand III, Archduke of Austria?)
Artemisia Gentileschi	1653	*History of Susanna*		50	Antonio Galise
Giuseppe Recco	1672	*Fruit and Flowers*	105 × 132	55	Giuseppe Cimino
Giovanni Battista Caracciolo	1612	*Samson*		60	Scipione Porzio

Artist	**Date**	**Subject**	**Dimensions (converted into cm from Neapolitan *palmi* where known)**	**Price in ducats**	**Purchaser**
Andrea Vaccaro	1660	Three histories: *Nativity*, *Sacrifice of Isaac*, Old Testament subject		60 × three	Presidente Diego Ugliola
Luca Giordano	1662	*Martyrdom of St Bartholomew*, *Martyrdom of St Andrew*		60 × two	Hierro de Castro on behalf of Marchese Fonseca
Viviano Codazzi	1645	Two [view] paintings		70 × two	Andrea de Ponte
Andrea Vaccaro	1655	*Story of Moses*, *Lot and his Daughters*	211 wide each	75 × two	Fra Pietro Turbolo
Giovanni Battista Caracciolo	1610	*Martyrdom of St Lawrence*		80	Lanfranco Massa on behalf of Marcantonio Doria
Giovanni Battista Caracciolo	1614	*Christ Carrying the Cross*	183 × 132	80	Lanfranco Massa on behalf of Marcantonio Doria
Carlo Sellitto	1614	Portrait		100	Duchessa di Monteleone
Jusepe de Ribera	1618	*Martyrdom of St Bartholomew*		100	Vincenzo Vettori
Giuseppe Recco	1669	*Still Life with Fruit and a Fountain*, figures by Giordano; *Still life with Fisherman Displaying his Catch*, figure of the fisherman by Giordano	237 × 185	100 × two	Giuseppe Paravagna, marchese di Noja
Luca Giordano	1677	*Crucifixion*, in the style of Dürer	105 wide, on panel	130	Antonio Coppola, payment made to Antonio Giordano
Jusepe de Ribera	1623	*Pietà*		150	Lanfranco Massa on behalf of Marcantonio Doria
Luca Giordano	1661	Two paintings by his hand in imitation of Ribera		150 × two	Hierro de Castro
Luca Giordano	1669	*Europa and the Bull*	237 × 342	150	Gugliemo Samuele on behalf of Simon Giogali
Andrea Vaccaro	1668	*Nativity*		150	Giovanni Battista Fusco
Artemisia Gentileschi	1649	*Galatea*, on a shell with five tritons and two dolphins	211 × 264	160 [45 for frame, acquired separately]	Don Flavio Ruffo, abate di San Bartolomeo, on behalf of Don Antonio Ruffo of Messina

Artist	Date	Subject	Dimensions (converted into cm from Neapolitan *palmi* where known)	Price in ducats	Purchaser
Artemisia Gentileschi	1636	*Bathsheba, Lucretia, Susanna*	303 wide each	200 × three	Lorenzo Cambi and Simone Verzone on behalf of the Prince of Liechtenstein, Karl Eusebius III (1611–1684)
Giuseppe Recco	1684	Two paintings with flowers	263 × 211 (actual dimensions of work at Burghley House: 265.5 × 201)	200 × two	George Davies on behalf of the Earl of Exeter
Jusepe de Ribera	1645–6	*Apollo and Marsyas*	Approx. 182 × 232 (on basis of other known works of this subject)	200	Cornelio Spinola and Dottor Paulo Spirito on behalf of the Marchese Serra
Artemisia Gentileschi	1649–50	*Diana and Actaeon*, including five nymphs and two dogs	264 × 211	230	Don Flavio Ruffo, abate di San Bartolomeo, on behalf of Don Antonio Ruffo of Messina
Jusepe de Ribera	1649–50	*Pietà*, close to the sepulchre with the Virgin, Nicodemus, St John and the Magdalene	237 × 290	270	Don Flavio Ruffo, abate di San Bartolomeo, on behalf of Don Antonio Ruffo of Messina
Andrea Vaccaro	1643	*Story of Abigail*		280	Alonso Vargas, duca di Cagnano
Massimo Stanzione	1635	*Rape of Persephone*, with other figures		300	Francesco d'Allegria
Massimo Stanzione	1651	*Judgement of Paris*, showing the three gods, Paris and two *putti*, life-size figures	264 × 211	300	Don Flavio Ruffo, abate di San Bartolomeo, on behalf of Don Antonio Ruffo of Messina
Luca Giordano	1688	*Battle of the Lapiths and Centaurs*	263 × 396 (dimensions of painting identified with this payment which is now in the Hermitage: 255 × 390, for which see Ferrari and Scavizzi 2003, cat. no. A290)	600	George Davies on behalf of the Count of Kingston

Table 3

PRICES FOR PRIVATELY ACQUIRED PAINTINGS, II: PAINTINGS COSTING LESS THAN 10 DUCATS

Artist	Date	Subject	Dimensions (converted into cm from Neapolitan *palmi* where known)	Price in ducats	Purchaser
Domenico d'Aquino	1623	100 paintings of saints		0.5 per painting × 100, 50 ducats in total for 100 paintings of single saints on copper, cost of materials to be incurred by the artist	Giuseppe de Torcalina
Antonio Giordano	1637	*St Nicholas* × five		1.5 × five	Francesco Maria Vagliese
Giovanni Bernardino Azzolino	1615	Ten landscapes and a painting of a saint	Ten small (landscapes) + one large (saint)	24 total for ten small landscapes and one large painting of a saint (2.2 per painting average)	Michele Salas
Onofrio Ricca	1643	One full-length saint (*St Dominic Soriano*) and three half-length saints (*Joseph, Januarius, John the Baptist*)	One full length, three half length	3.5 × four (14 ducats total)	Domenico Grimaldi

Artist	Date	Subject	Dimensions (converted into cm from Neapolitan *palmi* where known)	Price in ducats	Purchaser
Francesco Magliulo	1666	Two architectural paintings	79 × 132	4 × two (plus 8 ducats monthly stipend)	Giuseppe Rodeoro
Giovanni Ametrano	1685	Four paintings of fruit		4 × four	Domenico Antonio d'Azedo on behalf of 'his master' Don Giacomo Marchese
Principio de Concilio	1617	Four history paintings: *Noah's Ark*, *Destruction of Troy*, *Expulsion of the Rebel Angels*, *Great Flood*	Large	5 × four (20 ducats total)	Pomponio Clauso
Loys Croys	1616	Twelve paintings of emperors	Large	5.8 × twelve (70 ducats total)	Giovanni de Aragon
Loys Croys	1613	*The Seasons* × four, and two landscapes		5.8 × six (35 ducats total)	Principe di San Severo
Andrea de Leone	1679	Two roundel (*tondo*) paintings, probably battle pieces	Small	6 × two	Giacomo Capece Galeota
Aniello de Letizia	1678	Two copies after Preti: *Decollation of the Baptist/ Liberation of St Peter*	211 × 132 each	6.5 × two	Giovanni Serio de Micco
Carlo Coppola	1659	Landscape and figure contributions to six architectural view paintings		6.66 per painted contribution for a total price of 40 ducats for working on six paintings	Giulio Cesare de Virgiliis, paid on behalf of Antonio Francesco Fontana of Madrid
Andrea de Leone	1685	Battle painting	Small	7	Carlo Antonio de Rosa
Giuseppe Ruoppolo	1686	Four paintings of fruit	105 × 79 each	7.5 each (30 ducats total)	Nicola Grassi
Cornelio Ghesenz	1606	Six landscapes with figures		8.3 × six per painting (50 ducats total)	Conte di Montemiletto

Artist	**Date**	**Subject**	**Dimensions (converted into cm from Neapolitan *palmi* where known)**	**Price in ducats**	**Purchaser**
Giuseppe Trombatore	1687	*Portrait of Duchess of Sicignano*		8	Vincenzo Laudati on behalf of the Duchess of Sicignano
François de Nomé	1616	Eight architectural paintings	Large	8.1 × eight (65 ducats total)	Federico Gentile
Ferrante Maccario	1613	*St Sebastian*		8	Principe di Sansevero
Filippo Vitale	1621	Two landscapes		9 × two	Santi Francucci

Table 4

NEAPOLITAN SECONDARY ART MARKET SALES, 1603–1695

Date	Artist/s, subject/s (where known)	Price in ducats	Buyer	Seller
1603	*Christ Bearing the Cross* by Bassano, includes the undertaking that Sellitto will not retain a copy of the painting	20	Giovanni Battista Ròta (collector)	Carlo Sellitto (painter/dealer)
1630	Seven paintings: three landscapes by Tassi, one landscape by Napoletano, one large *Crucifixion with Saints* by Vouet, *Christ Ministered to by the Angels* by Jean Ducamps, *Ecce Homo* 'antico'	230 (33 average per painting)	Gaspar Roomer (merchant collector/dealer)	Grazia d'Angelo (widow of painter/dealer)
1631	Thirty-four paintings, large and small	300 (9 average per painting)	Paolo Finoglio and Giovanni Casolano (painter/dealers)	Grazia d'Angelo (widow of painter/dealer)
1637	A small framed painting of the *Crucifixion*	40	Pietro d'Amore (collector)	Giacomo de Castro (painter/dealer)
1637	*Christ Washing the Feet of his Disciples* by 'Giovanni Castiglietti'/G.B. Castiglione?	48	Pietro d'Amore (collector)	Giacomo de Castro (painter/dealer)
1644	Twenty-seven framed paintings	210 (8 average per painting)	Donato Cafaro (architect/engineer)	Domenico Gargiulo (painter/dealer)

Date	Artist/s, subject/s (where known)	Price in ducats	Buyer	Seller
1646	An octagonal framed painting	30	Pietro d'Amore (collector)	Giacomo de Castro (painter/dealer)
1652	Five paintings: Cavallino × four, Giovanni Battista Spinelli × one	160 (32 average per painting)	Gaspar Roomer (merchant collector/ dealer)	Giuseppe Labruto (collector)
1653	An unspecified number of paintings that includes a *Bacchus* by Ribera, 9 × 7 *palmi* (237 × 184 cm)	550	Gaspar Roomer (merchant collector/ dealer)	Giacomo de Castro (painter/dealer)
1653	Cesare Fracanzano, *Christ before Pilate*	20	Francesco Gentile (collector)	Principe di Montecorvino (collector)
1656	Cesare Fracanzano, two paintings, one of *Roman Charity*, one of *Cain Killing Abel*	50 (25 × two)	Principe di Cursi, G. B. Ciciniello (collector)	Domenico Testa (collector?)
1656	Massimo Stanzione, *St Cecilia*	15	Giuseppe della Peruta (collector?)	Pietro Aniello Guarino (collector?)
1657	Jusepe de Ribera, *Nativity*, on wood	200	Gennaro Patrone (collector?)	Giulia Gonzaga (collector)
1658	Four paintings: two landscapes, one *St Thomas* by Massimo Stanzione and one 'prospettiva' with figures	15	Antonio Testa (collector?)	Ascanio Luciano (painter/ dealer)
1659	Three paintings: one by Scipione Compagno of *St John the Baptist Preaching in the Desert*, two by François de Nomé, one of *Belshazzar's Feast*, and one of *Presentation of the Virgin*	130 (43 average per painting)	Matteo Angelo Sparano (collector?)	Costanza d'Aulisio (collector?)
1662	Two paintings by Fabrizio Santafede, one of the *Archangel Michael*, one of *St Stephen*	120 (60 × two)	Pietro de Florio (collector)	Ippolita Milano (collector?)
1664	Seventeen framed paintings, including a ruin scene by François de Nomé with figures by Cornelio Brusco, two paintings of *St Lucy* and *St Francis of Assisi* by Massimo Stanzione, four paintings of virgin saints by Giovanni Rusca	300 (18 average per painting)	Carlo de Mari, Marchese di Stigliano (collector)	Reverend Fra Giacinto Julis (manager of charitable endowment?)
1668	Andrea Vaccaro, *Nativity*, 7 × 9 *palmi* (184 × 237 cm)	50	Angelo Maria Petagna (collector?)	Aniello Mele (dealer)

Date	Artist/s, subject/s (where known)	Price in ducats	Buyer	Seller
1670	Six paintings: two by Giovanni Battista Spinelli of *St John* and *St Jerome*, four by Beinaschi of the *Four Evangelists*	70 (12 average per painting)	Santi Maria Celli (collector)	Ignazio Riccio (collector?)
1674	Eight paintings: *Virgin and Child* by Mola, *Angel* by Lanfranco, three paintings by Caroselli, comprising two small paintings and one depicting the *Triumph of the Love of Death,* two battle paintings by Jacques Courtois (Il Borgognone), one battle painting by a pupil of Borgognone	125 (16 average per painting)	Carlo Tiani (collector?)	Francesco di Maria (painter/ dealer)
1675	Two battle pieces by Aniello Falcone	30 (15 × two)	Ferrante Capparella (collector?)	Antonio Mazzocca (collector?)
1675	Twenty-one paintings: four large, one medium, sixteen small	137.67 (6 average per painting)	Rafaele de Vilosa (collector?)	Ascanio Luciano (painter/ dealer)
1676	Two paintings by Mattia Preti: *Wedding Feast at Cana, Christ and the Magdalene in the House of the Pharisees*	200 (100 × two)	Francesco de Simone (collector)	The heirs of the cleric Giovanni Antonio Milone
1683	Andrea Vaccaro, *St Sebastian*	40	Antonio Ciappa (merchant collector/ dealer)	Aniello Mele (dealer)
1686	Two small paintings, one by Reni	35 (18.5 × two)	Gaspare Lanzetta (collector)	Francesco di Maria (painter/ dealer)
1695	*Hercules and Deinara* by Giacomo Farelli	20	Antonio Billi (collector?)	Giuseppe Manna (collector?)

Table 5

PRICES FOR ALTARPIECE AND FRESCO COMMISSIONS IN NEAPOLITAN CHURCHES, 1589–1704

Date	Artist	Painting and location (all altarpieces in oil, unless otherwise indicated)	Dimensions in cm	Price in ducats
1589	Cavalier d'Arpino	Frescoes and oil paintings, choir, Certosa di San Martino	Various	800
1591	Belisario Corenzio	Frescoes, *Life of St Agatha*, St Nicholas chapel, Certosa di San Martino	Various	220
1599	Giovanni Bernardino Azzolino (in partnership with Giulio dell'Oca)	Cupola (*Trinity*) and pendentives (*Doctors of the Church*), frescoes, Chiesa dello Spirito Santo	Various	160
1601	Belisario Corenzio	Frescoes, chapel of the Nativity, Gesù Nuovo	Various	230
1602	Belisario Corenzio	Frescoes, cupola and pendentives, Santissima Annunziata	Various	637
1603	Girolamo Imparato	*Nativity*, chapel of the Nativity, Gesù Nuovo		200
1605	Belisario Corenzio	Frescoes, sacristy, Santissima Annunziata	Various	200
1605	Belisario Corenzio	Frescoes, choir, Santissima Annunziata	Various	250
1606	Caravaggio	*Seven Works of Mercy*, Pio Monte della Misericordia	387 × 256	400
1607	Giovanni Battista Caracciolo	*Immaculate Conception with Sts Dominic and Francesco di Paola*, Santa Maria della Stella	334 × 209	103

Date	Artist	Painting and location (all altarpieces in oil, unless otherwise indicated)	Dimensions in cm	Price in ducats
1612	Fabrizio Santafede	*The Raising of Tabitha*, Pio Monte della Misericordia	206 × 205	100
1615	Giovanni Battista Caracciolo	*Liberation of St Peter*, Pio Monte della Misericordia	310 × 207	100
1617	Giovanni Battista Caracciolo	*Earthly Trinity*, Chiesa della Pietà dei Turchini	340 × 230	150
1618	Filippo Vitale	*St Charles Borromeo and Franciscan Friars*, Sant'Anna dei Lombardi	Large	200
1622	Giovanni Battista Caracciolo	*Christ Washing the Feet of the Disciples*, choir painting, Certosa di San Martino	393 × 390	333
1626	Paolo Finoglio	*Circumcision*, chapter house, Certosa di San Martino	255 × 170	100
1630–37	Massimo Stanzione	Frescoes and three altarpieces, chapel of St Bruno, Certosa di San Martino	Various	2,000
1630–31	Paolo Finoglio	Frescoes and altarpiece (altarpiece subsequently rejected), St Martin chapel, church of the Certosa di San Martino	Various	1,200 (minus 120 ducats, subsequently returned for rejected altarpiece of *St Martin*)
1631	Giovanni Battista Caracciolo	*Assumption*, altarpiece, chapel of the Assumption, Certosa di San Martino	244 × 170	251
1631–41	Domenichino	*Scenes from the Life of St Januarius*, frescoes and altarpieces, Naples Cathedral	Various	22,500 (total fee, including frescoes and altarpieces)
1634–40	Giovanni Lanfranco	*Christ Blessing* (cupola), *Four Evangelists* (pendentives), frescoes, Gesù Nuovo	Various	10,000
1636	Andrea Vaccaro	*Penitent Magdalene*, Capitolo dei Frari Conversi, Certosa di San Martino	180 × 120	30
1636	Pacecco de Rosa	*St Nicholas*, altarpiece, chapel of St Nicholas, Certosa di San Martino	255 × 164	80
1637	Belisario Corenzio	Frescoes, chapel of St Hugh and St Anselm, chapel of St Nicholas and sacristy, Certosa di San Martino	Various	500
1637	Belisario Corenzio	Frescoes, chapel of St Ignatius, Gesù Nuovo	Various	915
1637	Belisario Corenzio	Frescoes, chapel of St Stephen, San Domenico Maggiore	Various	400

Date	Artist	Painting and location (all altarpieces in oil, unless otherwise indicated)	Dimensions in cm	Price in ducats
1637	Jusepe de Ribera	*Pietà*, sacristy (subsequently moved to the treasury), Certosa di San Martino	264 × 170	400
1637–8	Massimo Stanzione	*Pietà*, internal façade of the church of the Certosa di San Martino	240 × 320	300
1637–9	Giovanni Lanfranco	*Ascension*, *Apostles*, *Angels*, *Crucifixion*, nave and choir frescoes, Certosa di San Martino	Various	7,500
1638	Domenico Gargiulo	Lunette fresco, *Israelites' Gift for the Tabernacle*, Tesoro Vecchio, Certosa di San Martino	Various	80
1638–42	Massimo Stanzione	*Our Lady of Purgatory* Chiesa del Purgatorio ad Arco		450 + 25 for ultramarine
1638–43	Jusepe de Ribera	*Prophets* and *Patriarchs* × twelve, nave of the church of the Certosa di San Martino	236–54 × 266–72	960 (80 × twelve)
1638–46	Giovanni Lanfranco	Choir and nave frescoes, five oil paintings measuring 403 × 208–210 (× four) and 404 × 307 (one), Santi Apostoli	Various	10,000
1639	Massimo Stanzione	*Preparations for the Last Supper*, choir painting, Certosa di San Martino	393 × 393	1,000
1639–40	Massimo Stanzione	*Scenes from the Life of the Virgin* Gesù Nuovo, choir ceiling frescoes	Various	1,400
1639–40	Domenico Gargiulo	Coro dei Conversi, frescoes, Certosa di San Martino	Various	500
1640	Domenichino	*Martyrdom of St Januarius*, altarpiece, Naples Cathedral	355 × 220	1,575 (part of total fee of 22,500)
circa 1640–42	Guido Reni	*Adoration of the Shepherds*, choir painting, Certosa di San Martino	485 × 330	3,000 (as supposedly recounted by Reni and subsequently reported by Malvasia)
1640–47	Massimo Stanzione	*Life of the Virgin*, three soffits, Santa Maria Regina Coeli	Large	225 × three
1641	Domenico Gargiulo	*Last Supper*, Santa Maria della Sapienza	306 × 202	120
1641	Giovanni Ricca	*Transfiguration*, Santa Maria della Sapienza	330 × 220	130
1641	Belisario Corenzio	Frescoes, Santa Maria della Sapienza	Various	2,142
1641	Jusepe de Ribera	Three paintings of *Scenes of the Life of St Ignatius*, for Fanzago's chapel of St Ignatius, Gesù Nuovo		200 × three

Date	Artist	Painting and location (all altarpieces in oil, unless otherwise indicated)	Dimensions in cm	Price in ducats
1641	Cesare Fracanzano	*St Francis Xavier*, high altar, San Francesco Saverio (subsequently reconsecrated as San Ferdinando)		200
1642–4	Massimo Stanzione	*Scenes from the Lives of Sts Peter and Paul*, nave frescoes, San Paolo Maggiore	Various	3,500
1642–7	Domenico Gargiulo	Frescoes (and a small number of paintings on canvas and copper) for the Quarto del Priore, Certosa di San Martino	Various	416
1643	Giovanni Lanfranco	*Paradise*, cupola frescoes, Cappella del Tesoro, Naples Cathedral	Various	6,000
1643–6	Massimo Stanzione	*St Januarius Healing the Sick*, Cappella del Tesoro, Naples Cathedral	275 × 150, oil on copper	500
1644	Massimo Stanzione	*Christ Leaving the House of Pilate* (figures), sacristy, Certosa di San Martino	Various	600
1644–5	Agostino Beltrano	Cupola and pendentive frescoes, chapel of the Immaculate Conception, Santa Maria degli Angeli a Pizzofalcone	Various	400
1644–5	Viviano Codazzi	Perspectives × two (Colonnade and *Christ Leaving the House of Pilate*, with figures by Stanzione paid for separately), sacristy, Certosa di San Martino	Various	400
circa 1644–6	Massimo Stanzione	*Lamiozza* of sacristy, main altarpiece, chapel of St Hugh and St Anselm, Certosa di San Martino	Various	800
1645	Agostino Beltrano	Scenes from the *Life of St Nicholas of Bari*, frescoes, chapel of St Nicholas of Bari, Pietà dei Turchini	Various	100
1645	Charles Mellin	*Purification of the Virgin*, Santissima Annunziata		600
1645	Viviano Codazzi	Perspective, fresco, Tesoro Vecchio, Certosa di San Martino	Various	215 + 45 for ultramarine
1646	Giovanni Lanfranco	Vault frescoes, Casa Professa, Gesù Nuovo	Various	500
1646	Jusepe de Ribera	*Immaculate Conception*, Cappella Reale, Palazzo Reale (destroyed)	Large	530
1646	Agostino Beltrano	*Our Lady of Purgatory*, Chiesa delle Anime del Purgatorio, Nola	395 × 263	80
1646	Charles Mellin	*Immaculate Conception*, Santa Maria Donnaregina	352 × 230	170

Date	Artist	Painting and location (all altarpieces in oil, unless otherwise indicated)	Dimensions in cm	Price in ducats
1647	Jusepe de Ribera	*St Januarius Emerging Unscathed from the Furnace*, Naples Cathedral	320 × 200	1,400
circa 1647	Domenico Gargiulo	Tesoro Vecchio frescoes, ceiling oculus and spandrels, Certosa di San Martino	Various	300
1648–54	Domenico Gargiulo	Frescoes, including *View of Naples with Charles of Anjou and Queen Joanna I Presenting the Certosa di San Martino to St Martin*, Quarto del Priore and adjoining rooms, Certosa di San Martino	Various	393
1649	Agostino Beltrano	*St Jerome and the Angel*, Sant'Agostino degli Scalzi	Large	50
1649–59	Massimo Stanzione (completed by Sannino Santillo)	*Visitation*, Gesù Nuovo	338 × 205	250, artist to pay for ultramarine out of his own expenses
1651	Jusepe de Ribera	*Communion of the Apostles*, choir painting, Certosa di San Martino	400 × 400	900 or 1,000
1651	Jusepe de Ribera	Two half-length figures, *St Jerome*, *St Sebastian*, Quarto del Priore, Certosa di San Martino	125 × 100 (each)	100 (50 × two)
1652	Aniello Falcone	*Fall of the Rebel Angels*, *Sts Peter and Paul* (half-length figures), *Scenes from the Life of St Ignatius*, frescoes, sacristy ceiling, Gesù Nuovo	Various	800
1652	Andrea Vaccaro	*St Hugh Supervising the Construction of Lincoln Cathedral*, St Hugh chapel, Certosa di San Martino	205 × 305	200
1653	Mattia Preti	*St Nicholas of Bari, San Domenico Soriano*	217 × 157	50
1655	Agostino Beltrano	Cupola frescoes, Santa Maria Donnaregina Nuova	Various	700
1656	Mattia Preti	*Virgin and Child of the Immaculate Conception with Saints* (× seven), frescoes, city gates of Naples (now destroyed)	Various	1,500 ducats + ultramarine

Date	Artist	Painting and location (all altarpieces in oil, unless otherwise indicated)	Dimensions in cm	Price in ducats
1657–9	Mattia Preti	*Scenes from the Life of St Celestine and of St Catherine of Alexandria*, nave and transept, San Pietro a Maiella	Ten large canvases: five in the nave and five in the transept: two diameter 360, two 145 × 400, one 370 × 370, two diameter 370, two 300 × 150, one 450 × 500	1,100: 550 for the nave paintings and 550 for the transept paintings, 110 ducats average per painting
1657–60	Mattia Preti	*Crucifixion with Franciscan Saints, Virgin and Child Adored by Poor Clares*, San Lorenzo Maggiore	350 × 200 each	200 each
1660	Andrea Vaccaro	*Intercession of the Virgin for the Souls in Purgatory*, main altarpiece, Santa Maria del Pianto	350 × 250	100
1660–61	Luca Giordano	*Annunciation*, *Patron Saints of Naples*, organ, Naples Cathedral	Various	415
1661	Luca Giordano	*Crucifixion Adored by Patron Saints of Naples*, lateral altarpiece, Santa Maria del Pianto	400 × 315	100
1661	Luca Giordano	*Ecstasy of St Alexis*, Chiesa del Purgatorio ad Arco	214 × 138	65
1675	Luca Giordano	*Martyrdom of St Placido*, Santa Giustina, Padua	373 × 185	200
1678	Luca Giordano	Eight *Doctors of the Church*, six *Patron Saints* of the church, Naples Cathedral	Various	800
1684	Luca Giordano	Two *Scenes of the Passion: Christ Falls the First Time*, *Christ is Nailed to the Cross*, lateral altarpieces, Santa Maria Regina Coeli	152 × 204, 152 × 206	200 (100 each)
1684–5	Giovan Battista Beinaschi	*Crossing of the Red Sea* (cupola), *Four Prophets* (pendentives), frescoes, chapel of the Crucifixion, Gesù Nuovo	Various	500
1703–4	Luca Giordano	Cappella del Tesoro, frescoes, *Triumph of Judith*, *Old Testament Female Heroines*, *Fall of Manna*, *Moses Striking Water from the Rock*, *Serpent of Bronze*, *Furnace of Nebuchadnezzar*, *Sacrifice of Elijah*, Certosa di San Martino	Various	2,000

Table 6

PRICES FOR ALTARPIECE AND FRESCO COMMISSIONS AT THE CERTOSA DI SAN MARTINO, 1589–1704

Date	Artist	Painting and location (all oil altarpieces, unless otherwise indicated)	Dimensions in cm	Price in ducats
1589	Cavalier d'Arpino	Frescoes and oil paintings, sacristy	Various	800
1591	Belisario Corenzio	Frescoes, *Life of St Agatha*, St Nicholas chapel	Various	220
1622	Giovanni Battista Caracciolo	*Christ Washing the Feet of the Disciples*, choir painting	393 × 390	333
1626	Paolo Finoglio	*Circumcision*, chapter house	255 × 170	100
1630–31	Paolo Finoglio	Frescoes and altarpiece (altarpiece subsequently rejected), St Martin chapel	Various	1,200 (minus 120 ducats subsequently returned for rejected altarpiece of *St Martin*)
1630–37	Massimo Stanzione	Frescoes and three altarpieces, chapel of St Bruno	Various	2,000
1631	Giovanni Battista Caracciolo	*Assumption*, altarpiece, chapel of the Assumption	244 × 170	251
1632–4	Giovanni Battista Caracciolo	Frescoes, chapel of St Januarius	Various	100 + 500 (documentation for payments not complete)
1636	Pacecco de Rosa	*St Nicholas*, altarpiece, chapel of St Nicholas	255 × 164	80

Date	Artist	Painting and location (all oil altarpieces, unless otherwise indicated)	Dimensions in cm	Price in ducats
1636	Andrea Vaccaro	*Penitent Magdalene*, Capitolo dei Frari Conversi	180 × 120	30
1637	Belisario Corenzio	Frescoes, chapel of St Hugh and St Anselm, chapel of St Nicholas and sacristy	Various	500
1637	Jusepe de Ribera	*Pietà*, sacristy (subsequently moved to the treasury)	264 × 170	400
1637–9	Giovanni Lanfranco	*Ascension*, *Apostles*, *Angels*, *Crucifixion*, nave and choir frescoes	Various	7,500
1638	Jusepe de Ribera	Two half-length figures – *Moses, Elijah*, internal façade, church	168 × 97	100 (50 × two)
1638	Domenico Gargiulo	Lunette fresco, *Israelites' Gift for the Tabernacle*, Tesoro Vecchio	Various	80
1638	Massimo Stanzione	*Pietà*, internal façade of the church of the Certosa	240 × 320	300
1638–43	Jusepe de Ribera	*Prophets* and *Patriarchs* × twelve, nave of the church of the Certosa	236–54 × 266–72	960 (80 × 12)
1639	Massimo Stanzione	*Preparations for the Last Supper*, choir painting	393 × 393	1,000
1639–40	Domenico Gargiulo	Coro dei Conversi, frescoes	Various	500
circa 1640–42	Guido Reni	*Adoration of the Shepherds*, choir painting	485 × 330	3,000 (as supposedly recounted by Reni and subsequently reported by Malvasia)
1642–7	Domenico Gargiulo	Frescoes (and a small number of paintings on canvas and copper) for the Quarto del Priore	Various	416
1644	Massimo Stanzione	*Christ Leaving the House of Pilate* (figures), sacristy	Various	600
1644–5	Viviano Codazzi	Perspectives × two (*Colonnade* and *Christ Leaving the House of Pilate*, with figures by Stanzione paid for separately), sacristy	Various	400
circa 1644–6	Massimo Stanzione	*Lamiozza* of sacristy, main altarpiece, chapel of St Hugh and St Anselm	Various	800
1645	Viviano Codazzi	Perspective, fresco, Tesoro Vecchio	Various	215 + 45 for ultramarine

Date	**Artist**	**Painting and location (all oil altarpieces, unless otherwise indicated)**	**Dimensions in cm**	**Price in ducats**
circa 1647	Domenico Gargiulo	Tesoro Vecchio frescoes, ceiling oculus and spandrels	Various	300
1648–54	Domenico Gargiulo	Frescoes, including *View of Naples with Charles of Anjou and Queen Joanna I Presenting the Certosa di San Martino to St Martin*, Quarto del Priore and adjoining rooms	Various	393
1651	Jusepe de Ribera	*Communion of the Apostles*, choir painting	400 × 400	900 or 1,000
1651	Jusepe de Ribera	Two half-length figures, *St Jerome*, *St Sebastian*, Quarto del Priore	125 × 100 (each)	100 (50 × two)
1652	Andrea Vaccaro	*St Hugh Supervising the Construction of Lincoln Cathedral*, St Hugh chapel	205 × 305	200
1703–4	Luca Giordano	Cappella del Tesoro, frescoes, *Triumph of Judith*, *Old Testament Female Heroines*, *Fall of Manna*, *Moses Striking Water from the Rock*, *Serpent of Bronze*, *Furnace of Nebuchadnezzar*, *Sacrifice of Elijah*	Various	2,000

Notes

ABBREVIATIONS

AAR	Archivio dell'Accademia di San Luca, Rome
ASBN	Archivio Storico del Banco di Napoli
ASN	Archivio di Stato di Napoli

A NOTE ON SOURCES AND EQUIVALENCES

1 For an insightful overview and critical reappraisal of the historiography of the *Vite*, see Willette 1986. For a more recent analysis, reflective of the critical change in perception towards the usefulness of De' Dominici as a source more generally, see Pestilli 2013, chapter I, 'A Fabricated Life', pp. 9–38, with additional bibliography.

2 For which, see Ruotolo 1977, p. 74; Zupko 1981, p. 184; D. Marshall 1993, p. 576.

3 For a recent attempt to interpret local Italian currencies in relation to broader exchange trends, see Spear and Sohm 2010, pp. 34–5, 257–8, and pp. 119–20 for my own assessment of this issue in relation to the progressive devaluing of the Neapolitan ducat at foreign exchange.

4 E.g., Gentileschi cited in Garrard 1989, p. 390; and De' Dominici 1742–5, vol. II, p. 209 (life of Francesco Curia).

INTRODUCTION THE NEAPOLITAN BAROQUE ART WORLD: FROM BASEMENT TO BALCONY

1 For the anonymous *View of the Palazzo Gravina, Naples*, see D. Marshall 1993, cat. no. VC3, pp. 62–3.

2 Prota Giurleo 1952, pp. 16 and 23, citing a loan agreement of 1612 that documents the location of Sebastiano Sellitto's workshop with unusual precision.

3 For Michele Regolia's *Palace Interior*, see Naples 1984, vol. II, cat. no. 5.111, pp. 384–5; González-Palacios 1984, vol. I, pp. 284–5; Naples 2009, vol. II, cat. no. 4.1, p. 118.

4 Rubsamen 1980, passim.

5 Lattuada 2000, p. 17.

6 London 1982; Naples 1984.

7 Fort Worth 1982; Cleveland and Fort Worth 1984; Naples 1991; M. Nappi 1991; Naples 1992; Ferrari and Scavizzi 1992; Schütze and Willette 1992; Sestieri and Daprà 1994; Spike 1998; Catanzaro 1999; Naples 1999; Spike 1999; Conversano 2000; S. Causa 2000; Naples, Vienna and Los Angeles 2001; Naples 2002; Spinosa 2003; Ferrari and Scavizzi 2003; Pacelli 2008; Naples 2008c; Mariaclaudia and Lattuada 2009; S. Causa 2009; Farina 2010b; London and Fort Worth 2010; Naples 2011; Scavizzi and De Vito 2012; Tuck-Scala 2012; Spinosa 2013.

8 For surveys, see particularly Spinosa 1984b; Spinosa 2010; and Spinosa 2011. From the numerous survey exhibitions and collection catalogues on Neapolitan Baroque painting, see the following necessarily selective crucial examples: Athens 1984; Madrid 1985; Marseilles 1988; Barcelona 1990; Naples 1990; Naples 1994a; Prague 1995; Rimini 1996; Naples 1997a; Naples 1997b; Palermo 1997; Phoenix 2006; Naples 2008a; Naples 2008b; Naples 2009. For recent edited volumes devoted to various aspects of Neapolitan Baroque art and culture, see Pane 1984b; Chenault Porter and Munshower 1993; Abbate and Sricchia Santoro 1995; Bosse and Stoll 2001; Pestilli, Rowland and Schütze 2008; Colomer 2009a; Warr and Elliott 2010; Solinas and Schütze 2010; Calaresu and Hills 2013.

9 See the publications by De Vito, Delfino, Nappi, Rizzo, Ruotolo and others as listed in the bibliography. In 2013 this journal changed its title to *Ricerche sull'arte a Napoli in età moderna*.

10 Ann Percy in Cleveland and Fort Worth 1984, p. 22.
11 Portús Pérez 2005, p. 340.
12 Labrot 1992, inv. no. 7, pp. 69–71.

1 FROM THE STREET TO THE STUDIO

1 Letter from Cosimo del Sera to Andrea Cioli, 23 January 1618, cited in Parronchi 1980, p. 40: 'Hebbi lo schizzo del Quadro, che S.A. desidera da Fabbrizio Santa Fede il quale fu hieri da me con il Naccherini et ha promesso di mettervi mano molto presto volendo prima dar una rivista alla storia, perche in queste sorte di Materia, qua non hanno molta pratica.'

2 For this and the previous quotation, see letters from Cosimo del Sera to Andrea Cioli, 23 January 1618 and 13 February 1618, cited in Parronchi 1980, p. 40. Del Sera's comments on Ribera's talents are discussed briefly by Pérez Sánchez in New York 1992, p. 72.

3 José Milicua, 'From Játiva to Naples', in New York 1992, pp. 3–8.

4 For Santafede's *Our Lady of Grace with Saints*, see Leone de Castris in Naples 1997b, cat. no. 4, pp. 102–3, with bibliography. The documents for Santafede's career are surveyed in Leone de Castris 1991, pp. 334–6; and in E. Nappi 1992, pp. 98–100, with references to previous publications. Some more recently discovered documents are also discussed in Ioannou 2001, pp. 33–6.

5 For D'Errico, see Vargas 1988.

6 Labrot and Ruotolo 1980, pp. 25–7.

7 For Berardino Ròta and his collection, see Capaccio 1630, pp. 856–7. For discussion, see Morisani 1958, pp. 108–9; and Mormone 1954.

8 Labrot and Ruotolo 1980, p. 27.

9 Jusepe Martínez, *Discursos practicables del nobilísimo arte de la pintura* [*circa* 1675], Barcelona, 1950, cited and trans. in Haskell 1982, p. 60. Martínez's account of his relations with Ribera is translated in full in New York 1992, pp. 239–40.

10 For Balducci's *Annunciation*, see Leone de Castris 1991, p. 299.

11 Examples include a contract of 1587 between Fabrizio Santafede and the patron Berardino Inserò for an altarpiece and frame (the cost of which was to be subcontracted out of Santafede's earnings) that was to include 'uno cornicione di legname, con l'ornamento de la cimasa, et a li lati de detta cimasa che vi habbiano ad essere dua arpie, et tutto cio conforme al designo della detta cona come ne la sinistra parte si vede' (a wooden frame with an ornament at the upper part and on the sides of the upper section there are to be two harpies, and it is all to be done according to the drawing of the said altarpiece as in the left part one can see). The document later specifies that the drawing is to be 'de mano propria de esso m.co Berardino' (by Berardino's own hand) (Ioannou 2001, p. 35).

12 ASN, monasteri soppressi, vol. 1794, fols 2r–17r. The documents are discussed briefly by Faraglia 1878a, pp. 241–2; and by Mazzoleni 1964, p. 70 and n. 7, p. 76.

Other documents for Tramontano are published by D'Addosio 1912–13, p. 517.

13 Cimino's profession is not specified in the Tramontano documents, but he is variously identified in the previously cited published documents as an 'intagliatore', as a 'fabrilignaro' or even as 'mastro Paulo Cimmino de Neapoli squatratore di legname'.

14 Ioannou 2001, p. 34.

15 For Cimino's work in relation to that of painters and gilders, see the contracts of 1587 from the patron, Fabrizio di Sangro, for Cimino to provide Fabrizio Santafede with both the panels and the frame for a 'cona' that was to measure a massive 24 × 16 *palmi* (approx. 6.32 × 4.21 m); Ioannou 2001, p. 32.

16 See further the payments of 1593 and 1596 from the painter, Andrea Taurella, to Cimino which are for both 'una Cona de lignäme . . . et l'intagli de lignäme' (an altarpiece of wood . . . and for the carving of the wood); D'Addosio 1912–13, pp. 607–8. See further, the payment of 1603 from Belisario Corenzio to Cimino for the 'manifattura e lignäme e ogni altra cosa necessaria d'una Cona di palma 24, con le colone cornice e cimase tutte intagliate de ordine corintio' (the construction and the wood and everything else that is necessary for an altarpiece measuring 24 *palmi* [632 cm], with the columns and the carved upper section all done as in Corinthian columns); D'Addosio 1912–13, pp. 607–8, 51.

17 See the payment of 1619 to Nunzio Maresca for work on an altarpiece by Santafede produced for the convent of Santa Patrizia; published by D'Addosio 1920, p. 230.

18 For examples, see Filangieri 1883–91, vol. IV, pp. 464–5, 1560: contract between Leonardo Castellano and San Gaudioso; and see further Vargas 1988, doc. no. 3, pp. 157–8.

19 See the payment of 1598 from Santafede to the master carpenter Giovan Battista Vigliante, for the frame of an altarpiece that was to include elaborate mouldings and columns (Prota Giurleo 1952, p. 16). There are many other instances of contracts of this kind. See, for example, D'Addosio 1920, p. 382, which publishes a contract of 1600 for a privately commissioned devotional painting. The patron requires the painter, once he has completed the painting, 'da fare la cornice de noce negra larga 4 dita' (to make a frame in black walnut wood, 4 *palmi* wide). The same procedure was followed in a payment of 1593 from a private patron to the painter Andrea Taurella. The payment is for 'la fattura di una Cona de S.ta Caterina vergine con la sua historia' (the creation of an altarpiece with the story of St Catherine). The altarpiece is to measure 12 × 8 *palmi* (3.16 × 2.11 m) and is to be supplied with a gilded and painted, carved frame. All this is to be done within two months at the painter's own expense (D'Addosio 1912–13, p. 515).

20 Ioannou 2001, pp. 34–5.

21 Public fresco contracts commonly specify that the costs are to be incurred by the master painter (for an example, see the contract of 1609 between Corenzio and Santi Severino e Sossio noting that Corenzio promises to pay out of his own expenses the amounts required for the stucco, the gilding, etc., published by Faraglia 1878a, pp. 243–8).

22 Prota Giurleo 1952, p. 15.

23 For a discussion, see Prota Giurleo 1952, pp. 13–24, which provides the information for the presence of Rodriguez, Ardito, Cobergher, Croys, Giusto, Cafaro, Caracciolo, Greco and Rosa, Stanzione, Cavallino, Francesco and Agostino Beltrano, Pietro Bernini, Tommaso and Pacecco de Rosa and Filippo Vitale. For the other painters and for more specific reference to the location of the painters mentioned by Prota Giurleo, see also Ferrante 1898 (Rodriguez); Strazzullo 1986, doc. no. 18, p. 250 (Rodriguez); Stoughton 1978, pp. 208, 210, 212 (Tommaso de Rosa, De Arena and Caracciolo); Stoughton 1980b, pp. 191–2

(Caracciolo); Pacelli 1984b, p. 100 (Vitale); Amabile 1890, p. 58 (Van Swanenburgh); Prota Giurleo 1951a, pp. 20–22, 24 (Tommaso de Rosa, Filippo Vitale and Juan Do); Prota Giurleo 1951b, p. 137 (Passante); Delfino 1984, doc. no. 27, p. 159 (Antonio Cimino and Giacomo Recco); Prota Giurleo 1953, p. 130 (Azzolino); and D. Marshall 1993, p. 13 (Codazzi).

24 Prota Giurleo 1952, p. 15.

25 Stoughton 1978, p. 209.

26 The information on painters' marriages comes from Prota Giurleo 1951a, with the exception of Onofrio de Leone's and Candida Falcone's marriage, for which see Saxl 1939–40, n. 1, p. 77. De Vito (1996–7, p. 46 and pp. 56–7) has also published a full transcription of the *processetto matrimoniale* of 1626 between Juan Do and Grazia de Rosa referred to earlier in part by Prota Giurleo.

27 For Diana de Rosa and Agostino Beltrano's apprenticeship to Gaspare de Popolo, see Delfino 1989, doc. nos. 1 and 3, p. 30.

28 For Gaspare de Popolo's apprenticeship and marriage, see Prota Giurleo 1951a, p. 20.

29 Schütze and Willette 1992, pp. 123–4.

30 Prota Giurleo 1951a, pp. 26–7; and Pacelli 1984c, pp. 90–91, 96.

31 Letter from Giovanni Lanfranco to Ferrante Carlo, 11 November 1639, cited in Bernini 1982, p. 335. Finelli married Flavia Lanfranco in April 1638. The *processetto matrimoniale* was first published in Prota Giurleo 1957, and subsequently in greater detail in Strazzullo 1984, pp. 143–5.

32 De' Dominici 1742–5, vol. III, p. 161. The marriage is mentioned in passing by Rita Pastorelli in Naples 1984, vol. II, p. 193; and by Strazzullo 1984, who cites Lanfranco's letter to Ferrante Carlo.

33 For Lanfranco's *Virgin and Child with Sts Dominic and Januarius* (originally *St Anselm of Canterbury and St Hugh of Lincoln*), Afragola, Chiesa del Rosario, see Schleier in Naples 1984, vol. I, cat. no. 2.137, pp. 334–6. For Vitale's altarpiece of the *Virgin and Child with St Charles Borromeo and Franciscan Friars*, see Pacelli 1990.

34 For Finelli's activities in Naples, see Pastorelli in Naples 1984, vol. II, pp. 192–6; and Strazzullo 1984, with bibliography. For a brief discussion of the letter, see also Bernini 1982, n. 284, p. 150.

35 Prota Giurleo 1951a, pp. 21–2, 25.

36 Stoughton 1978, pp. 209–10.

37 See Prota Giurleo 1952, p. 23, for Sellitto's precise description of the location of his studio (the same information cited on p. 16, and a further description on p. 29).

38 Prota Giurleo 1952, pp. 16 and 29.

39 Prota Giurleo 1952, pp. 16–17.

40 Naples 1977, cat. no. 17, pp. 119–20; and Stoughton 1978, fig. 13, p. 209.

41 Stoughton 1978, p. 209. Documents published previously by Filangieri 1883–91, vol. VI, pp. 30–31; D'Addosio 1912–13, pp. 600–01; D'Addosio 1920, pp. 378–9; and Strazzullo 1954–5, p. 145.

42 ASN, Notai Seicento, notaio Francesco Antonio de Martino alla Sellaria, scheda 174, protocollo 14, 1636, fol. 290v: 'honofrio masturzo de neapolis Indoratore'; protocollo 15, 1637, fol. 425r: 'honofrio Masturzo pittore', unpublished. For Pietro Falcone's professional status as both a gilder and painter, see Saxl 1939–40, n. 3, p. 77. Vincenzo, Pietro and Nicola Falcone are also cited as 'pictores' in a document of 1635 (Faraglia 1905, n. 3, p. 18).

43 Document cited in Faraglia 1905, p. 17: 'excetto li pottini, di cui dovrà dipignere le incarnature'. For a definition and discussion of the *travacca*, see Stoughton 1980a, p. 167; and Pane 1984b.

44 Ioannou 2001, n. 77, p. 43.

45 Prota Giurleo 1952, pp. 19–20. For the documents, see also D'Addosio 1912–13, pp. 54–5; Previtali 1980, n. 4, p. 210; Delfino 1986, pp. 112–13; Vargas 1988, p. 164; M. Nappi 1991, n. 17, p. 21; E. Nappi 1992, pp. 42–3; and Ioannou 2002, p. 140.

46 Azzolino's high reputation is indicated by Giambattista Basile's poems in honour of his paintings and sculptures (for which, see Prota Giurleo 1953, pp. 150–51; F. Ferrante 1979, n. 5, p. 27; Schütze and Willette 1992, p. 37 and n. 83, p. 63).

47 See Rosa Petta in Naples 2009, vol. II, cat. no. 4.43a, p. 151, with bibliography.

48 Strazzullo 1954–5, pp. 77–8.

49 Azzolino's activities as a sculptor are also documented in bank payments of 1641 for a statue of St Francis Xavier (D'Addosio 1912–13, p. 604), and payments of 1638 and 1640 for statues of the baby Jesus (E. Nappi 1983b, p. 73). Prota Giurleo also discusses documents relating to his activities in this regard (Prota Giurleo 1953, pp. 147–8). For Azzolino's activities as a wax modeller, see further F. Ferrante 1979, n. 36, p. 28; Alvar González Palacios in Naples 1984, vol. II, pp. 289–90; and Sáez González 2008, pp. 114–15. Flavia Ferrante nonetheless rejects González Palacio's attribution to Azzolino of two wax sculptures in the Palazzo Pitti, Florence (F. Ferrante 1988, n. 6, p. 140).

50 Delfino 1985, n. 7, p. 91: 'A Lanfranco Massa D. trè et per lui à Giovanni Battista Spinello disse per fattura di 150 paternostelli d'oro che li ha fatto'.

51 De' Dominici 1742–5, vol. II, p. 317: 'non fu pittore di molta stima'.

52 For Onofrio de Leone's *St Januarius Emerging Unscathed from the Furnace*, see Brigitte Daprà in Naples 1997b, cat. no. 22, pp. 144–5, with bibliography.

53 Novelli Radice 1991, p. 203.

54 Missirini 1823, p. 81; Haskell 1980, p. 17.

55 Capaccio 1630, p. 859. For his collection, which was said to have included sculptures, medallions, vases and bronzes, see also De' Dominici 1742–5, vol. II, p. 377; Morisani 1958, p. 110.

56 Prota Giurleo 1952, p. 29; Stoughton 1978, p. 211.

57 Borrelli 1986, p. 80. For the *trabaccari*, see further, Pane 1984a, passim. For Gennaro Monte at San Giacomo degli Spagnoli, see Angela Catello in Naples 1984, vol. II, p. 305.

58 Ceci 1898, n. 1, p. 9.

59 Strazzullo 1961–2.

60 Ceci 1898; Strazzullo 1962, pp. 3–5. See also Ann Percy in Cleveland and Fort Worth 1984, n. 17, p. 29; and Pevsner 1940, n. 2, p. 115. Soon after 1634 the *rotellari* separated from the association. The gilders and playing card decorators separated from the painters a little before 1641, when the existing chapel at Sant'Agostino alla Zecca was demolished (Strazzullo 1962, pp. 4–5). The phrase 'per essere la professione nobilissima' comes from De' Dominici 1742–5, vol. III, p. 139, reporting a statement made by the painter Natalino Troncia, one of the founders of the Congregazione.

61 For this painting, see Stefano Causa in Naples 1991, cat. no. 2.35, pp. 282–3; and Ferdinando Bologna in ibid., pp. 78–80. John T. Spike's review of the exhibition (Spike 1992a, p. 141) further suggests that the head of St Charles Borromeo might have

been painted 'by an entirely different hand [who was perhaps] a specialist in the iconography of this newly canonized saint'.

62 Prota Giurleo 1951a, p. 20.

63 For Vitale's assistance in settling commissions left incomplete by Sellitto's early death, see De Vito 1987, pp. 106–7.

2 ALTARPIECES, FRESCOES AND THE LARGER WORKSHOPS, 1580–1620

1 For Caravaggio at the Pio Monte della Misericordia, see Pacelli 1984c; Bologna 2003; and Bologna in London 2005, pp. 22–4, and ibid., cat. no. 4, pp. 106–7 and 179, with further bibliography.

2 For Santafede's *The Raising of Tabitha*, see Spinosa 1984b, pl. 713.

3 For Caracciolo's *Liberation of St Peter*, see S. Causa 2000, cat. no. A33, pp. 182–3.

4 Letter from the deputies of the Cappella del Tesoro di San Gennaro to Francesco Lemos, conte di Castro, 27 September 1612, cited in Strazzullo 1978, pp. 11–12: 'per la scarsezza che è in questa Città di maestri et artefici sufficienti come bisognano in un opera di tanta qualità'.

5 Haskell 1982, p. 61.

6 Money from appraisals constituted a major source of revenue for professional associations of this kind. In the early 1590s the Accademia di San Luca, Rome, went one step further when it petitioned the papal authorities for it to be eligible to receive a 2 per cent tax on all appraisals costing 25 scudi or more, a stipulation that was finally approved in 1595 (Salvagni 2009, pp. 99–100).

7 Strazzullo 1962, pp. 39–45.

8 Catello 1975, p. 113.

9 Strazzullo 1955–6, pp. 42–3; Strazzullo 1965, p. 240.

10 Strazzullo 1961–2, p. 233.

11 Strazzullo 1961–2, p. 228.

12 ASN, Cappellano Maggiore, Statuti e Congregazioni, vol. B1183, fasciolo 10, Capitoli dell'Arte di Rivenditori, 19 July 1680; see Chapter Five for discussion.

13 D'Addosio 1920, p. 184: 'stimato da due pittori a sua scelta, che non ecceda la somma di D.ti 50 circa'.

14 D'Addosio 1920, p. 393.

15 Vargas 1988, doc. no. 4, p. 158; for discussion, ibid., p. 25.

16 Filangieri 1883–91, vol. VI, pp. 84–5; Vargas 1988, doc. no. 12, p. 161.

17 Vargas 1988, pp. 57–67.

18 For the *soffitto cassettonato* projects of the 1580s onwards, see Vargas 1988, chapters 2 and 5; and Leone de Castris 1991, pp. 58–60.

19 For this commission, see Spike 1999, cat. nos. 137–8, pp. 220–26.

20 Vargas 1988, doc. no. 8, pp. 159–60: 'per tutti li disegni che ha fatto et per le sue fatighe'.

21 For comparison with the tradition of Roman wooden church ceiling construction during the same period, see Anderson 1999. Anderson's research also highlights the collaborative nature of what were comparably large and involved undertakings. The greater proportion of wooden carving featured in the Roman ceilings meant, on the other hand, that these examples tended to be more heavily dominated by the participation of Roman carpenters/woodcarvers who would often work as project heads, overseeing the details of the commissions in question.

22 Vargas 1988, pp. 25, 37–8.

23 Röttgen 2002, pp. 22–30, 59–62, cat nos. 22, 30, 62, 64, pp. 242–5, 290–92, 297–303.

24 Röttgen 2002, pp. 28–9, 60, 522–3.

25 Leone de Castris 1991, pp. 186–9, 193–8.

26 D'Addosio 1912–13, p. 49. For a brief reference to the commission, see further Leone de Castris 1991, p. 324.

27 Faraglia 1878a, p. 244 (pp. 243–8, for the entire contract): 'Item se convene per speciale patto fra dette parti, che tutta detta pittura di qualsivoglia modo, o Istorie, o Figure in dette tre lamie, et mura se habbia a finire a gusto et soddisfattion edi detti R.[i] Padri ut supra, et farse per esso Bellisario di propria mano, et non farsi agiutare da altri, perchè detti Padri intendono, et volendo, et così sono convenuti con detto Bellisario, che detta pittura sia tutta di sua propria mano assolutamente; acciò se dica sempre che detta pittura è fatta assolutamente per mani de esso Bellisario, solo possa esso Bellisario fare fare da altri li frisi, campi, et prospettiva atteso altrimenti essi R.[i] Padri in nome di detto Monastero non haveriano contrattato con detto Bellisario.'

28 M. Nappi 1991, p. 20.

29 Mazzoleni 1964, fig. 70, p. 93.

30 For Corenzio's collaboration with 'Monsù Desiderio', see De' Dominici 1742–5, vol. I, p. 313. For De' Dominici's probable confusing of De Nomé with Barra, see Thuillier 1982, pp. 183–4; Stoughton 1988, n. 14, p. 165; and M. Nappi 1991, pp. 1, 19–20. Didier Barra appears to have arrived in Naples *circa* 1608 (he is first documented in Naples in 1619). He was probably too young to have collaborated with Corenzio in 1609, since he was born *circa* 1590. For a discussion of Barra's career and artistic personality, see Sluys 1961, pp. 14–16; Flavia Petrelli in London 1982, p. 108; Daprà in Naples 1990, pp. 364–5. For documentary references, see M. Nappi 1991, p. 330; and E. Nappi 1992, p. 27.

31 The document for Menens's collaboration with Corenzio at Sant'Andrea delle Dame was first published in part by Pacelli (1984a, n. 33, p. 529). Pacelli does not cite the date of the document, but it is subsequently discussed by Leone de Castris, who also connects it with Corenzio's other work at Sant'Andrea della Dame a few years earlier and who also provides the date of 1594 (Leone de Castris 1988, p. 500; Leone de Castris 1991, p. 324).

32 Pacelli 1984a, p. 179.

33 For the payment to Corenzio at Sant'Andrea delle Dame, see D'Addosio 1912–13, pp. 48–9; and Leone de Castris 1991, p. 324. For the payment to Corenzio at San Martino, see Filangieri 1883–91, vol. V, p. 141; and for discussion Leone de Castris 1991, p. 324.

34 Röttgen 2002, p. 242.

35 Prota Giurleo 1953, p. 144; Leone de Castris 1991, p. 320.

36 Strazzullo 1985, pp. 139–48.

37 Vargas 1988, pp. 159–60.

38 For a parallel case study concerning the high cost involved in gilding Roman late sixteenth-century ecclesiastical wooden ceiling commissions, see Anderson 1999, p. 97, and n. 104, p. 103. Anderson cites the example of the Oratorio dell'Arciconfraternita del Santissimo Crocifisso di San Marcello documentation, which cost 650 scudi to build and 470.93 scudi to gild – in other words, almost as much to decorate as to construct, a finding that Anderson notes as being consistent with other ceilings produced during the

period. The high cost of gilding these large wooden spaces meant that some patrons chose to leave portions of the ceilings in their original state of limewood carving in order, it seems, to economize on costs.

39 Vargas 1988, pp. 186–8.

40 Schütze and Willette 1992, p. 78.

41 Both De' Dominici and Giannone identify Andrea de Leone as Corenzio's pupil on the basis of the frescoes in the Palazzo Reale (De' Dominici 1742–5, vol. III, pp. 80, 144; Giannone 1941, p. 112). Their assertions were later confirmed by the discovery of documents identifying Onofrio de Leone as working with Corenzio on the Palazzo Reale frescoes in 1628 (for discussion, see Pacelli 1984a, p. 163; see further De Vito 1984, p. 10, nn. 25–6, figs 16–17; and Novelli Radice 1988, n. 2, p. 51).

42 Examples include the frescoes of 1651 by Onofrio de Leone in the sacristy of Santi Severino e Sossio (Novelli Radice 1976, p. 162; Spinosa 1984b, no. 244). See further the frescoes dating to the late 1640s in the chapel of St Anthony in Santa Maria la Nova attributed to Andrea de Leone by Novelli Radice (Novelli Radice 1988, p. 41). Andrea de Leone's frescoes in the Galeota chapel in the cathedral are also documented to 1679 (Rizzo 1984, p. 314).

43 De Vito in Delfino 1985, p. 89.

44 Röttgen 2002, pp. 117–18, and cat. no. 115, pp. 353–64.

45 Röttgen 2002, pp. 496–7.

46 The decision to abandon the format of ribs and a lantern and to remodel the dome as a continuous space was not taken until the time of Lanfranco's intervention at the Cappella del Tesoro in 1641, for which see Spear 1982, vol. I, p. 71; vol. II, cat. no. 109.XXV, pp. 299–302.

47 Naples 1997b, p. 50, and fig. 7, p. 28.

48 For Corenzio's negotiations with the monks of Montecassino, see Röttgen 2002, p. 364. For Corenzio's Greek origins, see Ioannou 2000, pp. 36–7.

49 Strazzullo 1954–5, p. 144. Corenzio's frescoes and D'Arpino's cartoons were destroyed during the bombing of Montecassino in 1944.

50 Celano 1692, vol. IV, p. 110; for discussion, see Strazzullo 1985, p. 139.

51 De' Dominici 1742–5, vol. II, p. 263.

52 Strazzullo 1978, pp. 49–50. Additional documents for the commission were published by E. Nappi 2001.

53 Strazzullo 1978, p. 108; E. Nappi 2001, doc. no. 5, p. 94.

54 Strazzullo 1978, p. 112: 'altra persona atta a far detta pittura, che sia valent'huomo et famoso'.

55 Spear 1982, vol. I, pp. 20–21.

56 See Erich Schleier, 'Note sul percorso artistico di Giovanni Lanfranco', in Parma, Naples and Rome 2001, pp. 46–52, with bibliography.

57 D'Addosio 1912–13, p. 256.

3 STANZIONE, RIBERA AND THE YEARS OF CONSOLIDATION, 1620–1656

1 Schütze and Willette 1992, cat. no. A1, p. 190.

2 S. Causa 2000, pp. 89–104, and see further the *regesto* published in ibid., pp. 351–7.

3 Schütze and Willette 1992, pp. 41–57.

4 De' Dominici 1742–5, vol. III, p. 150.

5 For Ribera's knighthood, see Chenault 1976. For Caracciolo's knighthood, see Stoughton 1973, p. 5; and S. Causa 2000, p. 356.

6 For Lanfranco and the Order of Christ, see Parma, Naples and Rome 2001, p. 268.

7 Schütze and Willette 1992, cat. no. A24, pp. 196–7; and Schütze 1993.

8 Novelli Radice 1974b, p. 100; Schütze and Willette 1992, pp. 56–7: 'quivi ha dato lavori veramente eccelenti ... A Napoli havete homini ottimi et esperti in dicta arte de pictura, sed lo Stantione è di molto superiore'.

9 Schütze and Willette 1992, n. 189, p. 68.

10 Schütze and Willette 1992, cat. no. A62, pp. 215–19; cat. no. A73, pp. 225–7; cat. no. A88, pp. 234–5; cat. no. A69, pp. 221–2; cat. no. A90, pp. 236–7.

11 For the fullest discussion of this issue, see Thomas C. Willette, 'La scuola stanzionesca', in Schütze and Willette 1992, pp. 121–51.

12 Schütze and Willette 1992, p. 130.

13 De' Dominici (1742–5, vol. III, pp. 32–6) recounts that Cavallino was apprenticed to Stanzione at the age of ten and that he stayed with Stanzione for eight or so years before attempting to strike out on his own sometime around 1630. Cavallino was nonetheless born eight years earlier than De' Dominici believed. The evidence of Cavallino's first paintings point, moreover, to a probable association with Stanzione in the early to mid-1630s, for example, the overtly Stanzionesque *Meeting of Anna and Joachim at the Golden Gate* (Cleveland and Fort Worth 1984, cat. no. 1, pp. 50–53, and p. 3 for a discussion of Cavallino's probable period spent within the workshop of Stanzione, plus see further Schütze and Willette 1992, p. 128; and, for a more recent critical re-evaluation of Cavallino's early development and relationship with Stanzione, see Spinosa 2013, 'Il giovane Cavallino, tra Falcone, Stanzione e Vaccaro', pp. 35–52).

14 For this issue, with particular reference to the influence of Ribera, see C. Marshall 2004, pp. 41–8.

15 For De Rosa's *Marriage of the Virgin*, see Giuseppe Porzio in Naples 2008a, cat. no. 40, pp. 132–3, with bibliography. For De Rosa's other secure works at the Chiesa della Pietà dei Turchini, see Spinosa 2010, cat. nos. 117a–b, p. 226, with bibliography. For Annella de Rosa, see further De' Dominici 1742–5, vol. III, pp. 98–9, 112–13; Prota Giurleo 1951a, pp. 20, 22–5; Prota Giurleo 1955c, pp. 30–32; Fiorillo 1984; Novelli Radice 1989; Ferdinando Bologna in Naples 1991, pp. 136–8; Schütze and Willette 1992, pp. 122–3; De Vito 1993a; Petrelli 2008.

16 Ruotolo 1973, p. 149: 'di Annella di Massimo copiata dalla Annunciata di Napoli'.

17 Labrot 1992, inv. no. 45, item 41, p. 226: 'Due quadri d'un palmo, et un'e mezzo con due vergini, e cornice dorata mano d'Annella ritoccati da Massimo'.

18 Labrot 1992, inventory of the collection of Francesco Montecorvino, 1698, inv. no. 38, item 48, p. 184; inventory of the collection of Pompilio Gagliano, 1699, inv. no. 41, item 79, p. 199; inventory of the collection of Don Giuseppe de Carafa di Maddaloni, 1648, inv. no. 9, item 57, p. 77; and 1649, inv. no. 12, item 5, p. 84.

19 Labrot 1992, inventory of the collection of Don Giuseppe de Carafa di Maddaloni, 1648, inv. no. 9, item 4, p. 76: 'figurata

di mano di Dianella, retoccata per mano di Massimo'. For Stanzione's *Martyrdom of St Agatha*, see Schütze and Willette 1992, cat. nos. A3 and A5, pp. 190–91.

20 For Beltrano's probable initial training under Corenzio, see Novelli Radice 1984, pp. 144–5.

21 For Beltrano's *Martyrdom of St Januarius* for Pozzuoli, see Novelli Radice 1974a, pp. 67–9, and p. 71, nn. 1–3, pp. 77–8.

22 For Beltrano's *Lot and his Daughters*, see Giuseppe Porzio in Florence 2014, cat. no. 82, pp. 264–5, with bibliography.

23 For Stanzione's *Lot and his Daughters* (Musée des Beaux-Arts, Besançon), together with its copy in the Palazzo Reale, attributed to Beltrano by Thomas Willette, see Schütze and Willette 1992, cat. no. A81, p. 230.

24 Delfino 1986, p. 115, n. 6, and p. 116 for commentary.

25 Labrot 1992, inv. no. 9, item 14, p. 76: 'Decisette quatri de tre palmi e dui [approx. 79 × 53 cm] con cornice alla Romana con l'Jstorie, che stando dentro S. Paolo, fatte per mano di Agostino, e con disegni di Massimo'.

26 Contract dated 27 October 1642, published by Schütze and Willette 1992, pp. 226–7: 'eccetto che per fare li campi e li panni, e sbozzare possa farlo fare da altri'.

27 For Beltrano's *St Paul on the Isle of Malta* (with Heim Gallery, London, 1967 [attributed to Cavallino]; sale Finarte, Rome, 27 May 1980, asta 333, lot 118 [attributed to Gargiulo]), see Cleveland and Fort Worth 1984, cat. no. 143, p. 241 (rejected attribution to Cavallino), and Schütze and Willette 1992, p. 226 (tentative attribution to Stanzione). Schütze and Willette have suggested that this and other *bozzetti* from the series may derive from another series produced by Stanzione himself. This tentative attribution is nonetheless to be rejected on the grounds that the dimensions of this painting match perfectly those listed in the Carafa inventory, and moreover its style seems much more consistent with Beltrano than with Stanzione.

28 Ambrosio 1988, n. 3, pp. 220–21, for the documents, and pp. 217–18 for a discussion of the frescoes.

29 Schütze and Willette 1992, cat. no. A99, pp. 240–41.

30 For the parallel example of some of the more senior pupils of the Carracci Academy in Bologna undertaking independent commissions from time to time, see Feigenbaum 1993, pp. 61–2.

31 Novelli Radice 1984, p. 143, and n. 4, p. 151.

32 Rizzo 1987, doc. no. 1, p. 153, illustrated ibid., fig. 44.

33 D'Addosio 1912–13, p. 608.

34 Delfino 1983, doc. nos. 20 and 21, pp. 110–11. For discussion, see further Ambrosio 1988, p. 217, with bibliography.

35 De Simone is listed as 'quondam' in a payment to Francesco di Maria of 8 August 1658 (De Vito 2003–4b, n. 17, p. 113).

36 Dalbono 1871, p. 114; Rolfs 1910, p. 282; Naples 1954, p. 44; Brejon de Lavergnée in Naples 1984, vol. I, p. 131.

37 Strazzullo 1954–5, p. 35; E. Nappi 1983a, doc. no. 174, p. 318.

38 For De Simone's *Martyrdom of St Potito* and his altarpiece in Santa Maria Antescula, see Novelli Radice 1978, n. 25, p. 28; and Creazzo 1988, n. 3, p. 231.

39 Ruotolo 1983, doc. no. 3, p. 59; and for illustrations, figs 30–36, pp. 65–71.

40 For the importance of this distinction in the work of Stanzione, see Schütze and Willette 1992, p. 80.

41 Pacelli 1986.

42 A. Mazzacane in *DBI*, vol. XXXII, p. 531.

43 For Fanzago's work at the Cacace chapel, see Cantone 1969b; and Pane 1984a.

44 For Bolgi's contribution to the Cacace chapel, see Ruotolo 1977, p. 75; Riccardo Lattuada in Naples 1984, vol. II, p. 160; Lillia Rocco in Naples 1984, vol. II, pp. 161–2.

45 For Stanzione at the Cacace chapel, see Schütze and Willette 1992, cat. no. A87, pp. 233–4.

46 Schütze and Willette 1992, doc. nos. 1–3, p. 234.

47 Letter from Giovan Camillo Cacace to D. Carlo Mauro de Aversa, 4 April 1656, published by Caravita 1869–70, vol. III, pp. 303–4: 'All'Illmo Rmo Padrone. Colmo il P. Abate D. Carlo Mauro de Aversa./Illmo Signor mio Li mesi passati pregai V. P. Rma mi havesse piacere di servirsi del Signor Nicolò Lolec di Simone fiamengo famoso pittore per l'opera si doveva fare nella Chiesa di Monte Casino, et V. P. Rma con la solita sua gentilezza mi disse che questo non stava a Lei ma al successore Abbate, con il quale per fare gratie a me si sarebbe operato acciò detto Signor Nicolò havesse conseguito il suo desiderio: Et perche ho inteso che già sia stato provisto il successore di V. P. Rma per questo con la presente vengo di nuovo a preparla che voglia favorire detto Signor Nicolò che oltre farà cosa di servitio al detto Monasterio, io neli resterò con obligo particolare, et per fine la riverisco augurandole dal Signor Iddio la buona Pasqua con cento altre felicitationi. Napoli li 4 di Aprile 1656. Di V. P. Rma:/Servitor obligatissimo Gio: Camillo.'

48 Schütze and Willette 1992, p. 233.

49 Porzio 2012–13; for Piscopo's work at the Cacace chapel, see Porzio 2012–13, pp. 101–2, 114–15; and Guida 2007–8, pp. 540–41.

50 Spear 1997, pp. 253–74.

51 Schütze and Willette 1992, cat. nos. A87.X and A87.III, p. 234.

52 De' Dominici 1742–5, vol. III, p. 34 (life of Cavallino) and p. 67 (life of Stanzione).

53 See Clifton 1995.

54 Jonathan Brown, 'Jusepe de Ribera as Printmaker', in New York 1992, pp. 168–9, and cat. nos. 77–9, pp. 179–82.

55 See the previously mentioned criticism made by Javier Portús of the lack of any extended discussion of the input of Ribera's workshop in the monograph of 2003 by Nicola Spinosa (Portús Pérez 2005, p. 340).

56 José Milicua, 'From Játiva to Naples', in New York 1992, pp. 9–18; Spinosa 2003, pp. 11–16, 34–9, 82–4.

57 Alfonso E. Pérez Sánchez, 'Ribera and Spain: His Spanish Patrons in Italy: The Influence of his Work on Spanish Artists', in New York 1992, pp. 35–49.

58 These paintings, still at Osuna, are the *St Jerome and the Angel of Judgement*, the *Penitence of St Peter*, *St Sebastian*, the *Martyrdom of St Bartholomew* and the *Crucifixion* (Spinosa 2003, cat. no. A4, p. 250, cat. nos. A35–7, pp. 260–61, and cat. no. A45, p. 264). For their original location, see further Pérez Sánchez in New York 1992, p. 71.

59 Ribera's 'dependence upon specifically Spanish patronage during his mature years in Naples' has also been emphasized by Michael Tomor (Tomor 1993, p. 313).

60 New York 1992, pp. 242 and 248.

61 New York 1992, p. 55.

62 De' Dominici 1742–5, vol. III, p. 5.

63 Prota Giurleo 1953, pp. 107–8.

64 Prota Giurleo 1953, pp. 106–7.

65 E. Nappi 1990, doc. nos. 65–6, p. 185.

66 Naples 1977, doc. no. 10, p. 130; doc. no. 43, p. 135; doc. no. 36, p. 134; doc. no. 47, p. 136.

67 Schütze and Willette 1992, cat. no. D24, pp. 264–5.
68 Pacelli 1990, n. 2, p. 189.
69 Vitale is not mentioned, for example, by Bernardo de' Dominici. For discussion, see further De Vito 1987; Bologna in Naples 1991, pp. 69–120; and S. Causa 1994.
70 Strazzullo 1954–5, p. 213.
71 A number of different proposals for dating the chapel have been advanced. For an overview, see Conversano 2000, cat. no. 14, p. 150; and Annachiara Alabiso, 'Paolo Finoglio a San Martino', in Conversano 2000, pp. 43–52. For the final payment, see E. Nappi 1988, p. 147.
72 This appraisal was originally published by Faraglia (1885–92, p. 659) and then republished with some important corrections by Gabriele Finaldi (in New York 1992, p. 242): 'non essendo riuscito a soddisfazione delli padri'.
73 For discussion, see Michele d'Elia, 'Paolo Finoglio a Conversano: la committenza Acquaviva', and Francesco Tateo, 'La cultura alla corte degli Acquaviva', in Conversano 2000, pp. 53–62.
74 For Ribera's *St Jerome* in Cleveland, see Spinosa 2003, cat. no. A219, p. 316, with bibliography.
75 Examples include Ribera's *Virgin and Child with St Bruno* of 1624 (a painting that seems to have been rejected or at least substituted with another painting by the Carthusians of San Martino), the *Trinitas Terrestris* of 1630 and the *Mystic Marriage of St Catherine* of 1648 (Spinosa 2003, cat. nos. A53, A64 and A293).
76 De' Dominici 1742–5, vol. III, pp. 22–5.
77 For the copious and hotly debated literature on the Master of the Annunciation to the Shepherds, see R. Causa 1972, p. 974; De Vito 1986; Spinosa 1988b; Bologna in Naples 1991, pp. 167–8; Spike 1992a, p. 140; Spike 1992b; Spinosa 1994–5; De Vito 1996–7; Spinosa 2000; De Vito 2003–4a; De Vito 2008; De Vito 2009; Spinosa in Naples 2009, vol. I, pp. 96–111; Spinosa 2010, pp. 37–8, nn. 27–8, pp. 59–60, cat. nos. 286–310, pp. 326–40; De Vito 2012–13b.
78 Prota Giurleo 1951b.
79 The most direct discussions of the issues created by this timeline remain Spike 1992b, passim; Prohaska, in Prague 1995, pp. 18–19; and Spinosa 1994–5, pp. 248–50.
80 Pietro Andrea Andreini, 'Nota de' Pittori, Scultori, et Architetti, che dall'anno 1640 sino al presente giorno hanno operato lodevolmente nella città e regno di Napoli', MS, 1675, cited in Ceci 1899, p. 165: 'Bartolomeo Passante imparò ed imitò molto da Giuseppe de Ribera suo maestro, anzi che le copie fatte de sua mano quasi non si distinguono dalli originali del detto Giuseppe.' The identity of the author of this 'nota' and the date of 1675 were established by Renato Ruotolo in 1982 (Ruotolo 1982, p. 10).
81 Celano 1692, vol. V, p. 1412.
82 De Vito 2000b, pp. 95–8.
83 For the literature on Hendrick van Somer, see Naples 1991, pp. 164–7, and cat. nos. 2.72–8, pp. 309–13; Bologna 1994–5, pp. 12–17; and Spinosa 1995.
84 For a survey, see the *regesto documentario* compiled by Renato Ruotolo and published in Naples, Vienna and Los Angeles 2001, pp. 479–94.
85 E. Nappi 1983b, p. 76.
86 Prota Giurleo 1951a, pp. 24–5. Do's marriage contract and deposition were subsequently transcribed and published in more complete form in De Vito 1996–7, pp. 46 and 56–7. For Do's other documents, see E. Nappi 1983b, p. 75; and E. Nappi 1992, pp. 65–6.
87 Bonazzi 1888, p. 126. For the painting, see Bologna in Naples 1991, cat. no. 2.76, p. 312.
88 For Ricca's *Elijah*, see Pérez Sánchez and Spinosa 1978, cat. no. 430a, p. 141; L. Galante 1992, pp. 40–44; and Bologna 1994–5, p. 12. For Ribera's *Elijah*, see Spinosa 2003, cat. no. A191, p. 308, with bibliography.
89 Faraglia 1885–92, p. 670.
90 Labrot 1992, inv. no. 19, pp. 113–15.
91 For Ribera's *Venus and Adonis*, see Spinosa 2003, cat. no. A165, p. 301, with bibliography. For Van Somer's *Venus and Adonis* (formerly Sotheby's, New York, sale, 24 March 1983, lot 64, attributed to Antonio de Bellis), see Teodoro Fittipaldi in Genoa and Salerno 2003, p. 140. The painting was formerly attributed to Antonio de Bellis by Nicola Spinosa (in Naples 1984, vol. I, p. 127), but then reattributed to Van Somer by the same author (Spinosa 1995, p. 229).
92 R. Causa 1972, p. 930: 'assolutamente personale ed inconfondibile, tutto spirito, vigore, intima coerenza di struttura'.
93 Originally published by E. Nappi 1990, doc. no. 63, p. 185: 'Giuseppe ... non havendolo possuto finire'.
94 For Ribera's *Apollo and Marsyas*, see Spinosa 2003, cat. no. A163, p. 300, with bibliography. For Giovanni d'Avalos and his probable commissioning of Ribera's *Apollo and Marsyas*, see Naples 1994b, p. 24.
95 For further discussion, see C. Marshall 2000, pp. 18–19.
96 For Ribera's work at the Certosa di San Martino, see Nicola Spinosa, 'Ribera a San Martino', in Naples 1992, pp. 290–313; and Spinosa, 'I profeti di Ribera', in Spinosa and Pagano 1992, particularly pp. 7–18.
97 Naples 1992, cat. nos. 114a–b, pp. 308 and 312–13.
98 Strazzullo 1979, pp. 342–4; and Pacelli 1979.
99 For the probable collaborative status of some of this series – most notably *Noah* – see Spinosa in Naples 1992, p. 300.
100 See particularly the two versions of the *Adoration of the Shepherds* in the Escorial, formerly attributed to Ribera and Juan Do (e.g., Spinosa 1984b, nos. 308–9), but now argued as entirely autograph by the same author (Pérez Sánchez in New York 1992, cat. no. 58, pp. 144–5; and Spinosa 2003, cat. nos. A233–A234, p. 321).
101 For this issue, see Spear 1997, pp. 253–74; and see further Spear 2004.
102 Nicola Spinosa, 'Ribera and Neapolitan Painting', in New York 1992, n. 19, p. 33.
103 For the events of 1647–8, with particular reference to their implications for Neapolitan Baroque painting, see C. Marshall 1998.
104 The paintings were delivered to San Martino on 15 February 1651.
105 These reported comments occur in a contemporary account drawn up by the Carthusians to prepare their case against the claims made by Ribera's heirs that he was owed money for the *Communion of the Apostles* as well as for the two half-lengths. The document was originally published by Faraglia 1885–92, p. 671, and then republished by Gabriele Finaldi, 'Documentary Appendix: The Life and Work of Jusepe de Ribera', in New York 1992, pp. 251–2: 'per far vedere al Mondo ch'era vivo e non morto, e ciò faceva con gusto grande per ricuperare la sua estinta fama'.

106 Jusepe de Ribera, letter to Andrea Cancelliere, 23 June 1651, cited in Faraglia 1885–92, p. 674: 'di molto gusto misaria pigliarmi tutta la summa insieme'.

107 This is made clear by an unpublished document of *circa* 1651–5 kept among the documents relating to payments for work at San Martino (ASN, Monasteri soppressi, vol. 2142, fols 47–8). The document is an itemized listing of the series of small instalment payments made to Ribera by the Carthusians over the course of 1651 while he was working on the *Last Communion*. It forms part of the claims drawn up against the Carthusians that was prepared during the early 1650s by Ribera's heirs (for discussion of which, see Finaldi in New York 1992, pp. 251–5). It reads as follows:

[fol. 48v] Conti di Gioseppe Rivera	
[fol. 47r] A 15 de febraro q.[do] si portonno le mezze figure ducati cento sisanta in Conto delle opere ______	D. 160
A 18 marzo d.[ti] ______	D. 40
A 3 de Aprile d.[ti] ______	D. 40
A 15 de Aprile per mano di espataro d.[ti] ______	D. 60
A 19 di maggio che si ando a S. Martino d.[ti] ______	D. 50
A 6 di Giugno vennero li padri procuratori d.[ti] ______	D. 50
A 22 di Giugno venne frà Bona Ventura il bolognese d.[ti] ______	D. 50
A 4 de Luglio alla Bona Anima che sa[...]i a S. martino d.[ti] __	D 100
A 29 de Luglio d.[ti] ______	D. 50
[fol. 47v] A 21 de Agosto d.[ti] ______	D. 50
A [blank] de Settembre ______	D. 100
	750

questi e quanto si tiene Riceuta in Conto delle opere che la bona anima faceva per San Martino e non in altra Verita che questo le mezze figure non sono e state pagate mai [unpublished].

108 Faraglia 1885–92, pp. 675–8; Finaldi in New York 1992, pp. 253–5.

4 ANIELLO FALCONE AND THE RISE OF NEAPOLITAN CABINET PAINTING

1 ASN, Notai del Seicento, Notaio Francesco de Martino, scheda 174, protocollo 14, 1636, fol. 22r–v. For discussion, see Saxl 1939–40, n. 3, p. 86; De Vito 1982, pp. 11–12.

2 For the payment of 1628 of 12 *giuli* a month for the life model of the Accademia di San Luca, see ASN, TNC, uff. 15, 1628, pt III, vol. 117, fol. 292r–v, transcribed at http://www.nga.gov/casva/accademia/html/eng/asrtncuff1516280829.shtm (accessed 15 November 2014). For a discussion, see Roccasecca 2009, p. 134.

3 For Celano's reference to Sellitto's model, also discussed by De' Dominici, see Celano 1692, III, p. 867; and De' Dominici 1742–5, vol. I, p. 249. For the painting itself – including its subsequent deattribution from Sellitto's oeuvre – see Naples 1977, cat. no. 15, pp. 115–18, with bibliography.

4 For Gentileschi's complaints about the high cost of models, see Garrard 1989, pp. 393, 397.

5 De' Dominici 1742–5, vol. III, pp. 45–6. For commentary, see Schütze and Willette 1992, n. 7, p. 176; and Andrea Zezza in De' Dominici 2003–8, vol. III, n. 4, p. 84.

6 For Poussin's attendance at Domenichino's life-drawing academy, see Blunt 1967, p. 57. For Domenichino's academy, see further Spear 1982, vol. I, pp. 105 and 107.

7 For the unlikelihood that Domenichino conducted an open studio in Naples, see Spear 1982, vol. I, p. 109. Percy's suggestion (in Cleveland and Fort Worth 1984, p. 4) that Cavallino may have studied life drawing under Domenichino should thus be discounted.

8 For these drawings, see Madrid 1984, pp. 52–66. For a discussion of the Del Carpio collection, including other drawings from the collection now dispersed in various private and public collections, see Prosperi Valenti Rodinò 2008; Farina 2010a, pp. 190–92. For the Falcone drawings more specifically, see Farina 2010a, pp. 187–90.

9 De' Dominici 1742–5, vol. III, pp. 73–4 (for the Accademia del Nudo), and p. 192 (landscape sketching sessions).

10 For Andrea de Leone's two nude drawings in the Museo e Gallerie Nazionali di Capodimonte, Naples, see Ascione in Gaeta 1985, cat. nos. 25–6, pp. 76–9; and Muzii Cavallo in Naples 1987, cat. no. 63, n.p., with bibliography. Of these, see, for example, Vitzthum in Naples 1966, p. 17, who notes that the drawings confirm De' Dominici's account of De Leone's imitation of the style of Falcone's nude drawings.

11 For an example of Gargiulo's Falconesque study after the nude, see the unpublished drawing that was formerly on the London art market: attributed to Domenico Gargiulo, *A Kneeling Male Nude*, 342 × 275 mm; red chalk over pencil on buff-coloured paper; sale Phillips, London, 5 December 1988, lot 41 (Gargiulo); inscribed upper left: 'per fare un' mendico, ovvero il paralitico santato da Giesú'; provenance: Armando Neerman, London, 1972 (exhibited: Armando Neerman, *Italian Old Master Drawings from the 16th to the 18th Century*, exh. cat., London, 1972, no. 33 [Gargiulo]; Ambron collection, Alexandria).

12 For Rosa's early nude drawings, see Mahoney 1977, vol. I, pp. 45–7, and cat. nos. 2.1–8, pp. 139–44; and Wallace 1979, pp. 3–4, both emphasizing Rosa's indebtedness to Falcone's nude drawings.

13 For Porpora and Falcone, see De' Dominici 1742–5, vol. III, p. 80; and for more recent commentary, see Viviana Farina in De' Dominici 2003–8, vol. III/1, n. 39, p. 145. For discussion of Porpora's development and artistic relationship to Falcone's paintings, see R. Causa 1951, pp. 31–3.

14 For Coppola and Falcone, see Maria Rosaria Nappi in Naples 1984, vol. I, p. 123; Creazzo in Naples 2009, vol. I, p. 220; and Spinosa 2010, p. 203. For Coppola's imitation of Falcone's battle pieces more specifically, see De' Dominici 1742–5, vol. III, p. 80; Creazzo in London 1982, p. 270; Nappi in Naples 1984, vol. I, p. 123; Consigli Valenti 1986, p. 350; and Sestieri 1999, pp. 296–307.

15 The documentary basis for Giuseppe Trombatore's association with Falcone is that he acted as one of the witnesses to the further negotiations concerning Orsola Vitale's dowry in 1646 (Pacelli 1984b, pp. 96–8). Trombatore's close dependence on Falcone's model is evident in his many battle paintings, for which see Consigli Valenti 1986, p. 429.

16 For De Simone and Falcone, see Creazzo 1988, pp. 226–8.

17 The documentary basis for Luca Forte's association with Falcone is that he acted as one of the witnesses to the declaration of Falcone's marriage to Orsola Vitale on 2 May 1639 (Prota Giurleo 1951a, p. 26; Pacelli 1984b, pp. 90–91, 96).

18 For Codazzi and Falcone, see De' Dominici 1742–5, vol. III, pp. 193–4 (where, however, Codazzi is identified not as a strict pupil but rather as a member of the so-called Compagnia della Morte, an association subsequently proved to have been an invention; for which see further D. Marshall 1993, p. 14, with bibliography).

19 For Piscopo and Falcone, see Willette in Schütze and Willette 1992, pp. 122–3; and Porzio 2012–13, pp. 102–3.

20 For Masturzo and Falcone, see R. Causa 1972, n. 94, p. 949.

21 The documentation for this was first published in Cleveland and Fort Worth 1984, n. 2, pp. 28–9. For discussion of Cavallino's artistic links with Falcone, see further Cleveland and Fort Worth 1984, pp. 4, 10–11 and 19, which concludes with the comment that Cavallino's few surviving preparatory drawings manifest a 'great emphasis on contours and on working up shadowed areas with shading or cross-hatching in a manner similar to the styles of drawing of Aniello Falcone and Andrea de Leone'. See further Muzii Cavallo in Naples 1987, cat. no. 69, n.p., noting the 'morbido sfumato affine al ductus grafico falconiano' of Cavallino's red chalk *Study of a Male Nude* (Museo e Gallerie Nazionali di Capodimonte, Naples).

22 Prota Giurleo 1951a, p. 26.

23 For Pietro Falcone, see Saxl 1939–40, n. 1, p. 77. For Nicola and Diego, see Prota Giurleo 1951a, p. 26.

24 Honofrio Masturzo is identified as a painter in the life-drawing contract of 1636, but as a gilder in an apprenticeship document from the same year (ASN, Notai del Seicento, Notaio Francesco de Martino, scheda 174, protocollo 14, 1636, fols 290v–291r).

25 For the documentation for the chapel, see Novelli Radice 1974b, n. 11, p. 102. For further discussion, see Spinosa 2010, cat. nos. 157a–b, pp. 250–51, with additional bibliography.

26 For Onofrio de Leone's contribution to Falcone's frescoes at the Gesù Nuovo, see E. Nappi 1984, p. 326.

27 For Giordano's description of Falcone as 'l'Oracolo delle battaglie', see De' Dominici 1742–5, vol. III, p. 80.

28 For the tradition of the battle painting, see Consigli Valenti 1986; and Sestieri 1999. For Van de Velde and the development of the Northern battle piece more specifically, see Keyes 1984, pp. 103–15.

29 For Falcone's *Sack of a City* (provenance: sale Christie's, New York, 6 June 1984, lot 156), see Alabiso 1988, fig. 5 and pp. 192–4.

30 For De Leone's *St James at the Battle of Clavijo* (sale Finarte, Milan, 25 November 1976, lot 26), see Bréjon de Lavergnée 1984, cat. no. 24, fig. 642; Sestieri 1999, no. 25, p. 320.

31 For De Leone's *Tobit Burying the Dead*, see Brejon de Lavergnée in Naples 2009, vol. I, cat. no. 1.83, pp. 178–9, with bibliography.

32 Leone de Castris 1989–90, p. 122.

33 E. Nappi 1992, p. 56.

34 D'Addosio 1912–13, p. 581: 'due Quatri che li deve fare della Prospettiva di Napoli et di tutto il Golfo'.

35 E. Nappi 1975, doc. no. 35, p. 123.

36 For Jacopo Coppola, Zoabio, Iumiello and 'Bartolomeo fiamengo', see E. Nappi 1983c, p. 43. For an additional payment to Coppola (identified as 'Iacovo Coppo fiamengo'), see D'Addosio 1920, p. 385. For Bartolomeo Ghesenz, see Delfino 1985, doc. nos. 27–8, pp. 100–01. For Cornelio Ghesenz, see Delfino 1984, doc. no. 2, p. 158, which includes the quote 'quadri de caccia di fiandra'.

37 Longhi 1950, p. 33. See further Longhi in Milan 1951, p. 55.

38 For Gargiulo's early career and development within Falcone's ambience, see Sestieri and Daprà 1994, pp. 12–18; and Naples 2002, pp. 33–9. For Gargiulo's *Inn Keeper*, see Sestieri and Daprà 1994, cat. no. 2, p. 64, with bibliography.

39 For Rosa's drawings, see Mahoney 1977, cat. nos. 1.1 and 1.2, vol. I, pp. 132–7. For Gargiulo's drawings, see Sestieri and Daprà 1994, cat. nos. D37, D52–4, D58, with bibliography. For Falcone's drawings, see Madrid 1984, cat. nos. 26–7, pp. 54–5. Mahoney (1977, vol. I, p. 135) notes in relation to Rosa's drawings that they are so reliant on Falcone's model 'that one can say with certainty that Rosa was more than casually exposed to Falcone's techniques; that the young artist was, in fact, Falcone's student'.

40 For Gargiulo's *Market in the Piazza del Mercato*, see Naples 2002, cat. no. 55, pp. 134–5, with bibliography.

41 For Gargiulo's *Revolt of Masaniello*, see Naples 2002, cat. no. 52, pp. 129–30, with bibliography. For these paintings more generally, see C. Marshall 1998.

42 For this tradition, with an emphasis also on the fundamental importance of Gargiulo for subsequent Neapolitan landscape painting more generally, see Ortolani 1970. For Gargiulo's *Landscape with Abraham Conducting Isaac to be Sacrificed*, see Naples 2002, cat. no. 27, p. 97, with bibliography.

43 D. Marshall 1993, p. 13.

44 For Codazzi's and Gargiulo's *Barrel-vaulted Doric Palace Portico* of 1641, see D. Marshall 1993, cat. no. VC 23, pp. 99–100, with bibliography.

45 For Ascanio Luciano, see D. Marshall 1988. For the Neapolitan legacy of Codazzi's and Gargiulo's work more generally, see D. Marshall 1993, pp. 53–4.

46 For the much-discussed association of early Neapolitan still-life practitioners with Falcone and his associates (most notably Luca Forte and Paolo Porpora), see Bottari 1966; R. Causa 1972, n. 93, pp. 978–9; De Vito 1982, pp. 8–10; Spinosa 1989, p. 860; De Vito 2000a, pp. 32–5 (where, however, the author attributes the figures in a painting by Luca Forte to Falcone, but for which the attribution has been reassigned more recently to Domenico Gargiulo – for which see Angela Tecce in Naples 2009, vol. I, cat. no. 1.207, p. 360). Luigi Salerno (1984, p. 105) goes so far as to assert that Falcone 'can be credited with devising the battle scene "without a hero" but also scenes of everyday life and, in all likelihood, the still life as well', a comment that probably overstates Falcone's significance in this regard, but that nonetheless correctly registers the importance of his ambience for the early development of the genre.

47 For Coppola's *Martyrdom of St Januarius*, see Maria Rosaria Nappi in Naples 1984, vol. I, cat. no. 2.45, p. 232; Damian in Paris 2007b, pp. 42–5; and Spinosa 2010, no. 80, pp. 202–4.

48 For background on Capecelatro, see Labrot 1992, p. 101.

49 For these three paintings, see Labrot 1992, inv. no. 19, Ettore Capecelatro, marchese di Torella, items 24, 25 and 42, p. 114.

50 For Pacecco de Rosa's *Finding of Moses*, see Pacelli 2008, cat. no. 74, p. 339, with bibliography.

51 Although no paintings of this type are known by Gargiulo and Codazzi, the inventory reference renders likely the possibility that the two artists might have collaborated on a painting of this kind following the model of the version of the *Revolt of Masaniello* painted in Rome by Codazzi with figures added by the Roman Bamboccianti painter Michelangelo Cerquozzi, for which see further C. Marshall 1998, pp. 478–9, 484–5.

52 For the prices paid for Don Antonio Ruffo's battle pieces by Falcone and De Leone, see Ruffo 1916, p. 32.

53 Labrot 1992, inv. no. 19, Ettore Capecelatro, marchese di Torrella, item 9, p. 113, and item 30, p. 114. For Gargiulo's *Lot Fleeing with his Daughters from Sodom and Gomorrah*, see Sestieri and Daprà 1994, cat. no. 177, pp. 328–9.

54 Labrot 1992, inv. no. 19, Ettore Capecelatro, marchese di Torrella, item 77, p. 115: 'sopra pietra di Genua di Pietro pesce di noce con cornice d'oro'.

55 For the foundation of the Congregazione dei Pittori in 1664 and the inauguration of the Accademia del Nudo in 1665, see De' Dominici 1742–5, vol. III, pp. 139 and 308; Ceci 1898; Strazzullo 1962, pp. 5–8.

56 De' Dominici 1742–5, vol. III, p. 308.

57 For Gargiulo's frescoes and probable early training under Corenzio, see De Vito in Delfino 1985, p. 89; D. Marshall 1993, n. 39, p. 13. De Leone's training as a frescoist under Corenzio was originally posited by De Dominici (1742–5, vol. III, p. 80). Onofrio de Leone is documented working under Corenzio on the Palazzo Reale frescoes in 1628, and this led Bréjon de Lavergnée, De Vito and Pacelli to concur with De' Dominici in attributing some of the Palazzo Reale frescoes to Andrea and Onofrio de Leone (Bréjon de Lavergnée in Paris 1983, p. 166; De Vito 1984, p. 10; Pacelli 1984a, p. 163). This hypothesis was thereafter accepted by Pasculli Ferrara and Novelli Radice (Pasculli Ferrara 1986, p. 205; and Novelli Radice 1988, p. 41, and n. 2, p. 51).

5 ART DEALING AT THE LOWER LEVELS OF THE MARKET

1 For Van Swanenburgh's *Crossing of the River Styx* and other *Hell* scenes, see Judson 1983.

2 Van Swanenburgh's importance as a model for Salvator Rosa's scenes of witches is emphasized by Helen Langdon in London and Fort Worth 2010, p. 165. For this tradition in Renaissance and Baroque art more generally, see Macioce et al. 2004.

3 Amabile 1890, pp. 17–23, 58–65. The quotations cited occur on pp. 58, 60 and 62: 'l'hò cavato fuori allo muro della mia poteca ... di dare piacere alle gente che lo vedessero'; 'per esserno cosa contra alla Fede cattolica ... perche moltitudine di gente lo stavano mirando con attentione'; 'molti padri spirituali sono venuti alla poteca mia et hanno visto detto quatro et non me hanno detto cosa alcuna'.

4 For Van Swanenburgh's transfer to Leiden (1615) and subsequent teaching of Rembrandt, see Golahny 2003, pp. 60–64.

5 De Simone 1976, p. 87 and tav. 31, pp. 136–7.

6 De Simone 1976, pp. 85–6.

7 Prota Giurleo 1952, p. 29, cites the example of the workshop of Sebastiano Sellitto costing 1,610 ducats in 1619; and De Simone 1976, p. 78, notes the example of a suite of four workshops with rooms above costing 10,000 ducats in 1616.

8 Borrelli 1988, pp. 38–9; Stoughton 1978, p. 210.

9 F. Baldinucci 1845–7, vol. II, pp. 240–41.

10 E. F. Gersaint, 'Abrége de la vie d'Antoine Watteau', in *Catalogue raisonné des diverses curiosités du cabinet de feu M. Quentin de Lorangère* (Paris, 1744), p. 173; trans. and cited in Crow 1985, p. 45.

11 E. Nappi 1990, doc. nos. 65–6, p. 185.

12 E. Nappi 1983b, p. 76.

13 Peter Cherry, 'Seventeenth-century Spanish Taste', in Burke and Cherry 1997, vol. I, pp. 78–85. For a discussion of the D'Aquino contract and its relationship to the Spanish trade in *pinturas ordinarias*, see further Labrot 2010, pp. 86–7.

14 E. Nappi 1992, p. 50.

15 Bertolotti 1876–8, vol. II, p. 30.

16 In the 1630s the copper for Domenichino's panels in the Cappella del Tesoro di San Gennaro was priced at 0.4 ducats per *libbra* (equivalent to about 321 grams). The copper used as the support for Domenichino's smaller panels for the Tesoro (278 × 151 cm) cost approximately 240 ducats (Spear 1982, vol. I, p. 297).

17 G. Mancini 1956–7, vol. I, p. 249. For discussion, see Haskell 1980, p. 120.

18 De' Dominici 1742–5, vol. III, p. 72. The reference to Di Martino as a 'negoziante di quadri' occurs on pp. 75–6.

19 De' Dominici 1742–5, vol. III, p. 72.

20 For Falcone's *Battle Scene* (Sotheby's London, 5 November 1986, lot 183; resold Sotheby's London, 18 February 1987, lot 25), see Alabiso in Naples 2009, vol. I, cat. no. 1.73, p. 164; and Spinosa 2010, no. 150, p. 246, with bibliography.

21 Falcone's baptism certificate was published by Prota Giurleo 1951a, p. 26.

22 Pickrell 1984, p. 312; the translation is Pickrell's.

23 Borrelli 1991, p. 7, and n. 1, p. 14. Majetti includes the 'Corporazione di rivenditori di quadri usati e vecchi' in his list of early Neapolitan guilds and associations (Majetti 1885, p. 87). The church of San Tommaso d'Aquino was deconsecrated in the late eighteenth century and eventually demolished in the 1930s (G. Galante 1985, p. 219; and Petrelli in G. Galante 1985, pp. 229–30).

24 ASN, Cappellano Maggiore, Statuti e Congregazioni, vol. B1183, fasciolo 1.

25 ASN, Cappellano Maggiore, Statuti e Congregazioni, vol. B1183, fasciolo 10. Capitoli dell'Arte di Rivenditori, statute XXI, fol. 6r–v, statute 21: 'nella recognitione della qualità del valore e dell'altre circostanze di tutte e singole robbe dell'istessa professione et Arte, come sono, Trabacche, matarazzi, seggie, Scrittorij, boffette, vetriate, quadri, pannamenti, così di lana, come di tela, drappi anco di seta, et finalmente ogn'altra sorte di mobili usati di qualsivoglia nome'. The passage cited later in the text occurs at statute 25. The statutes have been cited and summarized briefly by Borrelli 1991, n. 1, pp. 14–15.

26 For a discussion of the *rivenditori*'s broader trade in second-hand goods as well as in paintings in other cities, see Allerston 2003.

27 For the *rivenditori* and the development of a more exclusive market for Neapolitan Baroque painting, see further C. Marshall 2006.

28 Delfino 1993, doc. nos. 11–13, pp. 27–8.

29 De' Dominici 1742–5, vol. III, p. 35. For Cavallino's *Payment of the Tribute Money*, see Spinosa 2013, cat. no. 8, p. 276, with bibliography.
30 De' Dominici 1742–5, vol. III, pp. 35–6.
31 Haskell 1982, p. 64; Ann Percy in Cleveland and Fort Worth 1984, p. 21, although she concludes that 'the account of his spending his entire career in the service of second-hand dealers seems romanticized'.
32 Prota Giurleo 1953, pp. 44–5.
33 See Labrot 1992, inv. no. 56, Francesco de Palma, duca di Sant'Elia, item 5, p. 284: 'Due quadri di palmi 4 e 5 di Paese e marina, mano di Domenico Oliva, discepolo di Micco Spataro con cornici della stessa maniera [mischie]'. For De' Dominici's discussion of Oliva in reference to his status as a follower of Gargiulo (where he is nonetheless identified as Ignazio Oliva), see De' Dominici 1742–5, vol. III, p. 211.
34 E. Nappi 1992, p. 51. A certain Ignazio Oliva is also documented in payments of 1651, 1653, 1657 and 1659 (E. Nappi 1983c, p. 51; Delfino 1985, p. 102; E. Nappi 2005, pp. 81–2). Some of these payments are for paintings produced by Oliva himself, but others are for the restoration of paintings, as well as at least one payment for a painting by another artist (E. Nappi 2005, p. 82). It is unclear whether there were two – presumably related – artists or else the same artist identified variously in the documents by his first and middle names.
35 For the payment of 1679 to De Leone for 'due quadretti', see Rizzo 1984, p. 314. For the payment of 1685 of 7 ducats for a 'battagliola', see E. Nappi 1992, p. 51. For De Leone's *Battle Scene*, see Finarte, Rome, sale 646, 10 May 1988, lot 177 (sold as one of a pair of scenes of the same subject), unpublished.
36 Passeri 1772, p. 386. Also followed by Pascoli (1730–36, vol. I, p. 64). For discussion, see further Mahoney 1977, vol. I, pp. 48–9; Farina 2010b, pp. 26–7; Langdon in London and Fort Worth 2010, p. 14.
37 For Rosa's *Coastal Landscape*, see Spinosa 2010, cat. no. 385, pp. 381–2, with bibliography.
38 De' Dominici 1742–5, vol. III, p. 217.
39 De' Dominici 1742–5, vol. III, p. 217. For a more recent commentary and discussion of previous attempts to identify one of the paintings mentioned by Passeri, see Farina 2010b, pp. 26–7, 155–6, with bibliography.
40 The clearest information of Rosa's early circumstances is to be found in the marriage document between Francesco Fracanzano and Giovanna de Rosa published by Salazar (Salazar 1903, particularly p. 122). Salazar notes that this document corroborates De' Dominici's account of Rosa's early period, observing, for instance, that De' Dominici 'esattamente ricorda' the location of Greco's workshop where Rosa lived. For the death of Rosa's father and Rosa's estrangement from his mother, see Prota Giurleo 1929, pp. 11–13. This and other documents show that Rosa's father died young in 1621 (rather earlier than De' Dominici asserts), leaving the family in difficult circumstances; that Rosa was abandoned by his mother four years later; that he was educated in a charity school, from which he withdrew in 1631; that he lived, together with his brother and sister, with his uncle, Domenico Antonio Greco, in Naples in the later 1620s; and that he already identified himself as a painter in 1632, when, at the age of seventeen, he witnessed the marriage of his sister Giovanna de Rosa to Francesco Fracanzano. For further discussion, see Farina 2010b, pp. 11–18.
41 Delfino 1984, p. 158.
42 For Croys's payment of 1613, see E. Nappi 1975, doc. no. 35, p. 123. For Coppola's payment of 1610, see E. Nappi 1983c, p. 43.
43 E. Nappi 1992, p. 50.
44 For Cornelio Brusco's *Destruction of Troy* (formerly Alessandro Baratti collection, Naples), see M. Nappi 1986, p. 35, and figs 18–20.
45 E. Nappi 1992, p. 64.
46 For a comparison with Rome, see Richard E. Spear, 'Rome: Setting the Stage', in Spear and Sohm 2010, pp. 37–9.
47 For another attempt to calculate the relationship between annual earnings and cost of living expenses, see Renata Ago, 'Five Industrious Cities', in Spear and Sohm 2010, p. 259. Ago arrives at a directly comparable sum of 140 scudi annual expense requirements for reasonably successful merchants/painters. It should be recognized that these amounts are still relatively modest and would not be sufficient for those artists and merchants wishing to pursue a more overtly ostentatious lifestyle. Passeri, for example, commented approvingly that the Roman Bamboccianti painter Michelangelo Cerquozzi left his nephew a legacy that amounted to an annual income of 300 scudi, an amount that enabled one to live 'comfortably and in a dignified manner' in Rome in the 1660s (Passeri 1934, p. 290; for discussion, see Spear in Spear and Sohm 2010, p. 95, and n. 539, p. 315).
48 The price fluctuated at certain periods – particularly during the Revolt of Masaniello in 1647–8. See Faraglia 1878b, p. 174. The price cited here is arrived at by dividing by forty the prices paid for a *tomolo* of wheat (or 40 kg in weight).
49 Calabria 1991, n. 47, p. 17.
50 Faraglia 1878b, pp. 255–6, provides cumulative prices from 1550 to 1649.
51 This and the following information concerning food prices are taken from Faraglia 1878b, pp. 264–5.
52 For Recco's *Copper Vessels with Fish and Squid*, see Paris 2007a, cat. no. 23, pp. 90–91. For Giordano's and Recco's *Riches of the Sea with Neptune and Two Sea Nymphs*, see Naples 1997a, cat. no. 1.10, pp. 162–4.
53 E. Nappi 1990, doc. no. 35, p. 185.
54 The reference to Ribera's *alfiere* occurs in De' Dominici (1742–5, vol. III, p. 18), who notes that he was paid in 'cinquine' – an old type of money worth 1.25 *carlini*.
55 E. Nappi 1990.
56 For Ribera's 'casa palaziata', see Prota Giurleo 1953, p. 101. Prota Giurleo transcribed part of the purchase agreement only, minus the price, and subsequent researchers have not been able to trace his original notarial source (Finaldi in New York 1992, p. 246). The sum of 3,100 ducats, however, can be determined from another published document that cites the annual 1 per cent tax rate of 31 ducats that Ribera was required to pay on the property (E. Nappi 1990, doc. no. 46, p. 183). For Ribera charging 100 ducats rent on this property, see E. Nappi 1990, doc. no. 44, p. 183.
57 The marriage contract between Margarita Ribera and Giovanni Sersale is published in New York 1992, pp. 247–8.
58 Delfino 1987; republished in full in New York 1992, pp. 232–4.
59 For Corenzio's dowry, see D'Addosio 1912–13, p. 53. For a comparable dowry of this level, see E. Nappi 1996–7, doc. no. 139, p. 176.

60 Lofano 2014, p. 802.
61 ASN, Cappellano Maggiore, Statuti e Congregazioni, vol. B1183, fasciolo 10. Capitoli dell'Arte di Rivenditori, statute XXI, fol. 6r–v, statute 9.
62 Caracciolo, 1959, p. 32.
63 Spinosa in Naples 1992, n. 20, p. 55, where the illness is hypothetically diagnosed as arterial hypertension with cerebral reflexions.
64 Jusepe de Ribera to Andrea Cancelliere, 23 June 1651, cited in Faraglia 1885–92, pp. 673–4.
65 Faraglia 1885–92, pp. 673–4; and Finaldi in New York 1992, 'Documentary Appendix', p. 251, for discussion.
66 De' Dominici 1742–5, vol. III, p. 82.
67 De' Dominici 1742–5, vol. III, p. 85: 'si videro scarseggiari di commissioni a tal segno, che eran costretti a dipingere mezze figure per rigattieri, e talora nemmen trovandoli pronti a comperarle, erano necesitati mandarle per le Città vendendo a basso prezzo per comperare il vitto cotidiano; sicchè menando una infelicissima, e misera Vita s'indussero a dipingere ancora per Bottegai quelle teste di S. Anastasio, che sogliono porsi a capo le culle de' Bambini a fin di preservarli dale malìe. Questa miseria fece sì, che scemassero assai di bontà, e di riputazione l'opere loro, dappoichè per far presto dipingevo a caso, e senza studio.'
68 For Carracci's *Vende quadri*, see Molinari Pradelli 1984, p. 32. For itinerant traders of this kind in Rome, see Lorizzo 2003, p. 328.
69 For the *Head of St Anastasius*, see Giuseppe Porzio in Naples 2008a, cat. no. 47, p. 144.
70 For an attempt to separate fact from fiction within De' Dominici's account on the basis of what little is known about the Fracanzani's careers, see De Vito 2003–4b, passim.
71 For Cesare Fracanzano's *Dying Mother* (Kunsthistorisches Museum, Vienna), see Schütze 2001, pp. 428–34; and Schütze 2002–3.
72 For this document, see De Vito 2003–4b, n. 8, p. 13.
73 For Francesco Fracanzano's *Apostle*, see Lilia Rocco in Rimini 1996, pp. 90–91.
74 De' Dominici 1742–5, vol. III, pp. 72–5.
75 Capaccio 1630, pp. 863–5. The best discussion remains Vaes 1925, pp. 188–95.
76 Saxl 1939–40.

6 DEALING BY ARTISTS

1 Haskell 1980, p. 121; Montias 1988, p. 245.
2 AAR, vol. 69, 'Rivenditori de quadri e Pitture', no. 125, undated, fol. 3v; no. 129, undated, fol. 4r; no. 126, 1654; vol. 69, nos. 129, 145, 'Nota de Revenditori di pitture e Dorature'. For further discussion of this aspect of the Archivio di San Luca documents, see Lorizzo 2003.
3 ASN, Notai Seicento, notaio Pietro Giordano, vol. 1313, no. 21, 1703, unnumbered sheets facing fol. 192v. The inventory is also discussed by Borrelli 1987, pp. 42, 47.
4 The inventory is arranged according to inheritance rather than by location and so makes no distinction between items from Cautiero's living quarters and from his workshop, save for a passage at the end that itemizes furnishings from the workshop. That the earlier sections include objects from the workshop and for sale is indicated by the frequent reference to stock-in-trade items such as reliquaries and four frames without paintings (both fol. 192/xiiv), eight 'Fenestrelli di Balcone' (fol. 192/xiiiv) and unframed paintings (fols 192/xir and 192/xiiv). The references to paintings cited in the text occur on fols 192/xiv and 192/xiir.
5 For Nicola Cassisa, a pupil of Andrea Belvedere who died in 1731, see De' Dominici 1742–5, vol. III, p. 575; Giannone 1941, p. 189; Alvar González Palacios, 'Un adornamento vicereale per Napoli', and Linda Martino in Naples 1984, vol. II, pp. 294 and 422; and Spinosa 1988a, pp. 89 and 378–9. For Gaetano Brandi, 'famoso pittore di ornamenti', see De' Dominici 1742–5, vol. III, p. 560; and Prota Giurleo 1953, pp. 39–42.
6 For Costa, see D. Marshall 1988, n. 5, p. 38.
7 Rizzo 1987, doc. no. 7, pp. 154–5, which refers to 'alcune tele da pittare quadri'.
8 Delfino 1984, doc. no. 39, p. 161, who transcribes the name of the collector cited in the document as Panerato.
9 Naples 1977, doc. no. 30, p. 133: 'per lo prezzo di tante tele impremite che l'haverà da consignare'.
10 Hibbard 1983, pp. 16–17.
11 For background and discussion, see Missirini 1823, p. 126; Haskell 1980, p. 121; Lorizzo 2003, pp. 325–8.
12 AAR, vol. 43, fol. 103v. The full wording of the grant is as follows: 'Nella qual Congregatione dopo diversi discursi fatti dalli sudetti Congregatione circa li interessi dell'Accademia, e per servitio della nostra Chiesa di San Luca essendosi raggionato, e fatta instantia per parte del Signore Mario Nuzzi detto de fiori di havere dall'Accademia una patente di poter tenere aperta in Roma una Bottega di rivender quadri, e pitture. Fù risoluto da tutti viva voce che glie si facci la Patente da Pittore Bottegaro, et una licenza à parte di poter essercitare, et tenere aperta una delle quattro, ò sei Botteghe ordinate nelli ordini stampati dell 1619 à Cam. 38.' Mario's application grew out of a wider context of controversy between the academy and those painters and *rivenditori* who sold second-hand paintings from their workshops. For this background, see further Lorizzo 2003. Lorizzo refers in passing to the document discussed above, on p. 326.
13 Ruffo 1916, passim; Vaes 1925.
14 Labrot 1992, inv. no. 7, pp. 69–71.
15 The published Getty Inventories omit references to drawings, frames and other related items. In the De Anfora inventory these omitted references include 'dieci tunni indagliati grandi [item 14a] . . . tre dozzini di tonni picoli di ligniamo [item 16a] . . . uno tunno piccolo indagliato e dorato [item 19a]'.
16 For Pesce, see De' Dominici 1742–5, vol. III, p. 211; and Sestieri and Daprà 1994, pp. 47–9.
17 This item is also not included in the transcription of the inventory published by Labrot 1992. The full record (item 72a) is 'quatro disigni di chiaro scuri di tela di carino mano di pietro pescie'.
18 Labrot 1992, inv. no. 4, pp. 60–61.
19 For the perception that painters made the best-qualified experts in artistic matters, see further Schnapper 1994, pp. 84–5.
20 Delfino 1984, doc. no. 27, pp. 159–60, which refers to the pictures to be produced in the workshop as 'quadri di figure frutti fiori et di qualsivoglia altra maniera'. The contract is also discussed by Borrelli 1991, p. 8. Antonio Cimino's pro-

fession is specified as that of a painter in the contract, and he can be further identified with the painter 'Antonio Cemino' who is documented in 1633 and 1640 (E. Nappi 1992, p. 38). The text in Italian of the passage cited later in the text is: 'jn compra de diversi quadri de diverse pitture et qualità fuora della botecha conforme ad esso giacomo parerà et piacerà per commune utile, et beneficio et sempre che esso giacomo haverà fatta compra de quadri fuori detta botecha dopo sequita la compra debbia esso giacomo portarli alla botecha et là si debbiano vendere, et smaltire a qualsivoglia prezzo si potra convenire con maggior utile, et beneficio sarà possibile'.

21 Prota Giurleo 1953, p. 14: 'il vero caposcuola dei "generisti" napoletani'.

22 For Recco's *Still Life with the Arms of Cardinal Poli*, see Spinosa 1989, cat. no. 1053, pp. 880–81, with bibliography. For Forte's *Still Life with Apples and Pears*, see Rimini 1996, pp. 170–71, with bibliography.

23 For a discussion, see Spinosa 1989, pp. 852–3, 872–3, 880, 893. For the collecting of still-life painting, see Labrot 1992, pp. 21–2, 39–41; Labrot 2010, pp. 288–94, 308–10.

24 For the prices for Sellitto's work, see the documents collected together in Naples 1977, pp. 129ff., and the list of works in his workshop, ibid., pp. 149–52. For an example of Sellitto's portraiture, see Naples 2009, vol. I, cat. no. 1.9, pp. 72–3.

25 Naples 1977, pp. 150–51.

26 Naples 1977, doc. no. 60, p. 139.

27 Naples 1977, pp. 147–8.

28 Naples 1977, p. 149.

29 Naples 1977, doc. no. 86, p. 144.

30 Originally published by Strazzullo 1956, pp. 77–8; and subsequently more fully in Naples 1977, pp. 149–52.

31 For the identification of Bartolomeo's copy after Zingaro, see Naples 1977, p. 152. For Sellitto's workshop assistants, see Prota Giurleo 1952, p. 27.

32 For Sellitto's *St Anthony*, see Naples 1977, cat. no. 10, pp. 92–3; and Athens 1984, cat., p. 17.

33 Such as the *Penitent Magdalene* (Museo del Prado, Madrid; S. Causa 2000, cat. no. 2.11, p. 267, with bibliography), which is sometimes attributed to Giovanni Matteo Arciero.

34 In 1612 Sellitto transferred a payment of 50 ducats to Arciero (Naples 1977, doc. no. 28, p. 133). In 1613 Arciero declared that he had been working for Sellitto for three years (Prota Giurleo 1952, p. 26).

35 The purchaser, Francesco Albertino, had previously paid Sellitto for unspecified work in 1613 (Naples 1977, p. 149, doc. no. 35, p. 134, and pp. 99 and 108 for commentary).

36 E. Nappi 1992, p. 100: 24 December 1603, 'Da Giovan Battista Ròta D. 15 a compimento di D. 20 per prezzo di un quadro de un Cristo con la Croce in collo de mano del Bassano del quale ha promesso non retenersene copia'.

37 For Giovanni Battista Ròta, see Mormone 1954, p. 53. For his patronage, see Quarta 1939–40, p. 480; Vargas 1988, doc. nos. 13, 30–31, p. 161; E. Nappi 1992, pp. 43, 56, 57.

38 E. Nappi 1992, p. 100.

39 As suggested by Prota Giurleo (1952, p. 27), and followed by subsequent authors. For Napoletano's *Martyrdom of St Sebastian*, see Chiarini 2007, cat. no. 31, pp. 260–61, with bibliography, and which also emphasizes the importance of paintings of this kind for the early work of Gargiulo and his associates.

40 Naples 1977, pp. 150–52, for the pictures by Napoletano, and ibid., doc. no. 79, p. 142, and p. 96 for a brief commentary on the document of 1615.

41 Naples 1977, p. 152, and doc. no. 78, p. 142, for the payment of July 1615.

42 Finoglio's date of migration to Conversano was traditionally set at 1639, but his presence there in 1635 has been established more recently (D'Elia and Belli 1970, p. 30; Buono 1978–9, p. 103; Marangelli 1979; and all authors thereafter). For Finoglio's paintings in the Museo Civico, Conversano, and patronage by the Acquaviva court, see also Marangelli 1967; Buono 1984–9; Conversano 2000, cat. nos. 41a–l, pp. 166–8, with additional bibliography. For Acquaviva's inventory of *circa* 1666, see Conversano 1983.

43 Caracciolo 1959, vol. III, p. 37.

44 ASN, notai Seicento, notaio Pietro Ciampone, scheda 107, protocollo 20, 1631, fols 283v–286v (15 May), 391r–397r (14 July, incorrectly cited as 4 July by Marangelli 1967, doc. 2, p. 208): fols 397v–398r (14 July), 450r–453v (12 September), 453v–454r (12 September). The documents were cited by Prota Giurleo 1953, p. 45, and subsequently published by Marangelli 1967, doc. nos. 1–3, p. 208, where the notary's name is incorrectly transcribed as Pietro Giannone. A further useful discussion of the documents is Pugliese 1984, n. 172, p. 534.

45 For the rental agreement, see fol. 283v and fols 284v–285r. For the Ospedale di San Giacomo degli Spagnuoli, see De Seta 1981, p. 124.

46 Ruotolo 1982, n. 7, p. 19.

47 For Jean Ducamps, or Giovanni del Campo, see Briganti, Trezzani and Laureati 1983, pp. 32–3. Vouet is described in the payment of 1630 as 'Monsueto' and by Capaccio as 'Monsuitto Francese' (Capaccio 1630, cited in Vaes 1925, n. 2, p. 189) and subsequently identified as Vouet by Vaes (1925, p. 191), Ruotolo (in Naples 1984, vol. I, p. 44) and Schütze and Willette (1992, p. 37).

48 Capaccio 1630, cited in Vaes 1925, n. 2, pp. 188–9.

49 Ferrante in Naples 1984, vol. I, p. 181; Naples 1985, p. 202.

50 Longhi 1957, p. 55; Putaturo Murano 1975, p. 189; Maria Rosaria Nappi in Naples 1984, vol. I, p. 155. The suggestion (London 1982, p. 249) that Napoletano may have been in Naples from 1627–8 cannot, however, be correct since he was rector of the Accademia di San Luca from 1627 until his death.

51 De' Dominici 1742–5, vol. III, p. 309, and pp. 448–9 for Antonio di Simone (for whom see also Ruotolo 1987, p. 180; Strazzullo 1990, n. 4, p. 34; and Schütze and Willette 1992, n. 17, pp. 176–7).

52 Ferrante 1900, p. 28; D'Addosio 1912–13, p. 40.

53 For documentary references, see D'Addosio 1912–13, pp. 40–41; Ruffo 1916, pp. 288, 302–3; E. Nappi 1983b, p. 74; Delfino 1985, pp. 98–9; E. Nappi 1990, doc. no. 63, p. 185; and E. Nappi 1992, pp. 49, 66 and 95. For his date of death, see De' Dominici 1742–5, vol. II, p. 291, and pp. 288ff. for a biography of the artist.

54 De' Dominici 1742–5, vol. II, p. 289. See the payment of 1653 for an altarpiece for San Potito (Delfino 1985, doc. no. 12, p. 99) and the payment of 1655 for paintings in Santa Maria Regina Coeli (De' Rossi and Sartorius 1987, pp. 41–2).

55 Two further examples are the payment of 1616 of 9 ducats to Cesare Castellano for the restoration of an altarpiece (Strazzullo 1954–5, doc. no. 55, p. 144), and the payment of 1653

of 50 ducats to Carlo Coppola for the retouching of 118 paintings belonging to the principe di Monteleone (Delfino 1985, p. 99, no. 14).

56 D'Addosio 1912–13, p. 41. For De Castro and Cacace, see E. Nappi 1983b, p. 74. The payment of 1640 is 'in conto di alcuni quadri che sta facendo per servitio suo', but no paintings by De Castro figure in Cacace's inventory of 1658 (Labrot 1992, inv. no. 18, pp. 109–12).

57 Labrot 1992, inv. no. 10, pp. 79–81, and inv. no. 17, pp. 105–8 (collections of Giuseppe Francesco Salernitano, barone di Frosolone, and Pietro d'Amore).

58 E. Nappi 1983b, p. 74: 23 February 1637, drawn 23 August 1637, 'A Pietro Jacovo d'Amore D. quaranta e per lui à Jacomo di Castro, et seli pagano per prezzo di uno quattro piccolo di Crocifisso con cornice d'oro vendutoli, et consignatoli e per esso à Paolo Chianese per altre tanti' (republished in Delfino 1985, doc. no. 10, p. 98). Strazzullo 1954–5, doc. no. 58, p. 144: 18 March 1637, 'A Pietro Jacono d'Amore Duc. 48 et per lui a Jacono de Castro per lo prezzo di uno quadro di mano di Giovanni Castiglietti di Giesù Cristo che lava li piedi all'apostoli'. The painter has been identified as Castiglione by Timothy Standring in Genoa 1990, p. 16, and as possibly being identifiable with Castiglione by Percy in Cleveland and Fort Worth 1984, n. 108, p. 32. For Castiglione's movements during this period, see further Percy 1967, p. 677; Newcome 1978, n. 37, p. 171.

59 E. Nappi 1992, p. 49, and p. 36 for D'Allegria's patronage of Caracciolo. For D'Allegria's patronage of Stanzione, see E. Nappi 1983b, p. 78.

60 Delfino 1985, doc. no. 11, p. 99; 4 June 1646: 'A Pietro Jacovo d'Amore D. trenta e per esso a Giacomo di Castro disse esserno per il prezzo di uno quadro in otto Angioli con cornice di Argento, e d'oro a lui venduto, et consignato, et per lui ad Aniello de Castro per altri tanti'.

61 For the practice of collectors purchasing frames directly from gilders, see Strazzullo 1979, p. 335 (payment for a frame to fit a painting commissioned from Giovan Vincenzo Forlì); Delfino 1988, doc. no. 7, p. 60 (payment for a frame to fit a painting by Filippo Vitale); Rizzo 1987, doc. no. 37, p. 159 (payment for a frame to fit a painting commissioned from Ribera); Ruffo 1916, p. 32 (payment for a frame to fit a painting commissioned from Artemisia Gentileschi). For the rotation of frames, see Labrot and Ruotolo 1980, p. 38; and Labrot 1979, n. 60, p. 116.

62 Labrot 1992, inv. no. 17, item 19, p. 106 (De Castro); item 47, p. 107 (*Crucifixion*); item 61, p. 108 (paintings not itemized); item 58, p. 108 (Napoletano).

63 E. Nappi 1983b, p. 76

64 For Gentileschi's and Stanzione's commissions, see E. Nappi 1983b, pp. 76 and 78; and Ruffo 1916, p. 32 and n. 1, p. 54. For Ribera, see Ruffo 1916, n. 1, p. 46. For Vaccaro, see E. Nappi 1983b, p. 80. For Caracciolo's altarpiece, see Faraglia 1885–92, p. 661; Stoughton 1973, p. 145, and cat. no. 57; and Stefano Causa, 'Battistello', in Naples 1991, fig. 27, p. 200, and pp. 198–202 for discussion. For the organ of Naples Cathedral, see Romano 1980, p. 161. For the prices of Neapolitan Baroque paintings, see further C. Marshall 2010.

65 E. Nappi 1983b, p. 75, for a document of 1670; and Paolillo 1985, p. 128, and Labrot 1992, pp. 113–14, for valuations of Gargiulo's pictures in the 1640s and 1650s, including a number appraised by Gargiulo himself.

66 For Compagno, see D'Addosio 1912–13, p. 46. For Beltrano's and De Leone's pictures, see Ruffo 1916, pp. 30, 32.

67 Originally published by E. Nappi 1990, doc. no. 63, p. 185; and republished by Finaldi, in Naples 1992, p. 407: 'per tanti quadri venduti e consignati a tutta sua soddisfazione et fra essi un bacco grande de nove et sette palmi fatto a mano del quondam Gioseppe Rebiera spagnolo'.

68 For Ribera's *Drunken Silenus*, see Spinosa 2003, cat. no A54, p. 267, with bibliography.

69 Labrot 1992, inv. no. 10, item 5, p. 80.

70 Ruffo 1916, p. 288 (26 January 1664); pp. 290–91 (20 September 1670); p. 295 (25 July 1671); p. 296 (19 September 1671); pp. 296–7 (2 October 1671); pp. 302–3 (22 July 1673). For references to De Castro selling Ruffo items from his stock, see Ruffo 1916, pp. 288 and 295 (sale of a painting by D'Arpino and a painting of a relief by Francesco Fiammingo).

71 Vincenzo d'Onofrio, *Giornali di Fuidoro*, Naples, 1934, vol. I, pp. 238–40; cited in Wethey 1967, p. 681. See further, Vannugli 1989a, p. 30.

72 De' Dominici 1742–5, vol. II, p. 290; vol. III, p. 37.

73 Such as the painting saved from De Aragón in the Muscettola chapel, San Domenico Maggiore, believed by De' Dominici to be by Dürer but now attributed to an unknown sixteenth-century Flemish painter (Naples 1960, p. 50; and G. Galante 1985, n. 400, p. 158).

74 Wethey 1967, pp. 681, 685.

75 Celano 1692, vol. V, p. 1417. For the Falcone drawing, see Madrid 1984, cat. no. 25, p. 54.

76 Letter from Giacomo de Castro to Don Antonio Ruffo, 20 September 1670, published by Ruffo 1916, p. 290: 'qui poi con l'occasione che la dilettatione del Sig.r Vicerè siamo rimasti esausti di pitture e di marmi, sì che bisogna cercare come dice il proverbio con la lanterna di mezzodì, tuttavia non si manca di usar diligenza'.

77 For Di Maria's *St Gregory the Illuminator*, see Spinosa 2011, cat. no. 57, p. 166, with bibliography.

78 De' Dominici 1742–5, vol. III, p. 311: 'Mando dunque a V.S. la fede di credito, acciò mi notifichi la quantità per la quale debbia a far la poliza, o per dir meglio le mando la poliza, acciochè ella medesima vi apponga in essa la quantità per notarsi in detta fede; mentre che io protestandole la mia indelibile amicizia, e costante servitù, che di conservarmi il carattere di suo servitore; come non ho la consolazione maggiore, che di godere delle sue dolci maniere, a guisa di lei opera . . . e rendere immortale la mia divozione verso lei; giacchè da per se stessa la sua fama vola fastosa per ogni Cielo; e bagiandole caramente le mani etc.'

79 E. Nappi 1992, p. 56. Di Maria's activities as a dealer, with an emphasis on his contacts made during various periods of residence in Rome, are also underlined by Lorizzo (2010, p. 148).

80 Delfino 1984, doc. no. 26, p. 159.

81 E. Nappi 1992, p. 57.

82 Pagano de Divitiis 1982, n. 29, p. 386. The paintings are unlikely to have been by Di Maria since they averaged 22 ducats each. Di Maria's pictures commonly fetched far more than this (Pagano de Divitiis 1982, n. 27, p. 385, payment of 1669 of 100 ducats for a portrait; n. 28, p. 385, payment of 1670 of 80 ducats for a portrait; n. 49, p. 392, payment of 1683 of 210 ducats to complete 250 ducats for two paintings).

83 For the traditional perception regarding a lack of interest in drawing among seventeenth-century Neapolitan painters and

collectors, and changes to this during the later decades of the seventeenth century – particularly as a result of the concerted collecting efforts of the marchese del Carpio and his adviser Sebastiano Resta in the early 1680s – see Farina 2010a; and for an overview of significant collections of Neapolitan drawing prior to this period (as dominated initially by the 'professional' collections built up over the years by artists such as Fabrizio Santafede and Domenico Gargiulo), see further Meyer 1999.

84 In 1674 Cardinal Leopoldo de' Medici's agent in Naples, Pietro Andrea Andreini, wrote to inform his patron that most of the drawings that had been sent to Florence in the previous year had come from Di Maria's studio (Ruotolo 1982, p. 10 and n. 27, p. 22).

85 Galasso 1982, pp. 688, 690.

86 Delfino 1989, doc. no. 20, pp. 39–40.

87 Delfino 1989, p. 40.

88 De' Dominici 1742–5, vol. II, p. 280; vol. III, p. 313. De' Dominici notes that he had received this information from Di Maria's son.

7 THE RISE OF THE ART MERCHANTS

1 Giacomo de Castro, letter to Don Antonio Ruffo of Messina dated 26 January 1664, cited in Ruffo 1916, p. 288: 'qui poi non vi è occasione di applicare o spendere per che non comparisce cosa di gusto solamente certi pezzi che uno Luca Giordano contrafacendo ora Titiano ora Paolo Veronese . . . ce a fatto buona prratticha e poi ci da una tinta anticha che non fanno male vista il Signore Gaspare [Roomer] ne a molti altri mercanti molti però gia si è scoverto e così non si riceve piu.'

2 For further discussion of this letter in light of De Castro's professional rivalry with the Flemish dealers De Wael, Brueghel and Roomer, see Wethey 1969–75, vol. I, p. 4; and Vaes 1925, pp. 198–9.

3 For the manuscript of 1681, 'Relatione della vita di Luca Giordano pittore celebre fatta sotto li 13 agosto 1681', see Ceci 1899; Prota Giurleo 1955b, p. 24; Ruotolo 2003–4. The same anecdote was drawn on subsequently by Baldinucci in his early account of Giordano's life – for which, see Francesco Saverio Baldinucci, 'Notizie della vita dell'eccellentissimo pittore Luca Giordano', MS, *circa* 1710–21, published by Ferrari 1966. The suggestion that Giordano was the author of the 'Relatione' was initially suggested by Ceci and then argued more definitively by De Vito 1991, p. 36, and thereafter by subsequent authors. For Giordano's marriage to Margherita Dardi, see Prota Giurleo 1955b, p. 26.

4 E. Nappi 1991, doc. nos. 7–9, pp. 165–6.

5 De' Dominici 1742–5, vol. III, pp. 397–8. For a more recent assessment of the complex and much-debated issue of Giordano as 'falsario', see Scavizzi and De Vito 2012, pp. 13, 21–50, with bibliography. The lack of critical consensus concerning the extent to which Giordano's early derivations from the style of earlier artists might have been intentional forgeries or more generalized exercises *alla maniera di* is indicated by the continued differences of opinion contained within this publication. On the one hand, Scavizzi expresses the opinion that Luca's early work was almost certainly sold as originals by his father (p. 13), whereas De Vito (p. 32) argues, to the contrary, that arguments in favour of Giordano forging his work 'sono infondate'.

6 De' Dominici 1742–5, vol. III, p. 136 (for the sale in Malta), pp. 156, 283 (for Giuseppe Fatturuso), p. 443 (for the date of Raimondo's and Bernardo's return to Malta) and pp. 274–6 (for Raimondo's art dealing during the 1670s and 1680s). The translated passage occurs on p. 136: 'E chi queste cose scrive attesta, che Raimondo de Dominici, suo Padre avendo comperate diece Accademie dipinte in tele di misura circa tre palmi dalla credità di Giuseppe Fatturuso, con altre teste, e cose di studio lavorate da Andrea, le vendè poi in Malta ad un Cavalier Francese, dilettantissimo di quadri per pittura del Caravaggio, e ciò senza il minimo scrupolo di coscienza, dapoichè il valore del Vaccaro non è punto inferiore a quello dell'Amerigi.'

7 For a discussion of the contemporaneous case study of Pietro della Vecchia's and Pietro Liberi's paintings in the style of earlier Renaissance artists, see Loh 2006. For this tradition more broadly, see Kris and Kurz 1979, pp. 97–8; Muller 1989.

8 Condivi 1999, pp. 11–12. For discussion, see London 1995, pp. 20–28; and Barolsky 1999.

9 E. Nappi 1991, p. 169.

10 E. Nappi 1991, p. 172.

11 Moretti 2005, pp. 33–4. For further discussion of this collection, see Borean and Cecchini 2002.

12 E. Nappi 2000, doc. no. 129, p. 77.

13 Sandrart 1675, pp. 278, 290.

14 De' Dominici 1742–5, vol. III, p. 343.

15 Celano 1692, vol. V, p. 1412. See also De' Dominici 1742–5, vol. III, p. 23.

16 For Cavallino and Ruoppolo, see De' Dominici 1742–5, vol. III, pp. 37, 294; for which see also Vaes 1925, n. 2, p. 199.

17 De' Dominici 1742–5, vol. III, p. 73.

18 De' Dominici 1742–5, vol. III, p. 344

19 De' Dominici 1742–5, vol. III, p. 435; and Vaes 1925, n. 1, p. 199, who also associates this reference with Roomer's exporting business.

20 De' Dominici 1742–5, vol. III, p. 73.

21 For the identification of 'Jacobo Sibraut', see further Chapter Nine.

22 Vaes 1925, pp. 193, 195. Vaes suggests that it was through Roomer's export of Bramer's work that Rembrandt came into contact with Bramer.

23 For the presence of Falcone's *Schoolmistress* in the collection of Peter Wouters in Antwerp in 1673, see Denucé 1932, p. 264. For discussion, see Saxl 1939–40, n. 1, p. 81; n. 6, p. 86. For the painting more generally, see Spinosa 2010, no. 145, p. 242, with bibliography.

24 De' Dominici 1742–5, vol. III, pp. 73, 79. The painting is also mentioned by Sandrart (1675, p. 290). For Coppola's version of the *Martyrdom of St Januarius*, see Maria Rosaria Nappi in Naples 1984, vol. I, cat. no. 2.45, p. 232; Damian in Paris 2007b, pp. 42–5; and Spinosa 2010, no. 80, pp. 202–4.

25 E. Nappi 2000, doc. nos. 229–30, p. 83.

26 For Roomer and Vaccaro, see E. Nappi 2000, doc. nos. 233–40, p. 83; for Roomer and Preti, see E. Nappi 2000, doc. nos. 241–2, pp. 83–4; for Roomer and Farelli, see E. Nappi 2000, doc. no. 240, p. 83.

27 E. Nappi 2000, doc. no. 227, p. 83.

28 For Berardino Ròta and his collection, see Capaccio 1630, pp. 856–7. For discussion, see Morisani 1958, pp. 108–9; Mormone 1954; Leone de Castris 1991, pp. 44, 58, 68–9, 78.

29 Celano 1692, vol. II, p. 431. Roomer's paintings by Polidoro da Caravaggio are said to have been sold at his death to the viceroy, the marqués de los Vélez. This report is mentioned by Vaes 1925, pp. 195–6; Morisani 1958, n. 8, p. 109; and Borrelli 1989, n. 45, p. 23.

30 Reade 1947, pp. 70–75. For discussion, see Leone de Castris 2001, p. 269.

31 Ruffo 1916, pp. 30, 36. For the conversion rate between Messinese *onzie* and Neapolitan ducats, see Grabski 1985, p. 41.

32 De' Dominici 1742–5, vol. III, pp. 150–51.

33 De' Dominici 1742–5, vol. III, pp. 76, 151 and 206.

34 The principal study of Valletta remains Consoli Fiego 1922. Valletta's significance is also emphasized by Francis Haskell (1980, p. 204), and a document confirming his association with Ruoppolo and Abraham Brueghel has been published by Antonio Delfino (1987, doc. no. 6, p. 98). For Valletta's involvement in the academies and his role in the development of the new sciences in Naples, see Galasso 1982, pp. 405–8, 411 and 665–9.

35 A. Musi in *DBI*, vol. XVIII, pp. 434–5. For Capece Galeota's disgrace and temporary exile from Naples, see further Galasso 1982, pp. 250–53.

36 E. Nappi 1991, doc. no. 163, p. 176.

37 For Capece Galeota and Mattia Preti, see E. Nappi 1980, doc. no. 158, pp. 65–6; republished in Spike 1998, p. 91. For Galeota's patronage of Recco, Fracanzano and Vaccaro, see E. Nappi 1992, pp. 93, 73 and 167, which also documents his patronage of the other lesser-known artists Giuseppe Armetano, Nicolò Mercurio and Francesco Pisacane (pp. 24, 88, 92). For his patronage of De Leone, see Rizzo 1984, p. 314.

38 For Ciappa's position as *razionale* of Vandeneynden, see Borrelli 1991, p. 12; and Ferrari and Scavizzi 1992, vol. I, p. 395.

39 Borrelli 1991, n. 29, pp. 16–17, and pp. 12–13 for discussion.

40 De' Dominici 1742–5, vol. III, pp. 150–51, 343, 345, 398.

41 Labrot 1992, inv. no. 78, pp. 439–43. Although drawn up in the 1740s, the inventory contains no eighteenth-century paintings as one might expect were the collection still in formation at this time. A single possible exception is a painting by the school of Nicola Vaccaro (1637–1717), but this is just as likely to have been acquired during Carlo Arici's day. All the other attributions are to painters active from the 1630s to the end of the seventeenth century, together with a single sixteenth-century painting attributed to the school of Bassano.

42 E. Nappi 1992, p. 110. For Mele's activities, see further Labrot 2010, p. 325.

43 For an overview, see Alfonso E. Pérez Sánchez, 'Ribera e la Spagna', in Naples 1992, pp. 57–80.

44 Burke and Cherry 1997, vol. I, inv. no. 43, items 141, 155, 156, 171, 375, 376, 582 and 583.

45 Burke and Cherry 1997, vol. I, inv. no. 49, items 140–41; inv. no. 109, item 55. In Naples, De Haro subsequently acquired one of the most important collections of drawings by Falcone (Saxl 1939–40, pp. 75–6; New York 1979, pp. 128–30; Madrid 1984, pp. 52–65).

46 Golzio 1939, pp. 274, 285–6, 288. For the Ribera acquisition, organized by Simonelli, see Golzio 1939, pp. 286–7.

47 Letter from Salvatore Castiglione to Carlo II Gonzaga in Mantua, 2 June 1661, cited in Genoa 1971, doc. no. XIX, p. 48.

48 De Marchi 1987, pp. 102, 345, 347 and 429.

49 Saxl 1939–40, n. 6, p. 83; Annachiara Alabiso in Naples 1984, vol. I, cat. no. 2.73, pp. 260–61, with bibliography.

50 Saxl 1939–40, n. 2, p. 78: the now-lost inscription is recorded as having read 'pinxit cum magna Neapolitanorum laude decollationem S. Januarii in Galliam Belgium Hispaniam pro pictis tabulis cognitium'.

51 For Giordano and Venice, see De Vito 1991; Ferrari and Scavizzi 1992, vol. I, pp. 38–54; De Vito 1999b; and Ferrari in Naples, Vienna and Los Angeles 2001, p. 32.

52 For Giordano and Florence, see Ferrari in Naples, Vienna and Los Angeles 2001, pp. 33–7.

53 For Giordano and Spain, see Alfonso E. Pérez Sánchez, 'Le tracce di Giordano nella pittura spagnola', in Naples, Vienna and Los Angeles 2001, pp. 454–62; and Madrid 2002, passim. For Giordano and Genoa, see Piero Boccardo and Carlo Milano, 'I Luca Giordano di Genova: dai Grillo ai Balbi e ai Durazzo', in Naples, Vienna and Los Angeles 2001, pp. 222–34.

54 De' Dominici 1742–5, vol. III, pp. 434, 438.

55 De' Dominici 1742–5, vol. III, p. 37.

56 De' Dominici 1742–5, vol. III, p. 432.

57 Vincenzo Samuele is described as Guglielmo's heir in a document of 1677 (Delfino 1991, doc. no. 12, p. 27). For discussion, see further Borrelli 1989, p. 16, who suggests that Vincenzo must have lived with Guglielmo for some years before he took over the family business in 1677. This confirms the earlier hypotheses concerning Vincenzo's probable relationship with Guglielmo developed by Gérard Labrot (Labrot 1984). On that occasion Labrot had suggested that the Vincenzo Samuele (variant spellings: Samueli, Samuelli) mentioned in the Carlo della Torre document of 1684 must have either been a misspelling or mis-transcription of Guglielmo or else a close relation to Guglielmo. The other references to Vincenzo make it quite clear that he was, indeed, a separate person. Borrelli identifies Vincenzo as Guglielmo's nephew and provides additional information on the Samuele family (Borrelli 1989, p. 16).

58 Labrot 1984, pp. 138–40.

59 E. Nappi 1991, doc. nos. 119 and 121, p. 173.

60 For Giogali, see Prota Giurleo 1953, p. 61; Borrelli 1989, p. 16, and n. 81, p. 25; Ferrari and Scavizzi 1992, vol. I, p. 54, and n. 38, p. 227.

61 E. Nappi 1991, doc. no. 120, p. 173.

62 E. Nappi 1991, doc. no. 48, p. 168.

63 For *salme* and other Neapolitan weights and measures, see Calabria 1991, p. xii.

64 De' Dominici 1742–5, vol. III, p. 401.

65 Prota Giurleo (1953, p. 60); then republished with corrections and additions by Delfino 1991, pp. 19–20.

66 Borrelli 1989, p. 18: 'procacciatore di prestiti e mutui e suo mercante d'arte'.

67 See the inventory transcription dated 29 July 1682 held at the Getty Provenance Index database (inv-I 328, item 3). For discussion, see Delfino 1987, doc. no. 6, p. 98; and Valter Pinto in De' Dominici 2003–8, vol. III, n. 45, p. 768.

68 De' Dominici 1742–5, vol. III, p. 860; Labrot 1992, pp. 177, 183–8, 199.

69 For this trade, see Ruotolo 1999.

70 For Neapolitan and other southern Italian examples of the *stipo*, see González-Palacios 1984, vol. I, pp. 239–47, 283.
71 For paintings on glass, see Alvar González-Palacios and Linda Martino in Naples 1984, vol. II, pp. 293–6, 422–30; González-Palacios 1984, vol. I, pp. 231–2.
72 Delfino 1991, doc. no. 8, pp. 24–5; E. Nappi 1991, doc. nos. 41 and 47, p. 168.
73 E. Nappi 1991, doc. nos. 42 and 45, p. 168.
74 E. Nappi 1991, doc. no. 46, p. 168.
75 Delfino 1993, doc. nos. 11–13, pp. 27–8.
76 E. Nappi 1991, doc. no. 40, p. 168.
77 E. Nappi 1991, doc. no. 116, p. 173.
78 E. Nappi 1991, doc. no. 50, p. 168; E. Nappi 1992, p. 93.
79 E. Nappi 1991, doc. nos. 52–4, p. 169.
80 Prota Giurleo 1953, pp. 61–2; republished in Delfino 1991, doc. no. 17, p. 31.
81 For the florin to ducat exchange rate, see Calabria 1991, p. xv.
82 Prota Giurleo 1953, p. 61; Delfino 1991, pp. 30–31.
83 For Bertocchi, see Ferrari and Scavizzi 1992, vol. I, pp. 244–5, 399.
84 Borrelli 1989, p. 19, and n. 112. This individual was quite probably related to the subsequently documented Abraham Vandenheuvel. Vandenheuvel's inventory of 1708 is mentioned briefly by Labrot (2010, p. 452) as having contained a high proportion of still-life paintings.

8 PUBLIC COMMISSIONS

1 The fullest discussion of this now-lost commission is to be found in Cinotti 1983, pp. 572–3; Bologna 1992, pp. 97–107, 241, 243–5; S. Causa 2000, p. 43.
2 Scaramuccia 1674, p. 76.
3 De' Dominici 1742–5, vol. II, p. 275.
4 Celano 1692, vol. III, pp. 9–10.
5 For Vasari's *Resurrection*, see Arezzo 2011, cat. no. 7, pp. 82–3, with bibliography.
6 Porzio 2010–11. Porzio also notes the probable connection with Caravaggio's lost painting for Sant'Anna dei Lombardi and also tentatively identifies Sellitto's *St Francis* with a painting of this subject mentioned in the early guides as among the work produced by him for the Curtoni chapel in Sant'Anna dei Lombardi.
7 For Caracciolo's *St John the Baptist*, see Prohaska in Naples 2009, vol. I, cat. no. 1.6, p. 68.
8 London 2005, pp. 148–9, with bibliography.
9 Only the two scenes from the *Life of St Peter* are now extant, for which see Naples 1977, cat. nos. 1–1a, pp. 63–7.
10 Pacelli 1990, p. 187, and n. 1, p. 189, and n. 5, p. 190, illustrated fig. 42, p. 191.
11 G. Galante 1985, p. 78.
12 For an attempt to reconstruct the appearance of Caravaggio's lost *Resurrection*, see Moir 1976, n. 249, pp. 148–9.
13 De' Dominici 1742–5, vol. III, p. 437.
14 Gazzara 2003, with bibliography.
15 For Manso and Carlo Emmanuele I, see Schütze and Willette 1992, n. 6, p. 11.
16 For Manso and Annibale Carracci (as based on an anecdote recounted by De' Dominici), see Stoughton 1973, p. 5; S. Causa in Naples 1991, p. 188.
17 For discussion, see De Maio 1983, pp. 253–6; Clifton 1994, p. 491. The painting is undocumented and hardly discussed in the literature on Azzolino. The date of *circa* 1622–8 has been extrapolated from the date of the canonization of St Francis Xavier and the date of 1628, which is the year in which one of the witnesses to the miracle attests to having first seen the painting move its eyes.
18 "Breve racconto del prodigioso moto d'occhi dell'Imagine di San Francesco Saverio", cit. De Maio, 1983, pp. 253–56.
19 Evelyn, cited in Smith 1914, pp. 6, 56.
20 De Simone 1976, p. 85.
21 Strazzullo 1968, p. 102.
22 Bacco et al. 1671, pp. 50–55.
23 Giannone, *Istoria civile*, 1723, vol. III, Libro XXXVIII, cap. V, paragraph 1; cited in De Seta 1981, p. 137.
24 Ricciardi 2007, p. 87.
25 For an overview of the documentation, see E. Nappi 1988, pp. 132–41.
26 Carlo de Lellis, *Parte Seconda o'vero supplimento a Napoli sacra di D. Cesare d'Engenio Caracciolo*, Naples: Roberta Molo, 1654; cited in Ricciardi 2007, p. 87.
27 For a reproduction of Sarnelli's illustration and discussion of Massimo Stanzione's involvement in this now-lost commission, see Schütze and Willette 1992, cat. no. D12, pp. 260–61, 450.
28 For the documentation of Jesuit building and patronage initiatives, see E. Nappi 1984; as brought up to date with further archival discoveries in E. Nappi 2002. For a useful commentary, including important additional archival clarifications, see Iappelli 1985.
29 E. Nappi 1984, p. 318.
30 For the documentation and brief discussion of its patronage context, see Strazzullo 1961.
31 For further discussion of Gesualdo, see Gray 1926; Watkins 2010. For more detailed analysis in the context of Jesuit patronage initiatives, see Iappelli 1985, pp. 82–3.
32 E. Nappi 2002, p. 112.
33 E. Nappi 2002, p. 112; and see further Iappelli 1985, p. 25.
34 Bösel 1977, doc. no. 1, p. 102.
35 For Lanfranco's frescoes at the Palazzo delle Congregazioni, see E. Nappi 2002, p. 111. In October 1646 Lanfranco was paid on account 15 ducats towards a total of 500 ducats for his frescoes in this oratory.
36 Bonazzi 1888. Bonazzi's discoveries were subsequently amplified by E. Nappi 1989.
37 For background to the church and convent of Santa Maria della Sapienza, see further Hills 2004, pp. 134–6.
38 Strazzullo 1978, pp. 165–6.
39 Hills 2008, pp. 31–3.
40 Florence 1983, p. 202.
41 Florence 1983, p. 203.
42 Schütze and Willette 1992, cat. no. A73, pp. 225–7.
43 For which, see Ruotolo 1988.
44 For Finoglio's *Blessed Andrea Avellino*, see Leone de Castris in Conversano 2000, cat. no. 9, pp. 148–9.
45 Bruzelius and Tronzo 2011, p. 70.
46 Schütze and Willette 1992, cat. no. A88, pp. 234–5.
47 Puglisi 1995, pp. 409–10.
48 Conelli 2000, pp. 158–9, and pp. 153–83 more generally for the parallel case study of the Neapolitan triumphal columns – or *Guglie* – in light of inter-order rivalries of the period.

49 For background on the cult of St Rosalia as a plague protector, see Bailey 2005, pp. 118–36.
50 Clifton 1994, p. 493.
51 For St Philip Neri's addition to the ranks of the patron saints of Naples, see Strazzullo 1978, p. 166.
52 G. Galante 1985, p. 116.
53 Fabris 2007, p. 102.
54 For Caravaggio and the Oratorians, see Friedlander 1955, pp. 117–35; Chorpenning 1987, pp. 149–50. For Barocci and the Oratorians, see Verstegen 2003. For Roncalli and the Oratorians, see Melasecchi 1998. For Borromini and the Oratorians, see Connors 1980.
55 Spear 1982, vol. I, p. 287.
56 Spear 1982, vol. I, pp. 21–2.
57 Solimena's frescoes, for example, were not completed until 1733 (Roberto Middione in G. Galante 1985, n. 276, p. 125).
58 This understanding of the importance of Oratorians' bequests and donations is indebted to the recent studies of the rooms of St Philip Neri conducted by Glenys Adams (Adams 2013; and see further Adams 2009).
59 For Reni's *Meeting of Christ with St John the Baptist*, see Naples 1986a, p. 11. For further discussion, see Whitfield in London 1982, cat. no. 118, p. 225; Cira Zingone in Lecce 2013, cat. no. 14, pp. 76–7, with additional bibliography.
60 For Anna Colonna's education at San Giuseppe dei Ruffi, see Hills 2004, pp. 107–8.
61 For this event, see Anna lo Bianco in Rome 1995, p. 547; and Dunn 1994, p. 645.
62 Dunn 1994, n. 11, p. 645.
63 For Algardi's involvement in this now-lost commission, see Montagu 1985, pp. 390–91.
64 Spear 1982, vol. I, pp. 109–10.
65 For this painting and its patronage context, see Anna lo Bianco in Rome 1995, cat. no. 106, pp. 546–8.
66 For this commission, see Connors 1980, p. 202.
67 For Giordano's *Ecstasy of St Alexis* (1661; Chiesa del Purgatorio ad Arco), see Ferrari and Scavizzi 1992, cat. no. A155, vol. I, p. 275, who also note its indebtedness to Da Cortona's *St Alexis*.
68 For discussion, see Anna lo Bianco in Rome 1995, p. 547.
69 For Anna Colonna Barberini's patronage at Santa Maria Regina Coeli in Rome, see Dunn 1994 and Dunn 2000.
70 For discussion of this monument, see Dunn 1994, p. 651.
71 Napoli 2010, p. 113.
72 Sarnelli 1685, p. 78. For the Florentine emphasis of the Girolamini, see further Napoli 2010, pp. 116–17.
73 For Pietro Bernini's work at the Girolamini, see Middione in G. Galante 1985, n. 273, p. 125; and Fernanda Capobianco in Naples 1984, vol. II, pp. 154–5.
74 Naples 1986a, p. 6; Naples 1995, p. 45.
75 For discussion, see Adams 2013.
76 For the Quadreria dei Girolamini, see Naples 1986a; Naples 1995; Lecce 2013.
77 For the *quadreria* of the Pio Monte della Misericordia, see Naples 1970; Naples 2012.
78 For the appraised collection of Giovan Camillo Cacace of 1658, see Pacelli 1986; for the appraised collection of Don Cesare di Gennaro, principe di San Martino, of 1646, and its subsequent public auction at the Pio Monte della Misericordia, see Paolillo 1985.
79 Parrino 1700, pp. 121 and 125: 'il quanto bello tanto ricco monistero de'cartusiani . . . e quanto v'è; tutto è considerarsi come stupendo e maraviglioso'.
80 Sarnelli 1685, pp. 325–6.
81 ASN, Carta Visitationis, 1674, cited and translated in Napoli 2003, p. 249.
82 For a discussion of the social and cultural context to Gargiulo's *Thanksgiving after the Plague of 1656* see Clifton 1990.
83 Celano 1692, vol. VI, pp. 28–9: 'E cominciando dalla chiesa . . . per la pretiosità degli ornamenti non ha in che cedere ad ogni più ricco tempio d'Italia. Viene questa vestita, ne' pilastri e nelle cappelle, di gentilissimi marmi commessi a lavori che si ponno chiamare originali, perché, essendo stati inventati dal cavalier Cosimo Fansaga [sic], qui fu la prima volta che furono veduti in Italia'.
84 Napoli 2010.
85 See, for example, the payments cited by E. Nappi 1988, p. 148: 19 December 1634, payment of 430 ducats by Vincenzo Carrafa to the Certosa di San Martino for 400 *tomoli* of grain; this payment then transferred to Caracciolo for his work in the chapel of St Martino and payment of 13 February 1640 of 24 ducats to the Certosa di San Martino for rent on a workshop; this payment then transferred to Lanfranco to conclude his payments for work at the Certosa.
86 For the strong influence of Fanzago's architectural motifs on Gargiulo's Coro dei Conversi frescoes and the likelihood that Gargiulo was following Fanzago's drawings for this project, see R. Causa 1973, pp. 65–6. His suggestion has been followed by subsequent commentators, for which see Rocco in G. Galante 1985, n. 263, p. 286.
87 D. Marshall 1986, pp. 50–51; for documentation of Codazzi's requirement to produce the work 'secondo li disegni fatti dal signor Cosimo Fanzago', ibid., doc. no. 13, p. 66.
88 For discussion, see C. Marshall 2000, pp. 18–20.
89 For Lanfranco's letter recounting these complaints about Fanzago (dated 11 September 1639), see Florence 1983, p. 178.
90 For discussion, see Chapter Three.
91 For discussions concerning the issues surrounding Ribera's *God the Father* and *Trinitas Terrestris with Sts Bruno, Benedict, Bernardino of Siena and Bonaventura* (both formerly in Santissima Trinità delle Monache), which De' Dominici believed had been rejected by the Carthusians and donated by Ribera to the church of Santissima Trinità delle Monache, see Nicola Spinosa in Naples 1992, cat. nos. 1.24–5, pp. 158–61, with bibliography.
92 Faraglia 1885–92, p. 660.
93 For Caracciolo's *Christ Washing the Feet of the Disciples*, see S. Causa 2000, cat. no. A74, p. 193. For the chapel of the Assumption, see S. Causa 2000, cat. nos. A111–12, pp. 203–4; for the chapel of St Januarius, see S. Causa 2000, cat. nos. A123–7, pp. 206–8; for Caracciolo's replacement altarpiece of *St Martin and Four Angels*, see S. Causa 2000, cat. no. A104, pp. 201–2.
94 For Corenzio's now-lost paintings of the *Taking of Christ* and the *Crucifixion*, see Stoughton 1986, p. 238, and pp. 237–9 for the changes to the programme of the choir more generally.
95 Malvasia 1980, p. 118.
96 For Codazzi's litigation with the Carthusians, see D. Marshall 1986, pp. 49–57. Codazzi claimed to have completed work worth 900 ducats but to have been paid only 735. According to his calculations he was therefore owed 165 ducats.

97 Lanfranco's litigation with the Carthusians is briefly mentioned by Faraglia (1885–92, p. 442) and further discussed by Schleier in Florence 1983, p. 178. Lanfranco claimed to have been owed 880 ducats that he asserted had not been paid him following the 1,000-ducat extension in 1638 of his initial 7,500-ducat contract of 1637 for frescoes in the nave. The dispute seems particularly to have revolved around the issue of payment for and acceptance of Lanfranco's rejected altarpiece of the *Virgin and Child with Sts Dominic and Januarius* (originally *Sts Anselm of Canterbury and Hugh of Lincoln*).
98 The fullest discussion of the litigation of Ribera's heirs with the Carthusians remains Napoli 2012, pp. 22–4, with bibliography.
99 For Fanzago's litigation with the Carthusians, see Cantone 1969a and Cantone 1969b.
100 Ileana Creazzo in Buono, Campanelli and Cassani 1997, p. 256; Schütze 1993, p. 197.
101 For Caracciolo's career and commissions during this period, see the chronology and documentation brought together in S. Causa 2000, pp. 353–5.
102 For the popularity of Vaccaro's *Penitent Magdalene* and discussion in the context of his career more generally, see Tuck-Scala 2012, pp. 27, 58–60.
103 Gargiulo appears to have acquired his training in fresco while attached to the workshop of Belisario Corenzio in the early 1630s. From 1635 to 1637 Corenzio was working in the atrium of the Certosa, and this suggested to De Vito the possibility that Gargiulo's work in the atrium may have led to his being commissioned by the Carthusians in the years that followed (Giuseppe de Vito in Delfino 1985, p. 89).
104 For which, see Ortolani 1970, passim.
105 Courtright 1990, n. 33, p. 344.
106 J. Mabillon, *Museum Italicum* . . ., 1724, vol. I, p. 103; cited in Strazzullo 1983, p. 231.
107 Thomas Salmon, *Lo stato presente di tutti i paesi e popoli del mondo*, Venice, 1761, vol. XXIII, p. 68; cited in Strazzullo 1983, p. 233.
108 For the Quarto del Priore, see Naples 1986b. Knowledge of the paintings in the prior's quarters is limited by the fact that they were confiscated during the Napoleonic occupation of 1806 and dispersed throughout Naples and beyond. The inventory of 1806, which remains a precious documentation of the state of the collection at the time of its dispersal, was first published by Borzelli 1913, and thereafter used as the basis for subsequent reconstructions of the *quadreria* by Franco Strazzullo and Teodoro Fittipaldi, for which see Strazzullo 1983; Fittipaldi 1984; and Fittipaldi 1988.

9 PRIVATE COLLECTIONS OF PAINTING

1 For the activities of the Accademia degli Oziosi, see Minieri Riccio 1878–80, p. 174; Schütze and Willette 1992, pp. 33–40; Schütze 1992b; Schütze 2001, pp. 407–14.
2 Borzelli 1906, pp. 176–203; Mirollo 1963, pp. 86–93.
3 Fulco 1979.
4 For the *Tomb of Giambattista Marino*, see Rita Pastorelli in Naples 1984, vol. II, cat. no. 4.53, p. 237, with bibliography.
5 Labrot 1979, pp. 43–6; Labrot and Ruotolo 1980, pp. 25–7.
6 De Seta 1981, chapter 5, pp. 95–128.
7 For the Firrao chapel, see Pacelli 1987, pp. 236–41; De Vito 1999a; Abbate 2002, pp. 149–50.
8 For Firrao's litigation with Fanzago, see De Vito 1999a, passim.
9 For payments for work at the Merlino chapel, see E. Nappi 1984, pp. 322–4 and doc. nos. 22–9, p. 334.
10 For the lack in Naples of open spaces for *piazze* and the subsequent rarity of Neapolitan palaces with unified façades comparable to those of Florence or Rome, see Mazzoleni 1999, pp. 14–15.
11 For the decoration of the Palazzo Firrao, see Labrot 1993, p. 173, and nn. 49–52, p. 245.
12 For the *seggi*, see further Astarita 1992, pp. 24–5.
13 Labrot 1992, inv. no. 19, pp. 113–15.
14 Paolillo 1985.
15 Paolillo (1985, p. 113) surmised that Abate was probably a painter, but lacked further references to confirm this. Subsequent documents published by Eduardo Nappi establish that he was, indeed, a professional painter of at least middling rank (E. Nappi 1992, p. 23).
16 Ruotolo 1973, p. 118.
17 For Zurlo's collection, see Ruotolo 1973.
18 Labrot 1992, inv. no. 2, p. 55.
19 The inventory of the Capecelatro collection of 1655 is indicative, since it lists paintings in both the chapel and studio as well as in contiguous rooms (Labrot 1992, pp. 101–4).
20 For Claudio Milano's donation of his belongings to the Oratorians on 19 July 1631, which included his 'Galleria', see Naples 1986a, p. 65. For the reference of 1654 to Spinelli's 'galleria', see Labrot 1992, p. 95.
21 Labrot 1992, p. 41; Leone de Castris 1991, p. 78.
22 Paolillo 1985, pp. 123, 130–31.
23 For the architectural history of the Palazzo Gravina, see Divenuto 2003.
24 For the inventory references of 1707 and 1744, see Rubsamen 1980, passim. For a discussion and suggestions regarding the identification of these inventory references with extant paintings, see Lattuada 2000, pp. 298–301.
25 Lattuada 2000, cat. no. E36, pp. 214–15, with bibliography, and p. 301 for the identification with the Orsini di Gravina inventory reference. For the inventory reference itself, see Rubsamen 1980, inv. no. V, item 90, p. 54.
26 Lattuada 2000, cat. no. E60, pp. 238–40, with bibliography.
27 Lattuada 2000, cat. no. E63, pp. 242–3. Lattuada dates the canvas to *circa* 1650. It seems unlikely, however, to have been commissioned that late, given that the duchess was already married and a mother by that stage.
28 Rubsamen 1980, inv. no. 5, item 72, p. 52.
29 For the activities of Giangirolamo Acquaviva during the 1630s and 1640s, see Villari 1993, pp. 111–12, 127–30, 134, 136–7, 141. For the career and political affiliations of Acquaviva, see further Elena Fasano Guarini in *DBI*, vol. I.
30 Pierluigi Leone de Castris in Conversano 2000, cat. nos. 4a–4b, p. 146.
31 Fabrizio Vona, 'Paolo Finoglio a Conversano: le volte dipinte', in Conversano 2000, pp. 68–70.
32 Conversano 2000, cat. nos. 34–9, pp. 162–5.
33 Floro di Zenzo 1979.
34 For a biography and overview of the cultural activities and patronage of Andrea Matteo III Acquaviva (1458–1529), see Leone de Castris 1995–6.

35 For the listing of 1666 of the contents of the *galleria* of the Castello di Conversano, see Conversano 1983, pp. 44–9.

36 Vona in Conversano 2000, p. 66.

37 Conversano 2000, cat. no. 41h, p. 166, and pp. 166–8 for the series as a whole.

38 Lofano 2009, pp. 97–9. For Fracanzano's *Family of Satyrs*, see Spinosa 2010, cat. no. 204, p. 278, with bibliography.

39 The inventory of 1739 of the D'Avalos collection was originally published by De Martini 1994. It was subsequently republished, together with additional inventories and commentary, by Bugli 2003–4.

40 For the issue of the provenance of the Battle of Pavia tapestries, see Linda Martino in Naples 1994b, pp. 192–6, and cat. nos. 100–06, pp. 190–97.

41 For this portrait and for the patronage of Alfonso d'Avalos more generally, see Los Angeles 2005.

42 For Andrea d'Avalos's career and biography, see Gaspare de Caro in *DBI*, vol. IV; and Sirago 2009, pp. 149–51, with additional bibliography.

43 Bugli 2003–4, nos. 125 and 132 (1739), and nos. 202 and 208 (1776). The author is given as 'anonimo' in the inventory of 1739 and listed as Andrea Vaccaro in that of 1776. The painter is, however, more likely to be identified as one of the members of the circle of Aniello Falcone – such as Domenico Gargiulo and Andrea de Leone – who are known to have produced a number of portraits of the protagonists of the revolt in the years immediately following (for which, see further C. Marshall 1998, pp. 483 and 486).

44 Bugli 2003–4, no. 43 (1739) and no. 59 (1776). For the painting itself, see Leone de Castris in Naples 1994b, cat. no. 80, pp. 158–9.

45 Bugli 2003–4, nos. 171 and 222 (1739); nos. 79 and 148 (1776). For a reproduction of one of these portraits, see Bugli 2003–4, p. 151.

46 For Giovanni d'Avalos and Caracciolo, see S. Causa 2000, pp. 354 and 356 (Caracciolo was paid 12 ducats on account in 1621 for a *St Blaise* to be painted for Don Giovanni d'Avalos, and Caracciolo received on account payments in 1629 for an altarpiece of *St Ignatius*). For Giovanni d'Avalos and Ribera, see E. Nappi 1990, p. 183, which publishes a document of 24 August 1632 in which Ribera repaid Giovanni d'Avalos, principe di Montesarchio, 100 ducats paid to him earlier as a down payment for a painting of *St Lawrence* that he was not able to complete.

47 De' Dominici 1742–5, vol. III, p. 415: 'in cui Luca solea servirsi per modello della sua propria moglie ch'era ben formata di corpo, alta della persona, di membra proporzionate, e di vago sembiante, senza cercarne altri, e forse scandolosi'. For Giordano's D'Avalos *Venus* in the context of Artemisia Gentileschi's paintings of female nudes, see C. Marshall 2005, pp. 10–12.

48 Federica de Rosa in Phoenix 2006, pp. 92–3, with bibliography.

49 For the Genoese merchants and seventeenth-century Neapolitan trade and society more generally, see Dauverd 2007, passim.

50 For Andrea Doria and Naples, see Dauverd 2007, pp. 57, 203.

51 For Cornelio Spinola's payments to painters, see E. Nappi 1992, p. 26 (1638 payment to Azzolino), p. 49 (1639 payment to Giacomo de Castro) and p. 62 (1609 payment to Tommaso de Rosa).

52 For Cornelio Spinola's patronage at San Giorgio dei Genovesi, see Ioannou 2002, p. 144.

53 E. Nappi 1992, pp. 29, 35, 41, 48, 51, 64, 68 and 91.

54 For Massa's inventory, see Delfino 1985, pp. 90–97. Some of the paintings listed seem, nonetheless, to have been copies after the originals ordered by Massa on Doria's behalf, for which see De Vito 1994–5, pp. 64 and 69. For Massa's commissions to Belisario Corenzio and others for his family chapel at the Benedictine church of Santi Severino e Sossio, see Farina 2008.

55 For Massa's commissions to Caravaggio, see Pacelli 1980, pp. 44–5; Bologna 1992, pp. 263–80, and n. 94, p. 344. For Massa's commissions to Ribera, see Felton 1991; and Naples 1992, cat. no. 1.15, p. 136. For Massa's commissions to Caracciolo, see S. Causa 2000, n. 150, p. 131, and pp. 342, 352 and 354–6. For Massa's other commissions on behalf of Doria, see E. Nappi 1992, pp. 29 and 64.

56 For this aspect of Doria's Neapolitan interests, see Maristella Cavanna Ciappina in *DBI*, vol. XLI; and Pacelli 2011, p. 20.

57 For Roomer's dealings with Spinola, see E. Nappi 2000, p. 62.

58 E. Nappi 2000, Table 1, p. 67, provides a summary of financial transactions.

59 For Jean Ducamps, or Giovanni del Campo, see Kren 1978, p. 18; and Briganti, Trezzani and Laureati 1983, pp. 32–3. Vouet is described in the payment of 1630 as 'Monsueto' and by Capaccio as 'Monsuitto Francese' (Capaccio 1630, p. 189), and subsequently identified as Vouet by Vaes (1925, p. 191), Ruotolo (in Naples 1984, vol. I, p. 44) and Schütze and Willette (1992, p. 37).

60 E. Nappi 2000, doc. no. 227, p. 83.

61 E. Nappi 1990, doc. no. 63, p. 185; republished by Gabriele Finaldi, 'Appendice documentaria sulla vita e l'opera di Jusepe de Ribera', in Naples 1992, p. 407. For further discussion, see C. Marshall 2000, pp. 21–2.

62 Capaccio 1630, pp. 863–4. For a detailed analysis of the paintings mentioned by Capaccio and for the fullest account of Roomer's art collecting and career more generally, see Vaes 1925, pp. 185–202.

63 Celano 1692, 7th giornata, vol. V, p. 447.

64 For the identification of the Munich *Susanna* (the only known painting by Van Dyck of this subject) with the version in Roomer's collection, see Larsen 1988, p. 204, followed thereafter by the subsequent literature, e.g., Barnes et al. 2004, cat. no. II.1, pp. 150–51.

65 For a recent overview of the extensive literature on this topic and discussion of the influence of Van Dyck's work on Andrea Vaccaro and his ambience, see Riccardo Lattuada, 'I percorsi di Andrea Vaccaro', in Mariaclaudia and Lattuada 2009, pp. 73–7.

66 For the suggestion that Van Dyck might have stopped briefly in Naples en route to Genoa following his departure from Sicily in September 1625, see London 2012, p. 43.

67 For Vaccaro's *Susanna and the Elders*, see Naples 1994b, pp. 114–17.

68 Vaes 1925, pp. 148–55, 167–8. See further Bedoni 1983, p. 22.

69 Vaes 1925, p. 186.

70 De' Dominici 1742–5, vol. III, p. 35: 'il Cavallino per veder cosa di cui erasi sparsa così gran fama, e tanto bella gli parve, che quasi incantato dalla magia di que'vivi, e sanguigni colori con maravigliosa maestria adoperati, si propone imitarla.'

71 For Cavallino and Rubens, see Percy in Cleveland and Fort Worth 1984, pp. 17–19; and Spinosa 2013, pp. 102–3.

72 This artist is tentatively identified by Vaes (1925, p. 193) with Jacques Duyvelant, about whom almost nothing is known. He is almost certainly identifiable with the 'Giacobbe' who is listed as the author of a number of landscape and seascape paintings in the inventories of the collections of Ferrante Spinelli (1654), Pietro d'Amore (1656), Giovanni Pepe (1671), Alessandro de' Costanzo (1692), Ignazio Provenzale (1693), Agnesa Marciano (1702), Francesco de' Palma (1716) and Giovanna Battista d'Aragona Pignatelli (1723), for which see Labrot 1992, passim.

73 Haskell 1980, p. 205.

74 For Roomer and Pietro da Cortona, see Ruotolo 1982, p. 9. For Roomer and Poussin, see Alabiso 1989, pp. 32–3, which notes Falcone's quotation of Poussin's *Holy Family with St John and Twelve Angels* (private collection, New York) in his fresco at Barra of the *Crossing of the Red Sea*. In the past there has been some uncertainty as to whether to identify Poussin's *Holy Family* with early inventory references to the collections of either Ascanio Filomarino or Jan Vandeneynden (and through him to Roomer). The quotation at Barra should be read as a strong factor in favour of the latter possibility, since it seems intrinsically unlikely that Falcone would insert a quotation of a painting from another collector's works of art in a commission for a collector of Roomer's significance.

75 For Falcone's frescoes at Barra, see Alabiso 1989.

76 De' Dominici 1742–5, vol. III, p. 343.

77 See Elena Fumagalli in Florence 2009, cat. nos. 59a–b, pp. 168–71.

78 Scavizzi 2001, p. 166. For a discussion of Giordano's paintings of this kind, see Naples 1997a, cat. no. 1.9, p. 162.

79 See the two paintings by Snyders included in the early seventeenth-century inventories (*circa* 1625–41 and 1641) of the Doria collection published by Farina 2002, item C299, p. 210 and item D288, p. 227.

80 Ruotolo 1982, p. 27.

81 Ruotolo 1982, appendix I, pp. 27–39.

82 For Vandeneynden's patronage of Preti during the 1650s, see John T. Spike, 'La carriera pittorica di Mattia Preti', in Corace 1989, p. 28.

83 De' Dominici 1742–5, vol. III, pp. 344–5. For Preti's *Feast of Herod*, see Mariella Utili in Naples 1999, pp. 136–7; and Spike 1999, cat. no. 241, pp. 300–01.

84 For the original inventory reference, see Ruotolo 1982, p. 30. For Giordano's painting, see Mariella Utili in Naples, Vienna and Los Angeles 2001, cat. no. 44, pp. 166–9; and Naples 2008b, cat. no. 103, pp. 112–13, with bibliography. Utili nonetheless associates Giordano's *Apollo and Marsyas* in the Capodimonte with another version of the subject originally in the Stefano di Marinis collection, Genoa.

85 For an analysis of this theme, with particular reference to artistic and devotional cross-currents between Naples and Spain, see Padula and Seville 1996, pp. 13–31.

86 For the architectural history of Palazzo Zevallos Stigliano, see De Seta 2007, pp. 9–37.

87 The principal source on Filomarino's patronage remains the studies published by Loredana Lorizzo (2006), supplemented by her previous articles (Lorizzo 2001a, Lorizzo 2001b, Lorizzo 2003–4).

88 For Filomarino's biography and career, see Lorizzo 2006, passim; and Massimo Bray in *DBI*, vol. XLVII, with additional bibliography.

89 Innocenzo Fuidoro, *Giornali di Napoli dal 1660 al 1680*, Naples: Società Napoletana di storia patria, 1934, cited by Gino Benzoni in *DBI*, vol. XLVII.

90 The suggestion was originally made by Sebastian Schütze (1992a), and amplified thereafter by Lorizzo (2003–4, p. 123; Lorizzo 2006, p. 33).

91 For Marcantonio Filomarino's inventory of 1634, see Labrot 1992, inv. no. 33, pp. 160–65.

92 For the series of paintings of angels with the symbols of the Passion, see most recently Erich Schleier in Besançon 2008, p. 79, with bibliography, who writes in agreement with the suggestion that the Naples canvases are to be reattributed to the workshop of Vouet (Charles Mellin?).

93 For Filomarino and Vouet, see Lorizzo 2001b, p. 405; and Lorizzo 2006, pp. 34–40.

94 For Mellin, Filomarino and Barberini patronage of the 1620s, see Primarosa 2010, p. 58, and n. 95, p. 87.

95 For Filomarino and Mellin, see Lorizzo 2006, p. 111, and n. 22, p. 144. The suggestion that Filomarino might have facilitated Mellin's temporary residence in Naples was originally made by Doris Wild (Wild 1967, pp. 20–22).

96 Costello 1950, pp. 239–40.

97 Alabiso 1989, p. 34.

98 For this painting, preserved today in only fragmentary form, see Blunt 1947, p. 266; Blunt 1958, p. 76; Blunt 1966, no. 27; and Whitfield in Naples 1984, vol. I, cat. no. 2.168, p. 369.

99 For De Leone's version of the *Adoration of the Golden Calf*, see Spinosa 2010, cat. no. 104, pp. 218–19, with bibliography.

100 Lorizzo 2001b, pp. 405–8; Lorizzo 2006, pp. 40–46.

101 Blunt 1958, p. 86, and pp. 76–86 for Poussin's works in Neapolitan collections more generally.

102 De Reumont 1854, pp. 173–4.

103 Lorizzo 2006, p. 82.

104 Lorizzo 2006, p. 83.

105 Filomarino's diplomatic dispatches written to Pope Innocent X describing the events of the revolt remain one of its fundamental primary sources (for which see F. Palermo 1846, pp. 379–93).

106 For the doomed project of the so-called *epitaffio*, see Capasso 1897; Cantone 1984, pp. 420–21.

107 For this aspect of the revolt, see Villari 1993, pp. 130–35.

108 For Filomarino's patronage at the cathedral and the Palazzo Arcivescovile, see D'Andrea 1975, pp. 32–7.

109 Lorizzo 2006, pp. 53–5.

110 For this assertion, see De' Dominici 1742–5, vol. III, p. 83. For subsequent commentary, see De Reumont 1854, p. 333; and De Vito 2003–4b, p. 110, and n. 27, pp. 113 and 122.

111 For the Filomarino chapel, see Naples 1984, vol. II, pp. 303 and 451; Schütze 1989; Lorizzo 2001a; Lorizzo 2006, pp. 64–81.

112 Lorizzo 2006, p. 64.

113 For Scipione Filomarino, see Gino Benzoni in *DBI*, vol. XLVI, with bibliography.

114 For further commentary and analysis of Borromini's only other known Neapolitan commission, the now-destroyed high altar of the church of Santa Maria a Capella Nuova, sponsored by Filomarino's protector Cardinal Francesco Barberini, see Pasculli Ferrara 2000.

115 Francesco d'Andrea cited in Ruotolo 1987, p. 177.
116 A. Mazzacane in *DBI*, vol. XXXII, pp. 530–31.
117 Ruotolo 1987, p. 179; Labrot and Ruotolo 1980, p. 30.
118 A. Mazzacane in *DBI*, vol. XXXII, pp. 530–31; M. Biagetti in *DBI*, vol. XXXII, p. 536; Minieri Riccio 1878–80, p. 531; Quondam 1977, pp. 1080–81.
119 Galasso 1982, p. 108, citing Innocenzo Fuidoro (Vincenzo D'Onofrio), *Giornali di Napoli dal MCDLX al MDCLXXX*, Naples: Società napoletana di storia patria, 1934, vol. IV, p. 223; M. Biagetti in *DBI*, vol. XXXII, p. 537.
120 Celano 1692, vol. IV, pp. 581–2.
121 Galasso 1982, p. 411: 'indiubbiamente . . . la figura più significativa della cultura filosofica napoletana tra l'ultimo quindicennio del XVII e il primo quindicennio del XVIII secolo'; see also pp. 405–8, 665–9.
122 Willette 1986, p. 259; Minieri Riccio 1878–80, p. 387. For the Colonia Sebezia, see Minieri Riccio 1878–80, pp. 386–9.
123 Galasso 1982, p. 667; Ann Percy in Cleveland and Fort Worth 1984, n. 92, p. 32.
124 Consoli Fiego 1922, pp. 172–5, particularly pp. 173–5.
125 See the inventory transcription dated 29 July 1682 held at the Getty Provenance Index database (Inv-I 328). For discussion, see Delfino 1987, doc. no. 6, p. 98; and Valter Pinto in De' Dominici 2003–8, vol. III, n. 45, p. 768.
126 For the painted mirrors in the Galleria Colonna, see Rudolph 1979, pp. 13–14; and Rome 1981, cat. nos. 109–12, pp. 86–7.
127 For the argument that later seventeenth-century Neapolitan bourgeois collections should be regarded as 'expressions of autonomy and modernity in relation to other classes', see Borrelli 1986, pp. 77–80, and passim for the other publications by this author cited in the bibliography.
128 Labrot 1992, pp. 92–100.

10 THE VICEROYS

1 For the career and political connections of Niccolò Ludovisi (1610–1664), see Giampiero Brunelli in *DBI*, vol. LXVI, with bibliography.
2 Monterrey, 4 September 1632, cited in Anselmi 2000, p. 103. For the negotiations and sale of the Ludovisi *Bacchanals*, see further Zimmermann 2009, pp. 284–5; and García Cueto 2009, pp. 297–8.
3 For a useful entry point into this much-discussed aspect of Neapolitan Baroque painting, see Spinosa 1984a, especially pp. 35–8.
4 Boschini 1660/1674, pp. 168–75. The quotation attributed to Domenichino occurs on p. 171.
5 For this long-held view, see De' Dominici 1742–5, vol. II, p. 290; and more recently Labrot and Ruotolo 1980, pp. 44–5; and Haskell 1982, p. 62.
6 García Cueto 2009, pp. 299–303.
7 Colomer 2009b, pp. 31–2.
8 De Cunzo 1995, passim; De Cavi 2008.
9 De Cunzo 1995, p. 70; E. Nappi 1983c, p. 43; Pacelli 1984a; S. Causa 2000, cat. no. A23, p. 180; E. Nappi 2009, p. 107; Palos and Palumbo 2009.
10 For Ribera's *Immaculate Conception*, commissioned for the Cappella Reale in 1646 but subsequently removed to Spain and ultimately destroyed during the Spanish Civil War, see E. Nappi 1990, doc. nos. 54–6, p. 184. For Lanfranco's work at the Cappella Reale, see E. Nappi 1983c, pp. 47–8. For Mellin's cupola frescoes for the Cappella Reale, also documented to 1646, see E. Nappi 1983c, pp. 47–8.
11 G. Mancini 1956–7, vol. I, p. 249.
12 De' Dominici 1742–5, vol. III, p. 4. For Gibert's painting, see Naples 1992, p. 89.
13 Gabriele Finaldi, 'La serie di dipinti di Osuna', in Naples 2011, pp. 180–89.
14 For discussion, see Finaldi in Naples 2011, cat. no. 38, p. 186.
15 Lange 2009.
16 Lange 2009, pp. 259–62. For the likely identification of Ribera's now-lost paintings with the early commissions for the Alcázar, see further Gerard 1982, p. 14; and Madrid 2005, p. 174. For Gentileschi's *Hercules and Omphale*, see further Bissell 1999, cat. no. L-40, pp. 370–71, with bibliography.
17 Chenault 1976.
18 For the conferring of this order on Stanzione, see Schütze and Willette 1992, pp. 45–52. For Caracciolo's conferral, see Stoughton 1973, p. 5.
19 Ignacio Góngora, 'Claros varones en letres', Biblioteca Columbina, Seville; cited and trans. in Brown 1978, p. 38.
20 For Alcalá's collection, see Fitz Darby 1962; Brown and Kagan 1987; and Burke and Cherry 1997, vol. I, pp. 143–6.
21 Muñoz González 1999.
22 Brown and Kagan 1987, p. 243, for the suggestion that Alcalá might have invited Gentileschi to relocate to Naples, and pp. 239–40 for a discussion of Alcalá's paintings by Gentileschi. See further Bissell 1999, pp. 56–7, and n. 6, p. 406, citing other secondary writers' support of this hypothesis.
23 The most useful discussion remains Craig Felton in Fort Worth 1982, cat. no. 11, pp. 128–31.
24 For Cotan's painting, see Orozco Díaz 1993, cat. no. 16, p. 314, with bibliography; and Stoichita and Coderch 1999, p. 56. For this tradition more generally, with a particular emphasis on the paintings by Ribera and Velázquez, see B. Wind 1998, passim
25 New York 1992, cat. no. 22, pp. 89–90.
26 For Ribera's early paintings of philosophers, see Naples 2011, cat. no. 29, pp. 164–5; and Naples 1992, cat. no. 7, pp. 66–7.
27 Fitz Darby 1962, p. 288.
28 New York 1992, cat. nos. 35–40, pp. 112–19.
29 For the three copies after *Philosophers* by Ribera in the collection of Atanasio Jiménez de Arellano in 1657, see Burke and Cherry, vol. I, 1997, p. 548.
30 For the reference to a *Philosopher* by Ribera in the inventory of 1674 of the collection of the painter and art dealer Gerrit van Uylenburgh (the only Neapolitan painting in the collection), see Dudok van Heel 1982, p. 85.
31 For the ten *Philosophers* by Ribera in the inventory of 1677 of the Venetian collection of Giovanni Andrea Lumaga, see Moretti 2005.
32 For Doña Maria's journey to Vienna via Naples, see Bulifon 1932, pp. 142–3; Harris and Elliott 1976, p. 24; and Elliott 1986, pp. 369, 394–5 and 398. For Velázquez's stay in Naples during this period more specifically, see De Vito 2001.
33 Elliott 1986, pp. 18–19.
34 For Monterrey's collection, see Pérez Sánchez 1977; Burke and Cherry 1997, vol. I, pp. 146–9, 501–9.
35 Angela Madruga Real, 'Ribera, Monterrey e le Agostiniane di Salamanca', in Naples 1992, pp. 277–89; Zimmerman 2009, pp. 281–3.

36 See, for example, the comments of Haskell 1980, p. 171, who views Monterrey as 'the most conspicuous Spanish patron in Italy during the first half of the century'.

37 For these paintings, see Spinosa 2003, cat. nos. A122–3, pp. 286–7, with bibliography. For discussion, see further Naples 1992, cat. no. 26, pp. 95–8; Gabrielle Finaldi in Madrid 2005, cat. nos. 51–2, pp. 236–7; and Madrid 2014, pp. 101–8. The documentation for this commission is incomplete. They are first recorded being acquired for the Buen Retiro in Madrid in 1634 from the grandmother of one of the king's illegitimate children. As Finaldi has noted, however (Madrid 2005, p. 236), 'The document shows only the modality of payment and does not exclude the possibility that they were commissioned in Naples from the artist for the king. In fact, the combination of the pictures' subject matter and their enormous dimensions makes it extremely unlikely that they were not a royal commission.' The fact that the *Ixion* is signed and dated 1632 (Monterrey's second year as viceroy) points to Monterrey as the obvious candidate for this commission. Another factor linking him with the commission is the presence of two paintings by Ribera that are listed in Monterrey's collection of 1653 as 'two paintings by Joseph de Ribera of Tantalus and Sisyphus', appraised at the very high rate of 6,600 *reales* (Pérez Sánchez 1977, item 228, p. 456; and see further Burke and Cherry 1997, vol. II, p. 1594, for additional inventory references, where, however, the second painting is transcribed as 'fisico' rather than 'Ticio' as given by Pérez Sánchez). For the common confusion in transcribing the correct subjects depicted in these paintings, see further Finaldi in Madrid 2005, p. 236.

38 For the question of the other two paintings in the series, see, more recently, De Los Cobos in Madrid 2005, p. 186, and n. 76, p. 189, which notes the reference in the inventory of the Buen Retiro of 1701 to two additional paintings of *Sisyphus* and *Tantalus*, which are identified as copies after Ribera.

39 For a recent analysis of Titian's *Furias* series, with additional previous bibliography, see Madrid 2014, pp. 25–62. The discrepancy in the dating of Titian's *Tityus* today in the Prado (1560–65) with the series of the *Furias* originally installed in 1549 in the palace of Binche on the outskirts of Brussels is explained by the fact that the Prado's *Tityus* is, in fact, a second and subsequent autograph version of the subject painted by Titian for a Spanish private patron which was then subsequently swapped with the original version – at that stage in a poor state of conservation – following a request from Philip IV in 1626 (Madrid 2014, p. 30).

40 Spinosa 2003, cat. nos. B19–22, p. 351; and for discussion, see further De Vito 2000b, pp. 94–101.

41 For an overview of Van Uffel's patronage and collecting activities in Venice from 1616 to his return to Amsterdam in 1632, see Maartje van Gelder in Borean and Mason 2007, p. 320.

42 Sandrart 1675, p. 278. For commentary, see Keith Christiansen in New York 1992, p. 95.

43 Théophile Gautier, *Voyage en Espagne*, Paris: Flammarion, 1981; cited and trans. in Zwijnenberg 2003, p. 71; and see further, passim, for Ribera's reputation as a painter of grisly scenes of violence.

44 For this series, see Schütze and Willette 1992, pp. 200–02, with bibliography. For subsequent sources, with particular reference to Gentileschi's contribution to the series, see further Bissell 1999, cat. no. 32, pp. 249–56; Rome, New York and St Louis 2001, cat. no. 77, pp. 405–7; and Andrés Úbeda de los Cobos in Milan 2011, cat. no. 31, pp. 204–5. The last author proposes the slightly later date of *circa* 1635 and argues against Vannugli's suggestion (Vannugli 1989b) that the series was originally painted for the Ermita de San Juan.

45 Riccardo Lattuada, 'Artemisia and Naples, Naples and Artemisia', in Rome, New York and St Louis 2001, p. 382.

46 Guarino also paraphrased Stanzione's *Annunciation of the Birth of the Baptist* in a work produced for the Collegiata di San Michele at Solofra. For Guarino's indebtedness to the Buen Retiro series of the *Life of St John the Baptist*, see Mina Gregori in Naples 1984, vol. I, p. 304. For a more recent reappraisal, see Lattuada 2000, cat. no. E50, pp. 228–30.

47 For Cavallino's indebtedness to the series (as particularly evident in Cavallino's *Meeting of Anna and Joachim at the Golden Gate*, Szépművészeti Múzeum, Budapest), see Cleveland and Fort Worth 1984, pp. 9 and 53. For Falcone's indebtedness to Gentileschi's *Birth of the Baptist*, see Gregori in Naples 1984, vol. I, p. 304.

48 For the marqués de Castel-Rodrigo's role in commissioning the Roman component of the series, see Andrés Úbeda de los Cobos in Madrid 2005, p. 171. For the Buen Retiro landscape commissions, see further Giovanna Capitelli, 'The Landscapes for the Buen Retiro Palace', in Madrid 2005, pp. 241–61, with bibliography. Monterrey was also involved in this commission (pp. 242–5), so there was evidently a degree of crossover between each city, and their respective agents, in the apportioning of works for each of the two series.

49 Passeri, for example, clearly underlines the duque de Medina de las Torres's importance in this regard when he follows a reference to Monterrey's commissioning of Domenichino with 'the then viceroy, the Duke of Medina, who had replaced Monterrey, ordered him to leave this work [the commission for the Cappella di San Gennaro in Naples Cathedral] and commissioned him to paint several intricate paintings in oil for one of the king's galleries in Madrid. He also commissioned paintings from other artists'; Passeri 1772, pp. 38–9.

50 Bellori 1672, p. 389; Passeri 1772, p. 147; Giovanni Lanfranco, letter to Ferrante Carlo, dated 10 December 1637, cited in Bernini 1982, p. 333.

51 Gaya Nuno cited in Madrid 2005, n. 8, p. 203.

52 Annachiara Alabiso in Naples 1984, vol. I, cat. no 2.75, p. 262.

53 C. Marshall 1998, pp. 478–89.

54 For the social and political context of Oñate's vice-regency, see Coniglio 1967, pp. 267–71; Galasso 1982, pp. 23–4, 85–8.

55 Galasso 1982, pp. 21–4; E. Nappi 1983c, pp. 49–50; Palomares 2009, pp. 326–32.

56 Rubino, 'Notitia di quanto è occorso in Napoli dall'anno 1648 per tutto l'anno 1657', Naples, n.p., cited in Palomares 2009, p. 333: 'a i latti della quale sotto due archi vi erano inalzate due statue, a destra stava d'Amore con testa coronata et con un cornicopio in mano ripieno di ricchezze, significando l'amore che ci governa la Monarchia Spagnola, a sinistra stava la statua della Fedeltà con un scudo in mano ove si era dipinta la impresa del Popolo sotto la quale stava un cane dinotando la fedeltà napolitana verso i suoi Cattolici Regi.'

11 PUBLIC EXHIBITIONS, ARTISTIC RIVALRY AND THE INTERNATIONALIZATION OF NEAPOLITAN BAROQUE PAINTING

1 For the background to this commission, see Wethey 1967; and Ehlert 2007, passim.

2 For Vaccaro's *Intercession of the Virgin for the Souls in Purgatory*, see Ida Maietta in Naples 2008a, cat. no. 36, pp. 124–5, with bibliography.

3 For Giordano's altarpieces at Santa Maria del Pianto, see Mariella Utili in Naples, Vienna and Los Angeles 2001, cat. no. 31a–b, pp. 138–9, with bibliography.

4 For Gargiulo's *Piazza Mercatello during the Plague of 1656,* see Daprà in Naples 2002, cat. no. 66, pp. 150–51, with bibliography.

5 De' Dominici 1742–5, vol. III, p. 143.

6 De' Dominici 1742–5, vol. III, pp. 145–7 (life of Vaccaro); p. 399 (life of Giordano).

7 Stanzione is described in the 1650s as a 'competidor de Jusepe de Ribera' by the Spanish chronicler Lázaro Díaz del Valle. For this and a discussion of Ribera's and Stanzione's rivalry more generally, see Schütze and Willette 1992, pp. 158–9.

8 De' Dominici 1742–5, vol. III, p. 10.

9 For Ribera's *Noah*, see Spinosa 2003, cat. no. A193, p. 309, with bibliography.

10 For an attempt to sort out apparent fact from evident fiction, see Schütze and Willette 1992, pp. 158–9, 179–80, nn. 82ff., and n. 209; and Andrea Zezza in De' Dominici 2003–8, vol. III/1, n. 29, p. 24, and n. 35, p. 97.

11 For Renaissance rivalry, see Goffen 2002. For Italian Baroque rivalry, see Cropper 2005.

12 For the Festa dei Quattro Altari, see Ceva Grimaldi 1857, p. 660; F. Mancini 1968, p. 111; Raimondo 1973–4; Campanelli 1991, p. 498; Di Nola and Mancini 1985; and Naples 1997a, pp. 44, 150 ff.

13 Salomon 2010, p. 74.

14 Riccardo Lattuada, 'La stagione del Barocco a Napoli, 1683–1759', in Naples 1997a, p. 44.

15 For the departure of the procession from San Giacomo degli Spagnoli, see Raimondo 1973–4.

16 De' Dominici 1742–5, vol. III, p. 193. The purchaser of the painting is identified as Roderigo Messia di Pardo. Although Di Pardo (died *circa* 1702) was undoubtedly a significant patron of Gargiulo, he does not appear to have begun collecting until after the plague of 1656 and is unlikely, therefore, to have acquired one of Gargiulo's earliest exhibited paintings. A more likely candidate for this is probably the high-ranking councillor Ettore Capecelatro, since he is known to have commissioned a version of the *Massacre of the Innocents* from Gargiulo in 1636 (E. Nappi 1983b, p. 75; see further, Sricchia Santoro in De' Dominici 2003–8, vol. II, n. 11, p. 371, with bibliography).

17 De' Dominici 1742–5, vol. III, p. 194. For the presence of Gargiulo's *Triumph of Caesar* in the inventories of 1682 and 1716 of the collection of Francesco de Palma, duca di Sant'Elia, Naples, see Labrot 1992, inv. no. 31, item 1, p. 153, and inv. no. 56, item 56, p. 286.

18 Röttgen 2006, pp. 9, 19–36; Salomon 2010, pp. 79–80.

19 De' Dominici 1742–5, vol. III, p. 211.

20 For the rivalry between Giordano and Francesco di Maria, see further Maria Tamajo Contarini in Naples 2009, vol. I, cat. no. 1.138, pp. 262–3, with bibliography.

21 De' Dominici 1742–5, vol. III, pp. 307–8, 432. That the exhibition took place around 1678 is suggested by the fact that Giacomo del Po, who is said by De' Dominici to have come to Naples from Rome in that year, is securely documented as arriving in Naples in 1678 (for which, see Prota Giurleo 1955d, p. 260).

22 Haskell 1980, p. 126; and see further, Haskell 1960.

23 De' Dominici 1742–5, vol. III, p. 4.

24 For the varying accounts of Rosa's movements during this period, see Mahoney 1977, vol. I, pp. 50–61; Festa 1982, pp. 106–9; Scott 1995, pp. 7–14; Aurora Spinosa in Naples 2008c, pp. 18–19; Langdon in London and Fort Worth 2010, n. 32, p. 45.

25 For Simonelli, see Capitelli 2004, with bibliography.

26 For this and the previous quotation, see Passeri, 1772, p. 420.

27 For Rosa's *Prometheus*, see Caterina Volpi in Naples 2008c, cat. no. 30, pp. 148–9, with bibliography, as well as Miguel Falomir in Madrid 2014, pp. 128–32. For the various arguments concerning the relationship of the Corsini *Prometheus* to another now-lost painting of *Tityus* by Rosa formerly in the Gerini collection, Florence, and the question of which of these two paintings is to be identified with the painting exhibited at the Pantheon, see also Scott 1995, pp. 10–11; Salomon 2010, pp. 80–82.

28 For discussion, see Oreste Ferrari in Naples, Vienna and Los Angeles 2001, pp. 32–3, with bibliography.

29 For the dating of Giordano's *Nativity of the Virgin* and *Presentation of the Virgin in the Temple* to *circa* 1672–4, see Ferrari and Scavizzi 2003, cat. no. A0104, p. 48, with bibliography.

30 Letter from Paolo del Sera to Leopoldo de' Medici, Venice, 20 October 1668, in Fileti Mazza 1987, p. 439. For Giordano's Santa Maria della Salute paintings, see Ferrari and Scavizzi 1992, vol. I, cat. nos. A198, A223, pp. 282, 287; De Vito 1999b; and more recently, Ferrari and Scavizzi 2003, cat. no. A0104, p. 48.

31 Ferrari and Scavizzi 1992, vol. I, p. 58.

32 Vasari 1550/1568, vol. V, pp. 471–2.

33 De' Dominici 1742–5, vol. III, pp. 304–5, 401–2. The painting and ensuing dispute between Giordano and Di Maria is also discussed in an earlier manuscript compiled by Francesco Saverio Baldinucci between 1713 and 1721 on the basis of information provided by him from a range of sources – including information sent by De' Dominici in Naples (F. S. Baldinucci 1975, cc. 159f–160v; for which, see further Ferrari 1966, p. 95).

34 For Giordano's *Allegory of the Reintegration of Messina into Spain*, see Ferrari and Scavizzi 1992, vol. I, p. 62, n. 63, p. 228, cat. no. A258, p. 293, and p. 406; and Teresa Pugliatti in Messina and Rome 1994, p. 316. Ferrari and Scavizzi 1992 (followed by Pugliatti) identify the painting as a variant of the *Allegory* of 1678 on the basis of divergences between its composition and that described by De' Dominici and Baldinucci.

35 For this aspect of the *Allegory* exhibition of 1678, see further Ferrari in Naples, Vienna and Los Angeles 2001, n. 5, p. 68, who goes so far as to suggest that the *Allegory* may have formed part of an actual 'apparato effimero, promosso dallo stesso vicerè de Los Vélez'.

36 In 1670 Giordano received 80 ducats for assisting in the decoration of a catafalque to be erected in the Piazza della Selleria (Novelli Radice 1982–3, p. 183), and towards the end

of his life he is known to have contributed works to the Quarant'ore celebrations at the church of Santa Brigida (Lattuada in Naples 1997a, cat. no. 1.22, p. 179).

37 For the Pio Monte dei Poveri Vergognosi, founded in the early seventeenth century and closed in 1830, see Strazzullo 1954–5, n. 1, p. 145. It is not to be confused with the Monte e Banco della Poveri on the Via dei Tribunali. Giordano seems to have had a long-standing association with the Pio Monte dei Poveri Vergognosi. In 1670 he is documented at work on a modest commission to paint a number of unspecified portraits for the institution (E. Nappi 1991, doc. nos. 138–9, p. 174).

38 For Cassineses' *Triumphal Arch*, see Naples 1997a, p. 57; and Pisani 1992, pp. 30, 74.

39 For Celano, see Strazzullo 1995; and Pinto 1997, pp. 64–93.

40 De' Dominici 1742–5, vol. III, p. 401. For Artale, see Mirollo 1963, p. 218; Quondam 1972, p. 620; and Quondam 1977, p. 818, and n. 26, p. 1064. Artale's will of 1679 includes reference to paintings in his possession by Giuseppe Recco and Giuseppe Ruoppolo, together with a painting promised to him by Giordano that was probably a collaborative work since the document mentions that it was to have included figures by Giordano (Prota Giurleo 1955a). For further discussion of this and the still-life exhibition of 1684, see C. Marshall 2003.

41 De' Dominici 1742–5, vol. III, p. 402.

42 For the Neapolitan academies and the development of the new sciences, see further Stone 1997, passim.

43 Ferrari 1966, p. 95. For commentary, see Ferrari in Naples, Vienna and Los Angeles 2001, n. 5, p. 68.

44 For the complicated circumstances surrounding the exhibition of 1631 at Santa Maria di Costantinopoli, see Costello 1950; and Rome 1994, passim.

45 For the recent literature on the still-life exhibition and its dating to 1684 (initially suggested by Spike in New York 1983 and followed thereafter by Salerno and subsequent commentators), see New York 1983, n. 26, p. 19; Salerno 1989, p. 105, n. 28, p. 177 (noting the error made by Zeri in dating the exhibition to 1675); Riccardo Lattuada, 'Luca Giordano e i maestri napoletani di natura morta nelle tele per la Festa del Corpus Domini del 1684', in Naples 1997a, pp. 150–69; De Vito 2012–13a. For discussions of the paintings of 1684 in the wider context of Giordano's other still-life paintings, see further Ferrari and Scavizzi 1992, vol. I, pp. 119–22; De Vito 1993b, particularly pp. 44–5; Scavizzi 2001; Ferrari and Scavizzi 2003, pp. 63–4.

46 For De' Dominici's frequent references to this exhibition, see De' Dominici 1742–5, vol. III, pp. 296, 298, 442, 562–3.

47 The most comprehensive publication of Del Carpio's inventories and account of his activities as a patron and collector is Burke and Cherry 1997, vol. I, pp. 156–70, 462–83, 727–86, 815–77.

48 De' Dominici 1742–5, vol. III, p. 442.

49 For the two recently identified paintings and their measurements, see De Vito 2012–13a, p. 33.

50 Naples 1997a, cat. nos. 1.11 and 1.12, p. 166.

51 For Giordano's and Recco's *Riches of the Sea with Neptune and Two Sea Nymphs*, see Adelaide 1997, pp. 12–13, and n. 9, p. 24; Naples 1997a, cat. no. 1.10, pp. 162–4.

52 Lattuada (in Naples 1997a, pp. 162–4) cites information provided by Mauro Natale connecting the *Autumn* and *Summer* to an entry in a Del Carpio inventory of late 1687. This reference, however, cannot be connected with the *Autumn* and the *Summer* since the dimensions referred to in the inventory do not correspond with either painting. The *Autumn* and *Summer* each measure 2.44 × 3.48 m, whereas the Del Carpio inventory of 1687 records 'Quattro quadri di p.[mi] 4. e 3. Jnc.[a] con le quattro Stagioni di mano di Luca Giordano' (Burke and Cherry 1997, vol. I, item 202, p. 823). The dimensions of 4 × 3 Neapolitan *palmi* given in the inventory convert into approximately 1.05 × 0.79 m, which makes these paintings much too small to match either the *Autumn* or the *Summer*. A further factor dissociating the Del Carpio *Seasons* of 1687 from the still-life paintings of 1684 is that the *Seasons* are placed in the inventory in close sequence with two other presumably closely related series, which are listed as copies after Giordano, depicting the *Four Elements* and the *Four Continents* (Burke and Cherry 1997, vol. I, items 205 and 208, pp. 823–4). The *Four Seasons* of 1687 should thus be associated with the *Elements* and the *Continents* as having formed part of another, now-lost, series with no direct connection to the 1684 paintings.

53 C. Marshall 2003, passim.

54 For this exhibition, see Costello 1950, passim, as cited above; and for a more recent discussion, see London 2012, pp. 30–34.

55 George Davies, 'State Papers, Naples and Sicily', 1675, cited in Koenigsberger 1947, p. 315.

56 For this background, and for the growth of the English colony in Naples more generally, see Koenigsberger 1947, passim; and Coniglio 1955, pp. 111–22. For the English colony, with reference to their collecting and patronage activities more specifically, see further Borelli 1990, pp. 46–53.

57 Pagano de Divitiis 1982, n. 29, p. 386.

58 Pagano de Divitiis 1982, n. 27, p. 385.

59 Brigstocke 2004, pp. 337–8; Labrot 2010, p. 255. For Giordano and Exeter, see further Pagano de Divitiis 1982, p. 390; Ferrari and Scavizzi 1992, vol. I, p. 78, n. 15, p. 229, p. 244, and vol. II, cat. nos. A305–6, pp. 302–3. For Exeter's Neapolitan acquisitions more generally, see further Labrot 2010, p. 258.

60 For the Burghley House collections, see further Pittsburgh 1995; and Brigstocke 2004.

61 Pagano de Divitiis 1982, n. 21, p. 384.

62 Pagano de Divitiis 1982, n. 27, p. 385.

63 In 1670 Recco received payments from the marchese di Noja towards a total fee of 100 ducats for a painting of 'various sorts of fish' with an accompanying figure to be painted by Luca Giordano. The canvas is described as measuring 9 × 7 *palmi* (approx. 237 × 185 cm), D'Addosio 1912–13, p. 493.

64 For Recco's Burghley House still lifes, see Middione in London 1982, cat. nos. 116–17, pp. 223–4. For the payment documentation (which stipulates clearly a commission price of 200 ducats each), see D'Addosio 1912–13, p. 493; and further Brigstocke 2004, p. 340.

65 E. Nappi 1991, doc. no. 192, p. 178. For the painting, see Ferrari and Scavizzi 1992, vol. II, cat. no. A290, p. 299, with bibliography.

66 For Del Po's paintings after *Paradise Lost*, see Spinosa in Detroit and Chicago 1981, cat. nos. 41a–b, pp. 138–9; Spinosa 1988a, cat. no. 169, p. 142.

67 It was first translated into Italian in 1729, in partial form only, and then in 1735, *in toto*, for which see Dorris 1965.

68 For De Matteis's *Judgement of Hercules*, see O'Connell 1988, passim; Pestilli 2013, pp. 115–44, with additional bibliography.

69 O'Connell 1988, p. 152.

Catello 1975
Elio Catello, 'L'arte del ricamo a Napoli dal XVI al XIX secolo', *Campania sacra*, VI (1975), pp. 101–42

R. Causa 1951
Raffaello Causa, 'Paolo Porpora e il primo tempo della "Natura Morta" Napoletana', *Paragone*, II/15 (1951), pp. 30–36

R. Causa 1972
—, 'La pittura del Seicento a Napoli dal naturalismo al barocco', *Storia di Napoli*, vol. V, part 2, Naples: Società Editrice, 1972, pp. 915–94

R. Causa 1973
—, *L'arte nella Certosa di San Martino*, Cava dei Tirreni and Naples: Di Mauro, 1973

S. Causa 1994
Stefano Causa, 'Note di primo naturalismo: un contributo per Filippo Vitale', *Paragone*, XLV/529–33 (1994), pp. 203–11

S. Causa 2000
—, *Battistello Caracciolo: l'opera completa*, Naples: Electa, 2000

S. Causa 2009
—, *Meglio tacere: Salvator Rosa e i disagi della critica*, Naples: Arte'm, 2009

Ceci 1898
Giuseppe Ceci, 'La corporazione dei pittori', *Napoli nobilissima*, VII/21 (1898), pp. 8–13

Ceci 1899
—, 'Scrittori della storia dell'arte napoletana anteriori al De Dominici', *Napoli nobilissima*, VIII/21 (1899), pp. 163–8

Celano 1692
Carlo Celano, *Notizie del bello, dell'antico e del curioso della città di Napoli divise dall'autore in dieci giornate per guida e comodo dei viaggiatori*, Naples, 1692 (ed. Atanasio Mozzillo et al., 7 vols, Naples: Edizioni Scientifiche Italiane, 1974 [reprinted from the edition of 1856–60, ed. Giovan Battista Chiarini])

Ceva Grimaldi 1857
Francesco Ceva Grimaldi, *Memorie storiche della città di Napoli di Francesco Ceva Grimaldi*, Naples: Stamperia e Calcografia Vico Freddo Pignasecca, 1857

Chenault 1976
Jeanne Chenault, 'Jusepe de Ribera and the Order of Christ: New Documents', *Burlington Magazine*, CXVIII/878 (1976), pp. 305–7

Chenault Porter and Munshower 1993
Jeanne Chenault Porter and Susan Scott Munshower (eds), *Parthenope's Splendor: Art of the Golden Age in Naples*, University Park: Pennsylvania State University, 1993

Chiarini 2007
Marco Chiarini, *Teodoro Filippo di Liagno detto Filippo Napoletano, 1528–1629: vita e opere*, Florence: Centro Di, 2007

Chorpenning 1987
Joseph F. Chorpenning, 'Another Look at Caravaggio and Religion', *Artibus et historiae*, VIII/16 (1987), pp. 149–58

Cinotti 1983
Mia Cinotti, 'Michelangelo Merisi da Caravaggio', in *I pittori bergamaschi da XIII a XIX secolo: Il Seicento*, I, ed. Pietro Zampetti, Bergamo: Bolis, 1983, pp. 203–641

Cleveland and Fort Worth 1984
Bernardo Cavallino of Naples, 1616–1656, ed. Ann Percy and Ann T. Lurie (exh. cat., Cleveland Museum of Art and Kimbell Art Museum), Cleveland and Fort Worth: Cleveland Museum of Art and Kimbell Art Museum, 1984

Clifton 1990
James Clifton, 'Micco Spadaro at the Certosa di San Martino in Naples: The Plague Ex-Voto of 1656', *Ricerche sul '600 napoletano* (1990), pp. 85–99

Clifton 1994
—, 'Mattia Preti's Frescoes for the City Gates of Naples', *Art Bulletin*, LXXVI/3 (1994), pp. 479–501

Clifton 1995
—, "Ad vivum mire depinxit': Toward a Reconstruction of Ribera's Art Theory', *Storia dell'arte*, LXXXIII (1995), pp. 111–32

Colomer 2009a
José Luis Colomer (ed.), *España y Nápoles: coleccionismo y mecenazgo virreinales en el siglo XVII*, Madrid: Centro de Estudios Europa Hispanica, 2009

Colomer 2009b
— 'España, Nápoles y sus virreyes', in Colomer 2009a, pp. 13–37

Condivi 1999
Ascanio Condivi, *The Life of Michelangelo*, University Park: Pennsylvania State University Press, 1999

Conelli 2000
Maria Ann Conelli, 'The "Guglie" of Naples: Religious and Political Machinations of the Festival "Macchine"', *Memoirs of the American Academy in Rome*, XLV (2000), pp. 153–83

Coniglio 1955
Giuseppe Coniglio, *Il viceregno di Napoli nel sec. XVII: notizie sulla vita commerciale e finanziaria secondo nuove ricerche negli archivi italiani e spagnoli*, Rome: Edizioni di Storia e Letteratura, 1955

Coniglio 1967
—, *I vicerè Spagnoli di Napoli*, Naples: Fausto Fiorentino Editore, 1967

Connors 1980
Joseph Connors, *Borromini and the Roman Oratory: Style and Society*, Cambridge, MA: MIT Press, 1980

Consigli Valenti 1986
Patrizia Consigli Valenti, *La battaglia nella pittura del XVII e XVIII secolo*, Parma: Banco Emiliana, 1986

Consoli Fiego 1922
G. Consoli Fiego, 'Il museo Valletta', *Napoli nobilissima*, III/7–8, 11–12 (1922), pp. 105–10, 172–5

Conversano 1983
Comune di Conversano (ed.), *Inventario delli beni remasti nell'heredità del quondam eccellentissimo signor don Giovanni Geronimo Acquaviva di Aragona conte di Conversano*, Galantina: Congedo, 1983

Conversano 2000
Paolo Finoglio e il suo tempo: un pittore napoletano alla corte degli Acquaviva, ed. Cosimo Damiano Fonseca (exh. cat., Pinacoteca Comunale del Castello), Conversano: Electa, 2000

Corace 1989
Erminia Corace (ed.), *Mattia Preti*, Rome: Fratelli Palombi, 1989

Costello 1950
Jane Costello, 'The Twelve Pictures "Ordered by Velazquez" and the Trial of Valguarnera', *Journal of the Warburg and Courtauld Institutes*, XIII (1950), pp. 237–84

Courtright 1990
Nicola Courtright, 'Gregory XIII's Tower of the Winds in the Vatican', PhD dissertation, New York University, 1990

Creazzo 1988
Ileana Creazzo, 'Alcuni inediti di Niccolò de Simone e altre precisazioni sul pittore', in *Scritti di Storia dell'arte in onore di*

Raffaello Causa, ed. Pierluigi Leone de Castris, Naples: Electa, 1988, pp. 223–32
Cropper 2005
Elizabeth Cropper, *The Domenichino Affair: Novelty, Imitation and Theft in Seventeenth-century Rome*, New Haven and London: Yale University Press, 2005
Crow 1985
Thomas Crow, *Painters and Public Life in Eighteenth Century Paris*, New Haven and London: Yale University Press, 1985
D'Addosio 1912–13
Giambattista D'Addosio, 'Documenti inediti di artisti napoletani del XVI e XVII secolo (I. Pittori)', *Archivio storico per le province napoletane*, XXXVII/4 (1912), pp. 593–616; XXXVIII/1–4 (1913), pp. 36–72, 232–59, 483–524, 578–83
D'Addosio 1920
—, *Documenti inediti di artisti napoletani dei secoli XVI e XVII dalle polizze dei banchi*, Naples: Archivio Storico per le province napoletane, 1920; facsimile edition, Bologna: Arnaldo Forni Editore, 1991
Dalbono 1871
Carlo Tito Dalbono, *Massimo: i suoi tempi e la sua scuola*, Naples: Tipografia S. Pietro a Majella, 1871
D'Andrea 1975
Gioacchino D'Andrea, 'Il mecenatismo del Cardinale Ascanio Filomarino, arcivescovo di Napoli, 1641–1666', *Rivista di letteratura e di storia ecclesiastica*, VII/1 (1975), pp. 27–40
Dauverd 2007
Céline Dauverd, 'Mediterranean Symbiotic Empire: The Genoese Trade Diaspora of Spanish Naples, 1460–1640', PhD dissertation, University of California, Los Angeles, 2007
DBI
Dizionario biografico degli italiani, ed. Giovanni Treccani et al., 79 vols, Rome: Istituto della Enciclopedia Italiana, 1960–2014
De Cavi 2008
Sabina De Cavi, 'Il Palazzo Reale di Napoli (1600–1607): un edificio "spagnolo"?' in Pestilli, Rowland and Schütze 2008, pp. 147–70
De Cunzo 1995
Mario A. De Cunzo (ed.), *Il Palazzo Reale di Napoli*, Naples: Electa, 1995
De' Dominici 1742–5
Bernardo De' Dominici, *Vite de' pittori, scultori ed architetti napoletani*, 3 vols, Naples: Stamperia del Ricciardi, 1742–5 (facsimile edition, Bologna: Arnaldo Forni, 1979)
De' Dominici 2003–8
—, *Vite de' pittori, scultori ed architetti napoletani* [1742–5], ed. Fiorella Sricchia Santoro and Andrea Zezza, 3 vols, Naples: Paparo, 2003–8
D'Elia and Belli 1970
Michele D'Elia and Pina Belli, *I pittori del Guercio*, Bari: Quaderni di Terra di Bari, 2, 1970
Delfino 1983
Antonio Delfino, 'La chiesa di Donnaregina Nuova', *Ricerche sul '600 napoletano* (1983), pp. 81–117
Delfino 1984
—, 'Nuovi documenti sulla chiesa e sul monastero di Donnaregina nel Seicento: documenti inediti su alcuni pittori napoletani del Seicento', *Ricerche sul '600 napoletano* (1984), pp. 149–61
Delfino 1985
—, 'Documenti inediti per alcuni pittori napoletani del '600 e l'inventario dei beni lasciata da Lanfranco Massa con una sua breve biografia (tratti dall'Archivio di Stato di Napoli)', *Ricerche sul '600 napoletano* (1985), pp. 89–111 [introduction by Giuseppe de Vito]
Delfino 1986
—, 'Documenti inediti tratti dall'Archivio Storico del Banco di Napoli', *Ricerche sul '600 napoletano* (1986), pp. 111–17
Delfino 1987
—, 'Documenti inediti sui pittori del '600 tratti dall'Archivio Storico del Banco di Napoli (ASBN) e dall'Archivio di Stato di Napoli (ASN)', *Ricerche sul '600 napoletano* (1987), pp. 79–98
Delfino 1988
—, 'Documenti inediti sui pittori del '600 tratti dall'Archivio Storico del Banco di Napoli (ASBN) e dall'Archivio di Stato di Napoli (ASN)', *Ricerche sul '600 napoletano* (1988), pp. 57–64
Delfino 1989
—, 'Documenti inediti su artisti del '600 tratti dall'Archivio di Stato di Napoli (ASN) e dall'Archivio Storico del Banco di Napoli (ASBN)', *Ricerche sul '600 napoletano* (1989), pp. 29–40
Delfino 1991
—, 'Documenti inerenti a Luca Giordano tratti dall'Archivio di Stato di Napoli (ASN)', *Ricerche sul '600 napoletano* (1991), pp. 19–32
Delfino 1993
—, 'Documenti inediti tratti dall'Archivio di Stato di Napoli (ASN) e dall'Archivio Storico del Banco di Napoli (ASBN)', *Ricerche sul '600 napoletano* (1993), pp. 21–40
De Maio 1983
Romeo De Maio, *Pittura e controriforma a Napoli*, Rome: Laterza, 1983
De Marchi 1987
Giulia De Marchi, *Mostre di quadri a S. Salvatore in Lauro, 1682–1725: stime di collezioni romane*, Rome: Biblioteca Vallicelliana, 1987
De Martini 1994
Vega De Martini, 'Un inventario inedito della collezione d'Avalos', *Bollettino d'arte*, LXXIX/88 (1994), pp. 119–30
Denucé 1932
Jean Denucé, *The Antwerp Art Galleries: Inventories of the Art Collections in Antwerp in the 16th and 17th Centuries*, Antwerp: 'De Sikkel', 1932
De Reumont 1854
Alfred De Reumont, *The Carafas of Maddaloni: Naples under Spanish Dominion*, London: Henry G. Bohn, 1854
De' Rossi and Sartorius 1987
Ferdinando De' Rossi and Osvaldo Sartorius: *Santa Maria Regina Coeli: il monastero e la chiesa nella storia e nell'arte*, Naples: Editoriale Scientifica, 1987
De Seta 1981
Cesare De Seta, *Napoli* (Le città nella storia d'Italia), Bari: Laterza, 1981
De Seta 2007
— (ed.), *The Gallery of Palazzo Zevallos Stigliano*, Vicenza: Intesa Sanpaolo, 2007
De Simone 1976
Ennio De Simone, 'Case e botteghe a Napoli nei secoli XVII e XVIII', *Revue internationale d'histoire de la banque*, no. 12 (1976), pp. 77–140

Detroit and Chicago 1981
The Golden Age of Naples: Art and Civilization under the Bourbons, 1734–1805, ed. Frederick J. Cummings et al. (exh. cat., Detroit Institute of Arts and Art Institute of Chicago), Detroit: The Detroit Institute of Arts, 1981

De Vito 1982
Giuseppe De Vito, 'A. Falcone & Co.', in *Ricerche sul 600 napoletano: A. Falcone, B. Cavallino, A. De Bellis, M. Stanzione, N. Rossi*, Milan: L&T, 1982, pp. 7–35

De Vito 1984
—, 'Ritrovamenti e precisazioni a seguito della prima edizione della mostra del '600 napoletano', in *Ricerche sul '600 napoletano: saggi vari in memoria di Raffaello Causa*, Milan: L&T, 1984, pp. 7–17

De Vito 1986
—, 'Alla ricerca del "vello d'oro"', *Ricerche sul '600 napoletano* (1986), pp. 121–51

De Vito 1987
—, 'Un contributo per Filippo Vitale', *Ricerche sul '600 napoletano* (1987), pp. 105–43

De Vito 1991
—, 'Il viaggio di lavoro di Luca Giordano a Venezia e alcune motivazioni per la scelta riberesca', *Ricerche sul '600 napoletano* (1991), pp. 33–122

De Vito 1993a
—, 'Due postille alle "notizie" di Eduardo Nappi', *Ricerche sul '600 napoletano* (1993), pp. 129–41

De Vito 1993b
—, 'Luca Giordano e la pittura di genere: qualche riflessione', *Ricerche sul '600 napoletano* (1993), pp. 41–81

De Vito 1994–5
—, 'Appunti per Andrea Vaccaro con una nota su alcune copie del Caravaggio che esistevano a Napoli', in *Ricerche sul '600 napoletano: scritti in memoria di Raffaello Causa. Saggi e documenti per la storia dell'arte, 1994–1995*, Naples: Electa, 1996, pp. 63–144

De Vito 1996–7
—, 'Variazioni sul nome del Maestro dell'Annuncio ai pastori', in *Ricerche sul '600 napoletano: saggi e documenti, 1996–1997*, Naples: Electa, 1998, pp. 7–62

De Vito 1998
—, 'Il Rubens "pintado" da Luca Giordano: ma quando?', *Ricerche sul '600 napoletano: saggi e documenti, 1998*, Naples: Electa, 1999, pp. 118–37

De Vito 1999a
—, 'Cronaca di un travagliato rapporto fra Cosimo Fanzago e Cesare Firrao principe di Sant'Agata', in *Ricerche sul '600 napoletano: saggi e documenti, 1999*, Naples: Electa, 2000, pp. 15–17

De Vito 1999b
—, 'Le tele di Luca Giordano nella Basilica di Santa Maria della Salute a Venezia', in *Ricerche sul '600 napoletano: saggi e documenti, 1999*, Naples: Electa, 2000, pp. 118–29

De Vito 2000a
—, 'Una nota per Luca Forte', in *Ricerche sul '600 napoletano: saggi e documenti, 2000*, Naples: Electa, 2001, pp. 18–35

De Vito 2000b
—, 'Della contestualità di alcune opere di Luca Giordano', in *Ricerche sul '600 napoletano: saggi e documenti, 2000*, Naples: Electa, 2001, pp. 95–128

De Vito 2001
—, 'La durata del soggiorno a Napoli, alla fine del 1630, di Velázquez ed alcune possibili conseguenze', in *Ricerche sul '600 napoletano: saggi e documenti, 2001*, Naples: Electa, 2002, pp. 29–31

De Vito 2003–4a
—, 'Juan Dò riconfermato', in *Ricerche sul '600 napoletano: saggi e documenti, 2003–2004*, Naples: Electa, 2004, pp. 85–91

De Vito 2003–4b
—, 'Perifrasi fracanziane', in *Ricerche sul '600 napoletano: saggi e documenti, 2003–2004*, Naples: Electa, 2004, pp. 93–122

De Vito 2008
—, 'Alcuni dipinti inediti o poco noti di Juan Dò', in *Ricerche sul '600 napoletano: saggi e documenti, 2008*, Naples: Electa, 2009, pp. 33–38

De Vito 2009
—, 'Ritrovato il certificato di battesimo di Giovanni Dò', in *Ricerche sul '600 napoletano: saggi e documenti, 2009*, Naples: Electa, 2009, p. 71

De Vito 2012–13a
—, 'Due "quadroni" di Luca Giordano per la Festa dei quattro altari del 1684', in *Ricerche sull'arte a Napoli in età moderna: saggi e documenti, 2012–2013*, Naples: Arte'm, 2013, pp. 29–33

De Vito 2012–13b
—, 'Lettere e monogrammi: ancora sull'identificiazione del maestro dell'Annuncio ai pastori con Joan Dó', in *Ricerche sull'arte a Napoli in età moderna: saggi e documenti, 2012–2013*, Naples: Arte'm, 2013, pp. 34–9

Di Nola and Mancini 1985
Alfonso Di Nola and Franco Mancini: *La scena della festa: bozzetti e apparati scenografici per la festa dei Quattro Altari di Raffaele De Majo*, Naples: Guida Editori and Banca di Credito Popolare di Torre del Greco, 1985

Divenuto 2003
Francesco Divenuto, 'Il palazzo Orsini di Gravina a Napoli: dal cinquecento al ripristino novecentesco', *Palladio*, XVI (2003), pp. 32, 53–70

Dorris 1965
George E. Dorris, 'Paolo Rolli and the First Italian Translation of Paradise Lost', *Italica*, XLII/2 (1965), pp. 213–25

Dudok van Heel 1982
S.A.C. Dudok van Heel, 'Het "schilderhuis" van Govert Flinck en de Kunsthandel van Uylenburgh aan de Lauriergracht te Amsterdam', *Jaarboek van het Genootschap Amstelodamum*, LXXXIV (1982), pp. 70–90

Dunn 1994
Marilyn R. Dunn, 'Piety and Patronage in Seicento Rome: Two Noblewomen and their Convents', *Art Bulletin*, LXXVI/4 (1994), pp. 644–63

Dunn 2000
—, 'Spiritual Philanthropists: Women as Convent Patrons in Seventeenth Century Rome', in *Women and Art in Early Modern Europe: Patrons, Collectors and Connoisseurs*, ed. Cynthia Lawrence, Pennsylvania: Penn State University Press, 2000, pp. 168–75

Ehlert 2007
Rebecca Lisabeth Ehlert, 'S. Maria del Pianto: Loss, Remembrance and Legacy in Seventeenth Century Naples', MA dissertation, Queen's University, Kingston, Ontario, 2007

Elliott 1986
John Huxtable Elliott, *The Count Duke of Olivares: The Statesman in the Age of Decline*, New Haven and London: Yale University Press, 1986
Fabris 2007
Dinko Fabris, *Music in Seventeenth Century Naples: Francesco Provenzale, 1624–1704*, Aldershot: Ashgate, 2007
Faraglia 1878a
Nunzio Federigo Faraglia, 'Memorie artistiche della chiesa benedettina de' SS Severino e Sossio', *Archivio storico per le province napoletane*, III/1 (1878), pp. 235–52
Faraglia 1878b
—, *Storia dei prezzi in Napoli dal 1130 al 1860*, Naples: Pei Tipi del commendatore G. Novile Tipografico, 1878
Faraglia 1885–92
—, 'Notizie di alcuni artisti che lavoravano nella Chiesa di S. Martino e nel Tesoro di S. Gennaro', *Archivio storico per le province napoletane*, X (1885), pp. 435–61; XVII (1892), pp. 657–78
Faraglia 1905
—, 'Il testamento di Aniello Falcone', *Napoli nobilissima*, XIV/2 (1905), n. 3, pp. 17–20
Farina 2002
Viviana Farina, *Giovan Carlo Doria: promotore delle arti a Genova nel primo Seicento*, Florence: Edifir, 2002
Farina 2008
—, 'Un episodio di committenza Genovese nella Napoli del primo quarto del Seicento: La Cappella Massa ai Santi Severino e Sossio', in Pestilli, Rowland and Schütze 2008, pp. 171–84
Farina 2010a
—, 'La collezione del Viceré: il marchese del Carpio, padre Sebastiano Resta e la prima raccolta ragionata di disegni napoletani', in Solinas and Schütze 2010, pp. 183–98
Farina 2010b
—, *Il giovane Salvator Rosa, 1635–1640 circa*, Naples: Paparo, 2010
Feigenbaum 1993
Gail Feigenbaum, 'Practice in the Carracci Academy', in *The Artist's Workshop* (Studies in the History of Art, 38), ed. Peter M. Lukehart, National Gallery of Art, Washington, DC, 1993, pp. 59–76
Felton 1991
Craig Felton, 'Marcantonio Doria and Jusepe de Ribera's Early Commissions in Naples', *Ricerche sul '600 napoletano* (1991), pp. 123–8
Ferrante 1898
Don Ferrante [Giuseppe Ceci or Benedetto Croce, pseud.], 'Notizie ed osservazioni: la casa di Luigi Roderigo', *Napoli nobilissima*, VII/1 (1898), p. 15
Ferrante 1900
—, 'Notizie di artisti che lavoravano a Napoli nel secolo XVII, dal diario del Fuidoro', *Napoli nobilissima*, IX/5 (1900), pp. 27–31
F. Ferrante 1979
Flavia Ferrante, 'Aggiunte all'Azzolino', *Prospettiva*, XVII (1979), pp. 16–30
F. Ferrante 1988
—, 'Giovan Bernardino Azzolino tra tardomanierismo e protocaravaggismo: nuovi contributi e inediti', in *Scritti di storia dell'arte in onore di Raffaello Causa*, ed. Pierluigi Leone de Castris, Naples: Electa, 1988, pp. 133–41
Ferrari 1966
Oreste Ferrari, 'Una "Vita" inedita di Luca Giordano', *Napoli nobilissima*, V/1 (1966), pp. 89–96, 129–38
Ferrari 1979
—, 'Considerazioni sulle vicende artistiche a Napoli durante il viceregno austriaco (1707–1734)', *Storia dell'arte*, XXV–XXVII (1979), pp. 11–27
Ferrari and Scavizzi 1992
— and Giuseppe Scavizzi, *Luca Giordano: l'opera completa*, 2 vols, Naples: Electa, 1992
Ferrari and Scavizzi 2003
— and —, *Luca Giordano: nuove ricerche e inediti*, Naples: Electa, 2003
Festa 1982
Lucio Festa, 'Aspetti della vita e dell'arte di Salvator Rosa da documenti inediti', *Archivio storico per le province napoletane*, C (1982), pp. 101–25
Filangieri 1883–91
Gaetano Filangieri, *Documenti per la storia, le arti e le industrie delle provincie napoletane*, 6 vols, Naples: Tipografica dell'Accademia Reale delle Scienze, 1883–91
Fileti Mazza 1987
Miriam Fileti Mazza (ed.), *Il cardinal Leopoldo, volume primo: rapporti con il mercato veneto* (Archivio del collezionismo Mediceo), Milan: R. Ricciardi, 1987
Fiorillo 1984
Ciro Fiorillo, 'Sei tu Annella?', *Napoli nobilissima*, XXIII/5–6 (1984), pp. 208–11
Fittipaldi 1984
Teodoro Fittipaldi, 'Il "Quarto del Priore" e le sezioni storico-artistiche nella Certosa di San Martino di Napoli', *Arte cristiana*, LXXII (1984), pp. 267–355
Fittipaldi 1988
—, 'Inediti del Seicento nel quadreria del "Quarto del Priore" nella Certosa di San Martino di Napoli', *Arte cristiana*, LXXVI (1988), pp. 347–68, 405–28
Fitz Darby 1962
Delphine Fitz Darby, 'Ribera and the Wise Men', *Art Bulletin*, XCIV/4 (1962), pp. 279–307
Florence 1983
Disegni di Giovanni Lanfranco (1582–1647), ed. Eric Schleier (exh. cat., Gabinetto disegni e stampe degli Uffizi), Florence: Olschki, 1983
Florence 2009
Villa Medicea di Poggio a Caiano, Museo della Natura Morta: Catalogo dei dipinti, ed. Stefano Casciu (collection cat., Villa Medicea di Poggio a Caiano), Florence: Sillabe, 2009
Florence 2014
Le stanze delle muse: dipinti barocchi dalla collezione di Francesco Molinari Pradelli, ed. Cristina Acidini (exh. cat., Galleria degli Uffizi), Florence: Giunti, 2014
Floro di Zenzo 1979
Salvatore Floro di Zenzo, *Tasso a Napoli e il soggiorno claustrale*, Naples: Edizioni del Delfino, 1979
Fort Worth 1982
Jusepe de Ribera, lo Spagnoletto, 1591–1652, ed. Craig Felton and William Jordan (exh. cat., Kimbell Art Museum), Fort Worth: Kimbell Art Museum, 1982
Friedlander 1955
Walter Friedlander, *Caravaggio Studies*, Princeton: Princeton University Press, 1955

Fulco 1979
Giorgio Fulco, 'Il sogno di una "Galeria": nuovi documenti sul Marino collezionista', *Antologia di belle arti*, III/9–12 (1979), pp. 84–99
Gaeta 1985
Il disegno barocco a Napoli, ed. Gina Carlo Ascione (exh. cat., Palazzo Vio), Gaeta: Museo di Palazzo Vio, 1985
G. Galante 1985
Gennaro Aspreno Galante, *Guida sacra della Città di Napoli*, ed. Nicola Spinosa et al., Naples: Società Editrice, 1985
L. Galante 1992
Lucio Galante, *I dipinti napoletani della collezione D'Errico, secc. XVII–XVIII*, Galatina: Congedo, 1992
Galasso 1982
Giuseppe Galasso, *Napoli spagnola dopo Masaniello: politica, cultura, società*, Florence: Sansoni, 1982
García Cueto 2009
David García Cueto, 'Presentes de Nápoles: los virreyes y el envío de obras de arte y objetos suntuarios para la Corona durante el siglo XVII', in Colomer 2009a, pp. 293–321
Garrard 1989
Mary D. Garrard, *Artemisia Gentileschi: The Image of the Female Hero in Italian Baroque Art*, Lawrenceville: Princeton University Press, 1989
Gazzara 2003
Loredana Gazzara, 'Una lettura interpretativa sulla fondazione del Pio Monte della Misericordia in relazione alla sua commitenza artistica', *Napoli nobilissima*, series 5, IV (2003), pp. 51–67
Genoa 1971
Fonti per la storia della pittura, I: serie documentaria, *Lettere e altri documenti intorno alla storia della pittura: Giovanni Benedetto Castiglione detto il Grechetto, Giovan Francesco Castiglione, Salvatore Castiglione*, vol. I, Genoa: Edizioni per le fonti di storia della pittura, 1971
Genoa 1990
Il genio di Giovanni Benedetto Castiglione il Grechetto, ed. Gianvittorio Dillon et al. (exh. cat., Accademia Ligustica di Belle Arti), Genoa: Sagep, 1990
Genoa and Salerno 2003
Metamorfosi del mito: pittura barocca tra Napoli, Genova e Venezia, ed. Mario Alberto Pavone (exh. cat., Palazzo Ducale and Pinacoteca Provinciale), Genoa and Salerno: Electa, 2003
Gerard 1982
Véronique Gerard, 'Philip IV's Early Italian Commissions', *Oxford Art Journal*, V/1 (1982), pp. 9–14
Giannone 1941
Onofrio Giannone, *Giunte sulle vite de' pittori napoletani* [MS *c.* 1768–73], ed. Ottavio Morisani, Naples: R. Deputazione di Storia Patria, 1941
Goffen 2002
Rona Goffen, *Renaissance Rivals: Michelangelo, Leonardo, Raphael, Titian*, New Haven and London: Yale University Press, 2002
Golahny 2003
Amy Golahny, *Rembrandt's Reading: The Artist's Bookshelf of Ancient Poetry and History*, Amsterdam: Amsterdam University Press, 2003
Golzio 1939
Vincenzo Golzio, *Documenti artistici sul Seicento nell'Archivio Chigi*, Rome: Casa Editrice Fratelli Palombi, 1939
González-Palacios 1984
Alvar González-Palacios, *Il tempio del gusto: Roma e il Regno delle Due Sicilie: le arti decorative in Italia fra classicismi e barocco*, 2 vols, Milan: Longanesi, 1984
Grabski 1985
Józef Grabski, 'On Seicento Painting in Naples: Some Observations on Bernardo Cavallino, Artemisia Gentileschi and Others', *Artibus et historiae*, VI/2 (1985), pp. 23–64
Gray 1926
Cecil Heseltine Gray, *Carlo Gesualdo, Prince of Venosa: Musician and Murderer*, New York: Kegan Paul, 1926
Guida 2007–8
Gloria Guida, 'La chiesa di San Lorenzo Maggiore in Napoli nei documenti dell'Archivio Storico del Banco di Napoli-Fondazione e dell'Archivio di Stato di Napoli', *Quaderni dell'archivio storico* (2007–8), pp. 525–59
Harris and Elliott 1976
Enriqueta Harris and John Huxtable Elliott: 'Velázquez and the Queen of Hungary', *Burlington Magazine*, CXVIII/874 (1976), pp. 24–6
Haskell 1960
Francis Haskell, 'Art Exhibitions in Seventeenth Century Rome', *Studi secenteschi*, I (1960), pp. 102–21
Haskell 1980
—, *Patrons and Painters: A Study in the Relations between Italian Art and Society in the Age of the Baroque* [1963], rev. edition, New Haven and London: Yale University Press, 1980
Haskell 1982
—, 'The Patronage of Painting in Seicento Naples', in London 1982, pp. 60–64
Hibbard 1983
Howard Hibbard, *Caravaggio*, New York: Harper and Row, 1983
Hills 2004
Helen Hills, *Invisible City: The Architecture of Devotion in Seventeenth-century Neapolitan Convents*, Oxford: Oxford University Press, 2004
Hills 2008
—, 'Nuns and Relics: Spiritual Authority in Post-Tridentine Naples', in *Female Monasticism in Early Modern Europe: An Interdisciplinary View*, ed. Cordula van Wyhe, Aldershot: Ashgate, 2008, pp. 11–38
Iappelli 1985
Filippo Iappelli SJ, 'Gesuiti e Seicento napoletano', *Societas (Rivista bimistrale dei jesuiti dell'Italia meridionale)*, XXXIV/1–3 (1985), pp. 23–35, 73–91
Ioannou 2000
Pannayotis K. Ioannou, '"Dopo la sua varia fortuna": aggiunte e proposte sul primo periodo del pittore Belisario Corenzio', in *Ricerche sul '600 napoletano: saggi e documenti, 2000*, Naples: Electa, 2001, pp. 36–51
Ioannou 2001
—, 'Documenti inediti sulle arti a Napoli tra Cinque e Seicento', in *Ricerche sul '600 napoletano: saggi e documenti, 2001*, Naples: Electa, 2002, pp. 32–43
Ioannou 2002
—, 'Documenti inediti sulle arti a Napoli tra Cinque e Seicento (seconda parte)', *Ricerche sul '600 napoletano: saggi e documenti, 2002*, Naples: Electa, 2003, pp. 135–46
Judson 1983
J. Richard Judson, 'Jacob Isaacsz van Swanenburgh and the Phlegraean Fields', in *Essays in Northern European Art Pre-*

sented to Egbert Haverkamp-Begemann on his Sixtieth Birthday, ed. Ann-Maria Logan, Doornspijk: Davaco, 1983, pp. 119–22
Keyes 1984
George S. Keyes, *Esaias vanden Velde*, Doornspijk: Davaco, 1984
Koenigsberger 1947
H. Koenigsberger, 'English Merchants in Naples and Sicily in the Seventeenth Century', *English Historical Review*, LXII/244 (1947), pp. 304–26
Kren 1978
Thomas Kren, 'Jan Miel (1599–1664): A Flemish Painter in Rome', PhD dissertation, Yale University, 1978
Kris and Kurz 1979
Ernst Kris and Otto Kurz, *Legend, Myth and Magic in the Image of the Artist: A Historical Experiment*, New Haven: Yale University Press, 1979
Labrot 1979
Gérard Labrot, *Baroni in città: residenze e comportamenti dell'aristocrazia napoletana, 1530–1734*, Naples: Società Editrice Napoletana, 1979
Labrot 1984
—, 'Deux collectioneurs étrangers a Naples', *Ricerche sul '600 napoletano* (1984), pp. 135–42
Labrot 1992
—, *Collections of Paintings in Naples, 1600–1780* (Documents for the History of Collecting: Italian Inventories, I, The Provenance Index of the Getty Information Institute), Munich: K. G. Saur, 1992
Labrot 1993
—, *Palazzi napoletani: storie di nobili e cortigiani, 1520–1750*, Naples: Electa, 1993
Labrot 2010
—, *Peinture et société à Naples: XVIe–XVIIIe siècles, commandes, collections, marches*, Seyssel: Champ Vallon, 2010
Labrot and Ruotolo 1980
— and Renato Ruotolo: 'Pour une étude historique de la commande aristocratique dans le rouyaume de Naples espagnol', *Revue historique*, I (1980), pp. 25–48
Lange 2009
Justus Lange, 'El V duque de Alba como mecenas de las artes durante su virreinato en Nápoles (1622–29) y su relación con Jusepe de Ribera', in Colomer 2009a, pp. 253–66
Larsen 1988
Erik Larsen, *The Paintings of Anthony van Dyck*, Freren: Luca, 1988
Lattuada 2000
Riccardo Lattuada, *Francesco Guarino da Solofra nella pittura napoletana del Seicento, 1611–1651*, Naples: Paparo, 2000
Lecce 2013
Il racconto del cielo: capolavori dei Girolamini a Lecce, ed. Fabrizio Vona et al. (exh. cat., Chiesa di San Francesco della Scarpa), Naples: Arte'm, 2013
Leone de Castris 1988
Pierluigi Leone de Castris, 'La pittura del Cinquecento nell'Italia meridionale', in *La pittura in Italia: Il Cinquecento*, 2 vols, Milan: Electa, 1988, vol. II, pp. 472–514
Leone de Castris 1989–90
—, 'Teodoro d'Errico: i quadri "private"', *Prospettiva*, LVII–LX (1989–90), pp. 121–31
Leone de Castris 1991
—, *La pittura del Cinquecento a Napoli, 1573–1606: l'ultima maniera*, Naples: Electa, 1991
Leone de Castris 1995–6
—, 'Committenza Acquaviva e committenza D'Avalos al tempo dei primi viceré: un confronto', in *Territorio e feudalità nel Mezzogiorno rinascimentale: il ruolo degli Acquaviva tra XV e XVI secolo. Atti del primo Convegno internazionale di studi su 'La casa Acquaviva d'Atri e di Conversano': Conversano-Atri, 13–16 settembre 1991*, 2 vols, Galatina: Congedo, 1995–6, vol. II, pp. 393–415
Leone de Castris 2001
—, *Polidoro da Caravaggio: l'opera completa*, Naples: Electa, 2001
Lofano 2009
Francesco Lofano, 'La collezione Acquaviva d'Aragona nel Castello di Conversano: nuove opere rintracciate e alcune ipotesi', *Studi Bitontini*, LXXXVIII (2009), pp. 95–100
Lofano 2014
—, 'The Marriage Contract of Bernardo Cavallino', *Burlington Magazine*, CLVI/1341 (2014), pp. 801–2
Loh 2006
Maria H. Loh, 'Originals, Reproductions and a "Particular Taste" for Pastiche in the Seventeenth-century Republic of Painting', in *Mapping Markets for Paintings in Europe and the New World, 1450–1750*, ed. Neil de Marchi and Hans J. Van Miegroet, Brussels: Brepols, 2006, pp. 237–60
London 1982
Painting in Naples, 1606–1705: From Caravaggio to Giordano, ed. Clovis Whitfield and Jane Martineau (exh. cat., Royal Academy of Arts), London: Royal Academy, 1982
London 1995
Making and Meaning: The Young Michelangelo in Rome, ed. Michael Hirst (exh. cat., National Gallery), London: National Gallery Publications, 1995
London 2005
Caravaggio: The Final Years (exh. cat., National Gallery), Naples: Electa, 2005
London 2012
Van Dyck in Sicily, 1624–25: Painting and the Plague, ed. Xavier F. Salomon (exh. cat., Dulwich Picture Gallery), Milan: Silvana Editoriale, 2012
London and Fort Worth 2010
Salvator Rosa, ed. Helen Langdon, Xavier F. Salomon and Caterina Volpi (exh. cat., Dulwich Picture Gallery and Kimbell Art Museum), London and Fort Worth: Holberton, 2010
Longhi 1950
Roberto Longhi, 'Velázquez 1630: "La rissa all'ambasciata di Spagna"', *Paragone*, I/1 (1950), pp. 28–34
Longhi 1957
—, 'Una traccia per Filippo Napoletano', *Paragone*, VIII/95 (1957), pp. 33–62
Lorizzo 2001a
Loredana Lorizzo, 'L'altare della cappella Filomarino ai Santi Apostoli di Napoli alla luce di nuovi documenti romani', in *Ricerche sul '600 napoletano: saggi e documenti, 2001*, Naples: Electa, 2002, pp. 62–75
Lorizzo 2001b
—, 'Cardinal Ascanio Filomarino's Purchases of Works of Art in Rome: Poussin, Caravaggio, Vouet and Valentin', *Burlington Magazine*, CXLIII/1180 (2001), pp. 404–11
Lorizzo 2003
—, 'Il mercato dell'arte a Roma nel XVII secolo: "pittori bottegari" e "rivenditori di quadri" nei documenti dell'Archivio Storico dell'Accademia di San Luca', in *The Art Market in*

Italy, 15th–17th Centuries/Il mercato dell'arte in Italia, sec. XV–XVII, ed. Marcello Fantoni, Louisa Matthews and Sara Matthews-Grieco, Modena: Franco Cosimo Panini, 2003, pp. 325–36

Lorizzo 2003–4
—, 'Simon Vouet, Valentin e i Filomarino: nuove date e qualche ipotesi sugli scambi artistici tra Roma e Napoli', in *Ricerche sul '600 napoletano: saggi e documenti, 2003–2004*, Naples: Electa, 2004, pp. 123–36

Lorizzo 2006
—, *La collezione del cardinale Ascanio Filomarino: pittura, scultura e mercato dell'arte tra Roma e Napoli nel Seicento*, Naples: Electa, 2006

Lorizzo 2010
—, '"Impossessarsi del nudo": appunti per Francesco Di Maria disegnatore', in Solinas and Schütze 2010, pp. 147–52

Los Angeles 2005
Titian and the Commander: A Renaissance Artist and his Patron (exh. cat., Getty Center), Los Angeles: J. Paul Getty Trust, 2005

Macioce et al. 2004
Stefano Macioce et al., *L'incantesimo di Circe: temi di magia nella pittura da Dosso Dossi a Salvator Rosa*, Rome: Logart Press, 2004

Madrid 1984
Dibujos italianos de los siglos XVII y XVIII en la Biblioteca Nacional, by Manuela B. Mena Marqués (exh. cat., Biblioteca Nacional), Madrid, 1984

Madrid 1985
Pintura napolitana da Caravaggio a Giordano, ed. Alfonso Emilio Pérez Sánchez (exh. cat., Museo del Prado and Palacio de Villahermosa), Madrid: Museo del Prado, 1985

Madrid 2002
Luca Giordano y España, ed. Alfonso E. Pérez Sánchez (exh. cat., Palacio Real), Madrid: Patrimonio Nacional Servicio de Pub, 2002

Madrid 2005
Paintings for the Planet King: Philip IV and the Buen Retiro Palace, ed. Andrés Úbeda de los Cobos (exh. cat., Museo Nacional del Prado), London: Holberton, 2005

Madrid 2014
Las Furias: alegoría política y desafío artístico, ed. Miguel Falomir (exh. cat., Museo del Prado), Madrid: Museo del Prado, 2014

Mahoney 1977
Michael Mahoney, *The Drawings of Salvator Rosa*, 2 vols, New York and London: Garland, 1977

Majetti 1885
Raffaelle Majetti, *Associazioni di arti e mestieri per dritto romano: corporazioni di arti mestieri napolitane dal XIV al XIX secolo* (Memoria premiata nel concorso bandito dal Circolo Universitario Napolitano Antonio Genovesi per l'anno 1883 [Estratto dalla *Gazzetta del Procuratore*, Anno xx, no. 1, 1 a 3 e 7 a 10]), Naples: Carlola Cava Librajo, 1885

Malvasia 1980
Carlo Cesare Malvasia, *The Life of Guido Reni*, trans. and ed. Catherine Engass and Robert Engass, University Park and London: Pennsylvania State University Press, 1980

F. Mancini 1968
Franco Mancini, *Feste e apparati civile e religiosi in Napoli dal viceregno alla capitale*, Naples: Edizioni Scientifiche Italiane, 1968

G. Mancini 1956–7
Giulio Mancini, *Considerazioni sulla pittura*, 2 vols, ed. Adriana Marucchi Luigi Salerno, Rome: Accademia nazionale dei Lincei, 1956–7

Marangelli 1967
Francesca Marangelli, 'Paolo Finoglio', *Archivio storico pugliese*, xx (1967), pp. 195–210

Marangelli 1979
—, 'Paolo Finoglio attraverso i documenti', *Quaderni conversani* (1979), pp. 1–19

Mariaclaudia and Lattuada 2009
Izzo Mariaclaudia and Riccardo Lattuada, *Nicola Vaccaro (1640–1709): un artista a Napoli tra barocco e Arcadia*, Todi: Tau, 2009

Marseilles 1988
Escales du Baroque, ed. Arnauld Bréjon de Lavergnée et al. (exh. cat., Centre de la Vieille Charité), Marseilles: Biro, 1988

C. Marshall 1998
Christopher R. Marshall, '"Causa di Stravaganze": Order and Anarchy in Domenico Gargiulo's *Revolt of Masaniello*', *Art Bulletin*, LXXX/3 (1998), pp. 478–97

C. Marshall 2000
—, '"Senza il minimo scrupolo": Artists as Dealers in Seventeenth Century Naples', *Journal of the History of Collections*, XII/1 (2000), pp. 15–34

C. Marshall 2003
—, 'Appagare il pubblico: The Marketing Strategies of Luca Giordano, 1678–1684', in *The Art Market in Italy, 15th–17th Centuries/Il mercato dell'arte in Italia, sec. XV–XVII*, ed. Marcello Fantoni, Louisa Matthews and Sara Matthews-Grieco, Modena: Franco Cosimo Panini, 2003, pp. 245–52

C. Marshall 2004
—, 'Markets, Money and Artistic Manoeuvres: Bernardo Cavallino and the Grand Manner', in *'The Italians' in Australia: Studies in Renaissance and Baroque Art*, ed. David R. Marshall, Florence: Centro Di, 2004, pp. 41–8

C. Marshall 2005
—, 'The Spirit of Caesar in this Soul of a Woman: Artemisia Gentileschi and the Will to Succeed, 1629–54', *Melbourne Art Journal*, VIII (2005), pp. 4–27

C. Marshall 2006
—, 'Dispelling Negative Perceptions: Dealers Promoting Artists in Seventeenth-century Naples', in *Mapping Markets in Europe and the New World, 1450–1750*, ed. Neil de Marchi and Hans J. Van Miegroet, Brussels: Brepols, 2006, pp. 348–64

C. Marshall 2010
—, 'Naples', in *Painting for Profit: The Economic Lives of Seventeenth-century Italian Painters*, ed. Richard E. Spear and Philip Sohm, New Haven and London: Yale University Press, 2010, pp. 115–44

D. Marshall 1986
David Ryley Marshall, 'Viviano Codazzi as "Quadratura" Painter at the Certosa di San Martino, Naples, and Santa Maria in Via Lata, Rome', *Storia dell'arte*, LVI (1986), pp. 49–80

D. Marshall 1988
—, 'Ascanio Luciano: A Neapolitan Follower of Viviano Codazzi', *Paragone*, XXXIX/7 (1988), pp. 21–43

D. Marshall 1993
—, *Viviano and Niccolò Codazzi and the Baroque Architectural Fantasy*, Rome: Jandi Sapi, 1993

Mazzoleni 1964
Joel Mazzoleni, *Il monasterio benedettino dei SS Severino e Sossio sede dell'Archivio di Stato di Napoli*, Naples: Società napoletana di storia patria, 1964

Mazzoleni 1999
—, *Palaces of Naples*, New York: Rizzoli, 1999

Melasecchi 1998
Olga Melasecchi, 'Cristoforo Roncalli, Ludovico Leoni e la Congregazione dell'Oratorio Romano', *Storia dell'arte*, XCII (1998), pp. 5–26

Messina and Rome 1994
Messina: il ritorno della memoria, ed. Grazia Fallico (exh. cat., Museo Regionale, Museo Nazionale di Castel Sant'Angelo), Palermo: Novecento, 1994

Meyer 1999
Joachim Meyer, 'Le *Vite* di Bernardo De Dominici e il disegno napoletano', in *Ricerche sul '600 napoletano: saggi e documenti, 1999*, Naples: Electa, 2000, pp. 43–58

Milan 1951
Mostra del Caravaggio e dei caravaggeschi, ed. Roberto Longhi (exh. cat., Palazzo Reale), Florence: Sansoni, 1951

Milan 2011
Artemisia Gentileschi: The Story of a Passion, ed. Roberto Contini and Francesco Solinas (exh. cat., Palazzo Reale), Milan: 24 ORE Cultura, 2011

Minieri Riccio 1878–80
Camillo Minieri Riccio, 'Cenno storico delle accademie fiorite nella città di Napoli', *Archivio storico per le province napoletane*, III/4 (1878), pp. 745–58; IV/1–3 (1879), pp. 163–78, 379–94, 519–36; V/1–3 (1880), pp. 131–57, 349–73, 578–612

Mirollo 1963
James V. Mirollo, *The Poet of the Marvelous: Giambattista Marino*, New York and London: Columbia University Press, 1963

Missirini 1823
Melchior Missirini, *Memorie per servire alla storia della Romana Accademia di S. Luca*, Rome: De Romanis, 1823

Moir 1976
Alfred Moir, *Caravaggio and his Copyists*, New York: New York University Press, 1976

Molinari Pradelli 1984
Alessandro Molinari Pradelli (ed.), *Gli antichi mestieri di Bologna nelle incisioni di A. Carracci, G. M. Mitelli e G. M. Tamburini*, Rome: Newton Compton, 1984

Montagu 1985
Jennifer Montagu, *Alessandro Algardi*, New Haven: Yale University Press, 1985

Montias 1988
John Michael Montias, 'Art Dealers in the Seventeenth-century Netherlands', *Simiolus*, XVIII/4 (1988), pp. 244–56

Moretti 2005
Lino Moretti, 'La raccolta Lumaga: Giovanni Andrea Lumaga', in *Ricerche sul '600 napoletano: saggi e documenti, 2005*, Naples: Electa, 2005, pp. 27–64

Morisani 1958
Ottavio Morisani, *Letteratura artistica a Napoli*, Naples: Fausto Fiorentino, 1958

Mormone 1954
Raffaelle Mormone, 'La Cappella dei Rota in S. Domenico Maggiore', *Il Fuidoro*, I/3–4 (1954), pp. 52–5

Muller 1989
Jeffrey M. Muller, 'Measures of Authenticity: The Detection of Copies in the Early Literature on Connoisseurship', in *Retaining the Original: Multiple Originals, Copies and Reproductions* (Studies in the History of Art, 20), ed. Kathleen Preciado, National Gallery of Art, Washington, DC, 1989, pp. 141–5

Muñoz González 1999
María Jesús Muñoz González, 'Una nota sobra los intereses pictóricos del Virrey de Nápoles, duque de Alcalá (1629–31)', in *Ricerche sul '600 napoletano: saggi e documenti, 1999*, Naples: Electa, 2000, pp. 59–60

Naples 1954
La Madonna nella pittura del '600 a Napoli, ed. Raffaello Causa (exh. cat., Castel Nuovo), Naples, 1954

Naples 1960
IV Mostra di restauri, ed. Raffaello Causa, Oreste Ferrari and Marina Picone (exh. cat., Palazzo Reale), Naples, 1960

Naples 1966
Disegni napoletani del Sei e del Settecento nel Museo di Capodimonte, ed. Walter Vitzthum (exh. cat., Museo di Capodimonte), Naples: L'Arte Tipografica, 1966–67

Naples 1970
Opere d'arte nel Pio Monte della Misericordia a Napoli, by Raffaello Causa (collection cat., Pio Monte della Misericordia), Naples: Di Mauro, 1970

Naples 1977
Mostra didattica di Carlo Sellitto, primo caravaggesco napoletano, ed. Ferdinando Bologna and Raffaello Causa (exh. cat., Museo di Capodimonte), Naples: Museo di Capodimonte, 1977

Naples 1984
Civiltà del Seicento a Napoli, ed. Raffaello Causa et al. (exh. cat., Museo di Capodimonte and Museo Diego Aragona Pignatelli Cortes), 2 vols, Naples: Electa, 1984

Naples 1985
Bernardo Cavallino (1610–1656), ed. Nicola Spinosa et al. (exh. cat., Museo Pignatelli), Naples: Electa, 1985

Naples 1986a
La Quadreria dei Girolamini, by Pierluigi Leone de Castris and Roberto Middione (collection cat., Quadreria dei Girolamini), Naples: Guida Editori, 1986

Naples 1986b
Il Quarto del priore, ed. Luciana Arbace et al. (collection cat., Museo Nazionale di San Martino), Naples: Civita, 1986

Naples 1987
I grandi disegni italiani nella Collezione del Museo di Capodimonte a Napoli, ed. Rossana Muzii Cavallo (collection cat., Museo di Capodimonte), Milan: Silvana Editoriale, 1987

Naples 1990
All'ombra del Vesuvio: Napoli nella veduta europea dal Quattrocento all'Ottocento, ed. Nicola Spinosa et al. (exh. cat., Castel Sant'Elmo), Naples: Electa, 1990

Naples 1991
Battistello Caracciolo e il primo naturalismo a Napoli, ed. Ferdinando Bologna (exh. cat., Castel Sant'Elmo and Certosa di San Martino), Naples: Electa, 1991

Naples 1992
Jusepe de Ribera, 1591–1652, ed. Alfonso E. Peréz Sanchéz and Nicola Spinosa (exh. cat., Castel Sant'Elmo, Certosa di San Martino and Cappella del Tesoro di San Gennaro), Naples: Electa, 1992

Naples 1994a
Il secolo d'oro della pittura napoletana: da Battistello a Luca Giordano, pittori del Seicento nei musei di Napoli, ed. Lilia Rocco (exh. cat., Castel Sant'Elmo), Naples: De Rosa, 1994
Naples 1994b
I tesori dei d'Avalos: commitenza e collezionismo di una grande famiglia napoletana, ed. Pierluigi Leone di Castris (exh. cat., Castel Sant'Elmo), Naples: Fiorentino, 1994
Naples 1995
La Quadreria dei Girolamini, ed. Roberto Middione (collection cat., Quadreria dei Girolamini), Naples: De Rosa, 1995
Naples 1997a
Capolavori in festa: effimero barocco a Largo di Palazzo, 1683–1759, ed. Giuseppe Zampino (exh. cat., Palazzo Reale), Naples: Electa, 1997
Naples 1997b
San Gennaro tra fede, arte e mito, ed. Pierluigi Leone de Castris (exh. cat., Chiesa di Santa Maria Donnaregina Nuova), Naples: De Rosa, 1997
Naples 1999
Mattia Preti: tra Roma, Napoli e Malta, ed. Nicola Spinosa (exh. cat., Museo di Capodimonte), Naples: Electa, 1999
Naples 2002
Micco Spadaro: Napoli ai tempi di Masaniello, ed. Brigitte Daprà (exh. cat., Certosa di San Martino), Naples: Electa, 2002
Naples 2008a
Il Museo Diocesano di Napoli: percorsi di fede e arte, ed. Pierluigi Leone de Castris (collection cat), Naples: Elio de Rosa, 2008
Naples 2008b
Museo e gallerie nazionali di Capodimonte: dipinti del XVII secolo: la scuola napoletana, ed. Nicola Spinosa (collection cat., Museo di Capodimonte), Naples: Electa, 2008
Naples 2008c
Salvator Rosa: tra mito e magia, ed. Arnauld Bréjon de Lavergnée (exh. cat., Museo di Capodimonte), Naples: Electa, 2008
Naples 2009
Ritorno al barocco: da Caravaggio a Vanvitelli, ed. Nicola Spinosa (exh. cat., Museo di Capodimonte, Certosa e Museo di San Martino, Castel Sant'Elmo, Museo Pignatelli, Museo Duca di Martina and Palazzo Reale), 2 vols, Naples: Arte'm, 2009
Naples 2011
Il giovane Ribera tra Roma, Parma e Napoli, 1608–1624, ed. José Milicua and Jaiver Portús (exh. cat., Museo di Capodimonte), Naples: Arte'm, 2011
Naples 2012
The Pio Monte della Misericordia of Naples, ed. Raffaella Auriemma and Loredana Gazzara (collection cat., Pio Monte della Misericordia), Naples: Arte'm, 2012
Naples, Vienna and Los Angeles 2001
Luca Giordano, 1634–1705 (exh. cat., Castel Sant'Elmo and Museo di Capodimonte, Kunsthistorisches Museum and Los Angeles County Museum), Naples, Vienna and Los Angeles: Electa, 2001
Napoli 2003
John Nicholas Napoli, 'Fashioning the Certosa di San Martino: Ornament, Illusion and Artistic Collaboration in Early Modern Naples', PhD dissertation, Princeton University, 2003
Napoli 2010
—, 'From Social Virtue to Revetted Interior: Giovanni Antonio Dosio and Marble Inlay in Rome, Florence and Naples', in *Art and Architecture in Naples, 1266–1713: New Approaches*, ed. Cordelia Warr and Janis Elliott, Chichester: Wiley-Blackwell, 2010, pp. 101–24
Napoli 2012
—, 'Artists, Patrons and Trust in Seventeenth Century Naples: The Case of the Certosa di San Martino', *California Italian Studies*, III/1 (2012), pp. 1–31
E. Nappi 1975
Eduardo Nappi, 'La famiglia, il Palazzo e la Cappella dei Principi di Sanseverino', *Rivista internazionale di storia della banca*, II (1975), pp. 100–61
E. Nappi 1980
—, *Aspetti della società e dell'economia napoletana durante la peste del 1656: dai documenti dell'Archivio Storico del Banco di Napoli*, Naples: Edizioni del Banco di Napoli, 1980
E. Nappi 1983a
—, 'Documenti dell'Archivio Storico del Banco di Napoli', in *Arte napoletana in Puglia dal XVI al XVIII secolo: pittori, scultori, marmorai, architetti, ingegneri, riggiolari, organari, ferrari, ricamatori, bandenari, stuccatori*, ed. Mimma Pasculli Ferrara and Eduardo Nappi, Fasano di Puglia: Schena, 1983, pp. 289–330
E. Nappi 1983b
—, 'Pittori del '600 a Napoli: notizie inedite dai documenti dell'Archivio Storico del Banco di Napoli', in *Ricerche sul '600 napoletano: saggi vari*, Milan: L&T, 1983, pp. 73–80
E. Nappi 1983c
—, 'I vicere e l'arte a Napoli', *Napoli nobilissima*, XXII/1–2 (1983), pp. 41–57
E. Nappi 1984
—, 'Le chiese dei Gesuiti a Napoli', in Pane 1984c, pp. 318–37
E. Nappi 1988
—, 'Le chiese di Giovan Giacomo Conforto (dai documenti dell'Archivio Storico del Banco di Napoli)', in *Ricerche sul '600 napoletano: saggi e document per la storia dell'arte*, Milan: L&T, 1988, pp. 129–52
E. Nappi 1989
—, 'Giovan Giacomo Conforto e la Chiesa di S. M. della Sapienza di Napoli', *Ricerche sul '600 napoletano* (1989), pp. 113–34
E. Nappi 1990
—, 'Un regesto di documenti editi ed inediti, tratti prevalentemente dall'Archivio Storico del Banco di Napoli, riguardanti Giuseppe Ribera e una conferma della presenza a Napoli nel novembre 1630 di Velázquez', *Ricerche sul '600 napoletano* (1990), pp. 177–86
E. Nappi 1991
—, 'Momenti della vita di Luca Giordano nei documenti dell'Archivio Storico del Banco di Napoli', *Ricerche sul '600 napoletano* (1991), pp. 157–82
E. Nappi 1992
— (ed.), *Ricerche sul '600 napoletano: catalogo delle pubblicazioni edite dal 1883 al 1990, riguardanti le opere di architetti, pittori, scultori, marmorari ed intagliatori per i secoli XVI e XVII, pagate tramite gli antichi banchi pubblici napoletani*, Milan: L&T, 1992
E. Nappi 1996–7
—, 'La Chiesa della Anime del Purgatorio ad Arco nei secoli XVII–XVIII', in *Ricerche sul '600 napoletano: saggi e documenti, 1996–1997*, Naples: Electa, 1998, pp. 155–76

E. Nappi 2000
—, 'Le attività finanziarie e sociali di Gasparo de Roomer: nuovi documenti su Cosimo Fanzago', in *Ricerche sul '600 napoletano: saggi e documenti, 2000*, Naples: Electa, 2001, pp. 61–92
E. Nappi 2001
—, 'La cappella del Tesoro e la Guglia di San Gennaro: nuovi documenti e nuove fonti', in *Ricerche sul '600 napoletano: saggi e documenti, 2001*, Naples: Electa, 2002, pp. 91–9
E. Nappi 2002
—, 'I gesuiti a Napoli: nuovi documenti', in *Ricerche sul '600 napoletano Seicento napoletano: saggi e documenti, 2002*, Naples: Electa, 2003, pp. 111–33
E. Nappi 2005
—, 'Notizie su pittori che lavoravano a Napoli dal 1630 al 1656', in *Ricerche sul '600 napoletano: saggi e documenti, 2005*, Naples: Electa, 2005, pp. 77–83
E. Nappi 2009
—, 'I viceré spagnoli e l'arte a Napoli: Corpus documentale', in Colomer 2009a, pp. 95–128
M. Nappi 1986
Maria Rosaria Nappi, 'Il Filippo Napoletano di Roberto Longhi: Scipione Compagno o Cornelio Brusco?', *Paragone*, XLVII (1986), pp. 24–37
M. Nappi 1991
—, *François De Nomé e Didier Barra: l'enigma Monsù Desiderio*, Rome: Jandi Sapi, 1991
Newcome 1978
Mary Newcome, 'A Castiglione–Leone Problem', *Master Drawings*, XVI/2 (1978), pp. 163–72
New York 1979
17th Century Drawings in the Metropolitan Museum of Art, by Jacob Bean (collection cat., Metropolitan Museum of Art), New York: Abrams, 1979
New York 1983
Italian Still Life Paintings from Three Centuries, ed. John T. Spike (exh. cat., National Academy of Design), Florence: Centro Di, 1983
New York 1992
Jusepe de Ribera, 1591–1652, ed. Alfonso Emilio Pérez Sánchez and Nicola Spinosa (exh. cat., Metropolitan Museum of Art), New York: Abrams, 1992
Novelli Radice 1974a
Magda Novelli Radice, 'Agostino Beltrano, uno "stanzionesco" da riabilitare', *Paragone*, XXV/287 (1974), pp. 67–82
Novelli Radice 1974b
—, 'Precisazioni cronologiche su Massimo Stanzione', *Campania Sacra*, V (1974), pp. 98–103
Novelli Radice 1976
—, 'Contributi alla conscenza di Andrea e Onofrio de Leone', *Napoli nobilissima*, XV/5–6 (1976), pp. 162–9
Novelli Radice 1978
—, 'Appunti per il pittore Nicolò de Simone', *Napoli nobilissima*, XVII/1 (1978), pp. 21–9
Novelli Radice 1982–3
—, 'Notizie d'archivio sulla chiesa di S. Maria la Nova', *Campania sacra*, XII–XIV (1982–3), pp. 149–85
Novelli Radice 1984
—, 'Pittura napoletana del '600: inediti di Agostino Beltrano e Nunzio Russo', *Arte cristiana*, LXXII/702 (1984), pp. 143–52
Novelli Radice 1988
—, 'Andrea de Leone frescante e ipotesi sulla sua bottega', *Napoli nobilissima*, XXVII/1–2 (1988), pp. 41–53
Novelli Radice 1989
—, 'Una traccia per Annella de Rosa', *Napoli nobilissima*, XXVIII/1–6 (1989), pp. 147–54
Novelli Radice 1991
—, 'Documenti su Onofrio de Lione', *Napoli nobilissima*, XXX/5–6 (1991), pp. 201–4
O'Connell 1988
Sheila O'Connell, 'Lord Shaftesbury in Naples, 1711–1713', *Volume of the Walpole Society*, LIV (1988), pp. 149–219
Orozco Díaz 1993
Emilio Orozco Díaz, *El pintor Fray Juan Sánchez Cotán*, Granada: Universidad de Granada, 1993
Ortolani 1970
Sergio Ortolani, *Giacinto Gigante e la pittura di paesaggio a Napoli e in Italia del '600 all '800*, Naples: Montanino, 1970
Pacelli 1979
Vincenzo Pacelli, 'Processo tra Ribera e un committente', *Napoli nobilissima*, XVIII/1 (1979), pp. 28–36
Pacelli 1980
—, 'Caravaggio, 1610: La "Sant'Orsola confitta dal Tiranno" per Marcantonio Doria', *Prospettiva*, XXIII (1980), pp. 24–45
Pacelli 1984a
—, 'Affreschi storici in Palazzo Reale', in Pane 1984c, pp. 158–79
Pacelli 1984b
—, 'Testimonianze, considerazioni e problemi di restauro sui dipinti seicenteschi dell'Annunziata di Capua', *Ricerche sul '600 napoletano* (1984), pp. 85–100
Pacelli 1984c
—, *Caravaggio: le sette opere di Misericordia*, Salerno: Cooperativa Editrice, 1984
Pacelli 1986
—, 'La cappella Cacace in San Lorenzo Maggiore: un complesso barocco in una basilica gotica', *Ricerche sul '600 napoletano* (1986), pp. 171–81
Pacelli 1987
—, *L'ideologia del potere nella ritrattistica napoletana del Seicento*, Naples: Bibliopolis, 1987
Pacelli 1990
—, 'Filippo Vitale nel secondo decennio del Seicento al seguito di Carlo Sellitto', *Ricerche sul '600 napoletano* (1990), pp. 187–200
Pacelli 2008
—, *Giovan Francesco de Rosa detto Pacecco de Rosa, 1607–1656*, Naples: Paparo, 2008
Pacelli 2011
—, *Il martirio di Sant'Orsola di Caravaggio per Marcantonio Doria: ovvero uno renovatio iconografica*, Naples: Paparo, 2011
Padula and Seville 1996
Pathos ed estasi: opere d'arte tra Campania e Andalusia nel XVII e XVIII secolo, ed. Vega de Martini (exh. cat., Certosa di San Lorenzo and Real Monasterio de San Clemente), Naples: Electa, 1996
Pagano de Divitiis 1982
Gigliola Pagano de Divitiis, 'I due Recco di Burghley House: osservazioni sul collezionismo inglese e sul mercato delle opere d'arte nella Napoli del Seicento', *Prospettive settanta*, III–IV (1982), pp. 376–93

F. Palermo 1846
F. Palermo, 'Documenti diversi sulle novità accadute in Napoli l'anno 1647', *Archivio storico italiano*, IX (1846), pp. 357–401
Palermo 1997
Genio e passione: la pittura a Napoli da Battistello Caracciolo a Luca Giordano e le relazioni con la Sicilia, ed. Nicola Spinosa and Vincenzo Abbate (exh. cat., Palazzo Abatellis), Palermo: Electa, 1997
Palomares 2009
Ana Minguito Palomares, 'El Resurgir de la Corte: fiestas y actos públicos durante el virreinato del VIII conde de Oñate', in Colomer 2009a, pp. 323–38
Palos and Palumbo 2009
Joan Lluís Palos and Maria Laura Palumbo, 'La Sala del Gran Capitan en el Palacio Real de Nápoles y los orígenes del domino Español en Italia', in Colomer 2009a, pp. 133–48
Pane 1984a
Roberto Pane, 'La Cappella Cacace in San Lorenzo Maggiore', in Pane 1984c, pp. 100–11
Pane 1984b
—, 'Maestri di trabacche', in Pane 1984c, pp. 442–8
Pane 1984c
— (ed.), *Seicento napoletano: arte, costume, ambiente*, Milan: Edizioni di Comunità, 1984
Paolillo 1985
Ciro Paolillo, 'Un inventario dei beni del principe di San Martino redatto da Filippo Vitale ed Andrea Abate', *Ricerche sul '600 napoletano* (1985), pp. 113–32
Paris 1983
La peinture napolitaine de Caravage a Giordano (exh. cat., Galeries Nationales du Grand Palais), Paris: Editions de la Réunion des Musées Nationaux, 1983
Paris 2007a
L'oeil gourmand: A Journey through Neapolitan Still Life, ed. Véronique Damian (exh. cat., Galerie Canesso), Paris: Galerie Canesso, 2007
Paris 2007b
Tableaux napolitains: du naturalisme au Baroque, ed. Véronique Damian (exh. cat., Galerie Canesso), Paris: Galerie Canesso, 2007
Parma, Naples and Rome 2001
Giovanni Lanfranco: un pittore barocco tra Parma, Roma e Napoli, ed. Erich Schleier (exh. cat., Reggia di Colorno, Parma, Castel Sant'Elmo, Naples, and Palazzo Venezia, Rome), Naples: Electa, 2001
Parrino 1700
Domenico Antonio Parrino, *Napoli città nobilissima, antica e fedelissima, esposta agli occhi et alla mente de' curiosi. Parte prima*, Naples: Stampa del Parrino, 1700
Parronchi 1980
Alessandro Parronchi, 'Sculture e progetti di Michelangelo Naccherino', *Prospettiva*, XX (1980), pp. 34–46
Pascoli 1730–36
Lione Pascoli, *Vite de' pittori, scultori et architetti moderni*, 2 vols, Rome, 1730–36; facsimile edition, ed. C. Ricci, Rome: R. Istituto d'Archeologia e Storia dell'Arte, 1933
Pasculli Ferrara 1986
Mimma Pasculli Ferrara, 'Aggiunte a Fabrizio Santafede e Belisario Corenzio', in *Ricerche sul '600 napoletano* (1986), pp. 201–9
Pasculli Ferrara 2000
—, 'Borromini e Napoli: le committenze ed i cantieri artistico-architettonici', in *Francesco Borromini. Atti del convegno internazionale Roma, 13–15 gennaio 2000*, ed. Christoph Luitpold Frommel and Elisabeth Sladek, Milan: Electa, 2000, pp. 68–76
Passeri 1772
Giovanni Battista Passeri, *Vite de' Pittori, Scultori et Architetti che hanno lavorato in Rome, morti dal 1641 fino al 1673*, Rome, 1772
Passeri 1934
—, *Vite de' Pittori, Scultori et Architetti che hanno lavorato in Rome, morti dal 1641 fino al 1673*, ed. Jacob Hess, Leipzig and Vienna: Heinrich Keller/Antonio Schroll, 1934
Percy 1967
Ann Percy, 'Castiglione's Chronology: Some Documentary Notes', *Burlington Magazine*, CIX/777 (1967), pp. 672–7
Pérez Sánchez 1977
Alfonso Emilio Pérez Sánchez, 'Las collecciones del conde de Monterrey (1653)', *Boletín de la Real Academia de la Historia*, 174 (1977), pp. 427–59
Pérez Sánchez and Spinosa 1978
— and Nicola Spinosa: *L'opera completa del Ribera*, Milan: Rizzoli, 1978
Pestilli 2013
Livio Pestilli, *Paolo de Matteis: Neapolitan Painting and Cultural History in Baroque Naples*, Aldershot: Ashgate, 2013
Pestilli, Rowland and Schütze 2008
—, Ingrid D. Rowland and Sebastian Schütze (eds), *'Napoli è tutto il mondo': Neapolitan Art and Culture from Humanism to the Enlightenment*, Pisa and Rome: Fabrizio Serra, 2008
Petrelli 2008
Flavia Petrelli, 'Una luce su Diana de Rosa nota in arte come Annella', in *Ricerche sul '600 napoletano: saggi e documenti, 2008*, Naples: Electa, 2009, pp. 87–92
Pevsner 1940
Nikolaus Pevsner, *Academies of Art Past and Present*, Cambridge, 1940; reprinted New York: De Capo Press, 1973
Phoenix 2006
Fierce Reality: Italian Masters from Seventeenth Century Naples, ed. Thomas J. Loughman (exh. cat., Phoenix Art Museum), Milan: Skira, 2006
Pickrell 1984
Thomas Pickrell, 'The Case of Domenico Castiglione, "Mercante di Quadri"', *Art Bulletin*, LXVI/2 (1984), pp. 311–12
Pinto 1997
Valter Pinto, *Racconti di opere e racconti di uomini: la storiografia artistica a Napoli tra periegesi e biografia, 1685–1700*, Pozzuoli: Paparo, 1997
Pisani 1992
Massimo Pisani, *I Carafa di Roccella: storie di principe, cardinali, grandi dimore*, Naples: Electa, 1992
Pittsburgh 1995
Italian Paintings from Burghley House, ed. Hugh Brigstocke (exh. cat., Frick Art Museum), Alexandria: Art Services International, 1995
Portús Pérez 2005
Javier Portús Pérez, review of Nicola Spinosa, *Ribera: l'opera completa* (Naples: Electa, 2003), in *Burlington Magazine*, CXLVII/1226 (2005), pp. 339–40

Porzio 2010–11
Giuseppe Porzio, 'Un *San Francesco* di Carlo Sellitto da ritrovare', in *Ricerche sul '600 napoletano: saggi e documenti, 2010–2011*, Naples: Arte'm, 2011, pp. 147–52
Porzio 2012–13
—, 'Pittura e devozione nella Napoli del Seicento: ricerche su Giuseppe Piscopo', *Ricerche sull'arte a Napoli in età moderna: saggi e documenti, 2012–2013*, Naples: Arte'm, 2013, pp. 100–16
Prague 1995
Tra l'eruzione e la peste: la pittura a Napoli dal 1631 al 1656, ed. Ladislav Daniel (exh. cat., Národní galerie v Prazee), Prague: Národní galerie v Prazee, 1995
Previtali 1980
Giovanni Previtali, 'Fiamminghi a Napoli alle fine del Cinquecento: Cornelis Smet, Pietro Torres, Wenzel Cobergher', in *Relations artistiques entres les Pays-Bas et l'Italie à la Renaissance*, ed. Nicole Dacos, Brussels and Rome: Academia Belgica, 1980, pp. 209–17
Primarosa 2010
Yuri Primarosa, 'Giovanni Battista Muti Paparuzzi e Charles Mellin: un "nobile dilettante" e un pittore lorenese alla Corte dei Barberini', *Storia dell'arte*, XXVII (2010), pp. 41–92
Prosperi Valenti Rodinò 2008
Simonetta Prosperi Valenti Rodinò, 'Additions to the Drawings Collection of the Marqués del Carpio', *Master Drawings*, XLVI/1 (2008), pp. 3–35
Prota Giurleo 1929
Ulisse Prota Giurleo, *La famiglia e la giovinezza di Salvator Rosa*, Naples: privately published, 1929
Prota Giurleo 1951a
—, 'Un complesso familiare di artisti napoletani del secolo XVII', *Napoli: rivista municipale*, anno 77, serie II/7–8 (1951), pp. 19–32
Prota Giurleo 1951b
—, 'Del pittore Passante e del suo maestro Beato', *Il Fuidoro*, I/5–6 (1951), pp. 135–7
Prota Giurleo 1952
—, *Pittori montemurresi del '600*, Naples: Comune di Montemurro, 1952
Prota Giurleo 1953
—, *Pittori napoletani del Seicento*, Naples: Fausto Fiorentino Libraio, 1953
Prota Giurleo 1955a
—, 'Il cavalier Artale', *Il Fuidoro*, II/3–4 (1955), pp. 79–81
Prota Giurleo 1955b
—, 'Notizie su Luca Giordano e alcune sue pitture in Ispagna', *Napoli: rivista municipale*, LXXXI/9 (1955), pp. 21–32
Prota Giurleo 1955c
—, 'Notizie su Massimo Stanzione e sul presunto manoscritto falsificato dal De Dominici', *Napoli: rivista municipale*, LXXXI/11 (1955), pp. 17–32
Prota Giurleo 1955d
—, 'Notizie sui pittori del Po', *Il Fuidoro*, II/7–10 (1955), pp. 259–63
Prota Giurleo 1957
—, 'Notizie napoletane sugli scultori carraresi Vitale e Giuliano Finelli', *Archivi*, XXIV (1957), pp. 157–70
Pugliese 1984
Vincenzo Pugliese, 'Pittura napoletana in Puglia, I', in Pane 1984c, pp. 196–243
Puglisi 1995
Catherine R. Puglisi, 'Guido Reni's *Pallione del Voto* and the Plague of 1630', *Art Bulletin*, LXXVII/3 (1995), pp. 403–12
Putaturo Murano 1975
Antonella Putaturo Murano, 'Filippo Napoletano incisore', *Archivio storico per le province napoletane*, XIV (1975), pp. 185–201
Quarta 1939–40
Gaetano Quarta, 'Documenti estratti dall'Archivio Storico del Banco di Napoli dai Giornali copia-polizze dal Monte e Banco della Pietà: artisti napoletani o che operarono in Napoli tra la fine del sec. XVI e la prima metà del sec. XVII: pittori sec. XVI–XVII', *Rassegna economica del Banco di Napoli*, IX/10–12 (1939), pp. 477–80, 517–20, 557–60; X/1–2 (1940), pp. 42–4, 82–4
Quondam 1972
Amedeo Quondam, 'Dal manierismo al barocco', *Storia di Napoli*, vol. V, part 1, Naples: Società Editrice, 1972, pp. 351–640
Quondam 1977
—, 'Dal barocco all'Arcadia', *Storia di Napoli*, vol. VI, part 2, Naples: Società Editrice, 1977, pp. 811–1094
Raimondo 1973–4
Raffaele Raimondo, 'La festa dei quattro altari', *La Torre*, no. 12 (31 August 1973), no. 13 (23 September 1974), nos. 14–15 (12 October 1974), available at http://www.torreweb.it/raimondo/4altari.htm [accessed October 2015]
Reade 1947
Brian Reade, 'William Frizell and the Royal Collection', *Burlington Magazine*, LXXXIX/528 (1947), pp. 70–75
Ricciardi 2007
Emilio Ricciardi, 'I Carmelitani a Napoli: chiese, conventi e "santi deserti"', in *Ricerche sul '600 napoletano: saggi in memoria di Oreste Ferrari, 2007*, Naples: Electa, 2008, pp. 85–96
Rimini 1996
Tra luci e ombre: la pittura a Napoli da Battistello Caracciolo a Luca Giordano, ed. Denise Maria Pagano, Lilia Rocco and Nicola Spinosa (exh. cat., Museo della Città), Rimini: Electa, 1996
Rizzo 1984
Vincenzo Rizzo, 'Documenti su Cavallino, Corenzio, De Matteis, Giordano, Lanfranco, Solimena, Stanzione, Zamperi ed altri, del 1636 al 1715', in Pane 1984c, pp. 314–33
Rizzo 1987
—, 'Altre notizie su pittori, scultori ed architetti napoletani del Seicento (dai documenti dell'Archivio Storico del Banco di Napoli)', *Ricerche sul '600 napoletano* (1987), pp. 153–75
Roccasecca 2009
Pietro Roccasecca, 'Teaching in the Studio of the "Accademia del Disegno dei pittori, scultori e architetti di Roma" (1594–1636)', in *The Accademia Seminars: The Accademia di San Luca in Rome, c.1590–1635*, ed. Peter M. Lukehart, Washington, DC: CASVA/National Gallery of Art, 2009, pp. 123–59
Röttgen 2002
Herwarth Röttgen, *Il Cavalier Giuseppe Cesari d'Arpino: un grande pittore nella splendore della fama e nell'inconstanza della fortuna*, Rome: Ugo Bozzi, 2002
Röttgen 2006
—, *Caravaggio: l'amore terreno o la vittoria dell'amore carnale*, Modena: Franco Cosimo Panini, 2006

Rolfs 1910
Wilhelm Rolfs, *Geschichte der Malerei Neapels*, Leipzig: E. A. Seeman, 1910
Romano 1980
Stefano Romano, *L'arte organaria a Napoli dalle origini al secolo XIX*, Naples: Naples Società Editrice Napoletana, 1980
Rome 1981
Catalogo sommario della Galleria Colonna in Roma: Dipinti, ed. Eduard A. Safarik (collection cat., Galleria Colonna), Rome: Bramante Editrice, 1981
Rome 1994
Roma 1630: Il trionfo del pennello, ed. Michel Hochmann (exh. cat., Académie de France, Villa Medici), Milan: Electa, 1994
Rome 1995
La regola e la fama: San Filippo Neri e l'arte, ed. Claudio Strinati (exh. cat., Museo Nazionale del Palazzo di Venezia), Milan: Electa, 1995
Rome, New York and St Louis 2001
Orazio and Artemisia Gentileschi, ed. Keith Christiansen and Judith Mann (exh. cat., Palazzo Venezia, Metropolitan Museum of Art and St Louis Art Museum), New York: Yale University Press and Metropolitan Museum of Art, 2001
Rubsamen 1980
Gisela Rubsamen (ed.), *The Orsini Inventories*, Malibu: John Paul Getty Museum, 1980
Rudolph 1979
Stella Rudolph, 'Carlo Maratti: figurista per pittori di nature morte', *Antichità viva*, XVIII/2 (1979), pp. 12–20
Ruffo 1916
Vincenzo Ruffo, 'Galleria Ruffo nel secolo XVII in Messina (con lettere di pittori ed altri documenti inediti)', *Bollettino d'arte*, X/1–12 (1916), pp. 21–64, 95–128, 165–92, 237–56, 284–320, 369–88
Ruotolo 1973
Renato Ruotolo, 'Collezioni e mecenati napoletani del XVII secolo', *Napoli nobilissima*, XII/3–4 (1973), pp. 118–19, 145–53
Ruotolo 1977
—, 'Aspetti del collezionismo napoletano: il Cardinale Filomarino', *Antologia di belle arti*, 1 (1977), pp. 71–82
Ruotolo 1982
—, *Ricerche sul '600 napoletano: mercanti-collezionisti fiamminghi a Napoli: Gaspare Roomer e i Vandeneynden*, Massalubrense: G. Scarpati, 1982
Ruotolo 1983
—, 'Documenti sulla chiesa di S. Teresa agli Studi e su qualche pittore napoletano del Seicento', *Ricerche sul '600 napoletano* (1983), pp. 57–71
Ruotolo 1987
—, 'Artisti, dottori e mercanti napoletani del secondo Seicento: sulle tracce della committenza "Borghese"', *Ricerche sul '600 napoletano* (1987), pp. 177–89
Ruotolo 1988
—, 'Documenti sulla chiesa napoletana di S. Paolo Maggiore', in *Scritti di storia dell'arte in onore di Raffaello Causa*, ed. Pierluigi Leone de Castris, Naples: Electa, 1988, pp. 297–304
Ruotolo 1999
—, 'Sul mobile napoletano del secondo Seicento: rivenditori e scrittoriari, scrittoi con cristalli dipinti e pittori su vetro', in *Ricerche sul '600 napoletano: saggi e documenti, 1999*, Naples: Electa, 2000, pp. 111–16
Ruotolo 2003–4
—, 'Breve nota in margine alla "Relazione della vita di Luca Giordano" del 1681 ed alla datazione del suo affresco nella cupola di Santa Brigida di Napoli', in *Ricerche sul '600 napoletano: saggi e documenti, 2003–2004*, Naples: Electa, 2004, pp. 166–8
Sáez González 2008
Manuela Sáez González, 'La collección de pintura italiana del virrey Lemos, don Pedro Fernández de Castro, en la comarca de Monforte', in *Ricerche sul '600 napoletano: saggi e documenti, 2008*, Naples: Electa, 2009, pp. 111–20
Salazar 1903
Lorenzo Salazar, 'Salvator Rosa ed i Fracanzani (nuovi documenti)', *Napoli nobilissima*, XII/8 (1903), pp. 119–23
Salerno 1984
Luigi Salerno, *Still Life Painting in Italy, 1560–1805*, trans. Robert Wolf, Rome: Ugo Bozzi, 1984
Salerno 1989
—, *New Studies on Italian Still Life Painting*, trans. Robert Wolf, Rome: Ugo Bozzi, 1989
Salomon 2010
Xavier F. Salomon, '"Ho fatto spiritar Roma": Salvator Rosa and Seventeenth-century Exhibitions', in *Salvator Rosa*, ed. Helen Langdon, Xavier F. Salomon and Caterina Volpi (exh. cat., Dulwich Picture Gallery and Kimbell Art Museum), London and Fort Worth: Holberton, 2010, pp. 74–99
Salvagni 2009
Isabella Salvagni, 'The Università dei Pittori and the Accademia di San Luca: From the Installation in San Luca sull'Esquilino to the Reconstruction of Santa Martina al Foro Romano', in *The Accademia Seminars: The Accademia di San Luca in Rome, c. 1590–1635*, ed. Peter M. Lukehart, Washington, DC: CASVA/National Gallery of Art, 2009, pp. 69–121
Sandrart 1675
Joachim von Sandrart, *Academie der Bau-, Bild-, und Mahlerey-Künste*, Nuremberg, 1675; reissued with notes by A. R. Peltzer, Munich: G. Hirth, 1925
Sarnelli 1685
Pompeo Sarnelli, *Guida de' forestieri curiosi di vedere e d'intendere le cose più notabili della regal città di Napoli e del suo amenissimo distretto, ritrovata colla lettura dei buoni scrittori, e colla propria diligenza dell'abate Pompeo Sarnelli*, Naples: Bulifon, 1685
Saxl 1939–40
Fritz Saxl, 'The Battle Scene without a Hero: Aniello Falcone and his Patrons', *Journal of the Warburg and Courtauld Institutes*, III/1–2 (1939–40), pp. 70–87
Scaramuccia 1674
Luigi P. Scaramuccia, *Le finezze de pennelli italiani, ammirate, e studiate da Girupeno sotto la scorta e disciplina del genio di Raffaello d'Urbino*, Pavia: Magro, 1674
Scavizzi 2001
Giuseppe Scavizzi, 'La pittura di genere e Luca Giordano', in *Ricerche sul '600 napoletano: saggi e documenti, 2001*, Naples: Electa, 2002, pp. 166–74
Scavizzi and De Vito 2012
— and Giuseppe de Vito: *Luca Giordano giovane, 1650–1664*, Naples: Arte'm, 2012
Schnapper 1994
Antoine Schnapper, *Curieux du grand siècle: collections et collectionneurs dans la France du XVIIe siècle, II: oeuvres d'art*, Paris: Flammarion, 1994

Schütze 1989
Sebastian Schütze, 'Die Cappella Filomarino in SS Apostoli: ein Beitrag zur Entstehung und Deutung von Borrominis Projekt in Neapel', *Römisches Jahrbuch für Kunstgeschichte*, xxv (1989), pp. 296–327
Schütze 1992a
—, 'Observations sur l'oeuvre de jeunesse de Massimo Stanzione et ses liens avec Simon Vouet et les autres peintres français à Rome', in *Simon Vouet. Actes du colloque international: Galeries nationales du Grand Palais, 5/6/7 fevrier 1991*, Paris: Documentation Française, 1992, pp. 225–44
Schütze 1992b
—, 'Pittura parlante e poesia taciturna: il ritorno di Giovan Battista Marino a Napoli, il suo concetto di imitazione e una mirabile interpretazione pittorica', in *Documentary Culture: Florence and Rome from Grand-Duke Ferdinand I to Pope Alexander VII. Papers from a Colloquium Held at the Villa Spellman, Florence, 1990* (Villa Spellman Colloquia, III), ed. Elizabeth Cropper, Giovanna Perini and Francesco Solinas, Bologna: Nuova Alfa, 1992, pp. 209–26
Schütze 1993
—, 'The *Vita S. Brunonis Cartusianorum Patriarchae* and its Interpretation by Massimo Stanzione in the Certosa di S. Martino in Naples', in *Parthenope's Splendor: Art of the Golden Age in Naples*, ed. Jeanne Chenault Porter, University Park: Pennsylvania State University, 1993, pp. 194–229
Schütze 2001
—, 'Il nuovo parnaso napoletano: arti figurative e ambiente letterario nel primo Seicento', in *Napoli viceregno spagnolo: una capitale della cultura alle origini dell'Europa moderna, sec. XVI–XVII*, ed. Monika Bosse and André Stoll, 2 vols, Naples: Vivarium, 2001, vol. II, pp. 407–34
Schütze 2002–3
—, '"Die sterbende Mutter des Aristeides": ein Archetypus abendländischer Affektdarstellung und seine Restitution durch Cesare Fracanzano', *Jahrbuch der Kunsthistorischen Museums Wien*, IV–V (2002–3), pp. 164–89
Schütze and Willette 1992
— and Thomas C. Willette: *Massimo Stanzione: l'opera completa*, Naples: Electa, 1992
Scott 1995
Jonathan Scott, *Salvator Rosa: His Life and Times*, New Haven: Yale University Press, 1995
Sestieri 1999
Giancarlo Sestieri, *I pittori di battaglie: maestri italiani e stranieri del XVII e XVIII secolo*, Rome: De Luca, 1999
Sestieri and Daprà 1994
— and Brigitte Daprà: *Domenico Gargiulo detto Micco Spadaro: la vita e l'opera*, Rome: Jandi Sapi, 1994
Sirago 2009
Maria Sirago, 'La collezione di argenti di Andrea d'Avalos, principe di Montesarchio e generale dell'"Armada del Mar Oceano"', in *Ricerche sul '600 napoletano: saggi e documenti, 2009*, Naples: Electa, 2009, pp. 149–56
Sluys 1961
Felix Sluys, *Didier Barra et François de Nomé dit Monsu Desiderio*, Paris: Minotaure, 1961
Smith 1914
H. Maynard Smith (ed.), *John Evelyn in Naples, 1645*, Oxford: Blackwell, 1914
Solinas and Schütze 2010
Francesco Solinas and Sebastian Schütze (eds), *Le dessin napolitain. Actes du colloque international Ecole Normale Supérieure, 6–8 March 2008*, Rome: De Luca Editori d'Arte, 2010
Spear 1982
Richard E. Spear, *Domenichino*, 2 vols, New Haven and London: Yale University Press, 1982
Spear 1997
—, *The 'Divine' Guido: Religion, Sex, Money and Art in the World of Guido Reni*, New Haven and London: Yale University Press, 1997
Spear 2004
—, 'What is an Original?', in *'The Italians' in Australia: Studies in Renaissance and Baroque Art*, ed. David R. Marshall, Florence: Centro Di, 2004, pp. 15–32
Spear and Sohm 2010
— and Philip Sohm (eds), *Painting for Profit: The Economic Lives of Seventeenth-century Italian Painters*, New Haven and London: Yale University Press, 2010
Spike 1992a
John T. Spike, review of Naples 1991, *Burlington Magazine*, CXXXIV/1067 (1992), pp. 139–41
Spike 1992b
—, 'The Case of the Master of the Annunciation to the Shepherds, Alias Bartolomeo Passante', *Studi di storia dell'arte*, III (1992), pp. 203–16
Spike 1998
— (ed.), *Mattia Preti: i documenti/The Collected Documents*, Florence: Centro Di, 1998
Spike 1999
—, *Mattia Preti: catalogo ragionato dei dipinti*, Florence: Centro Di and Museo Civico di Taverna, 1999
Spinosa 1984a
Nicola Spinosa, 'Painting in Naples during Bernardo Cavallino's Lifetime', in *Bernardo Cavallino of Naples, 1616–1656*, ed. Ann Percy and Ann T. Lurie (exh. cat., Cleveland Museum of Art and Kimbell Art Museum), Cleveland and Fort Worth: Cleveland Museum of Art and Kimbell Art Museum, 1984, pp. 33–42
Spinosa 1984b
—, *La pittura napoletano del '600*, Milan: Longanesi, 1984
Spinosa 1988a
—, *Pittura napoletana del Settecento, dal Barocco al Rococò*, Naples: Electa, 1988
Spinosa 1988b
—, 'Qualche aggiunta e alcune precisazioni per il Maestro dell'Annuncio ai pastori', in *Scritti di storia dell'arte in onore di Raffaello Causa*, ed. Pierluigi Leone de Castris, Naples: Electa, 1988, pp. 181–8
Spinosa 1989
— (ed.), 'La natura morta a Napoli', in *La natura morta in Italia*, ed. Federico Zeri, 2 vols, Milan: Electa, 1989, vol. II, pp. 852–963
Spinosa 1994–5
—, 'Il Maestro dell'Annuncio ai pastori, Bartolomeo Bassante, Antonio de Bellis o Bernardo Cavallino? Riflessioni e dubbi sul primo Seicento a Napoli', in *Ricerche sul '600 napoletano: scritti in memoria di Raffaello Causa. Saggi e documenti per la storia dell'arte, 1994–1995,* Naples: Electa, 1996, pp. 242–56

Spinosa 1995
—, 'Aggiunte a Hendrick van Somer, "alias" Enrico Fiammingo', in *Napoli, l'Europa: ricerche di storia dell'arte in onore di Ferdinando Bologna*, ed. Francesco Abbate and Fiorella Sricchia Santoro, Catanzano: Merdiana Libri, 1995, pp. 223–30
Spinosa 2000
—, 'Ancora sul Maestro dell'Annuncio ai pastori: Bartolomeo Bassante e Antonio de Bellis', in *Studi di storia dell'arte in onore di Denis Mahon*, ed. Maria Grazia Bernardini and Silvia Danesi Squarzina, Milan: Electa, 2000, pp. 177–84
Spinosa 2003
—, *Ribera: L'opera completa*, Naples: Electa, 2003
Spinosa 2010
—, *Pittura del Seicento a Napoli: da Caravaggio a Massimo Stanzione*, Naples: Arte'm, 2010
Spinosa 2011
—, *Pittura del Seicento a Napoli: da Mattia Preti a Luca Giordano, natura in posa*, Naples: Arte'm, 2011
Spinosa 2013
—, *Grazia e tenerezza 'in posa': Bernardo Cavallino e il suo tempo, 1616–1656*, Rome: Ugo Bozzi, 2013
Spinosa and Pagano 1992
— and Denise Maria Pagano: *I profeti di Ribera a San Martino*, Naples: Elio de Rosa, 1992
Stoichita and Coderch 1999
Victor I. Stoichita and Anna Maria Coderch: *Goya: The Last Carnival*, London: Reaktion, 1999
Stone 1997
Harold Samuel Stone, *Vico's Cultural History: The Production and Transmission of Ideas in Naples, 1685–1750*, New York: Brill, 1997
Stoughton 1973
Michael Stoughton, 'The Paintings of Giovan Battistello Caracciolo', PhD dissertation, University of Michigan, Ann Arbor, 1973
Stoughton 1978
—, 'Giovanni Battista Caracciolo: New Biographical Documents', *Burlington Magazine*, CXX/901 (1978), pp. 204–15
Stoughton 1980a
—, 'Documentazione per la pittura di Giovan Battista Caracciolo nell'Archivio Storico del Banco di Napoli', *Colloqui del Sodalizio*, II–VI (1976–80), pp. 165–7
Stoughton 1980b
—, 'Giovan Battista Caracciolo and his Son Pompeo: Documents from the Archivio Storico del Banco di Napoli', *Antologia di belle arti*, IV/15–16 (1980), pp. 187–94
Stoughton 1986
—, 'The Choir of the Certosa di San Martino', *Ricerche sul '600 napoletano* (1986), pp. 237–39
Stoughton 1988
—, 'Two Paintings of the "Madonna and Child with Saints" by G. B. Caracciolo', in *Scritti di storia dell'arte in onore di Raffaello Causa*, ed. Pierluigi Leone de Castris, Naples: Electa, 1988, pp. 161–5
Strazzullo 1954–5
Franco Strazzullo, 'Documenti inediti per la storia dell'arte nella città di Napoli', *Il Fuidoro*, I/3–8 (1954), pp. 77–9, 143–5, 210–13; II/1–2 (1955), pp. 32–7
Strazzullo 1955–6
—, 'Le corporazioni d'arti e mestieri a Napoli nei secoli XVII e XVIII', *Arte cristiana*, XLIII–XLIV (1955–6), pp. 40–44
Strazzullo 1956
—, 'Precisazioni sul pittore Sellitto', *Il Fuidoro*, III/1–2 (1956), pp. 77–9
Strazzullo 1961
—, 'Documenti per il cappellone di S. Ignazio nel Gesù Nuovo', *Partenope*, II/1–3 (1961), pp. 76–9
Strazzullo 1961–2
—, 'Statuti della Corporazione degli Scultori e Marmorari Napoletani', *Atti della Accademia Pontaniana*, n.s., XI (1961–2), pp. 221–40
Strazzullo 1962
—, *La corporazione dei pittori napoletani*, Naples: G. D'Agostino, 1962
Strazzullo 1965
—, 'La corporazione napoletana dei fabbricatori, pipernieri e tagliamonti', in *Studi in memoria di Gino Chierici*, Caserta: De Luca, 1965, pp. 224–54
Strazzullo 1968
—, *Edilizia e urbanistica a Napoli dal '500 al '700*, Naples: Berisio, 1968
Strazzullo 1978
—, *La Real Cappella del Tesoro di S. Gennaro: documenti inediti*, Naples: Società Editrice Napoletana, 1978
Strazzullo 1979
—, 'Documenti per la storia dell'arte del '600 a Napoli', *Atti dell'Accademia Pontaniana*, XXVIII (1979), pp. 323–44
Strazzullo 1983
—, 'La Quadreria del "Quarto del Priore" nella Certosa di San Martino a Napoli', *Atti dell'Accademia Pontaniana*, XXXII (1983), pp. 227–42
Strazzullo 1984
—, 'Un documento per Giuliano Finelli', *Ricerche sul '600 napoletano* (1984), pp. 143–7
Strazzullo 1985
—, 'Belisario Corenzio in tribunale: affreschi perduti nel Carmine Maggiore di Napoli', *Ricerche sul '600 napoletano* (1985), pp. 139–48
Strazzullo 1986
—, 'Alcuni documenti inediti attinenti la storia dell'arte del '600 napoletano', *Ricerche sul '600 napoletano* (1986), pp. 243–50
Strazzullo 1990
—, 'Le collezioni artistiche del duca di S. Elia (1716)', *Napoli nobilissima*, XXIX/1–4 (1990), pp. 28–35
Strazzullo 1995
—, 'Carlo Celano descrittore di Napoli sulla fine del '600', *Atti della Accademia pontaniana*, XLIV (1995), pp. 39–63
Thuillier 1982
Jacques Thuillier, *Claude Lorrain e i pittori lorenesi in Italia nel XVII secolo*, Rome: Accademia di Francia, 1982
Tomor 1993
Michael Tomor, 'Jusepe de Ribera's *Isaac's Benediction of Jacob*: Spanish Cross-Currents in Seventeenth-century Naples', in Chenault Porter and Munshower 1993, pp. 313–21
Tuck-Scala 2012
Anna K. Tuck-Scala, *Andrea Vaccaro, Naples, 1604–1670: His Documented Life and Art*, Naples: Paparo, 2012

Vaes 1925
Maurice Vaes, 'Corneille De Wael (1592–1667)', *Bulletin de l'Institut Historique Belge de Rome*, v (1925), pp. 137–247
Vannugli 1989a
Antonio Vannugli, *La collezione Serra di Cassano*, Salerno: Edizioni 10/17, 1989
Vannugli 1989b
—, 'Stanzione, Gentileschi, Finoglia: serie de San Juan Bautista para el Buen Retiro', *Boletín del Museo del Prado,* x (1989), pp. 25–33
Vargas 1988
Carmela Vargas, *Teodoro d'Errico: la maniera fiamminga del Viceregno*, Naples: Electa, 1988
Vasari 1550/1568
Giorgio Vasari, *Le vite de' più eccellenti pittori scultori e architettori nelle redazioni del 1550 e 1568*, ed. Rosanna Bettarini and Paola Barocchi, 8 vols, Florence: Sansoni, 1966–87
Verstegen 2003
Ian Verstegen, 'Federico Barocci, Federico Borromeo and the Oratorian Orbit', *Renaissance Quarterly*, LVI (2003), pp. 56–87
Vienna and Naples 1994
Settecento napoletano: sulle ali dell'aquila imperiale, 1707–1734, ed. Wolfgang Prohaska and Nicola Spinosa (exh. cat., Kunstforum der Bank Austria and Castel Sant'Elmo), Naples: Electa, 1994
Villari 1993
Rosario Villari, *The Revolt of Naples*, trans. James Newell, Cambridge: Polity Press, 1993 [Italian original: *La rivolta antispagnola a Napoli: le origini, 1585–1647*, Bari: Editori Laterza, 1967]
Wallace 1979
Richard William Wallace, *The Etchings of Salvator Rosa*, Princeton: Princeton University Press, 1979
Warr and Elliott 2010
Cordelia Warr and Janis Elliott (eds), *Art and Architecture in Naples, 1266–1713: New Approaches*, Chichester: Wiley-Blackwell, 2010
Watkins 2010
Glenn Watkins, *The Gesualdo Hex: Music, Myth, and Memory*, New York: Norton, 2010
Wethey 1967
Harold E. Wethey, 'The Spanish Viceroy, Luca Giordano and Andrea Vaccaro', *Burlington Magazine*, CIX/777 (1967), pp. 678–87
Wethey 1969–75
—, *The Paintings of Titian,* 3 vols, London: Phaidon, 1969–75
Wild 1967
Doris Wild, 'Charles Mellin ou Nicolas Poussin', *Gazette des beaux-arts*, LXIX (1967), pp. 3–44
Willette 1986
Thomas Willette, 'Bernardo De Dominici e le Vite de pittori, scultori ed architetti napoletani: contributo alla riabilitazione di una fonte', *Ricerche sul '600 napoletano* (1986), pp. 255–73
B. Wind 1998
Barry Wind, *A Foul and Pestilent Congregation: Images of 'Freaks' in Baroque Art*, Aldershot: Ashgate, 1998
E. Wind 1938
Edgar Wind, 'Shaftesbury as a Patron of Art', *Journal of the Warburg and Courtauld Institutes*, II/2 (1938), pp. 185–8
Zimmermann 2009
Katrin Zimmermann, 'Il Viceré VI conte di Monterrey, mecenate e committente a Napoli, 1631–1637', in Colomer 2009a, pp. 277–92
Zupko 1981
Ronald Edward Zupko, *Italian Weights and Measures from the Middle Ages to the Nineteenth Century*, Philadelphia: American Philosophical Society, 1981
Zwijnenberg 2003
Robert Zwijnenberg, 'The Repulsive Body: Images of Torture in 17th-century Naples', in *Bodily Extremities: Preoccupations with the Human Body in Early Modern European Culture*, ed. Florike Egmond and Robert Zwijnenberg, Aldershot: Ashgate, 2003, pp. 68–91

Photograph Credits

Art Gallery of South Australia, Adelaide: 79
Ashmolean Museum, University of Oxford: 187
Courtesy the author: 9, 12, 15, 16, 17, 18, 19, 20, 21, 22, 23, 24, 25, 27, 30, 36, 40, 48, 51, 55, 65, 67, 80, 81, 91, 96, 103, 104, 105, 106, 107, 109, 110, 111, 112, 114, 115, 117, 118, 121, 124, 125, 127, 129, 130, 132, 133, 135, 136, 137, 138, 139, 140, 148, 156, 160, 163, 164, 167, 184
Burghley House Collection, Stamford: 185
Christie's, London: 52, 54
Christie's, New York: 57
The Cleveland Museum of Art, Cleveland: 41
Courtauld Institute of Art, London: 32, 92, 120
David R. Marshall: 1
Finarte, Rome: 34, 58, 74
Fratelli Alinari, Florence/Art Resource, New York: 97
Fundación Casa Ducal de Medinaceli, Palacio Lerma, Toledo: 61, 165
Galerie Canesso, Paris: 78
Istituto Centrale per il Catalogo e la Documentazione, Rome: 47, 181
Luciano Pedicini, Archivio dell'Arte: 2, 4, 5, 10, 11, 13, 45, 75, 86, 88, 89, 102, 108, 122, 128, 131, 141, 142, 143, 144, 146, 147, 149, 151, 154, 174, 177
Matthiesen Fine Arts Ltd., London: 64, 162
Metropolitan Museum of Art, New York: 8, 76
Museo del Prado, Madrid: 56, 161, 166, 168, 169, 170, 172, 173, 183
Private collection: 77, 95, 145
Sarah Campbell Blaffer Foundation, Houston: 188
Scala, Florence/Art Resource, New York: 39 71, 83, 123, 151, 153, 157, 180
Scottish National Gallery, Edinburgh: 152
Soprintendenza per i Beni Artistici e Storici di Firenze: 85
Soprintendenza per i Beni Artistici e Storici di Napoli: 3, 6, 7, 14, 26, 29, 31, 33, 35, 37, 38, 42, 43, 44, 49, 50, 53, 60, 62, 63, 66, 69, 73, 82, 84, 87, 93, 94, 98, 101, 113, 116, 119, 126, 134, 155, 158, 159, 171, 175, 176, 178, 179, 182, 186
Sotheby's, London: 72
Sotheby's, New York: 46, 59, 68
Szépmúvészeti Múzeum, Budapest: 28
Wildenstein, New York: 90

Index

Note: page references in *italics* indicate illustrations; those in **bold type** indicate tables.